FROMMER'S
IRELAND
ON $35 A DAY
Susan Poole

□

1989–1990

Copyright © 1967, 1968, 1969, 1971, 1973, 1975, 1977, 1979, 1981, 1983, 1985, 1987, 1989
by Simon & Schuster, Inc.

Published by Prentice Hall Trade Division
A Division of Simon & Schuster, Inc.
Gulf + Western Building
One Gulf + Western Plaza
New York, NY 10023

ISBN 0-13-506379-5
ISSN 0276-9026

Text Design: Levavi & Levavi, Inc.

Manufactured in the United States of America

*Although every effort was made to ensure the accuracy
of price information appearing in this book,
it should be kept in mind that prices
can and do fluctuate in the course of time.*

CONTENTS

MAPS

To Dee, who has found her own special love for Ireland.

ABOUT THIS BOOK

□ □ □

Having bought this book, you no doubt already *know* what it's about. Simply stated, it's about saving you money.

If you've already decided you're going to Ireland, let me say that *you* have taken the first step toward that money-saving goal. If you haven't yet made up your mind, I'll do my very best in the following chapters to convince you that you should—for the traveler with a keen eye on the budget, there are few places in this inflation-ridden world that so happily offer so magical an experience at anywhere near the bargain prices you'll find in the Emerald Isle. We'll deal with the magic on almost every page, but for now, let's get down to basics: value-for-dollar.

Basics are what you'll buy for the $35 in the title. A place to sleep and three meals a day can easily be budgeted for that amount without sacrificing comfort, diet, or enjoyment. In fact—and this is a big part of the magic—in Ireland, your room will be clean, comfortable, and more often than not include an enchanting view plus (for not one cent extra) some of the most charming and entertaining hosts you're likely to find anywhere on the face of the earth.

The key is to go the bed-and-breakfast, farmhouse, guesthouse route. The only thing you'll forgo is a private bathroom, although in more and more cases a toilet and shower *will* be available at only slightly more than the cost of just a room.

For about $16 a day, you'll be welcomed into an Irish family home and overwhelmed each morning with a breakfast so ample you'll be hard-pressed to eat another bite until dinnertime. That by no means implies you'll be giving up your midday meal: the $19 balance in our budget will easily cover a pub lunch (which runs about $5) and a more-than-adequate dinner (about $14).

Of course, if you're a hostel devotee or eligible for student discounts, you'll have money left over. I recently met a young American student just ending a three-week stay at an average cost of $16 a day. And she did *not* look malnourished!

Above our basics, you'll have to figure additional costs for travel, entertainment, shopping, and the like. But since our purpose is to save you money in *every* area, you will find in these pages reports on the best bargains I could find in each of these categories. I've quoted prices in both Irish pounds and American dollars to save you some mental arithmetic (be sure to read the Inflation Alert carefully, however, and keep an eagle eye on the current exchange rate when you travel).

Because Ireland is chock-a-block with special places—and not *all* come at budget prices—you'll also find "Big Splurges" in almost every region. You might consider my budget recommendations as the meat-and-potatoes of this book, while Big Splurges are like the out-of-season strawberries you treat yourself to no matter what they cost. Whether or not you indulge will be up to you, your personal inclination, and your budget. They are *not* included in our $35-a-day: they *are* worth a thought or two.

One last word about that magic. In all the years I've been visiting Ireland, I've found it in places as disparate as big, luxury hotels (so impersonal in most other places), B&Bs with just one or two bedrooms, and casual pub encounters. Most of all, though, it exists in stumbled-on, out-of-the-way places, be they accommodations, eateries, or scenic spots. You have my personal guarantee that, as a budget traveler lodging with Irish families, you'll be steered to many a favorite pub or local attraction or unforgettable character by your hosts, and that's the *best* bargain you'll find for your $35-a-day!

Enjoy!

Acknowledgments

MY HEARTFELT THANKS to the people of Ireland, who have—from the moment I first set foot in their country—made me very welcomed. Very special thanks to Bord Fáilté, whose marvelous staff should serve as a model for all other tourism organizations around the globe; to Aer Lingus, all that an Irish airline should be; and to good Irish friends like the John Flynns, Frank Lewis, Micheal Macgiobuin, John B. Keane, Mary and Noel McLoughlin, Angela and Tony Muckley, Brenda Weir, Pat Mackey, and scores of others who have joined in the researching of this book with typical Irish wit, good humor, and helpfulness. To Orla Carey in New York and Paddy Derivan in Dublin, my undying gratitude for special support and unfailing aid.

INFLATION ALERT

Ireland—for all its magic—is not immune to the ravages of inflation. Also, currency exchanges continue to fluctuate with international monetary trends.

While I have made every effort to quote the most reliable prices and price forecasts, in today's world conditions change so rapidly that during the second year of this edition—1990—the wise traveler will *add about 20%* to the prices quoted in Irish pounds throughout and will carefully *check the exchange rate* at the time of travel.

A DISCLAIMER

I have personally checked the recommendations contained in the main body of this book. You should note, however, that those establishments described under the title "Readers' Selections" have *not* in many cases been inspected by the author and are the opinions of individual readers only. They do not in any way represent the opinions of the publisher or author of this book.

INTRODUCTION

IRELAND ON $35 A DAY

□ □ □

1. IRELAND AND THE IRISH
2. A BRIEF HISTORY
3. IRELAND WITH THIS BOOK
4. THE BASICS OF BUDGETING
5. THE DOLLARWISE TRAVEL CLUB

You know about Ireland, of course—it's that lovely isle that appeared when "a little bit of heaven dropped from out the sky one day." Skeptical? Well, look around for the most hard-nosed skeptic you know who's *been* to Ireland and then get set to listen to hours of rapturous memories!

Ireland has that affect on people. All people. For me, it began back in 1973, when I first encountered the incredible beauty of this small country's landscape and learned with amazement that the magnificent sum of $2.40 would make me an instant member of warm Irish families who were anxious to share their fireside, friends, favorite pub, innumerable cups of tea, and the most enormous breakfasts I'd ever seen.

I stayed three weeks that year, and haven't missed going back for a part of every year since. That's been possible for me—a confirmed budget traveler—because Ireland is so *affordable*. Oh, prices have risen there quite as fast as they have everywhere else in the world, but Ireland is still one of the best travel buys I've come across.

But there's much, much more to it than that. There are some things that would be cheap at *any* price, and Ireland has more than its fair share of those priceless commodities. Each visit has brought fresh discoveries and new friends. There are always new tales to bring home, still more of the witty one-liners that spring so naturally to Irish lips to try to remember, more memories of nights of unplanned music and song that somehow just happened, still more miles of unbelievably beautiful coastline or mountains or rolling green fields suddenly unfolding around corners I'd not turned before, new Irish names to add to my Christmas list.

Perhaps even more important is the glow I bring back each year after spending a little time with people who have managed to hold on to basic values that in other parts of the world these days seem as elusive as a dream.

Blarney Stone blather? Not so. Just wait until you hear the ravings of your plane mates on the flight back home! I am just *one* of those Americans who every year head off to Ireland—a fan club hundreds of thousands strong. We're joined by thousands of enthusiastic English, French, Dutch, Germans, and a good number from countries as far away as Japan, New Zealand, and Australia, who send the total number of foreign visitors into the millions. Many Europeans return year after year for superb fishing or golfing or biking or horse racing or theater or music—or simply to soak up the unique atmosphere of this little country and the extraordinary personality of its people. And each of us leaves Ireland filled with its special kind of magic, eager to spread the word to all and sundry. I'm willing to wager you'll do the same.

It's a formidable task to write about Ireland and the Irish. Back in 1842, William Makepeace Thackeray wrote an English friend: "I am beginning to find out now that a man ought to be forty years in this country instead of three months, and *then* he wouldn't be able to write about it!" Far be it from me even to attempt to beat Thackeray—I can only try to tell you about the Ireland *I* have discovered in several years of exhaustive research, pass along the finds of other travelers who have been kind enough to write, and tell *you how it is not only possible* to visit Ireland on our $35 a day—it's the *best* way to go!

1. IRELAND AND THE IRISH

Before diving into a detailed discussion of what you can expect to find in Ireland, let's talk about what you *won't* find. First of all, you won't find the stereotyped "stage Irish" of so many comedy skits. Nor will you find a land peopled entirely by saints and scholars (although, Lord knows, there's a plentiful supply of both). Or a land ravaged by violence, as the news media would sometimes lead you to believe—sure, it *does* exist, but it does *not* pervade the country. And as the Irish are the first to point out, you won't find a telephone system that works with anything like the efficiency you're used to at home (which can, I suppose, drive you a little dotty if you're in a hurry, but which can also, I *know,* lead to some pretty interesting telephone conversations with operators while you both wait to get your call through). One thing more: You won't find a populace out to take you for every cent in your holiday purse—in my experience, the phrase "what the traffic will bear" just doesn't exist in Ireland.

Today's Ireland is a land still covered with small farms in unspoiled countryside but moving away from an economy wholly dependent on agriculture, with more and more hi-tech industries moving in and making scarcely a ripple on the smooth waters of the world's most relaxed way of life.

It's a land of cities whose antiquities live quite comfortably, elbow-to-elbow, with modern luxury hotels and an increasing number of sophisticated cabarets and nightclubs. A land filled with social centers that go by the name of pubs. Whose Tidy Towns competition each year rates even the tiniest hamlet on its success—or lack of it—in the ongoing battle against litter. Where there's never sweltering heat or bone-chilling cold, and a rainy day really *is* a soft day.

Ireland is where the word "friendly" probably originated. Where stopping to ask directions can land you in a family kitchen swapping tales over a "cuppa." Where the answer to every question is a short story. Where you may—as I once did—wind up as the Dublin house guest of an Irish lady you met quite casually over breakfast at a B&B in Kerry.

Today's Ireland will take over your heart the minute you land and send you away looking back over your shoulder with a head full of plans to come right back.

THE LAY OF THE LAND: To get the statistics out of the way: Ireland covers 32,524 square miles, stretched out 302 miles at its longest and 189 miles at its widest points. It's the "last parish before America," that is, the most westerly island of Europe, and its bowl-shaped contours are formed by a great limestone plain surrounded by mountains (Kerry's Carrantuohill is the highest at 3,414 feet).

Its coastline is so indented by jagged peninsulas that the sea is never more than 70 miles distant. That glorious coastline measures more than 3,000 miles and encircles 9,000 miles of meandering rivers (the 230-mile Shannon is the longest) and some 800 lakes, the largest of which is Lough Neagh (153 square miles).

To the east, Great Britain lies across the Irish Sea; to the south, France is on the other side of the Celtic Sea; and the Atlantic Ocean wraps around the southwest, west, and northern coasts.

THE WEATHER: The Atlantic brings along with it the Gulf Stream's warming currents to create a friendly climate that deals in moderation rather than extremes—seldom more than 65° in July or August (occasionally "soaring" to 70°), 40° in January or February.

Rave to the Irish about their glorious country and nine times out of ten the response will be, "Sure, it's nice enough, if it only weren't for the weather." It's no use trying to convince them that the weather really isn't *that* bad—they're apparently born with an apology complex about their climate, and that's that! However, that famous (or infamous) rainfall is heaviest and most frequent in the mountains of the west, and frequent enough in the rest of the country to keep at *least* 40 shades of green glowing. Showers come and go—sometimes several times in one day—but for the most part, they consist of a misty, almost ethereal sort of rain, nothing like the savage, slashing onslaught you might expect, one that adds an extra dimension to the landscape. If you want to see more sun than rain, you'll generally find it in May everywhere except in the midlands and southeast, where June is apt to be sunnier.

THE FLORA AND FAUNA: As for the flora of Ireland, the vast majority of trees today are imports. That's because back in Neolithic times large areas of the oak, ash, and rowan forests that covered much of the central limestone plain were cleared for cultivation or grazing. English landowners of the past few centuries can be faulted for many sins against Ireland, but one of the positive things they brought across the Irish Sea was their passion for planting exotic trees and gardens, which went a long way toward the re-greening of the countryside. Since the beginning of this century, reforestation efforts have concentrated on large plantings of conifers and other evergreens, many in more than 400 national forests and other wooded areas open to the public. In addition to the verdant forest areas, you'll find the lovely heathers of the bogs and the unique wildflower population of County Clare's Burren.

One of the everlasting joys of Ireland's environment for me, personally, is that I can walk through the woodlands, bogs, or Burren without watching every step for fear of snakes. The experts say that's because the country was cut off from mainland Europe during the retreat of the Ice Age before the serpents could make their venomous way across; any Irishman worth his salt will insist the good St. Patrick is solely responsible for this blessing. As far as *I* am concerned—me, with my deathly fear of the reptiles—it matters not one whit who or what brought it about: I'll take a snake-free environment any way I can get it! As for other fauna, no life-threatening species roam the countryside (thanks, again, to the last Ice Age), although fossils of several gigantic examples of same have been unearthed by archeologists. The quite harmless fox, hare, and stoat are about all you're likely to find around today.

GEOGRAPHIC DIVISIONS: From its early history, Ireland's 32 counties have been divided into four provinces (those "Four Green Fields" of song and story). To the north, **Ulster** is now divided into the six counties that form Northern Ireland—Derry, Antrim, Armagh, Down, Fermanagh, and Tyrone—and three that lie in the Republic—Donegal, Monaghan, and Cavan. In the east, **Leinster** is composed of the 12 counties of Dublin, Wicklow, Wexford, Kilkenny, Carlow, Kildare, Laois, Offaly, Westmeath, Longford, Meath, and Louth. **Munster,** in the south, consists of counties Waterford, Cork, Kerry, Limerick, Clare, and Tipperary. And the west's **Connaught**—of Cromwell's slanderous "To hell or . . ." remark—is made up of Roscommon, Leitrim, Sligo, Galway, and Mayo.

TO SUM UP: There, then, are the bare facts of Ireland—and believe me, they are *bare*.

It's only when you see the delicate play of light and shade on the mountains while driving from Glengarriff in County Cork to Kenmare in County Kerry, or ride through the lush greenness of County Waterford byways, or stand and drink in the mystical moonscape of County Clare's Burren, or watch a grassy hillside go from the brightest hue of green to silver-gray in the changing light, or gaze at a cloud-studded sky so enormous it makes eternity seem small, or stand on the rocky Dingle Peninsula shore at Ventry where legend says the King of the World went down to defeat at the hands of Fionn MacCumhaill ("Finn MacCool") and his Fianna warrior band—it's only then that the face of Ireland comes truly alive. Around every bend, that luminous, ever-changing landscape cries out for the poet, and many a poet has answered its call. Poor Thackeray—no *wonder* he was so frustrated!

George Bernard Shaw, however, put it quite simply:

> There is no magic like that of Ireland.
> There are no skies like Irish skies.
> There is no air like Irish air . . .
> The Irish climate will make the stiffest
> and slowest mind flexible for life.

Amen!

THE IRISH: If it's hard to find words for Ireland itself, it's well nigh *impossible* to capture the personality of the people who live there. Flexible they most certainly are, to the point of a complexity that simply defies description. Warmhearted, witty, sometimes devious, filled with curiosity about visitors, deeply religious at Sunday's mass but the very devil in the pub on Saturday night, great talkers and even greater listeners, sometimes argumentative to the point of combativeness—and with it all, *friendly*. That's the Irish, all right. But it's the *style* in which they are all of the above that so delights when you visit them at home.

There's a certain panache about the Irish. Take, for example, the time I walked into a store in Cork and asked for a certain address, confessing that I was lost. With a smiling, sweeping bow, the owner allowed as how "You're lost no more, darlin', come with me." Whereupon he walked me to the building I was looking for several blocks away, chatting a steady stream and asking questions all the way. Now, *that's* panache!

Which is not to say, however, that you're going to be greeted at the airport by Irishmen rushing to bowl you over with all that chatter and charm. If there's anything they're not, it's intrusive—yours will have to be the first conversational move. But ask the first question, make the first comment, and you're off and running, your American accent an open invitation for the inevitable "And where in America would you be from?" followed up by the equally inevitable "Well, now, and didn't my own uncle Pat [or brother Joe or great-aunt Mary] go out to Chicago [or New York or Savannah or wherever it is you hail from]." And you're taken over by stories of the wandering relatives, more often than not over a pint or a cuppa with this perfect stranger who will, in his own good time, get around to what it was you wanted to know in the first place.

All the foregoing takes place, of course, in English. But it's the most melodic, lilting rendition of the language you'll ever hear. "Sure, the English gave us their language," say the Irish with a grin, "then we showed them how to use it." And they did, with writers like Jonathan Swift, Edmund Burke, Oscar Wilde, George Bernard Shaw, William Butler Yeats, James Joyce, and a host of others pouring out masterpieces of English prose as easily as most men tip the whisky jar. They're still at it today—I'll tell you about some of my favorite modern writers in the next chapter. But your average Irishman—*or* woman—embellishes everyday conversation with all the eloquence of the greatest writers and colorful, image-making phrases that would make any writer weep with envy. And they string them together in yarns that may be wildly fanciful, but are never dull.

As for the celebrated Irish wit, Irish laughter creeps around words and phrases, then curls past curving lips to land in twinkling Irish eyes and a mischievous chuckle.

Tim Pat Coogan, in his excellent book *Ireland and the Arts,* suggests that the Irish have used their words and their wit as both a sly release from and effective weapon against cruel oppression suffered over long centuries of invasion and foreign rule. There's truth in that, for in today's Ireland—as another Irish writer in an *Inside Ireland* article stated categorically—"Exaggeration and lighthearted blasphemy are national pastimes."

There's more to the Irish, of course, than talk. There's the strong religious influence that passed from Celtic to Catholic rites without a hitch. And the fascinating mix of Celt, Viking, Norman, and Saxon blood that has melded into an "Irish" race of brunettes, blonds, and redheads. And the paradoxical nature that led Chesterton to write: "All their wars are merry, and all their songs are sad."

Mary Moran, up in Castlebar, County Mayo, passed along to me (and to other guests at her Lakeview House B&B) an unsigned poem that probably comes as close as anyone can to describing the Irish in these lines:

> He's wild and he's gentle,
> He's good and he's bad,
> He's proud and he's humble,
> He's happy and sad.
> He's in love with the ocean,
>   the earth and the skies,
> He's enamored with beauty
>   wherever it lies.
> He's victor and victim, a star and a clod,
> But mostly he's Irish,
> In love with his God.

As I said, that's *close.* But it's a safe bet you'll go home thinking of "the Irish" in terms of John or Kitty or Siubhan or Michael—and you'll be as close as any poet can ever come!

2. A BRIEF HISTORY

The landscape of Ireland is haunted by its history. Its ghosts lurk along every road, around every bend, behind every bush.

Stone Age Irish move eerily behind the mists of prehistory that cloak dolmens left in their wake. Visit the reconstructed crannog at Craggaunowen in County Clare and Bronze Age men and women almost materialize before your eyes. Iron Age forts make a quiet day ring with the sounds, just beyond your ears, of those who sheltered there. Great monastic crosses and ruined abbeys accent the tremendous influence of early Christians, while round towers tell of the dangers they faced from Viking raiders. Listen carefully in Dublin and Waterford and you may hear the echoing footsteps of their Viking founders. Norman spirits inhabit ruined castles that squat along riverbanks, atop lofty cliffs, and in lonely fields.

The multifaceted history that shaped the fascinating Irish character we know today travels with you wherever you go in Ireland.

IN THE BEGINNING: Ireland took on its present shape when the world's last Ice Age retreated and left the country with multitudes of scooped-out lakes and tumbled mountains plus a land bridge that connected it to Great Britain. Sometime around 6000 B.C., a race of Stone Age settlers crossed over that land bridge to Ireland—we don't know where they originally came from, only that they clustered around the seashore and along inland riverbanks, fashioning crude flint tools, and surviving by fishing and hunting.

Long after that land link to Britain disappeared and Ireland had become an island—about 2000 B.C.—newcomers brought with them cows and other domesticated animals. They also brought the skill to clear the land and plant crops, thus beginning Ireland's long tradition of farming and cattle raising. It was this Neolithic race who cremated their dead and created communal burial chambers beneath stone cairns or inside earthen, tunnel-filled mounds. Newgrange, in County Meath, a full acre in size, is today the best known of the surviving tumuli and the one most of us visit to give a tip of the hat to those long-ago Irish.

THE METAL WORKERS: While the farmers in Ireland were tending their fields, European tribes were beginning to work with metals, which led to an ever-widening search for copper to be used in fashioning bronze weapons and tools and gold for making exquisitely crafted ornaments and jewelry. The search eventually reached Ireland and its rich deposits of both metals. The Bronze Age had begun, an age that brought to this remote, primitive little island a whole slew of artisans, merchants, and peddlers who traveled all over western Europe, leaving examples of their arts and crafts scattered around the continent.

Those who came to Ireland during this period were probably of Mediterranean origin. They were short, dark-haired, and swarthy-skinned and may have been Picts. The Romans knew them as the Iberni, but they were called the Uib-Ernai in Ireland, where they were believed to be descendants of the fertility goddess Eire, whose name means "noble." The island country was very soon known by that noble name, and today it is the oldest existing national name in the world (never mind that it's been corrupted by dropping the initial letter and tacking on "land"—*officially*, the country is still "Eire").

As beautifully crafted as are the metal objects created by these early Irish settlers, they fade in significance when compared to the most important legacy they left us. A wealth of megalithic stone structures still stand in solid, silent testimony to incredible scientific knowledge and engineering skill. Great pillars and huge standing stones bear mute witness to feats of construction that must have required great organization, hundreds of workers, and a dedication that defies belief. The megaliths of Ireland are among her most valuable treasures, and to the traveler's delight, they stand in solitary splendor in the green fields and atop rocky hilltops with nary a neon sign or souvenir stand in sight!

AND THEN CAME THE CELTS: Tall, fair-skinned, and red-haired, the Celts were fierce, warlike people who roamed the face of Europe before migrating to Ireland in the 4th century B.C. They came with iron weapons and a military prowess that soon established them—and their language—as rulers of the land.

Some 100 tribes spread across the country, setting up small kingdoms under petty lords, or chieftains. Those smaller units, in turn, paid allegiance (at least in theory) to regional kings, and in time a High King of Ireland sat at Tara. The five regional kingdoms were known as Ulster, Munster, Leinster, Meath, and Connaught, which became the four provinces of Ireland as we know it when the Kingdom of Meath merged with Leinster.

Hot-blooded Celts were not, however, *about* to let any of those titles and divisions go unchallenged. The countryside rang with the sounds of battle as petty king fought petty king, regional kings embarked on expansionary expeditions, and the High King of the moment never sat easy on his honorary throne. Peasants and bondsmen toiled for whichever chieftain was in power at the moment, and the free farmer anted up both tribute and loyalty, while craftily throwing up a sturdy earthen ring-fort (also called a "rath" or "lis") as protection against roaming marauders. Those ring-forts are still around, and many of today's town names reflect their locations. For example, Lismore, in County Waterford, takes its name from just such a large lis on its outskirts.

As for any sort of unity, it existed in the strong bonds of a common culture and traditions held together by the common language. Petty kingdoms might be at war, but all paid strict obeyance to the traditional laws of the Brehons (lawyers), who traveled freely from one kingdom to another. Learned men in all professions were honored throughout the land and established schools that set intricate graded scales of achievement. Traveling bards who recited long, epic poems of past heroic deeds were much revered and richly rewarded when they came up with new compositions that put a poetic purpose behind the latest exploits of whichever chieftain might be offering hospitality at the moment. Only slightly less homage was paid to the most skilled of the many artists and craftsmen who labored for each chieftain and often shared his table. Above everyone, the Druids were heralded as *all* tribes' wisest men and they conducted or prescribed the most sacred ceremonies.

It was this strange mixture of barbarous warring and a highly developed culture that greeted the arrival of Christianity in the 5th century A.D. And all the foregoing is the story of how it evolved—at least, that's the way archeologists and historians *think* it evolved, based on their best assumptions from carbon datings, artifacts, and educated guesses.

But listen to another version of the same story.

THE LEGENDS: Those early bards and the *seanachies* (storytellers) who followed also tell of three distinct racial groups involved in Ireland's beginnings. Their story, however, is a delightful blend of fact, fancy, and mysticism and has nothing whatsoever to do with carbon dating.

There were, they say, the "men of the quiver" (the *Fir Bolg*), the "men of the territory" (the *Fir Domhnann*), and the "men of Gaul" (the *Fir Gaileoin*). In one of the oldest legends, telling of the coming of the Celts, the bards explained that it was their iron-bladed spears (*laighens*) that gave Leinster its name. From that point, the stories go on to speak of the brave deeds of Conaire Mor, King of Ireland in the 2nd century B.C. The hero we know as Finn MacCool was born as Fionn MacCumhail in a blaze of glorified chivalry and courage as gigantic as the fictitious man himself. His faithful Fianna warrior band matched their leader in feats of bravery and daring. There were tales of the Knights of the Red Branch in the north and of the Ulster hero, Cuchulainn. Queen Maeve, who ruled Connaught, and the tragic Deirdre of the Sorrows were chief among the heroines who figured in song and story.

Later on, the seanachies, in a fit of revisionist history, came up with a quite satisfactory rationale for the shared traits of Irish and Scottish Celts. All were, they reckoned, descended from one man, Mileadh (Milesius), and they could look back in their lineage to one Gadelius and a lady known as Scota!

Which version holds the most truth, archeologists' or that of the seanachies? Take your pick. But I can tell you that to my Irish friends, those legendary heroes are as alive and well in their minds and hearts today as when the bards of old spun their tales. Which version would *I* choose? Why, both, of course—with perhaps just the slightest leaning toward Finn MacCool and Cuchulainn.

SAINTS AND SCHOLARS: The Romans, rampaging in southern Britain, never did get around to conquering Ireland, but in the mid-5th century A.D. a conquest of quite another nature took place. A pagan religion that had flourished for centuries surprisingly embraced quickly and with enthusiasm the doctrines and rites of Christianity that landed on Irish shores along with St. Patrick. A Roman by birth, in his youth the budding saint had tended swine in Ulster as a slave, escaped, and made his way back to the continent, where he entered religious life. Even in those days, however, the magic of Ireland was at work, and he returned to his former captors as a missionary in 432 A.D.

Those early years among people who were to become his devout followers may well have given St. Patrick the insight to convert many pagan *practices* as well as pagan people, thus making it easier for them to make the switch than it might otherwise have been. Retaining just enough pagan roots to avoid hostile resistance, he managed to transplant rites and superstitions into Christian soil without a murmur—the healing powers of many Irish "holy wells," for example, are those attributed to them by ancient Celts long before St. Patrick arrived on the scene. His firsthand knowledge of Celtic love of the mystical—especially when applied to the natural world—perhaps inspired him to use the native shamrock to symbolize the Holy Trinity and become Ireland's most enduring national symbol.

Irish king after Irish king listened to the missionary and led his subjects into the new religion, although none went so far as to abandon such distinctly Celtic pastimes as intra-kingdom warfare and riotous revelry within his own court. In homage to their new God (or maybe in penance for their more unChristian practices?) kings and other large landowners endowed His earthly representatives with lavish gifts of precious metals, land on which to build churches and monasteries, and other valuables which helped fund St. Patrick's work.

With the coming of Christianity, Celtic culture took a giant step forward. Already deeply respectful of learning in its higher forms, in the hundreds the Irish devoted themselves to a cloistered life within great monasteries that taught all the learning of their time, both Celtic and Roman. As Europe entered its culturally deprived Dark Ages, Ireland's monastic universities kept the lights of philosophy, theology, astronomy, literature, poetry, and most of the known sciences brightly burning, attracting thousands of students who fled the continent during those centuries. Artistic achievement hit new heights inside their walls, as the exquisitely illustrated *Book of Kells* demonstrates. Until the end of the 8th century, Ireland's Golden Age was the brightest beacon in the western world.

Away from these seats of learning, monks of a more mystical leaning moved out to more remote parts of the country and to rocky, misty islands just offshore. There they lived austere lives of meditation, building the beehive-shaped stone dwellings still intact today and marvelously engineered little stone churches like Dingle's Gallarus Oratory, constructed entirely without mortar and watertight for the past 1,500 years. The impressive stone Celtic crosses that dot the landscape had their origins in the 7th century.

Eventually, Europe's age of darkness was forced into retreat, helped mightily by returning European scholars and Irish monks and scholars who left home to carry their teachings into cathedrals, royal courts, and great universities they helped establish.

VIKING INVADERS: The first invaders of Ireland's recorded history were terrifying Viking raiders who came by sea in A.D. 795 to launch fierce, lightning-fast strikes along the coastline, taking away hordes of plunder and captives and leaving behind only smoking ruins. Their superior mail battle dress and heavy arms made easy victims of even the most stout-hearted, battle-loving Irish, and their raids moved farther and farther inland, with rich monastic settlements yielding the most valuable prizes. Churchmen found an answer to the danger in tall, round towers with their only entrance high above the ground (they stored their most precious treasures there, then pulled up long ladders to make access impossible). I have, incidentally, run across more than one seanachie whose story is that Finn MacCool built the first of these and the doorway was simply put at his natural entry-level—the monks just latched on to what turned out to be a perfect protective device. You'll find one of the best preserved at the Rock of Cashel, in County Tipperary.

As the years went by, raiders turned into settlers, establishing the first of a string of coastal cities at Dublin in 841, followed by Wexford, Waterford, Cork, and Limerick. Vestiges of city walls, gates, and fortifications remain to this day— Reginald's Tower, in Waterford, is one of the most perfect examples. Former raiders turned to peaceful trading and—in a pattern to be followed by subsequent "conquerors"—they were soon intermarrying with natives and becoming as Irish as the Irish themselves.

Not a few resident Irish chieftains, after disastrous defeats, began to take note of successful Viking battle methods and turn them back against the victors. But it wasn't until 1014 that Brian Boru—the High King of Ireland at the time—engaged his enemies at Clontarf, just outside Dublin, and won a decisive victory after a full day of battle. Interestingly, so intermixed had the two races become by that time that while a large part of the Viking forces consisted of "Irish" allies, Brian Boru's loyal "Norse" warriors were among the most valiant on the field! Boru was mortally wounded and ascended into the rarefied stratosphere of Ireland's most revered heroes.

THE NORMANS MOVE IN: Brian Boru's death was followed by a century and a half of kingly tug-of-war to establish one central authority figure. It was one of those ambitious combatants who took the first step on Ireland's long path of involvement with the British. His name was Dermot MacMurrough, King of Leinster, and he made the fatal mistake of stealing the beautiful wife of O'Rourke, the King of Breffni, who promptly stirred up Leinster's minor chieftains and hounded MacMurrough out of Leinster.

MacMurrough crossed the Irish Sea to Britain, then under the rule of Norman conquerors from France for a little over a century, and followed King Henry II to France, finally persuading him to sponsor a volunteer army to help win back Dermot's lost throne. It arrived in 1169 and landed in Waterford under the command of the Earl of Pembroke, popularly known as Strongbow. By marrying MacMurrough's daughter in Reginald's Tower, the wily Norman became King of Leinster when his father-in-law died the very next year.

Strongbow's military prowess quickly brought most of Leinster and Munster under his domination. He defeated Rory O'Connor (buried at Conmacnois, County Offaly), the last High King of Ireland, and appeared to be well on his way to achieving power to rival that of King Henry II. Needless to say, from Henry's point of view, something had to be done. Espousing a sudden interest in the religious eccentricities of Irish Catholics (who sometimes showed faint regard for the edicts of Rome—their Easter fell on a date different from that proclaimed by the pope, for instance), Henry rushed to Ireland clutching a document from the pope (Adrian IV, the only *English* pope in the Church's history!) giving him feudal lordship over all of Ireland, Strongbow notwithstanding.

Under the guise of a religious reformer, Henry was able to win the support of most Irish bishops, and the papal authority gave him a potent lever to gain the submission of Irish kings, lords, and large landowners. Stating that he held absolute ownership of all lands, it granted him the undisputed right to rent it to such nobles as professed loyalty and withhold it from those who refused to do so. Many of the Irish kings, anxious to hold on to their territories even if it meant fealty to the English king, traveled to Dublin to make the required submission.

But that feudal lordship flew squarely in the face of long-established Irish law, which had insisted since the days of the Brehons that no king or lord had the right to take lands owned by individuals or groups and that any attempt to do so should be resisted, by force if necessary. That basic precept kept Anglo-Norman and Irish lords growling at each other across a legal chasm for the next 350 years. Although every English monarch who followed Henry laid claim to the Lordship of Ireland, each was too busy with civil wars and foreign conquest to send armies to enforce that claim. Normans acquired title to more than half the country, building most of those sturdy castles in which you'll sightsee, banquet, or even spend the night during your visit.

All the while, however, the same thing that happened to the Vikings was happening to the Normans. Quickly adapting to their new homeland, they intermarried with the Irish and strayed so far from their sacred loyalty to the English throne and all things English that laws had to be passed in Parliament against their use of Irish dress, manners, and the native language—to my knowledge, the only time in the world's history that a *language* has been banished! Those laws turned out to be about as useless as the armed forces that never arrived—Norman families evolved into *Irish*-Norman families, with more loyalty to their own land holdings than to either Irish or English rulers.

As for those Irish chieftains and kings who refused to recognize English rights to their land, they just couldn't get their act together to oppose English claims with a united front. Instead, each Irish faction battled independently, with no central authority. Incessant warfare *did,* however, serve to concentrate the beleaguered English Crown forces in a heavily fortified area around Dublin known as "The Pale" and a few garrison towns around the country. Had not a pervasive religious dimension been thrown into the Irish stew, the Irish might have eventually managed to wrest control of their ancient land from British rulers. But King Henry VIII and the Reformation changed all that in the late 16th century.

AN ENGLISH "KING OF IRELAND" AND THE FLIGHT OF THE EARLS: Henry VIII brought to the throne of England a new approach to English rule in Ireland. Breaking with Rome, in 1541 he proclaimed himself King

of Ireland by right of conquest rather than by papal decree. To convince those troublesome Irish and their Anglo-Irish cohorts of the legitimacy of his claim, he dubbed all opposition open rebellion against "their" king and set about driving rebel leaders from their lands, so that he might grant the properties to his loyal followers, be they English or Irish.

Enter religion on the scene in full battle array. By the time Elizabeth became queen, the Reformation was firmly entrenched in England and the staunchly Catholic Irish found themselves fighting for their religion with even more fervor than they had fought for their lands. The great chieftains led uprising after uprising and, when English forces proved too great, appealed to Spain for help in 1601 to make a decisive stand at Kinsale, in County Cork. The Spanish arrived and joined Irish forces to occupy the town, which was quickly surrounded by English troops. From up north, however, Irish chieftains O'Neill and O'Donnell mounted an epic winter march to come upon the British from behind. Hopes were high for an Irish victory, but it just wasn't in the cards.

As luck would have it, a drunken Irish soldier wandered into English hands and spilled the whole plan, enabling the English to win the day and send the brightest and best of the native chieftains into hiding, their lands in Ulster now confiscated *in toto* by the Crown and resettled by loyal—and Protestant— English and Scots. In 1608 the surviving Irish chieftains met in Rathmullen, County Donegal, and decided to set sail for the Continent as a body, vowing to return to fight another day—a vow never fulfilled. That "Flight of the Earls" marked the end of any effective organized resistance to English rule for generations.

Organized or not, the ornery Irish continued to harass the British with bloody attacks, always followed by even bloodier reprisals. Finally, in 1641, they mounted a long-planned offensive to retake the lands of Ulster, and thus brought down on the land one of the bloodiest episodes in Irish history, one mirrored across its landscape even today.

TO HELL OR CONNAUGHT: By 1649 Irish incursions into Ulster and the massacre of hundreds of its Protestant settlers had so ravaged the land that Puritan general Oliver Cromwell arrived in force to squelch the rebellious Irish once and for all. Driven by religious fervor as well as political motives, Cromwell embarked on a campaign of devastation kicked off by the brutal slaying of more than 30,000 Irish men, women, and children at Drogheda.

From there, his trail of blood and destruction led to Wexford and thence across the country, leaving in its wake thousands dead, churches and castles and homes demolished, forests burned, and a degree of horror greater than any the Irish had known. Irish who escaped with their lives were shipped in the hundreds to work as slave labor on English plantations in the Sugar Islands—banishment to a virtual "hell"—or driven to the bleak, stone-strewn hills of Connaught.

To his loyal soldiers and their commanding officers, Cromwell awarded vast estates in the choice and fertile counties of the country. In the end, less than one-ninth of Irish soil remained in the hands of natives.

KING BILLY, THE TREATY OF LIMERICK, AND THE PENAL LAWS: Irish spirits rose once more when a Catholic, James II, ascended to the English throne in 1688, and when he was deposed by supporters of William of Orange—King Billy—and fled to Ireland in 1689, they took up arms in his defense. In Ulster, Londonderry and Enniskillen became the major refuge for Protestants loyal to William, and the stout walls of Londonderry held against a 105-day siege by Jacobite forces. King Billy himself arrived in 1690 to lead his army to a resounding victory in the Battle of the Boyne, after which James once more took flight, leaving his Irish supporters to their own devices. Hoping to get the best possible terms of surrender, the Irish fought on under the leadership of Patrick Sarsfield until October of 1691, when they signed the Treaty of Limerick, which allegedly allowed them to retain both their religion and their land. Parliament, however, had no intention of sanctioning any sort of threat to the Protestant Ascendancy, and refused to ratify the treaty, instituting instead a series of measures so oppressive they became known as the Penal Laws.

Catholics, under the Penal Laws, were stripped of all civil and political rights —they could neither vote nor hold office; enter any of the professions, especially law; educate their children; own a horse valued at more than £5; bear arms; or (the origin of Ireland's tiny farmlands of today) will their land to only one son, being required instead to divide it into smaller plots for all male heirs. Forced to work the estates of absentee English landlords, Irish farmers paid enormous rents for the privilege of throwing up rude huts and using a small plot of ground to raise the potatoes that kept their families from starving.

It was a sorry state of affairs for the proud descendants of heroic kings and chieftains, and it was to last a full century.

UNITED IRISHMEN, UNION, FAMINE, AND EMIGRATION: In the
time-honored pattern of earlier Irish rulers, Anglo-Irish Protestants gradually came to feel a stronger allegiance to Ireland than to England, and in the late 1700s Henry Grattan led a Protestant Patriot party in demanding greater independence. What they got was a token Irish Parliament in 1782, which sat in Dublin but was controlled from London. Things seemed to be taking an upward turn as Penal Laws were gradually relaxed and trade began to flourish. Dublin's streets blossomed with the Georgian mansions and gracious squares that are still its most distinctive features.

Like a little learning, a little independence turned out to be a dangerous thing. With a newly independent France as a model, a group of Irishmen led by Protestant Wolfe Tone formed the Society of United Irishmen in 1791 to work for the establishment of a totally independent Irish republic. Enlisting military aid from France, Tone led a full-fledged insurrection in 1798 that ended in pure disaster on the battlefield and even greater disaster in the halls of the English Parliament.

British leaders now had the ammunition they needed to insist on ending any semblance of Irish parliamentary rule. Even so, it took considerable bribery, promises of seats in the London Parliament, and threats to get the Dublin MPs to vote the end of their supposed legislative power. But in 1800 the Act of Union passed and Ireland became an extension of British soil. That should have put Ireland in her proper place—again—but in 1803 the Irish were at it once more, and with Robert Emmet urging them on, they launched yet another uprising. It was the same old story, however, and ended with Emmet gallantly declaring from the gallows, "When my country takes her place among the nations of the earth, then, and not till then, let my epitaph be written."

In the 1820s a young Catholic named Daniel O'Connell started to make noises about Catholic Emancipation—a total repeal of the Penal Laws and the restoration of all Catholic civil rights. Elected to Parliament in 1828, he accomplished that goal the following year and embarked on a campaign for repeal of the Act of Union. About all he got for his efforts in that direction was the affectionate title of "The Liberator," and just as members of the Young Ireland movement were beginning to be heard on that score, tragedy struck and the Irish goal became one of simple survival.

It was in 1846 that a disastrous potato blight spread throughout the country, destroying the one food crop of most Irish families. Until 1849, crop after crop failed and a population of nearly nine million was reduced to a little over six million. Hundreds of thousands died of pure starvation—it became a common sight to see roadside ditches filled with bodies of famine victims who had nowhere else to die simply because they had been evicted from their wretched homes by landlords who continued to demand exorbitant rents from tenants who no longer had the means to pay them. Well over a million turned their backs on Ireland and set out for the United States and Canada on ships so overcrowded and filthy and disease-infested they were little more than floating coffins.

THE LAND LEAGUE, HOME RULE, AND SINN FEIN: By 1879 the Irish tenant farmers were so fed up with the oppressive rentals that some had literally paid with their lives during the four years of famine that they eagerly joined with Charles Stewart Parnell and Michael Davitt in forming a union known as the Land League. They enlisted farmers around the country to strike back at any landlord who evicted tenants by the simple, but deadly effective, method of "boycott" (so called for the Captain Boycott against whom it was used for the first time). With their families shunned by an entire community and services of any kind cut off, landlords began to rethink their policies and to reduce rents to a fair level, grant some degree of guaranteed occupancy to tenants, and eventually, to allow tenants to purchase their own acreage.

Far from being grateful for such small favors, the Irish continued to fan the flame of their inherited zeal for freedom from English rule. Parnell for years led an energetic campaign for Home Rule which would grant limited independence, but it wasn't until the eve of World War I that such a measure was adopted by the British. Even then, there was strong and vocal opposition by loyal Unionists in Ulster, Protestants all, who were determined to keep Ireland a part of the mother country. Outnumbered by Catholics, they feared Home Rule would become Rome Rule, and the Ulster Volunteers were formed to put up armed resistance against the equally determined Irish Republican Army, the military arm of Sinn Fein, a republican political party whose name is pronounced "shin fain" and means "ourselves alone." With the British army already firmly ensconced, the country fairly bristled with arms when everything was put on "hold" by the urgency of world conflict.

"A TERRIBLE BEAUTY" IS BORN: To the astonishment of almost everyone—most of all, the Irish people—Easter Monday of 1916 put the whole question of Irish independence right back on a *very* hot front burner. Leading a scruffy, badly outfitted, and poorly armed little band of fewer than 200 patriots, Patrick Pearse and James Connolly marched up Dublin's O'Connell Street to the General Post Office and proceeded to occupy it in the name of a Provisional Government. Standing between the front pillars of the impressive building, Pearse read in stirring tones "The Proclamation of the Irish Republic to the People of Ireland." Behind him, his valiant little "army" prepared to dig in and hold their position as long as was humanly possible. Hopelessly small contingents were stationed at St. Stephen's Green and one or two other strategic points.

For six days following Pearse's proclamation, the Post Office stood embattled under the ancient symbol of Ireland (a golden harp on a pennant of brilliant green) and the Sinn Fein banner of green, white, and orange. The rebels numbered only about 1,000 all told, and their remarkable courage as they faced overwhelming British military might is the stuff of heroic legends—and, indeed, the very stuff of which Ireland's history is made!

It was a bloody, but unbowed, band that finally surrendered and was marched back down O'Connell Street to a future of prison or execution. Dubliners, many of them uncertain of where their loyalties lay, watched and waited to learn their fate. When Pearse, Connolly, and 14 others were executed by a firing squad and hundreds of others were imprisoned or exiled, Irish loyalties united behind their new Republic and world opinion stood solidly behind the ideal of Irish independence.

It was at that moment—as the executioners' gunsmoke cleared in Kilmainham Jail's yard—that Yeats was to proclaim "A terrible beauty was born."

In the years between 1916 and 1921 Britain tried every means at her disposal—including sending the ruthless Black and Tan mercenaries to terrorize the citizenry as well as rebels—to quell the rebellion, which continued to rumble even in defeat. In 1919, when Sinn Fein won a huge majority of parliamentary seats, they refused to go to London, but set up the National Parliament of Ireland in Dublin, which they christened the Dail (pronounced "dawl" and meaning "meeting"). From then on, guerrilla warfare raged, replete with atrocities, ambush tactics, and assassinations. After two years of bitter bloodshed, a truce was finally called and negotiations began which ended in December of 1921 with the signing of the Anglo-Irish Treaty that named 26 counties as the Irish Free State. Still within the British Empire, it was to be self-governing in the same manner as Canada and other British dominions. Six counties in Ulster would remain—as they wished—an integral part of Great Britain and be ruled from London.

A Free State under the treaty terms was not, however, what many Irish believed they had been fighting for, and civil war raged until 1923. Eamon de Valera, at the head of the I.R.A., stood solidly against William Cosgrave's pro-treaty forces in the conviction that only a united Ireland which included all 32 counties was acceptable. Cosgrave and the newly formed government felt that the treaty terms were preferable to continued war with Britain and that in time the six counties of Northern Ireland would join the other 26 by constitutional means. That question still throws its divisive shadow over Ireland today.

Fighting between the two factions was made more bitter because it often pitted brother against brother and there was wholesale destruction of property. As it became clear that the Dublin government would endure, de Valera threw in the towel militarily and in three years' time had formed the Fianna Fail ("feena foil") party. When that party took office in 1932 the oath of allegiance to the British Crown was finally abolished, and in 1948 Great Britain formally declared Ireland outside the Commonwealth when a coalition government headed by John A. Costello declared that "the description of the State shall be the Republic of Ireland."

ONWARD AND UPWARD: Since the proud day it became truly independent, Ireland has set about catching up with the progress so long held at bay by her fight to become her own mistress. Efforts to develop Irish industry resulted in state companies such as Bord na Mona building a thriving business from one of the country's greatest natural resources, peat (or turf). Aer Lingus, the national airline, was established, and the Shannon Free Airport Development Company has developed one of the world's leading airports along with an industrial complex that attracts companies from all over the world. The Industrial Development Authority has assisted firms from the United States, Germany, Japan, Great Britain, and a score of other countries in setting up factories and processing plants (most of them remarkably *clean* industries) and providing employment opportunities for a new generation.

Along with all these developments, there have also been some interesting changes in demographics. In 1926, still feeling the decimation of its population by starvation and emigration that spanned a century following the famine of the 1840s, Ireland counted only 2.972 million inhabitants in its first official census. The vast majority lived in rural areas and looked to farming for a living.

A decline in population continued as recently as 1961, when the figures showed 2.818 million. Every census since then, however, showed a slight increase, with a 2.2% jump in the short period of 1979–1981. The 1981 report showed a population of 3.443 million and a shift in distribution. For example, Ireland now has one of Europe's youngest populations, with more than one-half under the age of 21, although the ranks of the young have been considerably thinned by emigration since 1986, as severe economic conditions have sent Irish youth abroad in search of jobs. More and more, the Irish are moving to towns and cities—or, to be more precise, to the metropolitan suburbs, since most Irish still cling to the notion of a private house with its own garden. Back in 1966, urban and rural populations were just about even, but in 1981 some 1.915 million lived in urban areas compared to 1.529 million in rural localities.

Luckily for you and me, along with industry, successive Irish governments have recognized the potential for tourism in this gloriously beautiful land. And why not, since they've been hosts to "visitors" in one form or another since the dawn of history! Bord Fáilte (the "board of welcomes") has worked closely with hoteliers, bed-and-breakfast ladies, restaurateurs, and entertainment facilities to see that we're well taken care of. And they've wisely insisted that the *character* of the country is as much an attraction for us as are the natural beauties and ancient relics we come to see.

On the cultural scene, the lilting Gaelic language was reinstated as the official tongue, reclaiming an Irish identity very nearly lost during long years of suppression. Called "Irish" to distinguish it from other forms of Gaelic, the language takes first place on street signs, city and town name signs, and in governmental titles such as Taoiseach ("tee-shuck") for the prime minister or gardai ("guardee") for police or guards. Aer Lingus (Gaelic for "air fleet") welcomes you aboard in rhythmic Irish, and radio and television stations sign off in the native tongue. Every schoolchild is required to study Irish in an attempt to revive its day-to-day use, and although the vast majority now use English as their first tongue, there are some 40,000 Irish speakers who use English only occasionally. Most live in closely knit communities called the Gaeltacht ("Gwale-tack-ta"), often in rural, rather isolated locations in the west. Donegal, Dingle, and Connemara form the largest part of the Gaeltacht, where natives will readily converse with you in English, with asides in Irish to their friends and neighbors.

Irish arts—theater, literature, painting, music—have also seen a heartwarming revival, and people practicing ancient Irish crafts are now producing works of beauty and utility to rival any in the world.

On the political front, Ireland steadfastly held on to its neutrality during World War II, even in the face of tremendous pressures from both Britain and U.S. Nevertheless, hundreds of Irishmen volunteered in the armed forces of both countries. Since 1955 Ireland has been a member of the United Nations and has sent peace-keeping forces to Cyprus, the Congo, the Sinai Desert, and Lebanon. As long as Northern Ireland remains under British rule, however, no Irish government has authorized NATO membership, since NATO is pledged to guarantee the territorial integrity of its members. As a member of the European Economic Community, Ireland shares in the joys and woes of that controversial alliance. (If you want to get a good "crack," or conversation, going almost anywhere in Ireland, just bring up the subject of EEC membership—there are as many views on its results as there are Irish to discuss it!)

NORTHERN IRELAND: It's always a temptation to oversimplify the underlying reasons for the tensions that have troubled Northern Ireland since that 1921 treaty set it apart from the rest of the country.

Certainly, all that history we've just gone through is *really* at the root of things, for it created an environment in which injustices of the past live in the memories of a Catholic minority who see themselves as victims of inequities of the present. Their strong yearning for a united Ireland that would improve their status takes the form of support for Irish nationalism. Protestants who now have centuries of family history firmly rooted in Ireland must contend with a status quo not of their making, yet one they are fearful of changing. Despite all this, the majority in each population segment live side by side, somewhat warily, but more interested in making a living and raising decent, law-abiding families than in having to profess loyalty to extremists on *either* side.

The tangled threads of political events in Northern Ireland over the years of its separation from the south weave a pattern almost too complex to follow. There was the Civil Rights movement that began in 1968, only to bog down as the current "troubles" erupted and the British army was called in to keep a peace that still eludes them. In 1973 hopes were raised when a Northern Ireland Assembly held out the promise of active participation in government by the minority, only to be dashed when it was violently opposed by extreme factions of both loyalists and nationalists. There was the Women's Peace Movement of 1976 which for a time looked as though it might bring an end to violence and let men of peace get on with a solution—and while it was useful to show the depth of revulsion on all sides for terrorism, it, too, bogged down and faded away. In 1974 there was an effort made to set up a power-sharing Executive, but it was too short-lived to make any headway. Today a Secretary of State for Northern Ireland is the chief administrator and reports directly to Parliament in London.

In May of 1984 a report was issued by the All Ireland Forum that seemed to hold out more real hope of an eventual solution than any other development thus far. The Forum consisted of leaders from political sectors both north and south of the border, and it met nearly 100 times over the course of a full year. Its final report contained detailed, well-thought-out discussions of several acceptable compromises. In 1986 a highly controversial Anglo-Irish Agreement was signed, giving the Republic limited participation in Northern Ireland affairs, and only time will tell if this, too, will be but another step along the long road to a free and peaceful Ireland.

In 1988 more frequent outbreaks of violence grabbed international headlines. And Americans all too often cut out of their Irish itinerary a corner of the country that has a unique dimension to add to any Irish visit. Travel north of the border presents no real problem for the tourist despite recent events, and I highly recommend that you read more about it in the chapter titled "Introducing Northern Ireland" before you make that same mistake.

3. IRELAND WITH THIS BOOK

An Irish friend once said to me, "Whenever I am with visitors, I always wish there were some way to show them all the nooks and crannies of Ireland as well as the highlights tourists usually see." It was a wistful, heartfelt wish, and one I heartily echo.

Ireland's highlights are, of course, numerous and spectacular. And because you and I are limited by the amount of time we have to travel, it is simply not possible to take in all of the country's charms on one trip. Add to that limitation the fact that even those who live there are constantly stumbling onto new nooks and crannies, and my friend's wish becomes even more wistful.

What this book will do is point you to those highlights you just must *not* miss and throw in a nook or cranny wherever I have found one. It's a safe bet, however, that you'll come home with fond memories of more than a few you've found on your own—it's the *unexpected* that will charm you most and send you home warbling "Danny Boy" in the closest thing you can manage to a brogue!

IRELAND:
PROVINCES AND COUNTIES

IRELAND REGION BY REGION: Historically, Ireland is divided into the four provinces of Leinster, Munster, Connaught, and Ulster. For the modern-day traveler, however, its geography falls naturally into somewhat different divisions. Bord Fáilté recognizes the following regions, and to make it as easy as possible to correlate what you'll find in this book and Bord Fáilté information you'll pick up on your travels, I have followed their lead. The map on pages 22 and 23 gives you an overview, and set out below are the regions and the counties encompassed by each.

Eastern	Southeast	Southern
Dublin	Waterford	Cork
Wicklow	Wexford	Kerry
Louth	South Tipperary	
Kildare	Kilkenny	
Meath	Carlow	

Shannonside	Western	Northwestern
Clare	Galway	Donegal
Limerick	Mayo	Sligo
North Tipperary		Leitrim

Midland	Northern Ireland
Cavan	Antrim
Laois	Derry
Longford	Tyrone
Monaghan	Fermanagh
Offaly	Armagh
Roscommon	Down
Westmeath	

Rather than follow a predetermined itinerary, this book is designed to give you the highlights (and *my* nooks and crannies) of each region, county by county. In Chapter II there are several suggested itineraries, including the two-week circular route favored by many first-time visitors to Ireland. It's a good way to catch a glimpse of highlights, but it doesn't allow very much time for the unexpected. So if you should find yourself bewitched by a particular area—or if you're going to be based in one town with Aunt Mary and Uncle Sean—you'll find in-depth information about the close environs and those within easy day-trip range. Add a few overnight trips, use day-trip itineraries from your overnight destination, and without dashing around the country at breakneck speed, you'll get in an amazing amount of sightseeing—a travel method, incidentally, that I highly recommend even if you're *not* staying with Aunt Mary and Uncle Sean!

TOWNS, VILLAGES, AND CITIES: No matter how you get around Ireland, take time to savor at least some of those small villages and towns you'll pass through. Almost all have a square, or mall, or green around which shops and homes cluster. Although not as numerous as they once were, you'll still find some wonderful examples of hand-carved storefronts with ornately painted signs. Many towns have canals or rivers flowing right through the center of town, crossed by lovely old stone bridges. Still others boast sturdy old towers or town halls or gracefully spired churches. Look for the local courthouse, market house, or tholsel, many of which are early-19th-century structures of fine cut limestone.

You might make it a point to park the car in one town each day to walk the streets, call into a pub, or purchase fresh-baked bread from the local baker and a hunk of good Irish cheese from the local grocer for picnic makings to be rounded out by a bottled lager or stout from the pub. You won't be charged for the friendly conversation that comes with each purchase, and you'll pick up a wealth of information about the locality.

What I'm trying to say is that Irish towns and villages, as well as cities, are for *loitering,* not rushing through!

One of the first things you'll notice in Ireland is that each village, town, and city name is signposted in both its Anglicized spelling and the original Gaelic. As noted earlier, the Irish language is not an easy one to get your tongue around, and since a fractured-Irish pronunciation is both awkward and embarrassing, I'll give you the correct pronunciation along with the original meaning of major place names. That way, when you're down in County Cork, you'll never once say "You-gal" for a town whose name is spelled Youghal, pronounced "Yawl," and means "Yew Wood."

All place names, of course, have some meaning, and in Ireland they often refer to a natural or man-made feature of the locality or to clans and leading families. Some of the Gaelic words used in place names that will tip you off as to the history, setting, or appearance of the village or town are:

Gaelic Word	Meaning
ard	height
áugh *(au)*	ford
bally or baile *(balla)*	town, place, or farm
béarna *(barna)*	gap between hills
boher *(bo-her)*	road
cashel	castle
carn	heap of stones
carraig or corrig	boulder
cahir *(care)*	castle
cill	church
cnoc or knock	hill
dun *(done)*	fort or protected house
inis, inch, or ennis	island or riverside field
lios *(lis)* or lis	circular fort
moin or moyne *(mine)*	bog
rath	circular fort
slieve *(sleeve)*	hill
teach *(chock)*	house
tobar or tubber	well
trá or tray	beach
tulach, tullow, or tully	small hill
uibh *(iv)*	family or tribe
uisce *(ish-ca),* isk, or isky	water

ABOUT THOSE RUINS: While we're on the subject of words and their meanings, here are a few terms you'll run across in descriptions of many archeological sites, monuments, and ruins in Ireland, along with the briefest of definitions.

Dolmens: These consist of standing stones (usually three) surmounted by a massive capstone. They are actually one of the earliest forms of megalithic tombs and probably date from 3000 to 2000 B.C.

Passage graves: Also a legacy of Ireland's Neolithic forebears, these are great stone tombs entered through a long passageway (the one at Newgrange is 65 feet in length), with a large burial chamber. These were probably built for persons of importance, although no one knows for certain exactly who was entombed in them.

Court cairns: Found mostly in the northern regions of Ireland, these are the earliest megalithic chambered tombs, and their name derives from the fact that there is generally a covered gallery for burial, with one or more unroofed courts, or forecourts, for rituals.

Stone circles: It is thought that these early Bronze Age relics served as temples of worship, as did large earthen circles.

Ring forts: Essentially dwelling places, these circular enclosures sometimes were built within earthen walls, sometimes behind stone walls. Within those walls was some manner of house—wood, wattle-and-daub, or stone—few of which have survived, although some 30,000 rings are spotted all over Ireland and called by a number of names—rath, lios, dun, caher, and cashel. The large number still to be found is due to the fact that this form of protected dwelling originated as early as the Bronze Age and continued to be built right up until the Norman invasion.

Crannogs: These artificial islands were constructed in lakes or marshy places, and have even earlier origins than the ring forts. Look for them in the midland counties and County Clare.

Clochans ("beehives"): These remarkable stone buildings of corbel construction were erected without mortar as tiny oratories, mostly in western Ireland where wood was not a readily available building material. Through the centuries, those that have survived have remained perfectly waterproof, and they are considered outstanding examples of early construction expertise.

4. THE BASICS OF BUDGETING

I touched on the most fundamental "basic" for budgeting in the very beginning of this book (see Preface, "About This Book"), that is, a place to lay your head at night. Now, let's look a little closer at the subject. No moaning or groaning, please—you're definitely *not* in for a lecture here on pulling in your belt or sacrificing comfort in any way, shape, or fashion. On the contrary, budgeting in Ireland, more than any other country I've encountered in my travels, turns out to be fun, and lots of it! It's all a matter of knowing what's available, what *you* are looking for, and how to go about finding it.

Take, first of all, that roof over your head. If you're *really* counting pence, Ireland will put you up in hostels that in some cases outshine some of the classiest hotels in the country. There's one in Killarney, for instance, that is the sort of magnificent old country mansion most travelers only glimpse from afar, wishing vainly they could step inside for a look at how the Ascendancy lived in those huge piles of stone. As a hosteler, *you'll* be living there. Others, on a more "plain folks living" plane, provide all the necessaries, albeit sans the gigantic marble fireplaces and soaring ceilings of mansions like the one in Killarney.

Now, don't get me wrong—as magnificent as some are to behold, both inside and out, no hostel is going to give you the luxurious modern conveniences of a fancy hotel. But neither is any hostel going to have you roughing it in such spartan fashion that you'll be aching for a decent night's sleep. If you are willing to purchase real savings at the expense of a private room, you'll sleep in comfort in dormitory-like space. More hostel savings come from the fact that you can buy dinner at the local grocer's and prepare it in a communal kitchen. In Chapter I, I'll give you details on just what to expect in terms of accommodations and prices, but for now, suffice it to say that hosteling is a very pleasant, rock-bottom-priced way to base your budgeting.

Before leaving the subject, I must add that there are intangible benefits to traveling around Ireland via its hostels. You'll meet fellow budgeteers from around the world, all eager to compare experiences and pass along budget tips. One of the neatest Irish conversations I've ever had was with two young Australian girls who were hosteling around Ireland for the second time. Not only had they a load of money-saving advice to share, they had discovered more "nooks and crannies" leads than most of us could expect to encounter, thanks in large part to their fellow hostelers.

There's also another facet of hosteling well worth considering. By sleeping in the company of other penny-pinchers *most* of the time, you can use the money saved to live it up for the one or two truly "Big Splurges" that would not be possible if your funds had to be averaged out over the entire trip. A night, say, in Waterford Castle (not to be considered by most budgeteers) would certainly counterbalance any sense of deprivation brought on by a week of dormitory living.

For those of us whose budgets stretch to include a room of our own, however, Ireland's biggest bargain is its goodly supply of bed-and-breakfast homes (in town and country) and farmhouses. I simply cannot sing their praises enough! So addicted to them have I become that even if they *didn't* provide attractive, comfortable sleeping accommodations, I'd suffer a less-than-perfect bed just to indulge in the friendly family life so graciously shared in all. Now, that's a *personal* bias, and I know many, many travelers who could care less about meeting and getting to know an Irish family and insist (in all too many cases) on hotel amenities at budget prices—until, that is, they experience firsthand a couple of B&B overnights, after which wild horses couldn't drag them back to the hotel route, amenities or no amenities. And I hasten to say that you won't be asked to make that exchange of a good bed for friendly hospitality—at least, not in the B&Bs listed in this book.

Let me say, right up front, that you can forget about hotel amenities unless you're also willing to forget about the budget. No B&B *I* know of is going to have a telephone in your room or offer room service or—in many cases—give you your own private bathroom. No, if you are serious about budgeting, the cardinal rule is: *private baths are something you have at home, not when you're saving money on the road.* A sacrifice, you say? Well, let me ask you this: When was the last time you stayed in a friend's home and were given your own bathroom? Point made. Chances are 99 out of 100 that before you leave your first B&B, you'll know you've stayed with *friends,* shared bath and all!

Having said all that, I must confess that while researching this edition, I became aware of a very curious phenomenon: all around the country, I found B&B hostesses installing private toilets and shower stalls in guest rooms, all available on a first-come, first-served basis at no additional cost. I don't know if this is a trend or simply an extension of the very Irish wish to make guests as comfortable as possible (and every Irishman or Irishwoman knows without doubt that all Americans want a private bath!). Also, I must tell you that in many cases, you'll be charged an extra IR£1 ($1.60) per night for a private bath. And if private facilities are that important to you, you're bound to view that as a very minimal charge. However, if you're willing to share the bath down the hall in order to save the IR£1, but in your heart of hearts would prefer private facilities, it's worth asking when you book if the en suite bath costs extra.

Another budget-stretching device is to base yourself at one B&B or farmhouse for an entire week and take advantage of the half-board rate which includes bed, breakfast, and dinner each night at a good reduction. I've already mentioned

my own preference for settling in for a few days in one place rather than moving every night. Well, if you book in for a solid week in or near, say, Waterford, using that as a base to explore the eastern and southeastern regions, then book for another week in the west, you'll realize not only the traveling benefits I spoke of, but a much healthier budget as well.

The next "basic" when traveling is eating three squares a day. The first of those will be more than adequately taken care of in your B&B. An Irish breakfast is, simply put, overwhelming. If you're not a breakfast person at home, I'll wager that when in Ireland you won't be able to resist the repast spread before your eyes every morning. Coffee and toast only, you say? I *defy* you to pass up the juice, cereal, bacon (not your shriveled up, fried-to-a-crisp pork, but a meaty, succulent offering much like what we call Canadian bacon in the U.S.), sausage, broiled tomato, brown bread, and golden butter set before you in an Irish B&B! If, in addition, black pudding (I won't tell you what it's made of) appears on your plate, my best advice is to try it—you'll probably like it.

As for the remaining two meals of the day, there are two approaches. Traditionally, the Irish have always had their heartiest meal at midday. That's primarily because as an agricultural nation, those working in the fields felt the need for sustenance to see them through a long afternoon. Travelers could, by making lunch their main meal of the day, save considerably. That still holds true today—a full lunch will provide as much to eat as most dinners, at several punts less in cost. That's the first option.

However, as more and more Irish have become urbanized, eating habits have changed. And I, personally, welcome that change. I simply am not *ready* for a full meal at midday after that sumptuous breakfast. Indeed, there are days on end when breakfast and dinner constitute my full diet because I cannot accommodate more food. If that's not the case with you, however, just look for the nearest pub offering pub grub, relish hearty soup and a sandwich or salad plate (at a "peanuts" price), and save your main meal for late afternoon or the evening. Even better, stop in a town or village, chat with the local grocer as you shop for picnic makings, then head for the country and lunch under the trees or at the shore.

Another option is to choose high tea instead of a dinner menu. In days gone by, because of the national eating habits described above, high tea *was* the evening meal. It was, for all intents and purposes, a "mini-dinner" that would, to most of us, constitute a full meal, especially following an ample midday repast. Nowadays, however, high tea is a rather ambiguous term. I have had a high tea (at about IR£4—$6.50—less than a dinner menu) that was more nourishment than I could comfortably handle; and on the other side of the coin, I've had a high tea that consisted of one or two skimpy sandwiches, and maybe a sweet, that most certainly would not see me through the night. My best advice is, if your B&B or a local restaurant offers high tea, *ask* what it consists of. High tea can save you as much as 50% of your dinner costs, but you *must* know what "high tea" means to those offering it.

On a more positive note, however, you'll find restaurants listed in this book in every region that offer dinner menus for $12 or under that are full dinners. Most offer the special Tourist Menu, which in 1988 consisted of a three-course meal at either IR£5.60 ($9) or IR£7.50 ($12). Prices have not been set for 1989 as we go to press, but you may be sure they'll remain a bargain. For a complete listing of all restaurants offering these specials, pick up the "Dining in Ireland" booklet from any Bord Fáilte office.

As for transportation costs, there are several money-saving ways to get around, all spelled out in detail in Chapter II. Train and bus travel come cheap and will get you most places you want to go, although perhaps not at the exact time you want to go. Cycling is one of the cheapest and most popular ways to get around; shank's mare (hiking) is, it goes without saying, the least expensive; and hitchhiking is an accepted and time-honored mode of transportation (although it is prudent for female hitchhikers to travel in pairs). Using one, or a combination, of these methods will save pence that quickly add up to punts.

DROP A LINE: As is the practice with all Frommer guides, you are invited to participate in future editions. All the judgments, opinions, and comments in the text of this edition are based on personal inspections and experiences, except for those listed under the heading "Readers' Selections." Change is the very nature of the travel world, however: accommodations and restaurants appear and disappear; change managements, ownership, and chefs; improve or go to pot. Should you find any of these conditions, please do let me know about it.

Most of all, don't be shy about sharing with me any especially good discoveries of your own. Some of the best listings in this edition have come from Readers' Selections I have looked into.

You have my word that each and every letter will be read by me, personally, although I find it well nigh impossible to *answer* each and every one. Just write: Susan Poole, Prentice Hall Press, Gulf + Western Building, One Gulf + Western Plaza, New York, NY 10023. You can rest assured I'll be listening to what you have to say!

5. FROMMER'S™ DOLLARWISE® TRAVEL CLUB— HOW TO SAVE MONEY ON ALL YOUR TRAVELS

In this book we'll be looking at how to discover your value-for-money in Ireland, but there is a "device" for saving money and determining value on *all* your trips. It's the popular, international Frommer's Dollarwise Travel Club, now in its 28th successful year of operation. The club was formed at the urging of numerous readers of the $-A-Day and Dollarwise Guides, who felt that such an organization could provide continuing travel information and a sense of community to value-minded travelers in all parts of the world. And so it does!

In keeping with the budget concept, the annual membership fee is low and is immediately exceeded by the value of your benefits. Upon receipt of $18 (U.S. residents), or $20 U.S. by check drawn on a U.S. bank or via international postal money order in U.S. funds (Canadian, Mexican, and other foreign residents) to cover one year's membership, we will send all new members the following items.

(1) Any *two* of the following books

Please designate in your letter which two you wish to receive:

Frommer's™ $-A-Day® Guides
Europe on $30 a Day
Australia on $30 a Day
Eastern Europe on $25 a Day
England on $40 a Day
Greece (including Istanbul and Turkey's Aegean Coast) on $30 a Day
Hawaii on $50 a Day
India on $25 a Day
Ireland on $35 a Day
Israel on $30 & $35 d Day
Mexico (plus Belize and Guatemala) on $25 a Day
New York on $50 a Day
New Zealand on $40 a Day
Scandinavia on $60 a Day
Scotland and Wales on $40 a Day
South America on $30 a Day

Spain and Morocco (plus the Canary Is.) on $40 a Day
Turkey on $25 a Day
Washington, D.C., & Historic Virginia on $40 a Day
($-A-Day Guides document hundreds of budget accommodations and facilities, helping you get the most for your travel dollars.)

Frommer's™ Dollarwise® Guides

Australia (avail. July 1989)
Austria and Hungary
Belgium, Holland, & Luxembourg
Bermuda and The Bahamas
Brazil
Canada
Caribbean
Egypt
England and Scotland
France
Germany
Italy
Japan and Hong Kong
Portugal, Madeira, and the Azores
South Pacific
Switzerland and Liechtenstein
Alaska
California and Las Vegas
Florida
Mid-Atlantic States
New England
New York State
Northwest
Skiing USA—East
Skiing USA—West
Southeast and New Orleans
Southeast Asia (avail. July 1989)
Southwest
Texas
USA

(Dollarwise Guides discuss accommodations and facilities in all price ranges, with emphasis on the medium-priced.)

Frommer's™ Touring Guides

Australia
Egypt
Florence
London
Paris
Scotland
Thailand
Venice

(These new, color illustrated guides include walking tours, cultural and historic sites, and other vital travel information.)

Gault Millau

Chicago (avail. April 1989)
France (avail. July 1989)

Italy (avail. July 1989)
Los Angeles
New England (avail. April 1989)
New York
San Francisco
Washington, D.C.

(Irreverent, savvy, and comprehensive, each of these renowned guides candidly reviews over 1,000 restaurants, hotels, shops, nightspots, museums, and sights.)

Serious Shopper's Guides
Italy
London
Los Angeles
Paris

(Practical and comprehensive, each of these handsomely illustrated guides lists hundreds of stores, selling everything from antiques to wine, conveniently organized alphabetically by category.)

A Shopper's Guide to the Caribbean
(Two experienced Caribbean hands guide you through this shopper's paradise, offering witty insights and helpful tips on the wares and emporia of more than 25 islands.)

Beat the High Cost of Travel
(This practical guide details how to save money on absolutely all travel items—accommodations, transportation, dining, sightseeing, shopping, taxes, and more. Includes special budget information for seniors, students, singles, and families.)

Bed & Breakfast—North America
(This guide contains a directory of over 150 organizations that offer bed & breakfast referrals and reservations throughout North America. The scenic attractions, and major schools and universities near the homes of each are also listed.)

Dollarwise Cruises
(This complete guide covers all the basics of cruising—ports of call, costs, fly-cruise package bargains, cabin selection booking, embarkation and debarkation and describes in detail over 60 or so ships cruising the waters of Alaska, the Caribbean, Mexico, Hawaii, Panama, Canada, and the United States.)

Dollarwise Skiing Europe
(Describes top ski resorts in Austria, France, Italy, and Switzerland. Illustrated with maps of each resort area. Includes supplement on Argentinian resorts.)

Guide to Honeymoon Destinations
(A special guide for that most romantic trip of your life, with full details on planning and choosing the destination that will be just right in the U.S. [California, New England, Hawaii, Florida, New York, South Carolina, etc.], Canada, Mexico, and the Caribbean.)

Marilyn Wood's Wonderful Weekends
(This very selective guide covers the best mini-vacation destinations within a 200-mile radius of New York City. It describes special country inns and other accommodations, restaurants, picnic spots, sights, and activities—all the information needed for a two- or three-day stay.)

Manhattan's Outdoor Sculpture
(A total guide, fully illustrated with black-and-white photos, to more than 300 sculptures and monuments that grace Manhattan's plazas, parks, and other public spaces.)

Motorist's Phrase Book
(A practical phrase book in French, German, and Spanish designed specifically for the English-speaking motorist touring abroad.)

Paris Rendez-Vous
(An amusing and *au courant* guide to the best meeting places in Paris, organized for hour-to-hour use: from power breakfasts and fun brunches, through tea at four or cocktails at five, to romantic dinners and dancing 'til dawn.)

Swap and Go—Home Exchanging Made Easy
(Two veteran home exchangers explain in detail all the money-saving benefits of a home exchange, and then describe precisely how to do it. Also includes information on home rentals and many tips on low-cost travel.)

The Candy Apple: New York for Kids
(A spirited guide to the wonders of the Big Apple by a savvy New York grandmother with a kid's-eye view to fun. Indispensable for visitors and residents alike.)

The New World of Travel
(From America's #1 travel expert, Arthur Frommer, an annual sourcebook with the hottest news and latest trends that's guaranteed to change the way you travel —and save you hundreds of dollars. Jam-packed with alternative new modes of travel that will lead you to vacations that cater to the mind, the spirit, and a sense of thrift.)

Travel Diary and Record Book
(A 96-page diary for personal travel notes plus a section for such vital data as passport and traveler's check numbers, itinerary, postcard list, special people and places to visit, and a reference section with temperature and conversion charts, and world maps with distance zones.)

Where to Stay USA
(By the Council on International Educational Exchange, this extraordinary guide is the first to list accommodations in all 50 states that cost anywhere from $3 to $30 per night.)

(2) Any one of Frommer's™ City Guides

Amsterdam
Athens
Atlantic City and Cape May
Boston
Cancún, Cozumel, and the Yucatán
Dublin and Ireland
Hawaii
Las Vegas
Lisbon, Madrid, and Costa del Sol
London
Los Angeles
Mexico City and Acapulco

Minneapolis and St. Paul
Montréal and Québec City
New Orleans
New York
Orlando, Disney World, and EPCOT
Paris
Philadelphia
Rio
Rome
San Francisco
Santa Fe and Taos (avail. April 1989)
Sydney
Washington, D.C.
(Pocket-size guides to hotels, restaurants, nightspots, and sightseeing attractions covering all price ranges.)

(3) A one-year subscription to *The Dollarwise® Traveler*

This quarterly eight-page tabloid newspaper keeps you up to date on fastbreaking developments in low-cost travel in all parts of the world bringing you the latest money-saving information—the kind of information you'd have to pay $35 a year to obtain elsewhere. This consumer-conscious publication also features columns of special interest to readers: **Hospitality Exchange** (members all over the world who are willing to provide hospitality to other members as they pass through their home cities); **Share-a-Trip** (offers and requests from members for travel companions who can share costs and help avoid the burdensome single supplement); and **Readers Ask . . . Readers Reply** (travel questions from members to which other members reply with authentic firsthand information).

(4) Your personal membership card

Membership entitles you to purchase through the club all Frommer publications for a third to a half off their regular retail prices during the term of your membership.

So why not join this hardy band of international budgeteers and participate in its exchange of travel information and hospitality? Simply send your name and address, together with your annual membership fee of $18 (U.S. residents) or $20 U.S. (Canadian, Mexican, and other foreign residents), by check drawn on a U.S. bank or via international postal money order in U.S. funds to: Frommer's Dollarwise Travel Club, Inc., Gulf + Western Building, One Gulf + Western Plaza, New York, NY 10023. And please remember to specify which *two* of the books in section (1) and which *one* in section (2) you wish to receive in your initial package of members' benefits. Or, if you prefer, use the order form at the end of the book and enclose $18 or $20 in U.S. currency.

> Once you are a member, there is no obligation to buy additional books. No books will be mailed to you without your specific order.

CHAPTER I

IRELAND: THE PRACTICALITIES

□ □ □

This chapter may well contain the most important words between the book's covers. Not the most exciting, perhaps, but certainly careful reading of this part of your "homework" can make all the difference in whether you get back home bubbling over with happy memories unmarred by uninformed mistakes (budgetary *and* trip-planning) or slightly bewildered that you never *did* get to do and see the things you really wanted to.

We'll talk about details you should know *before you leave home* if your trip is to be a carefree one. It is absolutely essential that you know about such things as currency, the rate of exchange, and travel documents. And it is equally desirable that you be well informed on what to expect by way of accommodations, restaurants, shopping, sightseeing, and a host of other activities.

Since finances are the bottom line for any budget traveler, let's begin with an examination of Ireland's currency.

1. THE CURRENCY

The 1970s saw two significant changes in Irish currency. First, in 1971 the country went on the decimal system; that is, the Irish pound was divided into 100 pence. It was certainly a step toward simplification for those accustomed to such arithmetic, but even in 1989 you'll hear references in Ireland to the "old money" system of pounds, shillings, and "old pence." Since the Irish pound maintained parity with the pound sterling, English notes and coins were interchangeable with Irish money (although the reverse was never true and Irish currency was not accepted in England).

In 1979, however, the second currency change occurred when, as a member of the European Monetary System, the Irish government linked its monetary values to those of major EEC currencies and the Irish pound officially became the "punt." As a result, although English notes are now accepted on the same basis as any other foreign currency by many shops, restaurants, hotels, etc., life is simpler for the traveler if all transactions are in Irish punts (often still referred to as the "Irish pound").

For safety's sake, you'll want to carry most of your money in the form of traveler's checks, not in cash. In the last year or so, however, exchange rates of foreign currencies against the U.S. dollar have fluctuated more sharply than in the past, and you may want to consider this up-to-date recommendation by Deak International (formerly Deak-Perera), one of the leading currency-exchange companies on the international scene: If you know your travel dates several months in advance, keep a sharp eye on U.S./Irish exchange rates and purchase punts when the rate is favorable. While they don't advise converting more than one-third to one-half of your travel currency in advance, you can still realize a substantial increase in buying power if you take advantage of periods when the dollar is at its strongest. Needless to say, when you travel, you'll want to keep your traveler's checks separate from the record of their numbers so that any lost checks can be readily replaced.

One further tip: One of the most useful items on any international trip is the handy calculator currency converter sold by Deak International. It's credit-card size and you set the exchange rate just once—it will remain constant even when you push the "off" button. As the rates change, it's a simple matter to set in the new rate. The International Currency Converter is available at most Deak International offices (over 60 in the U.S. and Canada), or by mail or telephone from Deak International, 630 Fifth Ave., New York, NY 10019 (tel. 212/757-6915).

The **Irish punt** is divided into 100 pence, and coins come in denominations of ½ pence, 1 pence, 2 pence, 5 pence, 10 pence, 20 pence, and 50 pence. All banks make exchanges on the basis of daily quotations, and it is wise to change your money always at a bank or an American Express office. It is true that some of the larger shops and hotels also work on daily quotations, but many more simply take a weekly average when figuring exchange rates, which can sometimes cost you more when changing notes. Bear in mind, too, that *you'll get a better rate with traveler's checks than with cash.*

The conversion chart below is based on an exchange rate of IR£1 = $1.60, the rate in effect at press time. Fluctuations have been almost daily in recent months, however, and these figures should be taken only as a guide. *Be sure to check with a bank at the time you travel for the current rate.*

IR£	U.S. $	IR£	U.S. $
1p	.02	£6	9.60
5p	.08	£7	11.20
10p	.16	£8	12.80
25p	.40	£9	14.40
50p	.80	£10	16.00
75p	1.20	£12.50	20.00
£1	1.60	£15	24.00
£2	3.20	£17.50	28.00
£2.50	4.00	£20	32.00
£3	4.80	£22.50	36.00
£4	6.40	£25	40.00
£5	8.00	£30	48.00

OTHER FROMMER TRAVEL GUIDES: *Frommer's Ireland on $35 a Day* complements other $-A-Day and Dollarwise Guides dealing with individual countries and areas in Europe: *Europe on $30 a Day; Eastern Europe on $25 a Day; England on $40 a Day; Greece on $30 a Day; Scandinavia on $60 a Day; Scotland and Wales on $40 a Day; Spain & Morocco on $40 a Day; Dollarwise Austria & Hungary; Dollarwise Belgium, Holland, & Luxembourg; Dollarwise England & Scotland; Dollarwise France; Dollarwise Germany; Dollarwise Italy; Dollarwise Portugal, Madeira, & the Azores; Dollarwise Switzerland & Liechtenstein.*

The Frommer series also boasts City Guides to several European destinations: *Frommer's Amsterdam; Frommer's Athens; Frommer's Dublin & Ireland; Frommer's Lisbon, Madrid, & Costa del Sol; Frommer's London; Frommer's Paris;* and *Frommer's Rome.*

There are two additional Frommer guides that will make traveling less expensive and more rewarding: *Beat the High Cost of Travel* provides practical strategies and useful tips to cut your travel costs; and *The New World of Travel* gives you the inside information and innovative ideas of America's travel expert, Arthur Frommer.

Frommer travel guides can be obtained at most bookstores, or by mailing the appropriate amount (turn to the last few pages of this guide) to Frommer Books, Prentice Hall Trade Division, One Gulf + Western Plaza, New York, NY 10023.

2. PREPARING FOR YOUR TRIP

Now, down to the nitty-gritty. There are the things you *must* do ahead, such as arming yourself with the necessary documents and wardrobe, and the things you will *want* to know and do in order to get every last bit of enjoyment from your trip.

TRAVEL DOCUMENTS: All that United States citizens need to travel in Ireland is a valid passport. It is no longer necessary even to show proof of smallpox vaccination when returning to this country. If you're a British citizen, you can travel freely in Ireland without a passport, but I'd strongly advise bringing it along if you have one, since on some occasions it may be the only acceptable form of identification (for picking up money orders sent from abroad, etc.). If you're a citizen of any other country, be sure to check with the Irish Embassy in your area as to what additional documents you may need.

WHAT CLOTHES TO BRING: You can really put off the final decision on what to pack until you have pretty firmly in mind just what sort of Irish holiday you plan on, but there is one item that is an absolute *must,* no matter what time of year you come or what you plan on doing. You guessed it, it's a raincoat.

Ireland's capricious weather can—and often does—skip from a drizzly morning to a sparkling, sunny afternoon to evening showers all in the space of one day. Mind you, the rain truly *is* a soft rain and you'll seldom, if ever, encounter a slashing, unfriendly onslaught of the sort that often attacks you here in the U.S. However, soft or not, Irish rain can be as *wet* as any other—and more unexpected than most. Also, I find that a lightweight raincoat comes in handy not only to keep dry, but as a wrap on chilly spring or fall evenings, as well.

As for the rest of your packing, keep in mind that Ireland is basically a very *casual* country. Even if you're planning to spend most of your time traipsing around the countryside, but refuse to leave the country without at least one night of Dublin theater or cabaret, you won't need to bring along a separate evening wardrobe. Women will find that a semi-dressy blouse to go with the same pants that traveled quite comfortably around the Ring of Kerry will see them through almost any Dublin evening. Personally, I like to take along an "old-faithful" long skirt for any unexpected invitation to a more formal function, but a simple skirt and dressy top does just as well. For men, a sports jacket and a tie will serve for any "dressy" occasion in the city. There are a few "Big Splurge" restaurants you may want to budget for in which you'll also be more comfortable with this type of attire.

There's just one exception to the above, however, and it probably goes without saying. I'll say it anyway: even though almost anything goes for after-dark Dublin, the theater, a dinner cabaret, or a posh restaurant are definitely *not* places for jeans! So, if you're a jeans-and-T-shirt traveler, stick in one outfit for your big-city night out.

One word of caution: All of the above holds true for any Irish holiday unless you plan to take in Dublin's swank Horse Show Week or Wexford's Opera Festival. In that case, women will want to have along a cocktail dress and appropriate shoes for the round of parties and receptions that are so much a part of those scenes. And their male escorts will be more comfortable with a dark suit for those occasions.

For traveling around the rest of the country, stick to every veteran traveler's tried-and-true formula of packing sensibly and *light*. No matter how much you'd love to take along that smashing pure cotton outfit or linen jacket, if it won't drip-dry or must be ironed every time you unpack, *leave it at home*. Interchangeable tops and bottoms (pants or skirts, depending on your personal preference—either is perfectly acceptable these days in Ireland) will lighten your load.

You may want to put in a lightweight sweater or shawl, since nights can sometimes be cool even in summer months, although my trusty raincoat usually sees me through and leaves room for another shirt or two in the suitcase. Remember, too, that unless you're steel-willed enough to resist those gorgeous Irish hand-knit sweaters, you'll no doubt acquire one during your travels, and it might as well begin its long years of service right on its own home turf.

You may or may not want to include a dressing gown for those trips down the hall to your B&B bathroom—again, if space is at a premium, I often use that same trusty old raincoat. However, if there's room in the suitcase, the robe goes in.

The mix-and-match principle applies to shoes as well as other clothing. Now, I'm not suggesting that your stout walking shoes will go waltzing out to dinner or the theater, but sandals or pumps that match a dressy top as well as a sports outfit do double duty easily. One more word about shoes: Stick in one pair more than you think you'll need. No, I'm not violating that pack-light principle, I'm just advising you to be practical. Those unexpected showers can leave your feet pretty soggy, and it's best to have along a spare pair. An inexpensive can of waterproofing spray to treat your shoes before leaving home is a good investment.

One of the most awkward items to pack is always my toiletries case, and I've learned to carry along only an initial supply of such things as toothpaste, shampoo, etc., and buy replacements as I go along. Ireland's pharmacies and department stores are well stocked with many of the same brands you'll be used to at home. As for medications, in addition to your anticipated needs, it's a good idea to bring along prescriptions (for eyeglasses, as well) from your local doctor just in case you need refills.

Far be it from me to set down a strict "how to pack" formula, but I do have some suggestions for a method that I've evolved over the years that works pretty well. First of all, the pack-light theme begins with my suitcase. A sturdy duffle bag or one of the marvelous lightweight (and flexible) nylon bags now on the market adds almost no weight and seems to have endless space in which to fit one more item. Zippers are all-important with this kind of luggage, so be sure you conduct a careful inspection before leaving home.

Bulky items like shoes or hairdryers or the toiletries case go in first and provide a firm bottom layer. Underwear and T-shirts go in next, followed by layers of blouses, shirts, trousers, and skirts. A commodious shoulder bag carries the items I'll need en route and traveling around the country (and I find it handy to stick in a traveling toothbrush and small tube of toothpaste for those times it's inconvenient to go scrounging around the suitcase).

There's one more thing I never leave home without—an extra nylon bag that folds into a tiny envelope cover. That's for all the things that I inevitably pick up along the way and for those things that just won't go back into their original place in the bag I brought over. I pack that at home simply because I happen to have one that has seen yeoman's service, but if you don't already have one, you can easily pick up an inexpensive nylon duffle bag or folding bag in one of the department stores in the larger cities of Ireland. Just thought I'd warn you that you'll probably be needing one.

TOURIST INFORMATION: The native hospitality of the Irish begins long before you embark on your visit to their shores, and few countries send you off as well prepared as Ireland. The friendly folk at any branch of the Irish Tourist Board (Bord Fáilté, in Ireland) take their literal name, Board of Welcomes, quite seriously. They're an official government agency that somehow seems to escape the impersonal, don't-care attitude that so often pervades bureaucratic institutions. My best advice (even if you're in the beginning stages of just *thinking* about an Irish holiday) is to hie yourself down to the ITB office (or contact them by mail or telephone) and plug in to one of the most helpful organizations in the ranks of international tourism.

On this side of the Atlantic, they'll supply you with literature to help with your initial planning, answer any questions that may come up, advise you on tracing your Irish ancestry, arrange for you to meet Irish families, and generally see to it that you're off to a good start.

You'll find the **Irish Tourist Board** office located at this address in the United States: 757 Third Ave., New York, NY 10017 (tel. 212/418-0800).

There are also offices in Toronto, London, Paris, Frankfurt-am-Main, Amsterdam, Sydney, and Belfast.

Study carefully the following list of their informative publications to request either at the United States office or when you're in Ireland:

Ireland (holiday planner that incorporates a Traveler's Guide with specific information on vacationing in Ireland).

Official Accommodation Guide (a complete listing of approved accommodations in hotels, town and country homes, and farmhouses).

Town and Country Homes Association Guest Accommodation (listing, with photos, of association member homes—small charge).

Farm Holidays in Ireland (descriptions and photos of members of Farm Holidays Association—small charge).

Ireland—Self-Catering (holidays in cottages, castles, houses, bungalows, chalets, flats, and apartments—with photos).

Be Our Guest (illustrated hotel and guesthouse guide).

Dining in Ireland (listings of all categories of restaurants).

Map of Ireland (detailed road map with scenic routes outlined—indispensable, even if you're not driving!).

Ireland's Heritage (castles, houses, and gardens open to the public).

Calendar of Events (dates and venues of happenings around the country all through the year).

That list is by no means complete. If you don't see a publication for your special interest, ask about Information Sheets on that aspect. Information Sheets are concise, detailed reports on everything from sailing schools to hiking to museums to folk music, and you'll almost certainly find that one has been issued on the subject in which you are interested.

Tourist Offices in Ireland

Irish Tourist Board headquarters are at Baggot Street Bridge, Dublin 2 (tel. 01/765871). The following regional offices are open year round, and they are supplemented by more than 50 others that are open only during summer months:

Athlone: 17 Church St. (tel. 0902/72866).
Cork: Tourist House, Grand Parade (tel. 021/273251; Telex 76131).
Dublin: 14 Upper O'Connell St., Dublin 1 (tel. 01/747733; Telex 32462).
Dublin Airport (tel. 01/376387 or 375533; Telex 32491).
Dundalk: Market Square (tel. 042/35484).
Dun Laoghaire: St. Michael's Wharf (tel. 01/806984 to 806986).
Galway: Aras Failte, Eyre Square (tel. 091/63081; Telex 50170).
Killarney: Town Hall (tel. 064/31633; Telex 73952).
Letterkenny: Derry Road (tel. 074/21160; Telex 42049).
Limerick: The Granary, Michael Street (tel. 061/317522; Telex 26904).
Mullingar: Dublin Road (tel. 044/48650; Telex 46003).
Shannon Airport (tel. 061/61664).
Skibbereen: Town Hall (tel. 028/21766; Telex 76067).
Sligo: Aras Reddan, Temple Street (tel. 071/61201; Telex 24301).
Tralee: Aras Siamsa, Godfrey Place (tel. 066/21288; Telex 73125).
Waterford: 41 The Quay (tel. 051/75788; Telex 80713).
Westport: The Mall (tel. 098/25711; Telex 53846).
Wexford: Crescent Quay (tel. 053/23111).

Others, only open seasonally, are easily spotted if you look for the green "i" sign that is posted in such diverse locations as a pub or grocer's out in the boondocks or along the Quay in Waterford or in the handsome modern quarters at 14 Upper O'Connell St. in Dublin. Wherever you find that sign, rest assured there are friendly, knowledgeable people who seem to exist for no other reason than to point you to the accommodations, restaurants, sightseeing attractions, local pubs, or sporting events that will make your holiday a pleasant one.

Hours vary according to location and season, but you can count on year-round offices being staffed from 10 a.m. to 5 p.m. weekdays during winter months, with weekend and longer evening hours during the summer season.

Room Reservation Service

One of the most used of all Irish Tourist Board services is their accommodations-booking service. It allows a flexibility of movement that frees you and me to move about as our fancy dictates, secure in the knowledge that, having rambled far off our intended itinerary, we have only to call into the nearest ITB office when we're ready to move on and they'll happily telephone ahead for the next night's lodgings. Not only that, they'll stick to the room rate we specify without a grumble or groan (always provided, of course, that we ask for a *reason-*

able rate). I have yet to hear a tourist office person attempt to pressure anyone into opting for a higher-priced accommodation than the limit specified just because that limit may be in short supply. They'll phone around until they have you settled in at the price you want to pay.

If you stray so far from a set travel plan (the best thing I could hope for you in Ireland!) that you arrive in town with no place to lay your head that night, the local tourist office will perform the same service in their own locality.

In every case, you'll be asked to pay the telephone charges, plus a small service charge. Caution: If you're booking ahead, be sure to get to the tourist office in time to wait up to a half-hour for the office at your next stop to find your room and get back to the office making the request.

WHEN TO BOOK AHEAD: By now, you must know that Ireland invites a delightful, spur-of-the-moment travel plan. That, in my opinion, leads to gloriously unpredictable holidays and treasured memories. I am *not*, however, enamored of stumbling off a transatlantic plane, numb with jet lag and faced with the prospect of having to hunt for a room, even with the helpful ITB crew. Nor, having done it once or twice, am I inclined to hop behind the wheel of a car and head off into the country before my body adjusts to the time change or my mind is clear enough to cope with left-side-of-the-road driving. Even less desirable would be to arrive in the country, present myself to the nearest car-rental agency and find there's no car available! Or plan on seeing a play at the Abbey Theater and find it booked out for the only night I'm in Dublin.

To put it succinctly, there are some advance reservations that are absolutely vital to a happy holiday, even for the most haphazard traveler. If you're of a temperament that gets very, very nervous if you don't know where you'll be sleeping a night or two down the road, then prearranged reservations become a must. With all that in mind, may I suggest the following minimal advance bookings.

At the top of the list is your first night's accommodation. Whether you're flying into Shannon or Dublin, I strongly recommend that you plan to spend the first day and night right there. Jet lag (yes, Virginia, there *is* such a thing as genuine jet lag—it is *not* a question of mind over matter!) is one strong reason for that recommendation, but there are others.

In the case of Shannon, for example, far too many visitors rush right through the Limerick area and miss one of Ireland's richest sightseeing spots. But if you're booked into a B&B and can catch a few hours' sleep soon after you arrive, you'll be refreshed and ready for Bunratty's medieval banquet that night (also booked ahead), a perfect introduction to the country. Or you might want to while away the evening at Durty Nellie's or one of Limerick's other great pubs. The next day could see you on your way around the country after short detours by the Cliffs of Moher, just a short drive away, or some of Shannonside's other outstanding attractions. For Dublin arrivals, what better first night (after that catnap to get your body straightened out) than a cabaret or pub crawl.

You can book your first night's stay through **Central Reservations Service,** Dublin Tourism, 14 Upper O'Connell St., Dublin 1 (tel. 01/735209; Telex 32462), but only by charging to MasterCard or Visa four weeks in advance. Or you can write directly to one of the accommodations listed in this book. If you choose the latter, you'll save time by enclosing a deposit and an International Reply Coupon for postage. The same applies if you're especially anxious to stay at any of the accommodations listed in this book and you're certain of the dates for each—during summer months you could be disappointed otherwise.

Then there's the matter of a car rental. Ireland is a small country, with most of its visitors descending during summer months, and there simply is not an inexhaustible supply of automobiles. Especially if you plan to come during the high season, it is absolutely essential to book your car as far in advance as possible.

For more specialized holidays, such as horse caravans or cabin cruisers, it is even more important that you get your reservation in early. Reserve through travel agents or by writing the rental company direct at the addresses listed in Chapters II (cars and caravans) and III (cruising).

As for special events, such as a castle banquet, hotel cabaret, Dublin theater, etc., Irish Tourist Board offices can make those bookings for you, but it is much more direct to write to each separately, enclose the International Reply Coupon for postage and a deposit (or the full price), and ask for immediate confirmation. Tickets for major festivals—Dublin Theatre, Wexford Opera, and the Dublin Spring and Horse Shows—can be booked directly by using the addresses for each shown in this book.

As I said at the beginning of this section, *some* advance bookings just must be made. But I want to end this section by stressing again that if you schedule your Irish stay *too* rigidly, you'll miss half the fun of Ireland!

READ BEFORE YOU GO: In the introductory pages to this book, I have tried to give some indication of the uniqueness of the Irish people and the country in which they live. But the characters of both are best illuminated by native writers, those luminary figures who have cast a glow across the world's literary scene for centuries. Their names are legion, and I would not even *attempt* to give you a definitive list of writings that would lend the most insight and color to your Irish experience.

I have always found that reading is a very personal choice, but I would like to share with you a few of the writings that have been most meaningful to me, personally, as I have come to know Ireland and its people. Beyond that, I can only say that such reading has always enriched *any* travel for me, and I hope you will take the time—either before or after your visit to Ireland—to explore the Irish dimensions available only through the country's literature.

There are, of course, the greats: Synge, O'Casey, Joyce, *ad infinitum*. For me, to capture the sheer poetry of the country, almost anything by Yeats can be recommended; the gutsy, gusty irreverence of Brendan Behan (I have especially enjoyed *Brendan Behan's Island—an Irish Sketchbook*) brings a sense of poignant hilarity to the Irish scene that I've found nowhere else; James Plunket's *Strumpet City* paints a rich, full portrait of Dublin that encompasses that city's multilayered society in the years leading up to World War I; and John B. Keane's writings, be they essays or plays, bare the soul of the Irish countryman in an honest, telling, and affectionate manner that lends understanding and depth to many an Irish encounter.

Further, I have a recommendation you won't find listed anywhere under Ireland's great writers, but which represents some of my most enjoyable and instructive Irish reading. Walter Macken, a native of Galway, was only 51 when he died in 1967, leaving a trilogy of Irish historical novels which have quite literally brought the country's history alive for me through characters and events that throb with reality. *Seek the Fair Land* is set in 1649, the Cromwell era; *The Silent People* tells of the famine years and British oppression; and *The Scorching Wind* is a tale of Ireland's Civil War. You'll find them in most Irish bookshops and at Shannon and Dublin airports, and I urge you to read any or all of them for the simple pleasure of a good story well told, as well as for a sort of "instant history" lesson.

3. DISCOUNTS FOR STUDENTS

For students, Ireland has so much going for it that I sometimes think it should be a compulsory part of any first-rate school curriculum. First of all, as pointed out in the Introduction, with half its population aged 25 and under, it is truly a haven for the young (*Tir na nog*, the ancient Celts called their version of heaven, and the Gaelic name translates to "land of youth"). Sports, music, dancing, and a host of other activities are geared for the young and available wherever you go in the country.

Not only are recreational and leisure pursuits at your fingertips in Ireland, but the ancient tradition and reverence for learning continue to this day, with all sorts of interesting educational experiences available.

BEFORE YOU COME: Any student traveling to Ireland will be literally missing the boat without an **International Student Identity Card,** which opens doors to marvelous events and activities aimed only at students as well as substantial discounts on almost every facet of travel. You must, however, arm yourself with this valuable document *before you leave home.* The cost in 1989 is $10, and you can obtain your card through **CIEE** (the Council on International Educational Exchange), 205 E. 42nd St., New York, NY 10017 (tel. 212/661-1414). With the card in hand, you'll be entitled to participate in all the listings below, as well as many, many more happenings you'll discover once you arrive on Irish soil.

For anyone between the ages of 15 and 26, CIE's **Youth/Student Rambler Ticket** is a budget godsend. It allows you unlimited travel on bus and rail services, standard class, for a cost of $82 for eight days, $111 for 15 days, or $145 for 30 days. It must, however, be purchased *before* your arrival in Ireland, and is available through travel agents or from CIE Tours International, 122 E. 42nd St., New York, NY 10168 (tel. 212/972-5600).

You should also obtain, well in advance, the Irish Tourist Board publication, *Discover Young Ireland: A Guide to Learning and Leisure Opportunities.* In its pages, you'll find full descriptions of budget holidays, whether of the just-for-fun or more studious variety. You should also request their **Student Group Accommodation List,** which is especially useful during school holiday periods (Easter and July and August) for student residence halls that offer accommodations at reduced rates to students.

WHEN YOU ARRIVE: The student's best friend in Ireland is the **Irish Student Travel Service** (USIT). If you deplane at Shannon, your very first Irish stop should be the Limerick office at Central Buildings, O'Connell Street (tel. 061/45064 or 48925). Hours are 10 a.m. to 2 p.m. and 3:15 to 6 p.m. on weekdays, and 10 a.m. to 1 p.m. on Saturday from May to September. The head office is in Dublin at 7 Anglesea St., off Dame Street (tel. 01/778117), with hours of 9:30 a.m. to 5:30 p.m. on weekdays and 10 a.m. to 1 p.m. on Saturday. In Waterford you'll find USIT at 33 O'Connell St. (tel. 051/72601).

USIT will arrange cut-rate travel between Ireland and other European destinations, help you plan itineraries both inside the country and beyond, advise you about accommodations, camping, summer jobs, and student bargains in every area you can think of.

TRANSPORTATION SAVINGS: One of USIT's most valuable services is the **Travelsave Stamp** that, affixed to your International Student Identity Card, entitles you to such benefits as a 50% discount on Dublin buses and trains, as well as 50% off all rail and bus travel throughout the country, and rail travel in Northern Ireland. In addition, students with a valid CIE stamp will be entitled to approximately one-third off round-trip weekend rail fares and 50% off the ferry service to the Aran Islands and the United Kingdom.

In Dublin, you can purchase an **Educational Travel Concession Ticket** through the Tourist Information Office, 14 Upper O'Connell St. (tel. 01/747733), that permits unlimited travel on Dublin bus and train services at a cost of IR£15 ($24) for two weeks or IR£24 ($38.50) for four weeks.

STUDY IN IRELAND: The aforementioned *Discover Young Ireland: A Guide* to Learning and Leisure Opportunities, published by the Irish Tourist Board, is a cornucopia of study possibilities in Ireland, many of which include accommodations in Irish homes, weekend travel, and cultural events. Subjects are as varied as Irish literature, drama, music, archeology, crafts, and the Irish language. Bookings for every course should be made as far in advance as possible, so you should write for the booklet and make your decision early (see ITB addressses listed in Section 2 of this chapter, or contact the Youth and Education Department, Irish Tourist Board, 757 Third Ave., New York, NY 10017; tel. 212/418-0800).

There are two excellent study programs in Ireland sponsored by U.S. organizations. The Council on International Educational Exchange (CIEE) offers **Encounter Ireland** to any full-time student of an American college or university. For four weeks, participants stay with an Irish family in Dublin and attend lectures, concerts, art exhibits, and other cultural events and visit the sightseeing highlights of the city and its environs. A fifth week is left free for you to travel around the country independently, using the rail pass that is included in the price. To qualify, you must send them a 500-word essay on your reasons for wanting to go to Ireland, two passport-type photos, a reference from one of your professors, and a completed application form. The price in 1988 (1989 costs are not available as we go to press), including round-trip air fare from New York, was $1,950, and dates are late June to mid-August. For full details and an application, contact CIEE, Encounter Ireland Program, 205 E. 42nd St., New York, NY 10017 (tel. 212/661-1414).

The second program is sponsored by the Irish American Cultural Institute and is called the **Irish Way**. It is for 9th- through 12th-graders. This gives you 5½ weeks in Ireland, all at Gormanston College in County Meath, some 25 miles north of Dublin. Studies during that time range from mythology, history, archeology, and drama to literature, folk music, and balladry. There are interesting and entertaining field trips, and for spare-time recreation, there's an indoor swimming pool, tennis courts, and facilities for golf, handball, and soccer. Also included are a nine-day home stay, in which students live with Irish families, and a five-night tour staying in hotels. The estimated cost for 1989 is $1,555 plus air fare, and some partial scholarships are available. The program begins in early July and runs into early August. For details, contact The Irish Way, Irish American Cultural Institute, 2115 Summit Ave., College of St. Thomas, St. Paul, MN 55105 (tel. 612/647-5678).

In addition to these, there are many other summer study programs available, and the comprehensive feature on **Irish Summer Schools Directory,** published as a supplement by *Inside Ireland* (see page 56), gives a complete picture of the possibilities, including details on courses (both credit and noncredit), prices, accommodations (campus or home stays), extracurricular activities, etc.

4. WHERE TO STAY

The most amazing single fact about Ireland's budget accommodations is that there's just isn't one *single* category of budget accommodations! Oh, I know I've sung the praises of the town and country B&Bs, and I'll keep right on doing that. But they are by no means the only budget accommodations on the Irish market. If your notion of budget travel is camping, there are good campgrounds located in just about every scenic section of the country; backpackers will find a marvelous supply of hostels at dirt-cheap rates; next up on the cost scale come those wonderful Irish family B&Bs; then there are the farmhouses, which range from modern bungalows to great Georgian mansions, all on working farms; if you lean toward the "small inn" type of home-away-from-home, there are the guesthouses a little higher up the price range; and for families or small groups traveling together, self-catering cottages may prove to be the most economical way of all to enjoy an Irish visit. There's even a countrywide holiday program that includes some very nice hotels with special midweek and weekend package rates that can only be called budget.

The selection within those ranges that you'll find in these pages have all been personally inspected, but you'll never be buying a pig in a poke even if you book into a place that *isn't* in this book. The ever-vigilant Bord Fáilté staff keeps a sharp eye on every accommodation they approve, with annual, unannounced inspections. That green shamrock approval sign is so highly coveted among Irish housewives that new wallpaper goes up at the first sign of wear and you may well find your hostess slapping a brand-new paint job on woodwork with a vengeance. (I sometimes think Irish women paint their woodwork far more frequently than I get around to washing mine!) And a quirk of the Irish vocabulary you're bound to notice is that every vacuum cleaner is known as a "hoover"; equally quirky is the fact that "hoovering" seems to take place several times a day—just let one speck of dirt or dust appear on the carpet, and out comes the "hoover."

What I'm trying to say is that wherever you see the Bord Fáilté–approved sign, you'll find *clean* premises. Not only that, but each approved accommodation is required to register its rate for the year with the Bord and cannot charge more than that unless higher rates for holidays or special events are also registered and appear in the Bord Fáilté listings. They also certify that you'll get the exact accommodation you bargained for when you booked and that you'll never be asked to share a room with a stranger. If, by chance, you run into what you think is a violation of these rules, you are expected to make your complaint known— first to the hostess, and failing satisfaction, to Bord Fáilté, Baggot Street Bridge, Dublin 2 (tel. 01/765871). If you think you've been overcharged, be sure to get a receipt to send on to Dublin.

Now, not all B&Bs, guesthouses, and hotels are approved, which isn't to say there aren't some very good unapproved accommodations out there. It's just that if you book into one that isn't, you're strictly on your own unless—as is the case in a very few listed herein—I've been there, tested facilities and hostess for you, and found them more than just adequate. Some of the warmest, most hospitable places I've stayed in have not been on Bord Fáilté's list, and to be honest, I have run into only one or two that were perfect horrors. All the same, it's a good rule of thumb to stick to the approved places unless you have a recommendation from someone whose judgment you trust.

One or two points should be made that I expect will make your stay in any of these even more enjoyable. First of all, when the Irish say "double room," they mean a room with a double bed; if a room has twin beds, it's called just that, a "twin-bedded" room. Now, in this book, I've used "double" to mean a room that will accommodate two *people,* whether they cozy up in a double bed or each claims a single bed. So if you have a decided preference about sleeping in the same bed as well as the same room with your traveling companion, best get that straight when you book.

When it comes to those lovely Irish breakfasts, there's one little point I'd like to make on behalf of your hosts and hostesses: if you're traveling in a party, try to agree the night before on a time when you'll *all* show up at the breakfast table; otherwise, the poor cook winds up trying to get four or five hot breakfasts on the table at staggered intervals and has to try to find room on the table for four or five separate pots of tea or coffee.

Finally, if you're staying in a guesthouse, lodge, or small hotel and an American accent colors everything you say, it's more than likely a small service tip will be welcomed, if not exactly expected. Actually, that's our own national fault— tipping is such a part of our culture that if we neglect it, there's the suspicion that service has not been up to par. Australians and some other nationalities who *never* tip are happily accepted on their own terms. Personally, I usually leave a 50p tip at breakfast, a punt or two at dinner (if, of course, service is not a part of the bill). In B&Bs, tipping is not really called for, and it's entirely up to you as to whether you'd *like* to leave a punt or two for someone who's been especially helpful—but that *never* includes your host!

CAMPGROUNDS: If the great outdoors holds such appeal for you that tenting is the only way to go in your book, then the very first item in your backpack should be Bord Fáilte's **Caravan & Camping Parks** booklet. It's available for a small charge from the Irish Tourist Board, 757 Third Ave., New York, NY 10017, and it lists approved campgrounds, camping equipment renters, and (for the less hardy) caravan—we know them as vans or recreational vehicles—renters.

To be approved, campgrounds must provide good toilet facilities, water-supply points, rubbish-disposal facilities, and properly spaced sites for tents and caravans. Many offer far more than these minimum requirements, with laundry and recreation facilities, a shop, or sometimes even a restaurant on the premises. Charges vary according to location and season, and can range from IR£4 ($6.50) to IR£6 ($9.50) per night for caravans or tents, with a small per-person additional charge; weekly rates offer a considerable savings over daily rates. Caravan rentals range from IR£85 ($136) to IR£190 ($304) per week, depending on size and season.

HOSTELS: The first thing to be said about hostels is that, although they're called *youth* hostels, you'll be welcomed if you're 6 or 60. The second thing to be said is that in order to use them, you must have an **International Youth Hostel Card,** which *must be purchased before you leave home.* They are available from **American Youth Hostels, Inc.,** P.O. Box 37613, Washington, DC 20013 (tel. 202/783-6161), and cost $10 for those under 18 or over 54, and $20 ages 18 to 54; a family membership costs $30. For another $8.95 (plus $2 postage and handling) you can purchase their *International Youth Hostel Handbook* (Vol. I—Europe and North Africa) in which you'll find Irish hostels listed.

An Oige is the Irish Youth Hostel Association's official name, and it's a voluntary organization dedicated to helping residents and visitors take full advantage of Ireland's outdoor splendors and to providing hostel accommodations at minimum rates. It also puts together such holiday bargain packages as the Rambler/Hostelling Holiday, which include an eight-day bus/train ticket plus eight overnights in hostels. There are cycling holidays and combination rail/cycling holidays, as well. For full details, contact An Oige, Irish Youth Hostel Association, 39 Mountjoy Square, Dublin 1 (tel. 01/363111).

Any office can furnish their *An Oige—Irish Youth Hostel Handbook* for a small charge, which details every one of the 53 hostels throughout the country, along with information on making reservations, rules and regulations to be observed, and such extras as travel discounts on certain ferry services available to hostel cardholders.

As for the hostels, you'll find them in locations convenient to all sightseeing and ideal for short hikes, bike day trips, and swimming and other sports activities. They come in all shapes and sizes, from Georgian mansions like the one in Killarney I mentioned earlier to hunting lodges, converted coast-guard cottages, old farmhouses, and former schoolhouses. All have separate sleeping and washing facilities for men and women, a self-catering kitchen, dining room, and common room. A warden is on duty at each, and the hostels are in use between the hours of 10:30 a.m. and midnight.

Pillows, blankets, cooking utensils, and dishes are provided, but you'll need to bring your own sheet bag or sleeping bag, cutlery, and tea towel and bath towel. Overnight charges are based on age, season, and location, and in 1988 ranged from IR£2.50 ($4) to IR£4 ($6.50) for Seniors (over 20); IR£2 ($3.25) to IR£3.50 ($5.50) for Juniors (18 to 20); and IR£1.50 ($2.50) to IR£3 ($4.75) for Juveniles (under 16). There will undoubtedly be slight increases in 1989 and 1990.

If you arrive in Ireland without an International Youth Hostel Card but still want to go the hostel route, contact Paddy and Josephine Moloney, **Irish Budget Hostels,** Doolin Village, Co. Clare (tel. 065/74006). This is a link of privately owned hostels for which you need no registration card, and there's no age limit. Facilities at each will vary, but all have both dormitory and private accommodations, hot showers, full kitchen facilities, blankets, and sleeping sheets on request. Most have been approved by the Tourist Board, and the Moloneys can provide you with a directory of locations in Counties Dublin, Wicklow, Wexford, Cork, Kerry, Limerick, Clare, Galway, Mayo, and Donegal. Rates range from IR£3 ($4.75) to IR£4 ($6.50).

TOWN AND COUNTRY HOMES: Absolutely *the* best travel buy in Ireland! It isn't only that the rates in Irish B&Bs stretch your budget so far; even more, it's that they offer the best possible way to get to know the Irish as they live in their own homes. It's that you become an integral part of those homes, sharing family life as a young daughter or son brings your breakfast or offers the loan of a bike or volunteers to show you the way to a very special local attraction you won't find in guidebooks (one of those nooks and crannies I talked about earlier), or explains how easy it is to rent a boat for a day's fishing on the lake. It's relaxing in a pretty, individually decorated room that has all the comforts, but not a smidgin of the "sameness" of a motel room. It's starting off the day with a breakfast to end all breakfasts and a friendly chat with your hostess, who really *is* interested in your plans for the day and eager to offer suggestions, directions, or whatever else you may need. It's coming in from an evening out to find a fire lit and the tea table set or, if your evening has been really late, a pot of tea in your room. In short, although it's budget prices you'll be paying, you'll be extended a brand of hospitality no amount of money could buy elsewhere.

One of the most delightful features of traveling via B&Bs is that no two are alike. One night you may stay in a gorgeous city town house, the next in a seaside bungalow, the next in an idyllic country home. Many have only three or four rooms to rent, while others have added extensions to accommodate their guests (my personal preference is for those smaller, homier places, although the extensions generally have been designed especially with the traveler in mind and sometimes have more amenities). Nor are any two hostesses alike except in their friendliness. You'll be staying with bustling mothers of a large brood, whose offspring wait tables, make beds, do the "hoovering," polish furniture, and help in the kitchen. Then there will be the lovely widow whose children have all grown up and fled the nest and who will tell you she gets far more from your company than she can ever repay. You'll be treated to a look at family life far different from our own, where the "telly" may draw an audience, but it is a fickle one that will switch it off in a second if there's the prospect of a good "crack" (chat) with someone from America. You'll be shown the cards that came last Christmas from guests of the previous season (with the not-so-subtle hint that your hostess would *love* to hear from you from time to time when you go back home).

As for the practicalities, your room may be so spacious you'd call it a mini-suite in the U.S., or it may be small and cozy. In most cases you'll share the bathroom with other guests, and sometimes with the family. In others you'll have your own toilet and/or shower or bathtub, and there will probably be a small charge for that luxury, although I encountered many while researching this edition in which all rooms cost the same, private facilities or not. Stay out as late as you please in the evening—you'll have your own front-door key. In fact, in some rural areas that won't even be necessary, for they still follow the tradition of leaving the key in the door all night.

I should add here a word about central heating: not all B&Bs have it, and you must remember that even where you do find it, Irish central heating is not like that at home. Where it doesn't exist, there's almost always a small heater in your room to take the chill off, if not exactly heat it up. What that means is that your room may tend to be chilly around the edges at times. My own solution is to throw on a light sweater, usually enough to keep me comfortable. And there's not a B&B lady in the whole of Ireland who won't gladly furnish a hot-water bottle to make your bed warm and toasty when you retire.

If you'd like to have dinner at your B&B, most will accommodate you if you let them know by noon, and you'll be served a wholesome, well-prepared meal for about the same price as your room rate. There's never any charge, however, for the endless cups of tea that appear magically when you drag in from a day's sightseeing or return from an evening out. Likely as not, the evening cuppa will come with hot scones or a bit of cake, and you'll share it in the lounge with the entire family. It is then that a spontaneous singing or storytelling session is apt to break out that often lasts until the wee hours and sends you to bed glowing with a new, heart-expanding Irish experience.

Babysitters can usually be arranged at very modest fees, and almost all B&Bs offer reductions for children sharing a room with parents. Single travelers may have a problem finding a single room—there just aren't very many, and if you're given a double room, there may be a small supplementary charge. Another thing to keep in mind is that many of these homes are two and three stories high, so if you're elderly, handicapped, or just plain don't like to climb stairs, it will pay you to ask about a ground-floor room (not a "first-floor" room, since the Irish consider that to be what we would call the second floor).

For all the above, you'll pay anywhere from IR£8 ($12.75) to IR£10 ($16) in the country and smaller towns, slightly more in cities. In Dublin, prices in the few B&Bs in the inner city are quite a bit higher, but there's a multitude of accommodations within easy suburban bus or train rides. Most B&Bs also offer a Partial Board rate, a weekly charge for bed-and-breakfast plus the evening meal, that is a real money-saver.

For a list of all approved town and country homes, plus farmhouses (see the next section), pick up or send for the Irish Tourist Board's booklet *Town and Country Homes & Farmhouses,* available for a small charge at any ITB office or by mail from the Irish Tourist Board, 757 Third Ave., New York, NY 10017. Also, the Town & Country Homes Association publishes a *Guest Accommodation* booklet with pictures of all member homes. It's available for a small charge from any Irish Tourist Board office. The association is nationwide, and its members can book you ahead to your next destination with any other member. I find standards exceptionally high in these homes and have yet to find one I couldn't recommend, both for facilities and friendly hospitality.

If you plan to book before leaving home (*especially* for that first night), you can do so through your travel agent; the Central Reservations Service, 14 Upper O'Connell St., Dublin 1 (tel. 01/735209) at least four weeks in advance, using a VISA or MasterCard credit card; or directly with one of the B&Bs listed in this book. If you choose the last option, be sure to write well in advance, state the exact dates you want to book, and enclose a deposit of one night's charge and an International Reply Coupon. If you book by telephone, have all the information right in front of you before you call, and then confirm by letter.

FARMHOUSES: You'll find the very same sort of hospitality in Irish farmhouses. And there's more: For an equally modest price range, they throw in country settings that can make you almost weep from the beauty of it all, the enchantment of a working farmyard, vegetables fresh from their own gardens, lamb or beef that not long ago was on the hoof in their own fields, fish caught that very morning in the river that flows through their land, perhaps a pony or horse to ride, and a day of sharing farm chores if you'd like to know what it's like to be a farmer. I can't imagine a more heavenly vacation for a child—or grownup—than one on an Irish farm.

Farm breakfasts are, if anything, even more massive than those in town and country homes, and very often there's the bonus of fresh fruit or berries, homemade butter, and homemade jams. Dinner is likely to be a whopper, with four courses and desserts swimming in rich, fresh cream. As with town and country homes, you'll have to let your hostess know by noon if you want to dine with her that evening.

The one essential for a farmhouse holiday is a car, since almost all are off the beaten track and cannot be reached by public transportation. A happy—and inexpensive—way to arrange both is through **Johnson & Perrott's Irish Farmhouse Holiday Program**. It combines a Ford Fiesta with unlimited mileage and farmhouse accommodation at any of the 38 participating locations around the country for seven nights for IR£148 ($236.75) per person from July through mid-September, IR£128 ($204.75) other months. That's for two people traveling together, and if you want a larger car, there's a supplementary charge. For details, contact Johnson & Perrott Rent-a-Car Ltd., Emmet Place, Cork (tel. 021/273295, or toll free in the U.S. 800/223-6764). Even if you don't go for the combination package, remember that Johnson & Perrott discounts basic car rentals by 15% for our readers (see Chapter II).

Prices for farmhouse accommodations usually run one or two punts higher than town and country homes, and they offer those budget-stretching Partial Board weekly rates as well. As stated above, they're listed in the ITB publication, and there's also an **Irish Farm Holidays Association (Fáilte Tuaithe)** publication (small charge) with pictures and a brief description of each member farmhouse. Standards seem to be just that little bit higher in association farmhouses, and they, too, will gladly book you with a fellow member along your itinerary.

Reservations procedures for farmhouses are the same as in the town and country section above.

GUESTHOUSES: I don't really know how to describe a "guesthouse" accurately—it always seems to me they fit the pattern of a traditional small inn. Suffice it to say that they combine many of the services you expect in hotels (some, for instance, have telephones in guest rooms) with the personalized service and informality of a B&B. Some have been built for this specific purpose, others are in period residences, others have just sort of grown into being as a popular B&B that expanded to meet the demand.

There are several advantages to staying in a guesthouse, even though you'll be paying a higher rate than in the B&Bs. For example, many have a restaurant right on the premises, which can be a real convenience. They are also allowed to sell wine (but not spirits) to guests. Ariel House, in Dublin, adds such personal conveniences as a hairdryer in every room.

Rates are based on both single-person occupancy as well as per-person-sharing. In the disadvantage column, all guesthouse rates are subject to a small Value Added Tax (VAT) for accommodation, food, drink, and other services. For all that, there are some guesthouses in Ireland whose sheer attractiveness, convenience, and charm make the added tax seem a small price to pay. The ones you'll find in these pages are those I consider exceptional and look forward to visiting again and again. Whether you're addicted to those extra little creature comforts or just plan to treat yourself to an occasional guesthouse stay, I can assure you of one thing: some of the intimacy of a B&B may be missing, but you'll find exactly the same brand of hospitality in both.

Guesthouse rates range all over the place, depending on facilities, location, and season, from a low of IR£21 ($33.50) to as high as IR£45 ($72) per-person-sharing. Not really budget, but good value, all the same. The Irish Tourist board includes all approved guesthouses in their *Guest Accommodations* booklet, available for a small charge, and their *Be Our Guest* booklet includes pictures. Also, through a Discover Ireland program, designed to encourage the Irish to explore their own country (you'd be surprised how many set off for foreign shores without a thought, but never venture beyond their own county's borders at home!), guesthouses, B&Bs, and hotels in some of the most scenic locations in the country offer astonishingly low midweek and weekend specials. Pick up the *Discover Ireland* booklet in any Tourist Office in Ireland (you won't find it outside the country), and you'll be as welcome as any native to take advantage of these savings and enjoy the luxury of accommodations well outside the budget at their usual rates.

HOTELS: Don't jump to any hasty conclusions—I'm not about to suggest that you can hotel it around Ireland on our $35-a-day budget. But because Ireland's hotels have gotten a rather bad press (largely deserved) in years gone by, I want to bring you up-to-date just in case you opt for a hotel night or two.

It is true that for many years most of the country's hotels were low- to sub-standard, with only a few Dublin shining examples along with the luxury castle hotels. In the past few years, however, that situation has changed drastically, and for the better. Today there are small, owner-operated hotels all around the country that feature clean, attractive guest rooms, good dining rooms, and service just one step away from being as personal as guesthouse or B&B hospitality. Surprisingly, I've even experienced that same B&B friendliness in some of the largest luxury establishments, where you'd expect the hustle and bustle of bus-tour traffic to make any sort of personal contact impossible. On second thought, given the ebullient Irish nature, that probably isn't surprising at all!

About those luxury hotels: They vary in style from long-established, comfortable "clubbiness" to sophisticated elegance that can hold its own on an international scale. If you do consider treating yourself to an overnight in one, you'll have a choice of décor and atmosphere. A good way to shop around for one that suits you is to go into the ones that catch your fancy and have a drink at the bar and look around the public rooms. And although the desk clerk may think you a bit "bold," he or she will be happy to show you a guest room if there are vacancies and you ask nicely—after all, this is *your* big moment, and you don't want to be disappointed.

As for prices, see the "Big Splurges" section later in this chapter for just what you can expect to pay for luxury hotels. Overnight in a good, small hotel such as the Blue Haven in Kinsale, County Cork, will run you about IR£44 ($70.50) for a double room. Almost all hotels offer some form of discount for weekends, longer stays, etc., so be sure to inquire when you make reservations.

SELF-CATERING: One of the most effective—and increasingly popular—money-saving devices is to rent your own "home" and eat in when it suits you. That doesn't necessarily mean that your travels are restricted, for it is quite possible to rent self-catering premises in a central location on Ireland's east coast for your first week, make easy day trips from that home base, then shift to another on the west coast for your second week. While you're trading in that lovely B&B hospitality for economy's sake, you'll be given a wonderful excuse to shop in the small markets, chat with local housewives doing the same, pop into the local pub on a regular basis, and—wonder of wonders!—have your own hearth around which to serve your own tea to the new friends you're bound to acquire.

Self-catering accommodations come in all guises, from inner-city town houses and flats to free-standing houses in small towns, country and seaside bungalows, thatched cottages, and chalets. In off-season months, it is possible in some locations to rent for a few midweek days or weekends only, but most rental periods run from Saturday (beginning 4 p.m.) to the following Saturday (ending before noon). There are three price periods: April, May, June, September (mid-range prices); July and August (peak prices); and all other months (lowest price). Rates can range from about IR£85 ($136) in the mid-price range to IR£200 ($320) in the high season for a cottage that accommodates seven. More luxurious accommodations run higher, but are still a very good buy. As you can see, if you're traveling with a gaggle of children or friends, your per-person costs can be cut to the very bone by self-catering.

Your basic rate will usually include all linens, and if not, they can almost always be rented for a small charge. Kitchens come fully equipped, and some premises even have central heating. In addition, you can expect extra charges for electricity, heating oil and cooking fuels, and in some cases, television. In projecting your costs, be sure to count those extras in. If you're uncertain about what they will be, ask at the time you book for an estimate by the landlord based on the number of people sharing the premises.

The Irish Tourist Board has compiled a book listing all approved self-catering accommodations except inner-city Dublin flats and the cottages listed below, entitled simply *Self-Catering*, and it's available for a small charge. For Dublin flats available, contact Dublin Tourism, 14 Upper O'Connell St., Dublin 1 (tel. 01/747733). This should be another part of your "homework" before catching that outward-bound plane. Study carefully the descriptions, terms, and photographs, book directly with your choice as far ahead as you possibly can, and you'll arrive fully prepared to be a temporary Irish resident.

All the above applies to privately owned self-catering accommodations, but there is one very special widespread scheme you should know about, especially if you get all dreamy-eyed at the thought of a traditional thatched cottage. Known as **Rent an Irish Cottage Ltd.,** the organization has put together small villages of rental cottages in the west of Ireland that combine the traditional hearth, half-door, and raftered ceilings you've dreamed about with modern conveniences like central heating (when you really don't want to bother with a turf fire), electric kitchens (no wood to chop or heavy pots to hang over an open fire), and shiny bathrooms with showers. The Irish lady who once lived in a thatched cottage *without* all those comforts would go all dreamy-eyed with wonder if she could see these!

The cottages are arranged much as in a small Irish village, and they're all located close to some of the country's most splendid scenic spots, never far from facilities for recreational activities like fishing, swimming, golfing, pony trekking, or long hikes through gorgeous countryside. Needless to say, what with grocery shopping, pubbing, etc., it won't take long for you to become a part of the local scene.

There are four types of cottage design, all hand-thatched, with accommodations for five to eight people. During peak season, weekly rentals range from IR£140 ($224) to IR£240 ($384), but they descend to a low of IR£90 ($144) in some months, IR£60 ($96) on weekends.

A brief rundown on the thirteen locations follows:

Corofin, Co. Clare (close to lakes, castles, the Burren, and underground caves).

Feakle, Co. Clare (24 miles from Shannon Airport, near woodlands, rivers, lakes, and the Cliffs of Moher).

Puckane, Co. Tipperary (two miles from the Shannon River in North Tipperary, with water sports, boating, and fishing nearby).

Kilfinane, Co. Limerick (27 miles from Limerick City near the Ballyhoura Mountains, with horseback riding and fishing available).

Ballyvaughan, Co. Clare (close to the shores of beautiful Galway Bay, with the ocean beach just three miles away).

Carrigaholt, Co. Clare (set at the mouth of the Shannon, with historic ruins and majestic cliff scenery close by).

Holycross, Co. Tipperary (Holy Cross Abbey, dating from the 12th century, is a stone's throw away, as is excellent fishing).

Murroe, Co. Limerick (just seven miles from the city, near historic castles and wooded glens).

Broadford, Co. Clare (Shannon Airport is only 14 miles away, near all Shannonside castle banquets and sightseeing attractions).

Renvyle, Co. Galway (right on the edge of Connemara's stark beauty, only a mile from the Atlantic).

Louisburg, Co. Mayo (a lovely little fishing village and a good jumping-off place for touring the western region).

Terryglass, Co. Tipperary (on the shores of lovely Lough Derg).

Ballycastle, Co. Mayo (on Mayo's northern coast, alongside a sandy beach, good fishing, and an excellent base for touring north to Sligo and beyond).

For complete details and booking information, contact **Rent an Irish Cottage Ltd.,** Shannon Airport, Shannon, Co. Clare (tel. 061/61588).

5. WHERE TO EAT

For centuries, the Irish—sometimes by choice, sometimes from necessity—seemed to eat simply to exist, without much thought to anything beyond a basic diet of little more than tons of boiled potatoes and gallons of buttermilk. Before you begin to pity them *too* much, however, wait until you've tasted a real Irish potato—its mealy innards have a taste far superior to any grown on this side of the Atlantic, and when slathered with rich, golden butter, there just isn't much better eating. I must confess I could make a meal of them any day.

Be that as it may, however, while most of my Irish friends still make the potato a main part of their daily diet, these days the old spud comes to the table roasted, baked, mashed, or in the form of french fries. And far from being the main dish, it is strictly an accompaniment to local veal, beef, and lamb, or salmon (fresh and or smoked), prawns, plaice, or trout from Ireland's abundant waters. Tender, sweet lettuce, tomatoes that taste of the sun, and cucumbers the size of our squash go into fresh salads, and vegetables both home-grown and from the gardens of Spain or Israel complete the heaping plates of "mains." Bread? It's that famous soda or brown bread, freshly baked and many times still warm, just waiting to be spread with pure, golden butter. Starters can be thick, tasty barley, beef, or vegetable soup or shrimp cocktail or homemade pâté or small portions of that wonderful smoked salmon. Desserts tend to be apple or rhubarb tart or sherry trifle, all topped with lashings of sweet, rich fresh cream. Tea, of course, comes in a bottomless pot to pour endless cups. All pretty plain foods, all wholesome, and all in *gigantic* portions.

That's in Irish homes. As for Irish restaurants, they've come a long way from the times when "chefs" were simply cooks who had moved from the home hearth into hotel dining rooms, small tea rooms, or the few fancy eateries concentrated mostly in Dublin. Today's chefs are likely to have been trained in leading culinary schools on the Continent or in one of Ireland's excellent hotel-training institutions. Menus are more varied than I ever thought I'd see in this land of plain-food eaters. International cuisine is available not only in Dublin, but in all the larger cities and many small villages tucked away beside the sea or in the basement of a mansion on the grounds of Bunratty Castle. French, Italian, Chinese, and even Russian restaurants are to be found, along with some very good ones that serve wonderfully prepared native dishes. It is even possible nowadays to get a decent cup of perked coffee in many restaurants, although I find (even as a confirmed coffeehound at home) the tea in Ireland is so much better that I seldom long for coffee.

There are several native foods you should be sure not to miss while you're in Ireland. For me, dairy products top the list: never have I tasted butter or cream to compare with Ireland's. And if you're a cheese lover, you'll find some excellent cheddars made by creamery co-ops as well as commercial firms (I make it a practice to ask the locals about cheeses made in their locality, and I've struck real gold in Kerry's mountains as well as Waterford's fertile fields). Smoked salmon is not only a delicacy, it's *affordable* in Ireland, and you can gorge yourself to your heart's content. Dublin Bay prawns are a "don't miss," as is plaice, a freshwater fish served all over the country. Small-town bakeries often have soda bread for sale fresh from the oven, as well as some cream-filled pastries that are as light as a feather and as sweet as heaven itself.

But as pennypinchers, our main interest is in satisfying each day's hunger on the budget we've set for ourselves, and believe me, you'll do that and eat *well*. So well, in fact, that I'll wager you'll be able to treat yourself to at least one pricey meal in the Big Splurge restaurant of your choice. Remember, you're going to begin every day with a mammoth breakfast that will either carry you over all the way to dinner or at the very least call for only a light midday repast. Remember, too, that if you're staying in B&Bs, it is probable that you'll be served tea and scones or cake along about ten o'clock in the evening, and it won't cost you a cent!

Incidentally, the tea you'll be served all along your Irish travels is downright habit forming, with a hearty, robust flavor that could make you foreswear coffee for all time. If you should find yourself addicted, you'll be glad to know that it can grace your own breakfast table (or midnight tray) when you get back home. Richard Bewley and his wife, Jo, members of the famed Bewley's tea and coffee shops family in Dublin, now live in the U.S. and have established a mail-order business for Bewley's tea and other Irish products. While they're primarily importers and wholesale distributors, they'll be happy to send you their mail-order catalog, as well as let you know if there's a shop in your area that carries their imports. Prices for the tea are quite reasonable, and there's no better memory-nudger than a steaming "cuppa" of the Bewley's brew. Contact Bewley Irish Imports, 606 Howard Rd., West Chester, PA 19380 (tel. 215/696-2682).

PICNICS: One of the most joyous dining experiences in Ireland is a picnic in that glorious outdoors. In the more than 400 forest areas open to the public you'll find picnic sites galore, many with tables and benches provided for your comfort. There are very good booklets available giving directions to all 400, and I always keep a publication called *The Open Forest: A Guide to Areas Open to the Public* in the car—that way, I can locate the nearest forest park quickly, no matter where I happen to be. That, plus several leaflets on nature trails, is available for a very small charge from the Amenity Section, Forest and Wildlife Service, Leeson Lane, Dublin 2. Pick up some fresh bread, a good Irish cheese, a bottle or two of lager or stout, and you're in business. If you're not near one of the forest parks, there's always the seashore or a riverbank or just a spot alongside the road (unless you're on one of the main highways, you won't be bothered by traffic). Need I add that you should leave the countryside as rubbish free and beautiful as you found it?

PUBS: Not all pubs serve food, and almost none serve it in the evening. But some of my best Irish lunches have been pub grub that has varied from soup and sandwiches to a heaping plate of hot roast beef, mashed potatoes, vegetables, and rolls, depending on my appetite at the moment. Some pubs also serve marvelous salad plates of chicken, beef, or salmon. A cup of hearty soup and rolls or a sandwich will run you about IR£2.50 ($4), and that hot meal will cost around IR£3.50 ($5.50). If you're not in the mood for an alcoholic brew, you'll almost always be able to get a pot of tea. One note of caution: Irish sandwiches, for the most part, are skimpy little things compared to those we're accustomed to in the U.S., so be sure you aren't really hungry before you settle for them. If the pub serves soup, brown bread, and butter, it's a much better choice—tasty and filling.

TOURIST MEALS: Ah, here's the heart of our dining budget. The Irish Tourist Board—God bless 'em—has organized a Tourist Menu program with restaurants all around the country. Sometimes called "special value meals," these menus offer a full three-course lunch or dinner at bargain prices. There were, in 1988, two price levels: for IR£5.60 ($9) you may be restricted to a limited choice of main course meats; for IR£7.50 ($12) the selections will be more varied. Either way, the food is the same the restaurant serves on its pricier menu and portions are never skimpy. You can identify those eateries serving these meals by a distinctive sign displaying a smiling Irish chef. However, you must be sure to ask specifically for the Tourist Menu, or you may wind up being surprised when the check is presented. Prices are not expected to rise by more than 50p in 1989.

BUDGET RESTAURANTS: There are many restaurants, pubs, tea rooms, and department store cafeterias, some of which do not offer the Tourist Menu, but do serve very good food at budget prices. You'll find many listed in this book, but a good IR£1.50 ($2.50) investment is the Irish Tourist Board's booklet *Dining in Ireland,* which gives details on eateries in all regions, including a brief description of the cuisine, hours, and prices. It has been a lifesaver in my travels, and I never have any difficulty in finding dinner for under $10.

GUESTHOUSE MEALS: A happy way to dine inexpensively is to book for dinner with your B&B, farmhouse, or guesthouse hostess. As I've said several times before, you must let her know by noon or shortly thereafter that you want the evening meal. What you're almost certain to get is a version of the meal described at the beginning of this section, with such huge portions you'll roll away from the table and head for an outdoor stroll to walk off some of the pounds you can feel piling up around your hips. Not a bad way to end the day, now is it? As a rule of thumb, you can count on the price of dinner being the same as your overnight B&B rate, but to be safe, ask the cost when you book for dinner.

IRISH RECIPES: Guaranteed not to taste exactly the same back home, but set down here anyway for all you good cooks out there are the following traditional Irish recipes, one given to me by a tried and true Irish friend who is a terrific cook, one by a delightful widow lady who runs a small-town bakery that's been in business over 200 years, and one by a publican whose expertise behind the bar is legendary.

Irish Stew

> 3 lbs. neck of lamb
> 3 onions
> 8 potatoes
> Salt and pepper to taste
> 2 cups water
> 1 teaspoon chopped mixed herbs
> 2 tablespoons chopped fresh parsley (for garnish)

Trim excess fat from meat and cut into small pieces. Peel and slice onions and potatoes (make thick slices). Layer sliced potatoes on bottom of casserole, add a layer of lamb and a layer of onions. Sprinkle seasonings and herbs over all and top with sliced potatoes. Add water, cover and cook in medium oven (350°) for 1½ hours, or until lamb is tender. Sprinkle parsley on top just before serving.

Irish Brown Bread

> 1 cup whole-wheat flour
> 1 cup white flour
> 4 tablespoons (½ stick) butter
> ½ tsp. bicarbonate of soda
> ½ tsp. cream of tartar
> Pinch of salt
> Dash of sugar (if desired)
> Milk (just enough to wet and mix dough)

Mix flour, soda, salt, cream of tartar, and sugar thoroughly in a large bowl. With fingers, crumble butter into dry ingredients and mix well. Add just enough milk to form a soft pasty dough easy to handle, but not sticky. Turn soft dough onto a floured board and knead it smooth. Shape into a round (not too flat) cake and cut an X across top (don't omit this step—the X is not just for ornament, but to help in the rising). Bake in a preheated 350° oven for about an hour, or until brown and firm. *Note:* For a tasty preview of this recipe, stop in at Barron's Bakery in Cappoquin, County Waterford, and pick up one of Mrs. Barron's freshly baked cakes.

Irish Coffee

Fill a large, stemmed glass with hot water, then empty when glass is warm. Pour in one full jigger of Irish whisky and add at least one teaspoon sugar (the more sugar, the more the cream rises to the top). Add hot black coffee (the hotter, the better) to about an inch from the top and stir. Top it off with lightly whipped cream—there's an art to doing that: just sort of float it off over the back of a spoon.

6. BIG SPLURGES

All through this book, you'll find "Big Splurge" accommodations and restaurants listed. For example, no budgeteer in his or her right mind would contemplate a night in one of Ireland's luxury hotels or the romantic castles now open to guests. Yet, where and when else are you and I going to indulge our fantasies? And what better time and place than in Ireland? So while I don't exactly advocate that you go all out and bust the budget, I'm not exactly dead set against at least one "bust-out" overnight in a dream setting!

I'll give you two examples of Big Splurges that I'll save for all year. The first is Waterford Castle, just outside Waterford City. For me, its crenellated turrets, massive entrance hall, and tower rooms are the stuff dreams are made of, and I'll dine on peanut-butter sandwiches for a month just to have an overnight there! The other is Fitzpatrick's Castle Hotel, in Killiney, just outside Dublin, where I revel in the friendliness of a family-run establishment that pampers my budget-ridden soul.

For that kind of luxury, I must pay IR£80 ($128) at Waterford Castle — doubles run IR£100 ($160) per person. At Fitzpatrick's, singles pay IR£48 ($76.75), doubles cost IR£39 ($62.50) per person, and breakfast is extra. That's a lot of peanut-butter sandwiches!

You'll find all hotels listed in the Irish Tourist Board's *Hotels & Guesthouses* book. For the crème-de-la-crème of country houses (also well above our travel budget), pick up copies of *Irish Country Houses and Restaurants* and *The Hidden Ireland* from any ITB office. In their pages you'll find pictures and full descriptions of such special places as Ard na Greine Inn, in Schull, Co. Cork, and Longueville House, in Mallow, Co. Cork, and Rathmullan House up in Rathmullan, Co. Donegal.

Luxury country houses will cost between IR£25 ($40) and IR£45 ($72) per person, and most rates include breakfast.

The above are just three of the Big Splurges listed in the chapters to follow, but there are scores more around the country, each special in one way or another —and unless you break out in hives at the mere thought of peanut-butter sandwiches, I heartily recommend that you include at least one in your plans for an Irish holiday.

All of the above applies equally to posh restaurants. My favorites are in the following pages; almost any listed in the *Irish Country Houses and Restaurants* are worthy of your "bust out" dollars; and if you feel the urge for a super—and expensive—dinner out but haven't a clue where to find one, just ask around, everyone in the neighborhood will know where your hoarded wealth will be well spent.

7. SHOPPING

Most of Ireland's shopping bargains are variations of arts or crafts carried down from ages past, from those wonderful Aran sweaters to soft Donegal tweeds to drawings in the Celtic style to the incomparable Waterford glass. You'll find many still done in their traditional forms, but there's much excitement in seeing how they've been adapted to modern times. Woolens come in highly sophisticated styles, and contemporary crafts carry the imprint of today combined with the skills of ancient days.

SHOPPING BASICS: In the following chapters, I'll tell you about the best buys I've located in each locality. But first there are some ground rules you should know before you set foot in any shop.

Customs

Customs regulations of both Ireland and the U.S. will determine what you bring into Ireland and what you may take home with you. Citizens of non-EEC countries may bring the following into the country: if you're over the age of 17, 200 cigarettes, 50 cigars, nine ounces of tobacco, and one liter of distilled beverages and spirits exceeding 38.5° proof or two liters of other spirits; all ages may bring other dutiable goods valued at up to IR£32 ($51.25); and as much currency as you wish—or have! On leaving, there are no restrictions on any Irish purchase you carry with you, but you may not take out of the country more than IR£100 ($160) in Irish currency (if you wind up with a surplus, be sure to have notes converted to traveler's checks—on which there is no restriction—at a bank prior to departure).

Upon reentering the U.S., you'll be allowed to bring back purchases valued up to $400 without paying Customs duties or filling out a declaration form. Anything in excess of that amount will be assessed a flat 10% on the next $1,000 and an average of 12% for all over $1,400. Antiques that are over 100 years old come in duty free, but you must have an authentication of age from the dealer from whom you bought them to present to U.S. Customs.

The very detailed, 15-page booklet *Know Before You Go* (Publication No. 512) is available without charge from the U.S. Customs Service, P.O. Box 7407, Washington, DC 20044, and if you plan to do a lot of shopping, be sure you have it before leaving home.

Value Added Tax

It has been true for many years that no items mailed or shipped out of the country were subject to the Value Added Tax (VAT), but in May of 1984 that relief was extended to those things you carry back home in your luggage. That is a big break and can make a difference—as much as 10% to 23%—in the cost of your Irish purchases.

When making your purchase, you must prove to the merchant that you are a nonresident of Ireland by presenting your passport or other documentation (U.S. driver's license, etc.). You'll be issued an invoice which must be stamped by Irish Customs to prove that you did, indeed, take the merchandise out of the country. That invoice *must be returned to the vendor,* whether he allows you the VAT exemption on the spot or sends you a refund upon receipt of the stamped invoice. One warning: It is possible—not *probable,* but possible—that you may be asked to produce the items you've bought as you're outward bound so the Customs officer actually *sees* that they are being taken out of the country. You can avoid having to search for them through all your luggage (as a friend of mine once did) by packing all in one bag.

When you get the exemption is strictly up to the vendor (I know, you'd rather have those extra percents to spend in Ireland instead of after you're home—so would I, and the Irish government is probably missing out by not putting it in our hot-to-buy hands right then and there). Any shop is liable for the amount of the tax if it makes the deduction and you don't return that stamped invoice. So don't hassle your salesperson—just try to be as charming and as reliable-looking as you can; then *be sure to return the invoice.* The whole refund procedure is simplified if you use credit cards instead of cash, of course, when it's a simple matter of issuing a credit to your account—another good reason for using plastic money as often as you can (see below).

You should also be aware that when your refund arrives, it will be in Irish currency. Your bank will exchange it, but there can be several weeks' delay, and almost all banks charge a service fee of around $10. If, however, you send your refund check to the New York Foreign Exchange, Public Relations Department (26 Broadway, Suite 767, New York, NY 10004) or Ruesch International Monetary Services, Inc. (1140 19th St. NW, Washington, DC 20036), they'll mail you the U.S. equivalent less a fee of around $2 within a few days. All offices of Deak International (formerly Deak-Perera) also offer this service.

Credit Cards

Aside from the obvious convenience of buying now and paying later, thus giving you more cash for immediate needs and pleasures, and the advantage pointed out above, you'll usually save a dollar or two when you use American Express or VISA credit cards (the two most widely accepted, along with Diners Club and Access). Your billing will be at each company's exchange rate, which almost always averages several cents better per dollar than banks.

You won't be able to use your credit cards in many small shops, but you'll find they're accepted in all major department stores, many souvenir shops, car-rental companies, hotels, some restaurants, and all duty-free shops.

SHANNON DUTY-FREE SHOPPING: Back in the 1950s the world's first duty-free shop opened at Shannon Airport, and today it has grown into a super supermarket offering an incredible array of international products plus—best of all—a wide selection of the best of Irish-made goods. You'll save a bundle on Aynsley, Wedgwood, and Royal Worcester bone china from England, perfumes from France, cameras and Hummel porcelain figures from Germany, watches from Switzerland, and even cigarettes from the U.S. From Ireland itself, there are bargains in hand-knit sweaters, woolens and tweeds, fine Belleek china, Water-ford glass (as well as that from Galway and Cavan), Irish linens, jewelry and other items of Connemara marble, records and books, and a host of craft items.

As for prices, they're far lower on *all* items than you'd pay at home, though not too much lower, if any, on *Irish* goods than those in Irish shops, since the object is not to compete with the home market. Prices are marked in both Irish punts and U.S. dollars, and I find this a good place to use up any leftover punts as I leave for home, as well as a convenience when I'm down to only U.S. currency. Credit cards are also accepted.

In view of all this, should you save your shopping for Shannon just before departure? Well, that depends. You could have your heart set on taking home that special piece of Waterford glass, only to find that it happens to be the one item missing from the large stock at that particular time. Or you may remember with regret a lower price on an Aran sweater that you passed up somewhere on your rambles through the west and wind up paying a bit more at Shannon.

You can, in fact, get your duty-free shopping off to a good start even before leaving home by ordering the very good catalog that illustrates a representative selection, with prices shown in U.S. dollars, plus shipping charges by surface or air. Send $2 to Shannon Mail Order Stores, Shannon International Free Airport, Ireland. If you order by mail (a foot- and time-saving device), you'll pay any Customs duty directly to your postman upon delivery, but you'll still come out way ahead of U.S. prices. Incidentally, you can request a catalog while you're at the airport and it will be mailed to your home address. The $2 is deductible from your first mail order.

OTHER SHOPS: The one absolute for me in Ireland is to *buy it when I see it*. Never mind comparative shopping. There isn't really a big difference in prices around the country, as a rule, and I've found just the right woolly sweater in a little shop in Glengarriff, a beaten brass plaque depicting St. Brendan's epic voyage in a Donegal shop, and a few other items I might never have been able to call my own had I waited to find a better price elsewhere, since I never came across them again. For that reason, I hesitate to tout one shop over any other. There are, however, the following which I have found to be reliable for both variety, quality, service, and price, and I can recommend each without any hesitation. You'll find them detailed in the appropriate regional chapters.

In Dublin, my first stop is always the **House of Ireland,** where I've found several unusual Irish-made products (they have a good mail-order service, as well); in Killarney, **Maybury's** carries on a long tradition of large stocks and good value, plus one of the friendliest, most helpful staffs in the country (they also have a mail-order service); in Galway, **Padraic O Maille's** is excellent for woolens; and just outside Galway, **Mairtin Standun's** can be depended on for bargain prices on a variety of items.

In addition to the excellent shopping guide available through the Tourist Board in Dublin, *Inside Ireland* (see "Ireland by Mail" at the end of this chapter) furnishes subscribers an excellent Shopping and Touring Guide that also includes cash vouchers for many of the shops listed.

ARAN SWEATERS: At the top of most visitors' shopping lists is one of Ireland's famed Aran knit sweaters. They are as much a part of the Irish landscape as stone walls and green fields, and they're perfect to buy early and use for chilly weather during your stay. They've been made in Ireland as far back as the 9th century, and originated with fishermen along the west coast (especially in the Aran Islands, hence the name), who valued their water resistance as well as their warmth. Today most of the heavy natural oil has been removed from the wool from which they're made, and they're much softer than they used to be.

Designs, however, have changed not one whit. And for good reason. Long ago, each stitch depicted a different part of Irish life: the cable stitch stood for the fisherman's strong rope (it's also supposed to bring good luck) and the trellis stitch represented familiar stone walls. Using a combination of many such symbolic stitches, fishing villages designed patterns unique to each community, making it possible to return any drowning victim to his hometown for burial. Interestingly, in the beginning the sweaters were knit by men—women were relegated to the spinning of the wool.

The vast majority of Aran sweaters are knit in creamy, off-white bainin ("bawneen") wool, but you'll also find them in soft browns or mottled grays that are undyed, just as they came from the sheep. Their making is still very much a cottage industry (although all the knitters are women these days), and a fast worker can produce about two sweaters a week. A delightful touch is the little slip of paper placed in a pocket of each finished sweater that tells you which Irish lady is responsible for keeping you warm. Most are handwritten, and it's amazing the instant link you feel between maker and wearer.

A word of caution is in order about these sweaters (called "jerseys" in Ireland), since not all the creamy, off-white, cable-stitched sweaters you see are handmade. More and more machine-knits are appearing in shops, and if price is the primary consideration or you prefer a lighter-weight garment, you may be just as happy with one of these. They will *not*, however, have anything like the wearing qualities of the real thing. Hand-knits wear like iron, and I have one I'm sure will be passed on for several generations when I'm long gone! You should be able to tell the difference by the sheer weight of a hand-knit (or by that little slip of paper in the pocket), but if you have any doubt, be sure to ask the salesperson.

You can expect to pay something like $60 to $95 for an adult hand-knit pullover, slightly more for cardigans, and anywhere from one-half to one-third less for children's sizes. **Standun's,** in Galway, has good stocks and prices, but if you find the one you like elsewhere, buy it when you see it!

WOOLENS AND TWEEDS: For centuries Donegal homes came complete with looms from which poured the lovely tweeds and other woolens that are known all over the world. It is rare, however, to find a home loom today, because most of the weaving is done in small factories concentrated in Donegal and a few spotted around the country. You can watch a weaver at work if you call in to **Donal Houlihan's Handcraft Shop** in Glengarriff, Co. Cork, or at **Avoca Handweavers,** in County Wicklow. All department stores carry woolens both by the yard and made up into coats, suits, capes, and skirts, but some of the best buys are to be found at **Gillespi Brothers** in the little County Donegal town of Mountcharles, **Magee** of Donegal, and **Padraic O Maille's** in Galway. The **House of Ireland,** in Dublin, has a stylish selection of woolen garments.

WATERFORD GLASS: Actually, Waterford "glass" is crystal, earning that distinction by the addition of 33% lead oxide to basic ingredients of silica sand

and potash (crystal must contain no less than 22%, no more than 33½%). It has been around for two centuries (although actually produced for only one), and it is both beautiful beyond words and expensive.

You can tour the factory in Waterford (see Chapter XII), and buy its products there, as well as in many shops and department stores all around Ireland. And if Waterford glass is your shopper's heart's desire, best buy it here, for prices virtually double when it's imported. **Shannon Duty-Free Shops** carry a pretty good selection, and you'll find extensive stocks and good prices at **Joyce's** in Wexford and the **House of Ireland** in Dublin.

IRISH LACE: There is no purchase more evocative of long-ago elegance and a more gracious age than Ireland's handmade lace from Limerick or Carrickmacross. Supplies are becoming more and more limited each year as the younger generation become less and less willing to spend their days doing the tedious, time-consuming, and exquisite handwork. You can, however, still purchase examples of both from the convents which have kept the art alive.

In Carrickmacross, County Monaghan (15 miles west of Dundalk, just off the road from Dublin to Belfast), it's **Carrickmacross Lace Co-op** (see Chapter XXVII), where a lovely collar and cuffs set will run about IR£40 ($64). In Limerick, a lace handkerchief will cost IR£50 ($80) and upward at the **Good Shepard Convent** on Clare Street (see Chapter XX).

CRAFTS: Back in the 12th century, a traveler to Ireland waxed lyrical about the country's fine craftsmen in these words, "Fine craftsmanship is all around you. . . . Look carefully at it, and you will penetrate to the very shrine of art. You will make out intricacies so delicate and subtle, so exact and compact, with colors so fresh and vivid that you might say all this was the work of an angel, not of a man." I'm happy to tell you that things haven't changed all that much over the intervening centuries. There are over 800 craftspeople working full time and more than 1,000 part-time craft workers throughout Ireland. There are over 44 craft guilds, associations, and organizations affiliated with the Crafts Council of Ireland, which in turn is a member of the World Crafts Council and the Crafts Council of Europe. And there is now a Minister for State responsible for crafts in the country.

What all the above means to you and me is that Ireland is, indeed, a happy hunting ground for superb workmanship demonstrated in one of the most widely varied range of crafts in any one country in the world. To those skills we've already discussed above, you can add beautiful woodwork, leathers, pottery, ceramics, artistic metalwork, and many, many others. They're scattered all over the face of Ireland, working in small workshops usually, but maintaining standards that would make their legendary Celtic ancestors—themselves no slouches when it came to gold and bronze!—beam with pride.

By all means obtain a free copy of the *Crafthunter's Pocket Guide* from one of the Irish Tourist Board's U.S. offices, and failing that, plunk down the small charge for a copy at any Tourist Office within Ireland itself. It tells you exactly where to find which craftspeople, and it is indispensable in searching out those particular crafts in which you are interested.

BOOKS: What better memento to carry home from Ireland than the printed word! After all, words have been pouring from those agile Irish minds to the printed page in a veritable flood since the beginning of recorded history. Any booklover is quite likely to go a bit mad at the sight of such a wealth of bookshops, and the bargain hunter will happily spend hours sifting through used-book stalls and bookstore basements with their tables of reduced volumes.

Dublin has lost a few of its oldest, most revered bookshops, which fell victim to increased taxes, rentals, and traffic. You'll still, however, find one or two family-run shops along the Liffey quays, and both **Greene's Bookshop** on Clare Street and **Parson's** on Baggot Street are havens to which I could repair for weeks on end. In addition to these traditional shops, there are bright, new, and *large* bookshops galore. In Galway, **Kenny's Bookshop** is virtually a national treasure, and a treat not to be missed. You'll find details on these and some others in the chapters that follow. Use them as a *beginning* in your quest for books to take home, but keep your eyes open as you travel around—bookshops are tucked away in some of the most amazing places, and the Irish who run them are kindred spirits who'll wrap some memorable conversations with the book you end up buying.

IRELAND BY MAIL: I don't rightly know if these two suggestions belong under the "shopping" heading, but it occurs to me that they both represent an ongoing connection with the country you'll have lost your heart to during your two weeks' stay, and at bargain prices.

The first is *Inside Ireland,* a quarterly newsletter written especially for the likes of you and me who live somewhere else but want to keep up with what's going on over there. Its publisher, Dubliner Brenda Weir, is an expert on such far-ranging subjects as politics, cooking, and travel and has an enthusiastic and intense interest in everything else. The newsletter is an eclectic collection of witty and informative tidbits, in-depth articles, humor, services such as restaurant and accommodation reviews, answers to subscribers' queries on costs of an Irish visit, advice to those thinking of retiring to Ireland, and genealogy research. Subscribers enjoy such free fringe benefits as an annual shopping guide, accommodations directory, and a genealogy reference booklet. They also publish supplements on real estate in Ireland and annual extended features on Irish summer schools and Irish cookery, as well as special offers for certain Irish craft items. A valuable discount voucher for mail order or direct purchase also goes to all members. There's seldom any advertising in the pages of *Inside Ireland,* and all reports are totally unbiased and fully researched. You can get a sample copy by sending $2, or $30 for a year's subscription, to *Inside Ireland,* Rookwood, Stocking Lane, Ballyboden, Dublin 16 (tel. 01/931906).

The second publication that will keep your Irish memories fresh is *Ireland of the Welcomes,* a travel magazine published bimonthly by the Irish Tourist Board. It's beautifully produced and illustrated, and each issue has writing by some of the country's leading writers, as well as those of other nationalities, but always on a subject intimately connected with Ireland. You might learn about postmen who go their appointed rounds via bike in one issue, the brave men of the Coast Guard in another, and an especially notable art collection in yet another. It's a grand way to transport yourself back to Ireland while sitting in America, and the cost is a mere $14 for a year's subscription, $22 for two years. Write: Irish Tourist Board, Baggot Street Bridge, Dublin 2.

MISCELLANEOUS: Ireland has such an embarrassment of riches when it comes to gifts and souvenirs that I can only touch on a few in this book. Among those things to look for: **Connemara marble** in anything from bookends to letter openers to ashtrays to jewelry; **Owen Irish Turf Crafts** pressed and molded turf that comes in inexpensive pendants and paperweights and pricier wall plaques, all adorned with Celtic designs; the **Claddagh ring,** with its traditional folk design of two hands clasping a heart that wears a crown (it was originally the Claddagh, County Galway, wedding ring) that comes in moderately priced silver versions as well as more costly gold; **records** of Irish traditional music groups (what a great way to ease the heart when it grows homesick for Ireland once you're back home!); authentically dressed **character dolls** depicting such historical figures as the lady emigrant dressed in bonnet and shawl, or Molly Malone, with her wheelbarrow of cockles and mussels (look for them at the House of Ireland in Dublin); the **Knockcroghery Dudeen,** an authentic replica of the clay pipes of Olde Ireland, now made by Anne Lally in her home, Mill House Pottery, Knockcroghery, Co. Roscommon, and sold in most good craft shops.

CHAPTER II

GETTING TO AND AROUND IRELAND

□ □ □

1. FROM AMERICA
2. FROM BRITAIN
3. FROM THE CONTINENT
4. GETTING AROUND IRELAND
5. SUGGESTED ITINERARIES

From New York to Shannon is a five-hour flight; from Shannon back to the States takes six hours; and there's a five-hour time difference, so you can count on having at least a touch of jet lag.

1. FROM AMERICA

In these days of fierce airline competition and fares that change almost daily, you'll have to take the following figures as *guidelines* only. I can promise that you'll get different quotations, but about the same categories, when you set out to book your Irish flights.

No matter *what* the figures, however, before you settle on a fare, be sure and ask about any current specials or packages available—from time to time, Aer Lingus runs short-term, promotional fares that can put considerably more money in your pocket to be spent on *being* there instead of *getting* there.

AIR FARES TO IRELAND: Because of those fluctuating fares, it is impossible to give you even projected 1989–1990 fares. I can, however, tell you those filed through 1988, and they serve as a pretty good basis for comparison between the different fare types. My best advice is to work with a tried-and-true travel agent. If you don't know of one, ask around or look for the Certified Travel Counselor certification (it means the agent has had specialized training and met rather high requirements). It will cost you no more and save a lot of time and mental strain. Having said that, I must add that *you* should be as well informed as possible before you sit down to talk to an agent—the more you know about what's available, the more intelligently you can assess what's best for the budget. In other words, if you're serious about this budget business, you'll get the best results by combining your own, informed, judgment with that of a good agent.

When you travel to Ireland is a very important money-saving factor. For example, travel from mid-September to mid-May eastbound, or mid-October to mid-June westbound, is considerably cheaper (it's called the "basic season" in airline jargon) than if you go during "peak season" (all other months). Specific dates for season changes can vary from one year to the next, so you should check with the airline before setting your departure date. You should be aware, too, of any restrictions concerning advance booking, stopovers, etc., that apply to some of the less expensive fares.

Airlines serving Ireland from the U.S. as we go to press are Aer Lingus, Delta, and Pan Am, which means it could pay you to shop around for lowest fares being offered when you plan to travel, since all feature special promotional fares for limited times.

Delta flies twice weekly only from Atlanta, a gateway that may be more convenient for those coming from the West Coast or Midwest.

Also, a Boston departure will cost you less than a New York departure, and flying on to Dublin rather than deplaning at Shannon will add extra dollars to your fare. Fares quoted below are the 1988 round-trip costs between New York and Shannon. (Add to all fares a $13 departure tax.)

First Class: $3,220 year round. Certainly not in the budget class, but it gives a very good idea of the savings available by making another choice.

Economy Class: $952 during basic season, $1,128 in peak. Ticket is good for one year, and there are no advance purchase requirements.

APEX: $429 during basic, $629 in peak. This one's good for six months only, and there's a 21-day advance-purchase requirement.

EUROPEAN CONNECTIONS FROM IRELAND: Aer Lingus can either

fly you on their planes or hook you up with other airlines to reach any European destination on either end of your Irish visit. For the budgeteer, a good plan is to book a one-way Economy flight to Ireland, use a Eurailpass or Eurail Youthpass (purchased on *this* side of the Atlantic) to travel around Ireland and some 16 other countries on the Continent, then fly back Economy Class from your final destination city. Details on the rail passes are given later in this chapter. If you're visiting only Ireland and Great Britain, Aer Lingus will book you for arrival in Shannon and departure from London, or the reverse, at the regular round-trip fare.

YOUR CHOICE OF AIRLINE: "I believe our greatest achievement lies in the

fact that we have captured the hearts and minds of the public." Those words were spoken in 1957 about the spirit of the **Aer Lingus** staff on the airline's 21st anniversary of its founding, by a man who had been general manager for 14 years. Well, I don't know about the *rest* of the flying public, but more than 30 years after Jerry Dempsey made that statement, I'm here to testify that Aer Lingus and its staff have certainly captured *my* heart and mind!

As far as I'm concerned, my Irish arrival begins at Kennedy Airport in New York the minute I walk up to the Aer Lingus check-in counter and am greeted by a smile and a lilt straight from the "auld sod." And if the lovely green-and-blue Boeing 747 proudly sporting a shamrock won't exactly provide a "flight of angels," at least it bears the name of a saint. Now, I ask you, could any such vehicle fail to be blessed? As a matter of fact, for years there's been an annual blessing of the fleet—something comforting in that tradition.

But it's not the aircraft that engages my affection, it's the lovely people who fly it: the pretty Irish colleens in their snappy green uniforms who walk a million miles up and down the aisles to keep me and my fellow passengers happy. And the little group of black-clad nuns giggling away at the prospect of getting back home for a visit. And the sons and daughters of Ireland with *their* sons and daughters in tow, headed back to report to the Mam and Da on their life in America. And the slightly inebriated footballer who joshes with the stewardess about his exploits on the field up at Gaelic Park in the Bronx. And the scores of excited Americans—like me—who smile and smile and smile with the contentment of being, if not quite in Ireland, at least surrounded by the Irish. Never mind that this is Ireland's state-owned airline and earns a bit of loyalty on that score—as the man said, it's the *spirit* that gets you!

It's a spirit that first reared its head back in May of 1936, when most European countries already had established airlines in full operation. The best Ireland could do (she was, after all, still struggling to be a nation in her own right) was to send a little wood-and-canvas De Havilland 84 Dragon biplane named *Iolar* from a galvanized hut at Baldonnel's military aerodrome to Bristol and back. The five passengers weighed in on huge scales, and the airline's entire stock of spare parts went along in a biscuit tin. It was a small, brave, and spirited beginning, but by 1951, one million passengers had flown with the saints and shamrocks. I couldn't tell you how many passengers now fly with Aer Lingus every year—I can only tell you I count myself lucky to be among them.

Sentiment aside, Aer Lingus also offers the most frequent service from the U.S. to Ireland and can fly you on to any place in Europe from Copenhagen to Rome. Reason enough to choose the country's national airline.

A BUDGETEER'S FANTASY—GETTING THERE BY SEA: Time was that the only way to travel between Ireland and the New World was by ship: if your ancestors immigrated to America during the last century or before, they endured an Atlantic crossing that lasted for weeks, probably in cramped quarters and under generally miserable conditions. Sea travel is a different story these days, of course, and as with any island country, there's just no more romantic and relaxing way to travel to or from Ireland than by sea. Unfortunately, there is no regularly scheduled passenger-ship service between the U.S. and Ireland. Still, if you travel during the summer months, it is possible to manage that sea crossing —and in the utmost luxury—*if you're willing to bust the budget and indulge a decidedly nonbudget travel fantasy.*

In 1988 Cunard's *Queen Elizabeth 2* had two sailings from Cork to New York, reviving what was once a Cunard tradition. As we go to press, tentative plans are in place for several more in 1989. Service from New York to Cork is still uncertain. Romance and relaxation are joined by the ultimate in luxury on the *QE2*, and Cunard offers terrific package fares that let you travel one way by air, the other by ship, at money-saving prices (as little as $1,259 to $2,175 in 1988). Should the Cork sailings not fit into your schedule, you can go in either direction from Southampton and travel via car-ferry or air between England and Ireland. The Atlantic crossing takes four days from Ireland, five from England.

Not for budgeteers? Well, why not! By pinching pennies most of the time, you just may find it possible to live out every closet seafarer's dream this one time.

For 1989 schedules and fares, contact travel agents or Cunard Line Limited, 555 Fifth Ave., New York, NY 10017.

PACKAGE TOURS: Dedicated budget watchers have long known that when it comes to travel, some of the best bargains going are chartered flights or tours (escorted or unescorted). Once upon a time, that meant you were herded around with a group of other Americans, with little opportunity to break out on your own and freewheel it through a country, the only *real* way to get to know it, in my humble opinion. That is no longer true, and you can now realize enormous savings on air fare and accommodations and never see those other American faces

except in the airplane going over and coming back. Not that I have anything against my countryfolk, you understand; it's just that I don't go to Ireland to be with Americans.

Aer Lingus offers a wide selection of such bargains. You can choose only the fly/drive combination and take care of your own accommodations; the fly/drive/farmhouse or B&B combination, which covers your room each night from a choice of over 800 accommodations; or one of the most popular, the Irish Heritage package that covers air and land arrangements plus the services of the Irish Genealogical Research Society, who will do the groundwork in finding your ancestors, then give you a map showing those places important in your family's history. All can be tailored to your particular needs, time available, and budget. Book through Aer Lingus or travel agents.

Irish-owned **CIE Tours International** maintains offices in New York, London, Paris, and Düsseldorf, with expert staffs who can help you decide between the many package tours offered by CIE, both escorted and unescorted. Their coach tours are among the best, with knowledgeable drivers and guides who add the sparkle of Irish wit to their expertise. Self-drive packages give you a car, accommodation listings, itinerary suggestions and maps, and reserved accommodations for your first night. After that, you're free to roam, staying as long as you wish at one destination before moving on. For full details, contact CIE Tours International, 122 E. 42nd St., New York, NY 10168 (tel. 212/972-5600, or toll free 800/243-8687).

When it comes to escorted tours, it's hard to beat the dollar-for-value tours offered by **Globus-Gateway,** a long-established tour company that operates excellent coach tours to Ireland from late-April through mid-October. The eight-day "Introduction to Ireland" tour circles the country from Dublin, and encompasses the Ring of Kerry, Killarney, Blarney Castle, Cork, Limerick, Tipperary, Galway, and Connemara. There are other sightseeing highlights, and optional activities include a medieval banquet, a jaunting car ride in Killarney, and cabaret in Dublin. Land prices in 1988 ranged from $428 to $468. There's also a 13-day "Emerald Isle" tour that includes all the above plus many other highlights and an extended itinerary. For full details of both tours, send for their "Europe and Britain" book: Globus-Gateway, 95-25 Queens Blvd., Rego Park, NY 11374 (tel. 718/268-1700, or toll free 800/221-0090 in the eastern U.S. outside New York State), or 150 S. Los Robles Ave., Pasadena, CA 91101 (tel. 818/449-2019, or toll free 800/556-5454 outside California in the western U.S., Alaska, and Hawaii). Book tours through travel agents.

A good travel agent is an invaluable aid in finding just the right package tour, and one I can recommend is the **Grimes Travel Agency,** with three offices: 54 Mamaroneck Ave., White Plains, NY 10601 (tel. 914/761-4550); 250 W. 57th St., Suite 510, New York, NY 10019 (tel. 212/307-7797); and 95 Madison Ave., Suite 500, Morristown, NJ 07960 (tel. 201/539-6674). Since 1921 this has been a family-owned and -operated agency, with personalized service to clients around the country. There's a family member in each of the agency offices, and they're always available to find just the right package tour to suit your needs. They can plan individual, special-interest tours (golf, history, genealogical search, etc.) with an expertise acquired over the years. They also sponsor the Claddagh Club, which offers discounts on car rentals, specialized help in tracing family history, and many other benefits; there's a $25 membership fee, which is waived if you purchase a ticket through their offices.

2. FROM BRITAIN

A holiday combination of Great Britain and Ireland is a simple matter, with good links between the two countries by both air and sea.

BY AIR: Fares from London are calculated in pounds sterling, not Irish punts, since you will, of course, be paying with English currency. As we go to press, 1989 prices are not available, and although the following figures will undoubtedly be different when you travel, the categories and savings will be the same.

The regular **Aer Lingus** one-way air fare between London and Dublin in 1988 was £75 ($131.25) sterling, and there were special summer round-trip fares as low as £78 ($136.50).

BY SEA: **Sealink** operates daily car-ferry service from Pembroke to Rosslare, Holyhead to Dun Laoghaire (Dublin), Fishguard to Rosslare, and Stranraer to Larne (Northern Ireland). In 1988 the fare for passengers without cars traveling to any of the Republic of Ireland ports was IR£32 ($51.25). A car with driver paid IR£68 ($108.75) to IR£92 ($147.25). There are bargain round-trip specials offered at certain times of the year, known as **Motoring Money Savers,** which can save you a considerable amount if you're coming to Ireland for weekends or short stays of up to five days. Fares for the Northern Ireland service ranged from £15 ($26.25) to £10 ($17.50) for foot passengers (depending on season and first- or second-class travel), and drivers paid an additional £45 ($78.75) to £70 ($122.50) depending on car length and time of year.

In the U.S., you can get current Sealink sailing schedules and rate information by contacting: Sealink, c/o Britrail, 630 Third Ave., New York, NY 10017 (tel. 212/599-5400).

B+I Line sails between Holyhead and Dublin and Liverpool and Dublin on a daily basis, and in 1988 one-way fares ranged from £28 ($49) to £74 ($129.50). For current rates and schedules when you plan to travel, contact: B+I Line, c/o Lynott Tours, 350 Fifth Ave., Suite 2619, New York, NY 10118 (tel. 212/760-0101).

READER'S TRAVEL SUGGESTION: "For those under 26, **Transalpino,** 24 Talbot St., Dublin 1 (tel. 01/723825 or 742382), offers discounted fares good for two months to many European destinations, with as many en-route breaks as you please." (P. Scully, Sharpsville, Pa.).

BY BUS: There's good express coach service between London and several cities in Ireland, including Dublin, Cork, and Killarney. Round-trip tickets are good for three months and can have open return dates. Fares range from about £25 ($43.75) to £35 ($61.25). "Superbus" bookings can be made at more than 3,000 **National Express** agents in the U.K. and at all National Coach stations.

Slattery's Coaches also has good service to leading Irish cities, with bookings through U.K. travel agents.

3. FROM THE CONTINENT

You can begin or end a European holiday in Ireland, with easy access either way by air or by ship.

BY AIR: Again, the fares quoted here are those in effect in 1988 and are quoted in French francs.

Aer Lingus, in 1988, would fly you from Paris to Dublin for a regular one-way fare of 1,985 French francs ($330). Round-trip excursion fares went for 1,090 French francs ($182).

BY SEA: Most travel agents can make ferry bookings for you before you leave home, and you'll find listings below for each company's U.S. representatives, who will be glad to furnish details to help in your holiday planning.

Irish Ferries lets you extend your Irish holiday into Europe, with frequent sailings from Rosslare (near Wexford) to Le Havre, Rosslare to Cherbourg, and —from June 23 to August 26 only—from Cork to Le Havre. Two ships, the *St. Patrick II* and the *St. Killian II,* operate alternately, and both can accommodate cars as well as foot passengers. On board, you'll find restaurants, cafeterias, lounge bars, discothèques, duty-free shops, a movie theater, and a delightful mixture of nationalities and ages.

The ships do not sail on a daily basis, so best check on current schedules before you make final plans. In 1988, one-way fares began at IR£42.50 ($68) for a foot passenger in a six-berth cabin, IR£118 ($188.75) for car and driver. Sailing time is 21 hours to Le Havre and 17 hours to Cherbourg.

The line also has some terrific holiday package plans that can mean real savings for a European holiday. For example, in 1988 their two-week Villa Holiday provided a three-bedroom villa in a Brittany beach resort, with prices starting at IR£147 ($235.25) per person in low season, and a seven-day "Drive as You Please" plan offered bed-and-breakfast plus dinner, with a choice of over 170 good hotels around the country and prices beginning at IR£154 ($246.50). There are similar plans covering Spain and Jersey Island. These packages change from year to year, but they offer very good value and are well worth looking into. (Ask for their *Ferrytours* booklet, which describes all current plans.)

For advance information on current schedules, fares, and holiday plans, contact: Irish Ferries, c/o CIE Tours International, 122 E. 42nd St., New York, NY 10168 (tel. 212/972-5600, or toll free 800/243-8687), or Irish Ferries, 2-4 Merrion Row, Dublin 2 (tel. 01/610511).

4. GETTING AROUND IRELAND

Whether you come for a day or two, a week, two weeks, or longer, you'll find it easy to get around Ireland. If you're here for only a few days, you'll want to settle into one city (or B&B in the country) and take day trips only, perhaps using the excellent Bus Eireann coach tours to save the expense of renting a car. For longer visits, you have a multitude of choices via hiking, biking, escorted coach tours, rail and bus travel with an unlimited travel ticket, or a rental car with unlimited mileage. Or you may decide to work out a combination of more than one means of transportation—for example, renting a bike to carry along in your rental car can pay off when you suddenly discover a nook or cranny that's inaccessible by car.

In the following sections, I'll tell you about several Information Sheets issued by the Irish Tourist Board on specific modes of transportation. It's a good idea to write in advance for those you'd like to have, since not all ITB offices in Ireland have complete stocks at all times.

BY FOOT OR BIKE: Hiking, hitchhiking, and cycling are all quite acceptable and very popular ways to get around Ireland. My only caution would be against hitchhiking alone. If you team up with a companion, however, there is certainly no risk.

If you are a hiker, you'll be drawn to off-the-main-thoroughfare spots of incredible beauty—and I'll have to warn you that they're numerous and frequent! The Irish Tourist Board issues an Information Sheet on "Hill Walking and Rock Climbing" (no. 26A) that highlights many of these spectacular climbs. Other Information sheets detail walks in Wicklow, Kerry, South Leinster, Kildare, Dingle, and Cavan.

As for biking, there are more than 100 Raleigh Rent-a-Bike dealers around the country that rent bikes at rates of IR£5 ($8) per day or IR£22 ($35.25) per week. You'll be asked for a deposit of IR£30 ($48) when you book. And speaking of booking, that is virtually a requirement if you plan a long bike trip during the months of July and August. Students can rent at a discount through USIT (see Chapter I). *Note:* Unless you make special arrangements, bikes must be returned to the office from which they were rented.

The following Information Sheets will be particularly helpful in planning your cycling itinerary: no. 14A, "A Cycling Tour of Ireland"; no. 14B, "Cycling Dublin and Ireland East"; no. 14C, "Cycling the South East"; no. 14D, "Cycling Cork and Kerry"; no. 14E, "Cycling Shannonside"; no. 14F, "Cycling Donegal/Leitrim/Sligo"; no. 14G, "Cycling the Lakelands"; and no. 14H, "Cycling Ireland West."

BY HORSE-DRAWN CARAVAN: Ireland is one of the few places left in the world where you can pamper the gypsy in your soul. (Breathes there a soul among us so dead it hasn't dreamed of gypsy caravans and campfires? I think not.) The gaily painted caravans are comfortably fitted out to accommodate up to four—in fact, you probably should have at least four in your party to travel this way—and your leisurely pace gives you many opportunities to drink in details of Ireland's gorgeous landscape that those traveling by car will never see.

You've never handled a horse? Well, unless you're just plain scared to death of the dear creatures, that's no problem at all. The caravan operator will give you a quick course in harnessing and unharnessing, as well as the care and upkeep of your animal companion. If you wish, he'll also take you for a test drive to be sure you and your horse are compatible. Also, the farmers along your route who are appointed to provide feed and give you a parking site for the night will be all too happy to help you with any questions that come up after you've hit the road.

With a caravan, you're not really free to ramble just any old where—some roads are too steep or too heavily traveled to be suitable for your slow conveyance. Instead, you'll be offered a choice of carefully selected routes to follow, with overnight stopping places clearly marked. At some, you'll find showers, and almost all have sanitary facilities. You probably won't average more than about nine or ten miles a day, which allows plenty of time for chatting with the locals as you plod along, stopping for a pint in a friendly pub and just dreaming away the time. Time, did I say? You won't know the meaning of the word after a day or two of gypsying!

Come dinnertime, you'll have the option of eating in (you'll have cooking facilities, utensils, eating ware, and a sink) or sprucing up for a meal in the best local eatery. As a caravaner, you'll have an instant conversation-opener, and you're more likely than not to be the last one out of restaurant or pub, with the talk still going strong.

What this idyllic journey will cost you depends on the season. In 1988 charges for a four-berther ranged from IR£200 ($320) to IR£400 ($640) per week—cheap enough on a per-person basis! Add to that an average of about IR£6 ($9.50) per night for overnight stops.

Information Sheet no. 16C details the delights of traveling in a horse-drawn caravan, and the following are operators with whom you can book directly:

Mr. David Slattery, Slattery's Horse-Drawn Caravans, **Slattery's Travel Agency,** 1 Russell St., Tralee, Co. Kerry (tel. 066/21722): To the Dingle Peninsula, North Kerry, and Killarney.

Mr. Dieter Clissmann, Dieter **Clissmann Horse-Drawn Caravan Holidays,** Carrigmore, Co. Wicklow (tel. 0404/8188): To the Wicklow mountains and coast.

BY BUS AND TRAIN: One of the best buys in the travel market is the **Eurailpass,** good for unlimited rail travel in Ireland and on the Continent (but not in Great Britain or Northern Ireland), as well as on Irish Continental Lines ferries between Ireland and France. The good news is that it can now be used on Ireland's Expressway Bus Network, which means you can get to virtually any city, town, or village with your pass. They're available to any non-European resident, and must be bought before you leave home. Costs for 1988 were: $298 for 15 days, $370 for 21 days, $470 for one month, $650 for two months, and $798 for three months. Those between the ages of 14 and 26 are eligible for the **Eurail Youthpass,** at considerable discounts. Purchase these passes through travel agents.

You won't be long in the Republic before "bus and train" disappear from your vocabulary, to be supplanted by **"Bus Eireann."** That's the Irish Transport System, which operates all bus services, trains, and the Aran Islands ferry from Galway.

Somehow, that bald statement just doesn't convey the essence of Bus Eireann. It is, literally, the lifeline of the country, transporting Irish housewives from Cappoquin to Cork for a day's shopping, businesspeople from Killarney to Dublin for the day, university students home for weekends, commuters from Bray or Howth to and from work each day in Dublin, and travelers like you and me to just about anywhere we want to go in the country. Natives and visitors alike take Bus Eireann day trips to Ireland's most scenic spots at bargain prices, and for those addicted to escorted coach tours as a means of seeing a country with the least amount of personal planning, Bus Eireann provides some of the best.

Bus Eireann's home office is at the Central Bus Station (Busaras), Store Street, Dublin 1, and the central number for schedule and fare information is 01/302222. Timetables and other travel information are available there, as well as at bus and train depots around the country. Second-class travel is best for the budget, but you can go first class for a small supplement. Children under 15 go for half fare, and ages 15 to 21 pay less than two-thirds of the adult fare. One thing more: Bus Eireann is constantly offering special fares—weekends, midweek, etc.—so whenever you travel, be sure to ask about the cheapest fare available at the time, as well as special deals such as the popular "Break-away" and "Short Holiday Breaks" that include bus or rail fare and accommodations for two- or three-day periods.

Armed with a **Train Timetable** and a **Provincial and Expressway Bus Timetable,** there are few places you won't be able to reach in Ireland. The country's not that large (Galway is just three hours from Dublin by train!), both buses and trains are modern and comfortable, and your only inconvenience may be schedules for remote places, some of which don't have daily service. Of course, all those things are not all there is to public transportation. Rubbing elbows with the Irish as they go about their daily business is an added bonus for which Bus Eireann doesn't charge you a cent extra, and I must confess that some of my most memorable Irish experiences (and eavesdropping) have come from bus or train trips. Like everything else in Ireland, this kind of travel is so informal you'll think you're riding along with friends and neighbors by the time you reach your destination.

Rail and Bus Passes

If you're not using a Eurailpass, Bus Eireann will sell you a money-saving **Rambler Pass** for unlimited travel on rail or bus. Prices in 1988 were IR£52 ($83.25) for 8 days and IR£77 ($123.25) for 15 days. A combination rail and bus Rambler Pass cost IR£66 ($105.50) for 8 days, IR£95 ($152) for 15 days. Students are eligible for the **Youth Student Pass** (see Chapter I). All passes are available from mainline railway stations in Ireland, or you may purchase them through travel agents in the States or CIE Tours International, 122 E. 42nd St., New York, NY 10168 (tel. 212/972-5600, or toll free 800/243-8687).

Local Buses

In Dublin (where its name changes to Dublin Bus), Cork, Waterford, Limerick, and Galway, Bus Eireann operates double-decker buses in the inner city and outlying areas, as well as frequent service from Shannon Airport into Limerick, from Cork Airport into the city, and from Dublin Airport into that city. Fares are computed on the distance you travel and are surprisingly low: airport buses average IR£2.20 ($3.50). There are special **shopping fares** available in Dublin (see Chapter IV), and students are eligible for weekly discount tickets (see Chapter I). If you're going to be in Dublin a few days, you'll want to pick up a **Dublin District Timetable,** available at most newsstands for a small charge.

You won't pay as you board a local bus. Just get aboard and find a seat—the conductor will be along to collect your fare based on how far you're going. Those big double-deckers will usually accommodate everyone, so there's no need for the pushing and shoving and elbowing we so often encounter at home—the Irish simply queue up politely and everyone boards in turn. Very civilized.

Sightseeing Tours

You can fill every day of your visit with Bus Eireann sightseeing tours around the country at prices that are better than bargain. For instance, city sightseeing excursions cost about IR£9 ($14.50); seven-hour trips are IR£11 ($17.50); and 12-hour, all-day tours go for IR£20 ($32).

The tours operate from tourist centers all around the country, and there are few scenic spots they miss. I sometimes think it's worth the price just to listen to the patter of your driver/narrator—he not only knows the terrain and everything about it, but also throws in an Irish tale or two you're not likely to forget. Brochures entitled "Day Trips" detailing tours available in a particular area are available from Tourist Offices and local bus and train stations.

In addition to day trips, Bus Eireann operates first-rate escorted coach tours, as well as two self-drive, go-as-you-please tours using either hotel or B&B accommodations. They represent exceptional value (in 1988, the land cost for a seven-day self-drive tour was $187 to $319 per person for a car, accommodations, and several sightseeing and shopping extras; and a seven-day escorted Irish Heritage tour loaded with cabaret, medieval banquet, and other bonuses, ranged from $599 to $819, depending on season). Some 1989 tours feature two- and three-night stopovers, a real boon to those who hate packing and unpacking every day. Every coach tour or fly/drive passenger has a chance to engage in an intriguing Bus Eireann Treasure Hunt, which could net you another Irish holiday at Bus Eireann's expense. You're given a list of rhymed clues to ten questions (example: name two towns in the U.S. named for Irish towns, giving the U.S. state and the Irish county), and half the fun is getting the Irish you meet in your travels to help you unravel the answers.

BY CAR: Budget or no budget, there's just no better way to travel around Ireland than by car. Total freedom comes with the keys. You can loiter over an afternoon pint; extend a B&B overnight to three days when the place starts to feel like "home"; pull over into a layby (we'd call it an overlook) for an hour or two to steep yourself in Irish skies, mountains, coastline, fields, and rivers; stop to give a hitchhiker a lift (he'd call it a spin) to the next town and gain yet another Irish friend; seek out the perfect picnic spot and stay as long as you please; and wander as your fancy dictates, with no regard for schedules of any sort.

About that budget: this is where this book can earn its cost many times over, for with it, you qualify for a 15% discount on car rentals, which have escalated greatly in the past few years. In fact, if you're traveling with a party of three or four, that discount could well bring the cost down into near-budget range. Details are spelled out in the section that follows, so have your trusty calculator handy.

You probably don't need me to tell you that driving is on the left in Ireland, but I'll pass along a few tips garnered from my 15 or so years of driving on the "wrong" side of the road. First, before you even turn the ignition key, take time to check the rear-view and side mirrors to be sure they'll give you a clear view of the road behind. Check your luggage to be sure it's secure and won't come tumbling down if you make a sudden stop. Go over the gear system to be sure you understand it (every other rental car seems to have a different position for reverse!), then check the light dimmer and windshield wiper. Elementary details, to be sure, but while you're doing all this, you'll be adjusting to the transition from plane to Customs to car. If your arrival is an early-morning one, it's a good idea to stop for a nice hot cuppa in the airport to help that transition along. Remember, this is Ireland—you don't have to rush.

You'll be reminded of the drive-on-the-left edict by frequent signs between Shannon and Limerick and the Dublin Airport and that city. Still, the very first time you make a sharp turn, your inclination is going to be to head for the right-hand side of the road. Also, when you stop for gas, a pint, or a meal, it's very, very easy to pull off on the right side (which is the wrong side in Ireland, of course). I make it a practice to stop the car headed in the direction in which I'll be going, which somehow makes it easier to pull off on the left side. No matter what precautions you take, however, you're bound to feel awkward the first day—and maybe the second. So try to set a little tape recorder up there in your head to play and replay "Drive left" until it becomes second nature.

Speed limits in towns and cities will be 30 or 40 miles per hour (they're prominently posted), and it's 55 on the open road. Mileage is signposted in both kilometers and miles (if it's green and white, it's kilometers; black and white, miles). See "Metric Measures" in Chapter XXXII for mileage and other conversions.

Gas will cost anywhere from IR£2.50 ($4) a gallon up, and you'll find the cheapest prices at Jet stations. Those are Imperial gallons—larger by volume than ours—and in a small car, you'll cover remarkable distances on a tankful of gas. Increasingly, gas (petrol, of course) is sold by the liter, and the following will give you a quick comparison between liters, imperial gallons, and those we're accustomed to at home:

Liters	Imp. Gallons	U.S. Gallons
1	0.22	0.26
5	1.10	1.32
10	2.20	2.64
25	5.50	6.60
40	8.80	10.56

You'll learn a whole new automotive vocabulary: your luggage will go into the boot, not the trunk; the hood is now the bonnet; the windshield becomes a windscreen; you'll park in a car park, not a parking lot; those are lorries, not trucks, you pass; and you're driving a car-for-hire, not a rental car, that runs on

MILEAGE BETWEEN IRELAND'S MAJOR CITIES
Distance in Miles

	Belfast	Cork	Derry	Donegal	Dublin	Dundalk	Galway	Kilkenny	Killarney	Limerick	Portlaoise	Roscommon	Rosslare Harbour	Shannon Airport	Sligo	Waterford	Wexford	Wicklow
Athlone	141	136	130	114	78	90	58	78	144	75	46	20	130	83	73	108	117	110
Belfast		264	112	104	104	52	190	177	271	201	157	139	205	215	128	207	192	136
Cork			266	250	160	202	130	92	54	65	108	156	129	80	209	78	116	166
Derry				43	147	97	169	208	274	204	175	131	247	218	84	238	235	179
Donegal					138	98	127	192	253	184	160	94	243	176	41	222	231	171
Dublin						53	136	73	192	123	52	91	101	138	135	98	88	32
Dundalk							148	123	219	150	94	94	153	165	104	141	157	85
Galway								107	120	65	93	51	170	57	86	137	157	168
Kilkenny									123	70	32	98	62	85	152	30	50	77
Killarney										69	140	164	171	84	213	120	158	208
Limerick											71	94	131	15	144	80	118	141
Portlaoise												66	84	86	119	62	71	77
Roscommon													150	96	53	129	138	123
Rosslare Harbour														146	203	51	12	72
Shannon Airport															136	95	133	156
Sligo																182	191	162
Waterford																	39	88
Wexford																		56

petrol, not gas. And those signs with bold Gaelic lettering reading "Geill Sli" mean "Give Way," and mean precisely that! Got it?

Now, about Irish roads—quite simply, I think they're wonderful! You may disagree. But, you see, I have an active dislike for huge, speedy double-laned highways (another new phrase, dual carriageways), and in spite of the fact that only about 5% of Ireland's roadways fall into that category, I grumble every time I see the bulldozers hard at it widening and straightening one of my beloved little country lanes. And they seem to be even harder at it with every visit. Of course, when you're trying to pass one of those gigantic trucks (excuse me, lorries), the wider roads do come in handy. But if you take my heartfelt advice, most of the roads you travel will fall into the 95% that are small, sometimes bumpy, and a hundredfold more interesting than the National Primary Routes. They always make me feel that I'm traveling right inside the landscape, not whizzing by it. One note of caution: U-turns can lead to disaster—on dual carriageways or country lanes.

There are some things you ought to know about those little roads. Like the fact that in early mornings and evenings, you're sure to meet at least one farmer and his hardworking dog driving the cows to or from the fields—right down the middle of the road. Don't panic! Just stop like everybody else, relax, give your man a nod or a wave, and let the sea of cattle wash right around you. Also, you're probably going to get lost at least once. That's because road signs sometimes mysteriously get turned around (leprechauns?), or you come to a junction with no signs. But let me tell you that getting lost in Ireland is a pleasant adventure. Stop at a pub to ask directions and you're in for some delightful conversation, especially if things are a little slow. An Irish friend tells me that the classic answer to such a request is "Well, if I were going there, I wouldn't be starting from here" —I'm still waiting to hear that one for myself!

But if it's directions you're after and there's more than one person present, the general discussion that erupts will enlighten you about all the alternative routes, the advantages and disadvantages of each, and a good many thumbnail sketches of the folks who live along the various ways. When everyone has had his say (and not until then!), you'll be sent on your way—if, that is, you don't accept a warm invitation to "stay over for the night and we'll have a bit of a singsong" —with detailed instructions on where *not* to go as well as the right route. Many's the time a stern "you'll come to a crossroad with a church, but pay no mind to it and keep to the road straight ahead" has kept me from making a wrong turn.

If the whole thing gets too complicated, don't be surprised if someone hops eagerly into the car to show you the way, brushing aside his return with an easy "And wasn't I wanting to go to the next town, anyway." And he won't think a thing about hitching all the way back home, for he was raised in a tradition that says if you've a roof over your head, a fire at your hearth, and a potato in the pot, it's very close to a mortal sin not to share them all with a stranger in need. More than that, he'll welcome the chance of a bit of conversation with someone from other parts—and he'll take the time for both the help and the "crack" (that's *Irish* "crack," nothing more addictive than a good chat).

Your car-hire company will provide you with a map, of course (not that it will keep you from getting lost), but most are not all that easy to follow. I highly recommend the **Holiday Maps** (regional, as well as for the entire country), which are much more detailed, have city maps (you'll need them), and give you a wealth of useful tourist information. They sell for about IR£3 ($4.75) and can be bought at most news agents. For quick itinerary planning, the following mileage chart will be helpful.

One last suggestion: **Comprehensive Communications, Inc. (CCI)**, has put together three **Auto-Tape Tours of Ireland** which follow a circular route around the country, beginning at Shannon. Commentators are both American and Irish, and along with a very good narration on the localities you're passing through, they throw in bits of folklore and music and odd bits of information that add color to your trip. They come with a map, and the tapes are timed for your probably rate of speed, but make suggestions for deviating from the prescribed itinerary to explore a nook or cranny or two. You don't have to buy all three if you're going to be in one section of the country only. Tape 1 takes you from Shannon to Sligo via Limerick, the cliffs of Moher, Galway, Yeats Country, and the prehistoric sites that dot this landscape. Tape 2 carries you on from Sligo through Dublin, Wicklow, Wexford, and Waterford to Cork. And Tape 3 completes the circle back to Shannon by way of West Cork's beautiful coastline and tiny villages, Kerry's mountains, Killarney, and Tralee. Actually, you'll enjoy your trip much more if you order these tapes ahead and listen to them before you leave for Ireland; when you return home, they're a lasting memento of your visit. Order from CCI, P.O. Box 385, Scarsdale, NY 10583 (tel. 914/472-5133); each tape costs $10.95 plus $1 for postage and handling.

Car Rentals

The first thing you must know about renting a car in Ireland is that it is absolutely necessary to book ahead. That's especially true from the first of July through the end of September, but in this small country, a run on the stock available can develop suddenly if there's a special event of some kind that draws lots of visitors. You should also know that you must be between the ages of 23 and 70 (top age with some companies is 65).

The rate you pay will depend on the size of the car and the season of the year. Seasonal dates may vary slightly from one company to another, but generally you'll find the highest charges from July through September, a more moderate rate in May, June, and October, and the lowest from November through April. Prices for the smaller, stick-shift cars are the best value; larger vehicles (the only ones available with automatic transmission) can run as much as a third more.

The rates quoted will include third-party and passenger liability insurance, but unless you add on collision damage waiver insurance, you'll be responsible for the full cost of repairs should you be involved in an accident. Even though that can add as much as IR£45 ($73) to your weekly costs, I strongly advise you to take it—otherwise, you'll be required by most companies to make a refundable payment of as much as IR£150 ($240). You may also be asked for a deposit at the time you book, but this is many times waived if you present a recognized credit card. Almost every company allows pickup at one airport and drop-off at another if you wish.

Three Discount Rates

Jim Thornton is general manager of **Johnson & Perrott Rent-a-Car Ltd.,** Emmet Place, Cork (tel. 021/273295, or toll free in the U.S. 800/223-6764), a highly reliable company that has for years given readers of this book a 15% discount on basic car rentals if they mention it when booking and have it with them when they pick up the car. That's a nice saving, but even nicer is the fact that it will get you to one of the most efficient and helpful car-hire companies in Ireland. To illustrate, let me tell you about my experience with J&P on my very first visit to Ireland back in 1973. I had requested a certain make car, which didn't happen to be available when I checked in with them at Shannon. However, a pretty colleen behind the desk—Maureen—assured me that one was due to be checked in later that afternoon and sure, wouldn't she be glad to drive me in to Limerick to my B&B for a bit of rest, then bring the car I wanted when it arrived. And sure, didn't she do it! The trip in included a running string of tips about where to go and what to do in the Shannonside area, as well as a lot of places around the country (that's how I first learned about Durty Nellie's)—places I might otherwise have missed. Came the late afternoon and came Maureen with my car, followed by a second J&P car to deliver her back to Shannon so I wouldn't have to drive her myself. At the time I was overwhelmed by such consideration, but in the ensuing years I've become almost blasé about that kind of courtesy—it seems to come naturally to the entire staff. They've helped me plan itineraries and choose the best routes all over Ireland, all the while as gracious and friendly as if they weren't putting themselves out at all.

Johnson & Perrott have pickup points at all air and sea ports, and in Dublin, Cork, Galway, and Limerick, with desks at the Dublin, Cork, Sligo, and Shannon airports. In those cities, they'll even deliver the car to your accommodation at no extra charge. There's no drop-off charge either at Shannon, Dublin, Sligo, and Cork airports (or they'll arrange to pick the car up at your guesthouse in those cities). Like all car-hire firms, they charge more during the high season, but it's a remarkably short one, July 1 to September 15, and the same Ford Fiesta that goes for IR£175 ($280) per week during that period drops to IR£130 ($208) other months. Both rates include unlimited mileage.

There are several money-saving specials available at Johnson & Perrott: I've already detailed their farmhouse holiday program (see Chapter I); there's a special "Businessman's Discount" for people coming to Ireland on a regular basis for business purposes. Be sure and inquire when you book about any specials in effect at the time. When booking, enclose a minimum $60 deposit. You can book through travel agents or with J&P directly.

Boland's Car Rentals, 206 Pearse St., Dublin 2 (tel. 01/770704), gives a 15% discount to readers when they mention this book when reserving and have it with them when they pick up the car. Boland's has offices at Dublin, Shannon, and Cork airports, and at Dun Laoghaire and Rosslare, all staffed by friendly, helpful personnel. They'll also deliver to most Dublin city hotels. With a good selection of Fords (several models), Opels, Suburus, and Renaults, their rates range from IR£25 ($40) to IR£82 ($131.25) per day, depending on the model car and the season. For rentals of 15 days or more, the range drops to IR£20 ($32) to IR£66 ($105.50), and all rates include unlimited mileage.

Dan Dooley Rent-A-Car, Knocklong, Co. Limerick (tel. 062/53103, or toll free in the U.S. 800/331-9301), is a family-run business, begun back in 1971, which will give our readers a 10% discount. Just mention this book when you reserve and have it with you when you pick up the car. They have one of the largest fleets of rental cars in Ireland, with a desk at Shannon, Cork, and Dublin airports as well as an office in Dublin city center, Cork, Dun Laughaire, and Rosslare. If your party is a large one, you will be glad to know they also offer nine-passenger minibuses. Timid drivers will find automatic-shift cars available. The 1988 rates ranged from IR£21 ($33.50) per day to IR£64 ($102) per day, with weekly rates ranging from IR£105 ($168) to IR£450 ($720). All rates include unlimited mileage.

Other Car-Hire Firms

Murray's Europcar, Baggot Street Bridge, Dublin 4 (tel. 01/681777), offers free delivery and collection within five miles of a local company office. Other offices are at Shannon, Cork, Galway, Wexford, Rosslare, Waterford, Sligo Airport, and Knock Airport. They have a wide variety of sizes and models, and weekly rates in low season start at IR£126 ($201.50) with unlimited mileage. Peak-season rates (in July and August) are about 25% higher. Murray's operates as official car-rental contractor to Aer Lingus and is the Irish agent for National Car Rental and Tilden, of Canada. Chauffeur Drive services are also available.

Both **Avis** and **Hertz** are represented in Ireland, each with offices around the country and free drop-off privileges from one office to the other. You can book through travel agents, but rates are considerably higher than at Johnson & Perrott, Boland's, Dooley, or Murray's.

5. SUGGESTED ITINERARIES

Set itineraries present a very real danger in Ireland. A 15-minute pub break in an afternoon's drive can easily turn into a two-day layover, all because your man behind the bar insists you'll be very welcome at the evening's singsong with such conviction that it is suddenly very clear that the Blarney Stone can wait another day—which turns into yet *another* day when you fall in with such convivial company at the singsong that nothing will do but that you stay over for the next night! Now, don't misunderstand me: it *is* possible to "do" a very good, circular tour of Ireland in two weeks. But whether or not you get all the way around will depend entirely on how determined you are to stay on that schedule.

Bearing all that in mind, you'll find some recommended tours set out below. The first, and longest, takes you around the outer rim of Ireland's cuplike terrain (see the map in the Introduction). This tour encompasses only the Republic: add another three to five days if you intend to visit Northern Ireland. Remember, this swing around the country will only touch the highlights, some of which you may wish to skip in favor of spending more time at a spot you find especially intriguing.

It's important to remember, too, that although mileages may *appear* short, these are *Irish* miles—distances, road conditions, and the usual driving considerations have absolutely nothing to do with how long it takes you to cover them.

There's an old Irish saying, "An Irish mile is long, but easy traveled." After one or two stops, you'll know the truth in that! Every pub or lunch or sightseeing stop will make it clearer, and you won't want to miss the photo "musts" that lurk around almost every bend.

Right here, I'd like to make a suggestion based purely on my personal choice of how to travel. The first of my suggested itineraries is a circular tour which anticipates that you will move from place to place almost every night. Well, I don't know about you, but I don't particularly enjoy packing and unpacking every single night. To avoid that, it is quite possible to select several major destinations along the route, settle in for a day or so and make longish day trips, returning to the same homey B&B in the evening. Besides, while Irish pubs are notoriously hospitable to visitors, if you return the *second* night, you're an instant "regular"—lots more fun! Of course, such a plan means longer stretches of driving when you do move along, but you will have taken in a lot of the sights along the way on your day trips, making those Irish miles go more quickly.

Shorter, regional itineraries can be incorporated into the circular route or taken on their own, depending on the time you have to spend and your own inclinations. To help you make any such adjustments, you will find full details for each region in the chapters that follow. One last time, I want to point out that these are *suggested* itineraries, and they are by no means cast in stone. Do as the Irish do and just "go with it," whatever "it" turns out to be, and you'll have a happy holiday.

TWO WEEKS—A CIRCULAR TOUR: The suggested starting point is Dublin. If you deplane at Shannon, however, you can simply begin with the Day 9 itinerary and follow the suggested route to the north or south, ending up again at Shannon for your flight home.

Days 1–2: *Dublin.* Allow arrival day for settling into your Dublin digs and getting the feel of the city. Devote the second day to exploring Dublin's fine historic buildings and Georgian squares, ending with a hotel cabaret or an evening's pub crawl.

Day 3: *Dublin to Waterford (or Tramore).* Get an early start and drive south to Enniskerry to visit the Powerscourt estate and gardens. Then on through Roundwood to Glendalough with its early-Christian ruins in a spectacular setting of mountains and lakes. Avoca is next, where Thomas Moore wrote his melodic "The Meeting of the Waters." South through Arklow to Enniscorthy, with time out to visit its small museum, and on straight through to Waterford, or detour over to historic Wexford's narrow, charming streets before continuing on to Waterford's Reginald's Tower (built in 1003) and its remarkable collection of city charters and other artifacts. Stop for the night in the city itself, or drive on to the seaside resort of Tramore with its three miles of sandy beaches.

Day 4: *Waterford to Cork.* Drive south through the old market town of Dungarvan, then westward to Youghal. Stop at the clock tower in the middle of town to visit its interesting museum, allowing ample time for the walking tour described in a brochure available there, which will take you along some of Ireland's oldest surviving city walls. On to Cork, where you can play the famous Shandon Bells at St. Mary's, visit the city's many historic sites, and enjoy an evening meal in one of its fine restaurants.

Day 5: *Cork to Killarney.* Stop by Blarney Castle to kiss the legendary stone, then head for Macroom, Ballingeary, and the Pass of Keimaneigh (you may want to make the short detour to Gougane Barra National Park). On to the lovely holiday resort of Glengarriff, then turn north through rugged mountain terrain to Kenmare and on to Killarney.

Days 6–7: *Killarney.* You'll want to spend one day visiting the famous lakes, islands, and ancient abbeys. On your second day, Killarney is the ideal base from which to make either the 109-mile Ring of Kerry drive or a 93-mile circuit of the bewitching Dingle Peninsula.

Day 8: *Killarney to Limerick.* If you opted for the Ring of Kerry on Day 7, you can swing around Dingle en route to Limerick (but it makes for a *long* day of driving—Dingle is, in fact, a perfect place for one of those itinerary adjustments to allow for an overnight stop). Then back through Rathkeal, Newcastle West, and the beautiful village of Adare to Limerick (only 16 miles from Shannon Airport). Save this evening for the Bunratty or Knappogue castle medieval banquet (which must be booked ahead).

Day 9: *Limerick to Galway.* Take time to explore Limerick's St. Mary's Cathedral before heading north, then add a few extra miles to take in the stunning Cliffs of Moher. Lisdoonvarna, the popular spa resort, is next, then the barren beauty of the Burren's limestone hills, Ballyvaughan, Clarinbridge, and Galway. Traditional music in a pub in Galway or nearby Salthill makes for a memorable evening.

Day 10: *Galway to Donegal.* A full day's drive will take you through Connemara to Moycullen, Oughterard, Recess, Clifden, Leenane, and along Clew Bay (with over 100 islands) into Westport. Not far away is Westport House, with its magnificent interior, beautiful gardens, and zoo park. Then head north through Castlebar, Pontoon, Ballina, and Enniscrone, a charming family seaside resort (stop for a swim or a walk along the strand). Then drive on to Sligo to see the 13th-century Franciscan Friary and the county library museum or just walk the narrow old streets and soak up the atmosphere so dear to Yeats's heart. You'll find the poet's burial place at nearby Drumcliff, then on to Bundoran, Ballyshannon, and Donegal.

Day 11: *Donegal.* Early in the day, explore Donegal town, with its Franciscan friary and castle. Then head off for a circular tour of County Donegal by driving west through Mountcharles, Killybegs, Ardara, Glenties, Maas, and Kincasslagh (Donegal tweed country). Push farther north through Annagry, Crolly, Bunbeg, Bloody Foreland, Gortahork, and into Dunfanaghy, nestled at the foot of steep cliffs along the shores of Sheephaven Bay. Drive south to

Letterkenny (and if you've an extra day, I strongly recommend the 120-mile loop around the Inishowen Peninsula to Buncrana, Malin Head, and Moville—the scenery is truly spectacular and well worth the drive), then through the picturesque Finn Valley back to Donegal Town.

Day 12: *Donegal to Carrick-on-Shannon.* Make this a leisurely driving day, south through Ballyshannon and Bundoran, then southeast to Manorhamilton (look for the ruins of a 1638 castle brooding over the town). Continue south through Drumkeeran and along the shores of lovely Lough Allen (a good day and place for a picnic lunch) to Drumshabo and Leitrim and into Carrick-on-Shannon, with its fleet of cruise boats bobbing at the wharves.

Day 13: *Carrick-on-Shannon to Dublin.* Drive through lake country to Cavan town by way of Mohill, Carrigallen, Killeshandra, and Crossdoney. On through Bailieborough and Carrickmacross to Drogheda. From Drogheda, visit the prehistoric tomb at Newgrange, then drive on through Slane into Navan. A further six miles will bring you to the Hill of Tara, home of ancient Irish high kings. From there, it's back to Dublin via historic Trim, Black Bull, Clonee, Blanchardstown, and the Phoenix Park.

Day 14: *Dublin.* A day for odds-and-ends and departure.

ONE WEEK—EAST COAST AND LAKELAND: Starting point for this tour is also Dublin, and **Day 1** is reserved for your arrival, settling in and perhaps a cabaret in the evening.

Day 2: Drive south through Dun Laoghaire, Dalkey, and Killiney along the Vico Road, with its spectacular views of Dublin Bay, into the seaside resort of Bray (leave the main road to detour along the seafront). Then on to Enniskerry beneath Sugarloaf Mountain. Visit nearby Powerscourt Estate and Gardens. Glendalough and its timeless ruins are next along the scenic mountain drive, then on to Rathdrum, Avoca, and Woodenbridge into Arklow. On to County Wexford's Gorey, Enniscorthy (stop in the museum), and into Wexford town, where an overnight stop will give you time to walk its narrow streets and relive its gallant history.

Day 3: From Wexford, head southwest to Ballyhack to catch the ferry across Waterford Harbor to Passage East in County Waterford (if you're enamored of tiny seaside villages, make the short detour to Dunmore East). See Waterford's 1003 Reginald's Tower and remnants of its Viking-built city walls. Kilkenny is next, where you should stop to see Kilkenny Castle, Rothe House, and the Kilkenny Design Workshops. Then it's on through Tullamore (home of the famous Tullamore Dew) to Athlone, "capital" of the midlands. Make this your overnight stop.

Day 4: Drive northwest to Roscommon to have a look at Roscommon Abbey, then on to the market town of Longford, with its 19th-century cathedral. Head southeast to Edgeworthstown (where you may want to visit the museum dedicated to novelist Maria Edgeworth) and through the angling center of Castlepollard to see nearby Tullynally Castle. Lough Derravaragh, in the immediate vicinity, is the setting of the Irish legend of the *Children of Lir.* Detour to Fore to see its Benedictine abbey and ancient crosses, then back to Castlepollard and south to Mullingar to spend the night.

Day 5: From Mullingar, drive through Kinnegad to Trim, with its impressive Norman castle, then head for Navan, where a short detour onto the Dublin road will bring you to the royal Hill of Tara. Back to Navan and on to Donaghmore and Slane. Look for Bronze Age cemeteries at Brugh na Boinne and visit Mellifonte Abbey and Monasterboice, then on north to Dunleer, Castlebellingham, and Dundalk. If there's time, drive a bit farther north to the rugged little Carlingford Peninsula, then back to Dundalk and along the coast through Clogher, Termonfeckin, Baltray, Drogheda, Balbriggan, Skerries, Rush,

Swords, and Howth (where there are marvelous views of the bay) and on to Dublin by way of Sutton.

Day 6: Spend this day exploring the city.

Day 7: Departure.

ONE WEEK—WEST COAST: A good tour for those deplaning at Shannon. Spend **Day 1** in Limerick, visit Bunratty Folk Park, and take in a castle banquet in the evening (must be booked ahead).

Day 2: Drive to Ennis, then southwest to the picturesque seaside resort towns of Kilrush and Kilkee. North to Lahinch and skirt Liscannor Bay to the mystical Cliffs of Moher. On to Lisdoonvarna, through the bleakly beautiful Burren to Black Head, Ballyvaughan, Kinvara, and Clarinbridge into Galway, where you'll spend the night.

Day 3: Head for Connemara by way of Spiddal, Costello, Screeb, Derryrush, Carna, Toombeola, Ballynahinch, and Clifden. Head northward to Letterfrack and Leenane, where a turn to the southeast will take you through Maam, Cong (setting of *The Quiet Man* movie), Ballinrobe, Patry, Ballintubber (stop to see the abbey), and into Castlebar. Visit Clonalis House, and make Castlebar your overnight stop.

Day 4: Drive to Westport and visit impressive Westport House with its magnificent mansion and zoo park. Take the road to Newport and travel through Mulrany to the Curraun Peninsula, Achill Sound, and on to the breathtaking views of Achill Island (reached by a causeway). Allow time to drive as far out as Keel and Dooagh. Stay overnight on Achill or return to Westport.

Day 5: Turn inland through a changing landscape to Castlebar, Claremorris (Knock and its celebrated shrine are a short detour away), Ballyhaunis, Castlerea, and Roscommon (visit its famous abbey) to Athlone for the night.

Day 6: Heading south from Athlone, drive to Birr and stop to visit the gardens at Birr Castle. Farther south, Nenagh's fine castle dates from about 1200. Turn due west for Portroe and drive along the shores of Lough Derg to Killaloe. From here, it's a short drive, via O'Brien's Bridge and Ardnacrusha, into Limerick.

Day 7: Departure.

THREE DAYS—SOUTHWEST: On **Day 1,** starting from Cork (but only after you've had time to visit some of the city's highlights), drive the five miles to Blarney Castle for the obligatory kiss of that magical stone, then back through Cork and south to the charming fishing town of Kinsale. Continue southwest through Timoleague, Clonakilty, Rosscarbery, Glandore, and Union Hall to the old town of Skibbereen. The route on through Ballydehob, Schull, Toormore, Durrus, and Bantry into Glengarriff is one of the loveliest in the country. In Glengarriff, visit Garnish Island, then climb through rugged mountains via the Tunnel Road to Kenmare and on to Killarney for the night.

Day 2: Allow the entire day to drive the Ring of Kerry (110 miles), since you won't want to rush through some of Ireland's most spectacular sea and mountain landscape. From Killarney, head for Killorglin, Glenbeigh, Cahirciveen, Waterville, Derrynane, Castlecove, Sneem, and Kenmare before returning to Killarney for the night.

Day 3: Devote this day to the Dingle Peninsula's very special charms. From Killarney, drive to Killorglin, then north to Castlemaine, west to Inch (where much of *Ryan's Daughter* was filmed), Annascaul, Dingle, Ventry, Slea Head, Dunquin, Ballyferriter, Murreagh, and back to Dingle. Cross Connor's Pass to the north side of the peninsula and Stradbally, Camp, and Tralee before heading back to Killarney. Alternatively, stay the night in one of the lovely B&Bs on the peninsula.

CHAPTER III

IRELAND, A TOURIST'S SURVEY

□ □ □

1. THINGS TO SEE AND DO
2. IRELAND AFTER DARK
3. TRACING YOUR IRISH ROOTS

My survey of Ireland's tourist treasures must, of necessity, be somewhat abbreviated—entire books have been written on each of the topics I'll cover in this chapter—but I'll talk about some of the highlights and point you in the direction of more complete details on the subjects that most take your individual fancy.

As I've said so many times already in the preceding chapters, if you give yourself up to Irish fate and just "go with it," you'll be ready to write a book or two yourself on the things you've discovered on your own that *aren't* covered in this book!

1. THINGS TO SEE AND DO

The Irish Tourist Board issues Information Sheets 5A and 5B listing most of the sightseeing attractions throughout Ireland, and in the regional sections that follow, you'll find my choices of things to see and do in almost every county. For now, though, I'll talk about generalities.

SPECIAL EVENTS: It may be a *slight* exaggeration to say there's a "special event" of one sort or another every other day in Ireland, but it's been my experience that the simplest, most ordinary occurrence can take on that air if two or more natives are present.

If you're lucky enough to arrive in a small town or village when its own special festival (sometimes called "pattern day") is in progress, you'll be in for a real treat. There is always at least one day, usually several, filled with the likes of fancy-dress parades, donkey races, traditional music and dance contests, and ending with a dance that draws locals from miles away. By all means stop, mingle with the Irish, and let the itinerary take care of itself. As far as I know, no one has ever compiled a list of these festivals and their dates, so you'll just have to be on the lookout for the homemade signs on the outskirts of town as you travel around.

Also, if you pick up a current copy of *Old Moore's Almanac* at a news agent, you'll find a listing of most fairs, festivals, and pattern days for the year.

From March through November, however, there are enough more formal, organized special events to set you thinking about an extended visit to take in more than one. Any Irish Tourist Board office can furnish a complete *Calendar of Events* to help you plan your travel dates around the ones most appealing. Some of the most outstanding and the months in which they usually fall are:

March
    St. Patrick's Week (his day is the 17th, of course)

April
    Cork International Choral and Folk Dance Festival

May
    Spring Show (Dublin)
    Pan Celtic Week (Killarney, Co. Kerry)
    Fleadh Nua (Ennis, Co. Clare; the national traditional music, song, and dance festival)

June
    Writers' Week (Listowel, Co. Kerry; Irish literature workshops, lectures, plays, etc.—you don't have to be a writer to attend)
    Festival of Music in Great Irish Houses (Dublin)

August
    Dublin Horse Show (*the* social event of the year—requires booking far in advance for accommodations in Dublin)
    Rose of Tralee (Killarney, Co. Kerry; sometimes held in early September)
    Fleadh Cheoll (a festival of traditional Irish music, with no set venue; check for current location)

September
    Waterford Festival of International Light Opera (Waterford)
    Gaelic Football and Hurling All-Ireland Finals
    Galway Oyster Festival (Galway)

October
    Dublin Theater Festival (future is uncertain—be sure to check if it's on the year you visit)
    Wexford Opera (Wexford)
    Cork Jazz International Festival (Cork City)
    Dublin City Marathon (Dublin)

In addition to scheduled events, Bord Fáilte is constantly coming up with off-season travel programs such as their "Springtime in Ireland" promotion that provides bargain air fare and accommodations, along with shopping discounts and several special activities. Then there's a "Christmas in Ireland" program most years and the annual St. Patrick's Week celebrations. Details vary from year to year on money-saving features, so you should check with any Irish Tourist Board office or travel agents to see what's up when you want to travel.

HISTORIC PLACES: There are more than 800 reminders of Ireland's antiquity scattered around the countryside that are labeled State Monuments, 100 high crosses, 120 round towers and *30,000* earthen ring forts! It's anybody's guess how many exist in unofficial splendor in green fields, on mountainsides, and along coastal indentations. Information Sheet no. 5B, published by the Irish Tourist Board, gives a good overall view of what to look for and how they came to be there. I also recommend for history and archeology buffs, Peter Harbison's excellent *Guide to the National Monuments of Ireland* (Gill and Macmillan, Publishers), available in most Irish bookshops.

To breathe life into the ancient times that left all those relics in their wake, the Irish have gone to great pains to preserve some in their state of ruin and restore others. The secluded full-scale Bronze Age lake dwelling on the grounds of **Craggaunowen Castle** in County Clare will send your imagination spinning right back to those dim and hazy days of Ireland's past. **Blarney Castle,** any one of the castle medieval banquets, **Bunratty Folk Park** in County Clare, the **Ulster Folk Museum** in Belfast, and **Glencolumbkille** in County Donegal bring you closer to modern times, and **Muckross House** in Killarney, County Kerry, recreates the life of a still later period.

In Dublin, look for those marvelous 18th-century **Georgian mansions,** as well as the gracious squares and crescents that give it such unique character. Outside of Dublin (many within easy reach of the city), there are splendid residences built by wealthy aristocrats, from medieval times right through to the last century representing Gaelic, Norman, and more recent Anglo-Irish cultures, to indulge their luxurious tastes and lifestyles. You can visit many of these castles and stately homes, as well as some of the most beautifully landscaped gardens in the world, for surprisingly small fees. There's **Malahide Castle,** Malahide, Co. Dublin; **Bantry House** in Bantry, Co. Cork; **Muckross House** in Killarney, Co. Kerry; **Clonalis House** in Castlerea, Co. Roscommon; and **Knappogue Castle** in Quin, Co. Clare, to name a few. Among the gardens you won't want to miss are those at **Mount Usher,** Ashford, Co. Wicklow; and **Powerscourt,** Enniskerry, Co. Wicklow. Check at Tourist Offices and bookshops for the illustrated booklet on those maintained by members of the **Historic Irish Tourist Houses and Gardens Association (HITHA),** or contact HITHA, 3A Castle St., Dalkey, Co. Dublin (tel. 01/859323), for full details.

ART GALLERIES: There are quite good art collections in galleries, some large and impressive, others small but still impressive. Dublin's **National Gallery,** Merrion Square West, and **Hugh Lane Municipal Gallery of Modern Art,** Parnell Square, are both on the "don't miss" list; **Malahide Castle,** Malahide, Co. Dublin, has an outstanding portrait collection; in Kilkenny, it's the **Kilkenny Castle Art Gallery**; in Waterford, the **Waterford Arts Center**; the **Cork Arts Society Gallery** is at 16 Lavitt's Quay; the **Fota Estate,** Carrigtwohill, Co. Cork, houses an extensive private collection of Irish landscape paintings; Limerick's **Belltable Arts Center,** in O'Connell Street, has regular shows by local artists; **Kenny's Bookshop and Art Gallery,** High Street, Galway, also exhibits works by local artists; and in Sligo, nearly 100 paintings by John and Jack Yeats, as well as other Irish artists, are shown at the **Sligo Art Gallery,** Stephen Street.

Check with the Irish Tourist Board (Information Sheet no. 5C is devoted to art galleries) and the Arts Council, 70 Merrion Square, Dublin 2 (tel. 01/611840), for further details about these and the many other galleries around the country.

MUSEUMS: Allow yourself plenty of time to visit the **National Museum** on Kildare Street in Dublin, **Kilmainham Jail Museum** in the Kilmainham section of Dublin, and the **James Joyce Museum** in the tower at Sandycove, Co. Dublin. And as you drive around the country, don't miss museums like **Reginald's Tower** in Waterford, **Rothe House** in Kilkenny, the **Clock Tower Museum** in Youghal, Co. Cork, the **museum at Craggaunowen,** Co. Clare (where Tim Severin's replica of St. Brendan's boat has found a permanent home), or **Glencolumbkille Folk Museum** in Co. Donegal.

If you're really into museum hopping, you can obtain an illustrated guide to the 150 museums in Ireland (including Northern Ireland) from many book-shops or direct from **The Irish Museums Trust,** Belfield House, University College, Dublin 4. It sells for IR£3.95 ($6.25), plus postage if you order by mail.

STATE FORESTS: Ireland's state forests—more than 300 of them—are for the most part small and undeveloped havens of nature trails, bird songs, and tranquility. Many have picnic sites, inviting the nice notion of an outdoor lunch in a different woodland every day. You can do that—or just plot a peaceful half-hour break each day—with the help of *The Open Forest, A Guide to Areas Open to the Public,* a publication of the **Forest Service,** Leeson Lane, Dublin 2 (tel. 01/615666). They can also furnish a whole bevy of detailed pamphlets on individual state forests.

You'll find the state forests well cared for and rubbish-free—you'll be on your honor to help keep them that way.

CRUISING: Ireland's hundreds of miles of inland waterways offer an ideal escape from the rigors of driving and one of the most peaceful travel experiences you could dream of. Cruising along the magnificent Shannon or from Belturbet to Belleek by way of Lower and Upper Lough Erne and its connecting river or on the Grand Canal from Dublin all the way to the Shannon or Barrow invokes a tranquility that just doesn't exist behind the wheel of an automobile. Add to that the delight of a unique view of the Irish countryside and stopovers at waterside towns and villages, and you have the holiday of a lifetime.

The beauty of such a holiday is that you don't have to be a seasoned sailor to hire a cabin cruiser from one of the 11 companies approved by the Irish Tourist Board. You'll be given free instruction on handling the craft, reading charts, etc., and I'm told most people are fully confident and ready to set sail after little more than an hour (if you're the least bit timid, however, your instructor will stay with you until your qualms have disappeared). It's a comfort, too, to know that especially during peak holiday seasons the waterways are constantly patrolled by professionals to keep an eye out for any holiday sailor who *might* get into difficulty. There's no license involved, but you must be over 21 years old and there must be one person other than the "Captain" who understands the controls and charts.

Cruisers range in size from two to eight berths and are fully outfitted with all the comforts of home (full kitchen, showers, hot water, etc.). For budget travelers, the savings from doing your own cooking and sharing the costs with a full passenger load make cruising a viable option.

The Tourist Board can furnish a full list of companies that rent cabin cruisers. Booking is done directly with the firm of your choice. As for costs, in 1988 those listed below charged rates of IR£65 ($104) to IR£115 ($184) per person per week, depending on the size of the cruiser and the season:

Carrick Craft, Carrick-on-Shannon, Co. Leitrim (tel. 078/20236)
Emerald Star Line, 37 Dawson St., Dublin 2 (tel. 01/718870)
Flagline (1972) Ltd., Rosebank Marina, Carrick-on-Shannon, Co. Leitrim (tel. 078/20172), and Shancurragh, Athlone, Co. Westmeath (tel. 0902/72892)
Athlone Cruisers Ltd., Shancurragh, Athlone, Co. Westmeath (tel. 0902/72892)
Shannon Castle Line, Ringsend, Dublin 4 (tel. 01/600964)

If a Shannon cruise is your idea of a Big Splurge, and you decide to do it in real style, you might consider the following. Surely one of the most relaxing and luxurious ways to enjoy Ireland's legendary landscape of castles, quaint villages, mountains, and misty green fields is from the deck of the 12-passenger *Shannon Princess* as it cruises the Shannon, stopping along the way to visit singing pubs or a castle or two, do some shopping, or take in a castle banquet. The elegantly appointed vessel has two suites, three twin-bedded staterooms, and two single staterooms, and meals on board fall into the gourmet class, accompanied by fine wines. Weekly departures are on Sunday from mid-April through October, and the itinerary is round trip from Killaloe up the Shannon and 25-mile-long Lough Derg.

Fares for 1989, which include all meals, open bar, sightseeing, and round-trip transfers from Shannon, range from $1,480 to $1,780 per person (based on double occupancy), according to season; singles pay $1,580. Early booking is advised. Contact **Horizon Cruises Ltd.,** 16000 Ventura Blvd., Suite 200, Encino, CA 91436 (tel. 818/906-8086, or toll free 800/421-0454, 800/367-8075 in Canada).

SPORTS: For the sports-minded, Ireland is a veritable banquet table loaded with goodies! Golfers will be welcomed guests at more than 180 golf courses (over 50 are championship class) around the country, be they professionals or bumbling amateurs who just like to whack the ball around. Greens fees run from around IR£8 ($19.25) to IR£15 ($24) per day. Courses range from 18-holers with such extras as a pro shop, resident pro to give instruction, and tea room to windswept greens overlooking the sea. *The Best of Irish Golf,* available from Tourist Offices in Ireland, lists them all and gives specific information on what's available to visitors at each.

Caddies are not generally available (although they can be booked ahead at some of the larger courses), and don't look for a golfmobile—the closest you'll come to that is a lightweight pull cart. Some courses have clubs for rent at about IR£3 ($4.75) per set per round, but most do not, so you'll be well advised to bring your own unless you have an Irish golfing buddy or two who's good for the loan of a set.

Irish Golfing Holidays can be arranged to include accommodations, golf clinics, and special golfing weekends with groups and societies. For full particulars—or for help in setting up a golf holiday itinerary on your own—consult travel agents or the Irish Tourist Board.

If there's such a thing as a fisherman's heaven, it must be located in the Emerald Isle! You can go **fishing** for such freshwater fish (coarse fishing) as bream, dace, pike, perch, and various hybrids in all those rivers, streams, and lakes, and never have to worry about a license or permit. Or stalk the famous Irish salmon from January 1 to September 30 in coastal rivers, their stillwaters and headwaters. Sea trout and brown trout are among the other challenging game fish. Sea anglers will find plentiful supplies of bass, whiting, mullet, flounder, plaice, pollack, and coalfish to be had from shore casting on rocks, piers, beaches, and promontories. Deep-sea angling for shark, skate, dogfish, pollack, ling, and conger is yours for incredibly low costs, all around the coast.

For help in planning a fishing holiday, contact the **Angler's Information Service,** Irish Tourist Board, Baggot Street Bridge, Dublin 2 (tel. 01/765871). You will no doubt want to send for one or all of the helpful Information Sheets (nos. 10A, 10B, and 10C) published by the Tourist Board for a nominal fee. Entitled "Sea Angling in Ireland," "Freshwater Coarse Angling," and "Game Fishing," they point you to the best fishing locations, boat rentals, fishing competitions, and bait stockists, and even provide angling maps.

Other water sports include **surfing, waterskiing,** and **boardsailing.** And of course there are all those lovely beaches for swimmers who don't demand summer temperatures much above 70. Personally, I find walking the sandy strands and deserted coves more fun than braving the waves—it is positively restorative to commune with sea and sun on long stretches when there's not another soul in sight. Seaside *resorts* can also be fun, from the lively, crowded Tramore in County Waterford to the quieter Kilkee in County Clare.

As for spectator sports, Irish **horseracing** has got to be close to the top of the list. A day at a race meet is very like a day at a country fair, with bookmakers vying for punters (bettors) while shouting out odds that change momentarily and punters shopping around to get their bets down when the odds are at their best. If your horse comes up a winner, you'll be paid from a big satchel at the book-maker's stand at the odds in existence at the time you placed your bet (so timing can be important, and it *pays* to do a little shopping around). Irish horses, of course, are world famous, and it's a thrilling sight to see them round the last bend of a grass course against a backdrop of mountains or seashore or rolling green fields.

There are over 250 race meets each year, the Big Five being the **Irish Grand National** at Fairyhouse on Easter Monday, the **Leopardstown Steeplechase** in February, **Punchestown Steeplechases** in April, the **Irish Derby** in the Curragh at the end of June or beginning of July, and (probably the most popular of all with the Irish) the **Galway Races** in July. Tourist Board offices can furnish exact dates, and if you should happen on a meet somewhere else in the course of your travels, there goes another itinerary change (one of the happiest Irish times in my personal memory was an evening race meet at Clonmel in County Tipperary when *my* itinerary called for me to be en route to Killarney!).

Gaelic football is a century old in its present, organized form, but it must have roots way back in the days of fierce tribal rivalries when encroaching civiliza-tion undoubtedly shoved all that competitive spirit from battleground to foot-ball pitch. None of the fervor of either participants or spectators has been lost in the shift, however, and for sheer excitement nothing quite matches that of shar-ing the stands at Croke Park in Dublin with upward of 90,000 fans roaring sup-port for their county teams in the All Ireland finals in early September.

Hurling is unique to Ireland, and I sometimes think it takes the Irish to fig-ure out its two-level scoring. There are goals and points (depending on whether the little leather ball is hit past the goaltender and over the goal line or over the goaltender's head between the upright goalposts). And right there ends my personal knowledge of the game's scoring. My ignorance notwithstanding, I find a Sunday-afternoon match irresistible—the skill and speed of agile athletes wielding hurleys (wooden sticks not unlike our hockey sticks) are wondrous to behold!

READER'S SPORTS SUGGESTION: "Irish foot races are different from those in the U.S., although the fun and enjoyment are the same. You can find out about upcoming races in Ireland by looking in any current copy of the Irish *Runner* magazine, sold at any news-stand and most sports stores or you can look in the telephone directory for the local chapter of the BLE (Bond Luthcleas Na H Eireann), the runners' association of Ireland. Registra-tion can be made through the mail or by telephone, and you pay a small registration fee at the race. This can be an excellent way for amateur runners to keep the waistline in shape and enjoy meeting Irish runners" (D. Imholte, Milpitas, Calif.).

2. IRELAND AFTER DARK

Because the Irish summer day is a long one, many of the "after dark" activi-ties described in this section actually take place while the sky is still light, so you may take that heading to mean evening hours, dark or not dark. You can also extend almost any of your daytime activities into the evening (except, of course, where sightseeing attractions are not open then), playing a round of golf, fishing, etc., after dinner until 9:30 or 10 p.m.

What I'll do here, however, is talk about those things you can do only in the evening hours. With one notable exception. You'll notice that pubbing tops the list below, but that's not to suggest—or even *hint*—that this particular activity should be limited to after dinner. Perish the thought that you miss Irish pubs in the afternoon! Things are slower then, with Dublin pubs catering mostly to foot-sore tourists, housewives taking a break from shopping (often with a tot or two in tow), and a few freewheeling Dubliners whose lifestyle does not confine them to an office. The publican is more relaxed, and the talk flows smoothly, ebbing around you, taking you in, and playing hob with a big chunk of your afternoon. In rural pubs, this is when you're likely to encounter those craggy oldtimers just itching for you to pose a question or otherwise open up a dialogue so they can proffer their philosophy and local expertise without being bold. So my reason for discussing pubs right up front is that no matter what *else* you plan of an evening, a pub stop is the very best way to begin and/or end it.

IRISH PUBS: A wise man once said that "a pub is the poor man's university." That it certainly is in Ireland! And it's an ongoing education as you encounter pubgoers from different walks of life and regions, each with an outlook on life, politics, religion, and any other subject as individual as his looks and a highly developed personal way with the words to expound on any of the above.

There's more to it than just that, however. Out in rural areas, the local pub is the social center around which everything revolves. What gossip and news isn't picked up at the creamery is dispensed as freely as a pint in the pub. Personal decisions that must be weighed and finally taken are a topic of general conversation in which everyone present lights up the problem with his own particular perspective. I once spent the better part of an afternoon in a small County Waterford pub absolutely fascinated by the dilemma posed by the fact that a wedding and a funeral were both scheduled for the following day—after about two hours of wrestling with the problem of which to attend, my fellow imbibers *still* hadn't reached a conclusion when I reluctantly picked myself up and moved on. But I can tell you that there are aspects to that agonizing decision I'd never dreamed of before that afternoon!

Pubs are, by and large, also where you're most likely to find traditional music and song in the "singing pubs" that bring in leading musical groups or give performing space to the local lads aiming in that direction. It must be added that you're just as likely to find the familiar twang of country and western hits as the impassioned lyrics of Ireland's native music. Even if a pub is *not* known for music, however, the lyrical Irish spirit frequently bursts its bounds in the country's drinking places, especially toward the end of the evening, when a fiddle or tin whistle suddenly appears and song just sort of erupts—along with reams of poetry that can be from the classics or entirely spontaneous, depending on the clientele.

The pubs themselves range over a wide spectrum of décor. In cities like Dublin and Belfast you can have a jar in an ornate, Victorian-style drinking establishment; a glitzed up chrome-and-mirrored abyss of pseudo sophistication; an oldtime pub replete with time-worn wood, etched glass, and touches of brass; an elegant hotel bar that is considered a pub despite its fancy getup; or a bare-bones drinking place which depends on its colorful "regulars" for whatever décor might exist. Out in the country, a pub might well be one half of a grocery or hardware store; a traditional-style pub that's been dispensing drink and hospitality since the days of coaching inns; a cozy, wallpapered, and carpeted appendage to a guesthouse or small hotel; or a large, barn-like room with linoleum on the floor and telly behind the bar.

There are still pubs around with little blocked off private rooms called "snugs" and lovely old etched-glass partitions along the bar to afford a bit of privacy. In some pubs, the dart board stays busy; in others, there's almost always a card game in progress; some keep the fireplace glowing. Most will have a main bar and an attached "lounge," which once was the only place you'd ever catch a female in what was exclusively a man's domain. Nowadays, the lounges are filled with couples of all ages, as well as singles (even males who, for one reason or another, prefer not to elbow it at the bar).

Pub etiquette is a delicate and complex matter, and your awareness of some of its intricacies can spell the difference between a night of unsurpassed conviviality and one of cool isolation that leaves you wondering where all that famed Irish pub joviality is to be found. Novelist and radio newscaster David Hanly once laid down the one vital ground rule that should see you safely through those first few minutes when you enter what many Irishmen consider their own personal club. He was writing about Dublin pubs, but the rule applies across the board: "If you are to be accompanied on this jaunt, choose a partner who is loud neither in dress nor in voice. Dubliners abominate strange noises in their pubs, and high, demanding voices—no matter what the accent—carry deadly imperial echoes." Need I comment that his reference to "partner" was a typically Irish, backdoor, way of saying that *you* should tread softly?

So keeping your voice and manners suitably moderated, you take your place at the bar, order your brew (*never* a fancy mixed cocktail unless you're in one of those city hotel bars mentioned above) and gradually—oh, so gradually—drift into conversation by way of a question. You're on your own as far as the question is concerned; it doesn't really matter so long as you project a real need for assistance that only a local can provide. Inquiries about the best place to eat, the best traditional music group around, etc., will do just fine and open up a general conversation likely to run the length of the bar, with everyone in attendance anxious to lend a hand to a visiting Yank.

The times and economic pressures are slowly eroding one facet of Irish drinking etiquette that was once inviolate, that of "buying the round." That ritual consisted of each member in a drinking group picking up the tab for a round of drinks for everybody. It was (still *is* in many places) as deadly a breach of manners to leave *after* you'd paid for your round as before your turn rolled around. Everybody drank until everybody had bought his round. Keep that in mind should you run into drinking companions, however casual your acquaintance, who insist that you'll not be permitted to pay for your first drink at all; the round-buying tradition requires that you hang in there until your check-paying turn arrives and stay the course.

The only exception to the above routine concerns women. In all my years of visiting Ireland, I've only insisted on buying my round once, and my male drinking companions were so uncomfortable with the whole thing that I've resolved to relax and go with local custom without the slightest twinge of guilt. As I said, however, what with the high price of the pint these days, round-buying is disappearing from the Irish pub scene, with everyone buying his own more often than not.

About prices: In some city bars you can pay as much as IR£1.40 ($2.25) for a pint of black, satiny smooth Guinness topped off with a creamy white head (which, in the well-pulled pint, lasts all the way to the bottom of that 20-ounce Imperial pint). By New York or Los Angeles standards, that's still a bargain, but many an Irishman nurses the one pint or orders by the glass (half-pint) to stretch things out through most of the evening for no other reason than the state of his purse. In suburban and rural pubs, you'll pay anywhere from IR£1.30 ($2) up. A "drop" of whisky will run a little less than a pint, and you should know that an Irish "drop" is a big one. Drinks in the lounge rather than at the bar generally cost around 2p more.

Pubs are open from 10 a.m. to 11 p.m. in the Republic during the winter, until 11:30 p.m. in summer months. On Sunday, it's 12:30 to 2 p.m. and 4 to 10 p.m. year round. Until 1988, you'd have been out of luck if you happened to develop a terrible thirst in Cork or Dublin on a weekday between 2:30 and 3:30 p.m.—pubs were closed up tight in observance of what was uniformly known as the "Holy Hour," which also meant you shouldn't plan on a late pub lunch in those two cities. These days, however, you can be as unholy as you please all day long.

One last word to the ladies: You'll be very welcome in Irish pubs, whether you're on your own, one of a bunch of females, or with a male escort. You may, however, be more comfortable in the lounge than at the bar (that varies from pub to pub, so try to size the place up when you first come in). Even being a nondrinker is no reason for missing out on pub sociability: all Irish pubs stock soft drinks (try the light, fizzy white lemonade) and nobody is going to look askance if you stick to those.

MUSICAL NIGHTS: Since the pre-Christian days when they revered their bards, the Irish have celebrated, mourned, exalted, damned, and lamented everything in their lives through music. Until the 1690s and Cromwell, songs and ballads were composed entirely in Irish; after that, English was the language meant to help erase any remaining traces of nationalism. Even the penal laws were unable to do that, however, for the wily Irish praised their country under the guise of singing about their sweethearts: "Roisin Dubh," "Kathleen Huallachain," and "Grainne Uail" speak of loved ones, but every Irishman knew they really were odes to Ireland herself. Those traditional songs and airs are still played frequently today, and if you listen closely to modern Irish ballads, you'll notice that a good few still concern themselves with celebrating, mourning, exalting, etc., etc., some facet of Ireland or Irish life.

The tones that spring from the harp, uilleann (elbow) pipes (played sitting down and developed to get around English law, which forbad the playing of any instrument while standing to prevent the pipes from playing troops into battle), the bodhran (a sort of drum made of goatskin stretched tightly over a round wooden frame), the tin whistle, fiddle, and accordion mix in a unique harmony that can break your heart or send your spirits (and your feet!) soaring. We've heard them on this side of the Atlantic in recent years most often from groups such as the Chieftains, and despite complaints to the contrary by American tourists in the past, they're to be found almost everywhere in Ireland itself.

The trick, of course, is to know where to look for them. Actually, it isn't much of a trick at all, for there's a central organization whose sole purpose is the promotion of traditional music, song, and dance. **Comhaltas Ceoltoiri Eireann** ("Kool-tus Kool-tura Airan," but universally known as **"coalthus"**) is based in the Dublin suburb of Monkstown, but has branches in every county. It organizes traditional entertainment in hotels, pubs, and at local branch meetings, all of which are open to the public, and you'll be very welcome as a visiting American.

At the Monkstown headquarters there are traditional music sessions on weekends all year round, with admission a paltry IR£1.50 ($2.50). During summer months they organize other events, like the **Fonntrai** (folk theater show featuring traditional music and dance), a **ceili** ("kay-lee," traditional set dancing as done in Irish homes in years gone by), and the **cois teallaigh** (musicians, singers, and dancers talk about and demonstrate their various arts). Admissions range from IR£1.50 ($2.50) to IR£4 ($6.50), and scheduled nights vary. You can usually enjoy a pre-show dinner of traditional, home-cooked recipes, in their traditional kitchen/restaurant by calling 01/800295 to book. Prices are moderate to cheap.

To learn what's on during your visit, both in Monkstown and around the country, contact Comhaltas Ceoltoiri Eireann, Belgrave Square, Monkstown, Co. Dublin (tel. 01/800295).

During the last weekend in August, look for the **All-Ireland Fleadh** ("flah"). It's a three-day traditional music and song festival held each year in a different town, and music lovers from around the world congregate in the pubs, hotels, private houses, and even in the streets to play, sing, and just listen to this music in a completely informal setting. A word of warning: Accommodations are generally booked for miles around once the venue is announced, so be prepared to book ahead, camp out, or stay up all night (not unheard of, I might add).

The **Fleadh Nua,** always held in Ennis, Co. Clare, on the last weekend in May, is another showcase for the best in traditional music. The caution mentioned above applies here as well.

No visit to the west of Ireland will be complete without taking in a performance of **Siamsa** ("sheemsa") **Tire,** the national folk theater of Ireland. It is based in Tralee, but performs regularly during summer months in Killarney and occasionally in other towns. Talented performers demonstrate such traditional Irish folk ways as thrashing and thatching the roof through music and dance. Information on performance schedules and the low admission charges (around IR£4 or $6.50) is available at most Tourist Offices (the Killarney office always has Siamsa information).

Another place to look for traditional Irish entertainment is **Seoda** ("shoda"), a dramatic and musical evening held in Galway's Gaelic theater, **Taibhdhearc** ("thive-yark"), on selected evenings during the summer.

BANQUETS AND CABARETS: An absolute standout among nighttime activities is any one of the medieval banquets held in **Bunratty** and **Knappogue** castles in County Clare and **Dunguaire** castle in County Galway. Each begins with a meal that harks back to the days when these were residences as well as fortifications, and each ends with superb entertainment that includes music, dance, song, and a bit of pageantry. Prices (about $42) are well above "budget," but this is the *one* Big Splurge I implore you not to miss.

For a different sort of musical evening that combines traditional and modern music, song, dance, and "stage Irish" comedy, look for the popular cabaret shows in leading city hotels. They're a bit sophisticated, a bit hokey, and loads of fun. Many include a pre-show dinner if you wish, although you can usually come along for the show alone if you prefer. A mark of the quality of these shows is the smattering of Irish you'll see in the audience (along with busloads of visiting tourists like ourselves). Prices are about $32 for the dinner/show combination, $20 for just the show.

THEATER: Think of Ireland and one of your first thoughts is of the theater. Think of Irish theater, and you immediately think of Dublin's **Abbey Theater.** It should be high on every visitor's "don't miss" list, and prices are so affordable even those of us who keep a tight rein on the budget can work in at least one performance. Admission at the better-known theaters will run from IR£7 ($11.25) to IR£10 ($16), and many smaller theaters charge even less.

Don't make the mistake of thinking that theater is to be found *only* in Dublin, however. There are good productions all around the country, some on a regular basis (like Cork's **Opera House),** others on a periodic basis. Look in local newspapers for productions, then go along, and for a pittance enjoy a night of good theater and—many times, though not always—a chat in the lobby after the show with the cast.

3. TRACING YOUR IRISH ROOTS

If you're one of the more than 40 million Americans whose forebears were Irish, it's a good bet you'll want to look into your family tree while in Ireland. What with some 14 of our presidents claiming Irish ancestry, our White House having been designed by Irishman James Hoban, and one of our states (Pennsylvania) bearing the name of a Corkman (William Penn), you're in very good company indeed.

Tracking down your Irish roots may not prove to be such a simple matter. More than 1,000 basic family names were established in Ireland between the 12th and 19th centuries, each of *those* having several variations. Not to be discouraged, however: there are descendants of families described in a 1201 account of Cathal O'Conor's inauguration as King of Connaught *still living on the same lands as their ancestors!*

To find your particular branch of a particular family, you'll want to know all you possibly can about your family history before you leave home. Search any and all records (letters, Bibles, relatives' memories, etc.) for the mention of specific townlands, villages, or counties from which your folks went out to America. The more you know about what they did, who they married, when they left home, and the like, the easier your job will be.

In Dublin, present yourself and your records to the **General Register Office of Births, Marriages, and Deaths** at Joyce House, 8/11 Lombard St. East, Dublin 2 (tel. 01/711000). Charges range from a low IR£5.50 ($8.75) for a Search Certificate, IR£2 ($3.25) for each extra copy, when you go through the records yourself for a five-year period in search of an individual. For six hours of unrestricted research, the charge is IR£11 ($17.50).

For genealogical and land tenure records dating as far back as the 17th century, check with the **Public Record Office**; land transactions back to 1708 are recorded with the **Registry of Deeds,** on Henrietta Street; there is a wealth of all manner of family information at the **Genealogical Office** on Kildare Street; and the **National Library** on Kildare Street holds journals and directories relating to Irish families.

Once you have basic data, it's off to the locality of your ancestors, where **parochial registers** often hold exactly what you're looking for and a talk with the parish priest may well send you off to shake the hand of a distant cousin or two still living in the neighborhood.

For Northern Ireland roots, consult the **Public Record Office of Northern Ireland,** 66 Balmoral Ave., Belfast, and the **Presbyterian Historical Society,** Church House, Fisherwick Place, Belfast.

Of course, the fastest way to get the search done is to join an Aer Lingus Irish Heritage Holiday tour (see Chapter II). They'll do the groundwork and furnish a list of local historians who can many times fill in the gaps.

No matter how you plan to go about your "roots" search, my best and strongest advice is to subscribe to *Inside Ireland* (see Chapter I) and receive their genealogical supplement with your very first issue. It is one of the most valuable aids available, and the helpful staff stands ready to help you reach Irish sources you might not otherwise find.

DUBLIN

□ □ □

1. ORIENTATION
2. USEFUL INFORMATION

Baile Atha Cliath ("the town of the ford of the hurdles") is its ancient Irish name (that ford was probably where the Father Matthew Bridge long ago replaced a frail wicker bridge—the "hurdles"—that once spanned the river); Norsemen called it Dubh-Linn ("black pool") when they founded the present city on the banks of the Liffey in 840; and a modern writer has called it "the most instantly talkative city in Europe."

Although Dublin was founded as a trading port by the Danes in 840, the *Irish Annals* relate that in 988 the Viking settlement was handed over to the High King of Ireland, and that's the date celebrated in 1988 when the city put on a year-long festival to commemorate its millennium.

By any name, Dublin is one of Europe's loveliest capital cities, with proud old Georgian buildings, elegantly groomed squares of greenery (Fitzwilliam, Parnell, Merrion, etc.), and acres of shaded leisure space (St. Stephen's Green and the Phoenix Park). Its heart beats to the rhythm of the Liffey, and its horizons extend to craggy Howth Head to the north, the softly curving shores of Dublin Bay to the east, and the slopes of the Dublin Mountains to the south. This sheltered setting along a natural transportation route has been the focal point of a long, rich, and complex history that has left its mark on the face of its landscape as well as its people. Indeed, Dubliners are happily convinced their city is not only the centerpiece of Ireland's Eastern Region, but of Ireland and the *universe* as well (and they just as happily skip off to "the country" at the merest hint of an excuse!).

Little remains nowadays of medieval Dublin, but it's easy to trace its outlines and see how the modern city has grown around it. On the south bank of the Liffey, you'll see Christ Church Cathedral's square tower—that was almost the exact center of the original city. To the east, Grattan Bridge stands near the "black pool" that marked its eastern boundary. Little Ship Street follows the course of the River Poddle (now underground), once a city boundary on the south bank of the river, and the quays along the north bank marked another outpost of the ancient city.

1. ORIENTATION

Today, as at its birth, Dublin is delineated by the brown waters of the **River Liffey,** which flows from west to east, passing beneath some ten bridges en route. **O'Connell Bridge** is probably the most important for you and me, since it connects those sections of the mile-long city center "north of the Liffey" (to Parnell Square at the northern end of O'Connell Street) and "south of the Liffey" (to St.

DUBLIN AND SUBURBS

Ward

Dublin Airport

Malahide

Portmarnock

Finglas

N2 N1

Coolock

Sutton

Howth

Glasnevin

Drumcondra

Raheny

North Bull I.
(Bird Sanctuary)

N4

Phoenix Park

Liffey R.

IRISH SEA

Dublin

Ballsbridge

Rathgar

N11

Blackrock

Dun Laoghaire
Car Ferry Terminal

Templeogue

Dundrum

Stillorgan

Stephen's Green at Grafton Street's southern end). Keep that firmly in mind, since Dubliners locate *everything* by its relation to the river—"north of" and "south of" are a part of the city's vocabulary you'll soon adopt as part of your own.

The main thoroughfare north of the river is **O'Connell Street,** an extension of the bridge. That's where you'll find the historic **General Post Office,** statues of Parnell, Father Matthew, and (who else!) Daniel O'Connell. At the base of his statue, look for the heroic "Victories," representing Fidelity, Eloquence, Courage, and Patriotism. The **Dublin and East Tourism Visitor Center** is also on O'Connell Street, along with several good hotels, shopping in one large department store and a jumble of smaller establishments, quick food eateries, and a number of important office buildings.

To the south of O'Connell Bridge, **Westmoreland Street** extends for only one block to the wide, statue-filled intersection known as **College Green,** which sprawls before the entrance to Trinity College. College Green, in turn, funnels into Dublin's most fashionable shopping thoroughfare, **Grafton Street,** so narrow that it is at times blocked off for pedestrian traffic only. If you've walked that city-center mile, by the time you reach the end of Grafton, you'll sigh with gratitude for the beautifully landscaped, restful refuge of **St. Stephen's Green.**

2. USEFUL INFORMATION

You'll find the **Dublin and East Tourism Visitor Center and Room Reservation Service** at 14 Upper O'Connell St. (tel. 01/747733), just across from the General Post Office. It's open Monday through Friday from late September to mid-March from 9:15 a.m. to 5:15 p.m.; Monday through Saturday mid-March to the end of June from 9 a.m. to 5 p.m.; and Monday through Saturday from the end of June to late September from 8:30 a.m. to 6 p.m.; closed New Year's Day, St. Patrick's Day, Easter Monday, October Public Holiday, and St. Stephen's Day (December 26). . . . For all **bus and rail information,** call 01/787777 from 9 a.m. to 9 p.m. daily, 10 a.m. to 7 p.m. on Sunday. . . . The **Central Bus Station** (Busaras) is on Store Street, north of the Liffey. . . . The three major **railway stations** are Connolly Station, on Amiens Street near Busaras; Heuston Station, near the Guinness Brewery on St. John's Road; and Pearse Station, on Westland Row (serves suburban rail lines). Irish Rail trains meet all ferries arriving at Dun Laoghaire ("Dun Leary") and the seven-mile ride into Dublin can be included in the boat fare if it is specified on the boat ticket.

Taxis operate from ranks at all bus and rail stations, in the center of O'Connell Street, at College Green, at St. Stephen's Green, and at several leading hotels (they're listed in the telephone directory under "Taxi-cab ranks"). You can telephone 783333 or 557777 for a taxi, but an extra service charge will be added to the fare. Minimum fare is IR£1.80 ($3) for the first mile, 10p (15¢) for each additional one-seventh of a mile or 1.3 minutes of waiting time. All taxis are metered, with a charge of 40p (65¢) for each additional passenger and each piece of luggage and 60p (95¢) on bank holidays, and between the hours of 8 p.m. and 8 a.m. there's an additional charge of 40p (65¢) per trip. **Dial-a-Merc** (tel. 373333) uses all Mercedes cars at regular rates.

The **General Post Office** is on O'Connell Street (across from the Dublin Tourist Center) and is open from 8 a.m. to 8 p.m. daily (to 7 p.m. only for mailing or receiving parcels, from 10:30 a.m. to 6:30 p.m. on Sunday and bank holidays). General Delivery mail can be picked up at the Post Restante desk until 8 p.m. Telegraph service is available at the GPO, as well as coin telephones. . . . Local telephone calls from coin phones cost 20p (30¢). For emergency calls, dial 999.

Shopping hours are 9 a.m. to 5:30 p.m. Monday through Saturday, with major shopping areas on Grafton Street, Henry Street, O'Connell Street, and South Great Georges Street.

The telephone prefix for Dublin is 01.

LOCAL BUSES AND TRAINS: There's excellent **bus service** to all parts of Dublin and outlying suburbs, making it easy to search out accommodations beyond the city center, where prices are considerably lower. Any bus marked "An Lar" (it means "the center") will be headed for the city center. Buses run from 7 a.m. (10 a.m. on Sunday) to 11:30 p.m. and that's 11:30 p.m. sharp to catch the last bus leaving the city center—if you're planning a late night in the city, better plan on taking a taxi to any outlying accommodation. Most buses depart from O'Connell Bridge, but you can check on your particular bus line by calling 01/787777 from 9 a.m. to 9 p.m. or by picking up a copy of the Dublin District Bus and Rail Timetable from the Central Bus Station on Store Street or almost any newsstand. Fares are graduated according to distance, with children under 16 traveling for halffare.

Bus discounts are offered during certain hours on certain lines, and one of the most useful is the shopping fare offered between 10 a.m. and 4:30 p.m. within center-city boundaries. Students can purchase discount tickets on a weekly basis from the Tourist Office at 14 Upper O'Connell St. by showing their ID.

The **electric train suburban service** that runs from Howth to Bray stops at some 25 stations en route. Operated by Irish Rail and called the Dublin Area Rapid Transit (DART), the service is fast, silent, and convenient, since departures are every 5 minutes during peak hours, every 15 minutes other times. Service begins at 7 a.m. and ends at about 11:30 p.m. Both the frequency and the speed now make it feasible to make your base at a resort like Bray or Dalkey and have easy access to all city attractions—a terrific, as well as money-saving, idea, since you'll be able to enjoy the seashore and the city equally. Some 19 feeder bus lines link up with the rail system, which stops at the following stations: Howth, Sutton, Bayside, Howth Junction, Kilbarrack, Raheny, Harmonstown, Killester, Connolly Station, Tara Street Station, Pearse Station, Lansdowne Road, Sandymount, Sydney Parade, Booterstown, Blackrock, Monkstown, Salthill, Dun Laoghaire, Sandycove, Glengeary, Dalkey, Killiney, Shankill, and Bray. Timetables can be obtained at most of these stations.

IF YOU'RE DRIVING: A word about driving in Dublin: *Don't!* Public transportation is so efficient and so frequent, traffic can be so heavy (especially in early-morning and late-afternoon hours), and Dublin's one-way streets can be so confusing that I urge you to drive directly to your accommodation, park the car, and leave it there until you're headed out of town! Parking can also present a real problem, since most spaces are metered for only two hours. All that is not to say, however, that it's impossible to drive around the city—it's just that even if you have to spring for a taxi occasionally (and I, for one, would opt for at least one taxi ride just for the conversation—Dublin taxi drivers are the most knowledgeable and entertaining in the world), you'll come out better and save both time and nerves if you leave the driving to someone else. Actually, once you reach the city center, most places are going to be within easy walking distance—and there's no better walking city than Dublin.

Note: One bit of warning if you're driving in Dublin. Recently there has been a rash of rental car break-ins, both on city streets and in guesthouse parking areas. The pattern has been for thieves to break the door lock, then gain access to the trunk with the trunk release on the driver's side. So you'd best leave all luggage, coats, cameras, purchases, etc., in your room and leave your locked car and its trunk bare-bones empty.

DUBLIN AIRPORT: Just seven miles north of the city center, Dublin Airport is in Collinstown. There's an ample supply of free luggage carts, so you won't need a porter (no tipping!). Should you land without a place to lay your weary head, help is at hand at the **Tourist Information Desk** located in the Arrival Terminal. It's open every day except Sunday from 8 a.m. to 6 p.m. during winter months (October through May), from 8 a.m. to 10:30 p.m. from June through August, and from 8 a.m. to 8 p.m. in September.

On the mezzanine, there's an inexpensive **cafeteria** for hot or cold snacks, as well as a **Grill Bar** for more substantial fare (a light meal for about IR£5 or $8, a four-course dinner for under IR£10 or $16). You'll also find bars and snackbars in both the arrival and departure halls. The **Bank of Ireland** is on hand in both halls to change your money, closed only on Christmas Day. For those flying on to Britain or the Continent, there's a duty-free shop selling a full range of goods; those headed to North America will be given a 45-minute shopping stopover at Shannon Airport (see Chapter I) to browse through the well-stocked duty-free shop there. There's also an Aer Lingus booking office in the airport.

Airport Bus fares into the Central Bus Station will run IR£2.30 ($3.75) for adults, half that for children. A **taxi** into town will run about IR£12 ($19.25).

DOWNTOWN DUBLIN

CHAPTER V

DUBLIN ACCOMMODATIONS

□ □ □

You'll probably pay your highest Irish accommodation rate in Dublin, which is not as intimidating as it may sound, for "highest" can still keep you within the daily budget limit of this book. However, you should know in advance that as distance from Dublin increases, prices decrease.

Accommodations in Dublin and its immediate environs are so numerous it's possible to stay in almost any section you like and in almost any price range you prefer (keeping in mind that the bottom range here is likely to be higher than elsewhere). There are good hostels, bed-and-breakfast homes, guesthouses, self-catering flats, small, intimate hotels, and large, luxury hotels. No problems, then, right? Not exactly. The greatest problem is that price range and locality do not *always* match up. For example, inexpensive B&Bs are not concentrated in the city center—for that location, you're going to have to pay more.

The alternative—and it is sometimes a very attractive one—is to book into one of the outlying suburbs (all with excellent transportation to the city) and enjoy the two different environments as you travel back and forth. You might book into Howth, Dalkey, Killiney, or Bray (in County Wicklow, but on the new rail service that makes it an easy commute) and spend mornings on the beach, afternoons or evenings in town. On the other hand, if (as is my personal inclination) you're a little lazy about all that getting about or want to be able to stay out later than those last bus and train departures with only the minimum taxi fare to get back to your lodgings, you will find it good value to skimp other places and pay more to stay right in the city.

Another thing to keep in mind is that prices in Dublin often soar during holidays and special events such as Easter, the Spring Show in May, the Horse Show in August, All-Ireland Finals in September, and international rugby matches. Best plan your visit to Dublin around those events unless you have a special interest in them—if you do plan to come during one of these periods, be sure to reserve well in advance.

In the recommendations below, you'll find a smattering of all the accommodation categories mentioned above, including some higher-priced guesthouses in the city proper which give readers of this book a substantial discount, along with one "Big Splurge" hotel that I have found well worth the extravagance. For your convenience, I have listed them by location.

Dublin is one place I do not advocate arriving without a firm reservation, but if you should arrive in that state and not find a place among the following recommendations, turn to the **Tourist Office Central Reservation Service,** 14 Upper O'Connell St., Dublin 1 (tel. 01/735209), or arm yourself with their publication *Town and Country Homes and Farmhouses* and start telephoning around.

Note: Prices shown below are those in effect in 1989—expect them to be higher in 1990.

1. IN THE CITY CENTER

HOSTELS: North of the Liffey, An Oige operates an excellent **hostel** at 39 Mountjoy Square South, Dublin 1 (tel. 01/363111), in a Georgian house that dates from 1798. There are accommodations for 22 men and 40 women in dormitory rooms. There's a common room and completely equipped communal kitchen (see Chapter I for what you will be expected to bring). City bus lines run along nearby O'Connell Street, and Connolly rail station is just ten minutes away. It is open daily until midnight. It is essential to book ahead, and you must claim your bed by 9 p.m. the first night of your stay. Book directly with Mrs. M. Sheridan, Warden. The hostel is open April 1 through September 30, and rates are IR£2.75 ($4.50) to IR£4 ($6.50) per night, depending on your age and when you come.

Just three blocks from St. Stephen's Green, the **YWCA Hostel** is at 64 Lower Baggot St., Dublin 2 (tel. 01/766273 or 608452). For most of the year the hostel is open to college students and working women, but tourists are welcomed during June, July, and August. Rooms are very like those of a motel (hot and cold water in each) and accommodate either two or three, for a total of 22. The door is locked at midnight, but you'll be given a key if you must be out later, although they prefer all guests to observe the closing hour. City buses nos. 4 and 10 provide convenient transportation. Bed-and-breakfast rates are IR£8 ($12.75).

A little farther out but also in the city center, a popular privately run hostel is **The Young Traveller,** St. Mary's Place, Dublin 7 (tel. 01/305000). There are 12 four-bedded rooms and one two-bedded room, each with its own shower. Amenities include an attractive lounge, TV lounge, launderette, and a self-service restaurant. Rates for bed-and-breakfast are IR£8 ($12.75).

GUESTHOUSES: One of two guesthouses listed here is south of the Liffey, the other on the north side. I must add that the neighborhood to the north is not what it once was, but is safe enough and just a short walk from buses on O'Connell Street. In Section 3 you will find center-city guesthouses in choice locations which discount their higher rates for our readers.

Centrally located just off St. Stephen's Green, the **Georgian House Guest House,** 20 Lower Baggot St., Dublin 2 (tel. 01/604300), is a restored Georgian town house right in the heart of the city. Annette O'Sullivan is owner and hostess at this four-story house, which has ten bedrooms, all with private bathrooms (with showers), TVs and radios, reached by way of rather narrow stairs. There's an off-street parking area in what was once the garden. The basement restaurant, the Ante Room, serves breakfast (included in rates), as well as lunch and dinner at moderate prices. Rates run from IR£26 ($41.50) to IR£33 ($52.75) per person.

Harvey's, 11 Upper Gardiner St., Dublin 1 (tel. 01/748384), built in 1785, is one of those four-storied Georgian homes. Mr. and Mrs. Harvey are pleasant and very helpful to guests, and their guesthouse is especially popular with young Americans. There are some interesting antiques mixed in with comfortable modern furnishings, and central heating has been installed. Drivers have the use of a private parking lot at no extra cost. Bed-and-breakfast rates are IR£13 ($20.75) for each guest.

HOTELS: I know budgeteers don't usually head for hotels, but there are two Dublin hotels that are so centrally located, with so much character and so relatively inexpensive, that I think you should know about them. While they're definitely not in the budget range, neither are they "Big Splurges," and their convenience and comfort make them well worth breaking over budget bounds.

The **Clarence Hotel,** Wellington Quay, Dublin 2 (tel. 01/776178), has for many years been a favorite with the Irish when they come to Dublin for business or pleasure, and it combines Grade A facilities with moderate prices, a comfortable and homey atmosphere, and a friendly staff. Its central location on the south bank of the Liffey puts you within walking distance of the entire center city, and the lounge (a gathering place for Dubliners as well as guests) is a haven of low-key conviviality when the day is done. The Grill Room (also favored by businesspeople, especially at lunch) serves delicious, inexpensive meals, while its pretty dining room is reputed to serve the best steaks in the city. Rooms are attractive and comfortable, and if you ask for one on the river side, you'll have a great view of port activity along the Liffey (others look down on city streets and the view can be just as fascinating). Rates are IR£24 ($38.50) to IR£31.50 ($50.50) for singles, IR£40 ($64) to IR£48 ($76.75) for doubles, plus a 15% service charge. There are attractive weekend and off-season specials, and all rates include a full Irish breakfast.

Kelly's Hotel, 36/37 S. Great George's St., Dublin 2 (tel. 01/779277 or 779688), has one of the most convenient locations in the city. It's a rather old-fashioned, upstairs hostelry with clean, comfortable rooms presided over by the friendly owners/operators, Paula and Tom Lynam. Of the 24 bedrooms, all but six have private baths, and there's a delightful old-style pub/bar with tall windows, leather seating, TV, and bar food. Dinner can be booked in advance for under IR£6 ($9.50). Bed-and-breakfast rates are IR£17 ($27.25) per person double occupancy, IR£21 ($33.50) single, and rooms with bath are an additional IR£2 ($3.25) per person.

2. IN THE SUBURBS

BALLSBRIDGE: Just a few blocks south of the city center, Ballsbridge is a residential neighborhood that holds several luxury hotels, the American Embassy, and rows of well-tended old homes. It is in this area that you'll find some of the nicest guesthouses that offer you, our readers, substantial discounts on rates (see Section 3 of this chapter).

Guesthouses

Convenient to the American Embassy, Royal Dublin Society grounds, and National Concert Hall, **Elva,** 5 Pembroke Park, Ballsbridge, Dublin 4 (tel. 01/602931), is the lovely Victorian home presided over by Mrs. Sheila Matthews. Three bedrooms have handbasins and three have private facilities; all have TVs. The private parking area is a real convenience, and there's good transportation into the city center (only a short ride away), as well as good restaurants within easy walking distance. Bed-and-breakfast rates are IR£16 ($25.50). Open Easter to mid-December. Take bus no. 10, 7, or 8.

Haddington Lodge, 49 Haddington Rd., Ballsbridge, Dublin 4 (tel. 01/600974 or 601637), is a restored Georgian house close to the Royal Dublin Society grounds. Mrs. Mary Egan is hostess here, and she can furnish dinner if you book in advance. There are three bedrooms with handbasins only, and three with private facilities. There are TVs in all rooms, and a private car park. Bed-and-breakfast rates are IR£16 ($25.50), and dinner is IR£9.50 ($15.25). Closed mid-December to mid-January. Take bus no. 10, 5, 6, 7, 7A, or 45.

MOUNT MERRION: Also southeast of the city center, Mount Merrion has good public transportation into town.

A Guesthouse

Mrs. Lily O'Shea is the popular hostess at **Sorbonne,** 54 Glen Abbey Rd., Mount Merrion, Co. Dublin (tel. 01/882750). It's a neat two-story home just off the N11 and Trees Road, convenient to the University College Dublin (UCD) campus, with off-street parking. The three bedrooms all have handbasins and TVs, and Mrs. O'Shea can provide a nice high tea. Bed-and-breakfast rates are IR£12 ($19.20) with a 20% reduction for children under 10. Open all year. Take bus no. 46A or 64A, or DART.

SANDYMOUNT: Sandymount is right on Dublin Bay, just a little to the east of Ballsbridge.

YWCA

Just two blocks from the sea, the **YWCA Radcliff Hall,** St. John's Road, Sandymount, Dublin 4 (tel. 01/694521), used to be a convent, and its renovation has retained the chapel as well as the well-tended 2½ acres of flower gardens, lawn, and fruit trees. There are some 40 high-ceilinged rooms in the main building which once housed nuns, and 20 more recently built chalets in the rear, all of which have twin beds and private bath. While the décor is simple, the rooms are attractive and comfortable. The light and airy modern dining room opens onto a patio, where meals are sometimes served in summer. There's a laundry room with irons, a TV and recreation room, and a library for guests' use. So you shouldn't feel too pampered in a setting of such beauty and comfort, you're required to make your bed in the morning. As you can imagine, Radcliff Hall is very popular with tourists. Also, this is the site of many conferences and it caters mainly to students during winter months, which simply means that advance booking—with a IR£10 ($16) deposit—is an absolute must, especially if you'd like a room with a private bath. Bed-and-breakfast rates of IR£12 ($19.25) per person for a twin-bedded chalet with bath and IR£10 ($16) per person for a single or double room in the main house without bath (add 10% to all rates) make this one of Dublin's best bargains. If you're staying an entire week, there's a half-board (breakfast and dinner) rate of IR£100 ($160) per person. City bus no. 3 passes the door, and you can also reach it on buses nos. 52, 6, 7A, 8, and 18.

Bed-and-Breakfast

Dolores and Tony Murphy are the delightful hosts at 14 Castle Park (off Guilford Park), Sandymount, Dublin 4 (tel. 01/698413). Their modern, semi-detached house is brightly decorated and neat as a pin, and guests are welcome to sit in the sun in the small garden out back. There are three rooms with built-in wardrobes and sinks. You'll meet at least one or two of the Murphy offspring (two boys and two girls), who often help serve meals, and the entire family seems dedicated to making guests feel at home. Dolores will be glad to prepare the evening meal if you give her sufficient advance notice. Rates for bed-and-breakfast are IR£11 ($17.50) per person, and they're open May through September. City bus nos. 2 or 3 will get you to the city center in ten minutes and there is a DART station just three minutes from the house.

BLACKROCK: In this pleasant Dublin suburb, you are never far from the city center, since there's frequent public transportation close by.

A Guesthouse

Set back in its own landscaped grounds, **Priory Lodge,** Grove Avenue, Blackrock, Co. Dublin (tel. 01/888221 or 832267), provides accommodations bordering on the elegant, while Dermot and Pauline Long provide warm Irish hospitality. There are five nice bedrooms with handbasins that come complete with TVs, radios, and direct-dial telephones. But you may want to opt for one of the three suites, each of which encompasses a private lounge, bedroom, and bath, but these will elevate Priory Lodge into the "Big Splurge" category with the additional charge of IR£10 ($16) per person—money well spent! There's a wine license, and Pauline can provide an exceptional evening meal for IR£12 ($19.25) with advance notice. She can also arrange babysitting. Bed-and-breakfast rates without private bath are IR£16 ($25.50), and there's a 20% reduction for children under 10. Open all year except for the Christmas holidays. Take bus no. 46A, 84, 6, 7, or 5 or DART.

DONNYBROOK: This suburb offers a fine choice for budget travelers.

A Hostel

One of An Oige's Dublin hostels is located at **Morehampton House,** 78 Morehampton Rd., Donnybrook, Dublin 4 (tel. 01/680325). There are dormitory accommodations for 44 men and 38 women, a completely equipped communal kitchen, and common room. It is carpeted throughout and has central heating. It's open all day until midnight. Rates range from IR£2.75 ($4.50) to IR£4 ($6.50) per person, depending on your age and the season. See Chapter I for the few items you'll be expected to furnish. City bus no. 10 will get you to and from the city center; no. 46A from Dun Laoghaire.

RATHGAR: To the southwest of the city, Rathgar is a residential section with exceptionally good bus transportation into the city center, about a ten-minute ride.

Guesthouses

Ann O'Dwyer presides over **St. Aidan's Guest House,** 32 Brighton Rd., Rathgar, Dublin 6 (tel. 01/906178 or 902011). Located on a tree-lined street, St. Aidan's is a large Victorian house that has been modernized and decorated in good taste. The lovely drawing room, complete with TV, has a tea and coffee trolly for the use of guests at any time of the day or night. The 12 bedrooms are done up in Laura Ashley decorator fabrics, have sinks, and are centrally heated. There are five with private bathrooms. All rooms have color TVs. One is a large double bed-sitter with a bay window, and four are singles. Amenities include ironing facilities, hairdryers, a playroom for small children, and a car park. Dinners cost IR£13 ($20.75). Bed-and-breakfast rates are IR£18 ($28.75) for a single with bath, IR£32 ($51.25) for a double with bath. Rooms without bath are IR£2 ($3.25) less. Discount for children is 20%. Take bus no. 15A, 15B, 15C, or 47.

Mrs. Mary Kennedy's **Abrae Court Guesthouse,** 9 Zion Rd., Rathgar, Dublin 6 (tel. 01/979944), is one of those lovely old Victorian homes in this residential section. Bedrooms all have shower and toilet as well as tea and coffee facilities. There's central heating, and Mrs. Kennedy is a warm, gracious hostess. Of special interest to our Jewish readers is the fact that Abrae Court is close by the Chief Rabbinate's office and the Terenure Synagogue. Rates for room only are IR£15 ($24) single, IR£13 ($20.75) per person double, and breakfast is an additional IR£4 ($6.50). There's a 20% reduction for children.

RANELAGH: Try this suburb to the southwest of town for a comfortable . . .

Bed-and-Breakfast
Mrs. Bird's brick Edwardian home, **St. Dunstan's,** 25a Oakley Rd., Ranelagh, Dublin 6 (tel. 01/972286), has been a favorite with readers for several years. In a lovely residential area near Rathgar, the house is also within walking distance of shopping and good restaurants. There's central heating, and the house is spotlessly clean. There are three attractive bedrooms, all with handbasins, and the rate for bed-and-breakfast is IR£11 ($17.50).

DUN LAOGHAIRE: This is where car-ferries arrive and depart for Great Britain, and with the new train service, as well as numerous bus lines, it offers great value as a Dublin area base.

Bed-and-Breakfast
Annesgrove, 28 Rosmeen Gardens, Dun Laoghaire, Co. Dublin (tel. 01/809801), is a pretty, two-story home in a cul-de-sac close to train and bus transportation, and a short walk from the car-ferry. Mrs. Anne D'alton is the gracious hostess here, and she is happy to provide an early breakfast for those with an early-morning departure. There are three nicely appointed bedrooms. For bed-and-breakfast, rates are IR£11 ($17.50); there's a 25% reduction for children. Open mid-February through November. Take bus 7, 7A, or 8, or DART.

In central Dun Laoghaire, Mrs. Doris Pittman presides over **Scarsdale,** 4 Tivoli Rd., Dun Laoghaire, Co. Dublin (tel. 01/806258). The modern house is nicely decorated and has three rooms, all with clock-radios as well as sinks. There is one room with a private shower and toilet at no extra cost. Meals are served in a pleasant dining room looking out onto the garden, where Mrs. Pittman grows both flowers and vegetables. She'll furnish the evening meal with adequate notice, and give an early breakfast for ferry passengers. Rates are IR£11 ($17.50) for bed-and-breakfast, IR£9 ($14.50) for dinner, and there's a 25% reduction for children.

Mrs. Marie de Voogd, 76 Lower Albert Rd., Sandycove, Dun Laoghaire, Co. Dublin (tel. 01/809005), welcomes guests to her lovely home, with four bedrooms which have tea-making facilities as well as handbasins. Electric blankets are furnished on chilly nights and the breakfast table features freshly ground coffee and natural bran cereals in addition to the usual tea and gigantic Irish breakfast. Rates for bed-and-breakfast are IR£12 ($19.25) and Mrs. de Voogd's home is open year round.

There's a warm, inviting atmosphere at **Cill Dara,** 5 Tivoli Rd., Dun Laoghaire, Co. Dublin (tel. 01/807355). Mrs. Mary Lehane will happily provide an early-morning breakfast for ferrygoers as well as dinner with advance notice. This is a lovely new house opposite the golf course and a short walk from the beach. It has three comfortable double bedrooms, a TV lounge, and a walled garden for relaxing in the sun, and it's convenient to bus and train service into the city center. Bed-and-breakfast rates are IR£11 ($17.50); 20% reduction for children. Parking facilities are available.

Rosmeen House, 13 Rosmeen Gardens, Dun Laoghaire, Co. Dublin (tel. 01/807613), has been popular with readers over the years, in large part because of its charming hostess, Mrs. Joan Murphy. The Mediterranean-style villa sits in its own grounds (with private parking), just minutes away from the car-ferry and train and bus transportation into town. Five bedrooms have handbasins, and one has private facilities (for IR£2, $3.25), per person extra); there's central heating, as well as electric blankets on all beds; and Mrs. Murphy is happy to provide an early breakfast if you have an early sailing. She can also provide an evening meal with advance notice for IR£10.50 ($16.75). Bed-and-breakfast rates are IR£11.50 ($18.50), with a 20% reduction for children. Open March through November. Take bus no. 7, 7A, or 8, or DART.

DALKEY: Another scenic seaside spot, Dalkey is seven miles outside town, but with easy bus and train access to the inner city.

A Bed-and-Breakfast

Rockview, Coliemore Road, Dalkey, Co. Dublin (tel. 01/858205), is in a quiet residential section situated on the coast. The car-ferry at Dun Laoghaire is just two miles away. Mrs. Seaver has four bedrooms, all with sinks. She doesn't serve evening meals, but there are good restaurants nearby. Bed-and-breakfast rates are IR£11 ($17.50) per person, with a 25% reduction for children. Bus no. 8 and the train run into town.

A Hotel

At rates just slightly above those at guesthouses, the **Dalkey Island Hotel,** Coliemor Harbour, Dalkey, Co. Dublin (tel. 01/850377), sits on the very edge of Dublin Bay looking out to Dalkey Island (boats are available right next door to take you out for an idyllic day on the uninhabited and very scenic island). The hotel is charm itself, with an Island Lounge featuring nightly entertainment in the summer and sea views all year long. The Sorrento Restaurant specializes in fresh seafood dishes at moderate prices and also has views of the sea. Both the lounge and restaurant are popular local gathering places. All guest rooms have private bath, telephone, color TV, and radio, and there are eight that front on the sea, most with terraces (five are glassed in for all-weather comfort). Rates, which include breakfast, run from IR£27 ($43.25) to IR£40 ($64) for singles, IR£45 ($72) to IR£66 ($105.50) for doubles, depending on the season. There's a 12½% service charge, and a 25% reduction for children. Dalkey is on the Dublin train route, and is also served by bus no. 8.

BRAY, CO. WICKLOW: By rights, the seaside resort of Bray should be listed in Chapter IX of this book. However, with the new electric train service into Dublin, it has moved into the "suburb" category and makes an ideal base if you want a little of both seashore and inner city. It is also convenient to County Wicklow sightseeing, such as Glendalough and Powerscourt.

A Bed-and-Breakfast

Strand House, Seafront, Bray, Co. Wicklow (tel. 01/868920), is a two-story, neo-Georgian house which faces the sea from its own set-back grounds (with convenient off-street parking). Mrs. Maeve O'Loughlin is the charming, helpful hostess, and her home is nicely decorated throughout. She keeps tourist literature on hand for guests and is quite knowledgeable about local restaurants as well as sightseeing highlights. Breakfast comes atop linen tablecloths, with a selection of dishes and perfect little butter curls, all of which probably reflect her long hotel experience. There are five bedrooms, all with sinks, one with private bath, and one rather small, cozy room overlooking the sea. Bed-and-breakfast costs IR£10 ($16), with IR£2.50 ($4) more per person for the room with private bath.

GLASNEVIN: This section is northwest of the city center in an area where several city bus lines provide frequent service.

A Bed-and-Breakfast

Mrs. Mary Murphy's **Hillcrest,** 13 Marlborough Rd., Dublin 7 (tel. 01/385340), is within walking distance of the Phoenix Park, with parking and good bus service to the city center. Mrs. Murphy has won high praise from readers for her hospitality over the years. Three rooms come complete with shower and toilet, and the other three have handbasins. Bed-and-breakfast rates are IR£12 ($19.25) with shower and toilet, and IR£11 ($17.50) without.

CLONTARF: To the northeast of the city, Clontarf is a pleasant residential section with several very good budget-priced accommodations.

Bed-and-Breakfast

Wavemount, 264 Clontarf Rd., Clontarf, Dublin 3 (tel. 01/331744), is a pretty, two-story home overlooking Dublin Bay. Pixie-faced Maura O'Driscoll and her husband, Raymond, have earned glowing accolades from readers over the years, and when I called on them, it was easy to see why. The house itself was spotless and shining, but even more impressive was the warmth with which this couple greet their guests. Breakfasts (featuring homemade bread) are overly generous and, to quote one reader, "magnificently presented" in a bright front room with a bay window looking out to the sea. There are three bedrooms (one with a bay window and that marvelous sea view), two with private shower and toilet. No extra charge for the private facilities and there's central heating. Bed-and-breakfast rates are IR£11 ($17.50), with a 25% reduction for children. Mrs. O'Driscoll will also provide the evening meal with sufficient notice. Open February to October. City bus no. 30 gets you into town in a quick ten minutes. Highly recommended.

Joe and Mary Mooney are hosts at **Aisling,** 19/20 St. Lawrence Rd., Clontarf, Dublin 3 (tel. 01/339097 or 338400). Their graciousness is matched only by the beauty of their home, which is composed of two adjoining period residences on a quiet street just off the Clontarf–Howth road. Furnishings include antiques such as the grandfather clock in the entrance hall, and the lovely dining room is lit by a Waterford glass chandelier. Breakfast comes on beautiful china set on linen tablecloths, with Galway crystal stemware and sterling flatware. In short, the Mooneys and their two daughters have a very special home which they happily share with guests. The nine bedrooms are spacious and attractively decorated; all have sinks, five have private baths, and there's a family room with shower. All have tea and coffee makers, and there's central heating. Rates for bed-and-breakfast are IR£11 ($17.50), with IR£3 ($4.75) per person extra for private facilities and a 10% reduction for children. A private parking area and gardens are added features.

Padua, 3 Hollybrook Park, Clontarf, Dublin 3 (tel. 01/333597), is a small, pleasant house presided over by the bubbly Mrs. McDonagh. There are four bedrooms, two of them triples and all with sinks. There are two shower rooms and one bathroom. Although the house is not centrally heated, there are electric heaters for the bedrooms. A lovely flower garden blooms out back. Rates are IR£11.50 ($18.50) for bed-and-breakfast. Bus service is via no. 28, 29, 31, 32, or 54 from Abbey Street.

Mrs. Eileen Kelly, 17 Seacourt, St. Gabriel's Rd., Clontarf, Dublin 3 (tel. 01/332547), is an outstanding hostess who welcomes guests into the family circle around a cozy open fire in the lounge. Her three large bedrooms are tastefully furnished, all with handbasins and one has private bath facilities. Bus transportation to the city center is close by, and there's central heating. Bed-and-breakfast rates are IR£11 ($17.50) and an additional IR£4 ($6.50) charge per room for private facilities. Open March to October.

3. ABOUT THOSE DISCOUNTS

The following guesthouses are all exceptional; all have especially good value-for-dollar rates, but are somewhat above our budget range; and all extend a 10% discount to readers of this book who *mention it when booking and have it with them when they check in.* The reduction is on *room rate only,* and such expenses as taxes, service charges, and meals (except breakfast) will be charged at the full rate. Advance reservations are necessary at each one. All have my highest recommendation and are well worth "busting the budget."

Ariel House, 52 Landsdowne Rd., Ballsbridge, Dublin 4 (tel. 01/685512), is one of Dublin's most popular guesthouses—and you can give the credit for *that* to Michael O'Brien, its genial owner/manager, who has a unique ability to put himself in the traveler's shoes, understand what will make traveling easier, more comfortable, and more fun, then proceed to furnish exactly that! He worked in some of San Francisco's leading hotels for several years and has done a fair bit of traveling himself, and his attitude toward his guests goes far beyond mere hospitality.

Ariel House's location is only five minutes from the city center, and major bus routes as well as a rail stop are just a few steps from the house. Landsdowne Football Stadium is just next door, and within easy walking distance are the American Embassy, the Royal Dublin Society, Chester Beatty Library, and the Berkeley Court and Jury's hotels (convenient if you want to take in an evening cabaret). The century-old red-brick house and its modern garden extension out back combine the graciousness of age with all the modern comforts you could possibly dream up. Guest rooms are models of good planning (the best-designed clothes-and-luggage space I've come across) and thoughtfulness—all have a built-in hairdryer, TV, telephone (soon to be direct-dial), and a private bath. Those in the main house have modern furnishings and high ceilings and are reached via a lovely old staircase. The garden extension rooms are ground level, and there's a ramp for wheelchairs. All rooms have either twin beds or one double and one single, and there are two large family rooms in the main house.

The pride of Ariel House, however, is the elegant Garden Suite, a very large bed-sitting room furnished with antiques, with wall-to-wall picture windows overlooking the garden at one end. The spacious bathroom holds a luxurious Jacuzzi. Needless to say, the Garden Suite is very popular and much in demand, especially by honeymoon couples, as well as romantic many-years-wed couples.

Breakfast, with a wide variety of choices from a printed menu, is served in a beautiful Victorian-style conservatory or the adjacent room that opens into the conservatory. Although full evening meals are not served, the O'Briens will furnish an attractive and filling salad plate ranging in price from IR£5 ($8) to IR£7 ($11.25) in the cozy wine bar.

Rates for a room with private bath and full Irish breakfast range from IR£55 ($88) single to IR£85 ($136), although they are lower at various times of the year, so be sure to ask for the best rate at the time of booking. The Garden Suite goes for IR£100 ($160).

Also in the convenient Ballsbridge section, the central portion of **Mount Herbert,** 7 Herbert Rd., Ballsbridge, Dublin 4 (tel. 01/684321), is a handsome three-story, slate-roofed white mansion with black trim, which was once the residence of Lord Robinson. Today it is joined by extensions to form a 120-room guesthouse run by the Loughran family, set back from the road, with a walled parking lot protected by an excellent security system. The full Irish breakfast included in rates is served in a pleasant window-walled dining room overlooking the garden, and moderately priced lunches and dinners are also available. In addition to the large lounge, there's a small, cozy sitting room that sports a fire in cool weather. The Health Centre helps keep you fit with its gymnasium, solarium, sauna, and badminton court, and you can keep your vanity intact in the beauty and hairdressing salons. There's also a very good gift shop.

Bedrooms are nicely furnished and come with private baths, direct-dial telephones, and color TVs with in-house movies. For the physically handicapped, two ground-floor rooms have wheelchair access to both bedroom and shower. Babysitting arrangements are available, as well and theater and car-rental bookings. Seasonal rates range from IR£16.75 ($26.75) per person to IR£20.95 ($33.50), and go up to IR£24.85 ($39.75) during special events and holidays. There are five singles and four doubles without private bath, with ample facilities close at hand, that run IR£3 ($4.75) less.

Just a five-minute walk from St. Stephen's Green, **Kilronan House,** 70 Adelaide Rd., Dublin 2 (tel. 01/755266), is a four-story town house with 11 guestrooms. Mrs. Josephine Murray, its gracious owner/manager, has years of hotel experience which are very evident in the smooth running of her attractive home. Tea and cookies are served each evening in the lounge, which has a TV and is a gathering point for guests, and breakfasts are highlighted by homemade brown bread and Mrs. Murray's homemade preserves. All guest rooms have a telephone, hairdryer, and tea and coffee makers, as well as private bath with shower. Bed-and-breakfast rates range from IR£22 ($35.25) to IR£24 ($38.50). Reduction for children is 25%. City buses nos. 14, 15, 19, 20, and 46A are nearby. Be sure to ask for the 10% discount to readers of this book when you reserve.

Iona House, 5 Iona Park, Glasnevin, Dublin 9 (tel. 01/306855, 306217, or 306473), is in a charming Victorian section and is a lovely old red-brick house built around the turn of the century. Karen and Jack Shouldice provide such extras as perked coffee and American-style bacon (crisp, rather than thick, like the Irish bacon) to make visiting Yanks feel at home. There's a homey lounge and a private garden, plus central heating. Guest rooms (which tend to be on the small side due to the installation of private baths) are attractive and comfortable, with private shower, color TV, radio, and self-dial telephone. Both German and French are spoken here. There is also a restaurant offering meals at good value. Rates are IR£22.45 ($36) single, IR£44.90 ($71.75) double, with a 50% reduction for children. Credit cards such as VISA, Amexco, Access, and Diners are accepted.

4. A BIG SPLURGE

This one *is* a "Big Splurge," and there's no discount involved. However, it is such a special place that I'll just let you know about it and you can let your conscience (and your budget) be your guide.

Fitzpatrick's Castle Hotel, Killiney, Co. Dublin (tel. 01/851533; in the U.S., 212/684-1820, or toll free 800/221-1074), is one of Dublin's finest luxury hotels, and is about a 20-minute drive from the city center on the outskirts of an ancient and charming village. Situated on nine landscaped acres, it was built in 1740 as a manor house and occupies the site of a much older building, whose huge 15th-century stone fireplace is now the dominant feature of the Dungeon Bar (which has nightly entertainment). The house, with its three turreted towers and white battlements, was pretty much a wreck when Paddy Fitzpatrick bought it and set about its transformation. These days the entire Fitzpatrick family is involved in running the place, which probably accounts for the graciousness and warmth that seem to extend to every member of the staff.

The 86 bedrooms all have private bath (tub *and* shower), TV, telephone, and radio. Those facing the front have little walk-on balconies set with a table and chairs, and those at the back all boast lovely canopied beds. There are seven luxury suites, some with a magnificent view of Dublin Bay, others with a Jacuzzi. There's an indoor swimming pool, indoor squash courts, saunas, hairdressing salon, and a very good giftshop. The popular bar is a gathering place for Killiney locals, and the dining room, Truffles, is a favorite of Dublin business people for lunch and families in the evening. In fact, you'll probably see as many Irish faces as tourists, since many make this their Dublin headquarters when coming from other parts of the country.

Adjoining the castle is a block of modern, luxury time-sharing holiday homes which are often available for weekly rentals, providing self-catering facilities along with all the amenities of the hotel (contact the hotel for rates and availability if you're interested).

Rates range from IR£49 ($78.50) to IR£77 ($123.25) single, IR£63.80 ($102) to IR£107.80 ($172.50) double, plus a 12½% service charge.

READERS' ACCOMMODATIONS SELECTIONS: Space will not permit us to publish all the good Dublin recommendations from our readers, but these appear to be outstanding. Remember, however, that I have not personally inspected any of the following.

"We stayed for a week with **Mrs. B. Geary,** Sliabh Bhui, 69 Hampton Court, Vernon Avenue, Clontarf, Dublin, Co. Dublin (tel. 01/331199). It was just like being home and the meals were fantastic" (Mrs. H. Kemp, Ottawa, Ontario, Canada). . . . "Mr. and Mrs. O'Connor, **St. John's House,** 23 Pembroke Park, Ballsbridge, Dublin 4, Co. Dublin (tel. 01/684847), are two delightful senior citizens who have been running this bed-and-breakfast for more than 25 years. Nice rooms, a lovely sitting room with TV, and all the interesting stories you want" (Helen Peterson). . . . "I want to enthusiastically recommend **Mrs. P. Doody,** 286 Clontarf Dr. (tel. 01/333470). The family was gracious and generous and the lodgings very comfortable" (S. Connell, Oakland, Calif.). . . . "I cannot recommend a better place than Mrs. Irene Blowers's **Jimire,** 19 Woodlawn Park, Mounttown, Dun Laoghaire (tel. 01/808228). Not only were we treated to an early breakfast (in order to catch an early ferry) that was hot, tasty, and hearty, but Mrs. Blowers set a beautiful table with lovely silver and china in her charming dining room. But that is only half the story. She and her husband helped us retrieve two Aran sweaters we had left on a bus in Waterford by tracking down the bus driver, who had them for us the next morning when he delivered passengers to the ferry. Then Mr. Blowers drove us to the ferry because our taxi was late and he wouldn't accept any money, saying only that it was his pleasure" (P. Vena, Lawrenceville, N.J.).

"Mrs. Colette O'Brien's **Arus Mhuire,** 8 Old Bridge Rd., Templeogue, Dublin 16 (tel. 01/944281), is four miles from the city center, but five different bus routes are nearby. There's a TV lounge for guests and five comfortable bedrooms, with a bath and shower in one. Mrs. O'Brien is hospitable and friendly" (P. Rogers, New York, N.Y.). . . . "Mrs. O'Connell, **San Vista,** 237 Clontarf Rd. (tel. 01/339582), is full of fun, a wonderful listener, kind, full of good information on where to go in Dublin, and the warm, friendly, caring kind of person I went to Ireland to meet. I highly recommend her clean, neat, and happy home. Excellent breakfasts served when you get up!" (R. Cantrell, Yamhill, Ore.). . . . "For budget travelers, let me recommend the **Dublin Tourist Hostel,** 2-5 Frenchman's Lane, Dublin 1 (tel. 01/749321 or 787227). Rates are dirt cheap for dormitory rooms, and single or double rooms are well below most other places to stay in Dublin. It's only a five-minute walk from O'Connell Street, and there's a budget restaurant" (M. Percival, Birmingham, Ala.). . . . "It's a little pricey, but we felt the **Lawrence Hotel,** Howth, Co. Dublin (tel. 01/322643), was worth every penny. There's a gorgeous view of the harbor, and we enjoyed the restaurant as well as our rooms" (Mary and Doug Clapman, Detroit, Mich.). . . . "If you enjoy a gracious, old-fashioned atmosphere in a beautiful setting by the sea, check into the **Howth Lodge Hotel,** Howth, Co. Dublin (tel. 01/390288). It even has open fires, and the Hanratty family, who own and operate it, couldn't be nicer to guests" (P. Noonan, Syracuse, N.Y.).

CHAPTER VI

WHERE TO EAT IN DUBLIN

□ □ □

1. SOUTH OF THE LIFFEY
2. NORTH OF THE LIFFEY
3. BIG SPLURGES

From picnics in St. Stephen's Green to pub grub to Tourist Menu meals to elegant Big Splurges, Dublin offers wide variety in cuisine as well as price. For convenience, the listings below are again by both location and category, that is, south or north of the Liffey.

1. SOUTH OF THE LIFFEY

PUB GRUB: Both hot and cold light meals are available in some of Dublin's most atmospheric pubs at midday—a good way to save money and do a little pub hopping at the same time.

The **Stag's Head,** 1 Dame Court, is a real beauty. Built in 1770, its last "modernization" was in 1895. Lots of gleaming wood, wrought-iron chandeliers, stained-glass skylights, huge mirrors, and (need I say it?) mounted stags' heads. Between 12:15 and 2:15 p.m. you can have soup and toasted sandwiches for about IR£3 ($4.75), or heaping hot platters of bacon, beef, or chicken plus two vegetables for IR£4 ($6.50).

The **Old Stand,** Exchequer Street (tel. 01/987123), is a Dublin tradition, especially among sports figures. A century and a half ago this was a forge, but today you'll find outstanding figures of the sporting world gathered to engage in "the crack" (talk) and exceptionally good pub grub. From 12:30 to 2:30 p.m. there are sandwiches and snacks for around IR£2 ($3.25), a daily special of soup, meat, vegetables, and tea or coffee for IR£4.50 ($7.25), omelets or salad plates for under IR£4 ($6.50), and hot platters of chicken, steak, or fish for IR£5 ($8) to IR£8.50 ($13.60).

In the Liberties section, near Christchurch, the **Lord Edward,** 23 Christchurch Pl., has a genuine old-world atmosphere, complete with stone fireplaces, beamed ceiling, and white stucco walls in the ground-floor pub. Upstairs is one of the city's finest (expensive, but well worth a splurge) seafood restaurants, but the same high-quality food and excellent service come at modest prices in the pub during lunch hours. You'll lunch well for IR£4 ($6.50) to IR£6 ($9.50).

The **Dubliner Bar,** in Jurys Hotel, Ballsbridge, serves up a carvery lunch ample enough to be your main meal of the day. The chef carves from a joint of beef and you help yourself to as much as you want from a wide variety of salads. Hours are 12:30 to 2 p.m. Monday through Friday, and best come early, since the place gets packed with Dubliners.

Paddy Cullen's, 14 Merrion Rd., is a character-filled, old-style pub presided over by the amiable Paddy himself, an ex-footballer of some fame. Good pub grub and lots of locals to keep you company.

RESTAURANTS: Place of honor among "south of" eateries would have to go to **Bewley's Café** for longevity, if nothing else. But never fear, the quality of food is never in doubt (nor has it ever been in the chain's 145-year history) at any of the five locations: 11/12 Westmoreland St., 78 Grafton St., 12 S. Great George's St., and the Dundrum and Stillorgan shopping centers. The devoutly Quaker Bewley family has, since 1972, shared ownership with all employees, which probably explains the courtesy and friendliness of the staff. Interiors are much like oldtime tea shops, and indeed you can purchase teas, coffees, fresh baked breads, and terrific pastries (for a St. Stephen's Green picnic, perhaps) to take away. A good three-course lunch will run you about IR£5 ($8) from the à la carte menu, and although lunch hours are noon to 3 p.m., you can get a full Irish breakfast starting at 8:15 a.m., and coffee, tea, and snacks right up to 6 p.m.

At the **National Gallery of Ireland,** Merrion Square, you'll dine against a background of classical music, at prices that give "budget" a good name. It's self-service and offers as many as five fish selections, six meat or poultry dishes, and a couple of vegetarian choices. Prices run about IR£4 ($6.50) for a main dish with side salads, less for vegetarian selections. Hours are 10 a.m. to 6 p.m. Monday through Saturday (until 9 p.m. on Thursday), and 2 to 5 p.m. on Sunday.

A longtime favorite with Dubliners is the **Unicorn Restaurant,** 11 Merrion Court, a lane just off Merrion Row (tel. 01/762182 or 688552). Not far from St. Stephen's Green, the Unicorn is owned and operated by Mr. and Mrs. Renato Sidoli, who came to Dublin from Bardi, Italy, some 30 years ago. Cuisine is, of course, Italian, with everything from traditional veal dishes to pastas to pizza. Italian wines are served (and also on sale to take away), and there's marvelous espresso and cappuccino. This is a cozy place with white walls, booths, and tables, and when the weather is fine, tables set outside in the sun. Lunch is about IR£6 ($9.50) and dinner runs about IR£10 ($16). You can drop in here any time you feel the onset of hunger pangs—hours are 11:30 a.m. to 10 p.m. on weekdays, noon to 3:30 p.m. and 6 to 10 p.m. on Saturday; closed Sunday and bank holidays.

Casper & Giumbini's Food & Drink Emporium, Wicklow Street (tel. 01/794347), is just across from Switzer department store's side entrance and has been a gathering place for some of Dublin's most attractive younger set (executives, students, office workers, etc.) since it opened in the basement of what was once the old Wicklow Hotel, replete with hand-carved mahogany, burnished brass, Tiffany lamps, and stained-glass windows on multilevel floors. This combination pub and restaurant is always lively with conversation, and at lunch and on weekends there's a resident pianist. At the handsome old bar (from the Wicklow), you can order any one of a dozen imported beers (including American brands) and soup, sandwiches, smoked salmon, bangers-and-mash, and other pub grub. Table service includes such full-meal items as seafood, chicken, veal, lamb, and steaks, as well as lighter fare like quiche, pizza, omelets, hamburgers, etc. Sunday brunch is a standout here, with two free drinks accompanying your selection of eggs Benedict; eggs with sausage, bacon, hash browns, black pudding, grilled tomatoes, and brown bread; smoked salmon and scrambled eggs with croissant; or steak and eggs with hash browns—all for IR£5.50 ($8.75). Bar-food prices are in the IR£2 ($3.25) to IR£4 ($6.50) range; à la carte selections, IR£4.50 ($7.25) to IR£8 ($12.75). Hours are noon to midnight seven days a week, and all major credit cards are honored.

Rajdoot Tandoori, 26/28 Clarendon St. (tel. 01/791122, ext. 132), is one of Dublin's newest Indian restaurant, and Mr. Sarda, its owner, opened his first restaurant in London's Chelsea back in 1966. You enter the elegant restaurant beneath a glittering 200-year-old crystal chandelier from a maharajah's palace in India. Inside, subdued lighting, brass tables, statues, and Indian prints provide a proper setting for excellent northern Indian specialties. Tandoori dishes such as pigeon breast, lamb, and fish appear along with curries and kebabs. Nan, roti/shapat, paratha, and other Indian breads are also delicious. The five-course set lunch is priced at IR£8 ($12.75), and dinner costs IR£20 ($32). The Rajdoot is just off Grafton Street in the Westbury Centre; hours are noon to 2:30 p.m. for lunch, 6:30 to 11:30 p.m. for dinner; closed Sunday.

The **Sandbank Restaurant,** in the Westbury Hotel, Clarendon Street (tel. 01/791122), serves up terrific seafood, along with a limited selection of nonfinny specialties, in a cozy, pubby setting on the lower level of the Westbury Hotel. Lunch entrees might include fresh plaice on the bone with anchovy-and-garlic butter, oak-smoked salmon served with lemon, onion, and capers, or a fisherman's platter, at prices that range from IR£5 ($8) to IR£6 ($9.50). For lighter eaters, there are soups, assorted hors d'oeuvres, and a delicious oak-smoked-salmon pâté that will run IR£1.50 ($2.50) to IR£4 ($6.50). Evening meals are in the IR£8 ($12.75) to IR£10 ($16) range. Service charge is 15%, and hours are 12:30 to 2:30 p.m. and 6:30 to 10:30 p.m. every day except Sunday, Good Friday, and Christmas.

Intimate is the word for **Shay Beano,** 37 Lr. Stephen's St. (tel. 01/776384), with its wickerwork chairs, black Chinese-style screens, and sparkling linen. The cuisine is French, and owner Eamonn O Cathain tries to keep his small staff French as well, maintaining that in the realm of waiters and chefs, the French are most professional. The menu changes daily (depending on the season and the chef's newest creation) and is limited to a choice from three starters, three main courses, and a wide selection of desserts. As for the wine list, it includes some 148 labels, with a concentration on reasonably priced Rhone Valley wines. The all-inclusive price (excluding wine, but including very good coffee) is IR£9 ($14.50) at lunch (served from noon to 2:30 p.m.) and IR£18 ($28.75) at dinner (from 7 to 10:45 p.m.). Shay Beano is open Monday through Saturday and seats only 38, so reservations are strongly advised at this popular place.

The cuisine is French at **Broph's,** 16 Merrion Rd., Ballsbridge (tel. 01/605288), an intimate little upstairs restaurant where the atmosphere is rustic and informal. If you're a fish lover, be sure to ask about their fresh fish dish of the day; otherwise, choose from selections that might include beef filet with whole-grain mustard (or with red wine and ginger), medallions of veal with kiwi fruit and green peppercorns, or breast of chicken with corn and basil. There's a good wine list, and the table d'hôte menu will run IR£11 ($17.50) to IR£15 ($24), depending on main course, plus a 10% service charge. Hours are 7 to 11 p.m. Monday through Saturday, and it's best to book ahead.

Kilmartin's Wine Bar, 19 Upper Baggot St. (tel. 01/686674), is a small, intimate restaurant located in a former bookmaker's shop. Mementos of that activity are displayed on exposed brick walls. The wine list here is excellent, and there's a good menu selection of lasagne, moussaka, fish, steak, veal, and chicken. Prices in this friendly place range from IR£8 ($12.75) to IR£14 ($22.50). Open from 12:30 to 2:30 p.m. and 6 p.m. to midnight, to 11 p.m. on Saturday; closed Sunday.

Through the South William Street entrance to Powerscourt Town House Centre, you'll find **Timmermans Wine Cellar,** ensconced in the original cellars of the mansion. Cozy alcoves hold hand-carved wooden booths brought in from an old chapel and these are also used in the courtyard area open to a parade of shoppers. There are more than 50 wines from which to choose (French, German, Italian, Spanish, Greek, and Californian, among others), as well as several sherries and ports. Food here is excellent, with salad platters and hot plates running IR£4 ($6.50) to IR£6 ($9.50). Brown bread and a very good pâté cost IR£2 ($3.25). As if that weren't enough, there's nighttime entertainment featuring jazz, ballads, or folk music on different days of the week. Hours are noon to midnight; closed Sunday and bank holidays.

Also in the Powerscourt Town House Centre, on the ground floor near the South William Street exit, is the **Periwinkle Seafood Bar,** which serves a terrific selection of hot and cold seafood dishes from noon to 5 p.m. Monday through Saturday, at minimal prices.

Dobbin's Wine Bistro, 15 Stephen's Lane (tel. 01/764679 and 764670), is one of those delightful, intimate spots so friendly that you begin enjoying a meal even before you're seated. It's a casual, attractive place that's a favorite with Dubliners, and best of all, the food is superb. The cuisine is best described as international, since in addition to succulent Irish lamb roasted with fresh herbs, you'll find Szechuan boned duckling, paupiettes of sole stuffed with fresh salmon and scallops, a lovely croustade of fresh seafood in sauce aux crevettes, and entrees of veal, pork, chicken, and steak. The wine list is one of Dublin's best. Prices are in the IR£10 ($16) to IR£16 ($25.50) range for a full lunch or dinner, but there's a nice selection of hors d'oeuvres (baked mushrooms in garlic butter, smoked salmon, fresh Dublin Bay prawns, etc.) and salads for much less that will do quite nicely for a less expensive lunch. Hours are 12:30 to 2:30 p.m. on Monday; 12:30 to 2:30 p.m. and 8 to 11:30 p.m. Tuesday through Friday; and 8 to 11:30 p.m. on Saturday; closed Sunday and holidays. It's a good idea to book ahead.

Rudyard's Restaurant and Wine Bar, 15 Crown Alley (tel. 01/710846), is just behind Dublin's Central Bank, and it's a refreshingly, attractive, rather Edwardian place, with lots of plants, soft background music, and an upstairs wine bar where light lunches are served. Downstairs, the menu features such inventive dishes as chicken biryani, a tasty concoction of fowl, spices, raisins, almonds, and rice. On hand also are standards such as an eight-ounce steak, rainbow trout, veal chops, and always a seafood special of the day. On Saturday evening there's jazz upstairs. Prices are surprisingly low, ranging from IR£6 ($9.50) to IR£9 ($14.50). Open for lunch and dinner, Monday through Saturday.

Barrels Trattoria & Wine Bar, 115 Grafton St. (tel. 01/801992), is a large, bustling pub-like eatery which serves a wide selection of fish, pasta, veal, and steaks at surprisingly low prices. Lunch, served from noon to 3 p.m., runs IR£3 ($4.75) to IR£6 ($9.50); dinner, from 6 to 9:30 p.m., will cost between IR£7 ($11.25) and IR£9 ($14.50); bar snacks (garlic bread, spareribs, mussels, etc.) are served continuously from 3 p.m. to closing and cost IR£1.50 ($2.50) to IR£3 ($4.75). Open seven days a week.

In all probability, you won't leave Ireland without at least one fish-and-chips meal, and let me tell you right here that you shouldn't leave Dublin without calling around to **Leo Burdocks,** 2 Werburgh St. (tel. 01/540306). For three generations Brian Burdock's family has been serving up what are probably the best versions of this traditional dish to be found in the country. Cabinet ministers, university students, poets, intellectuals, colorful natives of the Liberties (the old Dublin section in which you'll find them), Americans who've had the word passed by locals, and almost every other type to be found in Ireland—all queue up patiently for fish bought only that morning and those good Irish potatoes, both cooked on an old solid-fuel range in "drippings" (none of that modern cooking oil!). Great people-watching while you wait, and all that good eating costs a pittance: about IR£2 ($3.25) for the priciest choice (ray and chips; whiting and chips are at the bottom of the range). Open from 5:30 to 11 p.m. every day except Tuesday, Sunday, and holidays.

Dublin has one—and only one—23-hour restaurant (closed 5 to 6 a.m.), a handy place to know about at the end of a late evening or the early beginning of a day. The **Coffee Dock Grill,** in Jurys Hotel, Ballsbridge (tel. 01/605000), is also very much in the budget price range, with seafoods, salads, mixed grills, omelets, sandwiches, ravioli, and spaghetti available along with snacks and sweets at nominal prices—none over IR£10 ($16). Also, there's a good wine list.

Note: If you're staying out in or near Dalkey, an excellent choice for dinner is **Nieve's,** 26 Castle St., Dalkey (tel. 01/856156). It's a family-run restaurant with personal service in a cozy, intimate setting and has a resident pianist on weekends. The menu consists mainly of traditional Irish dishes, including seafood and a good wine list. Dinner will run IR£14 ($22.50) to IR£18 ($28.75). Hours are 6:30 p.m. to midnight daily. Very popular with the locals, so be sure to book.

2. NORTH OF THE LIFFEY

PUB GRUB: Just across from the Gate Theatre, **Patrick Conway's,** 70 Parnell St., dates from 1754. You'll often find theatrical people bending an elbow here before and after a show in the evening. At lunchtime, however, there's very good pub grub on offer (they're especially known for their hot apple tart). It's a large, rambling place, but do take notice (you can't really miss it!) of the huge circular bar just inside the entrance which encloses a carved wooden structure of Gothic proportions. For those visitors who need to know more about Dublin, just ask Frank, your host, who is a "mine" of information.

Daly's Lounge and Grill, 10 Eden Quay, is right on the Liffey. Downstairs is an oldtime pub, often lively with the chatter of newspaper people. Upstairs, you'll find lunches that go a bit beyond the usual pub grub, with several hot dishes as well as cold salad plates. Evening meals, too, are good and inexpensive. Lunch runs from 12:30 to 2:30 p.m. and dinner from 5:30 to 11 p.m. every day except Sunday.

A RESTAURANT: A very good place to eat north of the Liffey is the **self-service restaurant** downstairs at the Municipal Gallery of Modern Art, Parnell Square (tel. 01/788238). For around IR£5 ($8) you can choose from curries with rice, beef carbonnade with vegetables, a selection of salad plates, and desserts that include chocolate roulade, apple pie, and ice cream. There's wine by the glass. On Sunday, the popular lunch is a set IR£6 ($9.50) for adults, IR£4 ($6.50) for children. Hours are 10 a.m. to 5 p.m. Tuesday through Saturday and 12:30 a.m. to 4:30 p.m. on Sunday.

3. BIG SPLURGES

Dublin has a host of elegant restaurants, any one of which merits one of those memorable, kick-over-the-budget-traces splurges. The following, however, are some of my personal favorites. If your traces are just too tight to kick over for dinner, lunch will usually be sumptuous at about half the cost.

Locks Restaurant, 1 Windsor Terrace, Portobello (tel. 01/543391), sits on the banks of the Grand Canal not far from the city center. It's a delightful French provincial–style restaurant whose menu includes classic dishes as well as simpler choices. Only the freshest seasonal ingredients are used, and they come to table reflecting the touch of a master chef, both in taste (exquisite) and presentation (picture perfect). Among the fish dishes, you might choose filets of brill with a Noilly Prat and lettuce sauce, escalopes of wild salmon with a mint sauce, or their daily recommendation from the fish market. There's a lovely escalope of chicken with a tarragon-and-butter sauce, and grilled lamb cutlets are superb. Service is top-notch, and the informal, slightly rustic décor adds to the enjoyment of a meal here. It's open for lunch weekdays from 12:30 to 2 p.m., with a set menu of IR£11 ($17.50) and à la carte about IR£15 ($24); dinner is served Monday through Saturday from 7:15 to 11 p.m. and runs IR£18 ($28.75) for the set menu, about IR£22 ($35.25) à la carte. Dress is informal, and since Locks only seats 48, reservations are strongly advised.

The **Russell Room,** in the Westbury Hotel, Clarendon Street (tel. 01/791122), is, for my money, one of the most beautiful and relaxing restaurants in Dublin. Add to that classic dishes that are superbly prepared from the finest seasonal ingredients and attentive service, and you have a real winner. The spacious Westbury Terrace Lounge just outside is a perfect place for pre-dinner cocktails accompanied by pleasant piano music, and in the restaurant, soft shades of pink, green, and cream set the mood. Among standard favorites here are the crisp roast duckling with lemon, limes, and coriander; fresh sea trout filet with hazelnut-and-honey sauce; sliced beef filet with brandy, black peppercorns, and cream; and Irish salmon flavored with lemon balm, white wine, and cream. The wine list is extensive and moderate to expensive in price, coffee is freshly ground (decaffeinated as well as regular), and there's a nice selection of teas. Service is friendly and efficient.

Lunch is served daily from 12:30 to 2:30 p.m. and there's a set menu of four courses at IR£13 ($20.75); selections from the à la carte listings will run a little more. Dinner hours are 7 to 10:30 p.m. daily, with a IR£16 ($25.50) set menu of starter, soup, entree, vegetables, and dessert; à la carte selections average IR£30 ($48) for the same. There's a 15% service charge on all. Parking in the Westbury car park is available for IR£1 ($1.60) from 7:30 p.m. to midnight. Highly recommended.

The **Grey Door,** 23 Upper Pembroke St. (tel. 01/766890), has two faces, an informal bistro for lunch or pre-theater light supper and an elegant restaurant which owner Barry Wyse and his partner, P. J. Daly, have created in the drawing room of a Dublin town house. On the ground floor, the bistro is a charming setting of arched alcoves and nicely spaced tables. There is a sensible table d'hôte menu for lunch priced at IR£11 ($17.50), exclusive of taxes, with an extensive à la carte each evening. Dinner without wine will run about IR£20 ($32), and you should book in advance at this popular place. Dishes such as blinis, borscht, pelmini, steak Rasputin, chicken Kiev, salmon Severnaya, and galupsti sound like the food James Bond might eat in *From Russia with Love,* and of course you can eat this sort of food at the Grey Door, but for those who might find the idea of a different type of cooking slightly daunting be assured that once you have tasted the splendid dishes at this restaurant you will be back.

Blushes wine bar, downstairs at the Grey Door, offers a more moderately priced lunch and dinner menu in more informal surroundings.

Service throughout is as elegant as the setting and often there is a guitarist on hand softly strumming his native folk music. All major credit cards are accepted. Hours are 12:30 to 2:15 p.m. for lunch (both restaurants) and 6 p.m. to midnight (Blushes), 7 to 11 p.m. (Grey Door); closed Saturday lunch, Sunday, and bank holidays.

READERS' RESTAURANT SELECTIONS: "We were taken by Dublin friends to **White's on the Green,** 119 St. Stephen's Green (tel. 01/751975), and had a superb meal and a delightful evening. It's above budget prices, but a bargain considering the meal we had. It's very popular, so reservations should be made in advance" (S. Jones, New York,

N.Y.). . . . "The **Old Dublin Restaurant,** 90 Francis St., was a bit pricey, but a marvelous 'Big Splurge,' with delicious Russian and Scandinavian dishes prepared with all-fresh ingredients. It's in the Liberties, one of Dublin's oldest sections, and we had a meal and an evening long to be remembered" (S. Debnam, Norfolk, Va.). . . . "Our B&B hostess sent us to the restaurant downstairs at the **Carrick Hall Hotel,** 69 Orwell Rd., Rathgar, where we had an excellent meal of soup, main course, dessert, and coffee for about IR£5 ($8). We highly recommend it" (P. Shapiro, Wappingers Falls, N.Y.).

THINGS TO SEE AND DO IN DUBLIN

□ □ □

1. SEEING THE CITY
2. POINTS OF INTEREST
3. IN SEARCH OF LITERARY GREATS

Much of what you'll see in Dublin consists of the lines and wrinkles, blemishes and beauty spots left on her face by a long, rich, and colorful history. There were people living near the Liffey's hurdle bridge long before Vikings arrived in force in 840 to found a proper town. St. Patrick is said to have passed this way in 448; it is a fact that there were several small churches, and possibly there was a monastery. The Vikings, who had come as raiders, intermarried with the Irish and settled down to become merchants, traders, and craftsmen, but it wasn't until King Olaf was baptized shortly before his death in 979 that Christianity gained any sort of foothold. His son, Sitric, founded **Christ Church Cathedral** in 1038, one of three medieval buildings that have survived through the centuries. When Strongbow and his Normans captured Dublin in 1170, it was the beginning of another intercultural marriage, one sanctioned by King Henry II, who spent some time here in 1171 in a wicker palace that stood on present-day College Green. **St. Patrick's Cathedral,** the second medieval structure to survive, dates back to 1191, and in 1204 King John authorized the building of **Dublin Castle,** the last of the city's medieval relics still standing.

There were few substantial changes in Dublin after that until the 17th century, and those magnificent Georgian buildings began to appear in the 18th century. The Victorian age arrived in the mid-1800s, leaving traces in railway stations, banks, pubs, markets, and hospitals, as well as some commercial buildings in the College Green vicinity. From 1916 to 1922 Dublin's face was scarred by the ravages of uprising, although careful rebuilding and restoration have erased most of the scar tissue. In the 1960s came the "office revolution" and the advent of characterless glass-and-concrete boxes to hail Ireland's new progressive era. Indeed, in a fit of "progressive" zeal, the grand old city came close to demolishing many of her finest legacies from all that history, until concerned citizens halted the destruction at an early stage so that today's visitor may happily browse through treasures of the past along with modern monstrosities.

All this is by way of illuminating your path as you explore the charms of this fascinating place and the people who live here.

1. SEEING THE CITY

Before setting out to see Dublin, go by the Tourist Office at 14 Upper O'Connell St. and pick up a very good map of the inner city, as well as informative literature on the major buildings, museums, etc., that you will want to see. There's also an illustrated walking tour guide titled *Tourist Trail* that takes you along a sign-posted route (allow about 3½ hours) and tells you about the points of interest along the way. While you're there, take a look around the basement giftshop—it's one of the best you'll find anywhere in the country, with a wide selection of Irish crafts, souvenirs, books, etc.

SIGHTSEEING TOURS: If your time in Dublin is short, one of the best ways to make the most of it is by way of one of **Bus Eireann's half-day city tours** that leave from the Central Bus Station on Store Street every weekday morning and afternoon and Sunday, April to November (three days a week during the months of March and November). Not only will you see the greatest number of Dublin landmarks in the shortest possible time, but you'll be treated as well to a very informative and witty narrative, with all sorts of anecdotes thrown in—guides all seem to be chosen for the express purpose of proving they are the epitome of the proverbial Irish talent with words. Fare is IR£9 ($14.50) for adults, half that for children, and you book in advance at the Central Bus Station (Bus aras), Store Street (tel. 302222), on the day of travel. Bus Eireann also runs marvelous **day tours** to nearby scenic and historic spots such as Avondale and the Wicklow Hills, the North Dublin Coast and Malahide Castle, Glendalough and Avoca.

Grey Line Tours, Tourist Office, 3 Clanwilliam Terrace, Grand Canal Quay (tel. 01/619666), will collect passengers at all major city hotels for full- and half-day tours of Dublin city, Powerscourt, Malahide Castle, Boyne Valley and Newgrange, Glendalough and Wicklow, and the Hill of Tara, as well as Shannon River cruises. Prices range from IR£9.90 ($15.75) to IR£19.50 ($31.25). Nightlife tours also offer good value: Jurys and Doyles Irish Cabarets at a cost of IR£26.90 ($43) and IR£24.95 ($40). Call for reservations, exact times, hotel pickup times, etc. They'll give a 15% discount to readers who mention this book when making reservations and show it when joining the tour.

2. POINTS OF INTEREST

Dubliners will tell you that it takes years to take in all the city's treasures, and they're absolutely right. Let no one reading this book think they're going to "do" Dublin in a day or two! But you can cover a fair few of its highlights, and the following are my personal—and very subjective—recommendations on places not to miss.

SIGHTSEEING HIGHLIGHTS: One of the oldest and most beautiful of Dublin's buildings is **Christ Church Cathedral,** at the top of Lord Edward Street. Founded by King Sitric in 1038, it was originally a wooden structure, but was rebuilt in stone after the Norman invasion in 1169. Strongbow, the Anglo-Norman leader, who was instrumental in the rebuilding, lies here. Four Irish kings were knighted here by Richard II in 1394 when they pledged allegiance to that monarch, in 1689 James II prayed for divine protection before marching off to the Battle of the Boyne, and a victorious King William came back to offer thanks after that battle. There are lovely architectural details and stonework in the nave, transepts, choir, and chancel, and the crypt (the oldest section) is said to be one of the best of its kind in Europe. It is open May to August, Monday through Saturday from 10 a.m. to 5 p.m., with tours after services available on Sunday at

12:15 and 4:30 p.m. The hours vary throughout the rest of the year. Take bus no. 21, 21A, 50, 50A, or 50B.

St. Patrick's Cathedral, Patrick Street, was founded in 1190, and over its varied history has served purposes as disparate as a university (from 1320 to 1465) and a stable for the mounts of Cromwell's troops in the 17th century. Its best-known dean (from 1713 to 1745) was Jonathan Swift, who wrote *Gulliver's Travels* and a host of sharp-tongued attacks on the humbuggery of his times. His tomb is in the south aisle, while his beloved "Stella" (Esther Johnson in real life) lies nearby. It had fallen into near ruin by 1860, when a member of the Guinness family financed its restoration to its present magnificent state. Visitors are expected to give a contribution of 60p (95¢) per person. Hours are 9 a.m. to 6 p.m. (closed 12:30 to 1:30 p.m., November to February) Monday through Friday, to 4 p.m. on Saturday, and only during services on Sunday at 11:15 a.m. and 3:15 p.m.). All services are ecumenical, and there are some weekday choral services also open to the public—check with the Tourist Board for exact days and hours. Take bus no. 50, 50A, 50B, or 56.

North of the Liffey, the square tower at **St. Michan's Church** on Church Street dates back to the 1096 Danish church that stood on this site, although the present structure is of 17th-century origin. Handel is said to have played its organ (perhaps when he was in Dublin to conduct the first performance of his *Messiah* in 1742). But it's the perfectly preserved bodies that have lain in its vaults for centuries with no sign of decomposition that draw many visitors. The Sheare Brothers, executed during the 1798 rebellion, rest here, and on my last visit it was a young Crusader and a 15th-century nun whose mummified bodies could be viewed. Hours are 10 a.m. to 12:45 p.m. and 2 to 4:45 p.m. during the week, to 12:45 p.m. on Saturday, and the vaults are not open to the public on Sunday. There's an admission of IR£1 ($1.60) for adults, half that for children. Take bus no. 34 or 34A.

On College Green, **Trinity College** was founded by Elizabeth I in 1592, but its oldest surviving buildings are the red-brick structures put up in the early 1700s. The striking West Front is worthy of note, as are the 1740 Printing House and the Dining Hall dating to 1760. It is, however, the Old Library that you should be sure not to miss, for it holds a priceless link with Ireland's antiquity, the magnificently illustrated *Book of Kells.* The book, which consists of the four gospels laboriously handwritten in Latin by monks and discovered in the monastery at Kells, has been bound in four separate volumes, two of which are displayed in glass cases. The lofty, vaulted Long Room, the exquisite beauty of the open pages, and marble busts of famous Trinity graduates combine to create an awe-inspiring atmosphere you'll not soon forget. Pages are turned regularly to open a different page spread, and you may well find yourself returning for a second look. Other illustrated manuscripts are on display, as well as an ancient harp said to have accompanied Brian Boru into battle. Hours are 9:30 a.m. to 4:45 p.m. on weekdays, to 12:45 p.m. on Saturday; closed Sunday. There's an admission charge to view the book.

Just across College Green from Trinity, the **Bank of Ireland** building once was the seat of the Irish Parliament, and this is where the hated Act of Union was passed in 1800. An ailing Henry Grattan, whose statue now stands across the way, donned his worn Volunteer uniform and rose in these halls to bid an eloquent farewell to the independent Parliament. Today you can visit the House of Lords simply by asking directions from any of the Bank's uniformed attendants. Not so the House of Commons, however, for when the building was acquired by the bank, it was on the condition that the lower house be demolished to avoid any possible coup d'état.

To touch more recent Irish history, take a look around the imposing **General Post Office** on O'Connell Street that was built in 1818. The massive granite building with its six fluted columns is where Padraic Pearse in 1916 gathered his Volunteers, hoisted the Irish Tricolour, and from its portico proclaimed to the Irish people and the world that Ireland would henceforth be an independent Republic. From the nearby Liffey, an English gunboat shelled the building, starting a fire that gutted its interior, now completely restored. Its central hall holds a statue of Ireland's ancient mythical warrior hero Cuchulain, who tied himself upright to a stake in order to fight a superior force to the death. A memorial to the men who fought here, its marble base is inscribed with the words of Pearse's Proclamation.

One of Dublin's more impressive sights is the north bank of the Liffey at night when floodlights illuminate the noble outlines of the 1791 **Customs House** on Customs Quay and the dignified, domed **Four Courts** building on Inns Quay. Both were burned-out shells after the 1921 Troubles, but both have been totally restored and are now in use for their original functions.

Dublin Castle occupies an elevated position west of Dame Street, just off Lord Edward Street, the site of an earlier Danish fortress. The only remaining portions of the Dublin Castle built between 1208 and 1220 are a bit of a curtain wall and two towers. You can get a pretty good idea of the original outline, however, from the **Upper Castle Yard** (disrespectfully dubbed "The Devil's Half Acre" by Dubliners when this was the nerve center from which repressive British rule was administered for centuries). British viceroys resided in the opulent **State Apartments** (now restored to their former elegance), but during World War I they were converted into a Red Cross hospital. It was from there that the prisoner James Connolly, patriot leader of the 1916 Uprising, was taken by stretcher to Kilmainham Jail to be executed, thus arousing international outrage and hastening the goal for which he gave his life. Today every president of Ireland is inaugurated in these splendid quarters. Guided tours are conducted Monday through Friday from 10 a.m. to 12:15 p.m. and 2 to 5 p.m. for a small charge. However, because they are sometimes closed to the public for official functions, it is best to check with the Tourist Office before going. You'll also want to see the **Church of the Most Holy Trinity** (formerly the Chapel Royal), as well as the memorial outside the main gate honoring those Irish killed here during Easter Week of 1916 and standing on the spot where heads of Irish kings once were displayed publicly on high spikes. Take bus no. 50, 50A, 50B, 56, 78, 78A, or 78B.

To retrace James Connolly's final journey, save a Wednesday or Sunday afternoon to travel out to **Kilmainham Gaol Historical Museum** (tel. 01/535984), within whose walls political prisoners languished, were tortured and killed, from 1796 until 1924 when the late president Eamon de Valera left as its final prisoner. Its rolls held such names as the Sheares Brothers, executed for their part in the Rebellion of 1798; Robert Emmet, who went from here to his death, proclaiming, "When my country takes her place among the nations of the earth, then, and not till then, let my epitaph be written!"; Charles Parnell, who directed Land League boycott strategy from within Kilmainham's walls; the Invincibles of 1883, five of whom lie buried here where they were hanged; scores of Volunteers who rose up in rebellion during Easter Week of 1916, 14 summarily shot, the others sentenced to life imprisonment and later pardoned; and Eamon de Valera, who was imprisoned twice—once in 1916 and again in 1921 when he opposed the Treaty. It was Connolly and the 14 who died with him in May of 1916, however, whose sacrifice for Irish independence so fired their countrymen that the national will was united and, in the words of Yeats, "a terrible beauty" was born.

The old gaol lay abandoned from the time of De Valera's exit until 1960, when a group of dedicated volunteers determined to restore it as a national shrine to Ireland's fight for freedom. Fittingly, it was President de Valera who opened the museum at Easter 1966. To walk along its corridors, through the exercise yard, or into the Main Compound is a moving experience that lingers hauntingly in the memory. Guided tours are provided from 2 to 6 p.m. on Wednesday and Sunday year round under the auspices of the Parks and Monuments Service, who accepted the gaol back into state care in May 1986. There's a small admission charge, and if you'd like a tour on any other day, you can arrange it by phoning 01/535984. Take bus no. 21, 78, 78A, 78B, or 79 at O'Connell Bridge.

To visit the Parliament (Dail Eireann) that came into being when Ireland's long struggle finally brought liberty, go to **Leinster House** in Kildare Street. You'll have to be introduced by a member to gain admittance when the Dail (pronounced "Dawl") is in session. Check with the Tourist Board for hours when the Dail is not meeting.

MUSEUMS AND GALLERIES: The **National Museum of Ireland** (entrance on Kildare Street) holds collections of archeology, the fine arts, and history. A major renovation program is currently in progress in the Kildare Street building, and as we go to press a number of the exhibition rooms are closed to the public. Situated on the ground floor, the Treasury is the highlight of the archeological collections. This special exhibition traces the development of Irish art from the Iron Age to the 15th century and includes the Tara Brooch, the Ardagh Chalice, and the Cross of Cong, as well as a 20-minute audio-visual presentation. Adjoining the main hall in a large room there's a comprehensive study of the uprising of 1916. The second-floor gallery holds cases of Irish silver, coins, glass, and Irish lace. Also on the second floor, the Music Room features traditional instruments such as the Irish harp and the uileann pipes.

A second building, entered from Merrion Street, holds natural history exhibits, and a third, on Merrion Row, is devoted to medieval Dublin, with Viking relics and other mementos of the Middle Ages on display. All are closed Monday, but open from 10 a.m. to 5 p.m. other days (including bank holidays), except Sunday when hours are 2 to 5 p.m. Take bus no. 7A, 8, 10, 11, or 13.

The **National Gallery,** Merrion Square West (tel. 01/767571), is conveniently located in Leinster Lawn, and its collections include impressive works by Dutch masters, as well as ten major landscape paintings and portraits by Gainsborough, and canvasses by Rubens, Rembrandt, El Greco, Monet, Cézanne, and Degas. John Butler Yeats, perhaps Ireland's greatest modern portrait painter, is well represented, as are leading 18th- and 19th-century Irish artists. Portraits of Irish historical figures over the past three centuries are hung in the National Portrait Gallery. The young George Bernard Shaw spent much time browsing through the National Gallery and felt such a debt of gratitude for the education it afforded him that he bequeathed it a substantial monetary grant. The National Gallery is open from 10 a.m. to 6 p.m. Monday through Saturday (until 9 p.m. on Thursday) and 2 to 5 p.m. on Sunday, with free guided tours every half hour on Sunday; closed Christmas Eve, Christmas Day, and Good Friday. There's also a very good restaurant with low prices and a souvenir bookshop.

Near the top of O'Connell Street, the **Hugh Lane Municipal Gallery of Modern Art,** Parnell Square (tel. 01/741903), occupies a fine Georgian mansion which was once the residence of Lord Charlemont. A word of explanation is in order about the works you may find on view. Before his death by drowning on the *Lusitania* in 1915, and before Charlemont House was acquired as a permanent home for his paintings, Sir Hugh Lane lent his continental collection to the National Gallery in London. A codicil to his will, however, left the pictures to Dublin's Municipal Gallery, but lacked the two essential witnesses to his signature. After a long dispute, an agreement now has been reached to divide the 39 pictures into two groups, one to be housed in London, the other in Dublin, with exchanges to be made every 14 years. Among those you're likely to find in residence are works by Manet, Corot, Monet, Daumier, and contemporary works by

Irish artists. Hours are 9:30 a.m. to 6 p.m. Tuesday through Saturday and 11 a.m. to 5 p.m. on Sunday. There's an excellent downstairs restaurant (see Chapter VI), and just across the way is the beautiful **Garden of Remembrance,** dedicated in 1966 to those who died in the 1916 fight for liberty. Take bus no. 11, 12, 13, 16, 16A, 22, or 22A.

The **Irish Architectural Archive,** 63 Merrion Square (tel. 01/763430), while neither a museum nor an art gallery, will certainly intrigue anyone interested in Ireland's past. Since its establishment in 1976, the archive has become the central source of information on architecturally and historically significant Irish buildings from 1600 right up to the present. In addition to more than 30,000 pictures, the reference library holds a vast number of publications such as pamphlets, press cuttings, historical manuscripts, and engravings. While the emphasis is on architecture, as you would expect, all sorts of extraneous information can be gleaned from browsing through the box files of photos, many of which are fascinating shots of landscapes, period village street scenes, craftsmen like thatchers and masons at work, a hunt meet at a country mansion, etc. Who knows, the cottage from which your ancestors left for America, long demolished, may show up in one of these old pictures! Pamphlets from the past also make good reading, while giving a unique insight to Ireland's social history. The archive's collection is open to the public Monday through Friday from 10 a.m. to 1 p.m. and 2 to 5 p.m.

The **Royal Hospital,** Kilmainham (tel. 01/718666), now houses the Museum of Modern Art. Included in its collections are the more than 1,200 woodcuts, etchings, and engravings by 40 artists, including leading impressionists such as Manet, Degas, and Renoir, and masters like Rembrandt, Hogarth, and Goya. Hours are 2 to 5 p.m. Tuesday through Saturday and noon to 5 p.m. on Sunday.

THE GUINNESS BREWERY: A sightseeing attraction in a class by itself is the sprawling Guinness Brewery, set on 60 acres south of the Liffey. The largest brewery in Europe, Guinness exports more beer than any other company in the world. The rich, dark stout it has produced since 1759 is truly the "wine of Ireland," and you'll no doubt be a devout convert after your second pint (it is sometimes an acquired taste!).

Because of an extensive modernization and reconstruction program there are no tours of the plant at present, but you are cordially invited to call by the Guinness Hop Store (it's clearly signposted and just around the corner from the brewery front gate), where you'll be warmly welcomed Monday through Friday between 10 a.m. and 3 p.m., except on bank holidays. The historic four-story building—which, as its name suggests, was once used to store the hops used in brewing Guinness—has been carefully refurbished and restored, and you'll see a film about the brewing process, sample a glass or two of the dark stuff in a traditional-style bar, and browse through the Brewery Museum, which includes interesting sections on coopering and transport. If you'd like a souvenir of your visit, there's a very good shop on the premises.

THE IRISH WHISKEY CORNER: If you've done any homework at all before coming to Ireland (in the beverage department, that is), you probably already know that the unique blend of barley, yeast, and water that is Irish whiskey was first (back in the 6th century) called *uisce beatha* ("ish-ke ba-ha"), which translates to "the water of life." When King Henry II's soldiers spread its fame to England, the name took on an anglicised sound, *fuisce,* before eventually evolving into "whiskey." From the beginning, nothing about this blend was usual, and today it is still unique, even in the spelling of its name—it's the only European whisk(e)y that is spelled with an "e"!

If the subject interests you, there's a fascinating Dublin "See and Do" project you won't want to miss. The Irish Whiskey Corner, Bow Street (tel. 01/725566), has been set up by the Irish Distillers Group (which includes all seven of the great whiskey houses in Ireland) to present an all-encompassing picture of the history of Irish whiskey, as well as a demonstration of just how it is made. The old warehouse that was once used to mature whiskey has been spruced up into an exhibition center where you can view a short film on the good stuff's history, see a copper pot-still and distillery model and other implements of the trade, view the lifelike figure of a cooper fashioning the oak casks that are so important in its aging, and perhaps be chosen as one of four tasters to try various brands. To top things off, of course, everyone gets a sample in the Ball of Malt bar.

Tours are conducted every weekday, and they are absolutely free. Before you go trotting off north of the Liffey, however, I suggest you either call or check with the Tourist Board for exact hours. A reminder: When you bend an elbow, whether here or in any pub around the country, don't forget to turn to your neighbor and raise your glass in the traditional Irish toast, *Slainte* ("slawn-che")—it means "good health."

PARKS AND THE ZOO: Since 1690 **St. Stephen's Green,** at the top of Grafton Street, has been preserved as an open space to provide bucolic respite for Dubliners. Over the years it has evolved into the beautifully planted park that today finds city residents and visitors alike strolling along its paths, enjoying a lunch break picnic style, or simply soaking up its rustic charm as the city's traffic swirls around its edges. Formal flowerbeds, the arched stone bridge crossing one end of the artificial lake, shaded pathways, and statuary placed in pockets of shrubbery make this a very special place. Gates are open from 8 a.m. until dark Monday through Saturday, from 10 a.m. on Sunday.

The **National Botanic Gardens,** Botanic Road, Glasnevin (tel. 01/374388), were founded in 1795 by the Royal Dublin Society to "increase and foster taste for practical and scientific botany." Spread out over 50 acres of an estate that once was the home of the poet Thomas Tickell, they are now under the direction of the Department of Agriculture and Fisheries, and in addition to exotic trees, shrubbery, and tropical plants there is an Economic Garden (for economic and poisonous plants), a vegetable garden, and a lawn garden. Just inside the gates you'll find Thomas Moore's famous *Last Rose of Summer.* During summer months, hours are 9 a.m. to 6 p.m. (from 11 a.m. on Sunday), and in winter, they close at sunset. Greenhouses do not open until 2 p.m. on Sunday. Take bus no. 13, 19, 34, or 34A.

St. Anne's Park Rose Garden, Mount Prospect Avenue, Clontarf, is one of the prettiest in the city, with climbers, floribunda, hybrid tea, and old garden roses in profusion. In April and May, daffodils are in full bloom. Take bus no. 44A or 30.

The **Phoenix Park,** northwest of the city center, with its main entrance on Parkgate Street (tel. 213021), is one of the world's most beautiful, and is *always* referred to by Dubliners as "The" Phoenix Park. Within its nearly 2,000 acres are the residence of Ireland's president, that of the American ambassador, the lovely **People's Gardens,** the **Zoological Gardens** and **Dublin Zoo,** and the **Phoenix Park Racecourse.** Its lofty trees shade all manner of humans during daylight hours and a free-roaming herd of deer after dark.

The zoo is especially noted for breeding lions and other large cats, having bred the first lion cubs in captivity in 1857, but its fame also rests on the picturesque landscaping and gardens surrounding two natural lakes (alive with pelicans, flamingos, and scores of ornamental ducks and geese) and the spacious outdoor enclosures that house all manner of animals and birds. Youngsters will delight in the small **Children's Zoo** over in one corner, where they can take a pony ride, pet tame animals, and wish on the Wishing Seat. Treetops, the glass-enclosed fast-food restaurant, provides high-quality food at inexpensive prices, and the Pride of Lions' Coffee Shop and the Lakeside Ice Cream Parlour have outdoor umbrella-table service. Adults pay IR£3.20 ($5) admission; children from 3 to 14, IR£1.60 ($2.50); children under 3 are admitted free. During the summer months hours are 9:30 a.m. to 6 p.m. Monday through Saturday, from 11 a.m. on Sunday; in winter the zoo closes at sunset. Take bus no. 10, 25, 26, or 51.

3. IN SEARCH OF LITERARY GREATS

Ireland's greatest gift to the rest of the world may well be its writers, whose keen, sharp-witted, and uniquely phrased insights into the foibles of those who walk this earth are timeless and universal. From this sparsely populated little island have sprung an enormous proportion of civilization's greatest wordsmiths, and of them, a good many were born, lived, or died in Dublin. While some of the landmarks they left behind have disappeared and others have changed since they figured in their lives, the following will surely bring you closer to those whose legacy of such a wealth of words has prodded the minds and hearts of the rest of us.

The house at 7 Hoey's Court where **Jonathan Swift** was born is now gone, but it stood very near St. Patrick's Cathedral, where he was its most famous dean, serving 32 years, and where he was laid to rest. Listen for his footsteps, too, at Trinity College, where he was a student. **Thomas Moore** also studied at Trinity, and you'll find his birthplace at 12 Aungier St. Both **George Bernard Shaw** and **Oscar Wilde** began their tumultuous lives in Dublin in the year 1854, Wilde at 21 Westland Row and Shaw at 33 Synge St. The birthplace of **W. B. Yeats** was 5 Sandymount Ave., and 42 Fitzwilliam Square was his residence from 1928 to 1932.

James Joyce was born in Rathgar at 41 Brighton Square West, and from his self-imposed exile mapped the face of his native city in unremitting detail. The Martello Tower he occupied with Oliver St. John Gogarty in 1904 is now a Joyce museum (see Section 3 of Chapter IX), and his devoted followers can trace the Dublin meanderings of his Leopold Bloom as unerringly as if Joyce had written a guidebook rather than his *Ulysses* masterpiece. This is such an intriguing pastime for visitors that the Tourist Board has prepared a *Ulysses Map of Dublin* of the book's 18 episodes that is yours for a small charge.

Brendan Behan captured the heart and soul of modern Dublin in words that his countryfolk sometimes agonized over but never denied. He was born in Dublin in 1921 and remained its irreverent, wayward son until the early end of his life in 1964, when the president of Ireland led a huge crowd to Glasnevin Cemetery for the interment. His spirit no doubt still roams the city streets, reveling in the things that have changed and those that have remained the same.

While not a literary landmark, the **Moore Street market** was well known to Behan and no doubt to many another Dublin writer. It's just behind the GPO, and to go along Henry Street and then turn into the lively commerce of Moore Street is to walk into a never-changing bit of the kaleidoscope of color that characterizes this city and kept its writers busy. From 10 a.m. to 5 p.m. on week-days, fishmongers and greengrocers and vendors of a dozen other wares gather to haggle, gossip, and contemplate the vagaries of Dublin life. Not a literary land-mark, but surely a haunt of those with a literary bent!

CHAPTER VIII

DUBLIN AFTER DARK, SPECIAL EVENTS, AND SHOPPING

□ □ □

1. THE PUBS
2. THEATER
3. MUSIC
4. SPECIAL EVENTS
5. SHOPPING

While you certainly wouldn't say that Dublin "swings" after dark, you *can*
—just as certainly—say that it entertains. There's its internationally renowned
theater, traditional Irish **music** in traditional Irish settings, **cabaret, dancing,**
and above all, the **pubs.**

1. THE PUBS

Dublin pubs are, indeed, their own special kind of entertainment. It makes
no difference if you wander into one known for its conversation ("crack," as the
Irish say), its music, or its pint (actually, there probably isn't a pub in Dublin that
won't tell you they "pull the best pint in the city"), you'll not walk out of any one
of the above bored. As I have said before in these pages, the best possible beginning and/or end to a Dublin evening is the pubs.

If you're planning, however, on one of the "pub crawls" so often heard of on
this side of the Atlantic, better gear up your strongest will to move from one to
another: chances are *very* slim that you'll be able to walk out of the first one you
enter—and very good that you'll settle in with the first pint as a newly appointed
"regular," if only for that one night.

With more than 1,000 pubs to choose from, every Dubliner you ask will
come up with a different favorite (or list of favorites), and there probably won't be
a clunker in the lot. The problem is to be selective, and in the section below I'll
share with you the ones *I* have found most interesting. Whatever you do, however, don't confine yourself to *my* list—pop into the nearest establishment any-

where in the city when you're overcome with a terrible thirst, and you'll likely come home raving about your own list of favorites. One last word, and it's for nondrinkers: Irish pubs are centers of sociability, where you can get happily soused or chat the night away just as happily with nothing stronger than soda.

Pub hours are from 10:30 a.m. to 11:30 p.m. in summer, to 11 p.m. in winter.

SOUTH OF THE LIFFEY: This is pub country, where I dare say you can't walk a block without having a choice of pubs for the evening. One much favored by the natives is the **Stag's Head,** tucked away in Dame Court. Getting there is a bit complicated, but easy if you leave College Green on the left side of Dame Street and in the middle of the second block keep your eyes glued to the sidewalk, where you'll find a stag's head set in mosaic right in the pavement. It fronts a small alleyway on the left and at its end you emerge right at this beautiful old pub that's been here since 1770. An interesting mix of ages, occupations, and character types drink here in the evenings (for young executive types, tourists, etc., come for the excellent pub lunch—see "Where to Eat").

The **Old Stand,** in Exchequer Street, is named for the "old stand" at Lansdowne Road rugby ground, and it sometimes seems that half the rugby players (past and present) have congregated in this popular pub. Celebrated athletes like Moss Kene, Phil Orr, and Ollie Campbell are familiar faces here, and the talk centers around sports 90% of the time. The clientele is made up of all ages and occupations, and around five in the afternoon you'll find some of Dublin's most attractive younger set relaxing after a day of toiling in an inner-city office.

If you're a Brendan Behan devotee, you'll know about **McDaids,** 3 Harry St., the dark, high-ceilinged pub in which he claimed a corner for himself, his pint, and his typewriter. Patrick Kavanagh and Flann O'Brien are other literary lights who drank here, and the clientele is still very much of the written word and those doing the writing.

Neary's, 1 Chatham St., backs up to the Gaiety Theater's stage door, and both patrons and crack are many times centered around what's playing there, who's in the cast, and other things theatrical. You'll recognize Neary's by the two black sculptured bronze arms holding light globes at its entrance. Inside, décor is sort of neo-Edwardian, with a pink marble bar, brass gas lamps, mirrored walls, and lots of mahogany.

Doheny & Nesbitt, 5 Lower Baggot St., looks like a Dublin pub *should*—a great old wooden front with polished brass proclaiming the place a "Tea and Wine Merchant," high ceilings, mirrored partitions along the bar, iron and marble tables, and a snug. It's been here for more than 130 years, and no doubt has always enjoyed the popularity it does today, with Dubliners of every age and inclination claiming it as their "local," including the likes of journalists, politicians, artists, architects, etc., etc., etc. A great place for conversation and people-watching, equally good at the front bar or in the back room.

O'Donoghue's, 15 Merrion Row, is not strictly a "singing pub," but it is seldom without music of one sort or another, provided, not on a planned basis, by the hordes of bearded, bejeaned, and instrument-wielding clientele who crowd in here to play traditional Irish music, blue-grass, country-and-western, or whatever on guitars, uilleann pipes, bones, spoons, and I don't-know-what-all else. It's a lively, fun-filled gathering place if you don't mind the crush. Or you could take the advice of readers Ann and Brian O'Connell, who wrote me that they've found Sunday after church (12:45 p.m. to 2 p.m.) to be the most uncrowded hours, the time when they could relax and enjoy the conversation and music without someone's elbow in their faces.

Toner's, at 139 Lower Baggot St., is the hangout of art students and other cultural types. The long mahogany bar in this venerable old pub that's been around more than a century and a half is set with partitions to provide a bit of privacy at the bar. W. B. Yeats drank here.

There are still traces of its grocery-cum-pub beginnings at **Kehoe's,** 9 South Ann St., right in the heart of Dublin's shopping area. Presided over by longtime manager Nicholas Thorpe, Kehoe's still has grocery bins in front, and the soft patina of time cloaks the wooden fixtures inside. A good place for an afternoon pint, as well as a place to meet Dubliners who have been coming here for years in the evening.

Mulligan's on Poolbeg Street ("within an ass's roar of the Liffey and the Port of Dublin," according to Dublin writer David Hanly), next door to the *Irish Press* offices, is, quite simply, a Dublin institution. Since 1782 it's pulled pints for the likes of dockers, journalists, and in recent years, scores of students from nearby Trinity. Its front bar and four rooms still retain many of their original trappings, including 19th-century gas lights. As in the past, when the likes of James Joyce and other Dublin notables were regulars, there's the ring of clubby conversation, especially around five in the afternoon, then it settles down a bit as the evening progresses. Lots of newspaper types can be found hanging out among the students.

The oldest drinking place in Ireland was licensed by Charles II in 1666. It's the **Brazen Head,** 20 Lower Bridge St., said to have got its name in memory of a curious redheaded beauty who stuck her head out a window during one or the other of Dublin's public disturbances and promptly lost it to an English sword. Be that as it may, this ancient pub sits at what used to be the only place you could cross the Liffey by bridge, and it's tucked away at the back of a courtyard down an arched alleyway on the west side of Bridge Street, and the entrance is easily overlooked. Low ceilings, brass lanterns, and ancient, uneven wooden floors are the same as when Robert Emmet lodged here while plotting his ill-fated uprising (his writing desk is pointed to with pride) and patriots like Wolfe Tone and Daniel O'Connell came in to drink.

James Joyce fans may want to look up **Davy Byrnes**, 21 Duke St., the "moral pub" of *Ulysses* hero Leopold Bloom. Well, it's been modernized right out of Joyce's day and into a tastefully sophisticated sort of cocktail lounge that one writer has called the closest thing Dublin has to a singles' bar. The 1890s wall murals are still here, and you can still get a very good pint, but these days there are likely to be more orders for mixed drinks than for the old stuff.

One of Dublin's oldest pubs is the **Norseman,** 29 East Essex St. The old décor survives, but has been smartened up a bit to meet modern-day needs. It's situated just off Dame Street at the rear of the Olympia Theatre and not far from the Projects Arts Centre, which means you're likely to run into a gaggle of performers and theatergoers almost any evening. There are frequent ballad sessions, and the traditions of pub life mix companionably with Dublin's artistic traditions at the Norseman.

NORTH OF THE LIFFEY: One of Dublin's very special pubs is over in the Phoenix Park area. **Ryan's,** 28 Parkgate St., is a real gem—it's been in the Ryan family since 1920—and is largely undiscovered by tourists. I've heard Dubliners claim it is the finest pub in town, and they'll get no argument from me. It's a traditional place, with a marvelous old oak-and-mahogany central bar fixture that holds a double-faced mechanical clock. Then there's a superb collection of antique wall mirrors, and four antique brass lamp fittings mounted on the bar counter. That bar, incidentally, is partitioned with ornate dividers with beveled mirrors. To quote David Hanly again—and there's no better pub authority in all of Dublin!—"the decibel level is usually murmurously pleasant, and the staff is ridiculously polite." Those are sentiments shared by the many heads of state and celebrities from the movie and theater worlds who regularly pass through its doors. Great atmosphere, great staff, and a good place for a pub lunch.

Kavanagh's, 1 Prospect Square, Glasnevin, is just next to what was once the main gate to Glasnevin Cemetery. The pub has been there for a century and a half, and proprietor John Kavanagh is the eighth generation of his family to run the business. His fund of stories is endless, many of which concern the gravediggers who worked next door and who popped over to bang stones against the pub's wall, whereupon drinks were passed through an opening and placed on the poor man's shovel so he could get on with his work in a livelier state. (You can still see marks from those bangings on the wall outside.) For a long time Kavanagh's did more than dispense liquid refreshment, and all sorts of household goods were once sold from all the drawers in the place. This is, as it has always been, a workingman's pub—sawdust on the floor, worn wooden booths and cubbyholes, a dart game or two, and the relaxed chatter of men who've finished an honest day's work.

You might call **Patrick Conway's,** 70 Parnell St., a theater pub, since it's just across the street from the Gate Theatre, except that then you'd have to also call it a medical pub, since it is also across from the Rotunda Maternity Hospital. The fact is that you'll usually find a good mix of theater types and obstetricians welcoming friendly tourists like ourselves, along with a good many Dublin regulars. Some of my best pub conversations have been at Conway's, and the pub lunches are terrific (see Chapter VI). This claims to be Dublin's second-oldest pub, dating from 1745, and while it's been modernized into comfort, there's much of the traditional wood, brass, and convivial atmosphere remaining. Take note of the back bar, a marvel of carved mahogany. For visitors who need more information, just ask Frank, your jovial host, who knows Dublin inside out.

For sheer Victoriana, you can't beat the **Abbey Mooney,** 1 Lower Abbey St. You owe yourself at least one jar in this vast and splendid old pub, which is gleaming enough at eye level, with lots of brass and mahogany and stained glass. But look up to the high ceiling, and I can hear your gasp from here! Elaborate gilded garlands, cherubs, blossoms, and all manner of ornamentation form what is probably the most fanciful canopy in pubdom. The downstairs lounge is not quite so ornate, but both the O'Casey and Yeats lounges upstairs can almost hold their own. There's good pub grub (try the curries) at lunchtime and always a goodly crowd of theatergoers in the evening on their way to or from the nearby Abbey Theatre.

Frank Quinn, owner of the venerable Toner's south of the Liffey, also has two atmospheric pubs on the north side. **Barry Fitzgerald's,** 90-92 Marlborough St., and **Sean O'Casey's,** 105 Marlborough St., are both close to O'Connell St. and the Abbey Theatre, and both serve pub lunches and pre-theater meals.

PUBS WITH MUSIC: You won't find a better ballad club in all of Ireland than the **Abbey Tavern** out in Howth, some nine miles north of Dublin on the peninsula that curves around to form the northern end of Dublin Bay. The village itself is a beauty, with cliff walks, narrow little winding streets and pathways, gorgeous sea views, Howth Castle gardens with a collection of over 2,000 rhododendrons, and some very good seafood restaurants. A day exploring this pretty place— perhaps with a boat trip out to Ireland's Eye (an uninhabited island just offshore) thrown in—topped off with dinner and music at the Abbey is just about as good an Irish day as you could hope for! The bar/restaurant is low-ceilinged, candlelit, and has a fireplace glowing on cool nights, making it an informal, cozy place to eat. The big hall out back is anything but cozy, until it fills with music-loving souls, as it does every night of the week. They've all come to hear the Abbey Singers, who are instrumentalists as well as vocalists, and the 8:30 to 11 p.m. show calls on all their talents as they run through a whole host of ballads you've heard all your life, then go on to some you'll never hear anywhere except on Irish soil. It's a grand show, and so popular that *you must reserve at least a day ahead*, more than that in summer months (tel. 01/322006). They do, however, hold back some seats which go on a first-come, first-served basis—but the lines can be *very* long during July and August and you shouldn't count on getting in via this route.

There's a small admission charge to the hall, and drinks are at regular bar prices (you're not obliged to order drinks, however). There's good bus and train service out to Howth—just be sure you leave the Abbey in time to catch the last one back to town.

In the city proper, north of the Liffey, **Slattery's** on Capel Street features traditional Irish music nightly during the summer and on Sunday from 12:30 to 2 p.m. There's a small admission charge to their upstairs music lounge. South of the Liffey, you can find traditional music nightly and Sunday afternoons, plus jazz on Sunday nights, at **Foley's Lounge Bar,** Merrion Row.

Other Dublin pubs have sing-along nights from time to time, so check newspapers and *What's on in Dublin* (available from the Tourist Office) when you're there.

2. THEATER

Maybe you came to Ireland for the express purpose of experiencing Irish theater—many people do. Even if you didn't come just for that purpose, at least one of your Dublin nights should be spent at the **Abbey Theatre,** Lower Abbey Street (tel. 01/744505 or 787179). This is the national repertory company, born in 1898 when Augusta Lady Gregory, W. B. Yeats, and Edward Martyn determined to perform Irish plays with Irish casts to "show that Ireland is not the home of buffoonery and of easy sentiment, as it has been represented, but the home of an ancient idealism." And it did, indeed, provide a voice for such passionate writers as J. M. Synge and Sean O'Casey, sticking to its guns even when ultra-conservative Irish audiences rioted at the showing of Synge's *Playboy of the Western World.* Siobhan McKenna, Cyril Cusack, Sara Allgood, and Barry Fitzgerald (who held down a full-time job, rehearsed at lunch, then rushed back for evening performances) are just a few of the stage talents who blossomed to stardom through their training and experience at the Abbey. The original Abbey was quite small, and when it burned in 1951, members of the company cheered because the government would then have to provide them with quarters not so cramped. And they did gain a modern, functional theater with the best in stage equipment—but it took 15 years for the government to get the job done, and all the while the company performed in a variety theater to stay alive.

The theater may be new and cast names sometimes unfamiliar, but the emphasis is still on Irish playwrights (contemporary and classic) and Irish actors, with an occasional import (Tennessee Williams's *The Glass Menagerie* played there in 1984). This is theater at its best, with the surprisingly low prices of IR£5 ($8) to IR£10 ($16). Needless to say, the Abbey stays booked year round, and to avoid disappointment you should write them directly a minimum of three weeks in advance to book the performances you want to see.

Downstairs at the Abbey, the small **Peacock Theatre** hosts literary and poetry readings, experimental contemporary drama, and sometimes a retrospective of the classics. Ticket prices are IR£5 ($8) and IR£10 ($16).

The **Gate Theatre,** Parnell Square (tel. 01/744045), is housed in a beautifully restored 18th-century, European-style theater. Its resident company stages established and modern classics, with a bias toward Irish plays and plays with an especially visual appeal. It's a small, intimate place, with only 370 seats. Tickets run about the same as those at the Abbey, and there are free student tickets on a standby basis (for information, call 01/744368), as well as special group rates.

Located in an interesting old Dublin neighborhood that was once known as "Smock Alley," the **Project Arts Centre,** 39 East Essex St. (tel. 01/712321), is an artists' cooperative where anything might happen, from poetry readings to rock music to the best of new Irish writing and productions of European theater classics. Prices are kept at a bare minimum, about IR£5.50 ($8.75), with discounts for students, the unemployed, and senior citizens at 8 p.m. shows, and free admission to the gallery and to many other events such as contemporary music (most Saturday afternoons at 2:30 p.m.). Late-night shows at 11:30 p.m. on Friday and Saturday in the summer months cost around IR£4 ($6.50) and feature Irish and European left-wing cabaret artists. For the past three years the Project has won most of the principal Harveys (the Irish equivalent of the Oscars), including best actor, best music, best set design, and best costume design.

The **Gaiety Theatre,** South King Street (tel. 01/77117), and the **Olympia Theatre,** Dame Street (tel. 01/771020), both present mostly contemporary plays at moderate prices.

Tickets for all theaters can be purchased at box offices or through **Brown Thomas** (tel. 01/776861) and **Switzer's** (tel. 01/776821) department stores on Grafton Street.

3. MUSIC

TRADITIONAL IRISH MUSIC: It's sometimes hard to hear Irish music as it pours from the Irish heart in Ireland—with a very few exceptions, that's something you almost always have to stumble onto when the music and song is the totally unplanned, but irrepressible Irish spirit finding its own voice in its own environment. When you're in Dublin, however, that same joyous or melancholy or rebellious spirit in all its passionate glory is yours to share at **Culturlann na hEireann,** 32 Belgrave Square, Monkstown (tel. 01/80029). There's some kind of traditional entertainment on there every night of the week, but to hear some of the best musicians in the country, go along on Friday, Saturday, and Sunday. Fiddlers fiddle, pipers pipe, whistle players whistle, dancers take to the floor, and singers lift their fine Irish voices in informal sessions that bear little resemblance to the staged performances mentioned above. Things get under way about 9 p.m. and carry on until 12:30 a.m., and you'll be every bit as welcome as if you'd stumbled onto the sort of unplanned session I mentioned above. There's an admission charge of IR£1.50 ($2.50).

The **Piper's Club** makes Saturday nights special, when the members of this popular Dublin institution hold forth during those same hours. Other nights, there's ceili dancing that will get you out on the floor and stage shows featuring step dancers and traditional music. Call to find out what's on when you're there, then hightail it out to Monkstown. If you call 01/800295, you can book an inexpensive dinner of traditional, home-cooked Irish food in their kitchen/restaurant.

Comhaltas Ceoltoiri Eireann, the organization dedicated to preserving Irish culture in all its forms, sponsors all the above as well as some remarkable performing troupes of dancers, singers, and musicians who tour around the country during summer months. Keep an eye out for them as you travel, or inquire at local Tourist Offices. For IR£4 ($6.50), you'll be in for an authentic Irish treat!

CONCERTS: The **National Concert Hall,** Earlsfort Terrace (tel. 01/711888), is a splendid auditorium and features first-rate musical events. The prestigious (and excellent!) RTE Symphony and Concert Orchestras perform here regularly, as does the New Irish Chamber Orchestra. Visiting artists run the gamut from harpists to jazz stars. With tickets in the IR£4 ($6.40) to IR£7 ($11.20) range, this is superb entertainment at bargain-basement prices. Check with the Concert Hall or the Tourist Office to see what's on during your visit.

CABARET: Cabaret in Dublin is served up with distinctly Irish seasonings: "Danny Boy" and "The Rose of Tralee" are favorites of the audiences (mostly visitors, but with more than a few Irish families in from the country); there's an Irish comic telling Irish jokes; pretty, fresh-faced colleens dancing, singing, playing the harp, etc.; at least one Irish tenor or baritone; and usually one or more of those captivating Irish youngsters in traditional dress to step a lively jig or reel or hornpipe. It's Irish entertainment on the light side. No purists, these—but they're loads of fun and the performances are usually well above average. Most are held in hotels, and you can opt for dinner and the show or come along for the show alone. Dinners feature Irish specialties such as potato soup, salmon, or steak, colcannon (cabbage and potatoes), and perhaps an Irish Mist soufflé for dessert (that's the exact menu at the Burlington Hotel, and others are very similar). You'll pay about IR£20 ($32) for dinner and the show, IR£12.50 ($20) for the show alone. If you come just for the show, the price includes two drinks.

A handy way to take in cabaret without having to drive is by booking with **Dublin City Tours,** Tourist Office, 14 O'Connell St. (tel. 01/786682), for their Nightlife Tour. They'll pick you up and deliver you back to your hotel, and if you mention this book when telephoning, then present it when you join the tour, they'll give you a 10% discount off prices that range from IR£15 ($24) to IR£23 ($36.75), depending on the show and whether you have dinner.

The most popular cabarets are those at **Jurys Hotel,** Ballsbridge (tel. 01/605000); the **Burlington Hotel,** Upper Leeson Street (tel. 01/605222); and the **Braemor Rooms** at the Country Club, Churchtown (tel. 01/988664). You must book ahead, which can be done directly with the hotels or through the Tourist Office.

CRUISE AND BANQUET: For a delightful evening, consider the Robertstown cruise and banquet. After a leisurely cruise on the Grand Canal aboard a barge, sipping mulled wine along the way, you arrive around 8:30 p.m. back at the Old Canal Hotel for a banquet served up with traditional Irish entertainment. Bus Eireann can get you there and back for an all-inclusive (1988) price of IR£20 ($32), leaving the Central Bus Station around 6:30 p.m., returning around midnight. Book in advance at the Bus Eireann desk, Dublin East Tourism Office, 14 Upper O'Connell St. (tel. 01/744467); the Dublin Bus Office, 59 Upper O'Connell St. (tel. 01/720000); or Busarus, Store Street (tel. 01/302222, ext. 2485).

DANCING: Dancing is the national pastime among Ireland's youth (from time immemorial, it's been the boy-meets-girl turf). Although Dublin's discos and nightspots are constantly changing, you'll always find a cluster along Lower Leeson Street (sometimes called "The Strip"), with admission charges of about IR£5 ($8) weeknights and IR£6 ($9.50) weekends. Some are fully licensed, others sell wine only.

READERS' NIGHTLIFE SELECTIONS: "For a special evening in the Dublin area, we highly recommend either the regular restaurant or the cabaret at **Clontarf Castle.** We had a superb dinner in the tower dining room one evening and returned the next for the dinner and cabaret, which had good entertainment and which we enjoyed with more locals than tourists" (Harold and Mary Anne Ramsden, Anchorage, Alaska). . . . "The **Wexford Inn,** on Wexford Street, offers the best in popular Irish ballads, with the Wolfe Tones, the Furey

Brothers, the Dubliners, Dublin City Ramblers, and Paddy Reilly all performing there regularly. Owner Oliver Barden is a congenial host" (Frank McQueeney, Wayland, Mass.).

4. SPECIAL EVENTS

If you arrive in Dublin during one of these special events, you're in for a real treat—the entire city enters into the spirit of whatever is going on. You should check with the Irish Tourist Board about *specific* dates the year of your visit, and you should know that accommodations should be booked as far as possible in advance and will probably cost you a little more during these times when the city is packed with Irish from around the country as well as international visitors.

In May of each year, the annual **Spring Show** action is concentrated in the Royal Dublin Society's show grounds in Ballsbridge. It's a grand exhibition of agriculture and industry, with prizes for sheep and cattle and pig champions, butter and cheese judgings, sheep dog trials, pony shows, jumping competitions, and even fashion shows. For the young fry, there are Punch & Judy shows, magic shows, and a babysitting crèche to free parents for a ramble around the grounds. All in all, the atmosphere is that of a major country fair, and it draws farm families from around the country, as well as more than a few from across the Channel. In 1988 admission was IR£5 ($8).

The undisputed highlight of Ireland's social calendar each year comes with the **Dublin Horse Show** in August. For one glorious week, it draws a sophisticated international crowd, and the city dons its best duds to welcome them, with private and public parties scheduled around the goings on at the showgrounds of the Dublin Royal Society. There's much pomp and circumstance—and even more fun and frolic. As for the show itself, in what are acknowledged to be some of the finest jumping enclosures in the world, there are virtually nonstop jumping competitions; auctions net enormous sales figures for handsome horses with impeccable pedigrees; the Aga Khan Trophy competition raises the excitement level on Friday; and the whole thing winds up with the International Grand Prix of Ireland on Saturday. Side events include concerts by the army bands, a beautiful floral display is the handiwork of the Royal Horticultural Society, and Irish arts and crafts exhibits are supplemented by folkdancing on the lawn. It's a great week to be in Dublin, and even one day at the showgrounds is bound to net you a score of new Irish friends. It is also probably the most heavily booked week for Dublin accommodations, so make your plans early. You can buy a ticket for all events for around IR£20 ($32), or a one-day general admission ticket for about IR£6 ($9.50). For a detailed program of events and ticket information, contact the Royal Dublin Society, P.O. Box 121, Ballsbridge, Dublin 4 (tel. 01/680645).

The **Dublin Theatre Festival** takes place during the last week of September and the first week of October and is a unique theatrical celebration that incorporates all of Dublin's theaters and spreads onto the streets and university campuses and community halls, in a series of first nights which offer innovative Irish drama and major overseas theater and dance companies. Great Irish playwrights such as Behan, Leonard, Friel, and Murphy have been represented, and the festival has been the originator of classics like *Da, Philadelphia Here I Come!, The Importance of Being Oscar, Translations,* and *The Morning After Optimism,* which have gone on to grace the stages of the world.

The festival specializes in presenting new Irish work, and the central weekend of the festival offers visitors to Dublin the opportunity to see nine new Irish plays over a period of three days. Other highlights are international theater and dance of the highest standards from places such as Sweden, South Africa, the United States, Britain, France, Germany, and many others, representing all types of theater from comedy to classics, experimental theater, mime, and musicals. A Festival Club, where the theatergoers mingle with actors, directors, and members of the international press, as well as workshops, exhibitions, and an international theater conference, all make this a very special celebration. For details during your visit, contact Dublin Theatre Festival, 47 Nassau St., Dublin 2, and it is a good idea to contact them well in advance.

One more reminder to make your plans early for any of these events, then book your accommodations and send a deposit to hold them.

5. SHOPPING

The Tourist Board issues an excellent free booklet called *Shopping in Dublin* to help you find anything you could possibly want to buy in the city. It contains a very good center-city map, as well as a guide to sizes (many of which differ from those in America) and Customs regulations.

Speaking of Customs, you can mail gifts of any value duty free to any address outside Ireland. Also, be sure to save your receipts for the Value Added Tax refund for all purchases you are taking out of the country (see Chapter I).

A good place to begin your shopping—or just your browsing, for that matter—is the **Powerscourt Town House Centre,** Clarendon Street (look for the signpost on Grafton Street at Johnson's Court between Chatham and Wicklow Streets). If you just can't get excited about shopping centers, wait till you see this one! It's set in a 1774 mansion built by Lord Powerscourt, and the house and courtyard have been expertly renovated to accommodate small shops, wine bars, and restaurants. Among other shops, there's an Antiques Gallery, a Craftsman's Guild Gallery, high-fashion clothing shops, designer shoes and bags, and a hairdresser.

On Pearse Street, you'll find all manner of Irish craftspeople at work in the **Tower Design Craft Center** from 9:30 a.m. to 5 p.m., as well as a shop selling their products and a restaurant. Major department stores are **Brown Thomas** and **Switzer's,** on Grafton Street, and **Clery's,** on O'Connell Street.

The **House of Ireland,** 37/38 Nassau St. (tel. 01/777473 and 777949) is a stand-out for finding anything from Waterford glass to Belleek, Wedgwood, Aynsley, and Royal Tara china to fine tweeds, special cashmeres, knitcrafts, linens, Celtic jewelry, pottery, blackthorn walking sticks, and a wide range of quality souvenir items. Look for the porcelain dolls by Owencraft of Ballyshannon, in handmade costumes that illustrate the social history of Ireland (Molly Malone, complete with wheelbarrow of cockles and mussels, flower vendor, countrywoman dressed for Fair day, emigrant, etc.). Good prices and outstanding service from a friendly staff. They'll mail or ship overseas. . . . The best place to buy smoked Irish salmon to take home is **McConnell and Nelson,** 38 Grafton St. (tel. 01/774344). Sean Nelson and his staff will seal it for travel, and prices are considerably below those at the airport duty-free shops. . . . **Patricia's,** Grafton Arcade, is run by Patricia York, a noted authority on heraldry, and has a good stock of heraldic items.

Thomas Mullins Ltd., 28/32 Upper O'Connell St. (beside the Gresham Hotel), sells a long list of Irish-made goods—Waterford glass, Belleek china, Royal Tara, Avoca hand-knits, Aran's Irish product lines, and many other select gift items. . . . Some of the most unusual replicas of antique Irish jewelry, copper and wood handcrafts, and other top-quality items with historical emphasis are at **Fergus O'Farrell,** 62 Dawson St. . . . **Colette Modes,** 66 S. Great George's St., has one of the city's best collections of Donegal tweeds, cashmeres, knitwear, etc., and has frequent sales with good reductions. The staff here is especially helpful. . . . Tweed tailor-made jackets and suits for men are good value (last so long they're an investment rather than just a purchase) at **Kevin and Howlin,** 31 Nassau St. (at the bottom of Dawson Street, facing Trinity College). Also a large range of ready-made men's clothing. . . . **Monaghan's,** Grafton Arcade, has our highest recommendation for Aran sweaters to fit all members of the family, as well as lambswool, cashmere, and Shetland sweaters and a good stock of menswear. They ship worldwide and offer a mail-order catalog.

Blarney Woollen Mills, 21/23 Nassau St. (tel. 01/710068), specializes in Irish sweaters, Pallas linen womenswear, and Donegal tweed suits and coats styled by leading Irish designers. They have a good selection of Waterford glass and Belleek china and will mail anywhere in the world. . . . **Irish Cottage Industries,** 44 Dawson St. (tel. 01/713039), also has a good stock of tweeds and knitwear. . . . **Kilmainham Mills,** Kilmainham Lane (tel. 01/770051 or 773716), is reputed to be the oldest working mill in the world, and its products are exported to top designer houses in the U.S. and Europe. You can watch yarn being dyed and designs being laid out, and there's a shop featuring the finished goods. Open from 8:30 a.m. to 5 p.m. Monday through Friday and 1 to 5 p.m. on Sunday. . . . **Cleo,** 18 Kildare St. (around the corner from the Shelbourne Hotel), specializes in designer woolens, as well as linens. . . . The best all-around music store in Dublin is **Waltons Musical Gallery,** 2/5 N. Frederick St. (at the top of O'Connell Street). Their stock of Irish traditional records and sheet music is tremendous, and they sell a complete line of musical instruments. . . . Book lovers can browse for hours at **Greene & Co.,** 16 Clare St. (tel. 01/762554), through two floors of new and secondhand books, or the rows of trays out front on the sidewalk. They'll hunt down scarce or out-of-print books at no charge, and the staff is both friendly and helpful. . . . **Parsons,** Baggot Street Bridge, is another traditional bookshop, with a large selection of books of Irish interest. . . . **Waterstones Bookshop,** 7 Dawson St. (tel. 01/791415), is a branch of an English chain. Its stocks are extensive, there are special reading areas, and it stays open late to accommodate office workers (hours most weekdays are 8:30 a.m. to 8 p.m., with a 9 p.m. closing two days a week). They have a good book-search service, as well as mail- and telephone-order departments. . . . Inquire at the Tourist Office about the **Book Barrow Fair** held regularly in the Mansion House. About 30 booksellers come from all around the country to set up stalls for one day only, many selling old and rare volumes for bargain prices.

READERS' SHOPPING SELECTION: "**Patrick Flood, Gold and Silversmith,** located in the Powerscourt Town House Centre in downtown Dublin, does his own designing and crafting and has reasonable prices on silver Claddagh rings and other fine jewelry" (N. Rounsefell and S. Gilmore, Baton Rouge, La.).

AROUND THE EASTERN REGION

□ □ □

Counties Dublin, Wicklow, Louth, Kildare, and Meath

1. ACCOMMODATIONS
2. WHERE TO EAT
3. THINGS TO SEE AND DO

While the city of Dublin could keep you busy and thoroughly entertained for as long as your visit lasts, outside its boundaries the rest of the region is rich in attractions that will draw you like a magnet. The *county* of Dublin is blessed with a coastline sometimes soft and gentle, sometimes wild and rugged—the majestic curve of Dublin Bay from Howth on its rocky perch in the north to Dalky and its island at the crescent's southern tip, scenic fishing villages and pleasure-ridden seashore resorts north and south of the Bay all beckon invitingly to the visitor. Then there are the mountains that form a verdant, dramatic backdrop for bustling city, sleepy villages, and that enchanting seascape.

Wicklow glows with the greens and blues of a landscape often dubbed the "Garden of Ireland." Kildare's flat fields and bogs have seen historic figures come and go and today hold stables that have bred racehorses of international fame and the world-famous Curragh racecourse where modern-day sports-world history is written by home-grown champions of the sport. Counties Louth and Meath together hold enough historic sites to fill an entire book of their own—one the setting for Tara's home of Irish royalty, the other the scene of one of Cromwell's most devastating assaults on the Irish people.

In the sections that follow, we'll take an in-depth look at County Dublin and the Eastern Region, and I can only add a word of warning: you're likely to be so beguiled by this part of Ireland that you may forget there's a mother lode of treasures just as beguiling beyond its borders—it's easy to loiter too long around here, so read on before you even begin to draft an itinerary.

Whether you elect to make your base right in Dublin or opt for accommodations in a more relaxed country atmosphere, you'll be no more than an hour's drive from most of the sightseeing highlights of Counties Dublin, Wicklow,

Louth, Kildare, and Meath. This region has been at the center of so much Irish history that it is literally so strewn with relics that it's hard to venture far without tripping over at least one.

1. ACCOMMODATIONS

For convenience, the following are listed by county. All are ideal bases for day trips into Dublin and sightseeing around the region.

Note: Prices shown below are those in effect in 1989—expect them to be higher in 1990.

County Dublin

BED-AND-BREAKFAST. In a location beside Malahide Castle, **Mrs. Margaret Farrelly,** Lynfar, Kinsealy Lane, Kinsealy, Malahide, Co. Dublin (tel. 01/463897), has a comfortable, attractive house which is only ten minutes from Dublin Airport. The house is centrally heated and there is a lovely lounge for guests. Of the four bedrooms, three have handbasins, and both high tea and dinner are available. The rate for bed-and-breakfast is IR£11 ($17.50), high tea is IR£8 ($12.75), and there is a 25% reduction for children. Open February through October.

Mrs. M. Geraghty's house at 57 Biscayne, Coast Road, Malahide, Co. Dublin (tel. 01/451459), is a semi-detached end house with a lovely view overlooking the sea. It is a comfortable home and only a short drive from Dublin Airport. The three attractive bedrooms all have handbasins and high tea is available in the evening. The rate for bed-and-breakfast is IR£11 ($17.50) and high tea costs IR£7 ($11.25). There is a 25% reduction for children and her home is open all year.

A GUESTHOUSE. Maura and James Grogan's large, comfortable home, **Sea-View Guesthouse,** Strand Road, Portmarnock, Co. Dublin (tel. 01/462242), is convenient to Dublin Airport and B + I Ferry. The eight pretty bedrooms all have handbasins. They have a private car park and the house is centrally heated. The rate is IR£16 ($25.50) single and IR£25 ($40) double. A full Irish breakfast is IR£4 ($6.50), and dinner costs IR£9.50 ($15.25). There's a 25% reduction for children. Open all year.

County Wicklow

HOSTELS. You'll find hostels at **Glendaloch** (tel. 0404/5143) and **Aughrim** (tel. 0402/6102), as well as several other locations (consult the An Oige handbook for addresses).

BED-AND-BREAKFAST. See Section 2 of Chapter V for an exceptional B&B on the waterfront in Bray.

Mrs. Patricia Hackett is hostess at **Croghan View,** Ballyellen, Inch, Arklow (tel. 0402/7323). This two-story house is set in a lovely country area half a mile off the Dublin–Rosslare road just three miles from Arklow and is very near country pubs that encourage a singsong session at the drop of a note. The four bedrooms all have sinks, and there's central heating and ample parking. Rates are IR£10.50 ($16.75), with a 50% reduction for children. Open from June through mid-September.

Thomond House, St. Patrick's Road, Upper Wicklow (tel. 0404/67940), has splendid views of both the sea and the Wicklow Mountains. Mrs. Helen

Gorman is the charming owner, and her four bedrooms all have sinks. One comes with a private bath and shower. There's central heating and private parking. Wicklow is just one-half mile away (St. Patrick's Road is just off the main Wicklow–Wexford road, about half a mile past the Catholic church). It's located 30 minutes from Glendalough and 45 minutes from Dublin. B&B rates are IR£11 ($17.50), with a 50% reduction for children.

Ashdene, Knockanree Lower, Avoca (tel. 0402/5327), is a modern, tastefully appointed house in a beautiful setting near the Avoca hand-weavers, and not far from Glendalough. Mrs. Jackie Burns has elicited many letters of praise from readers for her friendly and thoughtful manner with guests. There are four bedrooms (two with sinks, two with private baths) and there's central heating. Rates are IR£11 ($17.50) for bed-and-breakfast, IR£9.50 ($15.25) for dinner, IR£7 ($11.25) for high tea, and children get a 25% reduction. Open Easter through October.

Mrs. May Caswell, **The Arbours,** Avoca, Co. Wicklow (tel. 0402/5294), is the lovely, hospitable hostess of this modern bungalow set in a forest, with a beautiful view of Avoca valley and river. Mrs. Caswell is well known for her good cooking, and dinner is available with advance notice. There are four attractive bedrooms and they all have handbasins. The rate for bed-and-breakfast is IR£11 ($17.50) and dinner costs IR£9 ($14.50). Open February to November.

Mrs. Cora Crennan, **Sea Crest House,** Ashtown Lane, Wicklow, Co. Wicklow (tel. 0404/67772), is the hospitable hostess of this modern bungalow set on lovely grounds overlooking Wicklow Bay. The house is centrally heated and there is a garden which guests may use. Of the six bedrooms, four have private facilities and all have handbasins. There is an extra charge of IR£2 ($3.25) for private facilities. The rate is IR£11 ($17.50) for bed-and-breakfast, and dinner costs IR£9.50 ($15.25); 50% reduction for children. Open March through October.

Abhainn Mor House, Corballis, Rathdrum, Co. Wicklow (tel. 0404/46630), is a very attractive, Georgian-style house run by Mrs. Esther O'Brien and is convenient to Glendalough and a forest park. The house is centrally heated and there is a garden for guests to use. There are six pretty bedrooms, three of which have private facilities and all of them have handbasins. The rate for bed-and-breakfast is IR£11 ($17.50) and dinner costs IR£9.50 ($15.25); 25% reduction for children. Open February through mid-November.

Mrs. Maura Byrne, **Escombe Cottage,** Lockstown, Valleymount, Blessington, Co. Wicklow (tel. 045/67157), is the charming hostess of this modern bungalow overlooking Blessington lakes. The house is centrally heated and dinner is available. There are six bedrooms and they all have handbasins; four have private baths. Her rate for bed-and-breakfast is IR£11 ($17.50) and dinner is IR£10 ($16); 20% reduction for children. Open March through October.

A FARMHOUSE. The Lane Family will welcome you warmly to their home, **Ballygriffin Farm,** Arklow, Co. Wicklow (tel. 0402/32251), which is set in the peaceful countryside two miles outside Arklow. The food is good, with homebaking, and they have a wine license. The house is centrally heated and there are six comfortable bedrooms, all with handbasins. The rate is IR£11 ($17.50) for bed-and-breakfast, and dinner costs IR£9 ($14.50); 40% reduction for children. Open March through October.

County Louth

A HOSTEL. There's a small hostel at **Port Oriel,** Clogherhead, Drogheda (tel. 041/22247), nine miles from Drogheda.

BED-AND-BREAKFAST. Just one mile from Drogheda, and convenient to Dublin Airport, **Harbour Villa,** Mornington Road, Drogheda (tel. 041/37441), is a beautiful two-story home in its own grounds right on the River Boyne. There's a pretty sun lounge and private tennis courts. Only three of the four bedrooms have sinks, but all are handy to bath facilities. Mrs. Sheila Dwyer extends a warm welcome to Americans. One reader heaped laurels on the Dwyers and their home, saying they were "among the most interesting and helpful people that we met in a country full of exceptionally interesting and helpful people. They were available and concerned but our privacy was never endangered for one moment. Mrs. Dwyer's food (at breakfast and especially at high tea) was the best we were served in Ireland. The house is attractively furnished, immaculately clean, set in beautifully landscaped grounds on the tidal estuary of the Boyne." I couldn't have said it better! Bed-and-breakfast rate is IR£12 ($19.25).

Mrs. Eileen McGeown's **Delamare,** Ballyoonan, Omeath, Co. Louth (tel. 042/75101), is a modern bungalow overlooking Carlingford Lough and the Mourne mountains. The house is set in beautiful surroundings and is very peaceful. There are three bedrooms and they all have handbasins. The rate is IR£10.50 ($16.75) for bed-and-breakfast and there is a 33% reduction for children. Open May to September.

Convenient to Dublin and overlooking the Boyne river is **Aisling House,** Baltray, Drogheda, Co. Louth (tel. 041/22376), a nice modern bungalow run by Mrs. Josephine McGinley. The house is centrally heated and just 100 yards from a good golf course and restaurant. There are five attractive bedrooms, three of which have private shower and they all have handbasins and color TVs. There is an extra charge of IR£1.50 ($2.50) for private facilities. The rate for bed-and-breakfast is IR£10.50 ($16.75) without private bath, and there's a 20% reduction for children. Open all year.

County Kildare

BED-AND-BREAKFAST. Overlooking the famous Curragh Racecourse, **Dara Lodge,** Curragh Racecourse, Pollardstown, Curragh (tel. 045/21770), is a strikingly modern bungalow 2½ miles from Newbridge. Mrs. Joan McCann has seven bedrooms, six with sinks and one with private bath. Her rates are IR£11 ($17.50), with 20% off for children. Central heating and private parking.

Joe and Sheila O'Brien's **Hillview House,** Prosperous, Naas, Co. Kildare (tel. 045/68252), is a large modern house with its own family-run restaurant. There is a comfortable lounge and a relaxed atmosphere, and a set dinner is available at six o'clock for IR£9 ($14.50). There are ten bedrooms, half of which have private facilities for which there is an extra charge of IR£2 ($3.25). The rate for bed-and-breakfast is IR£10.50 ($16.75) and there is a 20% reduction for children.

County Meath

A HOSTEL. A small hostel is located at **Bridge of Boyne,** Hayes, Navan, Co. Meath (tel. 046/24119).

BED-AND-BREAKFAST. Mrs. Peggy Downey is your hostess at **Ardilaun,** 41 Beach Park, Laytown (tel. 041/27033). Her modern two-story home is set on its own grounds and is convenient to Dublin Airport. There are three bedrooms with sinks, one with private bath and shower. Central heating and private parking are also among the amenities. B&B costs IR£10.50 ($16.75), with IR£1.50 ($2.50) extra for private bath, and there's a one-third reduction for children. Open April to October.

Mrs. Christina Woods, the lively proprietress of **Latimor House,** Old Castle Rd., Kells, Co. Meath (tel. 046/40133), welcomes guests into her modern bungalow just outside the historic town of Kells as though they were a part of her own family. Indeed, her seven grown children (always "coming and going," according to Mrs. Woods) join in the warm hospitality. The house is bright and cheerful, with a pretty living room, five attractive guestrooms, and central heat. There's a paved car park out front. Bed-and-breakfast rates are IR£10.50 ($16.75), and Mrs. Woods will gladly furnish an evening meal if ordered in advance.

On the main Dublin–Navan road is Mrs. Bridie McGowan's **Taraside House,** Growtown, Dunshaughln, Co. Meath (tel. 01/259721), a modern bungalow set on two acres of landscaped gardens. There is a good restaurant nearby and the house is centrally heated. There are five bedrooms, two of which have showers, and they all have handbasins. The rate for bed-and-breakfast is IR£10 ($16) and there is a one-third reduction for children. Open all year.

A FARMHOUSE. Pauline and Paul Mullan, **Lennoxbrook,** Kells, Co. Meath (tel. 046/45902), have opened up their rambling beef-farm home to guests, and pretty little red-haired Louise seems to second the motion, eager to show off her baby sister, Sally. The house has been Paul's family home for five generations, and there's an inviting, homey air about the place. Two of the five comfortable guest rooms have bay windows, and a real show place is the upstairs bathroom that Pauline has given a quaint country look. There's a good trout stream right on the grounds, so you can fish for your dinner if you wish. Only 40 miles from Dublin, and three miles outside Kells, Lennoxbrook is an ideal "home from home" when touring this historic area. Bed-and-breakfast rates are IR£10.50 ($16.75), and a dinner of home-grown meats is available for IR£9 ($14.50). Open April through October.

READERS' ACCOMMODATIONS SELECTIONS: "Raheenmore Stud, Wicklow, Co. Wicklow (tel. 0404/2156), is a delightful bed-and-breakfast on a working farm only two miles from the coast nearby. If you like being around horses, cows, pigs, chickens, sheep dogs, and cats, then this is the place for you. The breakfasts are enormous, with fresh milk, butter, eggs, and sausages from the farm" (D. McGrath, Long Island, N.Y.) . . . "I had the pleasure, again this year, of staying with Mrs. Cunnian and her lovely daughter, Marjorie, at **Ashford House,** Dublin Road, Arklow, Co. Wicklow. After four trips to Ireland Mrs. Cunnian's is still my favorite bed-and-breakfast and the most superior. Her warm hospitality and concern were great. We had a hot-water bottle on cool evenings, suggestions for sightseeing trips, and tea waiting at the end of the day" (Dr. J. Love, Crofton Woods, Md.).

"I recommend highly the home of **Mr. and Mrs. Malone,** Glen Gorse, St. Patrick's Rd., Wicklow (tel. 0404/3150). It is close to buses and trains and they will pick you up and deliver you back to the train. They also are full of information about the surrounding area" (Diann Castle, Calgary, Alberta, Canada). . . . **"Mrs. M. Leavy's** home at San Martino, The Maudlins, Trim, Co. Meath (tel. 046/31524), is on the edge of town. My substantial room with shared bathroom was quite inexpensive" (Leonard Wertheimer, Toronto, Ontario, Canada). . . . **"Moyglare Manor Hotel,** Maynooth, Co. Kildare (tel. 01/286501), is one Big Splurge we can both recommend wholeheartedly. It's a gorgeous Georgian house set in a beautiful park. All the rooms are large and nicely furnished, with views of the grounds and woodlands beyond. Best of all, there's a warm, relaxed atmosphere and very personal service" (Dee and Herb Appleman). . . . **"Beechmount House Hotel,** Navan, Co. Meath (tel. 046/21553), is less than an hour's drive from Dublin and is a good base for a leisurely holiday. The food and facilities are good and you will be warmly welcomed by Mr. T. McCluskey and his friendly, professional staff" (S. Caliri, Southern Pines, N.C.).

2. WHERE TO EAT

There are good restaurants scattered throughout the Eastern Region. Most of those listed below feature the Special Tourist Menu, with prices of IR£5 ($8) to IR£7 ($11.20) for three-course meals. There is one Big Splurge, however, and I highly recommend it as the place to wind up a full day of sightseeing (but be sure to book ahead).

County Wicklow

The **Grand Hotel,** Wicklow Town (tel. 0404/67337), has a lovely, moderately priced restaurant whose glass walls overlook the gardens. All three meals are served daily: breakfast (about IR£5, $8) from 8 to 10 a.m., lunch (around IR£8, $12.75) from 12:30 to 2:30 p.m., and dinner (about IR£13, $20.75) from 5:30 to 9:30 p.m. The lower-priced Tourist Menu is also served year round.

The **Coffee Shop,** Fitzwilliam Square, Wicklow (tel. 0404/3194), is a deli and restaurant specializing in home-cooked lunches. Soups, breads, cakes, scones, salads, and meats are all delicious and modestly priced. They will also fix picnic meals of filled rolls and sandwiches—a very good idea in this scenic county. The Special Tourist Menu is available year round, and a lunch from the à la carte menu will run around IR£5.60 ($9). Hours are 9:30 a.m. to 5:30 p.m.

In Glendalough, the **Royal Hotel** (tel. 0404/5135) has bar food as well as a good, inexpensive à la carte menu. There are marvelous views of the river and mountains from the dining-room windows, a pleasant place to eat. A Special Tourist Menu is available from mid-March through October. Hours are 12:15 to 2:45 p.m. and 6 to 8:45 p.m. daily.

County Louth

A good stopping place in Drogheda is **Walkers Hotel,** West Street (tel. 041/31017 or 31018). It's a first-class hotel, and its restaurant, open daily, serves good meals at moderate prices, and the lower-priced Tourist Menu is available in the bar from noon to 8 p.m. Lunch hours are 12:30 to 3 p.m., and lunch will run about IR£6 ($9.50); dinner is served from 7 to 11 p.m. at prices of around IR£11 ($17.50).

County Kildare

O'Brien's Hillview House is a family-run restaurant at Prosperous, Naas (tel. 045/68252), where an à la carte dinner costs about IR£10 ($16), unless you choose from the inexpensive Special Tourist Menu, available May through September. Dinner is served from 6 to 9 p.m.; closed Sunday and Monday.

County Meath

You can get just about anything from take-aways to steaks at **Monaghans Lounge,** Kells (tel. 046/40100). This is a pub-cum-health-club, with music on weekend nights during the summer. Lunch from the à la carte menu will average IR£5 ($8), dinner is anywhere from IR£10 ($16) to IR£12 ($19.25), and the Special Tourist Menu is available year round. Hours are 10:30 a.m. to 2:30 p.m. and 5 to 11:30 p.m.

Also in Kells, the **Murphy Inn Restaurant,** Market Street (tel. 046/40680), provides good, inexpensive meals prepared by the owner. Lunch will run about IR£4.50 ($7.25); dinner, around IR£9 ($14.50). Hours are 10:30 a.m. to 10 p.m.

BIG SPLURGE. If you're planning a day of sightseeing in the Boyne Valley (Trim, Newgrange, etc.), a great ending for the day is dinner at **Dunderry Lodge,** Dunderry, Robinstown Navan (tel. 046/31671). Best call at least one day (more if possible) in advance, however, for this popular restaurant is packed with Dubliners, who make the 45-minute drive for Catherine Healy's superb meals. The place itself, an old stone barn that Catherine and her husband, Nicholas, have converted to comfort but not to modernity, is loaded with charm, and if the weather is fine, you might eat outside in the rose-bordered courtyard. As for the menu, there's game in season, roast lamb, entrecôte steak with anchovy butter, salmon, and fresh fish from local waters. Vegetables are right out of the garden. In fact, freshness and a light hand with sauces and garnishes are the keynotes here. The wine cellar holds over 200 labels (Nicholas is on hand to help you select the one just right for your meal). Á la carte prices run IR£16 ($25.50) to IR£22 ($35.25). Hours are 7:30 to 9:30 p.m. Tuesday through Saturday, and lunch is served from 12:30 to 2 p.m. in summer. Closed one week at Christmas and Easter, as well as January 1 to February 15. Dunderry Lodge is actually about six miles from Navan, its entrance down a dirt lane—it's signposted, but to be safe, stop in the village and ask exact directions.

READERS' RESTAURANT SELECTIONS: "We had a gorgeous meal at **Slane Castle,** a lovely stately home overlooking the River Boyne in Slane, Co. Meath (tel. 041/24207). Expensive, but certainly worth every cent" (C. Ives, Raleigh, N.C.). . . . "We had a wonderful dinner, great service, and a rack of lamb for two plus wine for about $35 at **Eamon Sea,** a small restaurant in Bray recommended by our B&B hostess" (W. Scott, Villanova, Pa.).

3. THINGS TO SEE AND DO

Shades of James Joyce, King Billy, the High Kings of ancient Ireland, saints, and monks—they all roamed the hills and valleys of the Eastern Region, and their haunts are there for you to visit. For detailed information on sightseeing, accommodations, and any other subjects, contact the **Dublin and Eastern Regional Tourism Organization,** Tourist Office, St. Michael's Wharf, Dun Laoghaire (tel. 01/806984).

County Dublin

James Joyce Museum, Sandycove: Built during the Napoleonic Wars in the early 19th century, the Martello Tower that was home briefly in 1904 for James Joyce and Oliver St. John Gogarty is now a museum holding such Joyce memorabilia as personal letters and manuscripts, his walking stick and waistcoat, books, photographs, and other personal possessions. Lectures and poetry readings are held on the first floor, and there are marvelous sea views from the parapet. The tower is open Monday through Saturday from 10 a.m. to 1 p.m. and 2 to 5 p.m. April through October, and by appointment other months through the Dublin and Eastern Tourism Organization, 1 Clarinda Park North, Dun Laoghaire (tel. 01/808571). Admission charges are IR£1.20 ($2) for adults, 90p ($1.50) for students, and 60p (95¢) for children.

Malahide Castle, Malahide: This stately castellated residence was occupied until 1976 by the descendants of Lord Talbot de Malahide, its founder in 1185. One of the many historic happenings within its walls occurred on the morning in 1690 when some 14 Talbot cousins sat down to breakfast together before leaving to fight for King James in the Battle of the Boyne, a battle in which all lost their lives. Patrick Sarsfield and Oliver Plunkett were cousins of the Talbot family and visited the castle. Set in a 268-acre demesne whose formal gardens alone are worth a visit, the castle still retains traces of the original moat, and holds a rich collection of portraits of historical Irish figures as well as many fine examples of Irish period furniture. A separate building holds the **Fry Model Railway Muse-**

um, the first of its kind in Ireland. On display are model trains, trams, and railroad artifacts left by the late Cyril Fry. Hours April through October are 10 a.m. to 12:45 p.m. and 2 to 5 p.m. Monday through Friday, 11 a.m. to 6 p.m. on Saturday, and 2 to 6 p.m. on Sunday. The rest of the year, weekend and holiday hours are 2 to 5 p.m., with weekday hours the same as in summer months. Admission charges are IR£2.10 ($3.25) for adults, IR£1.45 ($2.25) for students and senior citizens, and IR£1.10 ($1.75) for children.

Newbridge House, Donabate, Co. Dublin (tel. 01/436534), set in a magnificent desmesne of some 120 acres, dates from the 1700s. Its great Red Drawing Room is just as it was when the Cobbe family was in residence here, giving you a perfect picture of how wealthy families entertained in this kind of Georgian home. To see how the "downstairs" staff kept the wheels turning, visit the kitchen and laundry, as well as the coach house and various workshops. April through October Newbridge House is open Monday through Friday from 10 a.m. to 1 p.m. and 2 to 5 p.m., on Sunday and bank holidays from 2 to 6 p.m. Other months, it's open only on Sunday and bank holidays from 2 to 5 p.m. Admission is IR£1.95 ($3) for adults, IR£1.35 ($2.25) for senior citizens and students, and IR£1 ($1.50) for children, with a family ticket for IR£5.75 ($9.25).

County Louth

Mellifont: To walk in the footsteps of monks who founded Ireland's first Cistercian monastery here on the banks of the Mattock River back in 1142 is to drink in the peacefulness of a setting that invites meditation. Their Chapter House and ruins of their cloister still remain from the structures built in the 13th century, but the foundations alone are left of the original building. There's no admission charge, and Mellifont is open year round.

Muiredach's 10th-Century Cross, Monasterboice: Standing a majestic 17 feet above this site which once held a large monastic community, this is universally recognized as the finest example of the sculptured high crosses. The unknown master carver who created its many figures and ornamental designs used one piece of stone for this memorial to Muiredach, about whom we know only that he ordered the inscription on the shaft that asks for prayers on his behalf. Those dents in the base were left by immigrants who took chips of the cross with them as they crossed the seas to new homes. There is no charge to visit the small churchyard with its round tower.

County Meath

Tara: From the time that pagans worshipped here, the **Hill of Tara** has figured in Irish history and legend. It was here that the High Kings were seated, and there's a rock that legend says roared when a new king was found to be acceptable. Burial mounds here go back some 4,000 years, and there are earthworks and low walls of earth left from a fortification of the Iron Age. All else of Tara's regal trappings must be left to your imagination as you view this low hillside with the mind's eye and feel the mystical presence of pagan priests and ancient royalty.

Newgrange: Even older than the burial mounds at Tara, Newgrange was probably built by the first settlers who came to Ireland from the Continent some 4,500 years ago. We know almost nothing about them, or what the ornamental spirals and other decorations at this impressive burial mound symbolized. We don't even know for whom the structure was built, whether holy men, chieftains, or kings. What we do know is that they were skilled builders, for the corbeled roof above the burial chamber has kept out the dampness of 40 centuries, and the 62-foot-long passage still serves quite well as an entry to the chamber, the stone at its entrance an enduring testament to prehistoric craftsmanship. Archeologists are constantly carrying out research at Newgrange in an effort to unravel such mysteries as the reason an opening above the doorway is so placed that the sun's rays reach the burial chamber only on the shortest day of the year, December 21, and then for exactly 17 minutes!

You can visit Newgrange daily from mid-June to mid-September from 10 a.m. to 7 p.m. There's a IR£1.50 ($2.50) admission charge for adults, 75p ($1.25) for students, children, and senior citizens.

Note: It's well worth your while to allow time to stop by **Newgrange Farm,** Slane, Co. Meath (tel. 041/24119), just 100 yards from the Tourist Offices and entrance to Newgrange. This is a traditional, 333-acre farm that grows barley, wheat, and other grains, but it is the farmyard, bustling with beef cows, bulls, heifers, goats, pigs, ponies, a horse, Hampshire Downs sheep (they're the ones that have a "teddy-bear" coat—children love them), rabbits, dogs, and poultry that are the main attraction for visitors. One of the farmers will lead you through this thriving menagerie, with a running commentary on just how the farm works. It's a delightful experience for all ages. Tours are conducted every day from April 1 to September 30, and admissions are 75p ($1.25) for children, IR£1 ($1.60) for students, and IR£3.50 ($5.50) for adults.

Trim Castle, Trim: Ireland's largest castle built by Normans is in this pretty little town. From its tall, gray central tower you can see across the river to ruins of town walls dating from the 14th century. The site of an abbey which once held a statue of the Virgin credited with miracles is marked by what is called locally the Yellow Steeple. The castle's drawbridge tower once hosted England's Prince Hal, and its grounds have yielded up a mass grave of skeletons minus their heads who may have been the unfortunate (and unsuccessful) defenders of the stronghold against the forces of Cromwell.

County Wicklow

The **County Wicklow Tourism Association** is in Market Square, Wicklow (tel. 0404/67904).

Powerscourt Demesne and Gardens, Enniskerry: The O'Tooles, Lords of Glencullen, once occupied a castle on the site of Powerscourt House, an impressive 18th-century mansion of hewn granite that was gutted by fire in 1974 and is no longer open to the public. From its perch on high ground with a view of Great Sugarloaf Mountain, however, magnificent Japanese and Italian gardens slope downward, dotted with statuary and ornamental lakes. The 14,000-acre demesne, which straddles the River Dargle, holds rare shrubs, massive rhododendrons, and a deer park. Its most noted feature, however, is the Powerscourt Waterfall which tumbles 400 feet from a clifftop and is the highest waterfall in Ireland and Great Britain—it is at its most magnificent after a rainy spell. Outside the fortified tower stand two cannon from the Spanish Armada. A tea room and a giftshop featuring Irish goods are housed in the mansion's outbuildings. From March to October the gardens are open every day from 9 a.m. to 5:30 p.m., and the waterfall (reached by its own gate, four miles from Enniskerry) is open from 10:30 a.m. to 8 p.m. in the summer and closes at dusk in wintertime. Admission to the gardens and demense is IR£2 ($3.25) for adults, IR£1 ($1.60) for children, with a small additional charge for the waterfall area.

In the town of Wicklow, there are traditional Irish music sessions one night a week during summer months at the **Boathouse.** Inquire at the Tourist Office for schedules.

Glendalough: "Valley of Two Lakes" is the literal translation of its name, and when St. Kevin came to this place of exquisite natural beauty, he found the solitude and spiritual atmosphere he was seeking. No visitor today can leave unaffected by that same peaceful atmosphere, which seems to cling to the hills and lakes and woods. For many years St. Kevin lived here as a hermit, sleeping sometimes in a tree, sometimes in a small cleft in the rocks. When his sanctity and wisdom began to draw disciples to his side, a great school grew up that attracted thousands of students from all over Ireland, Great Britain, and the Continent. By the time of his death in 617 at an advanced age, the school had already become recognized as a great institution of learning.

Scattered around the shores of Glendalough's Upper and Lower Lake are ruins that trace the history of this mystical glen. There are relics of its great European influx, the Danish plunderers, the skirmishes between Wicklow chieftains, Anglo-Norman invaders, and of the burning in 1398. On the south shore of the Upper Lake (and reached only by boat) stands the Church of the Rock (Tempall na Skellig), with St. Kevin's Bed (a tiny hollowed-out hole) to the east of the oratory and about 30 feet above the lake. The main group of ruins are just east of the Lower Lake and those farther east are near the mouth of the valley, where the monastic city developed long after St. Kevin's death.

"Meeting of the Waters": About four miles south of Rathdrum, the Avonmore and Avonbeg Rivers come together in an idyllic setting that inspired Thomas Moore's tribute:

> There is not in the wide world a valley so sweet
> As the vale in whose bosom the bright waters meet.

There's a flagstone path from the road down to the river banks, leading to a clearing which holds a bust of the poet, and the tree stump on which he sat while composing his famous lines is marked with a plaque.

Avoca: Not far from the junction of the two rivers, the little town of Avoca is where you'll find the oldest hand-weaving mill in Ireland. Do save time to stop by **Avoca Handweavers** (tel. 0402/5105), where second- and third-generation weavers man the mill that sits across a little bridge from the sales shop. The history of the mill is fascinating, and if you can find Jim Barry when he's not up to his neck filling orders, he can give you the account of how it has gone from near closing to its current humming state of good health. The patterns and weaves from this mill are marketed all over the world, and in the shop you'll find marvelous buys in bedspreads, cloaks, scarves, and a wide variety of other items, many fashioned by home workers from all over the country. Look for Dorothy Newman (who has been here nearly as long as Jim Barry). There's also another Avoca Handweavers shop on the Dublin road in Kilmacanogue, where tweeds are transformed into finished products right on the premises. But for my money, the original mill is the place to visit.

Arklow: Beautifully situated overlooking the sea, Arklow is a seaside resort town, a fishing village, and the site of **Arklow Pottery,** South Quay, Arklow, Co. Wicklow (tel. 0402/32401), makers of fine earthenware, tea sets, dinner sets, combination sets, and giftware, incorporating both modern and traditional designs. The retail shop attached to the factory carries a great selection of shapes and patterns, and is open from 10 a.m. to 5 p.m. daily. You can arrange a tour of the factory during the months of June, July, and August to watch the craftspeople at their trade.

Mount Usher Gardens: Located in Ashford, Co. Wicklow (tel. 0404/40116 or 40522), this privately owned garden ranks among the leading—and loveliest—horticultural centers in Ireland. Its 20 acres of flowers, trees, shrubs, and lawns lie in the sheltered Vartry River Valley, and although it is not a true botanical garden, its plants come from many parts of the globe. Spindle trees from China, North American sweet gum and swamp cypress, the New Zealand ti tree, African broom, and Burmese juniper are among those represented in a harmony of color in a magnificent setting of superb landscaping. There's also a tea room at the entrance (serving coffee, sandwiches, snacks, and afternoon tea), as well as a shopping courtyard. The gardens are open daily mid-March through October from 11 a.m. to 6 p.m., and admission is IR£1.80 ($3) for adults and IR£1.20 ($2) for senior citizens, students, and children.

READERS' SIGHTSEEING SUGGESTIONS: "We visited one of Ireland's most impressive stately homes, **Russborough House,** in Blessington, Co. Wicklow (tel. 045/65239). It's open only on Sunday and bank holidays from Easter through September from 2:30 to 5:30 p.m., and every day in June, July, and August. The main rooms are elegantly furnished, and the famous Beit art collection includes paintings by Rubens, Gainsborough, Vermeer, and many others. Lots of Irish silver, and interesting old Irish maps that date from 1592 to 1750" (C. Ives, Raleigh, N.C.). . . . "Not far from Dublin on the N4, in the small town of Leixlip, Co. Kildare, as we came through the outskirts, my eye caught a tiny green-and-white sign high up on a telephone pole on the right that read **'Whitecliff Industries—Factory Outlet—Placemats.'** Being a veteran outlet shopper, I insisted we investigate, and we found a small concrete-block building in which about a dozen women were making those lovely placemats you see all over Ireland. The 'seconds' I bought were really good, and they cost about one-third the price at Shannon Duty-Free Shop" (A. Trimble, Pittsburgh, Pa.). . . . "No one should miss **Castletown House** in County Kildare. It's the largest country house in Ireland, just 12 miles outside Dublin, and it was built alongside the Liffey by William Connolly, Speaker of the Irish Parliament back in the 1700s. It is truly magnificent, and the restoration is still going on because it fell into such disrepair the past few years. Check with the Tourist Board about hours, as it isn't always open every day" (B. Harris, Arlington, Va.).

CHAPTER X

WEXFORD

□   □   □

Wexford is a small, prosperous town with industry, agriculture, and tourism happily blending into a relaxed atmosphere that makes it virtually impossible for the visitor to hurry through. Because of its shallow harbor, it was named Waesfjord ("The Harbor of the Mud Flats") by the Vikings, but it was the legendary Fir Bolgs who christened the River Slaney after their leader Slaigne.

Today, although very much in touch with the modern world, the town also displays with pride the many marks of its colorful past. Westgate and the wall at Rowe Street Church are relics of the Danish town wall later reinforced by the Normans. The sturdy bronze pikeman in the Bull Ring commemorates the bravery of those freedom-loving natives who stood—and fell—against tyranny in 1798.

Either Wexford or Waterford—a mere 40 miles apart—will serve as a base from which to explore this part of the Southeast Region in easy day trips, and your decision may well rest on whether you prefer Wexford's small-town informality or Waterford's slightly (but ever so slightly!) more sophisticated big-town ambience (by no means, however, a big-city "bustle"). Whichever you choose, be sure not to neglect the other.

1. ORIENTATION

You can walk most of Wexford's streets in a half hour or so, which means it has never seen fit to install a public transportation system. **Main Street**—so narrow you can very nearly stand in the middle and touch shops on either side with outstretched arms—runs parallel to the line of the quay, one block from the water, always alive with the buzz of friendly commerce. The aforementioned **Bull Ring** (scene of a Cromwellian massacre in 1649 that left 200 survivors of the 2,000 populace) is a wide intersection at the northern end of Main Street (its name comes from the fact that the cruel sport of bull-baiting was practiced here by the Norman aristocracy). The **Quay** runs for six blocks along the water's edge, with an inset semicircular **Crescent Quay** near the center facing a statue of Commodore John Barry (presented to the people of Wexford by the American government to honor this native son who became the "Father of the American Navy"). Poet Thomas Moore's mother was a Wexford native, and her home is now Tom Moore's Tavern, in the Corn market.

2. USEFUL INFORMATION

You'll find the **Tourist Information Office** at Crescent Quay (tel. 053/23111), open every day except Sunday from 9 a.m. to 6 p.m. (later in summer months). . . . The **train and bus depot** is at the north end of town at Redmond Place (tel. 053/22522). . . . **Private for-hire cars** are available in lieu of taxis. They meet most trains and buses and can be called to pick up fares at hotels and guesthouses. There's no standard rate and no meter, so you should agree on a fare when you engage a car. . . . **Car and passenger ferries** from Fishguard, Wales, and Le Havre, France, dock at Rosslare Harbour, 13 miles to the southeast, and Irish Rail trains bring passengers into Wexford. . . . The **General Post Office** is on Anne Street, open from 9 a.m. to 5:30 p.m. every day except Sunday. . . . **Pubs and lounges** have hours of 10:30 a.m. to 11:30 p.m. (to 11 p.m. during the winter) every day except Sunday, when they're open from noon to 2 p.m. and 4 to 10 p.m. . . . Current activities are detailed in the free booklet *Welcome to Wexford*, published by the Junior Chamber of Commerce from June to October and distributed by the Tourist Board, shops, and hotels. . . . Wexford's **telephone prefix** is 053.

3. ACCOMMODATIONS

In addition to the listings below in or on the outskirts of Wexford, the county is literally bursting with marvelous farmhouses within an easy driving distance of the town. You'll find my selections in Chapter XI, "Around County Wexford."

Note: Prices shown below are those in effect in 1989—expect them to be higher in 1990. Also, Wexford prices are usually higher during the Opera Festival in October.

BED-AND-BREAKFAST: Mrs. Mary White, 11 High St. (tel. 053/23006), has been a favorite of readers for several years. Her guesthouse is located on one of Wexford's narrow old lanes (sometimes called McSwiney Street). Mrs. White, an enthusiastic hostess who offers both hospitality and good conversation, has five comfortably furnished bedrooms and all but one (next to the bathroom) have sinks. Tea and cookies appear regularly in the evening. B&B rates are IR£10 ($16), with a 20% reduction for children.

Mrs. O'Rourke, **Westgate House,** Westgate, Wexford (tel. 053/24428), has five comfortable rooms across from the rail and bus depot at the north end of town. Rates for bed-and-breakfast are IR£10 ($16). A car park is provided.

Just two miles from Wexford town, **The Anchorage,** Saunders Court, Ferrycarrig, Co. Wexford (tel. 053/44902), is the lovely modern home of Mary and Paddy Hatton, as hospitable hosts as you'll find in Ireland. Perched on a bluff overlooking the Slaney River estuary, its lounge has a gorgeous panoramic river view, and two of the guest rooms also look out to the river (the other faces the garden and green fields beyond). There are two twin-bedded rooms, and another with one double and a single bed, all nicely decorated by Mary. Incidentally, she graduated from the celebrated Ballymaloe Cookery School "with distinction," acquiring an expertise that shows up in the dinners or high teas she'll furnish with advance notice. Bed-and-breakfast rates are IR£11 ($17.50), dinner is IR£10 ($16), and high tea is IR£5.50 ($8.75). The Anchorage is signposted on the main

Wexford–Dublin road, on your right just after you pass the Ferrycarrig Hotel coming from Wexford town. Highly recommended.

Just two miles from town and about a half mile down the Johnstown Castle road (off the Wexford–Rosslare road), Mrs. Sarah Lee's **Rockcliffe,** Coolballow, Wexford (tel. 053/43130), is a pretty, modern home set high on an acre of landscaped grounds that feature huge, colorful roses in summer months. There are four nicely furnished and attractively decorated bedrooms, all with sinks. The Rosslare ferry is ten miles away, and Mrs. Lee is happy to fix an early breakfast for departing guests. B&B rates are IR£10.50 ($16.75), with a 20% reduction for children. There's central heat and private parking. Open Easter to October.

A FARMHOUSE: Also two miles out from town, one mile off the Wexford–Waterford road (signposted), **Clonard House,** Clonard Great, Wexford (tel. 053/23141), is a lovely old 1783 Georgian house that was John Hayes's family home, and its 120 acres are still operated as a dairy farm. His pretty wife, Kathleen, and their three lovely offspring now offer warm Irish hospitality to visitors in bedrooms that are unusually spacious and nicely appointed, with bucolic farm views out every window (my favorite is the top-floor room under the eaves overlooking the century-old farmyard with its interesting outbuildings). There are eight bedrooms, five with shower and toilet, three without. Don't try to ascend to the fourth floor, even though there's a stairway leading up from the third —it seems Johnny's forefathers were just getting into adding that extra floor when they marched off to fight in the 1798 uprising and never came back; to this day, it hasn't been completed. Log fires and a piano make the lounge a friendly gathering place for guests, and Kathleen's evening meals are fast gaining a faithful following (a five-course meal with wine available, at IR£10 or $16). B&B rates are IR£12 ($19.25) without shower, IR£13 ($20.75) with shower, with youngsters paying half. Open April through October.

BIG SPLURGE: Kay and Jim Whitty are the hospitable owners/managers of **Whitford House,** New Line Road (along the Duncannon Road), Wexford (tel. 053/43845 or 43444). The biggest surprise here is a full-size, heated indoor swimming pool, unique as far as I know among Irish guesthouses! The 19 bedrooms in the two-story white guesthouse are all beautifully decorated and all have private toilet and shower, two have full baths. There's a large TV lounge, and meals in the dining room are exceptional. The attractive Fortside Lounge Bar is open for guests and the general public. B&B rates are IR£18 ($28.75) single, IR£33 ($52.75) double.

4. WHERE TO EAT

One of the best places in Wexford for a good, inexpensive lunch is the **Wren's Nest,** Custom House Quay (tel. 053/22359). This is a good-looking bar whose backroom lounge features an attractive stone fireplace. A hot-plate special goes for under IR£3 ($4.75), salads run about IR£2.20 ($3.50), the house pâté and brown bread (excellent) costs IR£1.60 ($2.50), and sandwiches are under IR£1 ($1.60). Hot foods are served from noon to 3 p.m.; snacks, until around 7 p.m.

At the south end of Main Street, **Tim's Tavern,** 51 S. Main St. (tel. 053/23861), dishes up some of the town's best pub grub at budget prices. Ken and Margaret Martin run the Tudor-style pub, which features exposed beams, whitewashed walls, and a thatch-roofed bar, and you'll find one or the other on hand whenever you stop by. All soups, meats, vegetables, and desserts are homecooked, with portions more than ample. From noon to 2:30 p.m. Monday through Saturday, you can choose from a varied menu with everything from

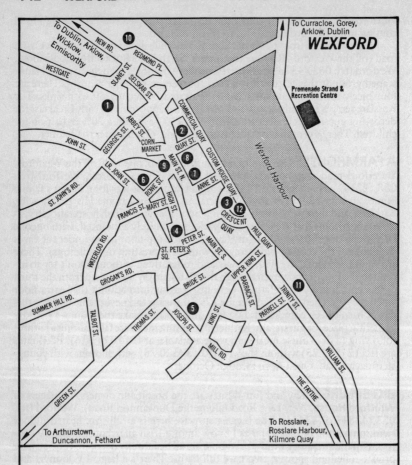

KEY TO NUMBERED SIGHTS:

1. **Westgate Tower**
   & St. Selskar Abbey
2. **The Bull Ring**
3. **Maritime Museum**
4. **St. Patrick's Church**
5. **Church of the Assumption**
6. **Church of the Immaculate**
   Conception
7. **Presbyterian Church**
8. **St. Iberius Church**
9. **Methodist Church**
10. **North Railway Station**
11. **South Railway Station**
12. **Tourist Information Office**

toasted sandwiches to open sandwiches of prawns, smoked or fresh salmon, or chicken to delicious salad plates of fresh or smoked salmon, prawns, or chicken at prices under IR£5 ($8). A hot, three-course lunch is IR£5.50 ($8.75). From July through October evening meals are served from 6 to 8 p.m., with a 12-ounce sirloin steak, french fries, and vegetables priced at IR£9.50 ($15.25), plus a good selection of salad plates. The food is exceptional, but even better is the clientele, many of whom lead off a singsong at the slightest provocation, and others (including Tim, himself) who are only too eager to share their expertise at betting the horses at Wexford race meets or others around the country. This is a place you well could come to dinner and wind up staying until Tim sings out, "Time, gentlemen, please."

At the opposite end of Main Street, the **Bohemian Girl,** North Main Street (tel. 053/24419), is another Tudor-style pub. It's a homey place, supervised by owner-chefs Kay and Seamus McMenamin, with a loyal local following and Bar Catering Competition Awards proudly displayed. Soups and brown bread are homemade, and on hand are pâté and smoked salmon and other seafood. Lunch prices start at IR£4.50 ($7.25), dinners begin at IR£8 ($12.75), and only snacks are served on Sunday.

By rights, I should list the **Oak Tavern,** Ferrycarrig, Wexford (tel. 053/22138), under a "Big Splurge" heading—that is, if you go for broke at dinner. However, this is such a special place that I heartily recommend you make the two-mile drive out the Wexford–Enniscorthy road to indulge in a marvelous bar lunch of soup, sandwiches, seafood snacks, or pâté for under IR£5 ($8) if you're pinching the pennies, or a mouthwatering dinner for about IR£12 ($19.25) if the time for splurging has arrived. (The Tourist Menu is available in the bar.) This old tavern has resided at the edge of the Slaney River for over a century and a half, and I must confess that I had a great fear it would disappear when a new bridge went up almost at its very entrance. John and Barbara Igoe, however, have not only kept the old place intact with not much more than a face scrubbing, but have added on an intimate little restaurant out back that fits right in with the tavern. It's in the two original front rooms, complete with open fire, piano, and lots of local faces, that you can indulge in bar food; or in fine weather, there's an outdoor terrace fashioned from a part of the old bridge, right at the water's edge. The charming **Ferry Restaurant** out back is lined with windows to take advantage of the river view, and also has an open fire as well as lovely tapestry upholstered seating. Specialties include a huge (ten-ounce) grilled salmon steak with parsley butter, river trout poached in tomato provençale concasse, and John's pride and joy, the well-aged steak cooked over charcoal. The Oak Tavern is open every day from 10:30 a.m. to 11:30 p.m., and the Ferry Restaurant serves dinner from 7 to 10 p.m., with advance booking absolutely necessary.

Two miles outside the other side of Wexford, on the Rosslare road, the **Farmer's Kitchen, Bar and Restaurant** is a fully licensed premises, and it is easily one of the nicest little restaurants in the Southeast. At lunch, salads and a daily special run about IR£5 ($8), and there's a full à la carte menu, as well as a quick-service grill menu, from 6 to 10 p.m. Dinner will average around IR£12 ($19.25).

The folks who publish *Inside Ireland* put me on to **Broom Cottage,** Drinagh, Wexford (tel. 053/24434), just down the road from the Farmer's Kitchen. Run by Teasie and John Devereux, it's a cozy restaurant in a charming, ivy-covered private home, with family knickknacks and lots of chintz in the small dining room. The Devereux children pitch in to help with table service, which adds to the homey feeling, and as for the food, it is, quite simply, superb! Everything is fresh and home-cooked, with seafood heading the list of specialties (plaice, trout, salmon, etc.), and pork, steak, and chicken are also on the menu. A full Irish breakfast is served from 6:30 to 10 a.m. for IR£4.50 ($7.25), and high tea/dinner, priced at about IR£10 ($16), from 5:30 to 9:30 p.m.

BIG SPLURGE: Worthy of anyone's Big Splurge dollars is the **Conservatory Restaurant,** in the Ferrycarrig Hotel, Ferrycarrig Bridge, Wexford (tel. 053/ 22999). Since Matt and Olive Britton arrived to manage this first-class hotel in 1987, they have developed the pretty, greenery-filled Conservatory into a leading restaurant in the Wexford region. With marvelous views of the River Slaney just across the lawn, the room exudes a warm, inviting glow, and the menu is as inviting as the setting. There's a comfortable and spacious lounge in which to have a before-dinner drink and place your order from selections such as poached Atlantic sea-fresh filet of pink salmon with Dutch-Gewurtz hollandaise garni, sautéed suprême of chicken with orange and lakeshore whole-grain-whisky mustard, and escalope of succulent veal au cinzano bianco style with saffron risotto. Desserts might include home-baked apple pie with that good fresh Irish cream, a crispy almond basket of assorted ice creams, or a selection of Irish farmhouse cheeses. The prix-fixe five-course dinner runs IR£17.50 ($28), plus a 10% service charge. A light lunch is available from 12:30 to 2:30 p.m., dinner hours are 7 to 9:30 p.m., and Sunday lunch is served from 12:45 to 2 p.m. Open daily.

5. THINGS TO SEE AND DO

The very first thing you should do is stop in at the **Tourist Office** and pick up a copy of *South Wexford,* a marvelous illustrated booklet that's one of a series by Pat Mackey, an official of the Southeastern Regional Tourism Organization, who knows the region like the back of his hand and will bring each town, village, and country lane vividly alive for you. It's available at a small charge. You can also get this and others in the series at the Waterford Tourist Office.

See the Tourist Office staff, too, for information on how you can participate in local hunting, fishing, boating, golfing, horseback riding, and just about any other sport you can think of—you think of it, and Wexford's probably got it! As for swimming, there's a good beach at **Rosslare,** although the Celtic Sea is not the warmest water you'll run across.

THE SIGHTS: Go by the wide intersection at the north end of Main Street known as the **Bull Ring** and spend a few minutes reflecting on the bravery of the pikemen who are portrayed by the bronze statue there. Until Cromwell visited his wrath on the town in 1649, a great high cross stood here, and when Cromwell destroyed it, he slew some 300 people who knelt in prayer before it. The house in which he stayed in Wexford stood on the present-day site of Woolworth & Co.

Westgate Tower, at the northern edge of town near the rail and bus station, is the only surviving gateway of five in the old town walls, and is pretty well preserved. Nearby, **Selskar Abbey** stands on the site of an ancient pagan temple dedicated to Odin and a later Viking church. Henry II came here in 1172 to do penance for his murder of the devout Thomas à Becket.

On **Crescent Quay,** take a look at the **Commodore John Barry statue,** and if you pass through Ballysampson, Tagoat (some ten miles from Wexford), tip your hat to his birthplace. Homage is due this seafaring Irishman from Americans, since he is credited with founding our navy after being appointed by George Washington in 1797.

Ask at the Tourist Office about what time and where to join the free **walking tour** conducted every summer evening by members of the **Old Wexford Society.** It's a labor of love for the dedicated group, and they'll point out such places as the birthplace of Oscar Wilde's mother next to the Bull Ring, the house in Cornmarket where poet Thomas Moore's mother lived, the house on North Main Street where the man who found the Northwest Passage, Robert McClure, was born, and many other historical spots. At the end of the tour, you'll look at Wexford with a different vision.

Some say that it was shipwrecked Cornish sailors who first brought **mumming** to Wexford. No matter how it arrived, however, it has survived, albeit with a decidedly Irish accent, down through the centuries, and it is unique to this country. The medieval folkdance with sword play was based on the Miracle Play triumph of good over evil, but today's mummers portray Irish patriots like Wolfe Tone and Robert Emmet. The three or four groups are composed of Wexford natives who have inherited their place in the ritualistic performances from family members going back several generations. They don't follow a regular schedule, but the Tourist Office will usually be able to tell you when the next appearance is likely to occur in one of the local pubs. If you can track one down, don't miss it.

You shouldn't leave Wexford without a visit to the **Irish National Heritage Park,** Ferrycarrig, Co. Wexford (tel. 053/41733, 22211, or 23111). Just three miles outside town, this marvelous park holds reconstructions of a campsite, farmstead, and portal dolmen from the Stone Age (7000–2000 B.C.); a cist burial and stone circle from the Bronze Age (2000–500 B.C.); an ogham stone, ringfort and souterrain, early Christian monastery, corn-drying kiln, horizontal water mill, Viking boathouse, and an artificial island habitat known as a crannog, all from the Celtic and early Christian ages (500 B.C. to 1169 A.D.); and a Norman motte and bailey, the first Norman fortification in Ireland, and a round tower, from the Early Norman Period (1169–1280 A.D.). There's also a nature walk of real beauty. Work is still continuing on this marvelous look back into Ireland's past, and there may well be many other reconstructions by the time you visit. It's open daily from April 1 to October 31, and there's a small admission charge.

A delightful way to reach the Heritage Park is via Paddy Hatton's hour-long **river cruise** on the Slaney River from Wexford Harbour to Ferrycarrig. To book, contact Paddy Hatton, The Anchorage, Saunderscourt, Crossabeg, Wexford, Co. Wexford (tel. 053/44902). The fare is IR£3 ($4.75) one way, IR£4.50 ($7.25) round trip. Departures are at 10 a.m. from Wexford Harbour and 1:30 p.m. from Ferrycarrig. Paddy also runs an evening cruise on the Slaney weekdays, as well as 45-minute cruises of Wexford Harbour from 3 to 5 p.m. weekdays during the summer months.

If you're a horseback rider, or would like to be one, the **Shelmalier Riding Stables,** Forth Mountain, Co. Wexford (tel. 053/39251), is a good detour from sightseeing. There's instruction for inexperienced or new riders, as well as pony trekking through forest and mountain country planned for every level of expertise, and a more exacting cross-country ride for experienced riders. A delightful offering is the periodic "pub ride" to imbibe a few jars in local establishments. The stables are five miles from Wexford town, open daily year round, and advance booking is essential.

SHOPPING: At 1 S. Main St., **Joyces China Shop** (tel. 053/22744) is an excellent place to shop for Waterford glass, Belleek, heraldic crests, and high-quality Irish souvenirs. Murt Joyce, who has visited the States and has a special fondness for Yanks, has a large stock of such items, competitive prices, and frequent specials on even the pricier merchandise.

Good gift selections are also available at **Barker's,** 36 S. Main St. (tel. 053/23159), and **Martin's,** 14 S. Main St. (tel. 053/22635)—both will ship overseas.

6. WEXFORD'S PUBS

The **Crown Bar** on Monck Street has been in the same family since it was established as a stagecoach inn in 1841, and Mrs. Annie Kelly, its present proprietor, and her sons, Paddy and Dick, are usually on hand to welcome visitors and show them around the Crown's unique collection of ancient weapons. The two small back lounges hold racks and cases filled with dueling pistols and flintlocks, pikes from the 1798 Vinegar Hill siege, brass blunderbusses, powder horns, and Michael Collins's revolver, among many, many other historical items. The Crown has become internationally known through televised appearances in England, France, Finland, and at home in Ireland. Lest you think this is more museum, let me hasten to assure you it's one of the best drinking and talking pubs in these parts!

Stop in the **Cape of Good Hope** pub on North Main Street, where Con Macken (uncle of international horseshow jumping champion Eddie Macken) holds forth as publican, greengrocer, and undertaker. It may be the only place left in Ireland where you'll find all three occupations under the same roof.

There's always a good crack going at **Tim's Tavern,** 51 S. Main St. (see "Where to Eat"), as well as sporadic singing nights. These folks are so good that they're sponsored by Guinness in the singing pub competitions during the Wexford Opera Festival. As yet they haven't won, but hope springs eternal and you'll find them in fine voice almost any night of the week.

7. WEXFORD OPERA FESTIVAL

I can't wish anything happier for you than that you should arrive in town in October for the Wexford Opera Festival—it's 11 days of music and revelry, with international and home-grown companies presenting both standard favorites and lesser-known operas. Three are performed through each week, along with recitals, workshops, and a host of other related activities. And the whole town gets into the act, with events like the singing pub competitions mentioned above, spontaneous "recitals" by anyone with a song in his heart and a pint in his hand, and a general "welcome to the world" attitude on the part of every resident. For detailed information on dates, scheduled performances and recitals, ticket prices, and booking, contact: **Wexford Festival of Opera,** Theatre Royal, Wexford (tel. 053/22144). Tickets vary from year to year, but run around IR£28 ($44.75) for Gala Night and weekends, and IR£23 ($36.75) for midweek performances.

CHAPTER XI

AROUND COUNTY WEXFORD

□ □ □

1. ACCOMMODATIONS
2. WHERE TO EAT
3. THINGS TO SEE AND DO

The "Sunny Southeast," they call it—there are more sunny days along this part of Ireland's coast than anywhere else in the country. The Southeast is also one of the most scenic regions, with lush greenery, good beaches, seascapes from cliff drives, wild mountain country, and some of the country's best fishing in rivers and coastal waters. The richness of its counties prompted Cromwell and other invaders to confiscate much of the land for themselves, and it was from here that many Irish were banished "To Hell or Connaught." Two American presidents, John F. Kennedy (County Wexford) and Ronald Reagan (County Tipperary), have family roots in this beautiful region.

County Wexford is pure charm, from the narrow old streets and lanes of Wexford town to solid stone ruins of Norman castles to whitewashed farmhouses overlooking rolling fields and wooded pastures to thatched cottages to fishing villages to sandy beaches. Vikings came to build a town at the edge of a shallow harbor to use as a base for plundering excursions on land and at sea. And there they stayed until the first Norman forces to land in Ireland arrived on Wexford's coast in 1169 and settled in. And *they* stayed, in spite of uprisings followed by bloody massacres and a liberty-loving native populace that gave them little peace. Father Murphy, of legend and song, led a valiant band of rebels to Vinegar Hill near Enniscorthy in 1798, where for nearly a month the ill-fed and ill-armed patriots held out against the English king's forces. Down on the Hook Peninsula, a light to guide sailing ships has burned continuously for more than 1,500 years, winking across the water to Crook Castle on the Waterford side and giving rise to Cromwell's declaration that he would sail up the river by Hook or by Crook. Today's invaders are tourists such as you and me who find the now-peaceful countryside a haven for sightseeing, sailing, fishing, and grand opera at the annual festival that draws international artists.

1. ACCOMMODATIONS

Town and country B&Bs, farmhouses, and guesthouses of very high quality abound throughout County Wexford.

Note: Prices shown below are those in effect in 1989—expect them to be higher in 1990.

A HOSTEL: Three cottages of the Coast Guard Station at Arthurstown, New Ross, are used for hostel accommodations.

BED-AND-BREAKFAST: Ivella, Rectory Road, Enniscorthy (tel. 054/ 33475), is a modern house perched on a hillside abloom with colorful garden flowers. Miss Ann Heffernan has three attractive guest rooms, two with double and single beds to accommodate families, and one double room on the front of the house which overlooks a terrific view. Breakfast comes with homemade brown bread and jam, and Miss Heffernan, who is as bright and sparkling as her home, also serves guests fresh strawberries from her own garden, topped with generous dollops of fresh cream. B&B rates are IR£10 ($16).

About 1½ miles from New Ross, Mrs. Noreen Fallon's **Killarney House,** The Maudlins, New Ross (tel. 051/21062), has two things to make it highly recommendable: guest rooms are on the ground floor, a boon for those troubled by stairs, and there's a breakfast menu with several selections. Then there's the peaceful country setting. All four bedrooms in this modern bungalow are equipped with sinks and electric blankets; there's a TV lounge for guests, central heating, and ample parking. Rates for bed-and-breakfast are IR£10 ($16), with a 50% reduction for children. Open May through September.

Mr. Sheil's **Ailsa Lodge,** Rosslare Harbour, Co. Wexford (tel. 053/33230), is a lovely large Edwardian house overlooking Wexford Bay and Rosslare Harbour. Mr. Sheil has seven nice bedrooms, all with handbasins and some with showers, and he serves an evening meal if you give him advance notice. The rate for bed-and-breakfast is IR£9.50 ($15.25) and dinner is IR£7.60 ($12.25); 25% reduction for children.

Mrs. Gough's **Ballyorley House** at Boolavogue, Co. Wexford (tel. 054/ 66287), is a lovely Georgian house about three miles off the Wexford–Dublin road. Mrs. Gough has proved a popular hostess with readers over the years. She has four nicely decorated bedrooms, all with handbasins, and an evening meal is available here if you want it. The rate for bed-and-breakfast is IR£10 ($16) and dinner costs IR£9.50 ($15.25). There is a 50% reduction for children.

FARMHOUSES: Some 15 miles outside Wexford town (to the west), the farming area around Foulksmills is fertile ground for farmhouse devotees. There are no fewer than five outstanding places to stay amid rolling pastures, tilled fields, and wooded countryside.

Mrs. Anne Redmond, of **Mill House,** Foulksmills (tel. 051/63683), opens her lovely old Georgian-style home to guests. Ivy-covered walls are the first hint of the traditional graciousness and hospitality to be found inside. The six bedrooms (four with sinks, the other two convenient to the bathroom) are all spacious, attractive, and furnished with many antique pieces. The water-powered mill that gives this place its name is a delight to adults and children alike, and Mrs. Redmond has set up croquet for the young fry, as well as providing an appealing little donkey for their amusement. Children, she says, are especially welcome, since she grew up as an only child and always longed for a large family (a dream now realized through her 14 offspring!). It's that "family" feeling that makes Mill House so special—along with marvelous Irish breakfasts and evening meals that feature homemade cream soups and tons of fresh strawberries in season. Wooded walks are handy after one of those sumptuous meals; the Mullinderry River lures fishermen; and both golf and tennis facilities are close by. Bed-and-breakfast rates are IR£10 ($16), with a 25% reduction for children aged 5 to 10, 50% for those under 5, and no charge for infants. Mrs. Redmond will be glad to send a brochure on request. Open from Easter to mid-September.

ACCOMMODATIONS □ 149

Mrs. Joan Crosbie's **Farm House,** Foulksmills (tel. 051/63616), is of 17th-century vintage, with a "newer" wing that only goes back to the 18th century. It's this part of the rambling, homey farmhouse that houses the ten comfortable guest rooms, all with sinks. There's central heating, and wood fires add a warmth of their own in both lounge and dining room. Mrs. Crosbie's sons, John and Jerry, are on hand to help manage the 150 acres, the large herd of cattle, and a fair few thoroughbred horses. The horses can be rented by guests, and you don't have to miss a ride through this lovely countryside just because you've never sat on a horse, for John is happy to give lessons to beginners. Rates for bed-and-breakfast are IR£10 ($16); add dinner and the daily rate is IR£18 ($28.75); or if you decide to settle down for a whole week, B&B plus dinner will cost IR£115 ($184). There's a 50% discount for children, and Mrs. Crosbie welcomes guests from March through October.

Just three miles outside Wexford town, a half mile off the main Wexford–Rosslare road, **Killiane Castle Farmhouse,** Drinagh, Wexford (tel. 053/42272), is John Mernagh's family home, which he and his lovely wife, Kathleen, now open to guests, who are assured of a warm welcome. It's hard to imagine a more romantic setting, with the farmhouse nestled next to a 13th-century Norman castle, huge old trees out front, and some 230 acres of pastureland creating an oasis of rural beauty. Inside, furnishings include many antiques, and on cool nights there's a fire glowing in the lounge, even though the house is centrally heated. The 12 guest rooms are large and nicely furnished, most looking out to lovely views of the countryside, and one is a single (sometimes very hard to come by). The Mernaghs and their five lively young sons offer such warm hospitality and comfort for their guests that they won the Farmhouse of the Year Award for the Southeast in 1982. Rates for bed-and-breakfast are IR£11 ($17.50), with a 20% reduction for children (babysitting is available); for a terrific home-cooked evening meal, the tariff is also IR£11 ($17.50), a very good and ample high tea (steak and vegetables are a typical meal) costs IR£9 ($14.50). Open March through October. Booking as far in advance as possible is strongly advised at this popular farmhouse.

Built in 1640, **Clone House,** Ferns, Co. Wexford (tel. 054/66113), a farmhouse with a spacious and pretty garden, won a National Garden Award in 1983. Mrs. Betty Breen and her family are very hospitable and the whole family has been very popular with readers for some years. One described them as "a super farm family." They are two miles from Ferns, five miles from Enniscorthy, and less than an hour's drive from Rosslare. The house is centrally heated, and electric blankets are supplied if needed. The four pretty bedrooms all have handbasins and two have private facilities and two have TVs. It is a working farm and excellent home-produced cuisine is guaranteed. A real convenience are the laundry facilities, available to any guest who may need them. A river running through the farm provides good trout fishing. The rate for bed-and-breakfast is IR£11 ($17.50), IR£2 ($3.25) extra for private bath. Dinner costs IR£10 ($16); 25% reduction for children. Open March through October.

Mrs. Phyllis O'Sullivan, **Woodlands House,** Killinierin, Gorey, Co. Wexford (tel. 0402/7125), is the hostess of this large farmhouse which includes a playroom, pool table, and amusements. There are spacious, pleasant lawns and gardens surrounded by a forest which has beautiful walks. It is centrally heated, but there's a log fire in the TV lounge. There are five bedrooms, four of which have private facilities, and some are traditionally furnished, as befits this 140-year-old Georgian house. Meals include fresh, home-grown ingredients and home-baking. The bed-and-breakfast rate is IR£11 ($17.50), with a 50% reduction for children, and for IR£10 ($16) Mrs. O'Sullivan will provide a full five-course dinner. Open Easter through October.

READERS' ACCOMMODATIONS SELECTIONS: "At **Mrs. O'Leay's Farm House,** Killilane, Kilrane (tel. 053/33134), the food and welcome were both excellent . . . **Carrignee House,** Carrigbyrne, New Bawn (tel. 051/24310), is a lovely guesthouse on the N25, convenient to J. F. Kennedy Park, Wexford, and New Ross. Mrs. French is a lovely and well-informed hostess" (Mary M. Wentz, Suffern, N.Y.). . . . "We stayed with Mrs. Mary Doyle, **Inishross House,** 96 Mary St., New Ross, Co. Wexford (tel. 051/21335), and we really feel this is a place that should be in your book. The hosts were friendly and helpful, the rooms were very nice, and breakfasts were superb" (Nicole Verleye and Roger Vandenberghe, Bruges, Belgium). . . . "Mrs. P. Threadgold's **St. Joseph's,** Kilrane Rosslare Harbor, Co. Wexford (tel. 053/33285), is only about a mile from the ferry landing and had the best bed we had in Ireland. There were two toilets on a floor, and lots of hot water. It was squeaky clean, with good food, and pleasant host and hostess" (Grace Craver, Keneohe, Hawaii).

2. WHERE TO EAT

That marvelous cruising restaurant is the **New Ross Gallery,** The Quay, New Ross (tel. 051/21723). Skipper Dick Fletcher conceived the idea several years ago, and now the *Galley* sets sail for lunches, afternoon teas, and dinners. Whichever cruise you select, you'll spend two to three hours relaxing over delicious specialties created from locally grown produce, meats, and fish in the comfortable, heated cruiser as you slide between the scenic banks of the River Barrow, Nore, or Suir. No canned music, no commentary—just the blissful comfort of good food, drink (the *Galley* is fully licensed), and conversation. If you're curious about the ancient stately homes, castles, and abbeys you glimpse along the shore, read the menu pages that give a detailed history of the area. There's seating for just 70, which makes for cozy intimacy, and the skipper is usually aboard in the role of gracious host.

In April and May and September and October, cruises depart according to demand from the Quay at New Ross at 12:30 p.m. for a two-hour cruise featuring a terrific lunch (many times a smörgåsbord buffet, so you can eat your fill) at an all-inclusive price of IR£10 ($16). During June, July, and August, there are daily departures. June through August there's an afternoon tea two-hour cruise departing daily at 3 p.m., at a cost of IR£4 ($6.50). And if you want to go all out for a truly memorable evening, from April through September you can book for the three-hour dinner cruise that leaves every day at 7 p.m. (6 p.m. in September), at a cost of IR£14 ($22.50) to IR£18 ($28.75). From June through August there are also afternoon and high tea cruises departing from Waterford, at prices of IR£4 ($6.50) to IR£8.50 ($13.50), but frequency can be uncertain, so best to check on days and times when you're there. It is possible on all the above to opt for the cruise only, at prices of IR£3 ($4.75) to IR£7 ($11.25). Reservations are absolutely essential, especially during the high season. Call 051/21723 or book through the Wexford or Waterford Tourist Office. This, in my book, is a don't-miss!

If you're wandering around the Hook Peninsula or taking the car-ferry from Ballyhack to Passage East, plan lunch or dinner at the **Neptune Restaurant,** Ballyhack Harbour, New Ross, Co. Wexford (tel. 051/89284). This attractive little restaurant sits next to a 15th-century tower house just across from the harbor, where the seafood comes right out of the water, most other meats come from local sources, and all are prepared by the owner himself. Service is friendly, and prices are a little higher than moderate, ranging from IR£8 ($12) to IR£15 ($19.25). Hours are 12:30 to 3 p.m. and 6 to 9:30 p.m. Tuesday through Saturday, on Sunday from 12:30 to 3 p.m. only. It only seats 30, so best call ahead to reserve. Closed Monday and November through March.

Elsewhere in County Wexford, you'll find the Tourist Menu at the following: **Hotel Saltees,** The Saltees, Kilmore Quay, Co. Wexford (tel. 053/29601), April through October; the **Coach House,** 1 Main St., Gorey, Co. Wexford (tel.

055/21280), June through September; and the **Crosbie Hotel,** 1 North St., New Ross, Co. Wexford (tel. 051/21457), year round.

The **Antique Tavern,** Enniscorthy, which has won "best pub" awards in both County Wexford and the entire Leinster province, serves some of the best lunches I've had in Ireland for under IR£5 ($8). Sandwiches, made with the freshest of breads and ingredients, are less, and soups have that unmistakable homemade flavor. It's a cozy, friendly place, with all the atmosphere of an old Irish pub.

3. THINGS TO SEE AND DO

In Enniscorthy, historic relics are displayed in a historic setting. The **Enniscorthy County Museum** is housed in a Norman castle built in 1172. It is said that Spenser wrote some of his epic *Faerie Queen* while living here. Cromwell gave it a battering, and it was on its way to becoming just another ruin until it was reconstructed in 1900. Today its rooms hold items that figured in the lives of Irish country people in years past, as well as mementos of the tragic 1798 uprising and the 1916 rebellion which had a happier outcome. There's a country "still" in such good condition it could still be put to work turning out Ireland's brand of moonshine, poteen ("pot-sheen"). Other interesting items include the collection of rush lights that were the first torches in the country. There's a small admission to the museum, and hours are 10 a.m. to 6 p.m. June through September, and 2 to 5:30 p.m. all other months. This small, interesting museum is well worth a stop en route to Wexford.

Two miles outside Wexford town, **Ferrycarrig** is the site of the first Norman earthwork and castle in Ireland.

County Wexford has a very special sightseeing attraction in the **Saltee Islands,** four miles off the pretty little fishing village of **Kilmore Quay,** 14 miles south of Wexford town, where local boatmen will take you out to the island after you've negotiated a fee (fishing trawlers will sometimes drop you off as they leave for the day's fishing and pick you up on the way home). A day on the Saltees can be soul-restoring even if you're not a birdwatcher, but if you qualify as the latter, you'll be treated to the sight of razorbills, kittiwakes, puffins, and thousands of gulls, along with hosts of seagoing species. It was in one of the Great Saltee's sea caves, incidentally, that the rebel leader of 1798, Begenal Havey, was captured and taken back to Wexford, where he was tortured and finally beheaded.

Berthed at Kilmore Quay, you'll find the former lightship, the *Guillemot,* which has been converted into a maritime museum. It is well worth a visit to view the many seafaring items, pictures, and models of famous ships and items of local history. As this is a community-run project, the price of admission is very reasonable: IR£1 ($1.60) for adults, 50p (80¢) for children, and IR£2.50 ($4) for a family ticket. Hours are 2 to 8 p.m. daily except Monday during the summer season. If you'd like to visit other times, contact Ann Kelly, Secretary, Kilmore Quay Maritime Society, Kilmore Quay, Co. Wexford (tel. 053/29714).

On your way to Kilmore Quay, you'll pass through **Kilmore Village,** a quaint little place with many traditional cottages crowned with roofs of thatch. Between the village and the quay, look for **Brandy Cross,** where you'll see a mound of little wooden crosses beside a certain bush. They've been put there by mourners on their way to the graveyard to bury a loved one—no one knows exactly why, but it's an ancient tradition.

Four miles southwest of Wexford town on the road to Murrintown, the interesting **Irish Agricultural Museum** (tel. 053/42888) is on the grounds of **Johnstown Castle** in early-19th-century farm buildings. This major museum of agriculture and Irish rural life houses displays on farming methods, life in the farmyard and the rural household (with a major collection of country furniture), and rural transport. Future plans call for reconstructions of workshops of rural craftsmen. There's a tea room, as well as a bookshop and an Irish-made-souvenir shop, open June through August. The museum is open from 9 a.m. to 5 p.m. weekdays, from 1 to 5 p.m. on Saturday and Sunday, June through August; 9 a.m. to 12:30 p.m. and 1:30 to 5 p.m. weekdays only, in May and September through April.

In 1848, when Patrick Kennedy left **Dunganstown** (near New Ross) for America, it was to escape the ravages of a devastating famine. He left behind a five-room thatched home set among stone farm buildings. A little more than a century later, his great-grandson, John Fitzgerald Kennedy, held the high office of president of the United States and returned to his ancestral home. The little thatched cottage had been replaced, but the outbuildings remained as they had been in his great-grandfather's time. Mrs. Ryan, a Kennedy by birth, and her daughter greeted the president and showed him around the place. Today the **Kennedy homestead,** on a pleasant river road, is marked by a small plaque on an outside wall, and if you'd like to take a look (from the road, please—Mrs. Ryan does not open the house to the public), make the short detour en route from Wexford to New Ross.

About six miles from New Ross, the **John F. Kennedy Park and Arboretum** is the tribute paid to the young slain president by the Irish government and United States citizens of Irish origin. It was officially opened by the late President Eamon de Valera in 1968 and covers some 623 acres, of which more than 300 are set aside as the arboretum. Already there are more than 4,500 species of shrubs, and the number is expected to reach 6,000. In the Forest Garden, there are trees from all five continents of the world. There are lovely shaded walks throughout the park, with shelters and convenient resting spots. If you follow the signposts to the top of Slieve Coillte, you'll be rewarded by a marvelous panorama of south Wexford and the splendid estuary of the Rivers Barrow, Nore, and Suir. Be sure to stop by the reception center and see the explanatory display fashioned in beaten copper. There's no admission fee to the park, only a IR£2 ($3.25) charge for parking. Open from 10 a.m. to 8 p.m. May through August, until 6:30 p.m. in April and September, to 5 p.m. in other months.

Take a drive down the **Hook Peninsula** (armed with Pat Mackey's informative booklet, *By Hook or By Crook,* available at the Tourist Office), through historic and quaint old villages. The ruins of the Knights Templars foundation still stand at **Templetown; Hook lighthouse** is the oldest in Europe, built over seven centuries ago; near Fethard-on-Sea, at the now-buried town of **Bannow,** the Normans first landed in Ireland; at **Ballyhack,** catch the car-ferry over to Passage East on the County Waterford side for ten minutes on the water to see these shores as they were seen by Viking and Norman invaders. The ferry runs continuously from 7:20 a.m. to 10 p.m. on weekdays, beginning at 9:30 a.m. on Sunday, April through September, with the last departure at 8 p.m. during other months. One-way fare is IR£3 ($4.75); round trip, IR£4.50 ($7.25).

WATERFORD

□ □ □

Just 40 miles from Wexford, Waterford is Ireland's fourth-largest city as well as one of the country's most fascinating. Every phase of Irish history has left its traces here, and the fine harbor today is as alive with freighters to-ing and fro-ing along the broad River Suir (as wide here as the Thames at Westminster Bridge) as in the days when Viking longships plied its waters.

Prehistoric dolmens, promontory forts, and passage graves in the area speak of the earliest settlers. Legends of valor and incredibly beautiful early Iron Age metalwork mirror the two sides of the flamboyant, battle-loving, and artistic Celtic clan of the Deise. The most extensive remains of Viking walls in the country and massive Reginald's Tower (which has stood intact for a thousand years) remind us of those fierce sea-raiders who came in 853 for a safe sea-haven from which to launch their plundering forays and stayed to become settlers and traders for over 300 years. Dozens of Norman towers like the "Half-Moon" on Stephen Street are legacies of the Normans, who claimed the city in 1170. And the modern Waterford Glass Factory, one of the city's most persistent claims to fame, is a descendant of the 1783 enterprise begun at the west end of the Quay by George and William Penrose.

The Irish call it Port Lairge ("Lairge's Landing-Place"), to the Vikings it was Vadrefjord, and always this city on the Suir has been the main seaport of the Southeast. It remains so today, maintaining a thriving shipping trade with the Continent and England. King John of England dubbed it in 1210 "a pearl of great price." Its walls withstood a siege by Oliver Cromwell in 1649, then fell to one of his generals the next year. James II was loyally received when he stopped in Waterford en route to Kinsale after a crushing defeat at the 1690 Battle of the Boyne—and hot on his heels came the victorious King William III to receive the city's surrender on honorable terms.

As for the *people* of Waterford—an amiable blend of all who came over the centuries as settlers, conquerors, and/or artisans—they are especially warm in their welcome to those of us who come only to visit. As far back as 1586 it was written of them by one Richard Stanihurst, "The people are cheerful in their entertainment of strangers." And so you will find them today!

1. ORIENTATION

As cities go, Waterford is a small one, easy to find your way around, with shank's mare the only vehicle you'll need for a good day's sightseeing. Its focal point is the broad quay that runs along the Suir's south bank and is named simply **The Quay.** Distinctive **Reginald's Tower** is at one end, the **Clock Tower** is at near-center (an important landmark), and a bridge crossing the Suir is at the other. Narrow streets and lanes, as well as somewhat wider **Barronstrand Street,** lead off the Quay to the half dozen or so streets on which are concentrated a great many of Waterford's sightseeing attractions, restaurants, pubs, and a few first-rate accommodations.

2. USEFUL INFORMATION

The **Irish Tourist Office** is at 41 The Quay (tel. 051/75788), open from 9 a.m. to 6 a.m. every day during summer, closed on Sunday during winter. This is one of the most helpful in the country, with facilities for booking accommodations, transportation, sightseeing—in short, as they say with pride, "anything that's bookable in Ireland." Accolades are due the staff in this efficient office for their friendly treatment of bewildered tourists in need of help. . . . At the northern end of the Suir Bridge, you'll find the **bus and rail depot.** . . . There's a **taxi** stand at the rail and bus station, and you can telephone 75222 for a cab to pick you up anywhere in the city. . . . The **General Post Office** is on the Quay a few blocks from Reginald's Tower, and hours are 9 a.m. to 6:30 p.m. during the week, until 1 p.m. on Saturday; closed Sunday. . . . Waterford's **telephone prefix** is 051.

3. ACCOMMODATIONS

You won't have any trouble sticking to our budget in Waterford—affordable accommodations are plentiful in just about any section of the city and its environs you prefer.

Note: Prices shown below are those in effect in 1989—expect them to be higher in 1990.

BED-AND-BREAKFAST: Just off the Waterford–Cork road (N25), **Annvill House,** The Orchard, Kingsmeadow, Waterford (tel. 051/73617), is a short walk from the Waterford Glass Factory. Alice and Eammon O'Brien welcome you to their modern two-story home and are happy to arrange tours and help with any other holiday plans. The five guest rooms are bright, attractive, and comfortable, with built-in wardrobes and sinks. A most unusual feature of the large, airy dining room is a case holding two walking sticks made of Waterford glass. There's central heat and off-the-street parking. B&B rates are IR£10 ($16), with a 10% reduction for children. Look for the Annvill signpost on the N25 as you approach the glass factory.

Right in the heart of the city, **Mrs. Mary Ryan,** 7 Cathedral Square (tel. 051/76677), is the attractive hostess in a three-story home that faces Christ Church Cathedral. Just one block up from the Quay, the old house has been nicely renovated, and the five bedrooms afford views of either the cathedral and historic district or the hills across the River Suir. There's plenty of parking space on this quiet little street (a real bonus for a center-city location), and you can, in fact, leave the car parked most of the time, since a great many places are within easy walking distance and you can catch a bus out to the Waterford Glass Factory just a block away. Rates for bed-and-breakfast are IR£10 ($16).

Americans with an historic bent of mind will be drawn to **Derrynane House,** 19 The Mall (tel. 051/75179)—it was in this house that Thomas Francis Meagher was arrested by the British in 1848 and sent off to Tasmania, from whence he escaped and made his way to America, eventually rising to the rank of

To Clonmel,
Kilkenny,
Dublin

NEWRATH RD.

To New Ross,
Wexford

ROSS RD.

DOCK RD.

MULGRAVE HILL

ABBEY RD.

N

BILBERRY RD.

THE BRIDGE

GRATTON QUAY

MERCHANTS QUAY

River Suir

O'CONNELL ST.

GRACEDIEU RD.

SUMMER HILL

ANNE ST.

THE QUAY

GT. GEORGE ST.

PARADE QUAY

THOMAS ST.

BARKER ST.

HIGH ST.

MILITARY RD.

MORGAN ST.

PETER ST.

ADELPHI TER.

LWR. YELLOW RD.

GREEN ST.

THE MALL

LOMBARD ST.

MORRISSON'S RD.

JOHN'S LA.

PARNELL ST.

CATHERINE ST.

WILLIAM ST.

GRIFFITH PL.

BARRACK ST.

CASTLE ST.

WATERSIDE

ST. JOHN'S TOWN

PARK RD.

MANOR HILL

MANOR ST.

John's River

WATER ST.

CANNON ST.

COLLEGE ST.

BATH ST.

LWR. NEWTOWN RD.

NEWTOWN RD.
To Waterford
Airport→

HENNESY'S RD.

POLLBERRY ST.

ST. JOHN'S HILL

CORK RD.

TRAMORE RD.

BALLYTRUCKLE RD.

To Dungarvan,
Cork

To
Tramore

WATERFORD

```
0          klms          ½
|————————————————————|
0          miles         ¼
```

KEY TO NUMBERED SIGHTS:

1. Railway Station
2. Bus Station
3. Tourist Information
4. Holy Trinity Cathedral
5. General Post Office
6. St. Olaf's
7. City Hall
8. Christ Church Cathedral
9. Reginald's Tower
10. People's Park
11. Waterpark College
12. Municipal Library, Art Gallery

brigadier general in the Fighting 69th Brigade during the Civil War. The four-story house is of Georgian style, with a wide, gracious entry hall. There's a large family room with its own bathroom, and six others have sinks and are served by two shower rooms and two bathrooms. Eilish O'Sullivan presides over this historic house and maintains a homey TV lounge for her guests. B&B rates are IR£11 ($17.50).

Mrs. Anne Carroll, **Roselda,** Cork Road, Waterford, Co. Waterford (tel. 051/73922), is an extremely helpful hostess, just three minutes from the Waterford Glass factory and always happy to arrange tours. She also has hand-cut crystal and Aran knit jackets available. She has four bedrooms, all of which have handbasins. Her bed-and-breakfast rate is IR£10.50 ($16.75) and dinner is available at a cost of IR£9 ($14.50). There's a 10% reduction for children and her home is open year round.

Mrs. Pauline Heenan, **San Michele,** Newtown Park, Waterford, Co. Waterford (tel. 051/73632), is the friendly lady who runs this clean, modern bungalow overlooking the River Suir. She is very helpful and will arrange tours of Waterford Glass. She is one mile from town and has three bedrooms, all of which have handbasins. Her B&B rate is IR£10 ($16) and there is a 25% reduction for children. Open June through August.

Mrs. Agnes Forrest, **Ashbourne House,** Milepost, Slieverue, Waterford, Co. Waterford (tel. 051/32037), is the gracious hostess of a lovely two-story, renovated farmhouse. Its scenic setting can be enjoyed from a garden which is for guests to use. There are seven immaculate bedrooms, three with handbasins and four with private bath facilities for which there is an extra charge of IR£1.50 ($2.50). The rate for bed-and-breakfast is IR£11 ($17.50) and dinner costs IR£9 ($14.50). There is a 25% reduction for children and Ashbourne House is open April to October.

I first learned of Mrs. Phyllis O'Reilly's **Saint Martins,** 24 Decies Ave., Lismore Lawn, Waterford, Co. Waterford (tel. 051/75713), when a reader wrote of the extraordinary warmth and charm of the O'Reillys. The modern, two-story home is only a few minutes away from the Waterford Glass factory and on a major bus route into the city center. There are three bedrooms with washbasins, and the odd "cuppa" appears magically just when you are in need of it. The bed-and-breakfast rate is IR£10 ($16), and dinner (with advance notice) is IR£9 ($14.50). For children, there's a 20% reduction. Saint Martins is open year round.

Only three miles from Waterford City, Carol and Willie Kinsella's attractive two-story bungalow **Halfway House,** Passage East Road, Waterford, Co. Waterford (tel. 051/76055), turns its back to the road, its front to gardens and rolling fields beyond. The four bedrooms, two with private facilities and two with handbasins and a shared bath, are nicely decorated, and the lounge and dining room are inviting public spaces. There's also a glassed-in back lounge that looks out to the garden, at the bottom of which is Willie's herb garden that sparks his many gourmet creations at the dinner table. Trained in Rockwell (Ireland), Luzanne (Switzerland), and London, Willie is the star of the kitchen here. His dinners feature the freshest local produce and seafood straight from the waters at Dunmore East. Bed-and-breakfast rates are IR£10.50 ($16.75) without private bath, IR£12.50 ($20) with. Those special dinners range from IR£10 ($16) to IR£12.50 ($20), depending on the menu, but all including sherry before dinner.

GUESTHOUSE: If you're driving into Waterford via the Rosslare road, about two miles before you reach the city start looking for **Diamond Hill,** Slieverue, Waterford (tel. 051/32855 and 32254), situated on a quiet side road at Slieverue Junction, approximately two miles from Waterford City just off the

N25 Rosslare road. It's a pretty, modern house set in lawns and gardens that have won the National Garden Award for guesthouses no fewer than four times. Its interior is as attractive as the exterior, with a nice lounge and beautifully decorated bedrooms featuring many built-ins and most with private shower/toilet. Mary and John Malone have won many devoted fans among our readers over the years, and now their charming daughter, Carmen, has joined them to run their excellent restaurant (see "Where to Eat") as well as help with the guesthouse. The hospitable Malones take a real interest in their guests, and in good weather set out chairs in the sunny gardens for a bit of outdoor relaxation. There is also a delightful craft shop displaying the best of Irish handcrafts at very reasonable prices. Rates for bed-and-breakfast run IR£12.50 ($20) to IR£15 ($24). There's a private parking lot, and the house is centrally heated. A real winner!

FARMHOUSES: Another perennial favorite with readers is **Foxmount Farm,** Halfway House, Waterford (tel. 051/74308). This 230-acre working farm is four miles out from town just off the Dunmore East road (well signposted), and the elegant old home, dating from 1700, sits on a slight rise overlooking a verdant lawn edged with flowering shrubs, pastures, and tilled acres. Margaret and David Kent are marvelous, caring hosts, always eager to accommodate their guests, whether by booking a glass-factory tour, explaining the history of the region, or simply showing them around the farm. Children delight in riding Nellie, the obliging resident donkey (there are also a horse and pony) and exploring the farmyard. Other amenities include table tennis and a tennis court. The house is furnished with lovely antiques, and evening tea around a glowing fire in the drawing room is a special event. The five guest rooms are also furnished with antiques and all have sinks. Meals are superb, featuring all fresh ingredients and home-baking (let Margaret know by noon if you want the evening meal). There's central heat and plenty of parking. Rates for bed-and-breakfast are IR£11 ($17.50), dinner is IR£10 ($16), and there's a 25% reduction for children. Open April through September.

The Gough Family's **Moat Farmhouse,** Faithlegg, Cheekpoint Road, Waterford, Co. Waterford (tel. 051/82166), is a 16th-century farmhouse which has been in the family for generations and is on the site of Faithlegg Castle and its 12th-century moat. The whole family is warm and hospitable, and the house is very comfortable. The meals are excellent and the house is centrally heated. All of the three attractive bedrooms have handbasins. The rate for bed-and-breakfast is IR£10 ($16) and dinner costs IR£9 ($14.50); 25% reduction for children. Open mid-March to mid-October.

HOTELS: **Dooley's Hotel,** 30 The Quay (tel. 051/73531), is a bit above budget rates, but its central location, friendly staff, and general character may well tempt you to view this as a "little splurge." This was a leading 19th-century coaching inn, and the grandniece of the Dooley family still books in whenever she's in Waterford, even though for more than 40 years the hotel has been owned and managed by Mrs. June Darrer and her family. The staff are longtimers who cater to guests as if the hotel were their own. The lobby and lounge bar (see "Where to Eat") are warm with rich reds and greens, stained glass, oil paintings, and leather circular booths. The attractive restaurant offers low-cost Tourist Menu meals from May to October as well as excellent, more expensive lunches and dinners. Guest rooms vary, according to whether they're in the older section, with its odd-shaped rooms (some small and cozy, others large and full of interesting nooks), or the newer wing, where rooms are more standard, although still furnished in the traditional style in keeping with the hotel's character. Most rooms have a private bath, and all have a radio, TV, and telephone. Rates begin at

IR£25 ($40) single, IR£35 ($56) double and vary according to size, location, and season. Add a 10% service charge. Children under 10 stay free in their parents' room.

A BIG SPLURGE: I can't think of a better place to spend those Big Splurge dollars than **Waterford Castle,** The Island, Ballinakill, Waterford (tel. 051/ 78203). For all the details, see the entry in Chapter XXXI.

READERS' ACCOMMODATIONS SELECTIONS: "Kay and John Ryder, **Mayor's Walk House,** 12 Mayor's Walk, Waterford, Co. Waterford (tel. 051/55427), have a conveniently located house in a quiet area of town. There is good personal service, because both Kay and her husband, John, are involved in running the bed-and-breakfast. There is good parking and it is only a short walk to the bus and rail stations and to the town center" (S. McGraw, New York, N.Y.). . . . "More than anything else, I was impressed by the hospitality of Mrs. Rena Power and her family, **Glencrea,** The Sweep, Kilmeaden, Co. Waterford (tel. 051/85240). Mrs. Power was kind enough to let her son accompany me while looking for the little parish church in which I thought my great-grandfather might be buried, and without his assistance I'm sure I would have been lost ten times over. She also gave my wife and me a night out at the Oak Room Restaurant alone together when she invited our three children to stay with her." (T. Quinlan, Cherry Hill, N.J.).

4. WHERE TO EAT

Fitzgeralds, The Mall (tel. 051/74656), serves a wide selection of budget-priced plates and half of Waterford's young working crowd at lunch. More than just pub grub, Fitzgeralds serves hot dishes of a meat and two vegetables in portions ample enough to be the main meal of the day. Heaping plates of roast beef, ham, or chicken with a potato and two vegetables are features. If you're not that hungry, there's soup and sandwiches, cold salad plates, and something called a "blaa" (lettuce, meat, onion, and tomato on a small roll), found only in Waterford, that goes for about IR£1 ($1.60). It's a large, attractive pub/eatery run by the same Fitzgeralds of the Munster Bar (see "Pubs"). Lunch hours are 12:30 to 2:30 p.m. Monday through Saturday, and prices run from IR£1.50 ($2.50) to IR£4 ($6.50).

T. & H. Doolans, Georges Street, is a century-and-a-half-old pub with much of its original décor and character still intact (see "Pubs") and a healthy local following for good pub lunches. Soup and sandwiches, salad plates, stews, and a variety of hot dishes are available from 12:30 to 2:30 p.m. at IR£1.50 ($2.50) to IR£4 ($6.50).

At the **Reginald Bar,** just behind Reginald's Tower on the Mall, you can choose from soup and sandwiches, salad plates, and hot dishes (meat plus two vegetables) for IR£1.50 ($2.50) to IR£4 ($6.50). At the award-winning **Reginald's Restaurant,** a four-course dinner will run about IR£4.50 ($7.20).

Such specialties as smoked salmon and brown bread are available in the pretty ground-floor bar of the **Granville Hotel,** The Quay, along with several tasty hot dishes, salad plates, and snacks. Hours are 12:30 to 2:30 p.m. daily.

Dooley's Hotel, The Quay (tel. 051/73531), offers good bar food in its cozy bar/lounge for IR£1.50 ($2.50) to IR£4 ($6.50), as well as a three-course Business Person's Luncheon Special in the main dining room for IR£5 ($8) and the Tourist Menu from May through October. There are also excellent four-course lunches from the regular menu at prices of IR£6 ($9.50) to IR£8 ($12.75). A children's menu is priced at IR£3 ($4.75). This pretty dining room is also a good place for the evening meal, with prices running from IR£9 ($14.50) to IR£13 ($20.75). Hours are 12:30 to 2:30 p.m. and 5:30 to 9:30 p.m. daily.

Manners Restaurant, George's Court and Barronstrand Street (tel. 051/ 78704), is a cheerful restaurant that serves breakfast, lunch, dinner, and morning and afternoon snacks, all at very reasonable prices. There's also a mouthwatering salad bar, as well as a wine bar and a ice-cream bar. Specialties include scampi, plaice meunière, trout amandine, filet steaks, chicken Cointreau, beef Stroganoff, pork filet Ludivic, and veal cooked with paprika and garlic in a creamy sauce. Breakfast will run around IR£3.50 ($5.50); lunch, IR£5 ($8); and dinner, IR£11 ($17.50). Tourist Menu prices are also available. Hours are 8:30 a.m. to 10:30 p.m. every day except Sunday, when it's noon to 10 p.m.

Both its traditional shopfront and the quality of its home-cooked food has brought awards to **Teaser's,** 124 The Quay (tel. 051/55908). It's self-service, with an appetizing delicatessen counter for morning and afternoon teas and a quick buffet lunch. In the evening there's table service, with a menu that includes authentic Italian dishes. Prices range upward from IR£1.50 ($2.50) for snacks, about IR£5.50 ($8.75) for lunch, and dinner will seldom run more than IR£9 ($14.50). Open from 10:30 a.m. to 8 p.m.; closed Sunday and public holidays.

The **Manor Court Lodge Restaurant,** Manor Court, Cork Road, Waterford (tel. 051/78851), was once the Gothic-style gate lodge to the Holy Ghost Friary, and its décor reflects its origin. Situated near the Waterford Glass factory, it offers something to ward off hunger pangs almost any time of day they attack. Breakfast, morning coffee, lunch, afternoon tea, and dinner are all tasty and attractively served. Oven-fresh scones are available with coffee and tea, and lunch might include lemon-baked chicken with crab. Among the dinner specialties are spiced silverside of beef, smoked haddock, and beef and seafood from local sources. There's also a good wine list with moderate prices. Lunch will run around IR£8 ($12); dinner, about IR£12.50 ($20). Hours are 8 a.m. to 10 p.m. seven days a week.

TWO VERY SPECIAL RESTAURANTS: Not really pricey enough to be labeled Big Splurges, but somewhat over our budget levels, the following two eateries are bargains in terms of value-for-money.

The **Oak Room Restaurant** in the Munster Bar, Bailey's New Street (tel. 051/74656), is, in my opinion, one of the loveliest dining rooms in Waterford. Dark-wood paneling, an impressive fireplace, and a service bar of carved wood set the tone, and the Fitzgerald family's warm, personalized service and culinary expertise keep alive the traditions of the Munster when it was a coaching inn two centuries ago. Only the freshest locally grown produce, meats, and seafood are used in creating superb specialties of the house, which change according to what's available daily. Prices will run about IR£10 ($16) to IR£15 ($24) without wine (a good wine list is available at moderate prices), and hours are 6:30 to 9:30 p.m. every day except Sunday and Monday. Advance booking is a must during summer months because of its popularity with locals as well as visitors.

Two miles outside the city on the Rosslare road, the **Diamond Hill** guesthouse (tel. 051/32254 and 32855—see "Accommodations") is another pretty place to dine. Pale-pink tablecloths and candles in silver holders add just the right touch of elegance, and Tiffany lamps complement the colors. Carmen Malone oversees everything, and both service and the Cordon Bleu cuisine are exceptional. Salmon from the Blackwater and Barrow Rivers are featured, as are lamb and other locally raised meats and fish, along with garden-fresh vegetables. Dinner without wine will run IR£8 ($12.75) to IR£12 ($19.25), and hours are 7 to 10 p.m. every day except Sunday. Again, advance booking is advisable.

5. THINGS TO SEE AND DO

The very *first* thing you should do is drop by the Tourist Office on the Quay to pick up two booklets that will bring this historic old town's streets alive with the ghosts of Celts, Vikings, and Normans. *Selected Walks Through Old Waterford* will send you prowling down narrow lanes and through impressive buildings to see the likes of **Christ Church Cathedral** (first established in 1050 by the same Reginald of "tower" fame), the French Church ruins, town walls, towers, and castles. The second booklet, *Reginald's Tower and the Story of Waterford,* gives you a very complete (and entertaining) history of the massive tower that dates from 1003 and of Waterford from its very beginning. Both are written and illustrated by Pat Mackey, a former official of the Tourist Board who knows and loves Waterford and the entire Southeast Region. While you're at it, look for his *City and County Guide to Kilkenny,* as well, and if you haven't yet been to Wexford, this is the time to get Pat's excellent *South Wexford* guide, which will make your journey several times more enjoyable. The books are inexpensive and will become treasured souvenirs of your Irish holiday. Pat has also written a marvelous book that gives the flavor of Waterford in the 1930s, '40s, and '50s. It's called *Talk of the Town,* and it opens up a view of Pat's hometown that has long since vanished— "cockle women," pawnshops, pig buyers, and street characters. You'll find it at the Tourist Office, and I heartily recommend it.

The Tourist Board also has the helpful *Waterford County Guide,* as well as an excellent selection of maps and Irish publications.

The Tourist Board will book you for a tour of the **Waterford Crystal Factory** (see below) and bring you up-to-date on what's going on in town during your stay and advise you on **Bus Eireann day trips** around the area. As I said, go there *first.*

REGINALD'S TOWER: At the end of the Quay, which turns into the Mall, Reginald's Tower stands sentinel as it has for a thousand years, though today as a museum it guards gems from Waterford's historical treasures. When Reginald McIvor, the Danish ruler, built this stronghold, its 12-foot-thick walls stood right at the river's edge, and it was constructed so that entrance could only be gained from inside the city walls. In the centuries since, the tower has proved its worth as the strongest fortification on the River Suir, having resisted attack from all sides (even Cromwell failed to conquer it, although the bitterly cold winter may have had as much to do with his lifting an unsuccessful siege as did the tower's impregnability). And it has witnessed events of major significance in Ireland's history, such as the marriage in 1170 of Strongbow to Eva, Irish King MacMurrough's daughter, which marked the beginning of England's entanglement with Irish affairs.

Today you enter the fascinating museum through what was once the tower's dungeon (wherein the Sitrics met their end and Reginald and O'Faolain were imprisoned). On the upper floors you'll find King John's mace and sword, along with many of the city's 30 royal charters. Interesting to Americans is the display on "Timbertoes," the wooden bridge across the Suir (now replaced by a modern structure) that was the work of Boston architect Lemuel Cox in 1797. The following year, rebels who participated in the uprising of 1798 were hanged from its beams. There's also a bronze plate over which currency changed hands back in the 18th century—it's called simply the "Nail," and has entered our vocabulary through the expression "paying on the nail." The tower is open from 9:30 a.m. to 12:30 p.m. and 2 to 5:30 p.m. Monday through Friday and to 12:30 p.m. on Saturday from mid-April to October. If you're in Waterford other months, ask at the City Hall (on the Mall) about winter hours. There's a small admission fee for adults, none for children.

THE WATERFORD CRYSTAL FACTORY: You will surely not want to leave Waterford without a trip out to the plant where some of the world's finest crystal is fashioned into works of art, so before we talk about what you'll see, let me warn you that if you're not to be disappointed, you should book as far in advance as possible during summer months. The half-hour tours are one of Ireland's most popular attractions and only small groups are allowed through at a time. You can write directly to Waterford Glass Ltd., Kilbarry, Waterford, if you're sure of your dates, or you can arrange a booking through most Tourist Offices around the country. Many Waterford B&B hostesses will be glad to book it for you when you make your accommodations reservation. Tours are scheduled at 10:15, 11, and 11:45 a.m. and 1:45 and 2:30 p.m., and no children under 10 are permitted, although they may wait in the showroom and watch a 20-minute film on the factory. Also, the factory is usually closed the last week in July and the first two weeks in August for its annual holiday (this can vary, so best check).

The modern industrial complex is a far cry from the premises on the Quay in which George and William Penrose began the whole thing back in 1783, but the brilliance of the crystal (a 33% lead content elevates Waterford "glass" into the crystal category, which accounts for its fire and sparkle, as well as for the difficulty in blowing) and the artistry with which it is fashioned and cut have changed not one whit. Despite its early beginnings, Waterford Glass has not accumulated a two-century history: horrendous taxes on raw materials (not much change there, either!) back in 1851 closed its doors, and when the Irish government moved to open them again in 1947 it took five years to gather the necessary artisans and build a proper home for the industry. Some 30 master glass blowers, cutters, and engravers were brought from Europe and set to work training Irish apprentices, and in 1952 Waterford Glass was once more in production. Today there's a staff of hundreds, all young Irishmen skilled in the exacting art and turning out 90,000 finished pieces of the beautiful crystal every week, of which about 70% is shipped to the U.S.

The tour begins in the Blowing Department, where teams of four to six work swiftly and expertly with molten glass as it emerges from the kiln, since in the space of three minutes it will become too hard to work. Once blown, the piece moves past checkers whose sole purpose is to spot even the slightest flaw—only two-thirds make it through this minute inspection, and they then go to the cutting department, where teams of six (four qualified cutters and two apprentices) cut the 35 basic Waterford patterns into wineglasses, bowls, decanters, etc. Some 15% of the pieces fall by the wayside at this stage, since one cut even slightly out of line makes the piece a reject. The still-dull cut surfaces are dipped into a mixture of acids, followed by a bath in soapy water and a final rinse in white vinegar, by which time the characteristic fire and sparkle of Waterford glass shine forth in all their glory. Except for the acids, the Waterford people advise that you follow much this same procedure in keeping your own pieces gleaming: that is, wash each piece separately in warm soapy water and rinse or rub with white vinegar, drying with one cloth, polishing with another. A bit of rice or coarse sand can be dropped into the soapy water and swirled around to clean the insides of decanters.

For years, Waterford glass was not available at its source. In 1986, however, the factory opened a showroom where the end products of all that fine workmanship are exhibited and are on sale. Don't expect any discounts, however—prices will be about the same as you find them around the country.

WATERFORD AFTER DARK: On Saturday and Sunday nights there's traditional Irish music (and a whale of a good time!) at the **Munster Bar,** Bailey's New Street behind Reginald's Tower. Call in around 9:30 or 10 p.m., when things should be just getting lively. Music is sometimes to be found in other Waterford pubs, but seldom on a regular basis, so check with the Tourist Office and in local papers.

The Pubs

You'd be hard-pressed to find elsewhere the tasteful mix of antiquity and modern comfort that has been achieved at the **Reginald Bar,** on the Mall directly behind Reginald's Tower. Its antiquity is attested to by a plaque on the left-hand wall as you enter which bears the inscription "Built Circa A.D. 850 by Sitric the Dane." One of the original city walls, it has deep recesses which once served the Vikings as "sally ports," through which small boats were launched to "sally forth" along the river that back then was just outside. These days the arched stone alcoves are fitted out with comfortable seating, and the only sallying forth that goes on is that of the attractive crowd that favors this lively pub. The peaked roof with its skylight and the modern fittings belie any image of musty reverence for history, and even such touches as gold and red Viking ships and a suit of polished armor have the look of today. For the most part the Reginald is a pub for congenial mingling, but there's music from time to time, and on most Sunday afternoons between 12:30 and 2 p.m. there are jazz sessions by very good local musicians. Visiting instrumentalists who have their horn, guitar, etc., along are welcome to the local group.

Just down Bailey's New Street (which runs alongside Reginald's Tower), the **Munster Bar** is a cozy, wood-paneled, etched-glass haven of conviviality, just as it has been for the past 200 years. It began life as a coaching inn, and the small room known as Peter's Bar (named for the Fitzgerald who took it over in the '50s) is a gathering place for some of Waterford's liveliest conversationalists. On cool evenings there's a coal fire in the small fireplace, reflecting off wall sconces and chandeliers of "old" Waterford glass (pre-1851). Peter's sons—Peter, Michael, and Tom—carry on their father's traditions of hospitality, and no matter which one is behind the bar, he'll see you're not long a stranger. On Saturday and Sunday nights the large upstairs room rings to the strains of traditional music, and singsongs erupt spontaneously.

What was probably the stables for the old Munster Inn (with an entrance from the Mall) and more recently a dilapidated garage has been converted by the enterprising Fitzgerald sons into a pub larger than the Munster, but featuring handcrafted woodwork and Waterford glass fixtures in the same style. **Fitzgerald's** is mobbed at lunchtime (see "Where to Eat"), and evening finds it filled again with convival Waterford imbibers.

On George's Street, you'll know **T. & H. Doolan's** by its Tudor-style front and frosted-glass door. Inside, there's a wonderfully eclectic collection of old farm implements, whiskey jars, stone crocks, mugs, copper jugs, and anything else the late Thomas Doolan took a fancy to hang from rough wooden beams or on the whitewashed walls. He was, of course, the "T" of the proprietorship, and if anything went amiss, blame promptly fell on the "H" of that partnership—and thereby hangs a tale. H. Doolan, it turns out, was purely a figment of T. Doolan's imagination, who came into being when Thomas was too long, T. and Tom too short, for the establishment's sign. The spirited characters of T. & H. still linger in this 150-year-old pub that was for many years a stagecoach stop. Conviviality reigns as always, whether you rest an elbow on the main bar or opt for the smaller lounge.

Gentlemen, leave your ladies behind when you head for **Thomas Maher's** pub on O'Connell Street! Surely one of a kind, this wonderful old pub that dates back to 1886 is presided over by one Thomas Maher, a small, white-haired, blue-eyed man who's been behind the bar some 56 years and knows his own mind when it comes to running his pub. "I don't want to see anyone too early, too late, or too long," he declares and then sets opening hours of noon to 2 p.m., 5 to 7 p.m. and 8:30 to 10 p.m. "That way," he says, "there's not time for anyone to get too drunk, and between five and seven I get them home for their dinner." He brooks no swearing, no singing—and no ladies. With those rules in force, you may well ask, who comes? Crowds of devoted "regulars," *that's* who comes. And well they might, for behind a traditional storefront that has won many an award for its design there's an interior that has changed little, if at all, over the years. You may drink your pint in a glass stamped with a '20s or '30s date (since 1928, all pint glasses must bear a date stamp), and if there's no date at all, chances are it is one left from as far back as 1916. If you like, you can purchase spirits bottled by Mr. Maher himself. And what does the publican do between those short opening hours? He grows apples, potatoes, and vegetables, distributing any surplus among some of his widow-lady friends rather than selling them. He keeps one foot in the country and one foot in town, which he says makes a nice balance, since "too many 'smart' drinkers can be wearying and too much country life makes for cobwebs." Mr. Maher and his pub are a Waterford institution you won't want to miss—if, that is, you're male.

A Special Event

Wexford has its Opera Festival, but Waterford has its **International Festival of Light Opera,** a lighthearted gathering of amateur companies who converge on the city in September from Europe, Great Britain, the U.S., and all parts of Ireland. Each of the 16 nights of the festival there are performances of such musicals as *Brigadoon* and *Showboat,* all of amazingly high standards, and things wind up with the presentation of a beautiful Waterford Glass trophy. But light opera is not the only thing going on during those 16 days: there are singing pub competitions (with all pubs granted an extension of hours up to 1 a.m.) and a host of auxiliary activities, with a special Festival Office set up especially to see that you get to the competition, performance, or sporting event of your choice. You can book tickets in advance (advisable) by writing: Booking Office, International Festival of Light Opera, Waterford. Prices for individual performances are in the IR£2.50 ($4) to IR£6 ($9.50) range.

SHOPPING: While Waterford is not exactly a shopping center, there are a few places you should know about. **Joseph Knox Ltd.,** 3/4 Barronstrand St., has long been one of Ireland's leading outlets for Waterford glass, fine bone china, and porcelain. They'll mail (a superb mail-order catalog is available on request), and they accept major credit cards. . . . Pipe smokers will love the old-fashioned shop called **Thomas Phelan,** 14 George's St. It's a relic of the days when gentlemen smokers were catered to by other gentlemen who loved the trade, and those behind the counter at Phelan's continue that tradition (catering just as happily to the odd *lady* pipe smoker like myself!). There's a good selection of pipes, as well as cigars, cigarettes, lighters, and tobacco.

If you're interested in crafts, you might drop by the **Waterford Trade Center** on the Mall to see who's in residence at the moment. On my last visit, there was a talented basket-maker and a stained-glass worker. Also, check out the **Waterford Craft Centre,** 28 Michael St. (tel. 051/55733).

CHAPTER XIII

AROUND COUNTY WATERFORD

□ □ □

1. ACCOMMODATIONS
2. WHERE TO EAT
3. THINGS TO SEE AND DO

Say "Waterford" to most Americans and they'll promptly reply "glass." And certainly a visit to the Waterford Glass factory is a highlight of any visit. But do save time for a ramble through the rest of this beautiful and picturesque county. Fishing villages like Passage East and Dunmore East have changed little over the years. The coastal drive from Waterford to Dungarvan dips from clifftop to secluded bathing coves. Lismore's castle looms over a site once occupied by a great monastic community and the River Blackwater, a salmon fisherman's dream. Ardmore is a pleasant mixture of historic ruins and modern resort comforts. And at Ring, Irish is the language of everyday life.

1. ACCOMMODATIONS

Note: Prices shown below are those in effect in 1989—expect them to be higher in 1990.

A HOSTEL: There's a **hostel** at Glengarra, Lismore (tel. 058/54390). It's 4 miles from Lismore, about 43 miles from Waterford City.

BED-AND-BREAKFAST: On the outskirts of Dunmore East (seven miles from Waterford City), **Beechmont,** Dunmore East (tel. 051/83293), is a pretty country bungalow set on a hill overlooking the village and harbor. You approach through a well-kept acre of lawn and garden that presage what's inside. Mrs. Rita Power's bright and sparkling home is furnished with interesting antiques (you may want to take your impressive bedroom pieces home!) that create a homey, rather than stuffy, atmosphere. The stone fireplace is a focal point in the lounge, whose windows look out to the garden. The three guest rooms (all with sinks) are as comfortable as they are attractive, and there's central heating. The two Power teenagers, William and Victoria, are great sailing and windsurfing fans and love to talk to guests about their favorite sports. B&B rates are IR£10 ($16), with a 25% discount for children, and there's central heating and a graveled car park. Open year round.

In the seaside resort of Tramore, eight miles south of Waterford City, Mrs.

Rita McGivney is the friendly hostess of **Rushmere House,** Tramore (tel. 051/ 81041). This century-old, three-story Georgian house is flanked by wide chimneys at each end and sits on a rise looking across Tramore Bay to Brownstown Head. The five guest rooms (three are family-size, with a double and a single with private bath) are spacious, with high ceilings and tall windows. All have sinks, and only one does not face the bay. Mrs. McGivney is the soul of Irish hospitality and takes a real personal interest in her guests. Rates for bed-and-breakfast are IR£10.50 ($16.75), IR£1.50 ($2.50) extra per person for rooms with private facilities, with a 25% reduction for children. There's central heating, and a large public car park just across the road. Open all year.

River View House, Cook Street, Cappoquin (tel. 058/54073), is a real charmer. It's a three-story rambling house built by the Sisters of Mercy as an orphanage in the late 19th century, and under the loving direction of Evelyn and John Flynn, it has blossomed as one of the most unusual and hospitable lodgings in the country. The house itself is fascinating, with multiple stairways and corridors, a private dining room in what was once the chapel, two lounges (color TV in the more informal one back of the dining room), and a game room with pool tables, table tennis, darts, and board games. Of the 21 rooms, my absolute favorites are the four on the top floor under the eaves, whose swing-out windows open up fantastic views of the town and the Blackwater River. All have sinks, and there are three singles, as well as a suite with one double bed, two twins, and a single and private bath. Outside, there's a small apple orchard set in a manicured lawn with benches for sitting in the sun and a play area with swings, swing balls, pitch-'n-putt, croquet, and a merry-go-round. As you can guess, children are very welcome here, and the four Flynn children—Caroline, Paul, Sandra, and Tracy—make certain that no River View guest, young or old, is neglected.

Personable Evelyn keeps her finger on the area's pulse and is always up-to-date on what's going on, the best fishing holes (the Blackwater is one of Ireland's best fishing rivers, and many River View guests return year after year for the sport), where entertainment may be found locally, etc. If you're planning a day trip, she'll gladly pack a lunch and Thermos bottle. Equally helpful, John will see that you have bait and fishing equipment if you decide on the spur of the moment to test your skill. Evening meals are very good, and tea and homemade scones (no charge) are a regular feature in the evening. B&B rates are IR£9.50 ($15.25), dinner is IR£4.50 ($7.25), and the weekly rate for full board is IR£95 ($152). Children get a one-third reduction. There's central heat and a paved car park. Open all year. You should book as far in advance as possible.

Jack and Eileen Landers, 2 Parks Rd., Lismore (tel. 058/54033), are positively habit forming! Since I first stayed in their shiny clean, attractive two-story home in 1973, I haven't missed a stay with them any year since. The house itself is bright, rooms are comfortable, and breakfasts are very good, but it is this pair who bring me back time and again. The teapot is ever on the ready, as is the sort of humor and fast-paced conversation that can only be Irish, and to say that guests are treated like family is a gross understatement. On the practical side, Jack and Eileen can point you to good eateries and special sightseeing in the area and take a special interest in seeing that your Lismore stay is a memorable one. There are three bedrooms, two doubles and one twin-bedded. Rates for bed-and-breakfast are IR£9 ($15.25), with a 25% reduction for children.

FARMHOUSES: The Castle, Millstreet, Cappagh (tel. 058/68049), incorporates into an attractive farmhouse an arched stone doorway and a few stone walls of a 350-year-old Irish castle. Joan and Emmet Nugent and their four children reign in this pleasant kingdom and extend warm, friendly hospitality to their guests. There's central heat and five bedrooms, all brightly furnished, all with sinks and electric blankets, some with private bath. Meals are a special treat, with Joan's fresh home-baked brown bread, lamb, and beef from the farm, salmon caught in local rivers, and vegetables straight from the farm fields. Guests are free to fish for trout right on the Nugents' land, and there's a pony for the young fry to ride. Located on the main Clonmel–Youghal road, the Castle is four miles north of the Dungarvan–Cappoquin road and is well signposted. Rates for bed-and-breakfast are IR£10 ($16), with 50% off for children. Dinner is IR£9 ($14.50).

Some 2½ miles south of Dungarvan, just off the main Dungarvan–Youghal road, **Ballyguiry Farm,** Dungarvan (tel. 058/41194), is a lovely Georgian house dating from the 1880s and set in the foothills of the Drum Hills. Kathleen and Sean Kiely make guests feel right at home, as do their four charming children. They delight in helping plan sightseeing forays around the area and will even map out itineraries on an ordnance survey map for your use on day trips. The six guest rooms are exceptionally pretty, with floral wallpaper and coordinated pastel bedspreads. Two family suites have private baths and are suitable for parents and up to three children. There's a playground, hard tennis court, and a pony for children to pet and ride. B&B rates are IR£10.50 ($16.75), and dinner (with farm-fresh ingredients) is IR£8 ($12.75). A week's stay with bed, breakfast, and dinner costs IR£120 ($192). Central heating, and electric blankets on all beds.

GUESTHOUSES: In Cappoquin, **The Toby Jug,** Main Street (tel. 058/54317), is a favorite with anglers who come to fish the Blackwater River, as well as with overseas visitors. Denise (everyone calls her "Dee") and John Noonan are the attractive young couple who have taken over its management from John's parents, who ran things for more than 30 years. Both know the area well and are happy to point visitors to scenic drives and sightseeing attractions nearby. John can organize fishing on the Blackwater and can furnish fishing gear for two. Denise is a graduate of the celebrated Ballymaloe Cookery School and turns out superb evening meals (see "Where to Eat," below). There are nine nicely decorated and comfortably furnished upstairs bedrooms, seven with handbasins and two with private baths, as well as a cozy TV lounge for guests. The pretty dining room and their popular public bar and snooker room occupy the ground floor. Rates are IR£10 ($16) for bed-and-breakfast, IR£11 ($17.50) with private bath; bed, breakfast, and dinner run IR£18 ($28.75); dinner is IR£9 ($14.50) and must be booked by 4:30 p.m., and Dee will fix a luncheon basket for IR£2.50 ($4) if requested the night before. Open February through October.

In Ardmore, **Melrose Guesthouse,** Ardmore, Co. Waterford (tel. 024/94208), is a beautiful Tudor-style family home that dates from the 1840s. Overlooking the pretty and historic little seaside village, Melrose is run by the Colbert family. Rooms are all nicely done up, and meals are served in a dining room whose windows overlook the town and countryside. Bed-and-breakfast rates are IR£10 ($16).

SELF-CATERING: Set right at the edge of Dungarvan Bay, **Gold Coast Holiday Homes,** Ballinacourty, Dungarvan (tel. 058/42249), are some of the most attractive cottages available in the Southeast Region. Arranged in a semicircle, each has its own garden area, and there's an outstanding restaurant and lounge bar on the premises, both very popular with locals. Each semi-detached, two-story cottage has a living/dining room with fireplace, fully equipped kitchen, two bedrooms on the ground floor and one upstairs, and bath. Bedrooms have built-in wardrobes and dressing tables and there's one double bed and four twins in each cottage. They're carpeted throughout, nicely furnished, and come complete with TV. Six people can be accommodated comfortably, and there's plenty of room to install an extra cot in the spacious upstairs bedroom. Weekly rates per cottage run from IR£105 ($168) to IR£250 ($400), depending on the season. From October to May, there are attractive midweek and weekend rates available. Rates include all linens, with an extra charge for electricity.

READERS' ACCOMMODATIONS SELECTIONS: "Mrs. M. Byron Casey, **Byron Lodge,** Ardmore, Co. Waterford (tel. 024/94157), is the hostess in a stately old mansion where you will sense the nostalgia of an era gone by in a most regal manner" (G. W. Howard, Silver Spring, Md.). . . . "Eileen and Larry Ryan, **Clonanav Farmhouse,** Ballymacarbry, Co. Waterford (tel. 052/36141), and their children are extremely accommodating and friendly. Meals were plentiful and extremely tasty. This is a dairy farm, so we had the cows to observe at our leisure. Our kids and theirs had many pleasant hours at night playing soccer and tag"(D. Keeney, Sudbury, Mass.). . . . "In Ardmore, we loved the **Ticauling** (tel. 024/94279). It is only a half block from the sea, and the low rates include a private shower. Mrs. Margarite Mulligan is the very nice hostess" (C. and D. Williams, St. Paul, Minn.).

2. WHERE TO EAT

Ballads and crubeen (boiled pigs' feet) hold center stage at **Rocketts Pub** on the coast road outside Tramore, but you'll also find such traditional favorites as colcannon (mashed potatoes and cabbage), spareribs, chicken, and stews, all at prices of IR£4.50 ($7.20) to IR£6 ($9.60).

In Dungarvan, the **Shamrock Restaurant,** O'Connell Street (tel. 058/42242), is a cozy, attractive restaurant upstairs (past the square on the Cappoquin route) that serves all three meals at prices which can only be called "bargain." It is one of the best values in the area, in fact, with the highest price on the menu being IR£7 ($11.25) for a T-bone steak with salad or vegetable. Other selections are buttered trout with two vegetables at IR£5 ($8), chicken curry rice, and roast stuffed chicken—all at IR£3 ($4.75) to IR£4 ($6.50). Burgers, quiche Lorraine, and a variety of other light meals go from IR£2 ($3.25) to IR£2.50 ($4). There's a full wine license, and hours are 9 a.m. to 9 p.m. with continuous service, making this a good place for an afternoon snack or one of their delicious and inexpensive (under IR£1) desserts and tea.

The same management runs the **Coffee Pot,** on The Square in Dungarvan, upstairs with windows overlooking the busy scene below. Luscious homemade pastries, pâté, light salads, quiches, and freshly brewed coffee are all moderately priced. Hours are 9 a.m. to 6 p.m. every day except Sunday, when they're noon to 6 p.m.

Right beside King John's castle, **The Moorings,** the Quay, Dungarvan (tel. 058/41461), is a 200-year-old pub and restaurant where Nora and Pat Spratt serve home-cooked meals from fresh ingredients in both the bar and the restaurant. Seafood, as you can imagine, is featured, and vegetarians are catered to. From time to time there's traditional and folk music. Bar food starts as low as IR£1.50 ($2.50), and dinner will run about IR£10 ($16). Hours for food service are noon to 9:30 p.m. *Note:* Even if you don't plan to eat here, you shouldn't miss this marvelous old-fashioned pub—stop in for a pint, if nothing else.

The **Gold Coast Restaurant,** Ballinacourty, Dungarvan (tel. 058/42249 or 42457), sits right at the water's edge on Dungarvan Bay. The glass-walled dining room is bright with blue, white, and red in tablecloths and napkins, and food here is exceptional, as well as very good value. Specialties are seafood dishes and locally grown meats and vegetables. Dinner will run around IR£14 ($22.50) without wine (the Gold Coast is fully licensed, and there's an attractive bar/lounge attached); lunch, about IR£7 ($11.25). The Special Tourist Menu is available at both meals. Hours are noon to 2:30 p.m. and 6 to 9:30 p.m., and it's very popular locally on weekends, so best book ahead.

Eammon's Place, Main Street, Lismore, is also a tremendous value, with some of the best home-cooking you'll find in Ireland. In this attractive bar and lounge, with its corner fireplace and three-legged iron pot for turf and wood, try Eammon Walsh's chicken liver pâté on Joan's homemade brown bread—scrumptious! And if salmon is available, I guarantee you'll get portions so ample you'll be hard-pressed to finish the plate. There's a set meal which varies from roast beef to bacon and cabbage, and your bill will never go over IR£5 ($8). Food is served from noon to 9 p.m. Monday through Friday, and you'll be missing a real treat if you don't stop in at least once.

In Cappoquin, the **Saddler's Tea Shop,** The Square (tel. 058/54045), is a bright, cozy place and very popular with locals, who drop in all during the day for tea and snacks. Its specialties are home-cooked meats and home-baking. Hot plates and cold salads are superb, as are the delicious scones and pastries. Breakfast runs about IR£1.25 ($2); lunch, no more than IR£4 ($6.50), many times less. Open from 9 a.m. to 6 p.m.

At **The Toby Jug Guesthouse,** Main Street, Cappoquin (tel. 058/54317), Denise Noonan, who took her culinary training at the Ballymaloe Cookery School, will serve dinner for IR£9 ($14.50) if notified by 4:30 p.m. of the same day. She offers a choice of three main courses, depending on what's available at the market, since she prides herself on using fresh native meats embellished with her special sauces. Among her specialties are tarragon chicken, lovely lamb marinated with herbs, and steak with pepper sauce. Desserts include a luscious chocolate mousse, a tart gooseberry fool, and apples with Irish mist (my personal favorite). Just let her know when you book the hour you'd like to dine.

If it's tradition you're looking for, as well as good food, keep a lookout for the **Seanachie Restaurant and Pub,** Pulla, Ring, Dungarvan (tel. 058/46285), just off the main Dungarvan–Youghal road. It began life as a public house back in 1847, at the peak of the Great Famine, and a mass grave from those pitiful times is just next to the parking lot. These—happier—days, however, there's pub food in the rustic bar (with soup and brown bread hearty enough to be a full meal), and a marvelous menu in the restaurant that features such delicacies as Helvick Head turbot, lobster, and Blackwater salmon. A measure of the excellence here is the fact that the Seanachie has won numerous national awards for its food and restoration of the premises. À la carte prices in the restaurant begin at IR£7.50 ($12), with complete meals starting at IR£8 ($12.75). In peak season, traditional music and dancing in the courtyard on Sunday afternoons are reminders that this was once the scene of crossroads dancing, when rural Irish gathered to dance away the shadows of oppression. Hours for lunch at the Seanachie are noon to 3 p.m., with continuous bar-food service from noon to 9 p.m. This is a good stop if you're driving from Dungarvan to Cork via Youghal.

3. THINGS TO SEE AND DO

DUNMORE EAST: The nine miles from Waterford city to Dunmore East are picturesque and historic, and when you reach the little town perched above its historic harbor (mail ships used to put in here, as did smugglers, pirates, and a variety of other characters), fine beaches and sheltered coves, you'll be tempted to stay a day or two for the fishing, swimming, sailing, and/or the good crack with some of the friendliest Irish in the country. You might lunch at the **Candlelight Inn,** the **Haven Hotel,** or the **Ocean Hotel,** or if it's a pint you're after, look for the **Strand Inn Pub,** where there's a small stone fireplace in the front room and good conversation in all three rooms. **The Butcher** is a pub in an old butcher shop and attracts mostly a youngish crowd. Spend some time on foot exploring the winding streets and going down to the quay to examine fishing and leisure boats, and when you're ready to get on with your journey, head for the coast drive to Tramore that winds along the clifftops with glimpses of the sea.

TRAMORE: Tramore, eight miles south of Waterford city, is a popular seaside resort with good swimming and lots of recreational development. That giant of a statue you'll notice looking down on the bay from Great Newtown Head is known hereabouts as the Metal Man, and legend has it that any unmarried female who hops three times around its base on one foot will hop down the aisle within the next 12 months. Can't vouch for that, so I'll just pass it on. From Tramore, the coast road continues climbing and dipping among spectacular views through picturesque little towns until you reach **Dungarvan.** I've driven this route in bright sunshine (the best of times) and in lashing rain (the worst of times), and it never fails to delight and unveil yet another vista.

CAPPOQUIN: Ten miles from Dungarvan, the small town of Cappoquin sits in a sharp bend of the Blackwater River, whose waters yield up vast quantities of roach, dace, sea and brown trout, and salmon. Fishermen descend on Cappoquin in droves, year after year, to try their luck. However, even if you're not a fisherman, I'd like to tempt you to stop a while in this quiet spot and learn something of the inner workings of all those "typical" Irish towns you've been passing through—this is a town I know well, and I'll share with you some of its daily life and some of the people who enrich it so.

Let me suggest that you take time to meander (that's slower than stroll!) down the short Main Street, taking in some of the traditional shopfronts that have not, as yet, been gussied up. Call in to the **small craft shop** and let the lovely proprietor tell you about the people who make the knits and pottery and Lord-only-knows-what-else you'll find heaped around in glorious confusion. This lady can tell you more about the history of this region and the people who live here than you'd get from any book. Then saunter on down to **Mary Five's shop,** with its wooden front adorned with a sign announcing that she has "Jewelry, Fishing Tackle & Souvenirs" to sell inside. Mary is a charmer, but more than that, she carries in the small shop an amazing amount of Waterford Glass, Belleek, Royal Tara, watches, silverware, etc., all at competitive prices. Stop in the **Toby Jug** for a pint and a chat with handsome young redhead John Noonan and locals who happen to be in residence at the time.

If, by then, you've begun to sink into the rhythm of this Irish town, it's time for a picnic. Still farther down Main Street, you'll come to **Maurice Kellerher's VG Supermarket,** which doesn't look a *bit* like the little greengrocer you'd imagine in a town like this, but resembles more the ones you left at home—until, that is, one of the pretty Irish lassies behind the counter smiles and inquires if you're having a good holiday. Pick up a bit of Irish cheese (cheddar from the West Waterford creamery, if you can get it), fruit, etc., and head back up Main Street and around the Allied Irish Bank corner (that's Cook Street, but nobody ever calls it that). Halfway down, you'll find **Mrs. Barron's bakery,** where you can pick up fresh-baked loaves of brown, soda, or white bread and mouthwatering pastries. There's been a member of the family baking here for over 200 years, and believe me, they've learned all the secrets of the trade. Then stop by the **Lonergan brothers' tailor shop** (they may be the only tailors who still sit in the window on a platform to do their work) and buy a small jar of their honey they gather from hives they keep in local fields. Now take all your goodies out to **Glenshelane Park,** about a quarter mile outside town. Known locally as "The Glen," it's a shaded spot on the banks of a tumbling stream that flows beneath a charming old stone bridge with a hump in its middle, and there's a picnic table where you can spread out your lunch. *Now,* if the peace of the ages doesn't descend on your head, there's no hope for you a'tall!

Note: Like so many small towns in Ireland, Cappoquin nurtures the creative spirit. Award-winning poet Thomas McCarthy (look for his books *The Sorrow*

Garden and *The First Convention)* was born and grew up here, although he now lives in Cork. Art still flourishes in the town, however, and to carry a bit of that gorgeous scenery home with you, look up Cappoquin's present resident artist, **Noel O'Donoghue,** O'Donoghue Terrace, Cappoquin (tel. 058/54344 or 54317). His paintings of local scenery are beautifully done, reasonably priced, and a perfect souvenir of your visit to this part of the country. Best to call ahead to make an appointment to see the paintings.

Four miles east of Cappoquin, in the foothills of the Knockmealdown Mountains, you'll find **Mount Mellary.** It's a monastic center for the Cistercian Order of the Strict Observance and was built over a century ago when the monks were banished from France. There's an impressive stone church and a cluster of other large stone buildings. The monks have turned a bare mountainside into productive fields and pastures, rising at 2 a.m. to do all their own work and retiring at 8 p.m. each evening. Until recently they observed a strict rule of silence, with only the guestmaster permitted to speak. Visitors are welcomed here, and many Irish Catholics come to stay for several days in the peaceful retreat.

LISMORE: West of Cappoquin, the town of Lismore is just four miles away on the south bank of the Blackwater, with the majestic lines of a picture-perfect **castle** looming over town and river. King John had it built in 1185 on the site of St. Carthach's monastery of the 7th century. It was, for centuries, one of the most renowned of Ireland's distinguished learning institutions, and it became the target for Viking raids, as well as Norman and English conquest. It was here that Henry II came to accept homage from Irish chieftains, but the monastic community was finally destroyed by Raymond le Gros in 1173. There are those in Lismore who will tell you that the shades of murdered monks still roam the castle grounds in the dark of night. Sir Walter Raleigh is listed among the castle's former owners, as is Richard Boyle, the Earl of Cork. Since 1753, however, it has been the Irish seat of the Dukes of Devonshire, one of whom married Lady Charlotte Boyle and thus acquired the property. Today it is certainly among the most impressive still-lived-in castles in the country, and along with its mass of square towers, crenelated walls, and great halls, there are comfortably furnished apartments. The people of Lismore recall with a special fondness the years that Fred Astaire's sister, Adele, lived here as a Duchess of Devonshire and was well loved in the town. The public is not admitted to the castle, but the beautifully tended gardens are open from 1:45 to 4:45 p.m. from early May to early September, for a small admission charge. Just don't go wandering about in the dark of night!

Another Lismore link with history is the **Cathedral of St. Carthach.** Although it was rebuilt in 1633, there are 9th- and 11th-century grave slabs with inscriptions in Irish in the west wall of the nave. An altar tomb is dated 1557. About a mile east of the town on the "back road" to Cappoquin, is the great **Lis,** or earthen ring fort, from which the town took its name—not really a sightseeing attraction, but a pretty impressive high conical mound.

For a quiet drink in an old-fashioned pub, stop in Michael and Eileen **O'Donnell's pub** on Bridge Street in Lismore. In the old tradition, there is a hardware shop on one side, a pub on the other—not too many left like that these days.

There are several scenic drives around the Cappoquin/Lismore area. One of the most breathtaking is that through a gap in the Knockmealdown Mountains known as **The Vee.** It's signposted from the outskirts of Lismore and climbs through mountainsides covered with heather to the V-shaped pass, with laybys that overlook sweeping views of Tipperary's Golden Vale, before descending to the little town of **Clogheen,** Co. Tipperary. Between the gap and Clogheen, keep a watch on the high side of the road for one of the most curious graves in the world, that of one Samuel Grubb, one-time owner of Castle Grace, who so loved his lands that he decreed he should be buried upright on the mountain slopes overlooking them. There's a small pathway leading up to the stone cairn that is his final resting place (if one can rest on one's feet).

Then there's the **Nire Valley** drive through the heart of the Comeragh Mountains among mountain peaks, wooded hillsides, and mountain pastures dotted with sheep and cattle. Turn off the Dungarvan–Cappoquin road onto the signposted **Clonmel** route—the road is well paved all the way. It is at **Ballymacarbry,** about halfway along the Nire Valley drive, that you'll find **Paddy Melody's Pony Trekking Center** (tel. 052/36147). Experienced rider or novice, you really should plan a stop here to explore this beautiful mountain country from horseback. Guide Ann McCarthy will see that you are seated correctly (even children are safe in her care); the horses are gentle and sure-footed; and there's a choice of paths from 5 to 12 miles, all through wooded mountainsides and bleaker slopes covered with gorse (or furze, as it is sometimes called locally) alongside rushing river waters and sparkling lakes. For those who absolutely refuse to sit a horse, there are jaunting cars. There are even longer treks available, as well as three- and four-day trekking holidays. Especially in July and August, it is advisable to phone ahead and book for these popular treks. Plan enough time before or after your ride (or even if you just stop by the attached pub for a jar) to browse through Paddy's five scrapbooks in which enthusiastic riders have waxed poetic with comments, couplets, jingles, and epic poetry over the beauties of the Nire Valley.

Paddy (or anyone at Melody's) can direct you to a mountainside shrine to Irish patriots and leaders who met in March of 1923 in what is now known as the **Knockanaffrin Republican Cottage** ("The Cottage in the Glen of the Secrets") to talk in well-guarded secrecy of plans to bring about an end to the bloody Civil War. Standing in the simple whitewashed cottage, the ghosts of De Valera, Liam Lynch, and others rise up unbidden to remind you that it is in secluded locales such as this that so much of Irish history was forged.

Golfers will find good courses that welcome visitors at **Lismore Golf Club** (tel. Lismore 78) and **Dungarvan** (tel. 058/41605). **Swimmers** will delight in broad strands and calm waters at Tramore, Ardmore, and Clonea Strand (on the coast road between Dungarvan and Tramore).

GLENMORE: At Glenmore, near Waterford City, **Pat and Cathleen Dolan's craft workshop** is a must if you're interested in fine silver objects. Pat, an accomplished silversmith, considers his work to be a continuation of Ireland's long tradition of working with precious metals. Cathleen is an artist, and their works are on display and for sale at their thatched cottage workshop. Look for the sign on the Waterford–New Ross road, or telephone 051/80185 for directions.

CHAPTER XIV

AROUND THE SOUTHEAST

□ □ □

Counties Kilkenny, Carlow, and South Tipperary

1. ACCOMMODATIONS
2. WHERE TO EAT
3. THINGS TO SEE AND DO

Kilkenny's lovely pastoral landscape is dotted with Norman castles and keeps, while massive 13th-century Kilkenny Castle is filled with priceless art treasures, its old stables now occupied by designers and craftspeople of the Kilkenny Design Centre.

Normans also left their stamp (and their castles) on the face of tiny County Carlow, no doubt drawn by land as fertile and productive as it is beautiful and rivers that teem with fish. Historic Carlow town, on the River Barrow, is a pleasant, mostly industrial, town.

In South Tipperary, Cashel is dominated by the ruins of a medieval church and friary, their dramatic perch atop the lofty Rock of Cashel, adding to the awe with which visitors approach the site. Farther south is Cahir and its remarkably preserved castle. From mountain passes, breathtaking views overlook the Golden Vale, whose fertile pastures produce that wonderful butter, cream, and cheese.

1. ACCOMMODATIONS

Note: Prices shown below are those in effect in 1989—expect them to be higher in 1990.

County Kilkenny

A HOSTEL. Sixteenth-century **Foulksrath Castle,** Jenkinstown (tel. 056/27674), provides hostel facilities eight miles from Kilkenny town.

BED-AND-BREAKFAST. The **Nore Valley Villa,** Inistioge (tel. 056/48418), is surrounded by scenic beauty. Located on the Rosslare–Kilkenny–Athlone road and overlooking the River Nore, this Georgian villa is close to Woodstock Forest. It makes an ideal base for day trips to historical sites nearby. Three bedrooms have handbasins, one has private facilities (IR£1.50, $2.50, extra), and there's central heat and plenty of parking space. B&B rates are IR£10.50 ($16.75), with 20% reduction for children.

Mrs. Milne, **Lunar Lodge,** Baunlusk, Cuffes Grange, Kilkenny, Co. Kilkenny (tel. 056/29925), is the charming hostess of this bungalow which is five miles outside Kilkenny. Her rose garden is interesting as well as beautiful, arranged to depict Irish subjects. There is an outside swimming pool and you can also have a game of croquet if you like. There are three bedrooms, all with private facilities, and electric blankets, hairdryers, and tea-making facilities are available. The rate for bed-and-breakfast is IR£13 ($20.75). Open April to September.

County Kilkenny

BED-AND-BREAKFAST. Mrs. Margaret Drennan, **Hillgrove,** Bennetts Bridge Road, Kilkenny, Co. Kilkenny (tel. 056/22890), is the delightful hostess of this luxurious country home, which is furnished with antiques and has an attractive garden that guests are free to use. There are four bedrooms—three with private facilities, all with handbasins. The rate for bed-and-breakfast is IR£10 ($16) without private bath, IR£11 ($17.50) with, and there's a 50% reduction for children. Open mid-March through October.

FARMHOUSES. Miss Patricia Cantlon, **Cullintra House,** The Rower, Inistioge, Co. Kilkenny (tel. 051/23614), is the lovely hostess of this pretty 200-year-old farmhouse some six miles from New Ross on the Kilkenny road. The house is centrally heated, the food is delicious, and dinner is by candlelight each evening. There are four comfortable bedrooms and one suite of three rooms, all with handbasins. The rate is IR£10.50 ($16.75) for bed-and-breakfast and the same price for dinner. There is a 20% reduction for children. Open all year.

Mrs. Alice McCabe and her family will welcome you warmly at **Brandon View House,** Ballyogan, Graignamanagh, Co. Kilkenny (tel. 0503/24191). Their 18th-century farmhouse is set in scenic surroundings with pretty gardens. Dinner is available and is made with fresh fruits and vegetables from the kitchen garden. The house is centrally heated and there are four bedrooms, one with private facilities and all with handbasins. The rate for bed-and-breakfast is IR£10 ($16) and dinner is the same price. There is a 20% reduction for children and they are open year round.

County Carlow

BED-AND-BREAKFAST. In the Brownshill section of Carlow town, **Mrs. Mary Ruane's** modern, two-story home on Link Road (tel. 0503/42473) has three bedrooms, all with handbasins. Rooms are spacious and well done up, and Mrs. Ruane will provide a nice high tea for under IR£5 ($8). Bed-and-breakfast costs IR£10 ($16), and her home is open in June, July, and August.

A FARMHOUSE. I can't imagine a more scenic place to stay than **Lorum,** Old Rectory, Kilgreaney, Bagenalstown, Co. Carlow (tel. 0503/75282). The Smith family's 150-year-old stone farmhouse is right in the middle of County Carlow's rich countryside, a mere 15 miles from Kilkenny. It's a good base for local sightseeing, and croquet, tennis, and lawn games will help while away your leisure hours. There are five bedrooms, including one of those hard-to-find singles. Home-grown fruits and vegetables grace the table, and there's central heating as well as electric blankets. B&B rates are IR£10.50 ($16.75), and dinner is IR£10 ($16).

South Tipperary

A HOSTEL. A lovely shooting lodge in scenic surroundings provides good hostel accommodations: **Ballydavid Wood House,** Glen of Aherlow (tel. 062/ 54148).

BED-AND-BREAKFAST. Mrs. Mary Quinn greets you at **Clonmore,** Cork–Galbally road, Tipperary town (tel. 062/51637). Her pretty bungalow sits in its own grounds, within sight of the Galtee mountains and a short walk from town. There are six bedrooms (all with handbasins, four with private facilities) and the house has central heat. Plenty of parking. Bed-and-breakfast rates are IR£10.50 ($16.75), with 25% off for children.

Mrs. Phelan, **Mullinarinka House,** Clonmel, Co. Tipperary (tel. 052/ 21374), is the very hospitable hostess of this lovely Georgian manor with its large, pretty gardens. Her husband, Eddie, is a great storyteller and is affectionately called "the Mayor of Mullinarinka." The house is furnished with beautiful antique furniture and is centrally heated. Dinner is available with advance notice. There are five pretty bedrooms and all have handbasins. The rate for bed-and-breakfast is IR£11 ($17.50) and the cost of dinner is IR£10 ($16); 25% reduction for children. Open Easter through September.

Mrs. O'Reilly, **Hill Crest,** Powerstown Rd., Clonmel, Co. Tipperary (tel. 052/21798), and her husband will welcome you warmly to their comfortable modern home which is convenient to town and the bus and railway station. Located in a nice quiet area, the house is centrally heated and there is a garden which guests can use. There are four bedrooms, all with handbasins, and an evening meal is available. The rate for bed-and-breakfast is IR£9 ($14.50) and dinner is the same price; 33% reduction for children. Open year round.

Mrs. Moira Foley, **Rahard Lodge,** Kilkenny Rd., Cashel, Co. Tipperary (tel. 062/61052), runs this pretty, modern farmhouse overlooking the Rock of Cashel, on the outskirts of town. It is set in a nice quiet area and has lovely gardens and lawns. The house is centrally heated as well as having an open fire, and electric blankets are available. Dinner is available with advance notice. There are six comfortable bedrooms, four with private facilities and all with handbasins. There is an extra charge of IR£1.50 ($2.40) per person for a room with private facilities. The bed-and-breakfast rate is IR£10 ($16) and dinner costs IR£10 ($16); 20% reduction for children. Open February through December.

County Tipperary

BED-AND-BREAKFAST. Mrs. Mary Kennedy, **Thornbrook House,** Kilkenny Road, Cashel, Co. Tipperary (tel. 062/61480), will welcome you warmly to her bungalow with antique furniture, peat fires, and a large lawn overlooking the Rock of Cashel. There are five bedrooms, two with handbasins and three with private facilities. Dinner is available with advance notice. The bed-and-breakfast rate is IR£10.50 ($16.75) and dinner costs IR£12 ($19.25); 20% reduction for children under 10. Open year round.

Six miles from Tipperary is Mrs. Mary Marnane, **Bansha House,** Bansha, Tipperary, Co. Tipperary (tel. 062/54194), the gracious hostess of a lovely Georgian house with beautiful views of the Glen of Aherlow and the Galtee mountains. The house is centrally heated and the food is delicious, cooked in traditional Irish style. There are seven bedrooms, all with handbasins. The rate for bed-and-breakfast is IR£10 ($16) and dinner costs IR£9 ($14.50); 25% reduction for children. Open March through November.

Peg and Sean Butler have turned Sean's ancestral home, **Carrigeen Castle,** Cork Road, Cahir, Co. Tipperary (tel. 052/41370), into a fitting representative of castle hospitality of old. The 1600 castle has a colorful past, having twice been used as a prison for rebellious Irish, but since Sean's father regained possession in 1919, it has taken back its function as family home, a function its present occupants now extend to paying guests. Bedrooms have been fashioned from the original upstairs rooms, and this may be the only B&B in Ireland in which you enter your bedroom through a centuries-old stone doorway. Vivacious Peg is a warm, thoughtful hostess, always ready with the extra cup of tea, as well as good advice about sightseeing in the area. Her young son, David, takes a special interest in greeting and assisting guests, there's a fire in the lounge on cool evenings, and just in case you've a musical itch, you can scratch it in a small lounge that holds a piano. The bedrooms include three singles, one triple, and a twin-bedded and double-bedded unit with private bath. Rates are IR£10 ($16) for bed-and-breakfast.

FARMHOUSES. The **Parkstown House,** Horse & Jockey, Co. Tipperary (tel. 0504/44315), is a 1770 Georgian manor house set in 200 acres of farmland eight miles north of Cashel. Its owner, the charming Mrs. Maher, has left her elegant touch all through the house, with gold velvet on the lovely seating grouped around the drawing room fireplace (made of fine Italian marble), matching wallpapers and fabrics, sprays of fresh flowers, and glowing wood fires. Many of the beautiful antique furnishings (including hand-carved wardrobes and dressers in guest bedrooms) are heirlooms in Mr. Maher's family. There's a cozy library with a TV and comfortable leather chairs. Four of the five guest rooms have handbasins, there are three hall bathrooms, and two rooms and a bath can be opened up as a family suite. Gracious is the word for house and hosts. B&B rates are IR£12 ($19.25), IR£13 ($20.75) per person in the private suite, 20% reduction for children. Central heat.

To reach **Killoran House,** Temple Tuohy, Thurles (tel. 0504/45271), look for the signpost on your right as you drive from Kilkenny on the main Dublin–Cork road. When you turn off the highway, it's a five-mile drive to Peg and Ned Cambie's large Georgian house that dates from the 1600s. This is Ned's family home, and among its antique furnishings are three stately grandfather clocks, two of which were crafted by his ancestors. There are four large bedrooms, comfortably furnished, with electric heaters in each. Log and peat fires glow in the drawing room. All meals feature farm-fresh ingredients. Killoran House sits in its own parklands, and just across the road is a round crenelated tower known as a "folly," which has an interesting history. Rates are IR£11 ($17.50) for bed-and-breakfast, with a 20% reduction for children. Dinner is IR£10 ($16) and high tea is IR£7 ($11.25).

BIG SPLURGE. About four miles from Clonmel on the scenic Ardfinnan road, **Knocklofty House Hotel,** Clonmel, Co. Tipperary (tel. 052/38222), is one of the most beautifully situated stately homes in Ireland's Southeast Region. Approached by a shaded avenue, the Georgian mansion enjoys superb views of landscaped lawns and gardens, and terraces lead down to the River Suir, which winds through the 105-acre estate. It has a long history, with strong connections to America, since it, along with vast landholdings in Counties Tipperary and Waterford, was presented to one Richard P. Hutchinson in the mid-1600s. A kinsman, Thomas Hutchinson, was the first governor of Massachusetts Bay, and Richard himself had sojourned in New England from 1633 to 1648. In 1783 his descendants became the Earls of Donoughmore, and Knocklofty House remained their family seat until the end of 1983. The beautiful galleried library dates from 1650, although the original house was considerably altered and refurbished in the mid-1700s, when a second floor was added. By the end of that century, north and south wings had been added. Records of all that history, along with photograph albums recording illustrious visitors, remain in the library to this day.

Nowadays it is Joyce and Paddy O'Keeffe who extend the gracious hospitality that is a tradition at Knocklofty House. Widely traveled, they have brought their expertise to bear in creating luxurious bedrooms and suites, as well as a recreation center that transforms the estate into a virtual self-contained holiday resort. There's a gymnasium, a 50-foot indoor heated swimming pool, Jacuzzi, sunbed, tennis court, squash court, table tennis, and clay pigeon trap. And there's excellent salmon and trout fishing just steps away in the River Suir, the nature woodlands invite leisurely walks, and horseback riding can be arranged. Within easy driving distance are the sightseeing attractions of Waterford city, Kilkenny, Ardmore, and Cashel.

It is perhaps in the beautiful oak-paneled dining room overlooking the river that the O'Keefes have outdone themselves, for it has gained no little renown as a first-class restaurant that draws bookings from far and near (see "Where to Eat").

Seasonal rates for bed-and-breakfast range from IR£30 ($48) to IR£40 ($64) per person, and there are special three-day and weekend rates available. Open year round.

READERS' ACCOMMODATION SELECTIONS: "Mrs. M. Trant, **Bawn,** Castlecomer Road, Kilkenny, Co. Kilkenny (tel. 056/65629), is warm, friendly, and can't do enough for you. Her bungalow is spotless, the rooms are very quiet, and she herself is a typical woman of Eire" (John Little). . . . "The **Lacken House,** Dublin Road, Kilkenny (tel. 056/65611) is run by the McSweeneys, and he is an award-winning chef. Their restaurant is open every day but Sunday and serves very good food at reasonable prices" (T. Taberco, Falls Church, VA).

2. WHERE TO EAT

County Kilkenny

It's no wonder the **Edward Langton Restaurant and Bar,** 69 John St., Kilkenny (tel. 056/65133 or 21728), has won national awards for three years running—quite simply, the food here is superb, it's great value-for-money, and the old-style setting is delightful. Morning coffee and afternoon teas are served in addition to lunch and dinner, with continuous food service from 10:30 a.m. to 10 p.m. (12:30 to 2 p.m. on Sunday). A special four-course dinner will set you back no more than IR£9 ($14.50). If you don't plan to eat here, at least nip in for a pint—it's worth the trip.

The temptation is great to list **Kyteler's Inn,** Kieran Street, Kilkenny (tel. 056/21064), as a sightseeing attraction, for the historic old building was once the home of Dame Alice Kyteler, a beautiful woman who grew rich by the successive deaths of her four husbands. When the Lord Justiciar of Ireland condemned her to death on charges of witchcraft, she was destined for a public whipping followed by burning at the stake. Dame Alice, however, took matters into her own hands and skipped town (nothing was ever heard of her again) and left her convicted accessories to go to the stake alone. When you enter this stolid stone house these days, it would behoove you to remember that within its walls were found a vast array of herbs, ointments, and other makings of magic spells. No magic potions in the food now, however, and a good lunch will run around IR£4 ($6.50), and dinner costs from IR£7.50 ($12). There's a Tourist Menu at lunch and dinner. Even if you don't make it for a meal here, do stop in for a drink and cast a leary eye at the "witchy" courtyard with its two wells that supplied Dame Alice with water to mix her deadly potions. Open from 10:30 a.m. to 11:30 p.m.

You'll also find the Tourist Menu offered in Kilkenny at **Mulhall's Restaurant,** 6 High St. (tel. 056/21329); and the **Club House Hotel,** Patrick Street (tel. 056/21994).

South Tipperary

Not for budgeteers is the main dining room at the **Cashel Palace Hotel,** Main Street, Cashel. This elegant, first-class hotel is a Georgian palace, erected in 1730 for the archbishop of Cashel, and the elegant drawing room overlooks gardens and a breathtaking view of the Rock of Cashel. There are also marvelous works of art, both oils and colored engravings, in its public rooms and along the corridors. But back to eating—down stone stairs, the flagstoned cellar holds the Derby Bar and the Bishop's Buttery, where you can hoist a pint before indulging in salad plates and hot dishes that run from IR£2.50 ($4) to IR£14 ($22.50).

A BIG SPLURGE. Some four miles from Clonmel, out a scenic country road, **Knocklofty House,** Knocklofty House Hotel, Clonmel, Co. Tipperary (tel. 052/38222), offers superb dining in a splendid room paneled in mellow oak overlooking lawns and gardens that slope down to the River Suir. The room is beautifully appointed, with a truly sophisticated elegance, and the menu features traditional dishes that reflect a French flavor in preparation. While selections change according to availability of fresh ingredients, typical choices are noisettes of lamb provençale, loin of veal with lemon and ginger, fresh local salmon with dill-cream sauce, and filet of mullet with a rosemary-butter sauce. Vegetables are always fresh and cooked to perfection, and vegetarians are catered to. There's a nice selection of wines at moderate prices. If you'd like a pre- or après-dinner drink, you'll be served in the balconied library that dates back to 1650, where a pianist often entertains during the high season.

A five-course table d'hôte dinner is IR£16 ($25.50) and is served from 7 to 10:30 p.m. (last orders at 9:30 p.m.); lunch, from 12:30 to 2:30 p.m., runs about IR£9 ($14.50). Reservations are strongly advised for dinner. Open daily. Highly recommended.

3. THINGS TO SEE AND DO

County Kilkenny

The town of Kilkenny is virtually a sightseeing destination in itself—its narrow, winding streets and well-preserved structures make it perhaps the most perfect example in Ireland today of a medieval town, and Pat Mackey has produced a splendid little illustrated booklet entitled *A City and County Guide to Kilkenny* which outlines walking tours of the town, as well as suggested day trips in the surrounding area. It's available at the Tourist Office in Waterford.

Sometimes called the "Marble City" because of the fine limestone quarried hereabouts, its Irish name is Cill Chainnigh, or St. Canice's Church, a little monastery established here by the good saint in the 6th century on the grounds of the present **St. Canice's Cathedral** (the round tower dates back to the original settlement). But it was the Normans, and later the Anglo-Normans, who built up the dignified town as a trading center that enjoyed the protection of royalty up until the mid-14th century. It was in 1366 that the infamous "Statutes of Kilkenny" forbade any mingling of Anglo-Normans with the native Irish, and by the time Oliver Cromwell arrived in 1649, the city's population was pretty well demoralized, making it an easy matter for him to seize the town, stable horses in the cathedral and smash its beautiful stained-glass windows, and slaughter many residents and banish others to Connaught in order to confiscate their property. Despite all its turbulent history, Kilkenny has held on to a cultural tradition that makes it a natural site for one of the most respected crafts centers in Ireland today, the Kilkenny Design Workshops, housed in the one-time stables of Kilkenny Castle. More about that later.

For a look at the home of a prosperous Tudor merchant, visit the **Rothe House,** on Parliament Street, built in 1594 and now a museum and library. There's a small admission fee, and hours are 10:30 a.m. to 12:30 p.m. and 3 to 5 p.m. Monday through Saturday and 3 to 5 p.m. on Sunday in the summer (on Sunday only during winter months).

The impressive 13th-century **Kilkenny Castle** that dominates the town was the seat of the Butler family. It was built in 1391, Cromwell made a mess of it during his stopover, it was restored and continued to be used as a residence until 1935, and in 1967 the Marquess of Ormonde gave it to the people of Kilkenny, who turned it over to the state two years later. Now almost fully restored, and rich in artworks—there are miles of oil portraits—and elegant furnishings, it is open to the public for tours conducted by guides well versed in stories of the people who lived and visited here. Ask around about Black Tom, then get set to hear some rather outrageous tales. Daily tours in May and June are at 10:30 a.m. to 12:45 p.m.; July through September, 10 a.m. to 7 p.m.; and there's a very small admission charge.

Created for the sole purpose of fostering good design in Irish industry, the **Kilkenny Design Workshops** are just across the street from the castle and occupy the former stables and coach houses. First-rate designers and craftspeople are provided equipment and work space to develop new designs of high standards for textiles, ceramics, glass, plastics, jewelery, and silver. Sadly, the workshops and crafts demonstrations are no longer open to the public, but there's a showroom where products based on these designs are for sale—a good place to do at least part of your shopping—and a friendly restaurant for lunch or coffee. Hours are 9 a.m. to 6 p.m. Monday through Saturday and 10 a.m. to 5 p.m. on Sunday.

Kyteler's Inn, Kieran Street, combines sightseeing with a pub-cum-restaurant (see "Where to Eat"), and is a don't-miss in Kilkenny. Two other pubs in which to put a terrible thirst to rest are **Tynan's,** John's Bridge (which won the "Best Pub in Ireland" award for its combination of polished brass, gleaming wood, etched glass, and interesting clientele), and the much plainer **Marble City Bar,** High Street, a congenial spot since 1789 for the "meetin' o' the drinkers" that continues to thrive under the friendly eye of Laurence Langton.

Smithwick's Brewery (call it "Smitticks" if you want to sound like a local) is in Kilkenny just across from the Rothe House, and they'll welcome you to tour the premises any afternoon at 3 p.m. Monday through Friday.

Elsewhere in County Kilkenny, the quaint town of **Thomastown** sits at the head of the Nore Valley, and among its interesting and ancient ruins are the remains of the 13th-century church where there are fragments of a high cross and some badly weathered effigies. Three miles away, the **Kilfane church** ruins have an impressive medieval stone effigy of a crusader in full armor. Nearby **Jerpoint Abbey** dates back to 1158 and the riverside ruins contain many monuments and effigies, as well as sculptures of saints and knights.

A Kilkenny miscellany: From **Tinacashel** crossroad (two miles from the town of Urlingford), you can count no fewer than a dozen Anglo-Norman castles. In the town of **Knocktopher,** the Carmelite Priory garden holds a flat-topped Mass Stone that was used during the long years when Catholics were forbidden to practice their religion. If you pass through **Castlecomer,** spare a thought to native son John Walker (uncle of New York's famous mayor, Jimmy Walker), who in 1899 invented the caterpillar track system which revolutionized so many phases of modern industry. And in **Rathosheen** townland (near the village of Johnstown), tradition says the Ring Fort is the final resting place of Ireland's legendary hero, Oisin.

About 4½ miles south of Kilkenny on the banks of the Nore, Nicholas

Mosse, a member of an old milling family, has set up a workshop for his award-winning pottery very near an old mill. His mother, who has a great interest in such things as old pine furniture, quilts, and antique household implements, runs the shop and a tiny museum of old Irish cottage pottery. She's so friendly that, to quote Nicholas, "Many's the visitor who gets a tour of the house and a cuppa." Look for **Nicholas Mosse Pottery,** Bennettsbridge, Co. Kilkenny (tel. 056/27126). Hours are 9 a.m. to 6 p.m. every day except Sunday, when they're open from 2 to 6 p.m.

County Carlow

In Carlow town, the 1833 Gothic-style **Cathedral of the Assumption,** off Tullow Street, holds a marble monument to a Bishop Doyle, who wrote extensively about 19th-century politics, using a pen name to stay out of trouble (the statue is by the celebrated Irish sculptor, Hogan). Near the Barrow bridge, you'll find the ruins of **Carlow Castle,** which was one of Cromwell's victims in 1650, but survived to be returned to the Earls of Thomond in the 1800s. Its final demise came about when a local doctor, who wanted to use it as a lunatic asylum, tried to thin its walls with explosives, rendering it so unsafe it finally had to be demolished. An interesting local museum, the **Haymarket,** is housed in an old theater and includes a reconstructed forge and kitchen, as well as tools and military and religious relics.

Two miles east of Carlow on the L7, **Browne's Hill Demesna** holds an impressive dolmen—its capstone weighs 100 tons, the largest in the country.

If you're driving from Carlow to Stradbally via the N80, **Windy Gap** opens up some truly outstanding views.

South Tipperary

Soaring above the South Tipperary town of Cashel (*Caiseal,* or stone fort) is Ireland's most majestic historical landmark, the lofty **Rock of Cashel.** It stands 300 feet above the surrounding plains, and since time immemorial has been intimately connected with royalty and mysticism. Its summit encompasses a full two acres; its view is measured in miles. Ancient Celts worshiped here, and Irish kings built their palace on the sacred site. In the 5th century the King of Munster erected a cashel, or stone fort, and it was there that St. Patrick came in the year 450 to preach to the current King of Munster, Aengus, using the humble shamrock as a symbol of the Christian trinity. Aengus (for Angus) saw the light and with his family accepted baptism. Murtough O'Brien presented the Cashel of the Kings to the church in 1101, and in 1127 Cormac MacCarthaigh (McCarthy), King of Desmond, built the little chapel that is his namesake, a miniature gem of Romanesque style. In the years that followed, construction on a massive cathedral was begun; King Henry II came to receive homage from such Irish princes as Donal O'Brien, King of Thomond; Edward the Bruce held a Parliament here; the first Protestant service was held in the cathedral; it was burned in 1495, restored, and damaged again by Cromwell's ruthless troops; and in 1748 the archbishop of the day left it abandoned and unroofed because—or so the Irish say—his coach and four could not make it up the steep incline to its great west door.

Somehow, all the foregoing cannot *begin* to convey the awe-inspiring presence of the Rock. Its mystical sense of all the ages past and those yet to come can only be experienced as you follow the guided tour, then leave it to wander on your own among the ancient stones and ruins, climb to the top of the cathedral tower to wonder at Tipperary's Golden Vale plains, and gaze at the stone Cross of Cashel with a base that may have been a pre-Christian sacrificial altar. The tours are conducted daily from 9 a.m. to 7:30 p.m. June through September, 10 a.m. to 4:30 p.m. daily in other months. There's a small admission fee.

South of Cashel in the town of Cahir, a rocky islet in the River Suir has been the natural site of fortifications as far back as the 3rd century, when the *Book of Lecan* reports that a fort here suffered utter destruction. Brian Boru maintained one of his residences here as High King of Ireland. The castle you see today on this ancient site was built by the Norman, de Berminghams, in the 13th century, and was held by the Anglo-Norman Butlers until 1599, when the Earl of Essex captured it after a short siege. In 1650 it was surrendered to Cromwell without a single shot, and within its walls, the articles to end the long Cromwellian wars were signed in 1652. Through all the centuries the Butler descendants held the castle title until the last of them died in 1961. After years of neglect the state took over in 1964, and it was opened to the public in 1971. Restored to near-original condition, **Cahir Castle** has figured in several motion pictures, but more important, with its residential apartments refurnished in authentic reproductions, it brings alive the life and times of all its centuries-old history. Guided tours are conducted during summer months, when there's a resident Tourist Office, and in winter there's an informative caretaker on hand. During the summer, hours are 10 a.m. to 8 p.m.; in winter you make your own arrangements. Small admission fee.

Just across from the castle, the **Crock of Gold** craft and tea shop has an excellent selection of crafts and books of Irish interest, and tea comes in Royal Tara cups.

Holycross Abbey is four miles south of Thurles (pronounced "Thurless") on the west bank of the River Suir. It was founded in 1168 and was a revered place of pilgrimage, since it held a particle of the True Cross preserved in a golden shrine set with precious stones which was presented to King Murtagh O'Brien, grandson of Brian Boru, in 1110. The shrine is now in the Ursuline Convent in Blackrock, Cork, but the abbey still contains many interesting and religiously significant ruins, and Sunday pilgrimages still take place from May to September.

Elsewhere in South Tipperary, visit **Carrick-on-Suir,** where the Ormond Manor House is believed to be the birthplace of poor Anne Boleyn, and the town is for sure that of the Clancy Brothers and cyclist Sean Kelly. And look for signposts that will guide you through the scenic Glen of Aherlow drive. **Clonmel,** the county town (in Irish, *Cluain Meala,* "Meadow of Honey"), was a garrison town on the River Suir and the home of Charles Bianconi, a poor Italian who built up the first public transport system in Ireland with a coaching service based here.

READER'S SIGHTSEEING SUGGESTIONS: "We found two folk museums of real interest. The first is **Fethard Folk and Transport Museum,** Cashel Road, Fethard (tel. 052/31516), about a 20-minute drive from the Rock of Cashel. The proprietors, Christopher and Margaret Mullins, live on the site and will open it at any time upon request. The second is **Bothan Scoir,** a 17th-century cottage museum, Upper Green, Cashel, just a ten-minute walk from the Rock. There are over 200 items in this restored laborer's cottage, which was opened in 1983 and has hours of 10 a.m. to 8 p.m." (S. McGraw, New York, N.Y.).

CHAPTER XV

CORK CITY

□ □ □

This grand old city that native son and gifted actor Niall Tobin has described as "an intimate higgledy-piggledy assemblage of steps, slopes, steeples, and bridges" is, to quote one visitor, "strewn like a bouquet along the valley."

> Limerick was, Dublin is, and Cork shall be
> The finest city of the three.

So says "The Old Prophecy" as quoted by Dean Hole in 1859. Well, never mind about *shall* be, any Corkman worth his salt will tell you that Cork *is,* and always has been, the finest city in Ireland! And with more than a little justification, I might add.

Enough of quotes. Suffice it to say that for you and me, Cork is friendly, cosmopolitan without the pseudo-sophistication of some large cities, and fun to visit. Its great age (its charter was conferred in 1185) imbues Cork with an enormous pride which assumes the right to be quite comfortable with itself. As a native once assured me with a perfectly straight face, "Sure, it's only an accident of geography that Dublin is the capital of Ireland." Not that anyone really cares if it is the capital: to be Cork is quite enough.

Its ancient Irish name is Corcaigh, or "Marshy Place," and in this place of marshes Druids once held their religious rites in the dense woods of the southern hills that rose above it. Celtic tribes built forts and fought battles over territorial rights in the hills to the north. And in the 7th century, St. Finbar came to establish a monastery on a small island in the swamp, asserting that there would be "an abundance of wisdom continually in Cork."

Attracted by the religious foundation's riches, the Vikings arrived in the 9th century to plunder, then settle in as they had in other Irish locations. Normans took over in the 12th century, fortified the city, and proceeded to build great churches and abbeys. But it was the advent of Oliver Cromwell, who captured Cork in December of 1649, that settled the hash of natives in the district, for unlike Danes and Normans who had assimilated happily with the resident populace, those who came after Cromwell held in contempt everything that was Irish and imposed harsh penalties on any who attempted to live with them amicably. No doubt it is from the strangling repression of this period that present-day Corkmen date their fierce sense of independence and abhorrence of injustice. Nor did being on the losing side ever lessen their fighting spirit—for a few centuries, in fact, they consistently allied themselves with defeat, standing behind pretender-to-the-throne Perkin Warbeck, Charles I, and James II.

That the blood has never stopped flowing hot in their veins at any hint of injustice is clear from the fact that when their Lord Mayor, Terence MacSwiney, died after a 74-day hunger strike, his comrades-in-arms locked the door in St. George's where the requiem mass was to be held, opened his coffin, clothed his body in his I.R.A. Commandant uniform, and inscribed on his coffin "Murdered by the Foreigners in Brixton Prison, London, England, on October 25th, 1920, the Fourth Year of the Republic." Blissful in his ignorance, the archbishop conducted the mass never knowing the message of the inscription, which was in Irish.

For centuries all that history slogged through acres of marshland, right up until the end of the 1700s. Vessels sailed up Patrick Street as late as 1760 (it was paved in 1791); in 1780 there was a canal down the center of the Grand Parade and a bridge where the Berwick Fountain now stands between Tuckey and Oliver Plunkett Streets.

Today the streets in Cork are dry, and its citizens are reckoned to be among the ablest merchants and traders in Ireland. Still, they are a lively, cultural bunch, much attuned to the arts, and quick to welcome strangers. Theater, ballet, and one of Europe's best jazz festivals are highlights of each year, while street musicians carry on the tradition of ballad singers down through the ages and the old piper who once trod Winthrop Street wheezing out "An' De Vallee Lay Smilin' Afore Me."

1. ORIENTATION

Cork's city center is on an island in the River Lee, which can be confusing when you suddenly encounter the river you thought you'd just left behind. Some 16 bridges cross the Lee, and the city center's maze of one-way streets and narrow lanes can—and do!—confound the best drivers in the world. My best advice to drivers (based on *long* experience) is to make your way to your accommodation, park the car, and leave it there. Public transportation (via lovely double-decker buses and a good taxi service) is excellent and can take you virtually anywhere you wish to go. Besides, Cork is a great town for walking.

Another bit of advice: Go by the Tourist Office and pick up one of their free city maps—it will save you a lot of grief in getting around Cork. Having said that, herewith are the basics of Cork orientation. The **River Lee** cuts across the city from east to west, the hills bound it on the north and south. Major points of reference are **St. Patrick's Street** (universally called simply Patrick's Street) and the **Grand Parade.** Other main arteries are **Washington Street** (which becomes Western Road as it runs past University College and heads out toward Killarney); **South Mall,** from which you turn into Anglesea Street en route to both Kinsale (and the airport) and Douglas Road; and **Glanmire Road,** leading out to Fota Park, Cobh, and the main Youghal–Waterford road, with a turnoff to the Dublin road. Just across **St. Patrick's Bridge** at the foot of Patrick Street, a hill so steep you'll swear your car is going front over back leads to the **Montenotte** section, where the cream of Cork's merchant crop built great Georgian houses on the hillside overlooking the river.

2. USEFUL INFORMATION

The **Tourist Office** is centrally located at Tourist House, 42 Grand Parade (tel. 021/273251). Hours are 9 a.m. to 7 p.m. Monday through Saturday and 3 to 5 p.m. Sunday in July and August; 9:30 a.m. to 5:30 p.m. weekdays and 9:30 a.m. to 1 p.m. on Saturday other months. . . . The **bus station** is one block down from St. Patrick's Bridge on Parnell Place, and the **railway station** is on Lower Glamire Road. For all **bus and rail** information, phone 021/504422. . . . **Cork Airport** is four miles south of the city on the Kinsale road, with connections to England and the Continent, as well as Irish destinations. There's good, inexpensive public **bus** transportation into town. . . . **Taxis** are stationed at the rank in the center of Patrick Street as well as at bus and railway stations and the airport, or you can telephone 961311 or 502211. They're metered, with a minimum fare of IR£1.80 ($2.90). . . . The **General Post Office** is on Oliver Plunkett Street, open from 9 a.m. to 6 p.m. every day but Sunday. . . . Current goings-on in Cork are reported in *Where to Go in Cork,* published weekly by the Junior Chamber of Commerce during summer months and available through the Tourist Office and most hotels. Also, check the *Cork Examiner.* . . . The **telephone prefix** for Cork is 021.

3. ACCOMMODATIONS

Some of Cork's best accommodations are in the Western Road area, very near University College. There's heavy truck traffic along this road, but those listed below are either on quiet side streets just off the Western Road or are set back from the street in their own grounds, so noise should not be a problem at any. While this area is within walking distance to the city center (a rather long walk, but with frequent bus service), other districts shown below are all convenient to bus lines running into town.

Note: Prices shown below are those in effect in 1989—expect them to be higher in 1990.

Western Road Area

A HOSTEL. The **hostel** facilities at Nos. 1 and 2 Redclyffe, Western Road (tel. 021/432891), are rated "superior," and city bus no. 8 runs right past the door.

BED-AND-BREAKFAST. On Western Road, **St. Kilda** (tel. 021/273095) is the three-story home of the charming Pauline Hickey and her husband, Pat. Set back behind a low wall, with ample parking out front, the old-style house has been completely refurbished and redecorated. There's carpeting throughout, and the six bedrooms have handbasins and built-in wardrobes. Some have showers. Most are doubles, but there's one small, cozy single. A piano in the lounge is frequently the focal point for guests in the evening. Bed-and-breakfast rates are IR£10 ($16). Take bus no. 5 or 8 to Cork University.

Hinse and Conor Luasa have won great praise for their **Garnish House,** 1 Aldergrove, Western Road, Cork (tel. 021/275111). The beautiful Georgian home is elegantly decorated, with six rooms with handbasins and two with private facilities. The Luasas are presently in the process of installing color TVs and tea makers in all rooms. Situated only about a five-minute walk from the city center, it has a private parking area, a great convenience along the Western Road.

Hinse has won compliments for her excellent breakfasts, and both she and Conor take a personal interest in their guests. The rate for bed-and-breakfast is IR£10.50 ($16.75), and Garnish House is open year round.

Ashford House, Donovan's Road (tel. 021/276324), is run by Mairead Smythe and her husband, Jack. The three-story house has guest rooms that are spacious and comfortably furnished. The Smythes also are eager to recommend places of interest as well as restaurants and entertainment centers. Rates, including a full Irish breakfast, are IR£9 ($14.50), with a 25% reduction for smallfry. Closed January.

KEY TO THE NUMBERED REFERENCES ON OUR MAP OF CORK: 1— Glanmire Road Station; 3—Prov. Bus Depot; 4—Cross-Channel Boats; 5—General Post Office; 6—City Hall; 7—Court House; 8—Irish Tourist Office; 9—School of Art; 10—Public Library; 11—Park and Museum; 12—University College; 13—Custom House; 14—St. Mary's Cathedral; 15—Shandon Church; 16—St. Finbar's Cathedral; 17—Greyhound Track; 18—G.A.A. and Show Grounds.

At the top of Donovan's Road, you'll find Connaught Avenue and **Ouvane House,** 2 Dunedin, Connaught Avenue (tel. 021/271822). Mrs. Maureen Vaughan makes guests very welcome, with a cuppa likely to appear whenever she thinks you have the need. The six bedrooms are unpretentious, comfortable, and home-like. There's central heat, and the lounge features a piano for guests' use. Rates are IR£9.50 ($15.25), with a 10% reduction for children.

Mrs. M. Barrett's **Villa Ronan,** Glasheen Road, Cork, Co. Cork (tel. 021/962459), is located on a pleasant, quiet road and has a garden which guests can use. She is very hospitable, and the location is convenient to the university as well as bus service in town. The house is centrally heated and there are four bedrooms, two of which have handbasins. The bed-and-breakfast rate is IR£10 ($16), and she is open Easter to October.

Just off the Killarney road, near the university, **Mrs. Rita O'Herlihy,** 55 Wilton Gardens, Wilton, Cork (tel. 021/541705), offers three bedrooms, two with private facilities. The modern, two-story home has a warm, welcoming air, and there's a very nice garden for relaxing in nice weather. Mrs. O'Herlihy's rates are IR£10 ($16) for bed-and-breakfast, and there's a one-third reduction for children. Central heating, and good parking.

Montenotte (Summerhill, St. Luke's) Area

BED-AND-BREAKFAST. At no. 2 Ardskeagh Villas, Gardiner's Hill, St. Luke's (tel. 021/501800), **Mrs. Leonard** has an old-style home in this district that is convenient to the railway station and within easy walking distance of the city center (although city bus lines are only a half block away). There are six homey rooms, all with handbasins, and Mrs. Leonard is a friendly, hospitable hostess. Rates for bed-and-breakfast are IR£10 ($16), with 20% off for children. Open April through September.

A GUESTHOUSE. Mrs. Monica King is the hostess at **Gabriel House,** Summerhill, Cork (tel. 021/500333). Close to the rail and bus station, and only a few minutes' walk from the city center, this gracious guesthouse has 22 guest rooms, all with private facilities, direct-dial telephones, and color TVs. There are large gardens, a private parking area, and magnificent views of the harbor. The bed-and-

CORK

breakfast rate is IR£18 ($28.75) per person sharing, and dinner runs IR£9 ($14.50).

Douglas Area

BED-AND-BREAKFAST. Convenient to the airport and Ringaskiddy ferry, **Fatima House,** Grange Road, Douglas, Cork (tel. 021/362536), is presided over by Mrs. Elizabeth O'Shea. A nice feature here for families is that Mrs. O'Shea is especially fond of children and welcomes them warmly. As you might expect, she's quite willing to provide babysitting. Her five bedrooms all have handbasins and are attractively furnished. Dinner is available with advance notice for IR£10 ($16); B&B rates are IR£10 ($16), with a 40% reduction for children. There's central heating and good parking.

Miss Joan Murphy's home, 1 Palm Grove, Ashdale Park, South Douglas Road, Cork (tel. 021/362281), is located in a quiet area, with good restaurants in the immediate vicinity. Two of her three nicely appointed bedrooms have private facilities, and there's central heating. Bed-and-breakfast rates are IR£10 ($16), with a 25% reduction for children. Good parking.

Blackrock Area

BED-AND-BREAKFAST. Mrs. Greta Murphy's **San Antonio,** 46 Maryville, Ballintemple, Cork (tel. 021/291849), is not far from Blackrock Castle in a nice residential area. There's a comfortable, "family" feeling about the place, and all three bedrooms are attractive. Central heating and private parking add to the comfort and convenience. Rates for bed-and-breakfast are IR£10 ($16), and Mrs. Murphy deducts 10% for children under 10. Open June to September.

At **Belrose,** 50 Maryville, Ballintemple, Cork (tel. 021/292219), Mrs. O'Leary has a warm, comfortable home in a quiet area, and opens three bedrooms (two with handbasins) to guests. She will arrange babysitting, and she allows a 10% reduction for children under 10. There's good parking, and the house is centrally heated. Her rates are IR£10 ($16) for bed-and-breakfast. Open April to October.

Kinsale Road (Airport)

BED-AND-BREAKFAST. You'll need a car for these two, since they're about five miles out from the city center. Both offer good value in rural surroundings close to the airport.

Au Soleil, Lisfehill, Ballinhassig, Cork Airport/Kinsale Road (tel. 021/888208), is a new bungalow with three attractive bedrooms, all with handbasins. Helen Deasy is a sister to Noreen Raftery, whose Shalom you'll find listed in the Western Region (County Mayo), and the Irish tradition of hospitality certainly runs strong in this family. Helen and husband Des will make you feel right at home. B&B rates are IR£10 ($16), with a one-third reduction for children. Open April through September.

Set in a terraced garden, Mrs. Kathleen O'Mahony's **Fuchsia,** Adamstown, Ballinhassig, Co. Cork (tel. 021/888198), overlooks hedgerows bordering green fields. There are two twin and two double-bedded rooms (one with private bath), all with feather comforters and handbasins. The lounge, with a bay window affording splendid views, has tourist literature on this area, and Mr. and Mrs. O'Mahony delight in recommending points of interest. Breakfasts feature her homemade jam and bread, as well as the delicious local sausage. Rates for bed-and-breakfast are IR£10.50 ($16.75), with a 25% reduction for children, and the evening meal is available with advance notice. Central heat. Open March through October.

READERS' ACCOMMODATIONS SELECTIONS: "We stayed in a wonderful private home with **Mrs. Noonan**, 8 King's Terrace (tel. 021/53810), a few short walking minutes from the center of Cork. Mrs. Noonan is a marvelous lady and served excellent breakfasts complete with homemade bread. The room was great, too." (Jury and Mike Rothschild, Sherman Oaks, Calif.). . . . "In the city of Cork I stayed with Mrs. G. Brien, **Sarto**, 2 Lislee Rd., Mayborough Estate, Rochestown Road, Douglas, Cork, Co. Cork (tel. 021/295579). She was extremely hospitable and her facilities were excellent" (M. Rich, Toronto, Ontario, Canada). . . . "Wonderful hospitality at **Tara Guest House**, 52 Lower Glanmire Rd., Cork (tel. 021/500294). Comfortable rooms are beautifully decorated, and breakfast is huge. It's only a block and a half from the train station" (L. and E. McDivitt, Mukilteo, Wash.). . . . "We found Mrs. Margaret O'Leary's **Killarney House**, Western Road, Cork (tel. 021/270179), to be outstanding, and we didn't hesitate a second to recommend it to other travelers we met" (Mr. and Mrs. D. Mulligan). . . . "Just two miles outside Cork city, we found **Evergreen House**, Rathpeacon, Co. Cork (tel. 021/505715). Noreen and Martin Curran are the very hospitable proprietors, and our bedroom had its own private bathroom. The house is clean and has bucolic views from each window" (M. Schoenstein, Napa, Calif.).

4. WHERE TO EAT

Cork has many good, inexpensive places to eat. One of my all-time favorites at lunch (or for a Big Splurge evening meal) is the **Oyster Tavern,** Market Lane, 56 St. Patrick's St. (tel. 021/272716). It's an old-world sort of place, with lots of wood, etched glass, old prints, and mirrors reflecting the centuries since its coachhouse days in 1792. The bar section is worth stopping by even if you don't eat. A bit complicated to find, the Oyster is signposted on the sidewalk on Patrick Street, which sign points you to Market Lane (one of Cork's last remaining cobbled laneways), leading into the block-long covered city market (worth a visit in itself before or after you eat). The à la carte lunch menu features the steaks and fish for which this place is famous, and you can put together a terrific lunch for about IR£6 ($9.50). Portions are so generous that this could well be your main meal of the day. Lunch hours are noon to 3 p.m. every day except Sunday, and it's a good idea to reserve. For dinner, come along from 6 to 10 p.m. and expect to pay around IR£14 ($22.50).

For less expensive but very good pub lunches, you can't do better than **Beecher's Inn,** Faulkners Lane (tel. 021/23144). Tucked away on this narrow old lane (enter from Emmet Place or Patrick Street), Beecher's also has the soft patina of time. The soft murmur of contented conversation fills the place as Cork regulars gather at lunchtime (12:30 to 2 p.m.). Seafood is a specialty, and a lunch of smoked salmon and brown bread washed down with a dark, creamy Guinness is memorable. There are hot plates and cold salads, none of which will run over IR£4 ($6.50).

De Lacy House, 74 Oliver Plunkett St. (tel. 021/20074), is large and lively, serving a good selection of hot plates and cold meats and salads for under IR£4 ($6.50) from 12:30 to 2:30 p.m. and 5:30 to 10 p.m. The Tourist Menu is offered from 12:45 to 7 p.m. Just one example of the good value here is a roast leg of lamb plate with two vegetables and potato for IR£4 ($6.50). Unusual for a grill bar and pub, De Lacy's accepts major credit cards. If you plan your evening meal here on any night Wednesday through Sunday, you might like to stick around for the traditional music sessions that get under way around 8:30 p.m. (see "Cork After Dark").

Shandon Tavern, 2/3 Lavitt's Quay (tel. 021/21807), offers a good lunch with table service from 12:30 to 2:30 p.m., but pub grub and snacks are available right up to closing time (11 p.m.). Snacks are in the neighborhood of IR£1.50 ($2.50), and lunch will run about IR£4 ($6.50).

In Queen's Oldcastle Shopping Centre, look for the **Periwinkle** (tel. 021/271199). As you'd expect, the specialty here is seafood, some of the freshest and best prepared you'll find in Cork. I especially like the seafood chowder, and there's a good seafood salad. There are always one or two nonseafood selections as well. It's self-service, and downstairs you eat at the blond-wood counters; upstairs, at tables overlooking the busy arcade. Prices can run anywhere from IR£2.50 ($4) to IR£8 ($12.75), and the Periwinkle is open every day except Sunday from 9:30 a.m. to 5:30 p.m.

David Halpin, owner of **Halpins Restaurant,** 14/15 Cook St. (tel. 021/277853), has used traditional materials of wood, slate, and stone to reconstruct this 300-year-old wax works into a very good eatery. It opens for lunch and serves food all day, seven days a week. This is a great favorite with locals, who find it good value, with prices running under IR£3 ($4.75) during the day, and about IR£8 ($12.75) in the evening.

Tung Sing Chinese Restaurant, 23A Patrick St. (tel. 021/24616 or 23793), offers excellent and inexpensive meals from noon to 12:30 a.m. Monday through Saturday and 1 p.m. to midnight on Sundays. Wine is available in this nice upstairs room.

A Big Splurge

Over on the Montenotte section's lofty heights, the **Arbutus Lodge Hotel Restaurant Montenotte** (tel. 021/501237) is known all over Ireland and the Continent for its legendary cuisine and exquisite service. The hotel was once an elegant town house, and the décor is that of subdued formality ("subdued" because the friendly service rescues it from "stuffy"). Large windows overlook the city below. Seafood, meats, and vegetables are the freshest—if your entree includes mushrooms, you may be sure they've been hand-gathered from the woods, not emptied from a can. Lunch in this very special place will run a minimum of IR£16 ($25.50), and dinner starts at about IR£24 ($38.50)—a Big Splurge, and very good value! If those prices are a bit steep for your budget, even in the Big Splurge department, the Gallery Bar at the Arbutus serves smoked salmon and delicious soups for prices that average about IR£10 ($16), and seafood selections in the bar and a garden patio from 12:30 to 2:30 p.m. Restaurant hours are 1 to 3 p.m. and 7 to 9:30 p.m.; closed Sunday. Major credit cards are accepted. Best to reserve (a few days ahead for dinner) at both the Restaurant and Gallery Bar.

READER'S RESTAURANT SELECTIONS: "Ruben's, on Marlboro Street, is cozy, convivial, and has good salad plates and other light fare at very low prices. The **Long Valley Pub** is very friendly and has good pub grub" (Rev. R.J. Goode, Eagle River, Wisc.).

5. THINGS TO SEE AND DO

One of Cork's chief charms is that it is so much a *walking* city, which is, of course, the best possible way to get around any city if you are to capture its true flavor and mingle with the people who give it life. My first recommendation, then, is to go by the **Tourist Office** and pick up their *Tourist Trail* guide to a signposted walking tour of Cork. It details a comprehensive route around the significant landmarks and tells you all about each one. Makes for a lovely day's ramble, with a stop whenever your fancy dictates for a jar, lunch, or whatever.

From time to time, there are also free evening **guided walking tours** departing from the Tourist Office two or three days a week during July and August. Inquire when you're there to see if they're on. For more personalized guided tours, contact Valerie Fleury, **Discover Cork,** Belmount, Douglas Road, Cork (tel. 021/293873). She has put together half-day tours in and around Cork for IR£14 ($22.50). Some of the more interesting that go outside the city are those to Blarney, followed by afternoon tea in a private home, Fota Park, and Kinsale. There's also a Kinsale trip, at a higher fee, that concludes with a six-course evening meal followed by a visit to a traditional Irish pub.

The **Blarney Stone**—I *know* that's uppermost in your mind!—is six miles from Cork city, and another outstanding attraction, **Fota Park,** is nine miles away. You'll find them listed in Chapter XVI in order that this section may be devoted to those things in the immediate vicinity.

I can't really say that the **Coal Quay** (pronounce it "kay" in this instance) qualifies as a sightseeing attraction, but I *do* know that it's a place unique to Cork and one I drop by on every visit. You won't find it listed anywhere under that name—the signposts say Corn Market Street—but no one in town will know what you're asking for unless you say "Coal Kay." Right in the heart of the city, it's to the right (opposite the Grand Parade which curves off to the left) at the end of Patrick Street, and it's as grand a collection of hardy Irish country-women as you're likely to run across. From stalls, tables, carts, or cardboard boxes on the sidewalk, these shrewd, witty ladies hawk everything from second-hand clothes to fresh vegetables to old shoes to old pieces of china to anything else they happen to have handy and can exchange for a "lop" or two ("lop" being, of course, a coin). I won't guarantee that you'll catch every nuance of conversation carried on in a language that's peculiar to this bunch, but I will guarantee that you'll catch a glimpse of genuine Irish folk life.

Not far from the Coal Quay, the red-brick **Crawford Art Gallery** on Emmet Place was built as the Custom House back in 1724 when ships unloaded where the sidewalk is now at the King's Dock. There's something almost homey about the big, rambling halls and exhibition rooms, and I've never been inside without encountering at least one art student diligently studying the masters. There are paintings and sculptures by modern Irish artists and an interesting collection of classical casts from the Vatican Galleries presented to Cork in 1818.

On Church Street, just off Shandon Street, **St. Ann's Church** is perhaps the most beloved of the city's many churches. What makes it so are the

> . . . bells of Shandon
> That sound so grand on
> The pleasant waters
> Of the river Lee. . . .

immortalized by Francis Sylvester Mahony in his 1830s poem "The Bells of Shandon," penned under the name of Father Prout. Shandon takes its name from the Irish *sean dun,* meaning "old fort." The Protestant church is distinguished architecturally only by its red-and-white "pepper pot" steeple which houses the bells. Its 170-foot height is crowned by an 11-foot 3-inch weathervane in the shape of a salmon (the symbol of wisdom), and the clocks set in its four sides are known affectionately as the "four-faced liar," since no two of them ever show the same time. Climb the steeple's winding stairs to see the famous bells, and for a small charge you can follow numbers on the bell strings that will send "The Bells of St. Mary's" pealing out over the city. Father Prout, incidentally, lies below in the small churchyard.

Cork's birthplace is three blocks past the South Main Street Bridge, where **St. Finn Barre's Cathedral,** on Bishop's Street, marks the spot on which the venerable saint founded his monastery in 650. As it grew in stature as a seat of learning, it became a mark of honor among Gaelic chieftains and Norman knights to be buried in its grounds. At the time of the Reformation, St. Finn Barre's became the seat of the bishopric of the Church of Ireland, as it is today. The French Gothic structure you see today was opening in 1870, and its great West Window is of particular note.

The magnificent **City Hall** on Albert Quay opened in 1936 to replace the one burned in 1920 during the War of Independence. This is where President Kennedy came to address an admiring throng during his visit in the 1960s.

Running parallel to the Western Road is **The Mardyke,** a mile-long, tree-shaded walk named after an Amsterdam walk called the "Meer Dyke" and bordered by **Fitzgerald Park,** where you'll find lovely landscaping, interesting sculptures, and a small museum.

For the best selection of Irish records, tapes, sheet music, books, and traditional musical instruments such as the tin whistle or bodhran, check **A. Shanahan & Co., Ltd.,** 53-54 Oliver Plunkett St. (tel. 021/271264). They're open Monday through Saturday from 9:30 a.m. to 5:30 p.m. and they have an excellent mail service.

A good many of the Irish books you browse through in bookshops around the country are published right here in Cork by **Mercier Press,** 4 Bridge St. Their inexpensive paperback editions are all by Irish writers on Irish subjects, fiction and nonfiction. These make good souvenirs as well as gifts.

During summer months, there are regular four-hour **harbor cruises** down the Lee. Hourly schedules vary, and they do not always run the same days every week, so check with the Tourist Office.

Golfers can rent clubs at the Cork Corporation–owned **Mahon Golf Course,** Mahon Peninsula, and if you have your own clubs, there are 18-hole courses at the **Douglas Golf Club,** Carr's Hill, Douglas, and **Monkstown Golf Club,** Monkstown.

This is a good place to enjoy one of Ireland's favorite spectator sports at the **Cork Greyhound Stadium** out on Western Road (tel. 021/43013). There's racing on Monday, Wednesday, and Saturday, starting at 8 p.m. Other nights, there are trial heats which you can attend at no charge (but no betting), but on race nights, admission is IR£1.50 ($2.50).

One last Cork sight that is sure to bring a smile to your lips is located in front of the Cork County Council offices on the "Straight Road" (just ask anybody where it is). Right in front of what is fondly called "the tallest building in Ireland" by locals (it beats the height of Liberty Hall in Dublin by all of six inches!), stand two figures who could only be **Corkmen.** Heads upraised, hands in pockets, they gaze quizzically up at this upstart of a building, trying to make sense of it. Ironically, these two, the work of the late Oisin Kelly, began life in Dublin, Cork's arch rival. It was only when that city treated them shabbily (they were found lying in a Dublin scrap yard and rescued by the County Council) that they came "home" to the city by the Lee. The people of Cork have affectionately dubbed them "Chah and Mial" after two beloved radio and television characters from the city, and any mention of the sculpture brings a smile to the lips of the locals. If you're driving by, slow down for a tip of the hat to these two embodiments of the Cork spirit—or as many tourists do, stop to snap a photo, surely one of your most unusual souvenirs of this spirited city.

6. CORK AFTER DARK

The people of Cork devote themselves to commerce with great acumen during the workday, but when the shop doors close, you'll find them just as busy in pursuit of cultural pleasure, whether it be highbrow or lowbrow.

Theater

There's almost always something on at the **Cork Opera House** in Emmet Place. It could be first-rate drama, a musical review, a comedy, a concert, or an artist's recital. Ticket prices are in the IR£4 ($6.40) to IR£6 ($9.50) range.

Cork's outstanding **Everyman Playhouse** has moved from its 12-year home on Father Matthew Street to the Old Palace Theatre, a lovely venue on Mac Curtain Street just beside the Metropole Hotel that was built in 1897 as a music hall, then used in later years as a cinema. Its gilt-and-gingerbread décor is protected by a preservation order, as well it might be, since it is so steeped in the theatrical history of the city. Due to reopen in 1989, its plans are to continue presenting a resident company performing productions of outstanding quality. Leading companies from Dublin, Belfast, Derry, Galway, Limerick, Great Britain, and America will play here as well, and if the past is any indication, standards will be high. A nice feature will be the intermission coffee service, and you'll still be able to hobnob with the actors after each production by dropping in at the Theatre Bar. For information and booking, contact Everyman Palace, Mac Curtain Street (tel. 021/501673).

Ballet

The **Irish Ballet Company,** Emmet Place, has distinguished itself internationally since it was formed in 1973 with a nucleus of a dozen dancers. Its ranks have grown considerably, and now include dancers from continental Europe, America, and Great Britain as well as Ireland. Classically trained, the troupe is equally at home with modern and Irish works. They're usually in Cork at the Cork Opera House in February and August, and in Dublin at the Abbey Theatre in June. If you can catch them, don't miss a brilliant dance company, and you'll really be in luck if they're performing Joan Denise Moriarty's *Playboy of the Western World,* with music by the Chieftains.

Other Entertainment

In the rear of the Tourist Office on the Grand Parade, the **Ivernia Theatre** has performances several times a week during summer months. Occasionally there's lunchtime theater as well. Check with the Tourist Office (tel. 021/273251), where you can buy tickets in advance, although they're also available at the door. Excellent entertainment at bargain prices.

De Lacy House, 74 Oliver Plunkett St. (see "Where to Eat"), has traditional music Wednesday through Sunday nights, and from time to time other forms of musical entertainment are offered on other nights.

The traditional music sessions at **An Bodhran** pub, 42 Oliver Plunkett St., are much more informal. The brick-walled century-and-a-half-old pub is a favorite with university students, most of whom take their traditional music quite seriously, while never losing that Irish twinkle of the eye. You'll usually find the ballads going Wednesday through Saturday nights, but you might drop in other nights to see what's doing.

7. THE PUBS OF CORK

Well, there is, according to some Cork experts, a pub for every 200 residents (including babes in arms): in a city populated by some 129,000 souls, that's a lot of pubs! You're just not likely to be seized by a terrible thirst without rescue close at hand, that's for certain. The pubs of Cork come in all sizes, styles, and décor, and I have no doubt you'll find your own "local" during your stay. The following few are some I've found appealing, with convivial conversation usually on tap along with libations.

An Bodhran, 42 Plunkett St., has been renovated, but with a great deal of attention to its original character. It's a small, cozy place with brick walls, dim lights, low ceiling, lots of timbered beams, and a lively clientele. It's a student hangout, but you'll usually find a mix of older types as well. Traditional music is loved here with all the fervor of a truly Irish heart (see above), as is stimulating conversation.

I first dropped in (literally) at **The Vineyard,** Market Lane (off Patrick Street), at the end of an exhausting afternoon of shopping. Things were pretty quiet except for a gaggle of Cork housewives, also exhausted for the same reason, who had sensibly decided there was nothing for it but a "drop" before heading off home to fix the dinner. It's an old, rambling place that dates back more than two centuries, but Liam Mackesy, the present owner, is the third generation of his family to run it. He has lightened it by installing a huge, high skylight in the center of the main bar. Rugby followers and players congregate in the Vineyard, where the crack (chat) leans a *lot* toward sports. Young, old, and in-between faces line up at the bar. It's a good pub in the evening, there's pub grub at lunch, and it can be a lifesaver in the late afternoon!

While I can't vouch for this personally, I have it on good authority (that is, from a kindred soul when it comes to pubs) that the **Mahon Tavern,** a small pub at the gates of Blackrock Castle, pulls a good pint and attracts a good clientele.

The above, of course, are just a hint of Cork's pub wealth. Others worth investigation include the following: The **Roundy House,** at the top of the Coal Quay, dates back to 1858 and is one of the oldest in the city, with pictures from the past adorning its walls. The **Swan & Cygnet,** at the foot of Patrick Street, goes back to 1870, and once during its long history was a boxing ring, although now you're more likely to run into musicians than pugilists. The **Mutton Lane Inn,** off Patrick Street, also goes back to the 19th century, and boasts a noteworthy old pewter collection. **Dan Lowrey's Sea-Food Tavern,** in Mac Curtain Street, was once a boarding house, and its décor now includes antique mirrors, a stained-glass front, and an open fire. That's a long enough list to get you started—let me know of any special discoveries of your own.

8. SPECIAL EVENTS

If you doubt that Cork is a party-loving town, just take a look at the festivals they put on every year. A festival in Cork, I might add, is a truly gala affair, with the entire city involved in the activities, and if you hit town in the middle of one, you're in for a treat. As this is written, firm dates are not available for 1989 and 1990, but the Tourist Board should be able to furnish them before you leave home.

My favorite of Cork's special events is the **Jazz International Festival,** usually in October. This is a *truly* international event, with some of the world's most outstanding musicians showing up for concerts held all around town, as well as impromptu jam sessions breaking out in pubs, B&B drawing rooms, and wherever two jazz devotees happen to meet. It's a joyous, free-spirited time.

In April or May, the **Cork International Choral and Folk Dance Festival** attracts top ranked performers from America, Great Britain, and the Continent. Come September, it's the **Cork Folk Festival.**

Now a word about a festival that may or may not come off—the **Cork Film Festival** which for years enjoyed a worldwide reputation as a showcase for independent filmmakers and was the gala of galas in Cork, but was cancelled for a year or two. Since 1986, however, it has been revived each year in late September or early October—very good news for those of us who have always looked forward to the festival as a time of great gaiety in the city. Check with the Tourist Office to see if it stays alive—if so, it's well worth a day or two to join in the festivities.

As if all those festivals weren't enough, Cork also goes all out for the **Boat Show** in February, the **Summer Show** in June, the **Irish Assembly of Veteran/ Vintage Motor Cycles** in September, and the **Cork 20 International Car Rally** in October! Pretty hard to miss a party, no matter *when* you come.

9. SHOPPING

Cork city is a major shopping center for the county, and the following are among its leading shops: **Cash's of Cork,** Patrick and Caroline Streets, is perhaps the leading department store, with everything from Waterford crystal, Belleek, Royal Tara, and Aran knits to the latest fashions for men and women. . . . **Roches Stores,** Patrick Street, also features giftware, travel goods, records, sports goods, and clothing. . . . **Fitzgeralds Menswear Shop,** 24 Patrick St., is Cork's only source of Burberry raincoats (with very competitive prices), and also stocks an excellent selection of Irish woolens, tweeds, and knits. . . . **Barry's Tea Shop,** on Princes Street, is where you'll find a good supply of that good Irish tea to take home, as well as a host of other hard-to-find food items. . . . **Easons,** on Patrick Street, stocks books of Irish interest, as well as a full line of current and classic fiction. . . . The aforementioned **A. Shanahan & Co. Ltd.,** 53-54 Oliver Plunkett St., is the best place to go for traditional music, records, and instruments. . . . For high-quality crafts, check **Crafts of Ireland,** 11 Winthrop St. . . . There's a whole collection of boutiques, specialty shops, and bookshops along a quaintly cobbled square just off Patrick Street (on Patrick Street, turn right at a store named Moderne).

CHAPTER XVI

INTRODUCING THE SOUTHWEST: AROUND COUNTY CORK

□ □ □

1. ACCOMMODATIONS
2. WHERE TO EAT
3. THINGS TO SEE AND DO

Only six miles from Cork city, Blarney Castle holds out the promise of silken phrases to those who will kiss its magic stone. Killarney is a testament to man's appreciation of nature's gifts; wooded Gougane Barra a testament to man's reaching out to his God in the midst of those gifts.

Scattered throughout all the above are quiet little villages peopled with strong characters and whimsical spirits. A Corkman is distinctive from other Irish, and a *West* Corkman is unique unto himself! A Kerryman combines wit, independence, and pride in a special blend like no other in the country.

The Southwest is, then, a region to be explored as fully as time will permit and savored in memory the rest of your natural life. We'll start with County Cork.

1. ACCOMMODATIONS

Note: Prices shown below are those in effect in 1989—expect them to be higher in 1990.

A HOSTEL: There's a superior-grade hostel in Summer Cove, Kinsale (tel. 021/72309). About a mile and a half out from Kinsale, the hostel has an extremely steep approach.

BED-AND-BREAKFAST: For an ideal two- or three-day base for sightseeing in Cork city, Blarney, Fota Park, and Youghal, consider a stay at **Cedar-Ville,** Carrigtwohill, Co. Cork (tel. 021/883246). Breda Hayes is the warm, bubbly hostess here, taking a keen interest in all her guests, and those lovely blooms that welcome you to the private car park out front are the handiwork of husband Dennis, a high school science teacher who must have been born with a green thumb. The house itself is spotless, and the five bedrooms are nicely decorated in soft pastels, all with handbasins (two with private facilities), as well as wide windows that look out to colorful flowers in front and back of the house. Meals here are superb, reflecting Breda's College of Catering training. The rate for bed-and-breakfast is IR£10 ($16), high tea is IR£5 ($8), and dinner is IR£9 ($14.50). Open March to November; signposted on the main Cork–Waterford road. Highly recommended.

Donal and Philomena (Phil) Brooks open their Georgian home, **Avonmore House,** South Abbey, Youghal (tel. 024/92617), to guests, with eight nicely done up guest rooms (all with showers) and superb meals. Donal is a forester and has a keen interest in traditional Irish music. Avonmore is conveniently located in the main residential section of Youghal and is only a short walk from the beach. B&B rates are IR£10.50 ($16.75), with a 25% reduction for children. Dinner is IR£9.40 ($15).

The **Strand House,** Front Strand, Youghal, Co. Cork (tel. 024/92755), sits right on the seafront in this quaint resort. Its Victorian style and period furnishings hark back to an earlier, more gracious, age, as does the hospitality extended by Margaret and Austin Flavin. There are six rooms, four of which are ideal for families, since they sleep up to four. Some come with private bath facilities at a small extra charge. B&B rates are IR£11.50 ($18.50). There's private parking, and it's open from early May through September.

The Lynch family will make you feel right at home at **The Gables,** Stoneview, Blarney (tel. 021/385330). This lovely period house is set in its own grounds and was once given to the parish priest by the owners of Blarney Castle. There are three attractive guest rooms, two with private facilities. Rates are IR£13 ($20.75) for bed-and-breakfast, with 50% off for children. Open March through October.

On the Blarney–Killarney road, you'll find **Glenview House,** Tower, Blarney (tel. 021/385370). This two-story stone house has been charmingly renovated with due regard to retaining its original character. Partly because of its structure, one of the three guest rooms does not have a handbasin, though the two bathrooms are handy. Mr. and Mrs. Finbarr O'Brien take a personal interest in all their guests, and Mr. O'Brien is especially helpful to those tracing their Irish ancestors. Bed-and-breakfast rates are IR£10 ($16), with a one-third discount for children. Open May through September.

Mrs. Kay O'Flynn, **St. Anthony's,** 3 Sunset Pl., Killeens, Commons Road, Blarney, Co. Cork (tel. 021/385151), is the charming hostess of this lovely bungalow just two miles from Blarney and three miles from Cork. The house is centrally heated and dinner is available in the evening. All six attractive bedrooms have handbasins and three have private facilities, for which there is an extra charge of IR£3 ($4.75). The rate for bed-and-breakfast is IR£10 ($16) and dinner is IR£10.50 ($16.75); 10% reduction for children. Open Easter to November.

Ms. Patricia Blanchfield, **Blanchfield House,** on the main Cork–Bandon road, Ballinhassig, Co. Cork (tel. 021/885167), is the gracious hostess of this beautiful country home with its own internationally known restaurant. The house is convenient to Blarney, Bandon, Kinsale, and Cork city. It is centrally heated and there is an attractive TV lounge for guest use. Guests enjoy private fishing for salmon and trout on the River Bandon, and riding and tennis are also available locally. Two of the six pretty rooms have private facilities and they all have handbasins. The rate for bed-and-breakfast is IR£13 ($20.75) and dinner costs between IR£8 ($12.75) and IR£16 ($25.50). Open all year.

Just three miles from Blarney Castle is Mrs. Ita O'Donovan's **Knockawn Wood,** Curraleigh, Inniscarra, Blarney, Co. Cork (tel. 021/870284), a lovely modern home. Mrs. O'Donovan is very hospitable and will provide an evening meal with no advance notice. The house is centrally heated and the four attractive bedrooms all have handbasins and two have private facilities. The rate for bed-and-breakfast is IR£10.50 ($16.75) and dinner is IR£8.50 ($13.50); 50% reduction for children. Open year round.

Miss Mary O'Driscoll, 1 Upper Park, Cobh, Co. Cork (tel. 021/811506), is hostess of an attractive Georgian home set in a private residential park overlooking Cork Harbour. All five pretty bedrooms have handbasins, and an evening meal is available with advance notice. The rate is IR£10 ($16) for bed-and-breakfast and high tea costs IR£6.50 ($10.40); 25% reduction for children. Open February to November.

Mrs. Carmel Hayes, **Dun Mhuire,** Kilbarry Road, Dunmanway, Co. Cork (tel. 023/45162), presides over this lovely, modern home and restaurant set in nice, peaceful surroundings. The food is excellent and the house is centrally heated. The four comfortable bedrooms all have handbasins and two have private facilities. The rate for bed-and-breakfast is IR£12 ($19.25) and there is a 50% reduction for children. Open May to September.

A little over four miles from Fermoy just off the main Cork–Dublin road (the N8), **Danmar House,** Ballyhindon, Fermoy, Co. Cork (tel. 025/31786), is a lovely modern bungalow. There are five nice bedrooms, four with handbasins and one with private shower. Mrs. Maureen Regan is the gracious hostess, and she'll provide high tea or dinner at reasonable rates with advance notice. Children under 12 get a 10% reduction on B&B rates of IR£10.50 ($16.75). Central heat and good parking.

Mrs. O'Regan, **Sirocco,** Ballyregan, Kinsale, Co. Cork (tel. 021/775129), is the charming hostess of this modern bungalow with magnificent views of the surrounding area. She and her family are lovely people and there is a garden for guests to use. There are three attractive rooms, all with handbasins, and high tea is available. The rate for bed-and-breakfast is IR£10 ($16) and high tea costs IR£7 ($11.25); 10% reduction for children. Open June to September.

About a mile outside Kinsale, Mrs. Griffin's **Hillside House,** Camp Hill, Kinsale (tel. 021/772315), has sea views and a pleasant garden. There are six bedrooms, all with handbasins, one with private facilities. This is an especially nice place to stay if you prefer the country but don't want to be too far from town. B&B rates are IR£10.50 ($16.75), with a 25% discount for children. Central heat and ample parking.

About an hour's drive southwest of Cork city, **Sea Court,** Butlerstown, Co. Cork (tel. 023/40151; in the U.S., 606/441-0291), is a beautiful Georgian country mansion that dates from 1760. Within easy driving distance of Kinsale, Bantry, and Killarney, the house sits in ten acres of wooded grounds on the Seven Heads peninsula jutting out into the Atlantic, and beaches are only a short walk away. Mr. and Mrs. David Elder bought this lovely place in 1983 and make their home here in summer, returning to the States in winter. While the house has been designated a historic structure by the Irish government and is open to the public at large during the summer season, the Elders have also opened it to paying guests. Rooms are spacious, well furnished, and some have private facilities (for a IR£1.50, $2.50, supplement); others have ocean views. Breakfasts are sumptuous, and David will happily pass along the recipe for the scones of which he is so proud. Bed-and-breakfast costs IR£12 ($19.25). Incidentally, should you be totally taken by Sea Court during a summer visit, it is available as a weekly or monthly rental in the off-season.

The Galvin Family, **Abbey Heights,** The Abbey, Skibbereen, Co. Cork (tel. 028/21615), are a lovely family and will welcome you to their pretty bungalow, less than a mile from town, with beautiful river views. The house is centrally heated and dinner is available with advance notice. The four comfortable bedrooms all have handbasins. The rates are IR£10 ($16) for bed-and-breakfast and IR£9 ($14.50) for dinner; one-third reduction for children. Open April to September.

Shangri-la, Bantry (tel. 027/50244), is a modern bungalow perched on a hill overlooking Bantry Bay. The glass-enclosed front porch affords gorgeous panoramic views of the bay, and chairs are often set out on the beautifully landscaped lawn for guests to savor spectacular sunsets. Guest rooms are comfortably furnished and each is decorated around one color, which gives it its name of Blue Room, Pink Room, etc. Four rooms have private facilities, and two have lovely semi-poster beds. Angela and Tony Muckley are gracious hosts who know the area well and love helping their guests plan their time here. Angela is a former president of the Town & Country Homes Association and is keenly interested in tourism. She is also known as a superior cook and her evening meals are memorable, with wine available. For breakfast, she many times offers guests a choice of the traditional Irish menu or pancakes or crumpets and honey (a nice change). Rates are IR£10 ($16) for bed-and-breakfast (20% reduction for children under 10, sharing room with parents), private facilities cost IR£1.50 ($2.50) more, and the single supplement is IR£3 ($4.75). It's IR£10 ($16) for the evening meal. There's central heating and a private car park.

Sea Front, Glengarriff, Co. Cork (tel. 027/63079), looks out over the harbor. Mrs. Ann Guerin knows the area well and is always happy to help her guests plan sightseeing, fishing, or other activities. Her four bedrooms in the centrally heated house all have handbasins, and rates are IR£10 ($16); 25% off for children under 12. She'll prepare an evening meal for IR£10 ($16), given enough notice. Open March to October.

FARMHOUSES: Lovely **Birch Hill House,** Grenagh, Blarney (tel. 021/886106), is a longtime favorite with readers. The lovely century-old Victorian home sits on a wooded bluff, part of a 105-acre farm. Mrs. Dawson is the friendly hostess, who is as interesting as her plant-filled home. The six guest rooms have handbasins, and some are quite large. All are nicely decorated and comfortably furnished. There are wood fires downstairs, electric heaters in guest rooms. B&B rates are IR£10 ($16), and there's a 25% discount for children. Open April through October.

Mrs. Fitzpatrick will welcome you to **Beechmount Farm,** Mallow (tel. 022/21764). The pretty Georgian house dates back to the 17th century and is partially furnished with antique pieces. Mrs. Fitzpatrick excels in the kitchen, and boasts that at Beechmount "you will never be cold or hungry." You'll sample her marvelous home-baking at afternoon tea. The 187 acres of green farm fields afford peaceful rural views, and the five simply furnished guest rooms feature electric blankets on all beds. Rates for B&B are IR£10 ($16), and high tea is IR£7 ($11.25). Open June to September.

GUESTHOUSES: Norma and Barry Twomey pride themselves on offering all the "traditional hospitality of a small inn" at **Whispering Pines Guesthouses,** Crosshaven (tel. 021/831843 or 831448), a popular boating resort village some 12 miles south of Cork city and 16 miles from the Blarney Stone. The two-story ultra-modern guesthouse certainly offers every convenience you can imagine, and it's just across the road from the Owenabwee River and Crosshaven Harbour,

with their pageantry of colorful sailboats. Guest rooms are beautifully decorated, have built-in wardrobes and a view of the river, and come with private baths. The dining room, with a fireplace for cool days, opens onto a patio, where breakfast is sometimes served in fine weather. In the lounge, large windows look out to the water, and a piano is on hand for guests (and Barry, when he can be prevailed upon to play). There are two deep-sea angling boats here which go out daily with anglers and return with fresh fish for the restaurant. You have a choice of no fewer than 12 pubs in the village, an easy walk from Whispering Pines. Bed-and-breakfast rates are IR£16 ($25.50) to IR£18 ($28.75), and dinner (there's a wine license) is IR£12 ($19.25).

In the little village of Myrtleville, about 12 miles southwest of Cork city, a marvelous and quite extraordinary guesthouse perches atop a high cliff overlooking the sea. **Bunnyconnelan** (ask for directions when you call for reservations; tel. 021/831237) was the holiday home built for a British diplomat back in 1830, but was not given its unusual name until a Scotsman bought it soon after World War II and christened it after his four daughters—Bunny, Connie, Nellie, and Ann. Now it's in the capable hands of Pat and Sheila O'Brien. The view is spectacular, with the Roches Point lighthouse blinking in the distance and award-winning gardens sloping down the cliffside. The ground floor holds an interesting bar/lounge which features stone fireplaces, beamed ceiling, and the most eclectic collection of decorations you can imagine, including bagpipes, barometers, a brass hunting horn, and tartan drapes. Outside, umbrella tables dot a flag-paved patio. On weekend nights this place is mobbed with people who've come down from Cork, often bringing their own music with them. The ground-floor dining room looks out to sea views through one wall of windows, and the meals are excellent, with seafood and steak starring on the moderately priced menu. Pub grub is available in the bar during the day. Upstairs, there are a dozen simply furnished rooms, most with that smashing view, that cost IR£12 ($19.25). Advance reservations are absolutely essential in summer months.

Ard-na-Greine, in Schull (tel. 028/28181), is pricey enough to qualify as a Big Splurge and special enough to warrant kicking over budget traces. Set on a hill a mile to the west of town, its peaceful, bucolic views are a tonic for travel-weary souls. The English translation of its name is "Height of the Sun," and the gorgeous blooms in gardens and front lawns attest to the abundance of sunshine it enjoys. Frank and Rena O'Sullivan have created a haven of comfort and semi-sophistication in an old inn that dates back two centuries. The O'Sullivans have managed to retain much of the inn's original character while installing amenities that would do a big-city luxury hotel proud. The beamed-ceilinged, white-walled dining room has a fireplace on each end wall and features evening meals that draw large local crowds. There's an excellent wine list as well. A lovely stone-floored bar which is open to the public and a cozy, private guests' bar are also featured. All bedrooms are beautifully decorated, and all have a private bath as well as tea and coffee makings. Rates, which include a full Irish breakfast, are from IR£28 ($44.75) per person, and dinner (which must be booked ahead) runs IR£18 ($28.75).

HOTELS: In the little West Cork village of Leap, a night in the comfortable, old-fashioned **Leap Inn** (tel. 028/33307) is like taking a giant step back to a time when friendliness and gracious hospitality was the mark of all country inns. The same family has run this place since 1834, and today Brian and Ann Sheahan continue the traditions of innkeeping that have grown with the years. Public rooms include a bar (which serves pub grub), lounge, and a pretty dining room, where a four-course dinner featuring fresh seafood runs about IR£8 ($12.75) and à la carte main courses are IR£5.50 ($8.75) and up. Upstairs, bedrooms are simply furnished but very comfortable. Only one of the ten has a private bath (no extra charge), and rates, which include a full Irish breakfast, are IR£10 ($16).

Here's another Big Splurge for your consideration. Set back from the road in spacious grounds, **Sea View House Hotel,** Ballylickey, Bantry (tel. 027/50073 or 50462), is a sparkling white three-story house built back in 1888. Miss Kathleen O'Sullivan, owner and manager, is known throughout Ireland for her hospitality, and her deft hand can be seen in every room, where antiques are not so much on display as placed for convenient use. Every room, in fact, fairly shouts "gracious." Sea View is also known for its excellent dining room, which has won several food awards, and its Sunday lunch is a great favorite with locals. Each bedroom is different in size and shape, and each is prettily decorated, and all have a telephone. Most have a private bath. Rates, which include private bath and full Irish breakfast, range from IR£25 ($40) to IR£32 ($51.25).

SELF-CATERING:

SELF-CATERING: You can relax into the peaceful Irish countryside in the very special holiday cottages at **Kinoith House,** Shanagarry, Midleton, Co. Cork (tel. 021/646785), spend your days sightseeing in the area or on the sandy strand at Shanagarry, a short drive away, and return at night for a meal in your cottage that includes freshly baked bread, free-range eggs, and fresh vegetables and fruits you can buy from the farm shop. Kinoith House Cottages are an adjunct of the internationally known Ballymaloe House nearby, and Myrtle Allen's famed cookery school is held here at Kinoith House under the tutelage of Darina Allen, her talented daughter-in-law. The proximity of Ballymaloe is a bonus for cottage renters, since one of Ireland's finest restaurants is right at hand for those times you'd really rather not cook.

The cottages are in what were once the outbuildings of the 18th-century farmhouse known as Kinoith. From the graveled courtyard, where vivid blooms are bright splashes of color, stroll through the garden and out into the apple orchard. Inside each the décor is country-pretty, with such modern conveniences as a dishwasher and television (and you have the use of laundry facilities), while there's the added, old-fashioned comfort of an open fire (the rent includes your firewood). The Pink Cottage sleeps eight to ten people, with a double bedroom, two twin-bedded rooms, and one double balcony bedroom; the White Cottage sleeps the same number, with one double bedroom, one twin-bedded room, and one room with double sets of bunk beds; and the Coach House sleeps eight, with a double and three twins. Weekly rates for these engaging cottages range from IR£295 ($472) to IR£350 ($560)—which makes them quite inexpensive on a per-person basis. Early reservations are advised to avoid disappointment.

READERS' ACCOMMODATIONS SELECTIONS: "Mr. and Mrs. A. Salinger, **The Lighthouse,** The Rock, Kinsale, Co. Cork (tel. 021/772734), are two lovely Americans who have settled in Kinsale. They have a lovely home furnished with antiques brought over from the States. The Salingers are extremely hospitable, quite willing to recommend places of interest and dining facilities" (Lois Powers). . . . "Mrs. A. Callaghan, **Ashlee Lodge,** Tower, Blarney, Co. Cork (tel. 021/385346), runs this outstanding guesthouse. It is beautifully decorated, immaculate and every possible convenience is thoughtfully anticipated and provided. . . . Mrs. B. Murphy, **Callas Farm,** Callas, Berrings, Blarney, Co. Cork (tel. 021/332114), was lovely to us, extending hospitality with a cup of tea and helpful information. This is a modern farmhouse with very clean, airy rooms" (Mrs. R. Reynolds, Sykesville, Md.). . . . "**Findus House,** Ballyvoige, Kilnamartyra, Macroom, Co. Cork (tel. 026/40023), run by Mrs. M. O'Sullivan, was truly a find! Exceptionally clean, and with an honest, warm hospitality, Findus House is a family-run, working farm. The children served us freshly baked bread and cakes that their mother had gotten up at dawn to prepare. It was a real delight" (H. and J. Armus, Toledo, Ohio).

2. WHERE TO EAT

The vast wooded, mountain, and seaside area of County Cork calls out for picnics, and I urge you to stop at a greengrocer's for provisions and have at least one meal under the skies. There are also several outstanding eateries in this region.

In Youghal, **Aherne's Pub and Seafood Bar,** 163 N. Main St. (tel. 024/92533 or 92424), serves bar food of such quality that it has won the National Bar Food award for several years. But pub grub is not its only distinction, for John and David Fitzgibbon have also installed an outstanding full restaurant in this old pub and enhanced its décor with such touches as oil paintings, wood paneling, and soft lighting. Seafood dishes, such as mussels in garlic butter, take star billing, but beef, lamb, and chicken dishes are equally well prepared. Except for bar food at IR£1.50 ($2.50) to IR£5.50 ($8.75), available all day prices in this attractive eatery will run slightly above budget, with lunch costing about IR£8 ($12.75) and dinner around IR£12 ($19.25). Restaurant hours are 12:30 to 2:15 p.m. and 6:30 to 9:30 p.m. Tuesday through Saturday. Major credit cards are accepted.

Bunnyconnelan, Myrtleville (tel. 021/831237) (see "Accommodations" above), serves fresh seafood, expertly prepared, at moderate prices in a window-walled dining room overlooking the gardens and the sea. Steaks, lamb, chicken, and pork are also on the menu, and there's a good wine list. Dinner hours are 7:30 to 11 p.m., with prices in the IR£8 ($12.75) to IR£10 ($16) range, and there's a very good Sunday lunch from 12:30 to 2 p.m., priced at around IR£10 ($16). Reservations are essential.

In Bantry, look for **O'Connor's Seafood Restaurant** on the Square (tel. 027/50221). Matt and Ann O'Connor run the cozy pub and restaurant, and their seafood dishes are truly special (try mussels à la Guinness!). There's a wide selection of steak, pork, lamb, and chicken for non-seafood lovers, and salads, sandwiches, shepherd's pie, and the like are on tap in the pub from 11:30 a.m. to early evening. Restaurant hours are 5:30 to 11:30 p.m. for full dinners, and 11:30 p.m. to 12:30 a.m. for light suppers. Main courses on the à la carte menu range from IR£8 ($12.50) to IR£11 ($17.50). Bar food prices are lower.

The **Vintage,** Main Street, Kinsale (tel. 021/772502), is a small restaurant, very cozy, very romantic, and totally delicious. There is an open fire in the dining room, 200-year-old beams and the original masts from sailing ships that came into Kinsale. Every evening, in a kitchen that is minuscule by restaurant standards, master chef Michael Riese, who was formerly head chef at the Four Seasons Hotel in his native Hamburg, conjures up a menu remarkable for its freshness of ingredients and approach. As much as possible Michael uses local foodstuffs—organically grown vegetables, free-range goose, duckling and rabbit, eggs from free-range chickens, and seafood caught just offshore. His Kinsale hot smoked salmon steak and his sole Véronique (filets stuffed with white wine, cream, and grapes) are superb. There's an excellent wine list and the Vintage is a member of the Kinsale Good Food Circle, as well as other prestigious professional organizations. Main courses average about IR£11 ($17.50). Hours are 7 to 10:30 p.m.; closed Sunday except holiday weekends. All credit cards are honored.

On the outskirts of Kinsale, **Man Friday,** Scilly (tel. 021/772260), is the sort of cozy eatery that invites you to relax from your first step inside. Its stone walls and pine paneling create a warm atmosphere, and its international menu will make your mouth water. Among the outstanding dishes are baked black sole with a seafood stuffing (as you might expect in this seaside spot, seafoods are a specialty), roast stuffed loin of lamb with mint and rosemary sauce, and Chinese beef, but anything you select will come to table at its very best, a fact testified to by the many awards and top ratings given Man Friday over the past few years. Dinner will run around IR£15 ($24). Hours are 7:30 to 10:30 p.m., and it's closed on Sunday and for two weeks in January.

In Kinsale, superior light lunches are served in the cozy **Blue Haven Hotel** lounge bar (lamb, corned beef, and sometimes very good lasagne) at inexpensive to moderate prices.

In the Bantry Bay area, one of the prettiest places for a meal that runs a little above budget is **Ballylickey House,** Ballylickey (tel. 027/50071). You'll find the suites and apartments here described in Chapter XXXI as a Big Splurge, and the restaurant is just as special, but only counts as a Minor Splurge. Its window wall overlooks the flower-bordered swimming pool, its lounge bar area has a country house air, and the dining room décor is that of a garden room, with an open-flame hearth in the rear on which all main meals are cooked. Your meal gets off to a good start when your order is taken in the lounge before a cheerful open fire as you sip a before-dinner drink from the bar. As for the food, chef Peter Brady is personally involved with everything, from marketing to find the best and freshest ingredients to overseeing the preparation of every dish. His experienced hand (he came here after long service at Dublin's Hibernian and Berkley Court hotels) is evident everywhere, and your biggest problem may be to choose among seafood, lamb, beef, and other main courses offered in tempting variations. So far, I haven't sampled a one that wasn't outstanding! It's open seven days a week, and lunch, served from 12:30 to 2:30 p.m., will run IR£8 ($12.75) to IR£10 ($16), and dinner (from 7 to 10 p.m.) will cost between IR£11 ($17.50) and IR£18 ($28.75). This one has my highest recommendation.

A similar but slightly bigger splurge, a few miles from Bantry, is **Blairs Cove Restaurant,** Durrus (tel. 027/61127), the loving creation of Phillippe and Sabine De Mey, who have converted the stone stables of a 250-year-old mansion overlooking Dunmanus Bay in West Cork into a casually elegant restaurant. In summer, meals are served on the covered terrace overlooking the courtyard. Specialties are fresh seafood, lamb, and beef grilled over a big oak log fire in the dining room, and there's an exceptionally good wine list. Candlelight and soft piano music complete the romantic setting. Dinners run IR£15 ($24) to IR£20 ($32), plus 10% service charge, and advance reservations are essential. Hours are 7 to 9:30 p.m., and it's closed Sunday and Monday.

READERS' RESTAURANT SELECTIONS: "The **Barn Restaurant,** Lotamore, Glanmire, Cork, Co. Cork (tel. 021/866211), is a beautiful family-run local-type restaurant. They made us feel very welcome and could not have been nicer. The food was great and the whole experience was lovely. Don't miss the dessert cart!" (S. Likavec, Pittsburgh, Pa.). . . . "The **Pink Elephant,** Kilbrittain (between Kinsale and Glengarrif), Co. Cork (tel. 023/49608), has excellent food and a nice atmosphere with classical music playing softly on tape. Lovely scenery seen from the restaurant" (N. Rounsefell and S. Gilmore, Baton Rouge, La.).

3. THINGS TO SEE AND DO

YOUGHAL: Be sure to allow time to linger in Youghal (it means "yew wood" and is pronounced "yawl"), the picturesque fishing harbor and seaside resort that has distinctive American connections. Movie buffs will be interested to know that this is where *Moby Dick* was filmed back in 1954, and there are still tales told in the town of Gregory Peck, the movie folks, and the giant white rubber whale that twice broke its moorings and drifted out to sea (local fishermen went to the rescue).

More important in the annals of history, however, is the fact that this was where Sir Walter Raleigh took his first puff on a pipe of American tobacco and it was here that he put the first spud into Irish soil. So important do the Irish consider this last event that from June 30 to July 7, 1985, they held a grand celebration of the 400th anniversary of that planting. There were cookery demonstrations and competitions (centered, of course, around the lowly potato), a Sir Walter Raleigh playlet, an "official" potato cookbook, and such ancillary events as a sea angling competition and the official opening of the newly restored old town walls. Although you missed the festivities, you can still see the Elizabethan house that sheltered the Englishman while he lived in Youghal. But first, go to the **Tourist Office,** Market House, Market Square, and pick up the *Tourist Trail* booklet. It features a walking tour of the town. You might plan to have lunch at **Aherne's** (see "Where to Eat," above), and you should definitely stop by the **Moby Dick pub** (which dates back to 1798) for a pint and some conversation with the locals who frequent the place. If you're lucky, owner Paddy Linehan will be on hand and you might prevail on him to break out the scrapbook that chronicles his many years as a publican and souvenirs of the *Moby Dick* crew who adopted the pub as its local during filming.

Note: If, when traveling from Youghal to Cork city, you should find yourself in the little seaside village of **Ballycotton** (on the road from Midleton to Shanagarry), do stop in at the bar of the two-centuries-old **Ballycotton Hotel**— it's an authentic Irish country bar, run by the friendly O'Sullivan family, and its décor has been described by fellow American writer J. Herbert Silverman as "vintage country classic."

FOTA ISLAND HOUSE AND WILDLIFE PARK: Eight miles east of Cork city on the main Cork–Cobh road, Fota Island is a 790-acre estate that was once the property of the Earls of Barrymore. The splendid Regency-style manor house was built in the 1820s, and its elegant rooms, with their exquisite woodwork and molded ceilings, hold an impressive collection of 18th- and 19th-century furnishings. Don't miss the outstanding Irish landscape paintings, said to be the most extensive collection in existence. Nor should you miss the magnificent gardens and world-renowned arboretum, begun back in the 1820s. A 70-acre wildlife park is set among woods and lagoons, a fitting setting for the zebras, cheetahs, kangaroos, etc., that now call this home.

Fota House, Fota Island, Carrigtwohill, Co. Cork (tel. 021/812555), is open April through October, Monday through Saturday from 11 a.m. to 6 p.m. and on Sunday from 2 to 6 p.m. Other months, it's open only on Sunday and public holidays from 2 to 6 p.m. Admission is IR£2 ($3.25) for adults, IR£1 ($1.60) for senior citizens, and 50p (80¢) for children. Fota Wildlife Park (tel. 021/812678) is open April through October, Monday through Saturday from 10 a.m. to 5:15 p.m. and on Sunday from 11 a.m. to 5:15 p.m., with admission charges of IR£2.10 ($3.25) for adults, IR£1.60 ($2.50) for students, and IR£1 ($1.60) for children, senior citizens, and disabled persons; children under 3, free. No dogs are allowed inside the park.

Train service to Fota Island is available from Kent Station in Cork city. Call 021/503399 for times and fares.

BLARNEY: Now, about that magical stone out at **Blarney Castle**—back in the 1830s, Father Prout wrote of it:

There is a stone there
That whoever kisses
Oh! he never misses
To grow eloquent.
'Tis he may clamber
To a lady's chamber
Or become a member
Of Parliament.

All that blather about the stone started, it is said, when the first Queen Elizabeth tried to elicit the fealty of one Cormac MacCarthy, an Irish chieftain who was then Lord of Blarney. The silver-tongued MacCarthy smiled and flattered and nodded his head, all the while keeping firm hold on his *own* sovereignty until the Queen, in exasperation, is reputed to have exclaimed, "This is nothing but Blarney—what he says, he never means!" Which may be the first *recorded* instance of that lovely Irish talent for concealing a wily mind behind inoffensive words.

At any rate, if you would like to acquire a bit of Irish eloquence, Blarney Castle is six miles northwest of Cork (there's bus service from Cork for nondrivers), and the castle is open from 9 a.m. to 6 p.m. daily year round, except for Christmas Eve and Christmas Day. Adults pay IR£2.50 ($4); children, half that. Be warned, however, that kissing the stone involves having a guard hold your feet as you lie on your back, bend far back until you can reach the magic rock—and by the time you've gone through all those contortions, you'll have *earned* a silver tongue! Magic aside, however, the old castle ruin is well worth the trip in its own right, and there's a lovely sense of tranquility about the grounds filled with ancient trees. You can also visit nearby **Blarney Castle House** and the gardens.

Dedicated shoppers may want to make the trek out from Cork for no other reason than to visit the **Blarney Woolen Mills** (tel. 021/85280), which date from 1824 and today carry lovely Blarney Castle Knitwear and literally hundreds of high-quality Irish gift items. They're open seven days a week from 9 a.m. to 5:30 p.m., until 10 p.m. during summer months.

KINSALE: A scenic 18 miles south of Cork city, the fishing village of Kinsale has figured prominently in Ireland's history since it received its charter in 1333. Back in 1601 it looked as though the Irish might prevail against their English rulers when Don Juan d'Aguila arrived from Spain with a large force to assist the Irish rebels. Even though Mountjoy threw some 12,000 soldiers into a siege of the town, his position seemed doomed when Irish chieftains O'Donnell and O'Neill massed their forces behind the English, thus leaving them surrounded. History might well have been dramatically changed had it not been for an Irish soldier (reportedly in his cups) who let slip vital information to Mountjoy, enabling him to successfully rout both Irish and Spanish. South of town, you can visit the remains of **King James Fort,** the very one that housed the Spanish in 1601.

In **Summer Cove,** on the east side of the bay, there's quite a lot left of **Charles Fort,** built by the English in 1677 and in constant use as late as the 1920s. It sits high on a clifftop, and the view of Kinsale Harbour is spectacular. (Summer Cove, incidentally, is where you'll find the popular **Bullman pub,** a hangout mostly for the younger generation, which gets quite lively at night.) You really should make the six-mile drive south to the **Old Head of Kinsale,** where a 12th-century **castle** sits in ruins atop high cliffs overlooking the spot where the

Lusitania lies in its deep-water grave, sent there (along with some 1,500 souls) in 1915 by a German submarine.

Other Kinsale tag ends of history to look for include the town stocks (no longer used, of course, but kept on view as a reminder of the long-ago fate of lawbreakers). They're in **St. Multose Church,** whose congregation worships today in a structure erected in the 12th century. A ruined 12th-century **Carmelite Friary** and 15th-century **Desmond Castle** provide interesting poking around. One bit of interesting Kinsale miscellany: it is here that the town's womenfolk once wore the long, black hooded cape that's known as the **Kinsale Cloak**— you'll see it copied in rich fabrics to be used as an elegant evening cloak, but these days it is rare to see it on Kinsale streets.

If, by this time in your travels, you've become an Irish pub addict, there are two in Kinsale you won't want to miss. My personal favorite is the **Seanachai Pub** on Market Street. It's tucked away on a picture-postcard-pretty street, uses a second, phonetic spelling of its name (Shanakee), and is over 200 years old. Brothers Vincent and Gerard McCarthy, both musical, are genial hosts to resident locals who come in scores and warmly welcome all visitors. If time permits, I'll warrant you won't be able to go along to the Seanachai just *once*—it's as habit-forming as peanuts! In the two small front rooms, you'll find original old stone walls, open fires, and a marvelous painting of the legendary Irish storytellers for whom the pub is named. The brothers McCarthy have added a larger backroom by means of opening up equally old adjacent buildings, retaining stone walls and restoring ceiling beams and crumbling fireplaces. During summer months there's music seven days a week. And that means traditional Irish music as well as the beloved sing-along ballads, which can seem a bit trite in other settings but never in the Seanachai. Michael Buckley, the beloved All-Ireland accordion player, performs regularly, as do other local musicians who seem to enjoy the crack almost as much as the music. There's also dancing in the backroom on weekends all through the summer, but absolutely *nothing* could draw yours truly from those front rooms where music and talk and the brown stuff flow easily until one of the McCarthys sings out "Time, gentlemen, please."

The second noteworthy pub is **The Spaniard,** an atmospheric converted stable where fishnets seem right at home in the horse-stall cubby holes. This is where you'll find a homogenous crowd of international sportsmen here for the world-famous shark fishing, guitar-toting students, and a fair smattering of local characters.

If you'd like to get in some fishing, arrangements can be made through the **Trident Angling Centre,** Trident Hotel, Kinsale (tel. 021/774099).

WEST CORK: You *can*, of course, make a beeline from Cork city to Killarney, and it'll be a scenic dash indeed. However, if it's humanly possible, try to take the long way around by swinging down through West Cork, an area of which it has been written, "West Cork is bigger than Ireland." Well, an hour or two of gazing at its wild, unspoiled and magnificent vistas of coastline, tiny villages, sheer cliffs, and miles and miles of emptiness will go a long way toward convincing you of the truth of that statement! The ghosts of Ireland past who roam this ruggedly beautiful region include that of independence fighter Gen. Michael Collins, who was ambushed at a place called Beal na Blath in August of 1922 (there's a memorial marking the spot on the Dunmanway–Crookstown road). And in **Castle-townend,** surely the shades of two Victorian ladies named Edith Somerville and Violet Martin Ross still haunt the hallways and grounds of their beloved Drishane House, where together they wrote gently humorous tales of their Irish neighbors. The entire English-speaking world has chuckled over the misadventures recounted in their most famous work, *The Experiences of an Irish R.M.*, either in print or on the television screen.

Drive through **Clonakilty** (where Michael Collins was born), where castles dot the shores of the bay. Look for the **West Cork Craft Centre,** Leap (tel. 028/33217), where Claire Thompson and her husband have converted one room of their home overlooking Glandore Harbour into a showroom for locally made crafts. Claire will tell you about the talented people who produced the pottery, tweeds, glass objects, paintings, etc., and show you her own toys and crocheted collars. Incidentally, Claire asks that you just ring the bell if you find the door locked—she's only stepped into another part of the house and didn't hear you drive up. Stop for lunch or dinner or overnight at **Leap** (see "Accommodations," above). Don't miss **Baltimore**, with its ruined O'Driscoll castle brooding over the town from a high cliff and its tales of the horror in 1631 when Algerian pirates massacred all but 200 of the inhabitants and carried those off for a life of slavery in North Africa. Lovely **Sherkin Island,** with its ancient, ruined Franciscan abbey and peaceful, lonely coves, can be visited by motorboat from Baltimore during the summer—for schedules and rates, phone Mr. D. Sheehy at Baltimore 25. Pass through villages like **Ballydehob**; linger a while at the picturesque fishing village of **Schull** and visit its waterfront; from Schull, travel the 18 miles to **Mizen Head** at land's end, through **Goleen,** with its sandy strand, **Crookhaven,** and around **Barley Cove**; return to Schull along Dunmanus Bay on the other side of **Mount Gabriel,** which rises 1,339 feet. It's a detour you'll long remember!

BANTRY AND GLENGARRIFF:
The little town of Bantry (named for an ancient Celtic chieftain) sits at the head of lovely **Bantry Bay,** surrounded by hills. The 21-mile-long inlet of the sea apparently had great appeal to the French, who twice (in 1689 and 1796) selected it for attempted naval invasions of Ireland. You'll see fishing boats tied up right at the foot of the town, and if you elect to stay over here, your B&B hostess will be able to arrange a trip on the water with Ken Minehan. During the summer, hour-and-a-half cruises of the bay take you past Whiddy Island and its oil terminal and castle ruins. Sea-angling trips can also be arranged. For schedules and rates, contact Ken Minehan (tel. 027/50318).

Bantry House, on the southern outskirts of the town, sits in a magnificent demesne and is the ancestral home of the Earls of Bantry. Beautifully landscaped lawns and gardens slope downward from the front of the Georgian mansion that looks out over the bay. Inside there is an impressive collection of European antiques, paintings, sculptures, and other items that caught the fancy of globe-trotting earls over the centuries. A tea room and a craft shop are open during summer months, and admission charges for the house are IR£2 ($3.25) for adults, IR£1 ($1.60) for students and senior citizens, and 50p (80¢) for children (under 6, free). There's no charge to visit the grounds. Newly added are B&B rooms with private baths at reasonable prices. Open daily year round.

There are lovely scenic drives and walks around Bantry, one of the most spectacular being to the top of Seskin Mountain, where there's a layby from which there are incredible views of Bantry Bay. The antiquity of the region's settlement is attested to by many stone circles, standing stones, and cairns dating to the Bronze Age.

If you're in Bantry in the evening, there's usually ballad singing and dancing at **Crowley's Bar** in the summer, and the **Bantry Bay Hotel** has entertainment every night (special Irish nights during the summer).

Shopping Note: **Philip J. Dix & Co. Ltd.,** on New Street (tel. 027/50112), has an exceptionally good range of Waterford crystal, Belleek, Donegal porcelain, Irish-made pewter, silver, and a host of other quality giftwear.

Between Bantry and Glengarriff, on the edge of the little town of **Ballylickey,** nestled in a curve of the road (on the side nearest the sea), if you look carefully you'll see an unpretentious sign reading "Artist's Studio, Paintings of Irish Scenes." That modest sign is little indication of the fine paintings you'll find inside **Raymond Klee's studio** (tel. 027/50157), which adjoins his home. The Welsh-born artist has lived and worked all over the world and has won such coveted awards as those bestowed by the French Salon and the Fine Arts Guild (in England), but has chosen to settle with his beautiful and talented wife, Florence, in this beauty spot and devote his time and his art to depicting the very scenes that have won your own heart since you first put foot on Irish soil. His landscape canvases are remarkable in that they capture the elusive colors and sweeping majesty of Irish skies as well as the earthbound beauties most often painted by other artists. Sunsets over a dune-rimmed strand, storm skies that set fishermen scurrying to bring curraghs to safety ashore, and graceful configurations of sun-touched clouds are there to perpetuate your memories of those same scenes. Stone-enclosed fishing harbors and mountain stretches are other subjects, and hanging on the walls of his studio are portraits of that craggy Irish farmer and fisherman you were talking to just last night over a friendly pint. Surprisingly, prices run from just under IR£60 ($96) to just under IR£100 ($160), and there are sizes small enough to wrap securely and take back home easily, as well as larger canvases that might well become the focal point of a Stateside room. Whether or not you buy a painting, do stop by to see these marvelous works and chat with an interesting and talented artist.

Glengarriff is set in a beautiful, mountain-ringed cove on Bantry Bay, and it's worth a stop at some of the craft shops you'll see lining the streets. I've found good values here over the years, but none as good as those at **Donal Houlihan's Handcraft Shop,** Glengarriff (tel. 027/63038). The shop is on the corner just across from the road that turns up a hill to go to Killarney. And in addition to the small showroom out front, there's a large store out back up a little hill that carries lovely knitwear, mohair, cashmere, linen, and caps, gloves, and scarves. The most outstanding buys here, however, are the tweeds which Donal weaves in the shed back of the shop. You're welcome to step in to see the loom in action if your timing is right. Not only are his tweeds beautiful blends of soft Irish colors, but prices are some of the best in the country. Another excellent shopping spot here is **Nicole's Boutique** at Falvey's (tel. 027/63043), where you can choose hand-knits to be made up to your own colors and designs.

You're not likely to get out of Glengarriff without taking the boat trip out to **Garnish Island,** about a mile offshore—bold boatmen have been known to stop cars in mid-road to hawk the trip. As in Killarney, however, I urge you to listen to their good-humored pitch and let yourself be hawked. The lovely little island is a riot of subtropical plants in gorgeous bloom, and there's a landscaped Italian garden you shouldn't miss. George Bernard Shaw loved the place and wrote portions of *St. Joan* here. The cost is nominal, and both time and money are well spent.

GOUGANE BARRA: One of the most beautiful spots in the country, Gougane Barra (which means "St. Finbar's Cleft"), is a still, dark, romantic lake a little northeast of the Pass of Keimaneigh (well signposted on the Macroom–Glengarriff road). The River Lee rises here, and all around are deeply wooded mountains. St. Finbar founded a monastery here, supposedly on the small island connected by a causeway which now holds a tiny chapel (nothing remains of the good saint's 6th-century community) and eight small circular cells, dating to the early 1700s, as well as a modern chapel. Its isolation and connection with St.

Finbar made this a natural refuge for Irish worshippers during Penal Law days when they were forbidden to hold mass and turned to the out-of-doors for their services. Today Gougane Barra is a national forest park, and there are signposted walks and drives through the wooded hills. There's a small admission charge per car to enter the park.

CHAPTER XVII

KILLARNEY AND ITS LAKES

□ □ □

Its ancient Irish name is Cill Airne (Church of the Sloe); it was aptly described by the poet Moore as "Heaven's Reflex"; and *Irish Echo* columnist Joe Murphy has written, with awe akin to reverence, "Assuredly, he or she who has not seen Kerry or Killarney knows not the beauty of nature." The sheer perfection of that beauty has defied the best efforts of many a writer, poet, and artist to capture its essence, and your first glimpse of the lakes in their magnificent setting is certain to leave you wonderstruck. Nor will that wonder be diminished by repeated viewings, for the mercurial nature of this splendid landscape colors its g⟨andeur with whimsical, ever-shifting nuances of sun and cloud and mist.

A broad valley holds the three main lakes, with Lough Leane (the Lower Lake) closest to Killarney and separated from the Middle Lake by Muckross Peninsula. It was on one of its 30 islands that dedicated monks faithfully recorded Irish history from the 11th to the 13th century in the *Annals of Innisfallen*. The Middle Lake covers 680 acres and holds four islands, and is connected to the small, narrow Upper Lake and its eight islands by a broad river called the Long Range. Each lake has several streams flowing into it, and the River Laune connects them to the Atlantic. Their waters reflect the shimmering reflections of birch and oak and mountain ash and arbutus, while hovering over all are the peaks of some of Ireland's finest mountains: Macgillycuddy's Reeks, with Carrantuohill, the country's highest mountain at 3,414 feet; the Tomies; the Mangerton range; and Torc. As a Killarney jarvey once said to me, "'Tis a grand sight, one of God's blessings."

And what of Killarney? Well, it was a quiet little country market town until a visiting Englishman named Arthur Young "discovered" it in the 18th century

and told the rest of the world about this natural beauty spot. Since then, of course, the rest of the world has arrived on Killarney's doorstep in droves, demanding accommodations, eateries, guides, entertainment, and a good deal more than a quiet little country market town could be expected to provide.

Right here, I'd like to dispel what seems to be a very popular myth about Killarney. It *is,* I grant you, more "commercial" than any other town in Ireland, but—and this is what I'd like to put to rest—if this is a "tourist trap," then the world could do with a few more like it! *Sure,* there are jarveys lined up ad infinitum, each hawking his own jaunting car ride. But no matter which car you climb aboard, you can do so in the sure knowledge that fees are carefully controlled (so you won't be "ripped off") and you'll hear at least one good story (like the one about the lad who plunged into the Devil's Punchbowl and was never heard from until his poor mother got a postcard from Australia asking would she please send along his clothes).

As for accommodations, Killarney has an abundance of high-quality, low-priced B&Bs and guesthouses as well as some pretty elegant luxury hotels whose prices are high but not exorbitant. Meals can be in any number of inexpensive and charming restaurants, in moderately priced establishments that bring near-gourmet dishes to table, or you can be as lavish as you please in the upper price range in one of the hotels. Shopping is good in Killarney, with competitive prices, well-stocked shops, and a number of craft workshops. As for entertainment, there are good singing pubs and hotel cabarets (and if your timing is right, the Killarney races). Killarney has also bred some of the best—and most entertaining—sightseeing guides in the world.

What I'm trying to get across is that you'll get your money's worth in Killarney. And you'll get it from some of Ireland's friendliest, most ebullient citizens. From your landlady to your waiter or waitress to the clerk behind a shop counter to your jarvey or boatman, everyone seems delighted that you've come and can't *wait* to see that you have a good time.

1. ORIENTATION

Killarney is a small town, easy to find your way around. **Main Street** is its chief artery and becomes **High Street** at its northern end. **New Street** runs to the west of Main Street, and **Plunkett Street** (which becomes **College Street**) runs east.

2. USEFUL INFORMATION

The **Tourist Office** is in the Town Hall on Main Street (tel. 064/31633), open from 9 a.m. to 8 p.m. weekdays, 10 a.m. to 1 p.m. on Monday through Saturday from July to September, and 9:15 a.m. to 5:30 other months. . . . The **bus and train station** is off East Avenue (across from the Great Southern Hotel). For all bus and train **information,** call 064/31067. . . . The **General Post Office** is on New Street, with hours of 9 a.m. to 5:30 p.m. every day but Sunday. . . . **Taxi** ranks are at the railway station and in College Square, and taxis are unmetered (tel. 31331 for hire). . . . There's no local bus service, but Bus Eireann runs several good day trips to nearby locations. . . . The **telephone prefix** for the area is **064.**

3. ACCOMMODATIONS

As I said above, Killarney is fairly broken out with good, inexpensive places to stay—you'll even find two hotels listed, both of which are slightly above our budget range, but so slightly as to be acceptable, and both so centrally located I felt you should know about them. Some of the "Out of Town" places are within reasonable walking distance of town, though not with heavy luggage, and if you're coming by bus or train, those under the "In Town" heading will be most convenient.

Note: Prices shown below are those in effect in 1989—expect them to be higher in 1990.

In Town

HOSTELS. Killarney's hostel, **Aghadoe House** (tel. 064/31240), is one of the best in the country. An impressive brick mansion set on its own grounds, it's about three miles from the town center, with a courtesy bus from the railway station. It is absolutely necessary to book in advance during July and August, and because many hostelers are hikers as well, the wardens here (Mr. and Mrs. Claffey) ask that you be reminded that the mountains in the area can be quite dangerous and if you intend hiking or climbing them, you should be sure to notify the Claffeys of your intended route.

The **Four Winds International Hostel**, 43 New St., Killarney (tel. 064/33094), is one of the nicer things to happen in Killarney in recent years. It provides comfortable, attractive, and inexpensive lodgings right in the center of town. There are sleeping accommodations for 80 in bunk-bedded dormitories, as well as four private rooms and sites for 14 tents, plus a lounge, dining room, and kitchen. Guides and maps to local outdoor activities are provided, and the 1989 rates are IR£4 ($6.50) and IR£6 ($9.50) per person.

BED-AND-BREAKFAST. Bridie and Don Long, of **Wind-Way,** New Road (tel. 064/32835), are young, charming, and enthusiastic about helping their guests get the fullest enjoyment from their Killarney stay. Their Old English sheepdogs, Kojac and his girlfriend, Tamiami (named after a happily remembered Florida trip), share in their hospitality. The four guest rooms are nicely done up in bright colors, with a bit of décor whimsey in some. All have private facilities. The Linden House restaurant (see "Where to Eat") is just across the road, a great convenience for the evening meal. There's central heat and a private car park. Bed-and-breakfast rates are IR£11 ($17.50). Highly recommended.

The **Hibernian,** 21 New St. (tel. 064/31258), is the three-story home of Maura Brosnan and her charming family. Mrs. Brosnan happily helps you book tours by jaunting car, coach, boat, or bike. The five guest rooms are comfortably furnished, and the location couldn't be more convenient. Rates are IR£9 ($14.50) per person, with a one-third discount for children.

Also very convenient, **The Orchard,** 65 New St. (tel. 064/31887), has eight bedrooms. Mrs. Joan O'Donoghue heads the friendly staff, all of whom take a personal interest in their guests. B&B rates are IR£9 ($14.50).

Marie and Sean O'Brien, Knockcullen, New Road (tel. 064/33915), have a sparkling-clean, two-story home on this tree-lined street. The four guest rooms are all attractively furnished, and Marie's table is laden with fresh and healthy fare —she even caters to vegetarians at breakfast. B&B rates are IR£9.50 ($15.25).

Mrs. O'Mahony, **Mystical Rose,** Woodlawn Road, Killarney, Co. Kerry (tel. 064/31453), is the friendly hostess of this bungalow with its beautiful rose garden which guests are free to use. The house is located near the Killarney lake district and she will arrange tours for guests who want it. She has three nice, clean rooms and they all have handbasins. Her rate is IR£9 ($14.50) for bed-and-breakfast and there is a 33% reduction for children. Open March to October.

Mrs. Connell, **St. Anthony's Villa,** Cork Road, Killarney, Co. Kerry (tel. 064/31534), is the friendly hostess of this attractive, modern bungalow which is convenient to town and the bus and railway station. She is very helpful and will arrange tours around Killarney for anyone who may want it. There are three bedrooms, all with private facilities and handbasins. The rate for bed-and-breakfast is IR£10 ($16), and there is a 25% reduction for children. Open March to November.

GUESTHOUSES. Perhaps the most popular in-town guesthouse with readers over the years is **Linden House,** New Road (tel. 064/31379). Set on this quiet residential street, just one block down from Main Street, its location is ideal, but much more appealing than location are the Knoblauch family, who have won special praise for the quality of their lodgings and the warmth of their hospitality. There's something of an old-world small-inn air about the three-story stucco house with many touches of wood, and bedrooms here are exceptionally comfortably and attractively appointed, all with private bath. There's central heat and one of the best moderately priced restaurants in Killarney, with a large local following (see "Where to Eat"). Popular with traveling Irish as well as tourists, Linden House is one place you must be certain to reserve ahead. Rates are IR£12 ($19.25) single, and IR£10 ($16) per person sharing, for bed-and-breakfast, and there's a 25% reduction for children. Closed from mid-December to mid-January.

The **Gardens,** Countess Road (tel. 064/31147), owned by Mary and Tom O'Reilly, is a charming place set in private grounds very convenient to the railway station and the town center. In the main two-story building, 20 bedrooms are nicely appointed, and all have a private bath. A boon to many travelers, a dozen are on the ground floor. There's central heat and good parking. Rates are IR£12 ($19.25) per person sharing, with a 25% discount for children under 10.

HOTELS. The three-story, distinctively Irish **Arbutus Hotel,** College Street (tel. 064/31037), once was favored by Franciscan monks when they came into town from their mountain meditations. For over 60 years it has been owned and operated by the Buckley family, and the present generation continues the hospitality that's been handed down. There's an old-fashioned air about the place, enhanced by such touches as lots of etched glass and stained glass, a fireplace in the lounge, and an intimate lounge-bar presided over by the amiable Dennis, who's been here many years, as has his wife, Sheila. I am particularly fond of the cozy dining room. All 40 bedrooms have private baths, and the rate for bed-and-breakfast is IR£18 ($28.75) in high season, IR£16 ($25.50) in low season. If you plan to use Killarney as a base for as long as a week, ask about special rates: *Note:* Connecting to the Arbutus is a low-priced coffeeshop called Pat's that offers very good value.

Owner Dermot O'Callaghan has refurbished the bar and restaurant of the small 14-room **Fáilté Hotel,** College Street (tel. 064/31893 or 33404), to make it an extremely popular gathering place for both locals and tourists for good, inexpensive meals. It specializes in fresh seafood and juicy steaks, with all meals personally supervised by Dermot's wife, Eileen. Bed-and-breakfast rates are IR£13 ($20.75) single, IR£22 ($35.25) double. Add 10% service charge.

Out of Town

BED-AND-BREAKFAST. The large, modern bungalow that is **Alpine Heights,** Gap of Dunloe, Co. Kerry (tel. 064/44284), is the home of young, pretty Teresa Ferris and her family, which includes five engaging children. Less than a half mile from the Gap of Dunloe, this pretty home, set behind white gateposts in a vibrantly green lawn, features guest rooms decorated in soft pastels (some with showers), built-in wardrobes, a bright, sunny dining room, central heating, and superb views of green fields and lofty mountains. The family-oriented Mrs. Ferris keeps a crib on hand for visiting youngsters. B&B rates are IR£10 ($16), with a 30% discount for children. Open from Easter through October.

Shillelagh House, Knockasarnett, Aghadoe, Killarney (tel. 064/31898 or 33583), is a modern two-story home about a mile and a half from the town center. Mrs. Mary O'Connor is its gracious hostess. The pretty guest rooms have handbasins and quilted headboards for the beds. There's a lounge with TV, and full Irish breakfasts are served in the bright dining room. Rates for bed-and-breakfast are IR£10.50 ($16.75).

Gallan (it means "standing stone"), Mangerton Road, Muckross, Killarney, Co. Kerry (tel. 064/31108 or 31570), is the domain of a very special family, Siubhan and Frank Lewis and their five lovely children. Their home sits amid spectacular scenery at the foot of Mangerton Mountain and overlooks the national park. Torc Mountain is nearby, and windows look out over the Killarney lakes. Each of the four guest rooms has a picture window from which to drink in all that beauty, and both lounge and patio open up marvelous panoramic views of the lakes, mountains, forest, and pastureland. The entire Lewis family are avid walkers and bikers, with intimate knowledge of the area and helpful advice and maps for visitors. Three rooms have a double and a single bed, one has two doubles. Siubhan is also happy to serve an evening meal with advance notice for IR£8 ($12.80). B&B rates are IR£9 ($14.50). Open April through October.

Marian House, Woodlawn Road (tel. 064/31275), is located just off Muckross Road and sits atop a small hill that looks out onto the mountains. It's a centrally heated, two-story house with six prettily decorated guest rooms. Mrs. Eileen Lucey is the hostess, and her B&B rates are IR£10 ($16), with a 25% discount for children. Open year round.

Mrs. Kathleen Doherty is the extremely helpful hostess of **White House,** Lissivigeen Cross, Killarney, Co. Kerry (tel. 064/32207), a luxurious, modern house with a beautiful view of the mountains. Located just two miles outside Killarney, it is convenient to shopping, restaurants, etc. There are four bedrooms, three with private facilities and all with handbasins. An evening meal is available with advance notice. The rate for bed-and-breakfast is IR£10 ($16) and dinner costs IR£8 ($12.75); 50% reduction for children. Open May through September.

FARMHOUSES. A beautiful 200-year-old country home, **Carriglea House,** Muckross Road (tel. 064/31116), is set on a rise overlooking the lakes a mile and a half from town. From the sweeping front lawn, approached by a tree-lined curving avenue, the view takes in the Lower Lake and Purple, Torc, and Mangerton Mountains. Marie and Michael Beasley own this working dairy farm and take great pleasure in helping guests plan their holiday time in Killarney. The lovely old centrally heated house has spacious rooms furnished with many antiques and tastefully decorated in restful colors. Particularly noteworthy is the dining room's chandelier of gold, blue, and pink porcelain. In addition to guest rooms in the main house, there are several in the adjoining coachhouse, whose entrance is paved with stone from Clare. One large coachhouse room has a bay window overlooking the front lawn. All guest rooms have handbasins, and some have private bath or shower. Rates for bed-and-breakfast are IR£11 ($17.50), with an additional IR£1.50 ($2.50) per person for rooms with private facilities.

Mrs. Kearney, **Gap View Farm,** Firies, Killarney, Co. Kerry (tel. 066/64378), is the delightful hostess of this large 18th-century farmhouse with its lovely views of the Gap of Dunloe and the Kerry mountains. The house is centrally heated as well as having turf fires, and fresh farm foods are served at every meal.

The house is eight miles outside Killarney and has a garden which guests can use. There are six lovely bedrooms and they all have handbasins. The rate for bed-and-breakfast is IR£10 ($16) and dinner costs IR£9.50 ($15.25); 40% reduction for children. Open Easter to October.

A GUESTHOUSE. Three miles from town on the main Ring of Kerry road, **Loch Lein,** Fossa (tel. 064/31260), is the domain of the delightful Kathleen Coffey. It is set in green lawns sloping down to the Lower Lake, and is approached via a country lane that's signposted on the main road just past the golf course (on your left as you approach from Killarney). The modern L-shaped guesthouse holds a dozen guest rooms that are exceptionally large and well furnished. All have handbasins and six have private baths or showers. Natural-wool bedspreads were woven in Kerry mills. There's a TV lounge with a fireplace and a bright, window-walled dining room. As attractive and sparkling as is the house, it is outshone by Mrs. Coffey, a small, pixie-like lady who is an accomplished conversationalist and storyteller. Her five sons and five daughters are all grown, but most live nearby and at least one is usually in attendance, as interested in guests' welfare as their mother. The family has been in this area for generations, giving the Coffeys a treasure trove of local legends they're only too happy to pass on to you, very special mementos of your Irish holiday. B&B rates begin at IR£11 ($17.50), with a 25% discount for children. There's central heating and a graveled car park.

READERS' ACCOMMODATIONS SELECTIONS: "Mrs. M. Hickey, 70 Countess Grove, Countess Road, Killarney, Co. Kerry (tel. 064/32651), has a suburban home just five minutes' walk from town. The rooms are very nice and you receive a generous breakfast" (Helen Peterson). . . . "Dromin, Lewis Road, is the very lovely home of Mrs. Mary O'Driscoll Harman. It's only a short walk to the main street and has off-street parking" (E. Henritzy, New Orleans, La.). . . . "Bridge View, Mill Road, is a quiet, clean, and comfortable small bungalow. Mrs. O'Shea is most pleasant and was kind enough to give us an early breakfast so we could be on the road early" (Gary Shaw, Rochester, N.Y.). . . . "The Silver Spruce, New Road (tel. 064/31376), is a modern, attractive, and immaculate place, and both Mr. and Mrs. Sheehan take a personal interest in their guests" (Agnes Dunne, Manitowoc, Wis.). . . . "We enjoyed staying at Hilltop Villa, Loreto Road (tel. 064/31084), with Mrs. Breda O'Sullivan. We had a spotless, comfortable room and the O'Sullivans were very helpful and friendly" (Mrs. Richard Danckert, Pittsfield, Mass.).

"Mrs. O'Donoghue, at Cum A Ciste, Cork Road (tel. 064/31271), is charming and helpful, and the modern house has central heating. Breakfast is served beautifully on bone china and silver" (Dr. J. M. King, Greenville, S.C.). . . . "Mr. and Mrs. Brosnan, Woodlawn Road (tel. 064/31328), couldn't have been friendlier. Their farmhouse is about a mile from town and the lovely rooms look out onto green fields" (Linda and John Penkalski, N. Arlington, N.J.). . . . "We stayed four days instead of one with Mrs. Noreen O'Sullivan, Lios Na Manach Farmhouse, off Mill Road, Killarney, Co. Kerry (tel. 064/31283), and we cannot say enough about her hospitality and the tranquility of her farm" (D. and S. Bissonnette, New York, N.Y.). . . . "Moira and Jim O'Gorman, Gorman's Farm House, Tralee Road, Killaney, Co. Kerry (tel. 064/33149), are two of the loveliest people you would want to meet. All rooms have private facilities, and the food was outstanding, as was its location. They also have horses for free use by their guests" (N. Morgan, San Bruno, Calif.).

Author's Note: Space does not permit full comments on the following, all of which have been enthusiastically endorsed by readers: Mrs. Noreen Landers' **Ardrinane,** Ballydowney, Killarney (tel. 064/31647); Mrs. O'Meara's **Breffni,** Cork Road (tel. 064/31413); **Kilgrove,** off Muckross Road (tel. 064/31472), the Dalys, owners; **St. Rita's Villa,** Mill Road (tel. 054/31517), home of Mrs. Peggie Cronin; Mrs. Dempsey's **Eagle House,** College Street (tel. 064/31351); Mrs. Mary Casey's **Direen House,** Tralee Road (tel. 064/31676); and **Woodlands,** Ballydowney, Killarney (tel. 064/31467), Mrs. Evelyn Moynihan, hostess.

4. WHERE TO EAT

The Laurels pub on Main Street serves terrific pub grub in old-style surroundings of low, beamed ceilings and rustic wooden tables. The food is good, the company congenial, and the "crack" (talk) stimulating.

Sheila's Restaurant, 75 High St. (tel. 064/31270), is a dark-green front and lots of light-blond wood inside. Good, inexpensive lunches (sandwiches, soups, quiches, and three-course hot meals) are served from noon to 3 p.m. at prices of IR£2.50 ($4) to IR£6 ($9.50). Four-course dinners of seafood, steaks, etc., will run IR£11 ($17.50), including wine, served from 6 to 10:30 p.m. Wine is always available by the glass or bottle.

The **Old Kentucky Restaurant and Bar,** New Street (tel. 064/31645), has a large menu of grills, salads, sandwiches, and snacks. There's also a children's menu and the Special Tourist Menu from noon to 3 p.m. Prices will run around IR£3 ($4.75) for lunch, IR£6 ($9.50) for dinner, and hours are 10 a.m. to 10 p.m. daily.

One of the best places in town for a delicious, home-cooked evening meal is **Linden House,** New Road (tel. 064/31379), described above under "Accommodations." Franz Knoblauch is German-born, married to the lovely Irish Anne, and together with their family they have created a Bavarian-type dining room of exposed brick and wooden booths. It's a cozy place, very popular with locals, and the menu is good, solid family fare. Son Peter supervises the spotless kitchen and insists on the freshest ingredients. Dinner will run about IR£10 ($16), and in July and August it's a good idea to book ahead—other months you'll usually have only a few minutes' wait at the most. There is also an à la carte menu available. Incidentally, residents are served a "House Special" menu at 6 p.m. at the reduced price of IR£8 ($12.75), and the restaurant is closed to nonresidents on Monday and from December through January. Highly recommended.

Another very special place to eat is **Foley's Steak & Seafood Restaurant,** 23 High St. (tel. 064/31217). This was a coaching inn many years ago, and there's an old-style air about the front bar lounge, where a fireplace adds to the coziness. The pretty backroom is more formal, decorated with soft shades of rose and green. Carol and Denis Hartnett are the family team responsible for turning out superb meals with the highest standards. Seafood is a specialty, and Carol (who does the cooking) uses only the freshest fish. Denis cuts all their steaks and buys only Kerry mountain lamb, using nothing but centerline cuts. Actually, this is a full-service eatery, serving all three meals (breakfast from 8 a.m.), and bar food is available from noon to 2:30 p.m. Lunch prices run about IR£7.50 ($12) and main courses on the dinner menu are in the IR£7.50 ($12) to IR£14 ($22.50) range. The Tourist Menu is available from noon to 3 p.m. Dinner hours are 5 to 10:30 p.m., and there's a pianist on Friday, Saturday, and Sunday nights during the summer. Open seven days, and reservations are advised in high season.

Kiely's Bar and Restaurant, College Street (tel. 064/31656), is a large, attractive place, and the bargain here is the carvery lunch that's served here daily from noon to 3 p.m. for under IR£5 ($8). There's a full à la carte and dinner menu from 6 to 9 p.m. at moderate prices.

Big Splurge

The **Strawberry Tree,** Plunkett Street (tel. 064/32688), exudes a warm, pubby feeling, as well it might since for well over a century that's exactly what occupied these premises. Frosted glass and the small bar up front attest to its former life, and comfortable sofas and low stools are grouped around the cheery fireplace just opposite the bar. It's a perfect spot to have a before-dinner drink and study the menu. You do, in fact, place your order from this oasis of warmth before being seated in the small dining room in the back done up in soft, restful pastels.

Owner Evan Doyle, who came to Killarney from a restaurant in Clifden, has produced an interesting menu using Irish fish, fowl, meats, and farm produce prepared with a slight French flavor. For starters, you might try baked St. Killian (Irish farmhouse cream cheese baked in filo pastry accompanied by a raspberry sauce) or "A Symphony of Smoked Delicasies" (smoked filet of venison, breast of duck, eel, salmon, and trout, with a chutney of fresh mangoes). Roast quail and chicken with pan-fried breast of woodpigeon with a sauce of strawberry vinegar and red currant is one of the more unusual entrees, and there are several fresh fish dishes, sirloin steak, pork, and even vegetable purses (pastry filled with diced root vegetables served over three rices surrounding a mousse of three vegetables and accompanied by a sorrel sauce). A standout among desserts is the "chocolate box," a luscious creation of rich chocolate cake, ice cream, and fresh cream that comes in the form of a box of chocolates. Portions are ample but not overwhelming, and presentation is well nigh perfect. Dinner from the à la carte menu will average around IR£16 ($25.60), and advance reservations are strongly advised, since the Strawberry Tree is small (only 26 seatings) and extremely popular. Light lunches are served from 12:30 to 2:30 p.m., and dinner hours are 6:30 to 10:30 p.m. Closed mid-January to mid-February. Highly recommended.

READERS' RESTAURANT SELECTIONS: "The **Sugan Kitchen,** Michael Collins Place (tel. 064/33104), was by far the friendliest and warmest eating place we discovered. As Irish songs played in the background, hostess Margaret O'Shea made us feel like part of the family. The small dining room of just seven tables and the country décor are homey, and traditional Irish and vegetarian portions are plentiful. The Sugan Kitchen is truly an extraordinary dining discovery" (Cathy and Paul Monsees, Washington, D.C.). . . . "I highly recommend **The Whaler** restaurant in the International Hotel, where dinners are moderately priced and specialize in the freshest seafood" (L. Won, San Francisco, Calif.). . . . "We highly recommend **Dingle's Restaurant.** What a treat! The food was excellent, and the owners made us feel we were dining at home" (A. Hatmaker, Glenely, Md.).

5. THINGS TO SEE AND DO

Killarney's wealth of natural beauties can be a bit overwhelming as you face the prospect of trying to get around to see as many as you have time for. Not to worry, the jarveys and boatmen and coach-tour people have it all worked out for you—their routes will take you to the high points, and although it is perfectly possible to wander around on your own, this is one time I highly recommend that you plan the budget around at least one or two of the guided tours, whether by jaunting car, boat, or coach. Fares are reasonable, and the guides know and love the scenery through which they escort you, embellishing every spot with the folklore that will make the experience even more memorable. After you've done that, I recommend just as highly that you go back on your own to linger and savor all that beauty and contemplate the things your guide has shared with you. The two experiences make a soul-restoring combination. Take time, too, to visit St. Mary's Cathedral, a splendid Gothic structure with interesting stained-glass windows. Then cross the road and commune with nature again in Knockreer Estate.

Note: In 1988, personally conducted walking tours of Killarney town left from the Tourist Office daily except Sunday for IR£2 ($3.25). Check with the Tourist Office to see if they are still available.

Seeing the Lakes

BY JAUNTING CAR. Uniform rates and routes are set each year for the season, and while the 1989 rates are not available as this is written, those listed are 1988 prices, which you can expect to rise by only a small amount, if at all. No need to stop by the Tourist Office to make arrangements—you'll be hassled by the long line of drivers down the street, and my advice is to look them all over and pick the Irish face and twinkling eye that tickles your fancy most. If you're strong-willed enough to hold out all the way to the last jaunting car, you're in for some entertaining conversation during the course of your "window shopping." In high season it's a good idea to reserve your seat on the wonderfully colorful trip the evening before you plan to go.

If the budget can possibly be stretched to include the **all-day trip,** you'll go home with glorious memories worth far more than the IR£20 ($32) fare. The day begins about 10 a.m., when you hop into a jaunting car, tucking a woolly car rug around your knees if there's a chill in the air (or you may be transported by bus). Then it's off at a trot to **Kate Kearney's Cottage** (which is not the traditional thatched cottage you might expect from its name, but a giftshop and snackbar) at the mouth of the **Gap of Dunloe.** Next comes a transfer to either a pony's back (for experienced riders only) or a pony trap to make the six-mile trek through wild, silent walls of granite so awesome you'll speak in whispers, if at all. Along the way there are still, mysterious lakes on either side, and it is in Black Lough that legend says the last snake in Ireland was drowned by the good St. Patrick—which explains, no doubt, why no fish have ever inhabited its depths. Lunch is a picnic at the end of the Gap (everyone brings his own) before meeting your boatman at the **Upper Lake.** The afternoon is a watery tour of all three lakes, ending when your boat docks at **Ross Castle,** where your jaunting car waits to return you to town about 5:30 p.m. A lovely day, and unrivaled by any other in my own travel experience.

Shorter tours (allow a half day for most) take you through the Killarney Estate along the lake shores to **Muckross Abbey,** home to Franciscan monks from 1448 until Cromwell ordered it burned in 1652. There's time to wander around **Muckross House** and its gardens, then on to view the lovely **Torc waterfall** before returning to town. The 1988 charge was IR£18 ($28.75). For the same fare, you can choose the heights of **Aghadoe Hill** for a breathtaking view of mountains, lakes, and the town below. A church and round tower date back to the 7th century. The return to town is by the way of the **Lower Lake** and **Ross Castle.** Various other routes are available at fares of IR£8 ($12.80) to IR£12 ($19.20).

BY BOAT. Killarney's boatmen are legendary for their skillful navigation of the lakes and their store of wondrous tales. Their numbers are also diminishing, but arrangements can be made for a day on the lakes with a party of four at fares that are set each year for the season. If you want to do the rowing yourself, rowboats are available at **Ross Castle** and **Muckross House;** call Torc Travel (tel. 064/32911) for rates.

The watercoach *Lily of Killarney* leaves the Ross Castle slipway several times daily to cruise the Lower Lake, with shuttle-bus service to the departure point available from Dero's Tours, Main Street (tel. 064/31251). The glass-enclosed cabin is completely heated, and there's a commentary on the history and legends of the lake as you pass Innisfallen Island, O'Sullivan's Cascade, Tomies Mountain, Darby's Garden, the old copper mines, Library Point, and many other points of interest. Fares in 1988 were IR£4 ($6.50) for adults, half that for children, and IR£10 ($16) for a family with two children. To book, contact Killarney Watercoach Cruises Ltd., 3 High St. (tel. 31068).

ON YOUR OWN. A delightful day can be spent biking along the **Lower Lake** and through the **national park** (entrance just off Muckross Road) or along the lakeside paths in **Ross Castle Western Demesne.** Cars are prohibited in both, and you'll feel very close to Mother Nature as you wheel along wooded paths, with stops to contemplate the timeless waters of the lake. Bicycles may be rented from **O'Callaghan's** on College Street, **O'Neill's** on Plunkett Street, and **O'Sullivan's** on Pawn Officer Lane, off High Street.

If you're an experienced rider and fairly fit (important if you don't want to cart sore muscles around the rest of Ireland), horses are available for day treks from the **Killarney Riding School** in Ballydowney (tel. 064/31686). They may also be hired at the **Gap of Dunloe** for the two-hour ride to the top of the Gap and back, but as sure-footed as are these steeds, you want to be a good rider before attempting it. Hikers who prefer the exhilaration of walking over the Gap should allow a minimum of three hours.

Muckross House

Set in some 11,500 acres of parkland and surrounded by marvelously landscaped gardens, the Tudor-style Muckross House dates back to 1843, when it was built by Henry Arthur Herbert, a wealthy Kerry M.P. Americans bought it in 1911, and in 1932 the entire estate was presented as a gift to the Irish people. The first two floors are furnished in the manner of the great houses of Ireland, while its upper floors hold some fascinating exhibits of maps, prints, and other documents, as well as a small wildlife and bird collection. Housed in its basement is a marvelous folk museum and crafts shops that bring to vivid life the Kerry country lifestyle of a time long past. Exhibits include a country pub, printshop, dairy, carpentry shop, and weaving shop. You'll see craftspeople at work in some, and you can purchase their products in the giftshop. There's a light, airy tea shop off the courtyard, a welcome respite for weary feet when you've toured the house and museum. There's no charge to wander about the park and gardens; adults pay IR£2 ($3.25), children pay 80p ($1.25), to tour the house and museum. It's open from 9 a.m. to 7 p.m. in July and August, various hours other times of the year—inquire at the Tourist Office.

Other Activities

You may **swim** in any of the lakes without charge, and you'll only need a license to **fish** for salmon—none needed to go after all those lovely brown trout (unless the controversial "rod license" fee is still in effect in 1989—be *sure* to inquire). Donie Brosnan, at the **Handy Store** in Kenmare Place, is the man to fix you up with bait and up-to-the-minute information about the best fishing spots. There are two 18-hole, championship **golf** courses along the northern shore of the Lower Lake, and clubs, caddies, and caddy-cars are available at the clubhouse. Check with the Tourist Office or the free *Weekly Killarney* to see if anything is on at Fitzgerald Stadium on Lewis Road, the venue for Sunday **hurling and Gaelic football** matches. Killarney **horserace** meets occur in May and July, and it's worth juggling your schedule to catch them—the town assumes a "country fair" air.

You'll find the **Ring of Kerry** drive described in the next chapter, "Around County Kerry," but, again, I strongly recommend that you stash the car and take a day off from driving to join one of the inexpensive coach tours. **Bus Eireann** (call 064/31067) has a day tour for IR£9 ($14.50) for adults, IR£5 ($8) for children. Barry O'Connor, of **O'Connor's Auto Tours,** Andross, Ross Road (tel. 064/31052), will give readers of this book a 12% discount on his mini-coach tour priced at IR£12 ($19.25). **Dero's Tours,** 22 Main St. (tel. 064/31251), will give readers a 15% discount on some tours, 10% or 5% on others. Tours of the Ring run daily from Easter to October, and you'll be collected at your accommodation in the morning and returned there in the evening. Be sure to mention the book when you book the tour and show it to the driver when he picks you up.

6. CRAFTS AND OTHER SHOPPING

As I mentioned earlier, Killarney is good shopping country. Also, in recent years several craft shops have opened in and near the town.

Crafts

Threads and Clay, College Street (tel. 064/33433), is a marvelous workshop run by John Joe and Mary Murphy. Located in an 18th-century granary down a little lane off College Street (look for the signpost), it holds a weaver's shed where you can watch the loom at work and a pottery. The shop sells products made on the premises as well as other interesting craft items and has a limited stock of Irish-interest books. They'll mail and insure any of your purchases. Hours are 9 a.m. to 6 p.m. Monday through Saturday. Students who present their ID card will be given a 5% discount.

A welcome addition to the Killarney scene is the **Frank Lewis Gallery** at 6 Bridewell Lane. Specialties are landscapes of the Killarney area, portraits, and sculptures by local artists, all of which are for sale. Tea and scones are also available. It's worth the walk just to take a look at this interesting little lane housing a variety of artisans. It's the only one in Killarney where all the more-than-a-century-old cottages are still lived in. Call 064/31570 for opening hours and days.

Vivid colors swirl in the heart of lovely paperweights, bowls, plates, miniature animals and birds, vases, and a host of other objects produced by **Kerry Glass Limited,** Fair Hill (tel. 064/32587). It's next to the Franciscan Friary opposite the Great Southern Hotel. The glassmakers work right in the showroom, and it is fascinating to watch them shape the liquid glass and apply the colors. The workshop is open from 8 a.m. to 1 p.m. and 2 to 4 p.m. Monday through Friday. There's also a shop on College Street that sells seconds.

The small **White Heather Home Crafts Shop,** 48 New St. (tel. 064/31145), is filled with attractive craft gift items, including bits of antique lace.

Other Shopping

Located just around the curve from the Town Hall and Tourist Office, **Tweeds & Crafts,** East Avenue Road (tel. 064/33306), carries a wide selection of high-quality tweed jackets and suits for men and women, cashmere jackets, hand-cut crystal, linen, Aran hand-knits, and a good many other items. The owner, personable young Geoff McCarthy, is usually on hand to assist you, but if he should be out when you call in, the staff is both friendly and helpful. Geoff also has the **Cashmere Shop,** just four doors away from Tweeds and Crafts, on the same street (tel. 064/33306), with a large and varied selection.

Maybury, Main Street (tel. 064/31888), is one of my favorite stores in the whole of Ireland. Maybe it's their huge stocks of Irish-made goods (over 3,000 pieces of Waterford crystal, umpteen hundred pieces of Belleek and Royal Tara, Irish porcelain character figures like the Rose of Tralee, and a whole host of other items) at terrific prices. But I suspect Maybury has gained my affection because of the likes of Jim Cronin, the manager, who always seems to be on hand to help with decisions, locate some special object, or simply give a little background information on something that has caught my interest. Ina Brosnan, in the glassware department, is of the same ilk, as are the rest of the staff in this busy shop—not surprising, since they are simply carrying on a tradition set back in 1846. They'll ship and insure any purchases, and you can write for their extensive mail-order catalog. Hours are 9 a.m. to 6 p.m., and in summer months, 7:30 to 10:30

p.m. Incidentally, if you've yearned to take home some of those lovely Irish lace curtains, they have a very fine selection.

7. KILLARNEY AFTER DARK

Killarney has two singing pubs to tempt your vocal cords. There's ballad singing and general hilarity (which can get pretty hokey if the likes of "Dixie" breaks out) in the backroom of **The Laurels** pub from May to October, and letters pour in from readers with enthusiastic endorsement of this liveliest of Killarney pubs. Go along about 9 p.m., when things are just tuning up. The larger and ever-so-slightly more subdued **Danny Mann** pub, on New Street, installs ballad groups every night right through the year, and in summer, it's likely to be packed with Yanks rendering heartfelt versions of such stock Irish exports as "Danny Boy" and "When Irish Eyes Are Smiling." The action starts about 9:30 p.m., and if you're not ready to end the evening at 11:30 p.m., a posh nightclub has been added to the pub, where things go on until 1:30 a.m.

During summer months there's ceili dancing (set dancing you'll recognize as the ancestor of our square dancing) and traditional Irish music every night of the week. The **White Gates Inn Hotel,** on Muckross Road, has a traditional music seisiun and sing-along on Friday night and other entertainment on Saturday during the season (call 064/31164 to see what's on). **O'Brien's Pub** on College Street has Irish music, and there's sophisticated music and dancing at Aghadoe Hotel.

A Very Special Irish Folk Pageant

Top of my own list of favorite nighttime entertainment in the Killarney area is at least one performance of **Siamsa,** the **National Folk Theatre** troupe that performs in their own Siamsa Tire Theatre in nearby Tralee. "Merrymaking" is the English translation of the Gaelic *siamsa,* and this is as merry a show as you'll come across, as it depicts through music, song, dance, and mime Irish country life of the past. In a stage setting of thatched cottage and farmyard, expert performers go about the business of thatching, churning, milking, harvesting, and other routine tasks that were the foundation of everyday life on the farm. It will no doubt surprise you, as it did me, to know that the troupe operates on a very limited budget, with just a handful of full-time performers and that most of those skilled-musicians, actors, singers, and dancers give hours and hours of their time to perfect the show and travel with it on a strictly voluntary basis. It's an inspiring as well as fun-filled evening of entertainment and puts you in close touch with an Irish lifestyle that has been the foundation of the nation for centuries. Having seen siamsa, you'll know intimately the source of the irrepressible Irish spirit that charms us so. You can book for both Killarney and Tralee performances at the Siamsa Tire Theatre, Godfrey Place, Tralee (tel. 066/23055), and tickets are under IR£5 ($8) in Tralee for adults, less for children. There's a special coach and theater ticket for IR£6 ($9.50), available at Deros Tours, 22 Main St., Killarney (tel. 064/31251). This is a definite "don't miss."

Cabaret

Out at the **GlenEagle Hotel and Country Club** on Muckross Road (tel. 064/31870), there's inexpensive Irish entertainment every night except Sunday during summer months. Ballads, folk songs, traditional music, and stories as only the Irish can tell them are on tap, with top-flight entertainers like the Wolfe Tones and Joe Dolan frequently on the bill. Admission is IR£6 ($9.50), and there's a free shuttle-bus service to the hotel from Kenmare Place between 8 p.m. and 1 a.m. There's dancing after the show until 1 a.m., or you might want to opt for the **Eagle's Nest,** a disco that often features jazz sessions or pub theater (small admission charge). A resident pianist and guitarist hold sway in the **Eagle's Whistle Lounge** (no cover charge), and they'll have you singing your heart out in a true Irish sing-along.

8. SPECIAL EVENTS

For one week in mid-May, Celts from six countries converge on Killarney to celebrate and preserve their ancient ties during **Pan-Celtic Week.** There are interesting exhibits on display, and the week's schedule includes sports competitions, workshops, concerts, pipe band competitions, informal seisiuns, dancing, and a marvelous Cornish Pen Gwyn torchlight procession led by a black-robed, jaw-snapping horse's skull, with musicians of all nationalities hypnotizing sidewalk spectators with ancient dance rhythms that inevitably draw them into the procession. Admission prices are minimal, and many events are free. Check the Tourist Board "Calendar of Events" for exact dates in 1989 and 1990.

Killarney is an ideal base from which to be a part of one of Ireland's major annual events, the **Rose of Tralee International Festival.** Tralee is just 20 miles to the north, and you'll find details in the next chapter.

AROUND COUNTY KERRY

□ □ □

1. ACCOMMODATIONS
2. WHERE TO EAT
3. THINGS TO SEE AND DO

Your entire visit could well be spent within the confines of County Kerry, and you'd still go home without seeing it all. No matter how much or how little you manage to get in, however, you will know beyond doubt that it well earns its honorary title, the Kingdom of Kerry.

1. ACCOMMODATIONS

Note: Prices shown below are those in effect in 1989—expect them to be higher in 1990.

HOSTELS: There's a very nice hostel on the Dingle Peninsula at Ballyferriter, about ten miles from Dingle Town. Contact **Dun Chaoin,** Ballyferriter, Tralee (tel. 066/56121).

Vincent Counihan, of **Waterville Leisure Ltd.,** Waterville, Co. Kerry (tel. 0667/4400), has converted a big old stone building that once housed the first cable station from Ireland to the U.S. and Europe into an outstanding privately owned hostel and outdoor adventure, sport, and leisure-training center. There are beds for 120, with bunk beds (continental quilts, pillows, and undersheet) in rooms for 2, 4, 6, 8, 10, and 12. Other facilities include shower rooms, washrooms, toilets, kitchen, dining room, laundry and drying room, two games rooms, a gym, and a TV lounge. The rate is a mere IR£5 ($8) per person. Best book before you arrive.

BED-AND-BREAKFAST: Some 13 miles east of Kenmare, **Sillerdane Lodge,** Coolnoohill, Kilgarvan (tel. 064/85359), offers a most unusual feature for an Irish B&B—a heated outdoor swimming pool! Set in a beautiful valley, the pretty bungalow has more than just that to offer, however, and perhaps its most appealing feature is the gracious Mrs. Joan McCarthy. This lovely lady takes a personal interest in all her guests and her home reflects her concern for their comfort. The bright dining room has huge windows to take advantage of gorgeous views, and bedrooms are beautifully decorated and spotless. All six have private facilities. Bed-and-breakfast rates are IR£11 ($17.50), with a 25% reduction for children. Central heat and plenty of room for parking. Closed Christmas Day.

On the outskirts of Kenmare, in a quiet street just off the main Kenmare–Ring of Kerry road, **Ardmore House,** Killarney Road, Kenmare (tel. 064/41406), is a modern one-story bungalow framed by a colorful rose garden. Toni and Tom Connor have six rooms with shower and toilet. Those on the front look out to the roses, and the back view is of peaceful green pastures, with mountains in the background. B&B rates are IR£10.50 ($16.75), children pay half that, and dinner is IR£9.50 ($15.25). Central heat and plenty of parking space.

If a mad dash around the Ring of Kerry is not your cup of tea, consider a stop at **Avonlea House,** Sportsfield Road, Sneem, Co. Kerry (tel. 064/45221), with Mrs. Maura Hussey. The lovely little village of Sneem won Ireland's Tidy Town Award in 1987 and is charming enough to warrant a stop on its own, even if it weren't on the Ring. Mrs. Maura provides four attractive bedrooms (one with private bath and toilet, three with showers only) on the outskirts of town. The food here is excellent, and there's a turf fire blazing in the Resident's Lounge most nights. The B&B rate is IR£10 ($16), with a 25% discount for children, and dinner is IR£9.50 ($15.25). Open mid-March to mid-November.

In Dingle, you'll get a very warm welcome from Mrs. Mary Leonard at **Dykegate House,** 8 Dykegate St. (tel. 066/51549). Conveniently located within walking distance of everything in town, the two-story house is rather plain but homey. Mrs. Leonard, a retired nurse, is the soul of hospitality and serves up one of the best breakfasts I've had in Ireland in a light and airy dining room. Guest rooms vary in size, but all are comfortably furnished. This has been a favorite of readers for years, and after a personal stay, I heartily concur in their endorsements. Rates for bed-and-breakfast are IR£10 ($16), with 50% off for children.

Also conveniently located in the heart of town, **Mrs. Betty Hand's** large two-story home on Green Street (tel. 066/51538) has four nicely appointed guest rooms, each with private shower. The friendliness of the Hand family is legendary, and they are always delighted to have American guests. There's central heat and a garden where guests are welcome to sit on a sunny afternoon. Rates for bed-and-breakfast are IR£10 ($16), with a 50% reduction for children. Travel vouchers accepted.

In a breathtakingly beautiful setting high on a hill overlooking Slea Head and the Blasket Islands, **Slea Head House,** Dunquin, Tralee (tel. 066/56234), first opened as a guesthouse in the 1930s when Mrs. Maureen O'Connell's grandmother took in students to teach them the Irish language. For many years now Maureen and husband Liam have continued the tradition of warm, personal hospitality that began back then. A more gracious, witty, or fun-loving couple would be hard to find. Guest rooms are all different in size and shape, all are fitted out with plain but comfortable furnishings, and most have that smashing view. Bed-and-breakfast will cost you IR£9 ($14.50).

In Ballyferriter, on the Dingle Peninsula, Miss Breda O'Sullivan's **Cois Abhann** (pronounce it "Cush Owen," and it means by the side of the river), Emila, Ballyferriter (tel. 066/56201), is a pretty, modern bungalow with floor-to-ceiling windows to frame magnificent mountain views. The six guest rooms are all done in pastel colors and all have private bath and shower. B&B rates are IR£10.50 ($16.75). There's central heat and plenty of parking space. Open March through September.

There are views of lofty Mount Brandon from all six guest rooms at **MacGearailt's Bungalow,** Bothar Bui, Ballydavid, Dingle (tel. 066/55142). The bright, modern bungalow is the home of Maura and Thomas MacGearailt, who delight in welcoming guests and pointing out the splendors of the Dingle Peninsula. All bedrooms have a private toilet and shower. Rates are IR£10.50

($16.75) for bed-and-breakfast and IR£10 ($16) for the evening meal, with 20% off for children. Central heat and parking. Open Easter through September.

A lovely modern bungalow named **Cliabhan** (it means "cradle," and is pronounced "clee-vaughn"), Dingle (tel. 066/51108), is about a ten-minute walk from Dingle town. Ursula and Tommy Sheehy are marvelous hosts, with a seemingly inexhaustible knowledge of the Dingle Peninsula and a keen desire to share it with their guests. From the pleasant lounge and dining room, there are views of green pastures dotted with grazing sheep and the hazy shapes of mountains beyond the bay. There's an ancient Ogham stone in the field out back and a ring fort down in the pasture. All five of the guest rooms have private shower facilities, and two have a bidet. Ursula is one of the few Irish hostesses to serve percolated coffee to Americans who've overdosed on tea. Bed-and-breakfast rates with this engaging couple are IR£9 ($14.50) per person sharing.

Rita and Gerald Brosnan, of **Drom House,** (it means "hilly"), Coumgaugh, Dingle (tel. 066/51134), are both Dingle Peninsula natives. Rita was born in a house just up the road, and Gerald is manager of the West Kerry Co-op that has resurrected farming as a viable occupation hereabouts. Their hillside home sits amid sweeping mountain vistas, and the modern bungalow is nicely decorated throughout. There are three pastel-hued guest rooms, and all have private bath facilities, clock-radios, TVs, and hairdryers. There's a TV/video lounge, as well as a playground for children. B&B rates are IR£10.50 ($16.75), with a 50% discount for children.

Mrs. Josephine Groarke, **Burntwood House,** Listowel, Co. Kerry (tel. 068/21516), is the pleasant hostess of this beautiful Georgian-style house set in very scenic countryside. The centrally heated house is comfortable and modernized. The food is delicious and the six attractive bedrooms all have handbasins. The rate for bed-and-breakfast is IR£10.50 ($16.75) and dinner costs IR£12 ($19.25); there is a 25% reduction for children. Open April to October.

Tim and Nancy O'Neill will welcome you to **Ashgrove House,** Ballybunion Road, Listowel, Co. Kerry (tel. 068/21268), about a half mile outside town. They're a charming couple, and their two teenagers, John and Carol, are very much a part of the hospitality they extend to guests. There are four pretty guest rooms, all with private facilities and all on the ground floor. The dining room overlooks the garden where there's a pleasant patio, and out front tea and scones are often served on the glassed-in sun porch. The B&B rate is IR£10.50 ($16.75), and Nancy will prepare a good high tea for IR£8.50 ($13.50). Open March through October.

A GUESTHOUSE: One of the prettiest guesthouses on the Dingle Peninsula is **Aisling,** Castlegregory (tel. 066/39134). The home of Dr. (retired) and Mrs. Healy, the two-story charmer is a mecca for visitors interested in Irish history and this unique region. The good doctor is an authority on both and delights in sharing his vast knowledge; both he and his wife, Helen, are also very helpful in directing their guests to good local eateries, craft workshops, etc. The house shines, with parquet floors, artistic arrangements of dried flowers, and examples of Irish pottery on display. The three upstairs bedrooms have washbasins, but share two bathrooms with showers, while two downstairs rooms off a patio have private baths. At breakfast, Mrs. Healy's justly famed brown scones star. Bed-and-breakfast rates are IR£12 ($18.20), with an additional charge of IR£1.50 ($2.40) for private facilities. For children there's 15% off regular rates. Open May through October.

FARMHOUSES: **Marino House,** Reen, Kenmare (tel. 064/41154 or 41501), has occupied one of Ireland's most scenic sites for over two centuries, a small, wooded finger of land extending out into Kenmare Bay. There's an old-fashioned air about the place, yet there's total modern comfort inside—an irresistible combination. Run by the O'Sullivans, Marino House has nine guest rooms in an extension, all with washbasins and central heating, and all comfortably furnished. Meals are served in a dining room overlooking the green lawn. Much patronized by regulars, this place gets booked quickly from year to year, so best reserve as far in advance as possible. B&B rates are IR£10 ($16), dinner is the same, and there's a 20% reduction for children. Open May through September.

Hawthorn Farm, Kilgarvan, Co. Kerry (tel. 064/85326), is a modern farmhouse, the domain of charming Kitty Dineen and her family. The hospitality, however, harks back to the strictly old-fashioned type and Kitty's table is widely known for its magnificent farm fare. Just wait until you taste her traditional Christmas cake (served year round), brown bread, and scones! Located just 12 miles from the sea, Hawthorn Farm has seven bedrooms with handbasins and three with private facilities. There's central heating, and it's open April through September. Bed-and-breakfast rate is IR£11 ($17.50) per person, dinner is IR£10.50 ($16.75), and weekly half board is IR£130 ($208) per person.

Mrs. Katherine O'Sullivan's **Sea View Farm,** Mountain Stage, Glenbeigh, Co. Kerry (tel. 066/68109), is an attractive, modern farmhouse with a beautiful view of Dingle Bay. There is a comfortable atmosphere here and the food is excellent. There are five bedrooms, all of which have handbasins. The rate for bed-and-breakfast is IR£10 ($16) and dinner costs IR£9 ($14.50); 25% reduction for children. Open April to October.

A HOTEL: There's a gem of an Irish country hotel on the Dingle Peninsula, and in many respects it is more a bed-and-breakfast place than a hotel. That's because of the informality and personal service you'll receive from Billy and Breege Granville at the **Ostan Granville,** Ballyferriter, Dingle (tel. 066/56116). *Ostan* is Irish for "hotel," but this 1838 Georgian house began life as a rectory, then was used by the Royal Irish Constabulary as a barracks until the 1920s, when it burned. That's when the Granville family took it over, restored it, and opened its doors to the public. There's an old-fashioned, homey look to the place, and its bar looks out to Mount Brandon, Ballydavid Head, Smerwick Harbour, and the Three Sisters—a wonderful place to bend an elbow before the fireplace while contemplating that sweeping view! Guest rooms are plain but comfortable. Some have private bath and shower, others only handbasins, but all have terrific views. A nice feature here is the attention given families with children; there's even a special tea each evening for the young fry, and babysitting is no problem at all. Meals are excellent and reasonably priced, with homemade soup and brown bread and fish straight from Dingle waters. Seasonal rates for bed-and-breakfast range from IR£12 ($19.25) to IR£16 ($25.50). There's central heat and plenty of parking.

SELF-CATERING: Overlooking the picturesque little village of Ventry and its harbor, 4½ miles from Dingle town on the coast road to Slea Head, **Ventry Holiday Cottages,** c/o John P. Moore, Green Street, Dingle, Co. Kerry (tel. 066/51588), are traditional in design, yet equipped with a fully fitted-out kitchen and other conveniences. Each features a large lounge/dining area, and there's a fireplace for cool days and nights. The three carpeted bedrooms will sleep six adults. There are eight cottages, and rates range seasonally from IR£90 ($144) to IR£300 ($480).

BIG SPLURGE: At **Doyle's Seafood Bar & Townhouse,** John Street, Dingle, Co. Kerry (tel. 066/51174), you're right in the heart of Dingle town. Over the past several years John and Stella Doyle have gained an international reputation for the quality of seafood served in their small, flagstone-paved restaurant in Dingle, a tribute to their single-mindedness in adhering to the highest standards in whatever they undertake. So it comes as no surprise that they have maintained that same high standard in renovating an adjacent 1830s house into eight attractive and comfortable bedrooms, all with private bath. Antique furnishings with a Victorian flavor add to their appeal, but comfort is not overlooked, with extra-size orthopedic beds, direct-dial telephones, and television. The two houses are interconnected, making access to the restaurant easy, while maintaining a high degree of privacy. Rates for bed-and-breakfast range from IR£22 ($35.25) to IR£27 ($43.25) per person, double occupancy, to IR£27 ($43.25) to IR£32 ($51.25) single. Open mid-March to mid-November. Highly recommended.

READERS' ACCOMMODATIONS SELECTIONS: "Mrs. M. O'Mahoney, **Reask View House,** Reask, Ballyferriter, Co. Kerry (tel. 066/56126), has superb modern accommodations in a truly rustic area. Outstanding amenities of golf and food nearby" (G. W. Howard, Silver Springs, Md.). . . . "**Sunset House,** Waterville, Co. Kerry (tel. 0667/4258), run by Mrs. P. Fitzgerald, is a lovely house overlooking Dingle Bay and Ballinskellig Island. Nice rooms and a comfortable atmosphere" (N. Rounsefell and S. Gilmore, Baton Rouge, La.). . . . "Mrs. Fitzgerald-O'Donnell, **Alpenrose,** Annascaul, Co. Kerry (tel. 066/57105), and her husband own and are proud of this immaculate, modern, and very comfortable inn. Dinner was delicious and breakfast was good and pleasant. It is a warm, clean, and cozy place to stay" (J. Grimshaw, Costa Mesa, Calif.).

"Mrs. Griffin's country farmhouse, **Goulane,** Castlegregory, Co. Kerry (tel. 066/39147), overlooks the bay, with a sandy beach. Our rooms were most comfortable, and there was that lovely smelling Irish soap at the sinks and plenty of large, clean towels. Mrs. Griffin is a delightful Irish mother of five and shared with us many wonderful stories of life in the country" (Tracy Shepard, Fort Lauderdale, Fla.). . . . "Mrs. M. McHugh, **Grianan Allach,** Kilcooley, Ballydavid, Co. Kerry (tel. 066/55157), and her family are friendly people always happy to assist you in seeing the local sights. The meals served family style are a great example of Irish country cooking, and the rooms and facilities are modern and very comfortable" (W.V. Steele, New York, N.Y.). . . . "The **Bank House,** North Square, Sneem (tel. 064/45226), was clean and cute and charming. Our room was light and airy and had a brass bed. They brought tea in the evening and went out of their way to make us comfortable. Margaret Harrington is the owner, and her husband owns a shop in town that sells hand-knit and hand-loomed sweaters that were very nice" (Lynn and Tim Jones, Wis.).

2. WHERE TO EAT

In Kenmare, the **Purple Heather,** Henry Street (tel. 064/41016), serves bistro food in a setting best described as eccentric. There's lots of wood, copper, hanging wine bottles, and an assortment of other items. Lunch specialties include excellent omelets as well as salads and smoked salmon and mackerel, the latter two served with fresh brown bread, at prices ranging from IR£4 ($6.50) to IR£7 ($11.25). Hours are 12:30 to 5:30 p.m. every day except Sunday, from Easter through October.

The owners of the Purple Heather also run the charming **Lime Tree Restaurant** in Kenmare (tel. 064/41225). Housed in an old stone schoolhouse, the Lime Tree is open in the evening only, and meals here are prepared with the same loving care as at the Purple Heather. Seafood figures prominently on the menu, and for a special treat, order the prawns, monkfish, and scallops in garlic butter. Lamb, steak, chicken, and veal are also available in tasty variations, and desserts are well nigh spectacular. Main-course prices on the à la carte menu are in the IR£8 ($12.75) to IR£12 ($19.25) range, and hours are 6 to 10 p.m. every day except Sunday, from Easter to the end of October.

In Killorglin, Nick and Ann Foley have converted what was once a butchershop into a charming multilevel steak-and-seafood restaurant with exposed-stone walls, lots of dark wood, open fires, oil paintings, and comfortable seating with plush upholstering in shades of red and green. **Nick's Restaurant,** Lower Bridge Street (tel. 066/61233 or 61219), serves only the best meats, since Nick is himself a master butcher. Prime beef comes in enormous steaks that actually earn the accolade "melt in your mouth." Lobsters, crayfish, and oysters reside in the restaurant's fish tank until they are to be cooked, and other fish dishes feature only same-day catches. The soups, be they beef and vegetable, mussel, or whatever, are thick and hearty with the unmistakable taste of "homemade." The menu is extensive, with ten starters and a choice from more than a dozen main courses, followed by a mouthwatering dessert trolley. But if you should have a yen for a special dish not listed—and if the makings are available—the Foleys are quite happy to prepare it for you. There's an extensive wine list, with all the varieties imported directly from France. Lunch salads of ham, beef, or seafood are featured on the special pub menu at prices under IR£5 ($8), from noon to 5 p.m. À la carte prices range upward from £9 ($14.50) for main courses. Music played on the grand piano can be enjoyed nightly. Nick's is open from noon to 10:30 p.m. seven days a week. Closed from Christmas Eve to New Year's Day.

Also in Killorglin, the **Old Forge,** Main Street (tel. 066/61231), is named for the huge forge, complete with bellows and anvil, which separates the pub and lounge. Home-cooked light meals are served in this atmospheric pub and eatery at very moderate prices, and there's traditional music in the lounge.

The **Bianconi Inn,** Killorglin (tel. 066/61146), serves very good meals in what was once an old coaching inn, with the owner as chef. Pub grub is available all day in the pub, and four-course dinners run about IR£12 ($19.25) to IR£14 ($22.50).

At **The Half Door,** John Street, Dingle, Co. Kerry (tel. 066/51600), John and Celeste Slye can count more awards than I have space to list. Residents of Dingle are as fond of the place as visitors, always the sign of a good eatery, and one meal in the bright, informal dining room or the skylighted arbor room out back will add to their list of boosters. But before I get into the food, let me say something about the atmosphere here: it's as friendly, relaxed, and jovial a place as you'll find anywhere, which makes every lunch or dinner something of a special occasion. Of course, in the final analysis it's the food that counts, and that's where all those awards come in. Celeste rules the kitchen, turning out mostly seafood dishes prepared with a marvelous simplicity that enhances their natural tastes. No need to worry about freshness—John has constructed huge tanks to hold several varieties until they're ready to pop into the pot, and others come right from Dingle's fishing fleet to the kitchen. I especially like the fresh sidesalads that come with main courses. As for the wine list, it is extensive and of such excellence that it won the Woodford Bourne National Wine Award two years running. The Half Door is open from 12:30 to 2 p.m. for lunch, 6 to 9 p.m. for dinner, every day except Tuesday. À la carte prices begin at £9.50 ($15.25). Closed November to mid-March.

John and Stella Doyle have created one of the best restaurants in Dingle, **Doyle's Seafood Bar,** John Street (tel. 066/51174). The cozy old pub has rock walls, a flagstone floor, and a blackboard menu showing a selection of seafood from local fishing boats' same-day catch. You'll find John up front at the bar, while Stella reigns in the kitchen. In addition to salmon, lobster, oysters, and other shellfish, there's good homemade soup and Stella's freshly baked scones. Prices range from IR£8 ($12.75) to IR£9.50 ($15.25), and you can expect a wait in this small, popular place (but that's no problem at all if you're ensconced at the friendly bar with other waitees). Don't plan to get there much after 7 p.m., however, to be sure of being seated. Hours are 12:30 to 2:15 p.m. and 6 to 9 p.m.; closed Sunday. Open mid-March to mid-November.

In Dingle, Mrs. Pat Moore runs the delightful **Beginish Restaurant** on Green Street (tel. 066/51588). She has managed to achieve a light and airy— and at the same time, cozy—look, and there's a lovely garden out back with tables for dining outside in fine weather. The food, with an emphasis on fresh seafood (what else, in Dingle!), is beautifully prepared and nicely served. She serves light lunches (but substantial enough to be the main meal of the day), then puts on very special evening meals from 6 to 9 p.m. Prices are quite reasonable, and this one is highly recommended. *Note:* Pat also owns one of Dingle's best craft and gift shops located just across the street and gives excellent service to Americans.

The **Armada Restaurant,** Strand Street, Dingle (tel. 066/51505), is a pleasant, moderately priced eatery run by Mark and Ann Kerry (Ann does the cooking). Meals feature seafood and local meats, and there's also a good vegetarian salad on the menu. The Special Tourist Menu is also offered. Salads are IR£5 ($8), and main courses are in the IR£6 ($9.50) to IR£9.50 ($15.25) range. Lunch hours are 12:30 to 2:15 p.m. and dinner is 6 to 9 p.m. (10 p.m. in high season), seven days a week.

Also in Dingle, **An Café Liteartha** (tel. 066/51380) is a very special kind of place, with a bookshop stocked with an impressive array of Irish-interest publications and records out front, and an inexpensive restaurant in back that serves all three meals. Food is plain but very good, and prices range from IR£2.50 ($4) for breakfast to IR£4 ($6.50) for lunch to IR£5 ($8) for dinner. Hours are 9:30 a.m. to 9:30 p.m. Monday through Saturday, 10 a.m. to 5:30 p.m. on Sunday.

READERS' RESTAURANT SELECTION: "We discovered a delightful restaurant in Listowel, Co. Kerry. The **Spinning Wheel** (tel. 068/21128) is a spotlessly clean, friendly restaurant with excellent food and reasonable prices" (Al and Eileen O'Sullivan, Long Beach, N.Y.).

3. THINGS TO SEE AND DO

An entire book could be written about this varied region, with its magnificent scenery, relics of prehistory, and population of highly individualistic people. I'll hit the highlights, but do take time to explore on your own—this is "nook and cranny" country!

FESTIVALS: For six days and nights in late August and early September the competition is fierce to see which of the international beauties gathered in Tralee best fits the time-honored description ". . . lovely and fair as the rose of the summer." Now, understand, the **Rose of Tralee International Festival** is a far cry from a lot of other such competitions, which usually amount to little more than beauty pageants that take themselves quite seriously—*this* festival is one of lighthearted fun and frolic that entails parades, pipe bands, street entertainment, inter-festival singing competitions for the **Folk Festival of Ireland** (I ask you, where else but Ireland would you find two festivals in full sway at the same place at the same time!) and, *finally,* the crowning of the Rose. It's six days and nights of sheer merriment, and it's a grand time to be in County Kerry. If you'd like to be part of the fun (and who wouldn't?), there are usually several package deals that cover transportation and accommodation, details of which can be obtained from the General Secretary, **Festival of Kerry Office,** 5 Lower Castle St., Tralee, Co. Kerry. If you're making your own arrangements, be sure to do it well in advance, whether you plan to stay in Tralee or in Killarney, 20 miles to the south.

In mid-August, Killorglin lets its hair down in three days of what many Irish call sheer madness disguised under the name of the **Puck Fair.** It's been held every year since 1613, and things get off to a right rowdy start when a tremendous male (or puck) goat is hauled up to a high platform in the square and crowned as King of the Fair. What follows is a sort of carnival/country fair/free-for-all, with most pubs staying open around the clock, all sorts of street entertainment, and over on the green, some pretty serious horse and cattle trading. Just how all this began is a matter of dispute: some say a goat bleated to alert a shepherd boy of approaching enemy forces and he, in turn, alerted the town about impending attack, while those of a more prosaic turn of mind say it dates back to one ill-fated fair when only one goat was put up for sale. No matter its origins, it is traditionally a gathering place for the country's traveling people, who come to drive some hard bargains in the horse-swapping business, catch up with tinker gossip, and indulge in nonstop revelry.

THE RING OF KERRY AND THE DINGLE PENINSULA: The famed scenic drive known as the Ring of Kerry circles the broad Iveragh Peninsula. A good starting point is **Kenmare,** ending up at **Killorglin,** but you can just as easily travel in the opposite direction. To cover the 110 miles properly, you should allow an entire day—it simply is not "dashing through" territory, and you'll want plenty of time for stops along the way—a picnic, a pint, or a pub lunch. The same applies to its neighbor to the north, the Dingle Peninsula, and both are worthy of a day from your travel schedule. If, however, *two* full days are out of the question, my top recommendation has to go to Dingle, which has a character totally unique that in some mystical way seems to touch the soul.

The Ring of Kerry

From **Kenmare,** travel west along the Kenmare River, looking across to the Caha and Slieve Miskish Mountains on the opposite shore. The pretty little village of **Sneem** is the last resting place of Fr. Michael Walsh, who was parish priest here for 38 years in the 1800s and is immortalized as "Father O'Flynn" in an Irish ballad. Two miles to the south, **Parknasilla** is the site of an elegant hotel whose rock gardens and colorful subtropical blooms are worth a stop. The road then turns inland through wild and gorgeous scenery before coming back to the coast at **Castlecove.** This is another loitering spot, for about a mile and a half north of the road stands Straigue Fort, one of the country's best-preserved stone forts built during the Iron Age. The circular stone walls, 13 feet wide and 18 feet high, have held over the centuries without benefit of mortar and along their interior are several flights of stairs of near perfect construction.

Near **Caherdaniel,** Daniel O'Connell, "The Liberator," lived most of his political life at his beloved Derrynane House, now a museum open to the public year round. The **Pass of Coomakista** lifts you some 700 feet above sea level, with breathtaking views of the bay, the Skelligs, and the coastline. It was on **Skellig Michael,** a massive rocky hulk that rises 700 feet above the sea, that a colony of early Christian monks built a retreat of stone beehive huts. From the little villages of **Ballinskelligs** and **Cahirciveen,** there are boat trips out to the ruins in good weather, and you reach them after a climb of no fewer than 640 steps. The rocky islands that make up the Skelligs are also bird sanctuaries, and thousands of puffins and other seabirds are in residence. Near Cahirciveen, **Valentia Island** is joined to the mainland by a causeway. The island's Irish name is Dairbhre, ("Place of Oaks") and it is from a romanticized pronunciation of the Irish *Beal Inse* (the name of a nearby sound) that "Valentia" evolved—not from the Spanish.

From Cahirciveen, you travel along the north coast of the peninsula through some of the Ring's most spectacular scenery, up a long valley to **Kells** at the edge of Dingle Bay, with the peaks of the Dingle Peninsula visible across the water, then up the steep sides of **Drung Hill** high above the bay and on through **Mountain Stage** and down again to **Glenbeigh** at the foot of **Seefin Mountain.** At **Killorglin,** you can return to Killarney, or turn west for the Dingle Peninsula, passing through **Castlemaine** (home of Jack Duggan, "The Wild Colonial Boy").

The Dingle Peninsula

This is the most westerly point of land in Europe, its offshore **Blasket Islands** the "last parish before New York." Its beginnings are shrouded in the mists of prehistory, which left its marks scattered over the face of the Slieve Mish mountains, along its coves and rocky cliffs and in the legends that persist to this day. Its ancient Irish name is An Daingean ("The Fortress"), and the remains of no fewer than seven earthen ring forts and two headland stone forts attest to the origin of that name. Its Glenagalt Valley translates as the "Valley of the Madmen," and is so called because as far back as the 12th century mentally afflicted came to roam its wilds, drink the waters of Tobernagalt ("The Well of the Madmen"), eat the watercress that grew along the stream, and return home sound in mind and body after a few months. Mystical? Oh, yes. I sometimes feel the very essence of Celtic magic has been distilled into the air of the Dingle Peninsula. Or perhaps it is only the soft, lyrical accents of the Gaelic that is the everyday language here that make it seem so.

Dingle town is a busy little market town, with a boat-building industry right in the middle of things. Among the craftspeople who sell their wares in the town is silversmith Brian de Staic. In his small **Seodoir an Daingin** shop on Green Street (tel. 066/51298) he fashions an unusual silver necklace in the shape of an Ogham stone with your name inscribed in the strokes of that ancient language. There's bar food during the day and music on summer nights at the **O Gairbhi pub** and **Garvey's Pub,** both on Strand Street. But for a night of traditional music and song that comes from true family tradition, look for the red-and-white pub on Bridge Street with the name **UaFlaibeartaig,** which translates to O'Flaherty's. The late father of the present O'Flaherty clan was recognized as one of the country's best traditional musicians, and now son Fergus and daughter Maire raise instruments and voice each night surrounded by locals and visitors who've come to hear the best. It's a warm, informal gathering in a setting that's as traditional as the music, with the haphazard collection of pictures, posters, and other assorted items that has accumulated here as in almost any country pub in Ireland.

Driving west from town, **Ventry Harbour** was, according to legend, the scene of a fierce battle between the King of the World, Daire Doon, and the King of Ireland, Fionn MacCumhaill. Still farther west, **Dunbeg Fort** perches on a high promontory, its landward side surrounded by earthen trenches, and its 22-foot-thick wall riddled with an elaborate souterrain (inner passage). It's at the high cliffs of **Sea Head** that you get the most sweeping view of sheltered coves below and across the water the **Blasket Islands.** The last of their tiny population was moved to the mainland in 1953, when the fishing industry failed to provide a living wage and the government gave land grants for small farm holdings on the peninsula. Visitors from Springfield, Massachusetts, in the U.S. may feel a special bond to the people of the Blaskets, since many islanders emigrated and settled in that city. Boats go out from **Dunquin Harbor** on an intermittent basis during summer months, and a student group has operated a guesthouse/hostel in one of the deserted houses in the summer on **Great Blasket.** If you're intrigued at the thought of staying overnight, call **Kruger's Pub** (tel. 066/56127) and make inquiries.

There are very good potteries on the peninsula, the first of which is **Dunquin Pottery** on the road between Slea Head and Dunquin. Operated by local people, Maureen, Eileen, and Sean Daly, who worked for founder Jean Oldfield for many years, the pottery turns out hand-thrown, ovenproof stoneware in shades of sand and browns and blues. The reasonable prices range from IR£2.75 ($4.40) for a ramekin to IR£44.50 ($71.20) for a lovely coffee set. The small café at the pottery serves Rambouts coffee, Irish porter cake, and other snacks.

At Ballyferriter, **Louis Mulcahy** (tel. 066/56229) operates a pottery studio/workshop, where he trains local potters in the production of many unusual items made from clay and finished with glazes developed in the workshop. There are the standard dinner sets, mugs, pitchers, and the like, but in addition, giant jugs and vases, unusual lamp bases, and beautiful wall plaques are on display in the studio. Louis's distinctive designs set his work apart from any other. Visitors are welcome to visit the workshop and kiln, and prices are quite reasonable for the unusually high quality. Open seven days a week.

Penny Sheehy is the potter at **Bradan Feasa Pottery**, Ventry (tel. 066/59962), who specializes in unique ceramic Celtic murals and explanation plaques of old Celtic myths. The old timbered-ceilinged building is almost a sightseeing attraction in itself, and they serve light meals of home-cooked food. You can also purchase good walking and motoring guides to Dingle.

In the center of Ballyferriter, stop at the old school that houses **Heritage Centre,** with "Treasures of the Dingle Peninsula." Ted Creedon, development officer of the exhibition, is usually on hand to expand on the story of Dingle's long history as illustrated by more than 200 photographs, artifacts, and text. You'll leave with more than a nodding acquaintance with the region's beehive huts, standing stones, mysterious graves, ring forts, and other relics. There's a tea and coffee shop at the Centre.

Also in Ballyferriter, go by the **West Kerry Co-op** office and purchase their excellent illustrated guidebook, which outlines a driving tour. They can also book you into local lodgings if you've fallen under Dingle's mystical spell and can't bear to leave just yet. The office is open from 9 a.m. to 5:30 p.m. Monday through Friday. The story behind the co-op is an inspiring one, which had its beginning in 1968, when young people were leaving in droves because much of the land was untillable, and there was great concern that the unique culture and heritage of the Gaelic-speaking region would wither and die. By banding together, 800 members of the farming community were able to import a special deep-plowing machine to break up the layer of iron that lay just inches beneath the surface of their land and turn it into productive acres. They have now reclaimed more than 12,000 acres, established an experimental nursery, and are raising some 200 tons of tomatoes hydroponically. They've also taken an active part in upgrading tourist facilities, as well as expanding the summer-school program that brings students to study Gaelic and live with local families who use the language in their everyday lives.

One of the peninsula's most astonishing relics is **Gallarus Oratory,** between Dunquin and Ballyferriter. It's a marvelous specimen of early Christian architecture. Built in an inverted boat shape, it has remained completely watertight for more than a thousand years, its stones perfectly fitted without benefit of any kind of mortar. Look, also, for the Alphabet Stone in the churchyard of **Cill Maolkeador,** an ancient ruined church. The pillar is carved with both the Roman alphabet and Ogham strokes.

At **Brandon Creek** (the legendary starting point of St. Brendan's voyage to the New World), stop in at **An Bother** (it means "The Road," and it sits right at the roadside), a pub that has for years been the gathering place of locals. It's a place to relax by the fire in the large lounge or sit at the bar in the small front room, with the constant flow of Gaelic conversation lulling you into a sense of the timelessness that is Dingle. It's mostly locals you'll meet here, and they welcome visitors warmly, breaking into English often enough to keep you from feeling excluded.

To reach the northern shores of the peninsula, take the **Connor Pass** road from Dingle town over to **Castlegregory.** Views from the pass and along the coastal road from Castlegregory on into **Tralee** go from best to better with each curve in the road, an embarrassment of scenic splendors that has quickly exhausted the film supply of many a camera buff.

In the little town of **Camp,** turn off the main road and drive up to **James Ashe's Pub.** This is the Irish pub you dreamed of before you came to Ireland— smoke-darkened wood, low ceilings, a peat fire glowing on the hearth, and Irish faces at home in the pub their families have frequented for generations. Margaret Ashe or her son, Thomas, will likely be behind the bar.

SHANNON CAR FERRY: If time is a factor—or, like me, you fancy a ferry ride any time one comes along—you can take the Shannon Car Ferry from **Tarbert** over to **Killimer** instead of driving the long coastal road to **Limerick** (although it is a beautiful drive, with many good views of Shannon). The crossing takes 20 minutes, aboard the *Shannon Willow* or *Shannon Heather,* and from April through September there are 30 sailings per day, beginning at 7 a.m. and ending at 9:30 p.m. (first sailing at 9 a.m. on Sunday). From October through March the last sailing is at 7:30 p.m. For your car and all passengers, you'll pay IR£6 ($9.50) each way. Those on foot pay IR£2.50 ($4) each way.

Note: If you have the time to opt for that scenic drive along the Shannon from Tarbert to Limerick, be sure to plan a stop at the **Castle Gate Shop,** Glin, Co. Limerick (tel. 068/34188). A former gate lodge of Glin Castle, it sits across from one of the most spectacular viewpoints of the mighty river, and after enjoying homemade scones, sandwiches, salad plates, or hot dishes, visitors often indulge in leisurely strolls to drink in the view and break the steady pace of travel. Run by one of the nicest Irish couples you're likely to meet, the Castle Gate Shop also sells odds and ends from Glin Castle (old silver, china, and even the occasional chamber pot), books on Irish subjects, and souvenirs. Prices are moderate to downright cheap, and they're open daily for breakfast, morning coffee, lunch, afternoon tea, and dinner.

READER'S SHOPPING SUGGESTION: "We found **McKenna's,** Main Street, Dingle, Co. Kerry (tel. 066/51198), to have the best buy in Waterford crystal. If you pay in cash (not with a credit card), you get a 10% discount. McKenna's also has many Irish sweaters and definitely is the cheapest we found anywhere" (D. Keeney, Sudbury, Mass.).

CHAPTER XIX

SHANNONSIDE AND SHANNON AIRPORT

□ □ □

1. INTRODUCING SHANNONSIDE: COUNTIES LIMERICK, CLARE, AND NORTH TIPPERARY
2. SHANNON AIRPORT

All too often, visitors rush through the Shannonside region, perhaps because so many deplane at Shannon and they're off and away without realizing that so many of Ireland's treasures lie right at their point of entry. Yet it is quite possible, as I once did, to spend two full, happy weeks in Ireland and not go far beyond the boundaries of the area that has been dubbed Shannonside.

1. INTRODUCING SHANNONSIDE: COUNTIES LIMERICK, CLARE, AND NORTH TIPPERARY

Limerick city is full of history, with fascinating sightseeing in and around town, from St. Mary's Cathedral to the Stone Age Centre at Lough Gur. As far as entertainment goes, there's theater and, of course, a choice of medieval banquets. In County Clare, from charming little seaside resorts like Kilkee day trips will take you to the lofty Cliffs of Moher, Knappogue Castle, and the intriguing Burren Display Centre that introduces that strange, lunar landscape. Northern Tipperary's Holy Cross Abbey is an enduring tribute to the dedication and devotion of early Christians and in Roscrea there's a beautiful home built within ancient castle walls.

There's much, much more in Shannonside, like the traditional music that lives so vigorously in generation after generation of County Clare fiddlers, whistle players, and pipers. And the crafts that flourish with such a flair in this part of the country. And the mighty River Shannon, with waters ideal for fishing, boating or just plain loafing.

With so many riches in such a small region, it would be a pity to make Limerick simply an overnight for first-day-in and last-day-out.

2. SHANNON AIRPORT

Chances are your first and last glimpses of Ireland will be from a plane arriving at or departing from Shannon Airport. It is, however, much more than a passing-through sort of airport. There's a **Tourist Information Desk** to help you book accommodations if you've arrived without them (I *implore* you not to in July or August!), to assist you with itineraries, and to be as generally helpful as Tourist Offices all around the country. Here, too, you can book the medieval banquet you'd decided to forgo but which grew irresistible on the flight over (look for the **Castle Tours** desk). **Bus Eireann** has a tour desk, where you can find out about tours around the country and book, if you choose. There's a post office, a bank, and scads of car-rental desks (again, please *don't* arrive in high season without having reserved a car in advance). See Chapter I for details on the Duty-Free Shop.

Budgeteers will find good, inexpensive food in the bright and attractive **Shannon Airport Grill.** It's self-service and offers a wide variety, from snacks to full meals, hot and cold. For a special meal, there's the buffet restaurant, the **Lindbergh Room,** named for our American aviator who had a hand in selecting Shannon as the site of this international airport. For bar snacks, drop in at the ground-floor **Burren Lounge and Bar.**

The airport is in County Clare, some 15 miles west of Limerick, with good bus service into town. **Buses** will drop you off at Ennis Road guesthouses (ask the driver when you get on) or take you to the bus terminal or any of the stops along O'Connell Street. If you're going from Limerick to the airport, there's a Shannon Airport bus stop on Henry Street, you can flag the bus down on Ennis Road, or you can catch it at the main bus terminal on Parnell Street. One-way fare is IR£3 ($4.75). **Taxi** fare will run around IR£12 ($19.25).

LIMERICK AND COUNTY LIMERICK

□ □ □

Limerick gets its name from the Irish *Luimneach,* meaning "Bare Spot," and centuries ago, that's just what was here—a barren, hilly bit of land on an island. Today you'll find a well-laid-out city with row after row of Georgian-style houses. In the intervening years, the site has been changed and molded by just about every group that has shaped the country's history. Because the island sat at the lowest ford of the Shannon, it is believed early Celts built an earthen fort at the island's highest point. Then came the Danes, in A.D. 831, to build a base from which to go aplundering. More than a century later Brian Boru sent them packing and installed the O'Briens as rulers. Next it was the Normans, with their stout city walls and castles. Portions of their walls remain to this day, as does King John's Castle. They were the first to bridge the Shannon (at the spot now crossed by the 1838 Thomond Bridge). Native Irish, of course, had no place in that Anglo-Norman stronghold, but were exiled to the south side of the river, where they eventually built their own walls and called their area Irish Town.

It was in 1691 that William III's siege of Limerick (which had once been abandoned as the city's stubbornly brave defenders prevented any breach of their walls) ended with the signing of a treaty of honorable and reasonable terms. You can see the stone on which it was signed at one end of Thomond Bridge, where it is enshrined as a memorial to a treaty whose terms were never carried out by the British. Even now Limerick is known as the "City of the Violated Treaty." During the 18th century Limerick took on its present-day form, with stylish town houses going up along broad avenues extending far beyond the old boundaries of Irish Town and English Town.

LIMERICK

1. Treaty Stone
2. King John's Castle
3. City Walls
4. Tourist Office
5. Limerick Lace
6. Museum
7. Town Hall
8. General Post Office
9. O'Connell Monument
10. Museum & Art Gallery
11. People's Park
12. St. John's Cathedral
13. St. Mary's Cathedral

1. ORIENTATION

Limerick's main street is the three-quarters-of-a-mile-long **O'Connell Street,** which becomes **Patrick Street** at its northern end. The west-to-east road that leads to **Shannon Airport** is called **Ennis Road** west of the Shannon, **Sarsfield Street** at its western end in the city, and **William Street** at its eastern end. The major intersection of O'Connell and Sarsfield is the center of most of the city's business and shopping, and all city bus lines pass this junction.

2. USEFUL INFORMATION

You'll find the **Tourist Office** on Michael Street (tel. 061/317522), in the Granary, a 1747 structure adjacent to the Dublin Road, overlooking the **Municipal Car Park** at Charlotte Quay, which has been beautifully converted into a tourism complex. Hours are 9 a.m. to 7 p.m. daily during summer months. . . . The **bus and railway station** is on Parnell Street on the southeast side of town, and the number to call for all **bus and rail information** is 061/48777. . . . **Taxi** ranks are at the railway station and at the corner of Thomas and Cecil Streets, just off O'Connell Street, and you can call 48844 or 46230 for a taxi. . . . The Limerick Junior Chamber of Commerce publishes a **Shannonside entertainment guide** weekly during summer months, which is available at most hotels as well as at the Tourist Office. . . . The **telephone prefix** for Limerick is 061.

3. ACCOMMODATIONS

A number of good, inexpensive accommodations are located on Ennis Road, the road that connects Limerick to Shannon Airport. Many of those listed below are within easy walking distance to the city center, across the Shannon River. All, however, are on bus lines that provide frequent service. Others are outside the city, and a few are in neighboring County Clare. They are, however, so convenient to Limerick city and to Shannon Airport that they warrant inclusion here.

Note: Prices shown below are those in effect in 1989—expect them to be higher in 1990.

A HOSTEL: The **An Oige hostel** in Limerick is a large old Georgian house at 1 Pery Square (tel. 061/314672). Right in the heart of the city center, it is located on a public park and has a fully equipped kitchen and showers. Advance booking is advisable during summer months. From the railway station, take city bus no. 1.

BED-AND-BREAKFAST: Convenient is one word for **St. Mary's,** Clancey's Strand (tel. 061/55919)—the city center is only about four minutes away by foot. Mrs. Walsh's two-story home sits behind neat flowerbeds and rose trees, and there's a sun lounge for guests' use. The four guest rooms are comfortably furnished, and two connect to accommodate a family. There's a spacious dining room that also serves as a lounge, a small breakfast room, and off-street parking. Rates for bed-and-breakfast are IR£10.50 ($16.75). Open April through October.

Mrs. Joan McSweeney's **Trebor,** Ennis Road (tel. 061/54632), is only about a five-minute walk from the city center. There are four nice guest rooms, all with handbasins and two with private facilities, and a TV lounge for guests. The centrally heated house also has parking facilities. Rates are IR£10.50 ($16.75) for bed-and-breakfast, IR£1.50 ($2.50) extra per person for private bath, with a 20% discount for children. Open year round except at Christmas.

Friendly Mrs. Power, of **Curraghgower,** Ennis Road (tel. 061/54716), makes visitors feel right at home in her three-story brick home. There are four guest rooms, all nicely decorated and comfortably furnished, and you'll breakfast with a view of the pretty back garden. B&B rate is IR£9.50 ($15.25), with a 10% discount for children. There's central heat and off-street parking.

Carole O'Toole, **Glen Eagles,** 12 Vereker Gardens, Ennis Road (tel. 061/55521), is the sort of caring hostess who will pack you a lunch to take along on a day trip. The O'Tooles can also arrange for car hire and chauffeur-driven guided tours in the region. The two-story house is in a quiet cul-de-sac off Ennis Road and only minutes from the city center. It is centrally heated, has five attractive guest rooms (two with private bath and all with handbasins), and there's a TV lounge, a pretty garden, and off-street parking. Rate for bed-and-breakfast is IR£10.50 ($16.80), IR£1.50 ($2.40) for private bath, with 20% off for children.

Bogside House, on Ennis Road opposite Dunne's Store (tel. 061/52703), is the modern home of Carmel Beresford, and has been one of my most popular recommendations with readers. The five guest rooms are spacious and decorated in shades of brown and beige, all with handbasins, three with private facilities. Carmel will gladly book banquets and help you arrange transport to them. The house is centrally heated, and there's good off-street parking. Airport and city buses stop just outside the door. The rate is IR£10 ($16) per person, double occupancy. Highly recommended.

The Misses Mary and Kathleen Collins, **St. Anthony's,** 8 Coolraine Terrace (tel. 061/52607), are delightful sisters first brought to my attention by a reader who wrote that "they really put themselves out to make a tourist's stay pleasant." The two-story house is their family home. It's neat as a pin and has a warm, homey atmosphere. Meals are served in a dining room overlooking a garden, and breakfast comes with homemade apricot and other fruit jams. They also serve a lovely afternoon tea with home-baking. The three guest rooms are comfortably furnished (one has three single beds) and have built-in wardrobes and washbasins. B&B rate is IR£10 ($16).

Mrs. Roche, **St. Martin's,** 4 Clanmorris Gardens (off the Ennis Road), Limerick, Co. Limerick (tel. 061/55013), is a warm, friendly woman and her home is situated in a quiet area close to the city center. Of her three lovely bedrooms, two have handbasins, and her breakfasts are delicious. Her rate is IR£9.50 ($15.25) for bed-and-breakfast and there is a 10% reduction for children. Open March to October.

Mrs. Feeney, **Dellastrada House,** 136 Upper Mayorstone Park, Ennis Road, Limerick, Co. Limerick (tel. 061/52300), is the friendly hostess of this semi-detached two-story house set in a nice, quiet area. The house is centrally heated and dinner is available in the evening. All three bedrooms have handbasins. The rate for bed-and-breakfast is IR£9.50 ($15.25) and high tea costs IR£8 ($12.75); 25% reduction for children. Open May through October.

One of the lodgings in this area most highly praised by readers, **Bunratty Lodge,** Bunratty, Co. Clare (tel. 061/72402), is a beautiful bungalow reached by the little country road that cuts between Durty Nelly's and Bunratty Castle (through the parking lot). Mrs. Mary Browne's hospitality accounts in large part for its popularity, which also means that you should book as far in advance as possible. The nine guest rooms have lovely pastoral views, and all have private facilities. A feature beloved by parents traveling with children is the alcove in two family rooms that provides privacy for the kids even while they share the room (works well, too, with that third friend, mother-in-law, etc.). The bed-and-breakfast rate is IR£12 ($19.25), and there's a 20% reduction for children. Open March through November.

Donal and Mary McKenna also offer a rather special brand of hospitality at **Gallows View,** Bunratty East, Co. Clare (tel. 061/72125). Reached by that same country road that runs through the Bunratty Castle parking area, the pretty two-story bungalow has five nicely done-up bedrooms, all with handbasins. One has private facilities, and more are planned for the near future. One family room and a double are on the ground floor, a blessing for those who have trouble with stairs. Several of Mary's interesting antique pieces are scattered throughout the house, and there's an inviting air to the lounge and dining room. Bed-and-breakfast costs IR£10 ($16), and there's a private car park. Open all year.

Mary and Noel Tobin's **Shannonside Country Home**, Newmarket-on-Fergus, Co. Clare (tel. 061/364191), is a favorite not only of our readers, but of airline personnel flying into and out of Shannon (which you can actually see from this hillside location). The large lounge, in which a peat fire is often lit, sports a snooker table and chess board, as well as several musical instruments, which often leads to impromptu singing sessions—Noel plays the accordion, daughter Dee Dee plays the mandolin, and daughter Geraldine is a dancer, as well as an art student. Mary will provide breakfast for those with early airline departures. There are eight bright, attractively furnished guest rooms, all with handbasins and private facilities. Bed-and-breakfast runs IR£12 ($19.25). Open all year.

Perched on a hilltop just outside the village, **Hill Serene House**, Carnakilla, Newmarket-on-Fergus, Co. Clare (tel. 061/71294), is a bright, modern bungalow. Carmel and Tim Murphy are the engaging couple who welcome guests here, and their three twin-bedded rooms are all attractively furnished, with handbasins and shaving points. The bed-and-breakfast rate here is IR£10.50 ($16.75). Open April through October.

In the pretty little village of Adare, Mrs. Mary Dundon's **Abbey Villa**, Kildimo Road, Adare, Co. Limerick (tel. 061/86113), has five nice guest rooms, all with private bathroom. It's a modern bungalow in a scenic setting, and Mrs. Dundon is a member of the Town & Country Homes Association, keenly interested in all her guests. Bed-and-breakfast rate is IR£12.50 ($20), with a one-third discount for children. You'll find central heat and plenty of parking.

Some three miles outside the picture-pretty village of Adare, Jennie and Michael Power's **Hillcrest**, Ballinvera, Croagh, Co. Limerick (tel. 061/86534), sits amid peaceful, bucolic beauty. The Powers are warm, hospitable hosts who take a keen interest in their visitors. Of the four spacious bedrooms, all have handbasins and electric blankets, and three have private facilities. The rate for bed-and-breakfast is IR£10.50 ($16.75), and with advance notice, Jennie will prepare dinner for IR£10 ($16). Open April to October.

Spa House, Castleconnell, Co. Limerick (tel. 061/377171), is a lovely 18th-century house about a half mile from the village of Castleconnell, about seven miles from Limerick. It sits on the banks of the Shannon, with its own historic spa well in the gardens. Mrs. Helen Wilson has five bedrooms, all attractive and comfortable, all with handbasins, and two with private facilities. There's central heat, plenty of parking, fishing, and marvelous scenic surroundings. The rate for bed-and-breakfast is IR£11 ($17.50), with 20% off for children. Open April through September.

FARMHOUSES: Cooleen House, Bruree, Co. Limerick (tel. 063/90584), is the Georgian-style home of Mrs. Eileen McDonogh. Set on a working dairy farm overlooking the Maigue River, the house is beautifully furnished, and Mrs. McDonogh is the soul of charm. There's private fishing on the grounds for salmon and trout, and in the village of Bruree the De Valera museum was the late president's first shrine in the country. There are four attractive guest rooms with handbasins, there's central heat, and guests are welcome to relax in the garden. The rate for bed-and-breakfast is IR£11 ($17.50). A discount of 10% is offered for children.

Sisters Ann and Maureen O'Shea's **Roseville**, Kilbreedy East, Kilmallock, Co. Limerick (tel. 063/88009), is just off a main road to Cork, Tipperary,

Dublin, and Lough Gur. The care the Misses O'Shea extend to their comfortable, homey farmhouse, which won the Tourist Board's "Most Attractive and Well-Kept Farmhouse" award for several years, spills over into the care and attention they give their guests. I've had nothing but praise from readers for their graciousness. The house has central heating and four guest rooms with handbasins. B&B rate is IR£9.50 ($15.20), and there's a 10% discount for children.

A HOTEL: Overlooking the picturesque little town of Killaloe, the **Lakeside Hotel,** Killaloe, Co. Clare (tel. 061/76122), sits on a slight hill surrounded by shady trees. Its rooms are rather plain, but very comfortable, and it's a favorite spot both for locals who come for meals and for holidaying Irish around the country. There's a nice lounge bar, and a dining room that offers both set meals and an à la carte menu. Rates range from IR£20 ($32) to IR£23 ($36.75) per person, depending on the season. It's one of the most relaxing places you could find, and a good headquarters for sightseeing around Shannonside.

READERS' ACCOMMODATIONS SELECTIONS: "Ray and Sheila Devine, **Shemond House,** Killaloe Road, Clonlara, Limerick, Co. Limerick (tel. 061/343767), have the cleanest house I have ever been in. We were greeted with an invitation for tea and after three days we hated to leave" (Mrs. H. Kemp, Ottawa, Ontario, Canada). . . . "I spent 13 days at **Boylans,** 22 Davis St. (tel. 061/48916), which is less than three minutes from the rail and bus terminal. Mrs. Teresa Boylan and family are the happiest and most accommodating people I have yet to meet, the rooms are immaculate, and the breakfast without comparison" (Evelyn Chorlton, Cambridge, Mass.). . . . "The best B&B we found was **Shannon View,** Bunratty, Co. Clare (tel. 061/74056), just 4½ miles from the airport. Mrs. Eileen Woulfe is a warm and charming lady who goes out of her way to accommodate guests. Her rooms are spotless and her breakfast is superb. We could not recommend a more delightful place to greet or bid farewell to lovely Ireland" (Barbara and George Finck, Santa Barbara, Calif.). . . . "**Shannon Grove House,** Athlunkard, Corbally, Killaloe Road, Co. Limerick (tel. 061/45756), is a great place to stay. Noreen Marsh has decorated her home beautifully, and her friendliness and helpfulness were outstanding" (M. McGrath, Bogota, N.J.).

4. WHERE TO EAT

The Tourist Office folks have done a superb job of restoring The Granary, Charlotte Quay, and one of the best things they did was to install the **Granary Tavern** (tel. 061/47266), retaining stone walls, vaulted ceilings, rough wood, and the general atmosphere of an old tavern. From June through September the Tourist Menu is served from 12:30 to 2:30 p.m., and in the adjacent **Mariner Restaurant,** there's a more expensive selection—around IR£6 ($9.50)—during those hours and at night, a very good dinner that goes a good bit above the budget, but is very good value, at around IR£12 ($19.25). Specialties are steaks, seafood, stuffed duck, lamb, and beef. In the tavern section, there's full bar service, and even if you don't plan a meal here, do stop by, bend an elbow, and enjoy the nightly ballads with no cover charge.

The **Chef's Cold Buffet,** Jurys Hotel, Ennis Road (tel. 061/55266), offers good value on weekdays from noon to 2:30 p.m. There's a wide range of cold meats and salads (with the chef's special dressing) served in the bar for around IR£5 ($8). For the evening meal, the **Coffee Dock** at Jurys gives good value in pleasant surroundings at about IR£9.50 ($15.25). Hours are 7 to 10:30 p.m. every day of the week. Both accept major credit cards if you want to conserve the cash.

In Todd's Bow, a small sort of alley just off William Street (near the Tourist Office), you'll find a bright and cheerful restaurant called the **Hi-Way City Centre** (tel. 061/42927). There are outdoor tables for fine weather, and inside lots of light wood and a very friendly staff. Meals and snacks are served from 10:30 a.m.

to 11 p.m., and it's a very popular lunch spot with locals. Hot light lunches such as poached filet of cod with cheese sauce or homemade shepherd's pie run under IR£5 ($8), sandwiches and snacks much less. In the evening, there's a set menu for four courses at IR£7.50 ($12). Snacks are served all day. Fully licensed and recommended.

The grill room in the **Royal George Hotel,** O'Connell Street (tel. 061/44566), serves moderately priced meals in an attractive setting. Lunch prices run about IR£5 ($8); dinner, around IR£10 ($16) or under. The Tourist Menu is served at lunchtime year round. Hours are noon to 10 p.m.; closed Sunday and Christmas Day.

Right in the center of the village of Newmarket-on-Fergus, Pat and Teresa Cronin have created the rather unique combination of a lively public bar and an adjoining restaurant that is the epitome of intimacy and superb food. **Cronin's Bar and Restaurant,** Newmarket-on-Fergus, Co. Clare (tel. 061/71157), specializes in Irish harvests from land and sea, using only the freshest ingredients and injecting a bit of provincial French flavor in their preparation. The bar serves snacks such as smoked salmon, seafood quiche, traditional Irish stew, sandwiches, and an Irish cheese platter, but it's in the lovely little restaurant that Cronin's really shines. There you'll find such dishes as poached escallops of salmon with leek sauce, Aran scallops in pastry with chive sauce, entrecôte Madagascar flambé, loin of lamb Athena, and breast of duckling in black-cherry sauce. There's also a very good wine list. Service is polished and professional, yet warm and friendly. There's a relaxed atmosphere that, along with the food, makes this one of the most popular eateries in the area with locals as well as visitors. Bar food ranges from IR£1 ($1.60) to IR£4 ($6.50), lunch averages about IR£7.50 ($12) from à la carte menu in the bar, and dinner is IR£16 ($25.50). Bar food is served daily except Sunday from 10:30 a.m. to 10 p.m.; lunch, from 12:30 to 3 p.m.; dinner, from 6 to 10 p.m. Best to reserve if you want to dine in the cozy restaurant—no need in the bar. There's a public parking lot just down the street, important in this village of tiny streets.

You will find the Tourist Menu served from 12:30 to 2:15 p.m. year round at the lovely old **Dunraven Arms Hotel** in Adare, Co. Limerick (tel. 061/86209), as well as inexpensive bar food in the pretty lounge overlooking gardens.

In Kilmallock, the **Bulgaden Castle Restaurant** (tel. 063/98209) is a delightful 18th-century tavern two miles east of town. Salads as well as hot lunches are under IR£5 ($8), and dinners featuring fresh seafood and local meats start at around IR£11 ($16.50). Hours are 12:20 to 10:30 p.m.

The plain, old-fashioned pub known as **Flannery's,** 20 Catherine St., at the corner of Cecil Street, serves pub grub and hot plates at the usual low pub prices.

BIG SPLURGE: MacCloskey's at Bunratty House, Bùnratty, Co. Clare (tel. 061/74082), is a relative newcomer to the Shannonside, and it makes a smashing Big Splurge! Bunratty House (just back of the castle) is an elegant mansion that dates back more than a century and a half. Its living quarters have seen comings and goings that would probably fill a book, but it's a sure bet that its arched-ceiling cellar has never before seen the likes of MacCloskey's gourmet restaurant. Gerry and Marie MacCloskey left West Cork and their award-winning Courtyard restaurant in Schull to bring their expertise to Shannonside, and the result is one of Ireland's most beautiful restaurants. The low ceilings and foot-and-a-half-thick walls have been whitewashed to a pristine white as a background for delicate shades of pink and rose, which are punctuated by the deep blue of tall candles at each table. The mansion's original wine cellar has been retained, and behind its ironwork gates rests an excellent selection of good wines.

Main courses of the set dinner change often to be sure that only the freshest produce, meats, and seafood are served. A typical five-course offering might include such starters as snails in garlic butter, a selection of melon with kiwi fruit, or smoked salmon; cream of lettuce soup or salad with Stilton cheese dressing; main courses of sea trout with hollandaise sauce, rod-caught salmon baked with herbs, leeks, and mushrooms, or black sole on the bone; fresh garden vegetables; and dessert of iced lemon-and-lime soufflé, rhubarb tart, or stuffed chocolate-covered pears. The price for such a feast comes to IR£22 ($35.25), plus 10% service charge. Hours are 6:30 to 10 p.m. every night except Sunday, Monday, and Christmas to February 1. Highly recommended.

5. THINGS TO SEE AND DO

The very *first* thing to do is go by the **Tourist Office** in the Granary on Charlotte Quay (tel. 061/317522). This is one of the best in the country, and they're prepared to book accommodations for you, steer you to eateries, help plan sightseeing excursions, tell you about craft shops in the area, alert you to any special events, festivals, or evening entertainment currently on, and send you away loaded down with maps and brochures to make your time in Shannonside a joy. There's also a very good selection of Irish publications for sale in the office. Daily except Sunday they conduct **walking tours** of Old Limerick. Ask about the Shannon Heritage Trail Explorer Ticket that saves you money on sightseeing admissions.

For sightseeing out of town, pick up the **Bus Eireann day trip** folder from the Tourist Office. There are some 17 tours during summer months, and they go as far afield as Connemara to the north and the Ring of Kerry to the south.

Grey Line Tours, in the Limerick Ryan Hotel, Ennis Road (tel. 061/326211), will pick up at all major hotels and guesthouses for full-day tours of Killarney and Muckross House, Galway City and Connemara, the Cliffs of Moher and the Burren, and Blarney Castle and Cork city. Each tour costs IR£19.50 ($31.25). There are also nightlife tours to Knappogue and Bunratty Castle medieval banquets at IR£27.90 ($44.75), and the Bunratty Ceili at IR£22.0 ($36.75). Call for bookings, schedules, pickup times, etc.

If your time in the Limerick area is short, **Valerie Sweeney,** Shannon Business Centre, Shannon, Co. Clare (tel. 061/62022), can meet your plane or collect you at your hotel to serve as a guide and save those precious hours by guiding you through sightseeing, shopping, golfing, or any other special interest. She can also arrange for a qualified driver to meet you and take the wheel of your rental car if you're a little timid about driving on the left immediately after a long flight.

IN THE CITY: Among the points of interest in the city, **St. Mary's Cathedral** ranks near the top. In the oldest part of the city, it was built in 1172 by Donal Mor O'Brien, the then King of Munster, on the site of his palace. It holds some intriguing antiquities, and the view from its bell tower is especially fine. There's no charge, and summer hours are 9 a.m. to 1 p.m. and 2:30 to 5:30 p.m. (in winter, it's only open in the mornings). From mid-June to mid-September, there's an excellent *son et lumière* light and audio show nightly inside the cathedral.

King John's Castle rises from the riverbank at one end of Thomond Bridge, and its ten-foot-thick walls include massive drum towers. The **Treaty Stone** is across the Shannon at the other end of the bridge.

At St. John's Square, the **Limerick Museum** exhibits artifacts from the Lough Gur area, as well as city charters, chains of office, the "nail" from the City Exchange on which merchants once struck their deals, currencies from periods in the city's history as far back as the Vikings, and a good deal more. It's free, and hours are 10 a.m. to 1 p.m. and 2:15 to 5 p.m. Tuesday through Saturday. Another interesting collection of ancient Irish metalwork, medieval bronzes, and enamels is in the **Hunt Museum,** at the National Institute for Higher Education, Plassey House (tel. 061/61511).

Limerick Lace

You're welcome to watch dedicated ladies making the famous and fine Limerick lace at the **Good Shepherd Convent** on Clare Street (it's out the Dublin road, across from the People's Park) from 9:30 a.m. to 1 p.m. and 2 to 5 p.m. Monday through Friday. Painstakingly made on very fine Brussels net, the lace may slowly fade away in the next decade or so, since there are so few young women willing to devote the time and care to such intricate work. At the convent, you can purchase items ranging from lace handkerchiefs at about IR£50 ($80) to bridal veils at IR£250 ($400) and up.

There is one note of optimism as we go to press. Nine young women in Limerick, under the guidance of Fr. Joe Young from the Southill Parish, are working to keep the skill alive. If their enterprise thrives, they will be able to fill mail orders from the United States as well as meet future demands in Ireland. I can only wish them well and hope that they prosper. Contact **Traditional Handmade Limerick Lace,** Unit 8, Tait Business Center, Dominick Street, Limerick; or in the U.S., Gerard South, c/o Sutton's Cache, 60 Kraft Ave., Bronxville, NY 10708 (tel. 914/337-6077).

BUNRATTY CASTLE AND FOLK PARK: You can drive or take a bus (it's the Shannon Airport bus, which makes a stop here) out to Bunratty Castle, and you really should allow a full morning or afternoon for the excursion. The marvelously restored 15th-century castle was built for the O'Briens, Earls of Thomond, and its restoration has included furnishings so complete the O'Briens who first lived here would feel right at home should their shades come back today. (That brings up a little aside: officially, Bunratty has no ghosts, but if you should chance to encounter a sad lady dressed in pink, or a soldier wearing a torn tunic and holding an empty scabbard, look quickly before they vanish—the lady threw herself into the courtyard upon learning that her lover had been killed the night before their wedding day, and from time to time they're spotted wandering the castle, though never together. As I said, *officially* the story is not true, but unofficially, it is widely believed.) There are heavy carved-wood chests, woven tapestries, ornate wooden chairs, and pieces that look as though they have been here forever. You enter over the drawbridge into the vast, vaulted Great Hall, the center of castle life and where the tradition of entertaining guests with elaborate feasts is re-created these days with nightly medieval banquets (see below). Narrow, winding stone steps lead to upper floors where family life went on.

You can visit Bunratty Castle from 9:30 a.m. to 5:30 p.m. daily, year round, and admission is IR£4 ($6.50) for adults, IR£2 ($3.25) for children.

The charming and authentic cluster of homes, shops, and workshops from early Irish life on the castle grounds came about almost by accident when a centuries-old farmhouse was moved from the Shannon Airport to make way for a longer runway, and it became the nucleus of a collection of traditional buildings that include a blacksmith shop (with the smithy hard at work inside), a fisherman's cottage, a coastal cottage with its thatch firmly tied against Atlantic gales, and several craft shops. Each is a "working" exhibit, with a costumed "housewife" baking brown bread in a covered iron pot on the hearth, weavers at their looms, and everybody going about daily chores. At one end of the park, a typical village street has been reconstructed, complete with post office, draper, tea room, and a tiny pub. All are occupied, and this is a good place to pick up gifts and souvenirs.

Also at Bunratty

You won't want to miss **Durty Nelly's** pub, even if you sip a non-alcoholic white lemonade. It's on a stone, arched bridge right at the entrance to Bunratty Castle grounds, and for centuries after it was built in 1620, it served the soldiers who were garrisoned there. Like the Earls of Thomond in the castle, those soldiers would feel perfectly at home in today's Durty Nellie's. The wooden chairs and benches are the same, peat still burns in the fireplaces, and some of the hodgepodge hanging on the walls and from the rafters look as though they were put there by one of the earl's protectors and haven't been moved since. Even the pigeon cote has survived in one room of the loft, just as it was when it bred delicacies for the castle table. Durty Nellie's draws huge crowds: tourists, you'd surely expect, but the amazing thing is the large number of locals who love the place. It's a grand place for a pint, and there's good pub grub as well (I never go past without stopping for a toasted corned beef and cheese sandwich or soup and brown bread). After about 9 p.m. things get pretty lively with music and singing, and even those drinking in the outside patio join in. Its Oyster Restaurant is open daily from 10:30 a.m. and the Loft Restaurant Monday through Saturday from 6 p.m. (tel. 061/364861 for reservations).

On the other side of Bunratty Castle, just beyond Fitzpatrick's Shannon Shamrock Hotel, **Mike McGlynn Antiques,** Bunratty, Co. Clare (tel. 061/ 62011), has an interesting collection of antiques housed in an old-style thatched cottage. Mike and his brother have something to offer everyone from the dedicated antique hunter to those of us who would simply like to bring back home some of Ireland's antiquity. For me, it was an elegant teak walking stick which undoubtedly reached these shores by way of an Irish seafarer. For you, it might be a small bit of fine porcelain or some bit of ironwork. There are works of art, china, paintings, furniture, and a host of other larger items. They'll gladly insure and ship any purchase too large to tote home.

Other shopping of interest at Bunratty is **Bunratty Cottage,** across from the castle, where designer Vonnie Reynolds displays her own designs as well as an exceptional stock of Irish woolens, tweeds, gifts, etc. **Avoca Handweavers** has also opened a large outlet alongside Mike McGlynn Antiques (see above).

Area Shopping Note

You'll see the **Ballycasey Craft Centre** signposted on the Limerick–Shannon road, and it's a don't-miss for crafts hunters. Clustered around the farmyard of the 18th-century Ballycaseymore House, individual workshops are home to artisans, from weaver to potter to fashion designer to silversmith to a host of other arts and crafts. The **Barn Restaurant** serves fresh, appetizing light lunches, with wine available, at modest prices.

LIMERICK'S PUBS: Sadly, a good many of the city's finest pubs have been

modernized right out of their character, but **W. J. South's** (also known as the **Crescent Bar**), on the Crescent (that's where Daniel O'Connell's statue commands the center of O'Connell Street), holds on to the trappings of its age with a firm grip. There's a long white marble bar up front, divided by wood and etched-glass partitions to give a bit of privacy. Faded tapestries hang on the wall opposite, and behind the bar there's an elaborate structure of mahogany, its arched niches framing old bottles and backed by mirrors speckled with age. Just back of the small front bar, a larger room is decidedly more casual, its walls displaying photos of rugby players (the Garyowen rugby team consider South's their "local"). Still another room is behind this, with tapestries of hunting scenes illuminated by a skylight. The best pint in Limerick is said to be pulled here, and you'll hear a *lot* about rugby and other sports.

The "aged" look at **Flannery's,** 20 Catherine St. (at the corner of Cecil Street), comes from woodwork that once graced an old distillery, and according to Jerry Flannery, "there's still plenty of whiskey salted in it." The pub itself is only a little more than 50 years old, but it has the comfortable atmosphere of a country pub, with a small snug at one end, and in the evening a core of regulars ever ready to converse with the visiting Yank, and at least one in the bunch who will hop right in to explain the game of rugby (this, too, is a sports pub) to the obviously ignorant. Flannery's also serves good pub grub at lunch.

My favorite of all Limerick pubs is neither aged nor particularly atmospheric, but it's very, very Irish. **Matt Fennessy's Pub,** New Street, Punches Cross, is the epitome of a neighborhood local, filled with convivial souls, a good pint pulled, and in general just the sort of place to pass a pleasant evening. A bit out from the city center, but easily reached via either a longish walk or a short bus ride, New Street turns off O'Connell (it's the intersection with Dan Ryan's Garage on one corner, Punches Pub on the opposite). Inside, there's an old-fashioned bar, a lounge, and a snug affectionately dubbed "The Senate" by regulars, since the affairs of the country are often debated and settled (sort of) within its walls. Every Saturday night there's sing-along music from 9 p.m. to closing. The clientele is almost all local, and they make Americans very welcome. Look for Mick Feerick behind the bar, one of Ireland's charmers. Incidentally, bar food is served from 12:30 to 2 p.m., should you find yourself in the neighborhood.

Nancy Blake's Bar, Denmark Street is a cozy, old-style pub popular for pub lunches and traditional music on Tuesday nights.

COUNTY LIMERICK SIGHTS: Tourist Offices in County Limerick are located at **Lough Gur Stone Age Centre,** Bruff (tel. 061/85186), open May through September, and the **Thatched Cottage and Craft Shop,** Main Street, Adare (tel. 061/86255), open June to early September.

Lough Gur: Some 17 miles southeast of Limerick city, Lough Gur is one of Ireland's most important archeological sites, and thousands of Stone Age relics have been found in and around it. The lifestyle of those long-ago Irishmen comes vividly alive in the **Stone Age Centre** at Lough Gur (tel. 061/85186). It's designed in the style of Neolithic period dwellings, and inside there are replicas of many of the artifacts discovered in this area, as well as models of burial chambers, stone circles, and dolmens. An audio-visual show tells you what we know of Stone and Bronze Age people and their habits, and periodically, walking tours are conducted to some of the more important archeological sites. The centre is open daily from 10 a.m. to 1 p.m. and 2 to 6 p.m. (on Sunday from 2 to 6 p.m.) May through September. Admission (which includes tea or coffee) is IR£1.50 ($2.50) for adults, half that for children.

Irish Dresden: The little town of Dromcollogher, southwest of Limerick City, is where you can visit the **Irish Dresden Ltd.** plant and shop (tel. Dromcollogher 30) Monday through Friday. Watch Exquisite Dresden figurines being made, then browse through their showroom.

Lough Derg and Killaloe: The 13-mile drive north of Limerick city to the charming little Lough Derg harbor village of Killaloe is delightful, and **St. Flannan's Cathedral** (12th century) is worth a visit to see the ornately carved Irish Romanesque doorway, Ogham stone (which also has Runic writings and a crude crucifix believed to be formed by a Viking who had converted to Christianity). Drive along the western shore of the lake to view magnificent scenery and ancient ruins on offshore islands. You're very welcome to **fish** or **swim** at no charge; **course fishing** is best at Plassy, and the Electricity Supply Board on O'Connell Street issues free permits for fishing.

6. LIMERICK AFTER DARK

From the Tourist Office, pick up the *What's On* booklet, which lists current goings on in Limerick and its environs, as well as a Calendar of Events published by the **Belltable Arts Centre,** 69 O'Connell St. (tel. 061/49866). The Belltable puts on very good concerts and plays at inexpensive prices. Also, the Glentworth Hotel, West County Inn, Lakeside Hotel in Killaloe, Clare Inn Hotel, and other hotels sometimes have cabaret, with or without dinner, during summer months, with dates, times, and prices listed in the *What's On* booklet (you can book through the Tourist Office or directly with the hotels).

The undisputed highlights of Limerick nighttime entertainment, however, are the medieval banquets in nearby Bunratty Castle and Knappogue Castle. Running a close second is the show at the Captain's Table in the Granary on Charlotte Quay. The banquets are Big Splurge experiences I suggest you budget for before leaving home, and it's a good idea to book for them as far in advance as you can during summer months. If you're flying in and out of Shannon Airport, another good idea is to book one on your first night in Ireland, the other on your last.

MEDIEVAL BANQUETS: Right here, I have to confess that for years I resisted the lure of the medieval banquet at **Bunratty Castle,** convinced of two things: that I'd spend the evening in the company of other tourists when I had come to Ireland to enjoy the company of the Irish; and that the whole show would be too "cute" to be wholesome. My second confession is that I was wrong, wrong, wrong, and that I've seldom missed attending one each trip since friends dragged me along a few years back. True, your fellow diners will almost surely be other tourists, but the great thing is that when you walk across the drawbridge into the Great Hall and are handed your first mug of hot mulled wine by a pretty, smiling Irish lass, the great good spirit of Irish fun takes over and Americans, French, German, Australians, Italians, and every other nationality represented lose their tourist trappings and become fellow conspirators in the evening's fantasy plot.

As for the show, *of course* it's hokey—it's meant to be! Blarney may have originated down there in County Cork, but there's lots of it afoot in Bunratty, as fresh-faced, lovely Irish girls in period costumes come around to cover your front with a protective bib, story follows story and song follows song from the Ladies of the Castle and their male cohorts (a merry group of entertainers, indeed), and the stuffiest, most "touristy" type turns mellow in the sometimes hilarious struggle to get through a meal without benefit of cutlery. The talent on stage is first-rate, and I defy you to keep a dry eye as the golden notes of an Irish harp wash over you in a massive room brought suddenly to a complete hush.

A typical banquet menu will begin with a cup of broth, followed by spareribs, half a roast chicken (sometimes a hunk of well-done beef), salad, vegetables, homemade bread torn into ragged chunks, and a dessert just dripping with calories. To top it all off, you quaff a mug of mead (the traditional honey-based drink). You'll be given a knife, and after that it's you and your fingers, just as in the old days. Between each course, one little bit of stage business or another goes on, the most popular of which is the appointment of the evening's "Earl of Thomond" from among the guests, who reigns at the top of the long banquet table. His "duties" include banishing another one of the guests to the dungeon and addressing his assembled guests with as flowery a bit of oratory as he can manage. It's a memorable night—the Earls of Thomond should have such a good time under their own roof!

The cost for all this merriment is IR£26 ($41.50), and there are two banquets each night, at 5:45 and 9 p.m., year round. You should reserve before leaving home if at all possible, either through a travel agent or by writing the Reservations Manager, Shannon Castle Tours, Shannon Airport, Co. Clare, Ireland (tel. 061/61788). Should you arrive without a reservation, any Tourist Office will try to get you a seat, or you can give the Reservations Manager a call to ask about an opening (sometimes there are cancellations). Just don't miss it!

Knappogue Castle: This massive 1467 stronghold is some 19 miles from Limerick city, which means you must have a car, since it is not served by local buses. The banquet here differs from that at Bunratty in that the group is smaller and more intimate and the entertainment tends to be somewhat less ribald, with sketches to bring to life myths and legends of Old Ireland and lots of song and dance. Many of my Irish friends prefer this to Bunratty (and there are usually a fair few Irish faces at the table), and in the best of all possible Irish holidays, you'd get to both. Prices, hours, and booking information is the same as for Bunratty, except that it runs from May through October only.

SHANNON CEILI:
While the banquets offer fun on a "lord and lady of the castle" level, over in the Bunratty Folk Park the merriment is more akin to that of the "downstairs" crew in those castles. There's traditional song and dance, with audience and performers engaging in lively back-and-forth joshing. And the dishes that come to table are likely to include Irish stew, apple pie, and soda bread. It's the fun and entertainment of Old Ireland's people *outside* the castles. The Shannon Ceili is held nightly at 5:45 and 9 p.m., May through September, with an admission of IR£21 ($33.50).

AROUND SHANNONSIDE

□ □ □

Counties Clare and North Tipperary

1. ACCOMMODATIONS
2. WHERE TO EAT
3. THINGS TO SEE AND DO

Within the Shannonside region, you can span Ireland's history from Stone Age relics around Lough Gur to Craggaunowen's Bronze Age lake dwelling and 15th-century castle to mementos of the 1800s in the Clare Heritage Centre. Traditional music thrives all through County Clare, and Mother Nature has turned up such wonders as the Aillwee Cave, the Cliffs of Moher, and the rocky expanse of the Burren. For the visitor, it's a great convenience that all are concentrated in an area compact enough to be seen on day trips from one base.

1. ACCOMMODATIONS

Shannonside has an abundance of good, inexpensive accommodations scattered over the entire region.

Note: Prices shown below are those in effect in 1989—expect them to be higher in 1990.

County Clare

HOSTELS. There's a fine **An Oige hostel** in Mountshannon, Co. Clare (tel. Mountshannon 9). It's a large old residence with many of its original furnishings, and sits right on the shores of Lough Derg. Boats may be hired in the vicinity to go out to the island of Inis Cealtra (Holy Island), where there is a round tower and other ruins.

The **Doolin Hostel,** Doolin Village, Co. Clare (tel. 065/74006), is privately owned and run by Josephine and Paddy Moloney and is sometimes known as the "Old Farmhouse Hostel." It is located on the Moloney dairy farm and provides hot showers, central heating, full kitchen facilities, a dining room, a laundry and drying room, and a hostel shop. The Moloneys also operate a bureau de change on the premises, and they provide farmhouse accommodations for nonhostelers. No registration card is required, and the hostel charge is IR£5 ($8) per person.

BED-AND-BREAKFAST. Kilkee is a small, quiet seaside resort, and Mrs. Mary Enright's **Aran House,** West End Kilkee, Co. Clare (tel. 065/56170), sits near the end of the curved bay, with a view of the cliffs across the water. Mrs. Enright is a warm, motherly sort who makes her guests feel right at home. Her buff-colored stucco house has twin bay windows in front and many antiques among its furnishings. There are six comfortable, homey guest rooms (one with private facilities), and the two singles overlook a small garden and rocky cliffside. Bed-and-breakfast costs IR£10.50 ($16.75), with a 20% discount for children.

    Aran View House, Doolin, Co. Clare (tel. 065/74061), is notable for its gorgeous sea view of the Aran Islands. Its gracious hostess is Theresa Linnane. The big two-story house, built in 1736, sits high on a hill, and a window-walled lounge takes full advantage of the view. The eight attractive, homey guest rooms include five with private bath facilities and the others with handbasins—all have lovely views. One large room has three single beds and private facilities, and there are two single rooms (sometimes very hard to find). Rates are IR£11 ($17.50) for bed-and-breakfast, and IR£12 ($19.25) for a room with private facilities.

    Leagard House, Miltown Malbay, Co. Clare (tel. 065/84324), is set in quiet, rural surroundings and is an interesting, rambling one-story house that once was run as a nursing home by Ireland's President Hillary before he went into politics. Suzanne and John Hannon, the present owners, take a personal interest in all their guests, and John is happy to give advice on such important matters as getting to the right pub at the right time to hear some of County Clare's fine traditional musicians. Suzanne excels in the kitchen, and her meals have won such praise that they now accept dinner reservations for nonguests; there's a wine license, and dinners are superb, with a IR£10 ($16) price. The six guest rooms are all light and airy, and I especially was drawn to the two up front which open onto a small, glass-enclosed room. All look out on peaceful country scenes, and the dining room opens to a windowed porch. The rate for bed-and-breakfast is IR£11 ($17.50), with 50% off for children.

    In Ennistymon, Tom and Mary McMahon have five homey guest rooms above **McMahon's Pub,** Church Street, Ennistymon, Co. Clare (tel. 065/71078). Mary is a cousin of a former Rhode Island governor, and Americans are given an especially warm welcome. Guest rooms are scattered about on several upstairs levels, and each has an individual size, shape, and character. Bed-and-breakfast costs IR£11 ($17.50), and Mary will cook an evening meal for IR£10 ($16). Pub grub is available in the pub (along with good conversation with the locals who favor this place) at lunchtime.

    Mrs. Eileen Carroll, **Tullamore Farm,** Kilshanny, Ennistymon, Co. Clare (tel. 065/71187), is the charming hostess of this large house which is set in lovely countryside. The house is centrally heated and there is a beautiful TV lounge with a view overlooking the hills. The food is excellent and there is a very relaxed atmosphere about the place. The four attractive bedrooms all have handbasins and three have private facilities. The rate for bed-and-breakfast is IR£10.50 ($16.75) and dinner costs the same; there is a 20% reduction for children. Open March through October.

    Jim and Eithne McGuire, **The Lodge,** Broadford, Co. Clare (tel. 061/73129), are the friendly owners of this beautiful, old, Victorian-style hunting lodge set in a state forest. You will receive lots of hospitality and attention here and they serve an excellent evening meal. The three lovely bedrooms all have handbasins and the house is centrally heated. The rate for bed-and-breakfast is IR£10.50 ($16.75) and dinner is IR£9.50 ($15.25); 20% reduction for children. Open April through September.

A FARMHOUSE. A marvelous old (200 years at least, according to Tess) farmhouse, **Tessie's Fernhill Farmhouse,** Doolin Road, Lisdoonvarna, Co. Clare (tel. 065/ 74040), is set on a hill overlooking fields and distant hills. It has twice won Best Farmhouse awards, and Tess Linnane, its owner, is a warm, enthusiastic hostess who takes great pleasure in making her guests feel at home. There's a large front lounge with picture windows looking out to the fields, and one guest room on the ground floor is ideal for the handicapped. Upstairs bedrooms have kept the character of the house, some with wooden peaked or slanted ceilings. All are nicely furnished, and all have handbasins. Bed-and-breakfast costs IR£11 ($17.50), and Tess serves a hearty Irish farm dinner for the same price. There's central heat and a paved car park.

HOTELS. The **Smyth Village Hotel,** Feakle, Co. Clare (tel. Feakle 2), is unique among Irish hotels. Located in the Rent-a-Cottage village of Feakle, the hotel is a sort of hotel/guesthouse, owned and operated by natives of the region, Mr. and Mrs. Con Smyth. The hotel consists of three connected two-story cottage-type buildings, and its bluff-top site overlooks the traditional cottages of the rental scheme. Hotel amenities include a full liquor license, tennis courts, a game room, and a dining room that is open to nonresidents for breakfast and dinner (lunch to guests only, if requested). Meals are served family style, with no choice of menu, but with "the very best quality done in the simplest way" and with Mrs. Smyth's home-baked bread. There's an old-fashioned pub that draws local musicians as well as visitors from the rental cottages below. All 12 bedrooms have private bath and are nicely decorated. Rates for bed-and-breakfast are IR£10 ($16) per person sharing a room and IR£11 ($17.50) for singles, with a service charge of 15% and a one-third discount for children. Special rates are available for stays of three days or longer. Open April through November.

    Hyland's Hotel, Ballyvaughan, Co. Clare (tel. 065/77037), is a real charmer. Dating back to the early 18th century, the two-story hotel is now in the hands of the eighth generation of the Hyland family, and the personal atmosphere is evident the minute you walk through the front door. The comfortable, attractive residents' lounge has a fireplace glowing with turf, as does the public lounge on the premises where local musicians gather nightly and in impromptu sessions uphold the County Clare tradition of good music and good spirits. Dunguaire Castle is just 15 miles away, and the hotel will arrange for you to attend the medieval banquet there if you wish. Bedrooms differ in size, but are quite nicely decorated. Seasonal rates range from IR£19 ($30.50) to IR£23 ($36.75) single, IR£30 ($48) to IR£36 ($57.50) double.

    Halpin's Hotel, 2 Erin St., Kilkee, Co. Clare (tel. 065/56032 or 56317), is a small (11 guest rooms), family-run hotel in this charming seaside resort. There are rooms both with and without private baths, the dining room serves good food at moderate prices, and there's entertainment in the bar during the summer season. Seasonal rates range from IR£15 ($24) to IR£17 ($27) per person.

County Tipperary

BED-AND-BREAKFAST. The **Country House,** Thurles Road, Kilkeary, Nenagh, Co. Tipperary (tel. 067/31193), is the modern bungalow home of Joan and Matt Kennedy. The family lounge, which guests are invited to share for TV or just visiting, has a peat-burning fireplace, and the house is set in scenic rural surroundings four miles out from Nenagh. Lough Derg is only about 20 minutes away. There are five nicely decorated guest rooms, all with handbasins, three with private showers, and one with private toilet and shower. B&B rate is IR£10 ($16), with one-third off for children. There's steam heat and good parking.

Mrs. Mary Fallon, **Cregganbell**, Birr Road, Roscrea, Co. Tipperary (tel. 0505/21421), has four guest rooms with handbasins and private showers. All beds have electric blankets. This is a lovely modern bungalow on the outskirts of town, with river fishing nearby. Rates for bed-and-breakfast are IR£9.50 ($15.25) with a 20% reduction for children. Centrally heated, and plenty of parking.

Gortalougha House, Ballinderry, Terryglass, Co. Tipperary (tel. 067/22080), is a lovely, large period house set in 100 acres of woodland just 20 yards from the shores of Lough Derg. Bessie and Michael Wilkinson are the hosts here, and they have their own boat for hire if you care to try your luck with the pike for which the Lough is renowned. The Wilkinsons will provide a packed lunch for fishermen or daytrippers. There are seven beautiful guest rooms, five with private baths and all with handbasins, and the house is centrally heated. Bed-and-breakfast costs IR£25 ($40) double, with one-third discount for children. Splurgy, but a real treat.

HOTEL. The charming **Waterside Hotel,** Dromineer Bay, Nenagh, Co. Tipperary (tel. 067/24114), sits on the shores of Lough Derg and is owned and operated by Barry Smyth, of the Smyth Village Hotel family (see County Clare, above), a pretty good recommendation in itself in light of their long record of happy visitors. The Waterside Restaurant specializes in freshwater fish, seafood, and fresh local produce, and the Captain's Bridge Bar, which has panoramic views of the lake, serves bar food all day. All 12 guest rooms have private facilities, and the rate, including a full Irish breakfast, is IR£16 ($25.50) per person.

READERS' ACCOMMODATIONS SELECTIONS: "A first-rate accommodation in Doolin, Co. Clare, was Mrs. K. Cullinan's **Harbour View** (tel. 065/74154). Her home is set on a hillside, with a magnificent view of the surrounding countryside. Mrs. Cullinan was very friendly and was helpful in recommending things to see and do in Doolin" (G. Wazeter and S. Strazzella, Bayonne, N.J.). . . . "Mrs. E. Woulfe, **Shannon View,** Bunratty West, Co. Clare (tel. 061/74056), is a wonderful, hospitable hostess, with beautifully appointed and comfortable rooms. A perfect beginning or end for Shannon Airport travelers" (Mr. and Mrs. W. Eich, Palo Alto, Calif.). . . . "I highly recommend **Carberry,** on Kilrush Road, Ennis, Co. Clare (tel. 065/24046). Mrs. Pauline Roberts provides a breakfast that can't be beat, and the rooms are immaculately clean and tastefully decorated" (Kate and Stan Katz, Albany, N.Y.). . . . "We found the most hospitable family in our Ireland experiences to be Nuala and Jimmy Clancy, of **Kilcarregh farmhouse,** a couple of miles out of Kilfenora in County Clare. Nuala served us sandwiches, homemade fruit cake, and tea soon after we arrived, and Jimmy played the accordion and tin whistle for us. He has won many prizes for his contributions to preserving the rich heritage of Irish folk music" (Dorothy Southall, La Fayette, Ky.). . . . "At Sixmilebridge, Co. Clare, **Riverview** is run by Tim and Martha Kearney. It is ideal for a first or last night's stay, since it is near Shannon Airport, and also for touring County Clare. Tim and Martha make you feel at home with coffee or tea always at hand" (Mrs. D. Weidenkeller, Santa Ana, Calif.). . . . **"Vaughn's Hotel** in Lisdoonvarna, Co. Clare, is a charming, spotless, 17-room haven in the center of this sweet little village. Irene Vaughn runs it and her husband runs the pub downstairs. No private baths, but very low rates" (Geraldine Levy, New York, N.Y.).

"The Avoca House, Cratloe, Co. Clare (tel. 061/97180), has bright, cheerful rooms with all facilities. Mrs. Mulcahy will give you efficient service at table and in looking after your bedroom. The house is just 1½ miles from Bunratty Castle on the road to Limerick"

(K. Shreenan, Montréal, Québec, Canada). . . . "Mrs. Joan Quinn's **Cratloe Heights,** Ballymorris, Cratloe, Co. Clare (tel. 061/87253), is only two miles from Bunratty Castle and registered with the Irish Tourist Board. She is a charming, warm person who cannot do enough to make your stay with her more comfortable and pleasant, and her home is truly a home away from home" (F. and J. Garsson, Los Angeles, Calif.). . . . **"Ballinalacken Castle,** Lisdoonvarna, Co. Clare (tel. 065/74025), is a 19th-century house (bed-and-breakfast) with the castle right next door. We enjoyed the luxury of the double rooms which were huge. There is a bar and dining room downstairs and the owners even offer to bring drinks to your room. We enjoyed free babysitting services there as well. If you ask the bar manager, he will give you the key to the castle next door so you may explore on your own" (K. O'Brien, Tujunga, Calif.). . . . "Mrs. V. O'Dea, **Fortwilliam,** Sixmilebridge, Co. Clare (tel. 061/72216), has a lovely home and is very nice. The place is nicely decorated and comfortable, with a quiet, relaxing atmosphere" (N. Rounsefell and S. Gilmore, Baton Rouge, La.). . . . "We enjoyed our stay at **Millbank,** Roslevar, Ennis, Co. Clare (tel. 065/22479). The Guilfoyles were friendly and hospitable and even arranged for us to go fishing" (M. Farley, Austin, Tex.).

2. WHERE TO EAT

Picnic spots abound in the Shannonside area, as do country pubs serving inexpensive pub grub.

County Clare

The **Visitors Centre** at the Cliffs of Moher has a bright and cheerful self-service tea room offering inexpensive soups, sandwiches, and assorted snacks.

For a very special lunch in a setting of old-world charm, stop by the **Old Ground Hotel** in Ennis (tel. 065/28127). In its Grill Room, superb seafood, salads, omelets, and locally grown meats are served at prices of IR£6 ($9.50) to IR£9 ($14.50). Hours are 12:30 to 2:15 p.m. Dinners here, featuring French cuisine and seafood, start at IR£16.50 ($26.50) and are served by candlelight in the hotel's pretty dining room.

Also in Ennis, **Brogans Restaurant and Bar** (tel. 065/29859 or 29480), serves bar food, as well as salads and hot or cold lunch plates for around IR£3.50 ($5.50) and grills in the evening in the same price ranges. Hours are 12:20 to 4 p.m. and 5 to 10:30 p.m. Soup and sandwiches are available in the bar continuously, beginning at 10:30 a.m.

In Doolin, alongside the Aille River you'll find **Bruach na hAille** ("Bank of the River") (tel. 065/74120). Helen and John Browne serve marvelous seafood and local dishes in a restored country house with flagstone floors and white-washed walls. The menu features everything from soup and salads to fresh mackerel, salmon, and local shellfish and a limited range of foreign specialties, with the emphasis on local seafood. Soups, desserts, and bread are all homemade. Wine is available by the glass, and prices run IR£6.50 ($10.50) to IR£12 ($19.25). Hours are 6 to 9:30 p.m., and from June through September the Tourist Menu is offered. Open May through October. Highly recommended.

Right on the strand at Kilkee, Doris and Klaus Meya have opened a bright, cozy café, **The Krazy Krauts,** The Strand, Kilkee, Co. Clare. For now, it's open from May to September (9 a.m. to 9 p.m.) only, since the Meyas spend winters in their native Germany, but their plans are to become "Irish" year round as soon as possible. In the meantime, their fully licensed place serves exceptionally fresh and well-prepared light meals all day for exceptionally moderate prices. An evening meal is served for under IR£10 ($16) if you order ahead. Don't miss the appealing little wine bar in the back with its tiny fireplace and paintings by local artists—specialties are German whites and French reds, and while you're there be sure to sample "Klaus's special" apéritif. The bar is open from 1 p.m. to 1 a.m.

In Corofin, Co. Clare, at **Maryse & Gilbert's** (tel. 065/27660), the cuisine is French and Italian. It's a small, intimate place set in lovely gardens. Dinner comes by candlelight and costs around IR£10 ($16). Hours are 7 to 10 p.m. daily except Sunday and Monday (closed Monday only in July and August).

North Tipperary

The **Waterside Restaurant,** in the Waterside Hotel, Dromineer, Nenagh (tel. 067/24114), has beautiful lakeside views and a menu that emphasizes Irish and international cuisine. Freshwater fish and seafood are the specialties, and there's also a bar-food menu. Prices are moderate, and hours are 12:30 to 3 p.m. and 7 to 10 p.m. daily. Bar food is served all day in the Captain's Bridge Bar.

Plain cooking, Irish style, is featured in the **Pathe Hotel,** Roscrea (tel. 0505/21301). In this family-run establishment, lunch costs about IR£5.50 ($8.80) and à la carte prices at dinner start at IR£8 ($12.75). Hours are noon to 3 p.m. and 6 to 10 p.m. daily. The Tourist Menu is available from June through August.

You'll also find the Tourist Menu available from 12:30 to 2:30 p.m. in Thurles at the **Hayes Hotel,** Liberty Square (tel. 0504/22122), with many Irish dishes listed on the menu.

READERS' RESTAURANT SELECTIONS: "The Piper's Chair, Doolin, Co. Clare, next to O'Connor's Pub, serves fine food in a charming atmosphere, specializing in local seafood and using only the freshest ingredients" (Otis and Jane Maclay, Houston, Tex.). . . . "We had a marvelous five-course meal, beautifully served by candlelight, with pretty china and silver, at **Mountcashel Castle Restaurant** in County Clare (tel. 061/72577). Our hosts, the Harringtons, were delightful, and we preferred our 'meal in a castle' to the medieval banquets" (Leila Morris, Columbus, Ga.). [*Author's Note:* Mountcashel Castle is on the main Bunratty–Knappogue route, two miles north of Sixmilebridge.] . . . "We especially enjoyed stopping in **Killilagh House,** a restaurant and craft shop in Doolin, Co. Clare (tel. 065/74183). The food was good, and there is a wine license. There's a peat fire in a cottage-like interior, and handcrafts on the walls" (S. Debnam, Virginia Beach, Va.).

3. THINGS TO SEE AND DO

County Clare

Tourist Offices are on Clare Road Ennis (tel. 065/28366), open year round, and at the **Cliffs of Moher Visitor Centre,** Liscannor (tel. 065/81171), open March through October.

THE CRAGGAUNOWEN PROJECT. One of County Clare's most interesting sightseeing stops is the Craggaunowen (pronounce it "Crag-an-owen") Project near Quin. Craggaunowen Castle has an interesting display of medieval art objects, and in the lake a short walk away, there's a fascinating re-creation of a crannog, a lake dwelling of the Bronze Age inhabitants of Ireland. The earthen ring fort on the grounds holds a reconstructed farmer's home of some 15 centuries ago. For me —thrilled as I have been at Tim Severin's daring voyage across the Atlantic to retrace St. Brendan's legendary route of A.D. 700—a highlight here is the glass shelter which has been constructed to house the tiny leather *St. Brendan* in which he made the voyage. The project is open daily May through September from 10 a.m. to 6 p.m., with an admission fee of IR£2.10 ($3.25) for adults, IR£1.30 ($2) for children.

KNAPPOGUE CASTLE. Also near Quin, Knappogue Castle (of the medieval banquets) is furnished in period pieces, somewhat more formally than Bunratty Castle. It's open daily from 9:30 a.m. to 5:30 p.m., with admission of IR£1.90 ($3) for adults, IR£1.15 ($1.75) for children.

CLARE HERITAGE CENTRE. If your family roots are in County Clare, you'll want to visit the Clare Heritage Centre at Corofin, near Ennis (tel. 065/27632), where you'll find a genealogical research service, thousands of family records, and interesting exhibits portraying life in County Clare in ages past. Open March through October from 10 a.m. to 6 p.m.; other months from 9 a.m. to 5 p.m. Small admission charge.

ENNIS. The bustling market town of Ennis has many interesting historical buildings, and the Tourist Office (see above) can give you a walking-tour guide through the more historic sections. Headquarters for traditional music, song, and dance is **Cois No hAbhna** (pronounced "Cush-na-how-na"), on Gort Road. Their shop has a large selection of records, tapes, and books on Irish traditional music, and they maintain a good schedule of happenings during summer months.

THE CLIFFS OF MOHER. Ireland's spectacular coastline really outdoes itself at the Cliffs of Moher near Liscannor. In Irish, they're named Ailltreacha Mothair ("The Cliffs of the Ruin"), and they stretch for five miles, rising at places to 700 feet. They're breathtaking and shouldn't be missed.

LOOP HEAD PENINSULA. A delightful day is one spent driving to seaside **Kilkee** with its curved bay and strand, then down the long finger of land that is the West Clare Peninsula to its end, where the Loop Head lighthouse holds solitary vigil. The coastline is one of clifftops, inlets and coves, sandy beaches, and a softly wild, unspoiled landscape. Along the way there are the ruins of forts, castles, and churches, and should you stop for a pint in a country pub, there are legends to be heard, like that of Kilstiffin Bank, a shoal that lies beneath the Shannon's waters. It was, so it is said hereabouts, at one time a part of the mainland, but was swept into the Shannon during a fierce storm in the 9th century, carrying people and their homes to a watery grave. But according to the older residents of this area, when sailing ships used to drop anchor off the Kisstiffin Bank, they'd be visited during the night by a small man from beneath the water who would climb the anchor cable and ask them to take up the anchor, for it had gone down his chimney. As you relax into the solitary beauty of the peninsula, you'll have no doubt at all about the truth in that story!

In the little Shannonside village of **Kilbaha** (Cill Bheathach, or "Birch Church"), the **Church of Moheen** holds a small wooden structure that is one of Ireland's most unusual testaments to the devotion of her people to their faith. It's a tiny three-sided chapel on wheels known as the Ark of Kilbaha which, during the years when English-imposed law forbade any landlord to permit a Catholic mass to be held on his land, was hidden away during the week, but pulled down to the shore of Kilbaha Bay on Sunday and placed below the high-tide mark on land that belonged to no man. There mass was said in safety, reverence, and peace. While you're in Kilbaha, look for **Jim Connolly's studio** Kilkee, Kilrush, Co. Clare (tel. Carrigholt 34). Jim lives and works in a thatched cottage, and his bronze sculptures are brilliant (the most noted is that of Eamon de Valera in Ennis). He's an interesting man to talk to, and while the bronzes are much too pricey and heavy to think of purchasing, he does have a ceramics shop with creative, inexpensive souvenirs. You might call before going, since he's often away.

DOOLIN. Doolin is a tiny coastal village that has gained international fame as a center for traditional Irish music. You'll find it in full sway most nights in **O'Connor's Pub,** a large, rustic place filled with musicians, singers, tellers of tales, students who may have hitchhiked across Europe to get here, and Yanks like us here to take it all in. There's regular boat service to the **Aran Islands** from here, only a 25-minute run, since Doolin is the closest point to the islands on the mainland. In fact, you'll sometimes meet Aran Islanders in O'Connor's of a Sunday night if the seas are calm. Boats leave from Doolin Pier daily, beginning at 10 a.m. during the summer, and the fare is IR£8 ($12.75).

THE PUBS OF COUNTY CLARE. If there's one thing County Clare has, it's traditional music and good fiddlers, tin whistle players, bodhran players, and pipers to play it. And their favorite venue by far is the local pub. The **Merriman Tavern,** in Scarriff, is an ancient place with a big ballad room that frequently hosts the likes of the Chieftains, with a small admission charge. The crowd in attendance is likely to include those cruising the Shannon who have pulled into Scarriff for the night, fishermen, and lots of locals.

On Friday nights, **Pat Donnlans,** in Kilkishen, rings with music. Other watering holes that regularly attract musicians are: **The Crab Tree** in Newmarket-on-Fergus; John Lynch's pub, **Do na ha** in Kilkee; **Hassets,** Quin; **John Minogues,** Tulla; **Lena Hanrahan,** Feakle; the **Smyth Village Hotel** in Feakle; and **Kennedy's Pub** in Puckane. The ancient **Crabtree Tavern,** Ballycar, Sixmilebridge, has ceili dancing and traditional music several nights a week during the summer. **Morrisey's Pub,** in Doonbeg, has traditional music and sing-alongs on Saturday nights during the summer.

THE BURREN. The northwestern hump of County Clare is a strange, barren moon-scape with no apparent signs of life. This is the Burren (An Bhoireann, "The Stony District"—the Irish call it "The Berne"). Those who walk its rocky hills, however, find that far from being sterile, it holds a wealth of tiny wildflowers, some of which are unique to this area. It was also inhabited in prehistoric times, and there are many dolmens, cairns, and ring forts left from that era. In Kilfenora, stop by the **Burren Display Centre** (tel. 065/88030) to see an enlightening audio-visual presentation. A tea shop and craft shop are also on the premises, and hours are 10 a.m. to 6 p.m. from mid-March through October. Small admission charge.

In the midst of the Burren, you'll find **Aillwee Cave** (tel. 065/77036), a fascinating underground wonderland of magnificent stalactites. There's a tea room as well as craft shops on the premises. Admission is IR£2.30 ($3.75) for adults, IR£1.20 ($2) for children.

One of the best ways to see the Burren is to join one of the **Burren Walking Tours** run by Collin Bunce (tel. 065/20885) from May 30 through September. The eight-mile walk begins at 10:30 a.m. and ends around 4:30 p.m., and costs a mere IR£3 ($4.75). You bring a picnic lunch, and *it's important to wear comfortable, sturdy walking shoes.* Pickup points vary with the day of the week, so be sure to check when you book.

In Ballyvaughan, stop by **Manus Walsh's Craft Workshop and Gallery** on the main Galway road. Manus's fascination with the Burren landscape is reflected in many of his paintings, and he also has a wide selection of enamelware of Celtic design, rings, necklaces, and wall hangings.

North Tipperary

HOLY CROSS ABBEY. Four miles south of Thurles, Holy Cross Abbey was founded in 1180, and before it was restored in 1976, had lain roofless for more than two centuries. It is open to visitors daily from 9 a.m. to 8 p.m.

ROSCREA. A large Georgian residence, **Damer House** was actually built within the curtain walls of Roscrea Castle. In the castle yard, the **Roscrea Heritage Centre** displays local artifacts. Open daily from 10 a.m. to 4:30 p.m., mid-April through September. Small admission charge.

GALWAY/SALTHILL

| 0 | m | 300 |
| 0 | ft | 990 |

1. University College
2. Salmon Weir Bridge
3. Court House
4. Town Hall
5. Franciscan Friary
6. Cathedral
7. Post Office
8. J.F.K. Memorial Garden
9. Lynch's Castle
10. St. Nicholas Church
11. Railway Station
12. Bus Terminal
13. Irish Tourist Office
14. O'Brien's Bridge
15. Claddagh Bridge
16. Spanish Arch
17. Aran Passenger Terminal
18. Port

one-third less. There's a charge of IR£1.50 ($2.25) per person for private facilities. Marless House has central heat and good parking.

A glowing fireplace takes the chill off cool evenings at Carmel and Tim O'Halloran's **Roncalli House,** 24 Whitestrand Ave., Lower Salthill (tel. 091/64159). Typical of the warm hospitality in this rambling two-story house overlooking Galway Bay is the fact that guests often wander in and out of Carmel's lovely modern kitchen as though it were their own home. There's a sunny front lounge and two outdoor patios for guests' use. There are two ground-floor bedrooms and four others upstairs, all with handbasins, private facilities, and built-in wardrobes; five of the rooms have private toilet and shower. Rates are IR£11 ($17.50) for bed-and-breakfast, and there's a 20% reduction for children. Add IR£1.50 ($2.40) for private facilities. Central heat and good parking.

Joe and Kathleen Stephens, **Inishmore House,** 109 Fr. Griffin Rd., Lower Salthill, Galway, Co. Galway (tel. 091/62639), are the very friendly hosts of this large, attractive house. The house is centrally heated and there is a TV in each bedroom. The meals are delicious, and the eight pretty bedrooms all have handbasins and five have private facilities. The rate for bed-and-breakfast is IR£10 ($16) and high tea costs IR£6 ($9.50); there is a 50% reduction for children. Open all year.

Mrs. Sara Davy is the very helpful and informative hostess of **Ross House,** 14 Whitestrand Ave., Lower Salthill, Galway, Co. Galway (tel. 091/67431). Her attractive home is located beside Galway Bay and is in a quiet cul-de-sac. The house is centrally heated and all four rooms have handbasins. Two of her rooms have private facilities and there is an extra charge of IR£1 ($1.50) for these. The rate for bed-and-breakfast is IR£10 ($16) and there is a 20% reduction for children. Open all year.

Mrs. Rushe, **Alkenver,** 39 Whitestrand Park, Lower Salthill, Galway, Co. Galway (tel. 091/68758), and her family will welcome you warmly to their home which is located in a quiet area and is convenient to Galway Bay and the city center. The house is centrally heated and there is an attractive TV lounge for guests to use. There are four comfortable bedrooms, two with private facilities and all with handbasins. There is an extra charge of IR£1.50 ($2.50) for rooms with private facilities. The rate for bed-and-breakfast is IR£10 ($16) and there is a 25% reduction for children. Open April to September.

Mrs. Maloney, **Loch Lurgan,** Barna Road, Knocknacarra, Galway, Co. Galway (tel. 091/22450), is the hospitable hostess of this bungalow overlooking Galway Bay and the Clare hills. The house is centrally heated and there is a garden which guests can use. There are four bedrooms, all with handbasins and two with private facilities, and an evening meal is available. The rate is IR£9.50 ($15.20) for bed-and-breakfast and dinner is the same price; 33% reduction for children. Open April to September.

GUESTHOUSES: Kay and Pat Conroy are the cheerful, hospitable hosts at **Adare Guest House,** Fr. Griffin Place (tel. 091/62638 or 63963), which is about halfway between the city center and Salthill. There's private parking out front, and in the lovely dining room you'll eat from Royal Tara china. The three-story centrally heated house has ten guest rooms, all with built-in handbasins and six with private baths. B&B rates are IR£12 ($19.25) with an additional IR£2 ($3.25) for private facilities, and a 25% reduction for children.

Glendawn House, Upper Salthill (tel. 091/22872), sits right in the heart of Salthill, just off the coast road and adjacent to a bus stop. There are some 14 guest rooms, all with handbasins, some with shower and toilet en suite, all nicely decorated. Run by Mr. and Mrs. Mullaney, the low two-story building has an entrance hall paved with Connemara marble. Rates for B&B are IR£10.50 ($17.50), with a 25% reduction for children.

In northeastern Salthill, **Knockrea,** Lower Salthill (tel. 091/21794), sits in its own grounds and garden on a quiet street. The nine attractive guest rooms all have handbasins, and rates for bed-and-breakfast are IR£11 ($17.50), 10% less for children.

BIG SPLURGE: The **Connemara Coast Hotel,** Furbo, Co. Galway (tel. 091/92108; or toll free in U.S., 800/223-6510), is an excellent base for exploring Galway and Connemara. Furbo is only 6½ miles west of Galway city, but it's the beginning of the unique Connemara landscape of small fields encompassed by stone walls and miles and miles of untamed acres strewn with stone too stubborn to be subdued. On this rugged coastline, the Connemara Coast Hotel is the custodian of a long tradition of Irish culture in this location. It was originally the site of Marino Cottage, home of a highly respected teacher of the Irish language and Gaelic culture who ultimately was instrumental in establishing a College of Gaelic Studies near Spiddal when his students outgrew his home. Among his visitors was the American film director John Ford, whose reaction to the view from what is now the hotel dining room was, "It would be very hard to find a more spectacular 'shot' than this to capture the sheer beauty of Galway Bay and the atmosphere of this lovely part of Ireland."

Today owner Charles Sinnott has honored that respect for tradition while making the Connemara Coast Hotel an oasis of comfort bordering on luxury and an ideal base for exploration of one of Ireland's most intriguing regions. Delightfully mixing tradition with modern-day convenience, the Connemara Coast welcomes guests with a turf fire burning in the reception area, as well as in the two-tier bar, where traditional folk music adds to the ambience. The 52 bedrooms are nicely decorated and comfortably furnished, with private bath, tea and coffee facilities, telephone, and color television in each. Set in grounds of more than two acres the hotel also has some 1½ miles of private shoreline.

Its lovely two-tiered dining room overlooks this magnificent setting through a large window wall. So rooted in Irish tradition is this establishment that its menu is printed in Irish—with English translations, thank goodness, for those of us who don't have the native tongue. Fresh seafood from local waters is featured, with delights such as lobster cooked in garlic, Irish whiskey, cream, or breaded escalopes of salmon with cream-and-dill sauce. There are also various landlubber entrees, like Connemara lamb, steak, duckling, and chicken. Service is of as high a standard as is the food, and entertainment might be either classical piano or traditional Irish music. There's a set-dinner menu at IR£15 ($24), and the meal will average a little more from the à la carte selections. All prices include tax and service charge. Hours are 7 to 10 p.m. seven days a week, and breakfast is served daily with the same panoramic view from 7:45 to 10 a.m. for IR£6.50 ($10.50).

As if the setting and dining were not enough, there is also sightseeing and activities along this picturesque coast; activities include boat trips to Aran Islands, scenic golf courses, sea and freshwater fishing, riding, and a wealth of nearby craft shops.

Seasonal rates for 1989 range from IR£29 ($46.50) to IR£35 ($56) single, IR£51 ($81.50) to IR£59 ($94.50) double. Rates increase during special events and holidays, but there are reduced rates for longer stays and several attractive holiday package rates, which in 1988 included three nights bed-and-breakfast plus three dinners for seasonal rates of IR£91 ($145.50) to IR£115 ($184). Highly recommended.

SELF-CATERING: Galway Bay Cottages, Barna, Co. Galway (tel. 091/ 69491), are on the main road leading out to Connemara. They feature town house-style cottages that sleep as many as seven, with completely furnished kitchens, turf-burning fireplaces, and electric heating. There's good local bus service to Galway's city center, just five miles distant, and good views of Galway Bay. Rates range from IR£150 ($240) to IR£370 ($592) per week, depending on season, and electricity is extra. *Note:* These cottages can be booked in the U.S. through Round Tower Travel, 745 Fifth Ave., New York, NY 10151 (tel. 212/ 371-1064).

READERS' ACCOMMODATIONS SELECTIONS: "Dermot and Margaret Walsh, **De Soto,** 54 New Castle Rd., Galway city, Co. Galway (tel. 091/65064), own this new and very superior modern family home. There are six comfortable and sparkling bedrooms, TV in the lounge, central heat, and small favors over and above the usual, to say nothing of the marvelous Irish breakfast and private off-street parking. Located right in the city center" (Bill and Mary Treacy, Fort Walton Beach, Fla.). . . . "Mrs. N. Guilfoyle, **Bay View,** Gentian Hill, Salthill, Galway, Co. Galway (tel. 091/22116), presides over this delightful, clean, hospitable, and picturesque bed-and-breakfast home located on a hill overlooking Galway Bay" (James and Gwen McColm, Venice, Fla.). . . . "Mrs. M. Duffy, **Ashbrook,** 59 Dalysfort Rd., Salthill, Galway, Co. Galway (tel. 091/23743), is the gracious proprietress of this immaculately clean, cheerful, and well-appointed guesthouse. It is also accessible to the main bus route to Eyre Square, the heart of the city" (Mr. and Mrs. E. Lavan, Staten Island, N.Y.). . . . "Mrs. Margaret Walsh, **Lawndale,** 5 Beechcourt, Grattan Road, Salthill, Galway, Co. Galway (tel. 091/66676), truly lavishes tender loving care on her guests as I can attest to. When I got quite ill in the wilds of Donegal a quick phone call assured us of her best room. On arrival the bed was turned down and waiting, she loaned me her own hot-water bottle, and she kept the heat on day and night (in the middle of May). After I had rested she prepared a special meal on a tray so I didn't have to stir" (M. Erdvig, Roswell, Ga.).

4. WHERE TO EAT

Although these first two listings are not in Galway town, they are not far away and are such favorites that residents often drive out for a meal. Either is a good stop en route between Galway and Limerick, and either warrants a special trip out from town.

Right on the main Galway–Limerick road, some ten miles south of Galway in Clarenbridge, **Paddy Burkes Oyster Inn** (tel. 091/96107) is a local institution. The old pub dates back three centuries, and beamed ceilings, wooden benches, copper, and brass give the place a settled, comfortable feeling. It has been the hangout of such celebrities as John Huston, Paul Newman, and Burl Ives, to say nothing of half the population of Galway. Needless to say, oysters get star billing, and in fact, Paddy Burkes is headquarters for Galway's annual Oyster Festival. In addition to the succulent bivalves, the menu includes smoked salmon prawn cocktail, fish chowder, and fresh cockles and mussels in garlic sauce. For non-seafood lovers, there are cold and hot platters of chicken, ham, and beef. Prices range from IR£1.50 ($2.50) for hot, homemade apple pie with fresh cream to IR£9 ($14.50) for steak. A dozen oysters cost IR£6 ($9.50). Food is served continuously during pub hours.

About two miles farther out along the Galway–Limerick road, look for the signpost at Kilcolgan that directs you down a sideroad to **Moran's of the Weir** (tel. 091/96113). The 200-year-old thatched pub is in the capable hands of the fifth generation of Morans to run the place, and at least a part of their success stems from the fact that oysters come straight from their own oyster beds close at hand. They're served with home-baked brown bread, as are smoked salmon, mussel soup, and other seafood items. Oysters go for IR£4.50 ($7.25) a dozen, smoked salmon plate for IR£5 ($8), and there's food service all through normal pub hours.

Very popular with Galway locals, **Rabbitt's Bar and Restaurant,** 23 Forster St. (tel. 091/66490), is a congenial, family-run bar that serves the Tourist Menu as well as bar food. It's a friendly place in which you'll seldom pay more than IR£5 ($8) for a meal.

Lydon's of Shop Street, 5 Shop St. (tel. 091/61131), is an attractive, pleasant upstairs restaurant with a touch of "Old Galway" ambience. The décor harks back to the days of Galway's thriving sea trade with Spain. It's famed for fast, friendly service and geared to budgeteers, with a three-course lunch costing around IR£5 ($8), with a daily special priced at IR£4 ($6.50); there's a "Kiddie Korner" menu for under IR£2 ($3.25). The special-value Tourist Menu is served from April through September and the hours are noon to 9 p.m.

On the ground floor, Lydon's has it's own in-store bakery, a delicatessen, and a modern self-service eatery offering a good selection of burgers, with Lydon's own sauce. Also on offer is a wide selection of tempting salads, home-made pâté, and fresh-baked croissants. A good cold plate will cost around IR£2.50 ($4) and there's a take-away service. Hours are 9:30 a.m. to 7 p.m. every day except Sunday.

The small cozy **Galleon Grill,** on the coast road in the village of Salthill beside the church (tel. 091/22963), is a popular spot with locals, and is one of the few late-night eating spots in Galway. Prices range from IR£3 ($4.75) on a wide and varied menu which offers burgers, omelets, grills, steaks, fish dishes, and curries. Hours are noon to midnight seven days a week.

Just off Eyre Square the fully licensed **Cellar Restaurant,** Williamsgate Street (tel. 091/65727), is a centrally located ground-floor, family-style restaurant offering a wide variety of food at reasonable prices. The moderate prices range from IR£4 ($6.50) for the daily special to IR£5 ($8) for a three-course lunch to under IR£7.50 ($12) for a satisfying evening meal. Open seven days a week from 10 a.m. to 9 p.m.

The **Park House Restaurant and Cocktail Bar,** Forster Street (tel. 091/ 64924 or 68293), is a lovely new restaurant whose décor manages to be both sophisticated and warmly inviting. Lunchtime brings hordes of locals to settle in for specialties like chicken and mushroom vol-au-vent, osso buco (braised veal on the bone with garlic, white wine, onions, celery, carrots, and tomatoes), freshly caught fish, and roast rib of beef. There are daily specials priced at just IR£3 ($4.75), a real bargain in this lovely place. Dinner menus feature entrees as sophisticated as the setting—for instance, roast stuffed duckling normande or escalope of veal Cordon Bleu—and are priced around IR£15 ($24). It's fully licensed, of course.

In Barna (on the Spiddal road), the **Twelve Pins Restaurant** (tel. 091/ 92368 or 92485) is an attractive place for lunch or dinner, with white stucco walls, low ceilings, lots of wood, and a small lounge area with a fire lit on cool evenings. There's a daily lunch special of steak, lamb, or chicken for IR£5 ($8) and salad plates of cold meats, smoked salmon, or prawns for about the same price. Dinner, with seafood specialties as well as steaks, veal, and roast duckling, will run between IR£8 ($19.25) and IR£11 ($17.50). Hours are 1 to 2:30 p.m. and 7 to 10 p.m. except in summer, when it's open all day. Fully licensed.

BIG SPLURGES: Emer and John J. ("J.J." to all and sundry) Coppinger have converted space in old stone warehouses into the charming **Malt House Restaurant,** Olde Malte Arcade, High Street (tel. 091/67866 or 163993). Amid stone walls and arches they've created a bar area, a cozy cubbyhole lounge, and an attractive restaurant. The food has won all sorts of accolades, with such specialties as sirloin steak Café de Paris, peppered monkfish, scampi rolls, scallops au gratin, and veal steak St. Augustine. Fresh seafood is the house specialty. They also serve homemade ice cream, and for a special treat, order the Irish-coffee flavor. There's an excellent wine list, and a friendly, efficient staff. If the IR£15 ($24) plus 10% service charge set price for dinner is beyond your means, try to get by for lunch, which runs about IR£6.50 ($10.50), or sample the bar menu for less. Hours are 12:30 to 2:30 p.m. and 7 to 9:30 p.m. This popular place is packed at lunch, so come early or late. It's an absolute must to book for dinner.

5. THINGS TO SEE AND DO

To catch the full flavor of Galway's rich and colorful history, go by the Tourist Board and pick up their booklet, *Tourist Trail of Old Galway* (small charge), which will lead you along a signposted route through medieval streets with an informative and entertaining narrative filled with legends and anecdotes associated with places along your way.

TOURS: Bus Eireann runs several worthwhile **day tours** from Galway and Salthill: Clew Bay and Killary Harbor; the Maam Valley and Cong; Knock Shrine; Carraroe and South Connemara, etc. Some are half-day trips; others last the entire day. All are moderately priced, and you can book at the Tourist Office in Galway or Salthill or the railway station.

For an interesting **walking tour** of Old Galway, just show up outside the Tourist Office at 11 a.m. Monday to Friday, and poet Rita Ann Higgins will lead you through two hours of Galway history and legend. The charge is IR£3 ($4.75), and Rita warns that you should wear comfortable walking shoes.

A pleasant way to see Galway and its environs is the 90-minute cruise on the River Corrib aboard the 72-passenger *Corrib Princess.* Its full-length sunroof lets you enjoy the scenery no matter what the weather. You'll cruise along a traditional trade route, past historical points of interest, castles, and scenes of great natural beauty, with an interesting commentary all the way. There's full bar service, and tea and coffee. There are morning and afternoon sailings from Woodquay daily, and the fare is IR£4 ($6.50). For exact times and to book, contact the Tourist Office, Eyre Square, Galway (tel. 091/61962 or 92447).

IN THE CITY: Things to look for include the Civic Sword and Great Mace on display in the **Bank of Ireland** on Eyre Square. You'll want to see the **Spanish Arch** and the somewhat cramped **Galway City Museum** just beside it. Not only is the museum filled with interesting artifacts, but its spiral staircase leads to a gallery that, in turn, leads to an open terrace from which there are great views of the city and harbor.

On **Market Street,** look for two interesting "marriage stones" set into the walls of houses there. The stones are carved with the coats-of-arms of two families united in marriage, and these two date from the early 1600s. Of even more interest is the **Lynch Memorial Window,** which immortalizes a legend that historians swear has no truth in it and most citizens of Galway swear just as vehemently is an event that added the word "lynch" to the English language. Be that as it may, the window points out that it was on this site (though not necessarily from this window) that Mayor James Lynch FitzStephen carried out a harsh sentence against his own son in 1493. The story goes that the Lord Mayor's 19-year-old son, Walter, was much enamored of a lovely girl named Agnes. He was also very good friends with a young Spanish lad, son of one of his father's Spanish friends, who had come to stay a while in Galway—good friends, that is, until Walter developed an acute case of jealousy when he thought the young Spaniard was courting Agnes. In a fit of rage he murdered his friend, then filled with remorse turned himself in to the police. It was his own father who sat as magistrate and condemned the boy to death when he entered a plea of guilty. The town executioner, however, refused to perform his grisly duty, a tribute to the boy's local popularity, and the sorrowing father gave his son a last embrace and did the deed himself. From this tragic hanging—so the legend says—came the term "Lynch Law."

If you're a James Joyce fan, you'll find the girlhood home of his lady love, Nora Barnacle, in **Bowling Green**—it's the second house on the left as you enter the lane from Market Street.

Take a stroll through Galway's version of the "Left Bank," the **High Street / Quay Street** quarter of old buildings being given new life these days.

Out at **Salthill,** give the young set and yourself a break by dropping them off at the **Leisureland Amusement Park.** There's a heated indoor pool, a super waterslide, and lots of rides.

THE ARAN ISLANDS:
THE ARAN ISLANDS: Lying almost directly across the mouth of Galway Bay, the Aran Islands group consists of **Inishere** (Inis Oirr, "eastern island"), the smallest and nearest to the mainland (Doolin, Co. Clare, is six miles away); **Inishmaan** (Inis Meain "middle island"), three miles distant from each of the other two and three miles long by two miles wide; and **Inishmore** (Inis Mor, "big island"), seven sea miles from the Connemara coast, eight miles long and 2½ miles wide, with the only safe harbor suitable for steamer docking at **Kilronan,** its main village.

Life has been made easier on the islands with the introduction of electricity, modern plumbing, and regular sea and air service to the mainland. Still, much of the culture and old customs remain, and the hardy islanders are a breed apart, conditioned by generations who have braved the seas in their frail curraghs and laboriously built up the rocky soil with seaweed and sand in which to grow their meager crops. You'll debark at Kilronan pier on Inishmore, to be greeted by lines of jaunting cars for hire to explore the island, with delightful and informative narratives by your driver/guide and a terrific vantage point from which to view the network of small stone fields marked off by meandering stone walls. You'll ride through the village and down the one main road that runs the length of the island past an ancient stone ring fort, ecclesiastical ruins, and tiny hamlets on the **Dun Aengus,** an 11-acre stone fort perched on a cliff some 300 feet above the sea. The jaunting-car fare runs about IR£15 ($24). There are bikes for rent as well, and if you're a walker, this is the country for it, with stops to chat a bit with an old man smoking his pipe in an open doorway or a housewife hurrying along a lane to the village. Although Gaelic is the everyday language, the courteous islanders will speak to you in English.

If you have a yen to visit Inishere or Inishmaan (where you're much more likely to see the traditional Aran style of dress than on Inishmore), ask any of the fishermen at the Kilronan pier and they'll arrange to take you over by curragh or other small boat. And if you're really taken with the islands, the Tourist Board lists several good accommodations, and one of these is sure to match your pocketbook as well as your penchant.

Bus Eireann operates regular service to the Aran Islands from the Galway docks, and you can book the day before at the railway station or the Tourist Office, or pay at the dockside kiosk. The round-trip fare in 1988 was IR£15 ($24), half that for children under 16. Inquire about their special family fares. It takes just over 2½ hours for the trip, and the water can be choppy, so if you're not sure you're a good sailor, it pays to take Dramamine or some other motion-sickness remedy about 20 minutes before you embark. The ferries dock only at Inishmore, but are met by curraghs from the other two islands to take off cargo. A shorter boat trip is that from **Rossaveal** (on the coastal road past Spiddal), which takes only 45 minutes and is run by **Aran Ferries**. The round-trip fare in 1988 was IR£12 ($19.25), half fare for children, with special family and student fares. Book at the Galway Tourist Office or call 091/68904 (091/95036 or 92447 after hours). You can fly out with **Aer Arann** (tel. 091/55437, 55448, or 55480) in a nine-seat, twin-engined aircraft from Caranmore Airfield on the Monivea road four miles out from Galway. The round-trip fare is about IR£42 ($67.25), and you can also book through the Tourist Office. Ask about their special packages that include an overnight stay on the islands.

6. GALWAY AFTER DARK

Be it a castle banquet, a night of theater, or a pint in a pub, you'll find plenty to do in Galway in the evening.

A LITERARY BANQUET: Much more intimate than the medieval banquets at Bunratty and Knappogue, the **Banquet and Literary Evening at Dunguaire Castle** is certainly not a budget item, but it is special enough to warrant a Big Splurge from the most devoted budgetcer. The castle is a small 16th-century keep, with banquet seating limited to 62. You'll learn its legend when you enter the reception hall and quaff a cup of mead as a pretty girl in medieval dress relates the story. In the upstairs banquet hall you'll dine by candlelight on such delicacies as smoked salmon, "chekyn supreme," and sumptuous desserts, accompanied by a plentiful supply of wine. When dinner is over, your costumed waiters and waitresses repair to the stage and bring to vivid life Ireland's literary heroes and heroines through their stories, plays, and poems.

Because attendance is so limited, this is one banquet you *must* reserve well in advance (through a travel agent before you leave home if possible, through the Galway Tourist Office, or the Tours Manager at Shannon Airport, tel. 061/61788 or 61444). There are two banquets each night from mid-May through September, at 5:45 and 9 p.m., and the all-inclusive price is IR£25.75 ($41.25). The easiest way to go is to book with Bus Eireann for their tour which leaves from both Salthill Promenade and the railway station (tel. 091/62141).

THEATER: Since 1928, Galway's **Taibhdhearc** ("thive-yark") **Theatre,** Middle Street (tel. 091/62024), has existed for the sole purpose of preserving Gaelic drama, and several nights a week during summer months it presents a one-act play in Gaelic, with music, song, poetry, and dance both before and after the performance. Following the action is no problem, not withstanding the language, and the musical program is simply spectacular, with step dancing that will leave you breathless, even as a spectator. This is where Siobhan McKenna began her training and career, and you'll see talent of much the same caliber on the stage almost any night. It's a very, very "Irish" entertainment, and very good value-for-money, as well, with tickets about IR£4 ($6.50). You can book through the Tourist Office or at the theater.

There's good drama, too, at the **Druid Theatre,** Chapel Lane (tel. 091/68617), where the resident professional company mounts productions like *The Beggars Opera,* avant-garde plays, and Anglo-Irish classics presented nightly year round. There are frequent lunchtime and late-night shows, and local newspapers usually publish the schedule. Tickets are in the IR£5 ($8) to IR£6 ($9.50) range, and you can book by telephone or at the theater

TRADITIONAL MUSIC: For the very best in traditional Irish music, check with the Tourist Board to see if your visit coincides with a Galway appearance of **Seisiun,** the troupe that tours the country during July and August.

In Galway, **Flanagan's Corner Bar and Lounge,** Henry Street and William Street West (tel. 091/63220), has traditional and folk music from Wednesday through Sunday nights, and they invite musicians to bring along their instruments and join in. The upstairs ballad room at the **Crane Bar** on Sea Road is often packed out, and the music here is very good. Galway's oldest family-run pub is **Rabbitt's,** 23 Forster St. (tel. 091/62215), just off Eyre Square. More locals than tourists, and a place for good conversation and conviviality as well as moderately priced food.

In Salthill, it's **O'Connors Pub** or the **Sacré Coeur Hotel** bar for singing pubs, and in nearby Spiddal, **An Cruiscin Lan** pub is much favored by the locals. In all, you'll pay only for the pint, with no charge for music and song.

SPECIAL EVENTS: The Irish, of course, can come up with an instant party on an occasion no more auspicious than two friends happening to be in the same place at the same time. And if there's a *race meet,* the party often turns into a gala! The folks in Galway have, in fact, perfected their party-throwing skills to such an extent that it sometimes seems the entire country shuts down to travel up this way for the six-day **Race Week** in late July or early August. There's music everywhere, food stalls, private parties (to which strangers are often warmly welcomed), honest-to-goodness horse trading, and lots of activity at the track. Because so many Irish descend on the town during that week, best book *way* ahead if you'll be arriving during the festivities.

The other "biggie" in Galway—and one which draws as many Irish as Race Week—is the **September Oyster Festival.** Actually, it's an international affair, with oyster-openers gathering from around the world to enter competitions for opening the most oysters in the shortest period of time. In a colorful ceremony, the Lord Mayor of Galway gets things under way by opening and eating the first oyster of the season. After that, it's two solid days (usually a weekend) of eating and drinking: oysters, salmon, prawns, and almost anything else that comes from the sea are washed down with buckets of champagne or Guinness. The action centers around Moran's of the Weir, Paddy Burkes, and the Great Southern Hotel, and a ticket to all the scheduled partying is costly—around IR£100 ($160) for the two days—but since the entire town *becomes* a party, the general gaiety spills over into the streets and pubs at no cost at all. Again, advance booking is an absolute must. It's usually the third or fourth weekend in September, but you should check the Tourist Board's Calendar of Events.

To open the herring season in mid-August, there's a lovely **Blessing of the Sea** ceremony on the waters of Galway Bay. Fishing boats form a procession as they sail out of the harbor, and leading them is an entire boatload of priests who petition heaven for a good and profitable season.

7. SHOPPING

One of Ireland's best tweed shops is **Padraic O Maille's,** on Dominick Street (tel. 091/62696). There's a vast stock of gorgeous hand-woven tweeds by the yard to be tailored by the shop, as well as ready-made jackets, men's and ladies' suits, ladies' cashmere knits and tweed coats, scarves, Irish "paddy" hats, and much more. This is also a good place to shop for Aran hand-knit sweaters (O Maille's was, in fact, the first place ever to market them commercially). Prices are competitive, and the staff in this family-run store are among the most helpful and friendliest in the country, which probably accounts somewhat for their patronage by the likes of John Ford, John Wayne, Maureen O'Hara, and Peter Ustinov. There's another, smaller shop, in the Tourist Office building, but do go by the original store, to browse if nothing else.

In 1938 the late Mr. Padraic O'Maille opened his shop to the public. He pioneered the commercial marketing of traditional Aran hand-knit sweaters and hand-woven tweeds that have been made in local cottages for centuries. Today his sister and nephew carry on the tradition he began. The business gained international recognition when O'Maille's made the costumes for *The Quiet Man*. The family-run shop also features the best in Irish-designed knitwear, ladies' suits, coats, and capes, men's tweed jackets, caps, hats, and ties. There's a good mail-order catalog, and major credit cards are accepted. Shop hours are 9 a.m. to 6:30 p.m. Monday through Saturday.

Fallers, Williamsgate Street (tel. 091/61226), began as a jewelry shop back in 1879 and today carries a huge stock of crystal, silver, china, porcelain, linen, jewelry, and quality souvenirs. They do an international mail-order business, and you can write for their color catalog (with prices in U.S. dollars).

It's hard to know just what to call **Kenny's,** High Street (tel. 091/62739, 61014, or 61021). It is, of course, just about the best bookshop and art gallery in the country—but it's also an institution! Begun back in the 1930s, the small bookshop has grown into a fascinating multilevel maze of rooms in ancient buildings lovingly restored by the Kenny family. There are marvelous works of Irish art, antiquarian maps and prints, old magazine issues, rare books on Irish subjects—and there are the Kennys. You'll nearly always find Mrs. Kenny behind the counter up front, and at least one of her sons on hand. They'll search for a specific book, and if necessary, mail it on to you in the U.S., and they even have their own bindery to wrap a prized edition in fine, hand-tooled covers. Periodically, they issue catalogs of Irish-interest publications, and many of the volumes in their stock come from private libraries they've purchased. Do go by to browse and look for that special Irish book to carry home, but be warned—this is not an easy shop to leave!

The **Browne Doorway Ltd.** gift boutique, 17 Eyre Square, has an excellent selection of crystal, china, and knitwear, and owner Helen Royliston is especially welcoming to Americans.

On the outskirts of town, the **Galway Irish Crystal** factory, Merlin Park, Galway (tel. 091/57311), sells beautiful crystal at one-third off prices you'd pay in shops. In the showroom it's a joy to watch Master Cutter John Wynne at work creating pieces just like those displayed on the shelves. The showroom is open from 9 a.m. to 5 p.m. seven days a week, and John is on hand Monday through Friday.

You can tour the **Royal Tara China** factory and watch master craftspeople creating fine bone china. It's located off the Dublin road at Flannery's Motel, and tours are at 11 a.m. and 3 p.m. Monday through Friday, by video on weekends. The showroom and shop are open seven days a week from 9 a.m. to 6 p.m. October through April, from 9 a.m. to 9 p.m. May through September, and there's a full-service restaurant on the premises. Considerable savings on purchases here as compared to shops elsewhere.

The **Abbey Hand Crafts,** Clarenbridge, Co. Galway, is some eight miles from Galway city on the road to Shannon, just outside the village of Clarenbridge. Over the years the Abbey has attracted a wide and loyal clientele who return year after year to purchase quality crafts and at the same time support a very worthy cause. It all began two decades ago, when the local secondary school closed down and villagers came together to help the Irish Sisters of Charity use the building to start a local knitting industry. Nowadays lay people run the Craft Shop, while the sisters teach blind people to knit and do much of the crochet and embroidery themselves. Profits from the shop help run their convent, but also provide for the poor in Ireland and in Third World countries.

There's a wealth of Irish handmade items on sale: tweeds, linens, woven bedspreads, Aran Handknit Bawneen (a specialty), blackthorn sticks, shillelaghs, handmade dolls, Waterford crystal, and Belleek porcelain and many others, in all price ranges. Many of the items on sale are made under the supervision of the sisters or in Galway homes and those in surrounding counties. Just back of the shop is the charmingly simple Cottage Tea Room, where you can rest your feet and enjoy traditional Irish home baking and tea.

On the Galway–Spiddal road, **Mairtin Standun,** Spiddal, Co. Galway (tel. 091/83108), grew from a small drapery and grocery shop into the large, bright store in which you can find very good bargains today. It's still very much a family business, but the stocks of Aran sweaters, tweed coats and jackets, glassware, china, souvenirs, and gifts is incredibly large. In the rear of the shop there's a pleasant tea room, a welcome refuge for weary shoppers. Standun's is open from 9:30 a.m. to 6:30 p.m. Monday to Saturday, from March to December.

AROUND THE WESTERN REGION

□ □ □

Counties Galway and Mayo

1. ACCOMMODATIONS
2. WHERE TO EAT
3. THINGS TO SEE AND DO

The west of Ireland. A simple phrase, yet one that conjures up an immediate and vivid image—brooding mountains, stony fields, windswept cliffs along a rugged coastline dotted with offshore islands, and air so heady that to breathe it is akin to drinking champagne. Oliver St. John Gogarty put it this way:

> There's something sleeping in my breast
> That wakens only in the West;
> There's something in the core of me
> That needs the West to set it free.

Counties Galway and Mayo make up Ireland's Western Region, and within their boundaries lie such distinct geographic divisions as Connemara, the Aran Islands, and Achill Island. Galway's landscape in the east is made up of flat, fertile plains that reach from Lough Derg and the Shannon Valley north to County Roscommon, while to the northwest, lumpy mountains push the mainland into a great elbow bent against the Atlantic. Lough Corrib stretches its 27 miles along an invisible line that marks the change.

Some 30 miles offshore, where Galway Bay empties into the sea, the Aran Islands are an outpost of rugged fishermen and their families who perpetuate a heritage of self-sufficiency and culture passed from generation to generation through the centuries. The walls of pre-Christian stone forts have endured the ravages of time to remind islanders of their "Celtic Twilight" origin. Round towers, oratories, and tiny churches tell of early Christians who spoke the musical Gaelic language, as do today's islanders. Menfolk still put out to sea in lightweight, tough little wood-and-canvas curraghs, as they have done over the ages, while their womenfolk spin and weave and knit the clothing that is so distinctly theirs. Visitors come by steamer or small aircraft, welcomed and entertained by natives who remain untouched by their foreign ways.

In Connemara, the serried Twelve Bens (sometimes called the Twelve Pins) look across a lake-filled valley at the misty peaks of the Maamturk range, and the jagged coastline is a solitary place of rocks and tiny hamlets and stark, silent beauty. This is a Gaeltacht area, where government grants make possible the survival of a language and the people who speak it. Among its rocky, untillable fields wander the spirits of Irishmen banished by Cromwell "to Hell or Connaught." Farther north, the long, narrow finger of Killary Harbour marks the County Mayo border.

Eastern County Mayo is also flat, and it was near Cong, on the Plain of Southern Moytura, that a prehistoric battle raged between Tuatha De Danann and the Firbolgs, ending in the first defeat of the latter, who declined in power afterward until they were crushed forever seven years later in Sligo. Northeast of Cong is the small village of Knock, a shrine to the many visions reported here and a place of pilgrimage for thousands of Christians. Pilgrims gather on the last Sunday in July each year to walk barefoot in the steps of St. Patrick to the summit of Croagh Patrick on Clew Bay's southern shore. Connected to the mainland by a causeway, Achill Island presents a mountainous face to the sea, its feet ringed by golden sandy strands.

1. ACCOMMODATIONS

Whether you choose the short, direct route from Galway town to Sligo via Tuam or the longer, coastal drive through Connemara's starkly beautiful landscape, you won't lack for excellent and inexpensive places to rest your head.

Note: Prices shown below are those in effect in 1989—expect them to be higher in 1990.

County Galway

HOSTELS. Superior hostel accommodations are available at **Inverin** (tel. 091/93154), some five miles from Rossaveal, and hostelers are eligible for reduced fares on the Aran Islands ferry. There's good, regular bus service to Galway, 19 miles away.

The **Twelve Bens Youth Hostel,** Ben Lettery, Ballinafad, Co. Galway (tel. Ballinafad 18), is set in mountains seven miles outside Clifden, and hikers are warned that climbing can be dangerous and should not be attempted without notifying the hostel warden of your intended route.

Farther north, some 51 miles from Galway, there are very good hostel accommodations at **Rosroe,** Renvyle.

BED-AND-BREAKFAST. Most people pass right through the Burren, but a lovely place to spend a night or two in the middle of this unique area is **Teac Caoilte,** Galway Bay View, Geehy North, Duras, Kinvara, Co. Galway (tel. 091/37214). The modern bungalow is the home of Anne and Joseph Quilty and it looks out over the Burren on one side, across Galway Bay to Galway town on the other. Mr. Quilty is an artist at the easel, and Mrs. Quilty is an artist in the kitchen, serving up superb meals. There's an excellent beach just down from the house, and the Quiltys enjoy steering guests to places of historical, botanical, and geological interest. The three guest rooms are all doubles, and all have handbasins. There's central heating, never a problem with parking, and the lounge features a lovely fireplace. Bed-and-breakfast runs IR£10 ($16), dinner costs the same, and there's a 10% reduction for children. Open April through October.

On the Galway Bay coastal road, just a half mile from Spiddal, Mrs. Vera Feeney's **Ardmore Country House,** Greenhill, Spiddal, Co. Galway (tel. 091/83145), is a modern bungalow overlooking the bay and the Aran Islands. The Cliffs of Moher are clearly visible on clear days and the panoramic view is framed by large windows in the lounge, or you can relax in the sun outside on the terrace to enjoy the landscaped gardens in proximity to the bay. The eight spacious guest rooms are attractively decorated and seven of them have private facilities. The gracious Mrs. Feeney has thoughtfully provided washing and drying facilities to renew your travel-weary clothes. Evening meals are a specialty here (be sure and book by noon), and you're offered a choice of menu at breakfast. The rate for bed-and-breakfast is IR£10.50 ($16.75), and dinner is the same. There's an IR£2 ($3.25) supplement for rooms en suite and a discount on stays of three days or more. Central heating and good parking. Open March through November.

Charming Mrs. Frances Tiernan's **Heather Lodge,** Westport Road, Clifden, Co. Galway (tel. 095/21331), has magnificent views of a mountain lake and the Twelve Bens range, all framed by huge picture windows in the lounge, which also has a fireplace. The pretty modern bungalow is about a mile from town, set back from the road on a slight rise, and the eight lovely bedrooms all have handbasins and built-in wardrobes. Two have a private shower, and another two have both private toilet and shower (no extra charge). There are two on the ground floor, and one has three single beds. B&B costs IR£10.50 ($16.75), with a 25% reduction for children. Central heating and car park. Open April through September.

Ard Mhuire guesthouse, Clifden, Co. Galway (tel. 095/21450), is a large, two-story house set in attractive gardens. Run by the O'Grady family who are known for their seafood restaurant in Clifden, its rooms all come with private bath, and there's a heated swimming pool and a tennis court on the grounds, as well as a private car park. The rate for bed-and-breakfast is IR£12 ($19.25).

Ben View House, Bridge Street, Clifden, Co. Galway (tel. 095/21256), is the comfortable two-story home of Mrs. Morris, a hospitable and helpful hostess. This is an ideal touring base for Connemara. The house is centrally heated and the four attractive bedrooms all have private toilets and showers. The rate for bed-and-breakfast is IR£11 ($17.50) and there is a 25% reduction for children. Open year round.

At the **Boat Inn Guest House,** Oughterard, Co. Galway (tel. 091/82196), owner Margaret Donnellan greets visitors with a warmth born of experience in tourism (she was long a member of the Tourist Office staff) and her own sparkling personality. The upstairs rooms are nicely done up, and they couldn't be more convenient at meal time—downstairs is a fine restaurant run by Margaret herself. There's even live folk music in the bar every night during summer months. The rate is IR£13.50 ($21.50) for bed-and-breakfast. Highly recommended.

Lakeland Country Home, Portacarron, Oughterard, Co. Galway (tel. 091/82121 or 82146), is the lovely lakeside home of Lal and Mary Faherty. It is a great place for relaxing and there are nice scenic walks nearby. The house is centrally heated as well as having turf fires, and electric blankets are supplied. Mary Faherty serves a delicious five-course dinner with advance notice. Of the nine attractive bedrooms, five have private facilities and all have handbasins. There is an extra charge of IR£2 ($3.25) per person for private facilities. The rate for bed-and-breakfast is IR£10.50 ($16.75) and dinner costs IR£12 ($19.25); 20% reduction for children. Open March to October.

Mrs. McDonagh, **Balrickard Farm,** Headford, Co. Galway (tel. 093/35421), is the hospitable hostess of this lovely farmhouse less than a mile from town on the Galway road. It is set in beautiful countryside and the house is centrally heated as well as having open turf fires. The three attractive bedrooms all have handbasins. The rate for bed-and-breakfast is IR£10 ($16) and there is a 25% reduction for children. Open March through November.

Mr. Stephen Dirrane's **Gilbert Cottage,** Oatquarter, Kilronan, Inishmore, Aran Islands, Co. Galway (tel. 099/61146), is a lovely house with a peaceful, relaxing atmosphere. Mr. Dirrane spent 20 years working in New York restaurants and his meals are excellent. The house is centrally heated and there are seven pretty bedrooms, all with handbasins. The rate for bed-and-breakfast is IR£10.50 ($16.75) and dinner is the same price. Open all year.

The **Cliff House,** Inishmore, Aran Islands, Co. Galway (tel. 099/61286), is a delightful place for an overnight stay on these offshore islands. Maura and David Dennis are hosts at the modern bungalow that perches on a site near Kilronan overlooking the sea and with sweeping views of the entire island. There are six attractive guest rooms with handbasins. There's one family room with private bath. B&B costs IR£10 ($16), the evening meal (there's a wine license) is IR£8 ($12.75), and there's a 33⅓% reduction for children.

FARMHOUSES. Get set for a rave! Actually, two raves—one for **Knockferry Lodge,** Knockferry, Roscahill, Co. Galway (tel. 091/80122), and one for the delightful Des Moran who runs it. Set in a secluded spot on the shores of Lough Corrib, just 14 miles north of Galway town, the lodge was originally occupied by the author of *Galway Bay,* Dr. Arthur Colohan. It was also Des's family home, to which he returned after several years in the hotel business in Europe to expand the house and establish a first-class accommodation with a superior cuisine. It is his own irrepressible personality which also added an element of fun that has attracted a loyal following of fishermen and relaxation-seekers who return again and again. There are turf fires in both of the large lounges, and there's a spacious dining room for outstanding meals (with such specialties as Corrib salmon, trout, and pike, Viennese goulash, Connemara lamb and spiced beef, among others). A game room provides table tennis and bar billiards. Fishing boats are available for hire, and the lodge can supply tackle (no charge for fishing except for salmon). Guest rooms are lovely, most with lake views. All have private bath facilities; the Lake Room and Galway Bay Room are furnished with antiques; and there's one huge room with four beds, wash basin, bidet, toilet, shower, and bath. Bed-and-breakfast costs IR£14.50 ($23.25), with additional charges for private facilities ranging from IR£1.50 ($3.25) to IR£4 ($6.50), dinner is IR£12 ($19.25); 25% off for children. There's central heating, plenty of parking, and Des wants guests who have been here before to know that the "presence remains on the bridge"— newcomers should be sure to ask for the tall tale that goes with that statement!

Leckavrea View Farmhouse, Maam (tel. 092/48040), is the comfortable home of John and Breege Gavin, on the Maam–Cong road about two miles from Maam village, with marvelous views of Lough Corrib and a little island crowned by Castle Kirk ("Hen's Castle") just offshore. Fishing on the lough is free (the Gavins have boats for hire), and if Castle Kirk intrigues you, John will (for a small fee) row you over to the island for a bit of exploring. In consideration for her guests who've come for peace and quiet, Breege keeps the TV in a separate lounge and usually keeps a fire glowing in the main lounge. The rate for bed-and-breakfast is IR£10 ($16), dinner is IR£10 ($16), with a 25% discount for children.

SELF-CATERING. Two warm, comfortably furnished traditional cottages in Connemara are ideal for family holidays in the west of Ireland. One is adjacent to a safe, sandy beach, with spectacular sea and mountain views; the other sits on the shore of a small lake with swans and good trout fishing. Each will sleep eight in three bedrooms, and fuel and heating are included in the weekly rate at the lake cottage. Electricity is extra. Rates are IR£245 ($392) per week during June, July, and August and public holidays; IR£130 ($208) in other months. For booking information, contact Mrs. Brenda Weir, **Rookwood,** Stocking Lane, Ballyboden, Dublin 16 (tel. 01/931906).

A BIG SPLURGE. If there is such a thing as casual elegance, **Ballynahinch Castle,** Ballinafad, Connemara, Co. Galway (tel. 095/31006), has it. Set in lush woodlands at the base of Ben Lettry in the Twelve Bens mountain range, the impressive manor house overlooks the Owenmore River and is surrounded by lovely gardens. This was the ancestral home of the O'Flaherty chieftains, and in more recent years the sporting home of an Indian maharajah. There's excellent fishing on the grounds, with boats available for hire, and miles of walking or biking paths, with bicycles for hire. Log fires, oil paintings, and wall tapestries give a warm, comfortable air to the two beautifully furnished lounges, and the dining room overlooks the river and gardens. The Castle Pub is a favorite gathering place for residents of the locality, with traditional music on tap often during summer months. All 20 guest rooms have a private bath, and some have a fireplace. Rates are seasonal, ranging from IR£30 ($48) to IR£42 ($67.25). Open year round.

County Mayo

HOSTELS. Five miles from Westport, **Traenlaur Lodge,** Lough Feeagh, Newport (tel. 098/41358), overlooks a harbor on Lough Feeagh.

Maigh Mhuillinn, Currane, Achill Sound, Westport (tel. 098/45280), sits on the mainland shore of Achill Sound, some 32 miles from Westport.

BED-AND-BREAKFAST. On the main Westport–Castlebar road, Mary and Joe Moran's **Lakeview House,** Westport Road, Castlebar (tel. 094/22374), sits on spacious grounds, with a large, sloping lawn out front. This was Mary's family home area, and both lounge (with fireplace) and dining room look out to green fields and rolling hills. Mary, whose warm personality bubbles with enthusiasm, bakes her own brown bread and scones and is always happy to share the recipe with guests (a frequent request). The four pretty guest rooms all have handbasins, and there's a twin-bedded room with private shower and a family-size room (two double beds) with private shower. The rate for bed-and-breakfast is IR£10 ($16); 20% reduction for children. The evening meal is IR£7 ($11.25). Central heating and a paved parking area.

Shalom, Westport Road, Castlebar (tel. 094/21471), is the home of Noreen Raftery, who has the fresh beauty of an Irish schoolgirl. She and Liam, who is a Garda, take a personal interest in their guests—as does Bruno, their gorgeous Collie dog. Conversation around the turf fire in their lounge has brought glowing letters from readers, who have nothing but praise for the Rafterys. The three nice guest rooms all have handbasins and built-in wardrobes, and there's one family-sized room with a double and twin bed. B&B costs IR£10 ($16), with a 50% reduction for children. Central heating and good parking. Open May to mid-October.

Mrs. Catherine Fitzpatrick is the wonderful hostess of **Ard-Mhuire,** Castlebar Road (N60), Newtown, Claremorris, Co. Mayo (tel. 094/71587), a comfortable, modern house set in a quiet, pleasant area. The house is centrally heated and there is an attractive TV lounge with a peat fire. Three of her four bedrooms have handbasins. The rate for bed-and-breakfast is IR£9.50 ($15.25); 50% reduction for children. Open March through September.

Mrs. Ann Coakley, **Hazel Grove,** Drumsheel, Cong, Co. Mayo (tel. Cong

60), will welcome you warmly to her luxurious, modern bungalow with its pretty garden. There are beautiful views of the Connemara mountains and the ruins of Ahaland Castle. The house is centrally heated. Two of the four comfortable bedrooms have private facilities and they all have handbasins. The rate for bed-and-breakfast is IR£9.50 ($15.25) and high tea is available for IR£5.50 ($8.75); 20% reduction for children. Open May to September.

In Charlestown there is Mrs. Evelyn O'Hara, **Riverside,** Charlestown, Co. Mayo (tel. 094/54200), the delightful hostess of this attractive, century-old, family home. There is also a restaurant which is open from February to December and an enclosed car park. The seven pretty bedrooms all have handbasins and the house is centrally heated. The rate for bed-and-breakfast is IR£10.50 ($16.75) and dinner costs IR£9 ($14.50); 33% reduction for children. Open February to December.

At the center of Achill is **The Grove,** Bunnacurry, Achill Island, Co. Mayo (tel. 098/47108), run by the charming and helpful Mrs. Philomena McHugh. Her home is convenient to everything and families are welcome. The house is centrally heated and the home-cooked meals are delicious. There are four attractive bedrooms, all with handbasins and complete with tea-making facilities. The rate is IR£9.50 ($15.25) for bed-and-breakfast and dinner is IR£9 ($14.40). There is a 50% reduction for children. Open March through October.

Rockmount, Achill Island, Co. Mayo (tel. 098/45272), is a modern bungalow convenient to the village and a bus stop. Mrs. Frances Masterson is the friendly, helpful hostess, who happily shares her knowledge of the island with guests, and the four Masterson youngsters are a delight. The four homey, comfortable guest rooms all have handbasins, and during my recent stay, other guests included natives who had come from other parts of the country to holiday here, making for lively Irish conversation. The rate for bed-and-breakfast is IR£9.50 ($15.25), with a 25% discount for children. Central heating and off-street parking.

Across the sound from Achill Island, **Teach Mweewillin,** Currane, Achill Island, Co. Mayo (tel. 098/45134), is a modern bungalow set on a hill overlooking sound and island. Mrs. Margo Cannon keeps a pony for children to ride, and gladly helps guests arrange fishing, sailing, or golf. There are four attractive guest rooms, all with handbasins. B&B costs IR£9.50 ($15.25), with a 50% reduction for children. Central heating and parking; open Easter through September.

Mrs. Carmel Lydon, Cong, Co. Mayo (tel. 092/46053), is the gracious hostess in her large, modern house built in the Georgian style. Set on Lough Corrib (boats available for hire) and near Ashford Castle, the house has seven very attractive guest rooms, all with handbasins and four with private bath and shower. Bed-and-breakfast costs IR£10 ($16); dinner is IR£9 ($14.50). Central heating and good parking; open May through September.

FARMHOUSES. Two miles from Westport on the main Louisburgh road, **Rath-A-Rosa,** Rosbeg, Westport, Co. Mayo (tel. 098/25348), has magnificent views across a lawn bordered with flowers to a small cove and across Clew Bay to the mountains of Achill Island. Large picture windows in the modern bungalow's lounge frame the vista outside. Mrs. O'Brien, the lady of the house, is known far and wide for her cooking, using the freshest of ingredients and locally grown meats, with fish straight from local waters. Dinners are superb, and must be booked before noon. Breakfast often features just-caught mackerel along with Mrs. O'Brien's special mustard sauce. Mr. O'Brien, a fluent Gaelic speaker, is very much a part of the warm hospitality here, with witty and informative conversation his specialty. The six guest rooms all have handbasins, one has its own bathroom, and two come with shower and toilet. There's central heating and never a problem with parking. The rate for bed-and-breakfast is IR£10 ($16), and dinner costs IR£11 ($17.50). Open mid-March through October.

Mrs. Agnes Cronin's **Sea Call,** Carn, Belmullet, Co. Mayo (tel. 097/ 81064), sits on a dairy farm right at the sea's edge, and it houses the kind of warm, Irish hospitality that brings guests back year after year (as do Mrs. Cronin's apple tart and homemade brown bread). The two-story bungalow is centrally heated and has three homey guest rooms, all with handbasins. The rate here is IR£10 ($16) for bed-and-breakfast, and you should book as far in advance as possible, since she's often filled with repeat guests.

READERS' ACCOMMODATIONS SELECTIONS: "Mr. and Mrs. O'Neill made us at home in their beautiful country place, **Creeve,** Oughterard, Co. Galway (tel. 091/82210). Located on a private road bordering the lake, the place is a paradise for salmon and trout fishermen, and the O'Neills have their own boats for guests. Their breakfast is excellent, and the beds were the best we slept in" (Alice Leonard, Alexandria, Va.). . . . "On **Inishmore,** I stayed at Bridget and Sonny Johnston-Hernon's manor house in Kilmurvey (tel. 099/ 61218), and in the evenings enjoyed the company of the neighbors by a roaring fire. Bridget's meals are glorious" (Carol Smallenberg, Vancouver, British Columbia, Canada). . . . "Mrs. O'Connor, **Burren View Farm,** Doorus, Kinvara, Co. Galway (tel. 091/ 37142), was very friendly and helpful, as were the girls who served us breakfast in the morning. Breakfast was delicious and more varied than we had had in some time" (D. Keeney, Sudbury, Mass.).

2. WHERE TO EAT

Picnic spots abound in the wilds of Connemara and Achill Island, and country pubs often serve delicious, hearty bar food.

County Galway

The **Boat Inn Guest House,** right in the center of Oughterard (tel. 091/ 82196), can take care of hunger pangs, no matter if they're large or small or when they take you over. The bar and lounge serves quality bar food throughout the day, there's a marvelous cold salad selection that includes oak-smoked salmon, smoked mackerel, cold chicken, etc., and hot dishes that feature traditional Irish stew, roast chicken, and even hamburgers. In the restaurant, many of the same dishes are available from 6 to 9:30 p.m., as well as lamb, steak, and fresh fish courses. Lunch prices are IR£4 ($6.50) and under; dinner runs IR£5 ($8) to IR£11 ($17.50).

The picturesque little village of Craughwell, Co. Galway, is the burial place of the famous 19th-century poet Anthony Raftery, but in these parts, it's better known locally as the location of the **Blazers Bar** (tel. 091/41674). The name comes from the Galway Blazers Hunt, who have their headquarters and kennels just behind the pub, and in winter, this is the meeting place before and after hunts. Run by Teresa and Donal Raftery (to answer your question, I don't know if they're related to the poet—forgot to ask), the pub has a fantastically warm atmosphere, and inside you'll find a glorious mixture of rural personalities, gentlemen farmers, and visitors like yourself. Do stop in for a pint, or if you get there at tea time, you'll be served on beautiful china from a menu of seafood, soup, and sandwiches. Hot lunches are served Monday through Friday from 12:30 to 2:30 p.m.

The **Boluisce Seafood Bar,** Spiddal Village, Connemara (tel. 091/83286), is a true "Irish" restaurant, piling your plate high with generous portions at moderate prices. You can choose anything from soup right up to lobster and other delicacies. A full dinner from the à la carte menu will run about IR£8.50 ($13.50). Hours are noon to 2:30 p.m. and 5:30 to 10 p.m.

On the coastal drive from Galway to Clifden, the **Hotel Carna** on the outskirts of the little village of Carna (the Clifden side) serves good bar food at inexpensive prices. It also offers budget accommodations, and there's periodic entertainment.

In Clifden, **O'Grady's Seafood Restaurant,** Market Street (tel. 095/ 21450), is an attractive family-run restaurant that's been around a long time, earning an international reputation for their excellent seafood dishes. They have their own fishing boats, so you may be sure the fish you eat is not long out of Atlantic waters. On Saturday night there are candlelight dinners, and from Halloween to Easter they feature game as well as seafood. Business lunches are served at moderate prices every day, and dinner will run IR£8 ($12.75) to IR£14 ($22.50). The Tourist Menu is offered up to 2:30 p.m. Hours are 12:30 to 8 p.m. in winter, until 9:30 p.m. in June, July, and August. Closed January and February.

On the outskirts of Clifden, **The Pantry,** Westport Road, Clifden (tel. 095/ 21389), is a large two-story white stucco building with black trim. Also family run, its menu is extensive, offering a good variety of fish, fowl, beef, lamb, and pork. This is a relaxing, attractive place with friendly service, and it is fully licensed. Lunch will run about IR£6 ($9.50), dinner is around IR£11 ($17.50), and they accept major credit cards. Hours are 1 to 2:30 p.m. and 6 to 10:30 p.m.

The **Doon Restaurant,** Moyard (tel. 095/41139), is on the road from Clifden to Westport and it's a terrific place to stop for a super seafood lunch. It's a tiny place and very popular, so it might pay to call ahead and reserve. There's a wine license, and lunch will run about IR£8.50 ($13.50). Hours are 12:15 to 3 p.m., and they're closed Wednesday and from November to mid-April.

Des Moran's **Knockferry Lodge,** Knockferry, Rosscahill (tel. 091/80122) (see "Accommodations"), serves marvelous evening meals, but it is absolutely necessary to book by midday. You can look forward to such unusual offerings (for Ireland) as smoked pâté and gazpacho, and whatever Des has on the menu on a particular night, you may be sure it will be well prepared, fresh, and delicious. There's a wine license, and both the red and white vin ordinaire carafes are exceptional. Serving hours are 7 to 8 p.m. Monday through Thursday, 7 to 9 p.m. on Friday and Saturday; closed Sunday. Dinner will run about IR£12 ($19.25), and major credit cards are accepted.

County Mayo

For an inexpensive lunch in elegant surroundings, go by the **Breaffy House Hotel** in Castlebar (tel. 094/22033), an impressive graystone edifice set in beautiful formal gardens and lawns. Its Mulberry Bar is a gracious room in the Tudor style, and a very good three-course businessman's lunch is served every day from 12:30 to 2:30 p.m., featuring the joint of the day and fresh vegetables, with smoked salmon or Irish stew frequently among other choices, all at prices of IR£3.50 ($5.50) to IR£4.50 ($7.25). If you can get a seat by the window, you'll be able to enjoy the beauty both inside and out.

On Achill Island, the **Amethyst Restaurant** in Keel (tel. Keel 4) is in an old-fashioned resort hotel run by the Irish novelist Noel Scanlon, whose books are also published in America, and his wife. It's a large, comfortable room furnished with antiques and serviceable pieces that are merely old. There's a fireplace at one end, a peaked, beamed ceiling, oil paintings and prints of Achill scenes, and you dine to the accompaniment of classical music. The menu is quite extensive, with seafood featured (as you might imagine in this setting), but there are other specialties such as tandoori chicken and several vegetarian selections.

There's a wine license, and complete dinner prices range from IR£8 ($12.75) to IR£9 ($14.50). Hours are 9 a.m. to 9 p.m., and it's closed from October to May.

The **Asgard Tavern,** Westport Quay, Westport (tel. 098/25319), is a delightful nautical pub where owners Mary and Michael Cadden serve award-winning seafood dishes as well as bar snacks. If you're in Westport in the evening, you'll usually find traditional or folk music here. Pub grub is served from noon until 8 p.m., and the restaurant serves dinner from 6:30 to 10 p.m. at prices that run around IR£11 ($17.60) from the à la carte menu. Major credit cards are accepted. Closed Monday all year, and Sunday in the winter.

In Castlebar, the **Davitt Restaurant,** Rush Street (tel. 094/22233), has a good lunch menu at around IR£4.50 ($7.25). Dinner, featuring French and English dishes, goes for about IR£7 ($11.25). Fully licensed. Hours are 12:30 to 10:30 p.m. seven days a week.

Mulligan's Pub, James Street, Claremorris (tel. 094/71792), serves full meals as well as pub grub. This traditional-style pub also offers the Tourist Menu at both lunch and dinner. Lunch prices start IR£3 ($4.75), dinner at IR£5 ($8), and hours are 10:30 a.m. to 9 p.m. Bar hours are 10:30 a.m. to 11:30 p.m.

READERS' RESTAURANT SELECTIONS: "**Ardmore House,** Westport, Co. Mayo, is a fine restaurant which has received culinary awards. It has an attractive atmosphere, good service, and excellent food—among the best we had in Ireland" (Margaret and Donald Lawrence, New York, N.Y.). . . . "**Crooklog House Restaurant,** Furbo, Co. Galway (tel. 091/69211), owned by Patrick and Margaret Moylan was a big-splurge meal, but the helpings were large (too large), everything was fresh, and the table was set with real sterling silver. It was the best I have eaten anywhere I have traveled" (Mrs. H. Kemp, Ottawa, Ontario, Canada).

3. THINGS TO SEE AND DO

For the most part, it's the scenery that stars in the Western Region—the scenery and the host of ancient archeological sites that attest to just how long people have inhabited this lovely, but inhospitable, landscape.

County Galway

If you're a dedicated fan of the poet William Butler Yeats (and most Yeats fans *are* dedicated), you won't want to miss a visit to **Thoor Ballylee,** Gort, Co. Galway. From 1917 to 1929 Yeats spent his summers in this square 16th-century castle keep, having bought it in ruins for a paltry £35 and restored it to living condition. On one wall is inscribed a poem that ends with the words:

> And may these characters remain
> When all is ruin once again.

Fortunately, the tower has not reverted to ruins, and you can visit daily between 10 a.m. to 6 p.m., May to September. There's a resident information staff, as well as sound guides to follow through the tower and grounds.

In Clarenbridge, just across the bridge (toward Limerick) from Paddy Burke's Oyster Inn, the **Abbey Hand Crafts** (see "Shopping" in Chapter XXII) is run by the Sisters of Charity. They feature a large selection of many-hued sweaters, woolens, exquisite hand-crocheted bedspreads and pillows, Waterford glass, Irish linen, Belleek china, Donegal porcelain, and many other gift items. Prices are good and service is helpful and friendly.

In Spiddal, look for the **Spiddal Craft Centre,** a delightful complex of workshops for weavers, potters, silversmiths, etc.

About two miles south of Oughterard, you'll find the impressive ruins of

Aughnanure Castle near the shores of Loch Corribe. It's a well-preserved example of an Irish tower house and was once a heavily fortified residence. That comes as no surprise when you learn that this was a stronghold of the battling O'Flaherty clan between the 14th and 15th centuries. The castle is open from 10:30 a.m. to 6 p.m. Monday through Friday.

If time is a factor, you may want to drive through the heart of Connemara via Moycullen, Oughterard, and Recess to reach Clifden. Or you might follow this route through Moycullen and Oughterard as far as Maam Cross, then cut south to Screeb and west along the coast. If you choose this route, try to stop by the factory and showroom of **Celtic Crystal Ltd.** in Moycullen (tel. 091/85172). They specialize in the use of Celtic designs and motifs in their hand-cut crystal glassware, and they're open to the public every day from May to October from 9 a.m. to 6 p.m. Also in Moycullen, the **Connemara Marble Products** (tel. 091/85102) factory offers a tremendous stock of items made from polished marble, ranging from inexpensive souvenirs to moderately expensive items like jewelry, bookends, clocks, etc. Prices are better here than in shops, and hours are 9 a.m. to 5:30 p.m. daily during summer months, weekdays only the rest of the year. Across the road, there's a tea room serving tea, coffee, and cookies. Take a look, while you're in town, at the good buys at **Moycullen Crafts and Antiques.**

A much more memorable Connemara experience is the **coastal drive** from Galway to Clifden, which will add perhaps as much as three hours to your travel time, but will leave photographs upon your heart to be examined and re-examined for years to come.

CONNEMARA. The drive I strongly urge you to take runs along the coast from Galway to **Spiddal, Inverin, Costelloe, Carraroe, Screeb, Derryrush, Kilkieran, Carna, Glinsk,** and **Ballynahinch** (where a ruined castle keep on an island in Ballynahinch Lake is said to be where the Martin clan imprisoned their enemy captives). At Ballynahinch you can join the main Galway–Clifden road for a quick run into **Clifden,** or continue to meander around the coastline through **Roundstone, Ballyconneely,** and **Ballinaboy** (look for the signposted memorial to Alcock and Brown, who landed near here on the first transatlantic flight in 1919—it's on a high hill with magnificent panoramic views) before reaching Clifden. (In Ballyconneely, look for Mrs. Nonie Walsh's **West Coast Handcrafts** shop.) It's a journey through silence and largely unpopulated spaces, through a landscape made beautiful by incredibly shifting light and shade and the starkness of rock-strewn fields and hills. Glimpses of sandy strands at the sea's edge and the tiny villages that dot your route add another dimension to the experience.

Pleasures are simple in Connemara, most often associated with the natural rhythms of country life. For a glimpse of some of these, keep your eyes open as you travel through for **turf** being cut and dried in the boglands from April through June, and especially along the coastal road you may see donkeys with loaded creels transporting the dried turf to be stacked against the winter's cold. **Sheep shearing** is done by hand, often within the roofless walls of ruined cottages, and if you come across sheep being herded through the fields in June and July, they're probably on their way to be shorn. Between Ballyconneely and Kilkieran, you can sometimes watch **seaweed** being harvested (done at the full and new moons for four hours only in the middle of the day). **Thatchers** are usually at work in September and October, and the biggest concentration of thatched cottages is between Ballyconneely and Roundstone and between Cleggan and the Clifden road by way of Claddaghduff. At Roundstone and Cleggan, small trawlers fish year round, with open lobster boats and currachs setting out only in summer months. The **Connemara Pony Show** in Clifden is held in August and buyers come from around the world to bid on the sturdy little animals; the town takes on a country fair look, with much revelry, handcraft demonstrations, etc. Sometimes spontaneous, there are "flapper races," in which children race Connemara ponies while families gather for a great day of eating and drinking in the out-of-doors. Little villages all along the coast hold frequent currach races, a splendid sight if you're lucky enough to come across one. As I said, finding the when and where of the above is a matter of keeping your eyes open—and of a well-placed inquiry over a pint at the local pub.

One thing you won't want to miss in Clifden is the spectacular **Sky Drive,** a cliff road that forms a nine-mile circle around a peninsula and opens up vast seascapes. It's well signposted from Clifden. Boats are also available (through most accommodations) for **deep-sea fishing** for mackerel, blue shark, conger, cod, ling, and many other varieties. Summer evenings bring **traditional music** in many of Clifden's hotel bars and pubs; check with the Tourist Office or your accommodation hostess.

Millar's Connemara Tweeds (tel. 095/21038) has long been a Clifden landmark, with shop shelves filled with beautifully colored pure-wool lengths produced by weavers in the locality. A whole raft of other Irish-made craft items —glass, pottery, and others—complete the downstairs displays, and when you ascend iron spiral stairs, there's a gorgeous display of Connemara scenes depicted by Irish painters. In a stone-walled wing of the shop, you can browse through Irish fashions in a setting that includes a turf fire on the stone hearth and furnishings such as an old spinning wheel. Patchwork quilts are beautifully executed and much sought after, thus not always available. In short, this is a happy hunting ground for almost anything Irish-made. Hours are 9 a.m. to 6 p.m. every day except Sunday.

Clifden is also the setting for week-long sessions of the **Irish School of Landscape Painting,** founded and conducted by master painter Kenneth Webb, now assisted by his daughter, Susan. Individual instruction is given, with emphasis on techniques to catch the shimmering Connemara light shadings. You can attend for the day only by paying a tuition, IR£20 ($32) in 1988, or for the week, with accommodations and two meals a day thrown in, for IR£233 ($373) to IR£285 ($456)—1988 prices. For details on dates and 1989/1990 costs, contact Miss C. Cryan, Blue Door Studio, 16 Prince of Wales Terrace, Ballsbridge, Dublin 4 (tel. 01/685548).

Letterfrack is where **Kylemore Abbey** sits in a picture-postcard setting of woodlands on the banks of Pollacappal Lough, its impressive façade reflected by the lake's mirror surface. The stone mansion dates from the 19th century, and is home to an order of teaching nuns. They have established a thriving pottery industry, and they welcome visitors to the shop. There's a tea room for refreshment, and you can stroll the lovely grounds to your heart's content.

Just outside Letterfrack, **Connemara Handcrafts** (tel. 095/41058), is one of the best craft shops in the country. Its displays feature items you will see in few other places, and each craft is given its own display space. There's even a good selection of Irish publications and records. The shopping is good, whether you're looking for inexpensive souvenirs and gifts of good-quality or pricier works of art, jewelry, or crystal, and they'll gladly ship any purchases, thus saving the VAT. Upstairs, a tea room overlooks the garden, where light lunches are available in addition to tea and snacks (such as homemade buttered barm brack, the traditional Irish fruitcake). From mid-March to June, hours are 9:30 a.m. to 6 p.m. weekdays and Saturday; during June, July, and August, closing time is 7 p.m., and Sunday hours are 11 a.m. to 6 p.m. Closed November to mid-March.

On the Leenane–Maam Bridge road, look for **Maam Valley Pottery and Sweater Shop,** Maam Valley, Co. Galway (tel. 091/71109). The well-stocked shop features hand-loomed ties, hats, scarves, wool knitwear, and a host of other items, all produced within roughly a 20-mile area of the shop. The pottery workroom is open to visitors, and it is fascinating to see the potters throwing the items displayed on shop shelves. Dublin escapees Ann and Dennis Kendrick are the helpful owner/operators. Tea and snacks are served on the premises.

From Leenane, you can continue northward to Westport, or turn east for a drive along the shores of Lough Corrib to Cong, just over the County Mayo line.

County Mayo

There are several good reasons to turn toward Cong—the magnificent ruins of an Augustinian abbey, Ashford Castle, and the fact that it was in this locale that most of the film classic *The Quiet Man* was filmed.

CONG, ASHFORD CASTLE, AND *THE QUIET MAN*. Cong is a picturesque little village where, in a phenomenon known as "The Rising of the Waters," the waters of Lough Mask, which go underground three miles to the north, come rushing to the surface to surge through the center of town before they dissipate into several streams that empty into Lough Corrib. At the edge of town, the **Royal Abbey of Cong** was built by Turlough Mor O'Connor, High King of Ireland, in 1120 on the site of an earlier 7th-century St. Fechin community. Considered to be one of the finest early-Christian architectural relics in the country, it is also the final resting place of Rory O'Connor, the last High King, who was buried here in 1198. You'll find **Ashford Castle** just outside Cong on the shores of Lough Corrib. The oldest part of the castle was built by the de Burgoes, an Anglo-Norman family, in 1228, and its keep is now a part of the impressive, slightly eccentric Ashford Castle Hotel, which also incorporates a French-château-style mansion of the Oranmore and Browne families built in the early 1700s and the additions made by Sir Benjamin Guinness in the mid-1800s (undertaken as much to provide employment for famine-starved natives as to improve the property). It's a marvelous, fairyland sort of concoction that makes a superb luxury hotel favored by international celebrities (President and Mrs. Reagan stayed here during their 1984 visit). No less marvelous are its grounds, with beautifully landscaped lawns sloping down to the island-dotted lake. While its rates are definitely out of reach for budgeteers, not so for a stroll through its elegant public rooms with massive fireplaces and wall-high oil paintings, or a drink in the **Dungeon Bar.** Not a penny charged to soak in all that luxurious beauty!

Now, about *The Quiet Man:* Successive generations of Americans have loved Ireland as a direct result of the antics of John Wayne, Maureen O'Hara, and Barry Fitzgerald as they romped through this film that has become a classic. So I've done a little research, and if you want to track down some of the locales, look for these. (Also, if you can get a good crack going in one of Cong's pubs, there's bound to be a local there who remembers the filming and has tales to tell, like how some scenes had to be reshot many times because the inquisitive head of a local "extra" would be seen peering out from a hedge in the background.) Many of the exterior shots were taken on the grounds of Ashford Castle—the woodlands, the church, Squire Danaher's house, and the salmon river with its arched bridge. The main village street scenes took place near the cross in the market square of Cong, and the nearby general store was transformed into Cohan's Bar for the picture. Over in front of the abbey, that pretty house you see at the side of the bridge was the Reverend Playfair's house. Many other locales, such as John Wayne's ancestral cottage (now a ruin near Maam Bridge) were shot on the hillsides of the Maam Valley in County Galway, and the village of Inishfree as seen from a distance at the very beginning of the film is actually a shot of Clifden, taken from the Sky Road. There, that should get you started—and one simple comment in a Cong pub will carry you a long way in the footsteps of *The Quiet Man*.

Immediately east of Cong toward Cross lies the Plain of Moytura, where you'll find the **Ballymagibbon Cairn**. Dating from about 3,000 B.C., the 60-foot-high, 129-yard-circumference cairn was erected to commemorate a fierce prehistoric battle between the Firbolg and de Danann tribes. It seems that the Firbolgs carried the day during the early fighting, and that first evening each presented a stone and the head of a Danann to his king, who used the stones to build the cairn in honor of the grisly tribute. On a happier note, nearby Moytura House (privately owned and not open to the public) was once the home of Sir William Wilde and his wife, Speranza, parents of Oscar Wilde.

BALLINTUBBER ABBEY. The route north from Cong to Castlebar passes through the little town of Partry, four miles north of which you will find Ballintubber Abbey. It is the only church in the English-speaking world with a 7½-century history of uninterrupted services. What makes this all the more remarkable is that mass has been said within its walls since 1216 despite years of religious suppression, two burnings, and the assault of Cromwellian troops. At times during those centuries it was necessary for supplicants to kneel before the altar in secret and under open skies when there was no roof. That it has now been completely restored is due almost solely to the devoted efforts of its pastor, Father Egan, who labored from 1963 to 1966 to push the project forward. The abbey's doors are open every day and visitors are welcomed.

KNOCK. Twenty-five miles southeast of Castlebar, the little church in the village of Knock has become a shrine to which thousands of pilgrims come each year, for it was here that there were a number of apparitions during the 19th century.

CROAGH PATRICK AND WESTPORT. If your northward route from Connemara heads directly for Westport, I suggest you take the road that passes through stony, barren hillsides to **Louisburgh**, where **Clew Bay** opens before you. Between Louisburgh and Westport, the drive touches the bay at several points, and on the other side of the road rises 2,510-foot-high Croagh Patrick, where St. Patrick is believed to have fasted for 40 days and modern-day pilgrims climb the stony paths in their bare feet in July for a 4 a.m. mass at its top.

Westport House (tel. 098/25141) dates back to 1731, but it sits on the grounds of an earlier O'Malley castle, the dungeons of which are now visited by children who are happily "terrified" by the terrors that have been installed for their entertainment. The lovely old Georgian mansion house is a virtual museum of Irish memorabilia and craftsmanship, with a magnificent drawing room, two dining rooms (one large, one small), a long gallery, and a grand entrance hall. Up the marble staircase, four bedrooms hold such treasures as state robes and coronets and 200-year-old Chinese wallpaper.

Lord and Lady Altamont and their five daughters are in residence here, and over the years they have turned their estate into a stylish visitor attraction as a means of maintaining such an expensive operation. A full dozen shops feature quality Irish products, heraldic items, historic Irish scrolls, Irish art, fashion, gifts, and antiques. On the grounds there's a marvelous children's zoo, a playground, tea room, and boating and fishing on a lake and a river. **Connemara Horse Caravans** operate from the old stone stables, and there are self-catering holiday homes for rent, some right on the estate grounds. You can pick up a brochure detailing all these enterprises, or get one in advance by writing Westport House Country Estate, Westport, Co. Mayo.

From mid-May to mid-September, the house and grounds are open daily from 2 to 5 p.m., until 6 p.m. during June, July, and August. Adults pay IR£4 ($4.50); admission for children is IR£1.50 ($2.50).

ACHILL ISLAND. Achill is Ireland's largest island, and its 57 square miles are connected to the mainland by a causeway that takes you into breathtakingly beautiful, unspoiled, and varied scenery. High cliffs overlook tiny villages of whitewashed cottages, golden beaches, and heathery boglands. The signposted **Atlantic Drive** is spectacular, and will whet your appetite to explore more of the island's well-surfaced roadways. This is a wild and at the same time profoundly peaceful place, peopled by friendly, hardy natives who welcome visitors warmly. In late May the entire island is covered by such a profusion of rhododendrons that my bed-and-breakfast landlady smilingly told me, "every car that leaves will be loaded with those blooms, and we won't even miss them!" Achill has long been a favorite holiday spot for the Irish from other parts of the country, and there are good accommodations available in most of the beach villages. If time permits, I highly recommend an overnight stay on Achill (in summer there's traditional music in many of the pubs), but if you can only spare a part of a day, this is one off-the-beaten-track place you really shouldn't miss.

READERS' SIGHTSEEING SUGGESTIONS: "The **Belmullet Peninsula** and the **Inishkea Islands,** only 2½ miles off County Mayo's coast, are well worth a visit because of their wild beauty and fascinating history" (William Moynihan, Nashville, Tenn.). . . . "**O'Donnellan's Craft Shop,** 6 Quay St., Galway, Co. Galway (tel. 091/65698), is a very small shop run by a mother and daughter who are extremely helpful. The prices are most reasonable especially if you are looking for hand-crocheted Irish lace" (F. Sherlock, New York, N.Y.).

CHAPTER XXIV

SLIGO AND COUNTY SLIGO

□ □ □

The Northwest holds some of Ireland's most wondrous scenery—the sort of sea and mountains and far-flung vistas that shaped the poet Yeats's life and work. His words about this mystical, magical part of Ireland cannot, of course, be bested, and you will find yourself recalling them again and again as you travel the Northwest.

It was County Sligo that nurtured Yeats, from boyhood stays in Magheraboy with his grandparents to the end of his life, when he was laid to rest in Drumcliffe Churchyard. His imagination was fired by local legends of ancient heroes and heroines who lived out their sagas in this part of Ireland and left the countryside strewn with mementos of their passing. Beautiful Lough Gill is where you'll find his *Isle of Inisfree,* and at Knocknarea's summit is the cairn where according to legend (and Yeats) "passionate Maeve is stony-still." All through the county are countless other cairns, dolmens, passage graves, and other prehistoric relics, bearing silent witness to the lives that so engaged the poet. Along the western part of the county are the Ox Mountains; the north holds high, flat-topped limestone hills like Benbulben; and for the pleasure-bent traveler, there's a fine beach at Strandhill, a golf course at Rosses Point, and good fishing in any number of rivers and lakes.

Sligo (Sligeach, "Shelly Place") grew up around a ford of the River Garavogue, which rises in Lough Gill and tumbles over swift rapids as it approaches its estuary. The town's strategic position gave it early prominence as a seaport, and as a religious center, it is the cathedral town of both a Catholic and Protestant diocese. For Yeats devotees and scholars, it offers a wealth of information and memorabilia, and all visitors will find a friendly welcome and accommodations that are friendly to the budget.

1. ORIENTATION

Sligo sits astraddle the **River Garavogue,** and the **Hyde Bridge** at Stephen Street is a central point of reference. **O'Connell Street** runs south of the bridge and holds the major shopping and business district of the town. The beach resort of **Strandhill** is five miles to the west; **Rosses Point,** five miles to the north; and there are several buses a day to each from the main bus station. **Magheraboy,** where Yeats spent many childhood summers, is a short distance from town to the southwest, and **Drumcliffe Churchyard** is five miles north of town.

2. USEFUL INFORMATION

You'll find the **Tourist Office** on Temple Street (tel. 071/61201), open from 9 a.m. to 6 p.m. daily in summer. . . . The **bus and railway station** is just above Lord Edward Street on the western edge of town. For all **bus information,** call 071/62051. . . . For **taxi** service, call 2596 or 3740; there's a taxi rank at the train station. There are preset fares to most points of interest, and cabs are not metered, so be sure to ask the fare. . . . The **General Post Office** is on Wine Street, west of the bridge, with hours of 9 a.m. to 5:30 p.m. Monday through Saturday; closed Sunday. . . . The *Sligo Champion* carries notices of current goings on in town and the area. . . . The **telephone prefix** for Sligo is 071.

3. ACCOMMODATIONS

Accommodations listed here are in and around Sligo town, all convenient bases for exploring Yeats Country.

Note: Prices shown below are those in effect in 1989—expect them to be higher in 1990.

HOSTEL: The only An Oige hostel in County Sligo is at the **E Vocational School,** Easkey (tel. Easkey 21). It is 26 miles from Sligo, 18 miles from Ballina, and is open only July and August.

BED-AND-BREAKFAST: Mrs. Mazie Rooney's modern, centrally heated bungalow, **Castletown House,** Drumcliffe, Co. Sligo (tel. 071/63204), is just off the N15 Donegal road, near W.B. Yeats's grave, and is ideal for touring Yeats Country. The three bedrooms are comfortably furnished; all have handbasins and one has a private bath with shower. Bed-and-breakfast costs IR£10 ($16), with a 20% reduction for children. Open Easter through October.

Near the railway and bus station, **Renate Central House,** Upper John Street (tel. 071/62014), is a small gabled house you'll recognize by its colorful windowbox blooms. Mrs. Hunt, whose husband is a former mayor of Sligo, has five attractive guest rooms, all with handbasins, and she takes a personal interest in her guests. There's a pretty dining room, and color TV in the drawing room. The B&B rate is IR£11 ($17.50), with 20% reduction for children. Central heating.

Mrs. Mary Whooley's **Ardenode,** Cartron Hill, Rosses Point Road, Sligo (tel. 071/43570), is a sparkling bright two-story house filled with flowers from the pretty gardens outside. Décor in the five guest rooms includes bedspreads and drapes that match floral wallpaper, and all have handbasins, built-in wardrobes, and full-length mirrors. The L-shaped dining room opens onto a pleasant patio out back. The centrally heated house is located in a peaceful cul-de-sac, and the widowed Mrs. Whooley and her three lovely children make guests feel right at home. The rate for bed-and-breakfast is IR£10 ($16), with a 20% discount for children.

Rathnashee (it means "Fort of the Fairies"), Teesan, Donegal Road, N15 (tel. 071/3376), is the home of Tess and Sean Haughey, and it's the kind of place where guests often wind up sitting around the kitchen table for long conversations in which the Haugheys share their extensive knowledge of what to see in Sligo. They also have one of the best private libraries in Sligo, with all types of literature and poetry, and they can arrange sightseeing tours with archeologists. Tess serves traditional Irish food and homemade preserves. The centrally heated modern bungalow is about two miles out from town, and there are four nice bedrooms, all with handbasins and two with private toilet and shower. B&B costs IR£10.50 ($16.75), dinner is IR£9 ($14.50), and there's good parking off the road.

Just off the Dublin–Galway road, **Aisling,** Cairns Hill, Sligo (tel. 071/60704), is a centrally heated modern bungalow overlooking Benbulben and Knocknare. The five guest rooms have handbasins and electric blankets, and three have private baths. Mrs. Nan Faul is the charming hostess. The rate for bed-and-breakfast is IR£10.50 ($16.75).

Mrs. Nellie Cogan gives guests a warm welcome at **Mountain View,** Upper Pearse Road, Sligo (tel. 071/3731). All four guest rooms have lovely views of Knocknarea and Benbulben, and the sea is only ten minutes away. Mrs. Cogan often ends the day over an evening cuppa and friendly chat with guests, giving helpful suggestions on where to go and what to do so that visitors won't miss out on anything in the area. The rate for B&B is IR£9.50 ($15.25).

Mrs. Doreen MacEvilly, **Tree Tops,** Cleveragh Road, Sligo, Co. Sligo (tel. 071/60160), is the charming hostess of this attractive home situated near the town center. It is on the road to Lough Gill, Innisfree, and Holy Well. The house is centrally heated and an evening meal is available. All of her five comfortable bedrooms have handbasins and four of these have private facilities, for which there is an extra charge of IR£1 ($1.60) per person. The rate for bed-and-breakfast is IR£10.50 ($16.75), and dinner costs the same; 20% reduction for children. Open all year.

Mrs. Carmel Carr, **St. Martin's,** Cummeen, Strandhill Road, Sligo, Co. Sligo (tel. 071/60614), will welcome you warmly to her attractive modern bungalow. The house is centrally heated and there is a garden for guests to use. Of the five rooms, four have private facilities and there is an extra charge of IR£1.50 ($2.40) for these. Her rate is IR£9.50 ($15.25) for bed-and-breakfast and there is a 50% reduction for children. Open March to November.

Mrs. Phil Clancy, **Seisnaun,** Kintogher, Sligo, Co. Sligo (tel. 071/43938), is the very warm and friendly hostess of this luxury modern bungalow which is convenient to Rosses Point, Yeats Country, and Drumcliffe. Situated in a peaceful area, it has beautiful views of Benbulben mountain and Yeats Country. The house is centrally heated and the food is delicious, complete with home-baking. All five attractive bedrooms have handbasins and one has private facilities, for which there is an extra charge of IR£1.50 ($2.50) per person. The rate is IR£10 ($16) for bed-and-breakfast, and dinner costs IR£10 ($16); 25% reduction for children. Open April to September.

Two miles from Grange, Mrs. Mary Cadden welcomes you to **Cloonaghbawn,** Ballinful, Co. Sligo (tel. 071/73205). Set in a quiet, scenic location near Lissadell House and Ellen's Pub (traditional music), the centrally heated white bungalow has three nice guest rooms with handbasins. The rate is IR£9 ($14.50), with a 40% discount for children. Open April through October.

My mail has been full of praise for Mrs. Maeve Walsh and her modern, centrally heated **Cruckawn House,** Ballymote Road, Tubbercurry, Co. Sligo (tel. 071/85188). Many readers write that they have returned to Cruckawn because of Mrs. Walsh's friendliness and helpfulness, and you'll understand why after staying in her relaxed, comfortable home. The two-story house is nicely deco-

SLIGO

To Carrowmore
To Strandhill
WOLFE TONE ST.
LORD EDWARD ST.
COLLEGE RD.
UNION PL.
HARBOUR RD.
ADELAIDE ST.
UNION ST.
QUAY ST.
LOWER
TEMPLE
CHARLES ST.
JOHN ST.
WINE ST.
QUAY ST.
River Garavogue
MARKIEVICZ RD.
To Rosses Point,
Drumcliff,
Bundoran
O'CONNELL ST.
GRATTAN ST.
POUND ST.
HIGH ST.
MARKET ST.
CASTLE ST.
TEELING ST.
THOMAS ST.
BRIDGE ST.
To Ballysodare,
Enniscrore,
Dublin
PEARSE RD.
CHAPEL HILL
ABBEY ST.
KENNEDY PARADE
CRANMORE (MASS LANE)
CHAPEL ST.
RIVERSIDE
THE MALL
To Lough Gill,
Manorhamilton,
Dromahair

—N→

KEY TO NUMBERED SIGHTS:

1. Railway Station
2. Methodist Church
3. Town Hall
4. Yeats Museum
5. Sligo County Museum
6. Church of Ireland
7. Sligo Abbey
8. St. John's Cathedral (Ch. of Ire.)
9. Cathedral of the Immaculate Conception (R.C.)
10. Presbyterian Church
11. Tourist Information Office
12. Dominican Friary

rated and has good views of the Ox Mountains. It sits on its own grounds, with a large garden and paved parking area, overlooking a golf course that visitors may use. Meals are superb, and there's a wine license. Guest rooms have built-in bookshelf/headboards and handbasins, and four have private bath facilities. There's a sun lounge, games room, and laundry facilities for guests' use. Rates are IR£10 ($16), and IR£2 ($3.25) extra for private bath.

Mrs. Anna McKiernan, **Glenwood,** Carrowmore, Sligo, Co. Sligo (tel. 071/61449), is the hospitable hostess of the lovely, new two-story house set in award-winning gardens on the Sligo–Carrowmore road beside a riding school. It is convenient to Knocknarea, Yeats Country, and Strandhill, and is surrounded by megalithic tombs. The house is centrally heated and dinner is available with advance notice. The five pretty bedrooms all have handbasins and two have private facilities, for which there is an extra charge of IR£1 ($1.50) per person. The rate for bed-and-breakfast is IR£10 ($16) and dinner costs IR£11 ($17.50); 25% reduction for children. Open April through September.

Mrs. Lindsay, **La Mer,** Luffertan, Strandhill, Co. Sligo (tel. 071/68182), has a lovely modern bungalow set in beautiful surroundings and overlooking Ballisodare Bay. It is located on the Ballisodare–Strandhill road and is two miles from town. The house is centrally heated and the three attractive bedrooms all have handbasins. The rate for bed-and-breakfast is IR£9 ($14.50) and there is a 25% reduction for children. Open May to September.

Mrs. O'Malley, **Rinroe House,** Quay Road, Inniscrone, Co. Sligo (tel. 096/36183), is the charming hostess of this beautiful Georgian-style house overlooking the sea and the River Moy. The house is centrally heated and there is a lovely sun lounge for guests to use. The four comfortable bedrooms all have handbasins and an evening meal is available. The rate is IR£10.50 ($16.75) for bed-and-breakfast and dinner costs IR£8 ($12.75); 25% reduction for children. Open June to September.

Just a mile outside Drumcliffe is Mrs. Healy's **Urlar House,** Drumcliffe, Co. Sligo (tel. 071/63110), a large, attractive, centrally heated farmhouse located on the Sligo–Bundoran road, right next to Benbulben mountain. There is beautiful scenery all around the house. There are five bedrooms and they all have handbasins. Dinner is available with advance notice. The rate for bed-and-breakfast is IR£10 ($16) and dinner costs the same; 25% reduction for children. Open March to November.

The McDonagh Family, **Westway,** Castletown, Drumcliffe, Co. Sligo (tel. 071/63178), are charming and hospitable and their modern farm bungalow overlooks Drumcliffe Bay and lies at the foot of Benbulben mountain. The house is centrally heated and electric blankets are supplied. There is a lovely sitting room with a log and peat fire. The three pretty bedrooms all have handbasins and an evening meal is available. The rate is IR£9.50 ($15.25) for bed-and-breakfast, and the same price for dinner; 20% reduction for children. Open April to August.

Big Splurge B&B

Charles and Mary Cooper, who have built the Knockmuldowney Restaurant, Glen Lodge, Culleenamore, Co. Sligo (tel. 071/68122), into one of the finest in Ireland, have now opened the upper floors of their home to guests. The same loving care and attention that have characterized the restaurant shine through in every one of the six luxury rooms above. Each room has its own private bath and shower, and each is decorated in colors and fabrics that exactly match the style of the old Georgian country house. Best of all, perhaps, is their size—all are large enough to give you the feeling of having your own suite, and there's comfortable seating for lounging. Those in the front of the house overlook the bay and mountains beyond, while the view from others is of lawns and gardens. Bed-and-breakfast here costs IR£26 ($41.50) per person sharing, and there's no Big Splurge I'd recommend more highly.

A HOTEL: Out in Strandhill, the **Sancta Maria Hotel,** Strandhill, Co. Sligo (tel. 071/68113), is a small, old-fashioned country inn, with the sort of comfortable, homey air that only comes from caring hosts like Brigid and Nace O'Dowd. The attention at the Sancta Maria is very personal, and the O'Dowds will happily help you plan your travels around the area, fill you in on local stories to embellish your journey, and otherwise make your stay pure pleasure. The nine guest rooms are comfortably furnished, with built-in closets and handbasins, and there's central heating. The O'Dowds plan Gaelic Nights on weekends through the summer months, when there's always a complement of nearby locals to join in the singing and dancing. The hotel is also fully licensed. All in all, it's a pleasant, relaxed "home from home," not at all hotel-like! Seasonal rates range from IR£10.50 ($16.75) to IR£11.50 ($18.50) plus 10% service, with a 10% reduction for children. Open Easter through December.

READERS' ACCOMMODATIONS SELECTIONS: "**Carrowkeel House** (tel. 071/ 2432) is a farmhouse about two miles from Sligo. Mrs. Hunter cannot be praised enough for her true Irish hospitality that makes one feel a part of the family" (Mrs. Gerti Elling, Mannheim, Germany). . . . "Mrs. Kearney, whose farmhouse **Avondale-Breeogue,** Knocknahur (tel. 071/78192), is four miles from Sligo, is a charming, thoughtful hostess, and her rooms are clean and very modern" (Mrs. J. Rothwell, Rolling Hills, Calif.). . . . "Mrs. Rita Monaghan, at **Cedarville,** Mail Coach Road, off Pearse Road (tel. 071/3080), won a major bread-baking championship, and her spotless guesthouse is very homey and comfortable. She is one of the friendliest and kindest people I've ever met" (Mary Raleigh, Limerick, Ireland). . . . "We stayed at **Lisadorn,** Strandhill, Co. Sligo (tel. 071/78210), with Lily and Paddy Diamond and were treated so grand we felt really special. They helped us with suggestions of what to see and look for along the way" (Peggy Moran, Fort Wayne, Ind.). . . . "I would like to recommend **Cillard farmhouse,** run by Mrs. Dillon (tel. 071/ 72801), for outstanding hospitality and the best breakfast we had on our trip. It is located in Carrowmore, only a five-minute walk from Sligo Riding Centre" (Sharlin McCabe, Houston, Tex.). . . . "**St. Ann's,** Keash Road, Ballymote, Co. Sligo (tel. 071/83432), is run by the Harrison family. Within minutes of our arrival, tea and biscuits were served as we relaxed at an outdoor table. We visited with the family till late at night in their kitchen. Our room and the bathroom were bright and spotless. Breakfast included jellies and preserves made from fruits raised in their garden" (Shirley Fisher, Portland, Ore.).

4. WHERE TO EAT

There are picnic tables scattered throughout lovely **Dooney Wood,** some four miles outside Sligo. Beside the car park, flat-topped Dooney Rock is where Yeats wrote of the fiddler playing. There are also parking areas and picnic tables at **Carns,** setting of many cairns and giants' graves, a mile and a half from Sligo out the Holywell road, as well as **Deerpark,** on the old road to Manorhamilton.

Bonne Chere, 45 High St. (tel. 071/42014), has been a favorite of Sligo families for years. It's a large room, with exposed beams and white arches, made cheerful by paintings of Yeats Country and potted plants. The menu features good, plain cooking, and there's a children's menu and a Tourist Menu. Prices run about IR£5 ($8) at lunch, around IR£10 ($16) at dinner. Hours are 8 a.m. to 11 p.m.

Beezies, 45 O'Connell St. (tel. 3031), is worth a visit, if only for a drink or a look around. The turn-of-the-century marble counters, bar partitions of Tiffany glass, and lamps with tulip-shaped shades give a real 19th-century look to the place. In back there's a full restaurant serving lunches starting at IR£5 ($8) and five-course dinners for IR£8 ($12.75).

Four miles southwest of Sligo, under Knocknarea, **Coolera House Pub-Restaurant** (tel. 071/68204 or 68177) serves an à la carte menu from 6:30 to 10 p.m., and a satisfying dinner (fresh fish are a specialty) should run around IR£11 ($17.50). During summer months, there's traditional music weeknights.

The **Traditional Restaurant/Lounge,** Teeling Street, Tubbercurry (tel. 071/85111), is a restaurant plus a bar/lounge, and the service by owners Anne and Tommie Killoran is pleasant and personal. Antiques (like the old butter churns) carry out the traditional theme, and the menu is varied and the dishes well prepared. There are quick snacks as well as full meals, and prices are moderate. Lunch will run around IR£5 ($8); dinner, about IR£7 ($11.25). They offer the Tourist Menu, and hours are 9 a.m. (they also serve a good breakfast) to 11:30 p.m. seven days a week. From June to September, Thursday night is Irish music night here.

BIG SPLURGE: Charles and Mary Cooper have, since 1978, built a reputation for their **Knockmuldowney Restaurant,** Glen Lodge, Culleenamore, Co. Sligo (tel. 071/68122), as one of Ireland's finest restaurants. Located five miles from Sligo town at the foot of Knocknarea, the restaurant is in a Georgian country house in the midst of a small estate and lovely gardens. As much as possible, the Coopers use vegetables and fruits grown on their own grounds, and from neighboring farms they gather the freshest lamb, poultry, pork, beef, and game. Salmon, sea trout, and other seafood come from the local Ballisodare fishery, some of which they smoke right at Knockmuldowney. The list of awards won by their outstanding creations is as long as your arm, and especially in summer months, advance reservations are absolutely necessary. Needless to say, the atmosphere is one of relaxed elegance, and the table d'hôte dinner price of IR£12.50 ($20) makes this a Big Splurge for budgeteers and is extremely good value for the money. Hours are 7:30 to 9:30 p.m. every day from mid-March to November. This restaurant has my highest recommendation.

To reach Knockmuldowney, take the Sligo–Strandhill road and at Strandhill continue 2½ miles on the Ballisodare road, where it's signposted.

5. THINGS TO SEE AND DO

While many visitors come to Sligo and head straight out to those spots associated with Yeats, it would be a mistake not to see the highlights of the old town itself.

SLIGO TOWN: To get the most out of a stay in Sligo town, join one of the **walking tours** conducted during July and August by young student guides who love the town and are intimately acquainted with such points of interest as St. John's Church, which was designed by the same architect as Leinster House, the seat of the Irish government in Dublin. Tours leave the Tourist Office at 11 a.m. and last an hour and 15 minutes. It's perfectly in order to tip your enthusiastic young guide a minimum of IR£2 ($3.25). The Tourist Office also has an excellent booklet that outlines a signposted *Tourist Trail* do-it-yourself walking tour (a nice souvenir, even if you go along with the guided tour).

On Stephen Street you'll find the **Sligo County Museum and Art Gallery,** which includes many exhibits relating to the poet W. B. Yeats and an extensive collection of paintings and drawings by his artist brother, Jack Yeats. Open Tuesday through Friday from May to September and by arrangement with the Tourist Board from October to April.

Sligo has always intrigued painters quite as much as writers, and the *poet* Yeats had no family monopoly on fascination with this countryside—his *painter* brother, Jack Yeats, sought to capture it on canvas. There's an excellent exhibition of his work in a gallery at the **Sligo Library.** The Sligo Art Gallery at the Yeats Memorial Building houses regular exhibitions by contemporary Irish artists.

Rental bikes are available from **Conway Bros., Wine Street** (tel. 071/ 61240).

The local Irish Countrywoman's Association has rescued and restored **Dolly's Cottage,** in Strandhill, the last thatched house in Sligo. Dolly was a well-loved resident of the area, and now you can visit her home from 3 to 5 p.m. weekdays to see the dresser with its delph-chinawear collection, a pouch bed with its patchwork quilt, spinning wheel, and other authentic period furnishings. Hand-crafted knit, wool, and leather items are on sale, as are sheepskin rugs and pottery. During summer months, country markets are held every Wednesday afternoon.

One of the most delightful ways I can think of to visit the beaches, *Ben Bulben,* Lissadell House, etc., is via horse and trap, and the **Moneygold Riding and Horse Driving Centre,** Grange, Co. Sligo (tel. 071/63337), can arrange it for you. They also have a variety of other horse-related activities, such as pony trekking, fast beach rides, and special holidays in an "organic" farmhouse and youth hostel, with rates beginning at IR£4 ($6.50).

YEATS COUNTRY: One of the best ways to get an overall feeling for the country that so stirred the poet's soul is to take Bus Eireann's **Yeats Country Tour,** conducted on specific days during summer months. It's a nearly four-hour trip, with a very good commentary, and the low fare (about IR£5 or $8) includes a visit to **Lissadell House,** where Countess Mankievicz (an important figure in the 1916 uprising) spent much of her childhood.

If you're rambling through Yeats Country on your own (which you might want to do even after taking the above conducted tour), go by the Tourist Office or a Sligo bookshop and pick up the excellent booklet *The Yeats Country,* which tells you which poems were written about which places. You'll also find those places associated with the great poet marked by simple signposts inscribed with the appropriate verses. One suggested route is to drive east along Lough Gill's northern shore to the **Holy Well,** a grotto where devout Catholics met during the years of the penal laws to celebrate mass in secret. Its stone altar is more than 300 years old. Look out over the lake to the southeast and the small *Lake Isle of Innisfree.* From there, drive to **Glencar Lake** and leave your car to walk across the fields to **Glencar Falls,** where there are steps built up the left side of what Yeats called "pools' among the rushes." As you return across the field, you can glimpse the little thatched cottage where Yeats called in for tea quite often as a young man. Just before you reach Sligo's town limits, you'll see the turnoff for **Drumcliffe** to the north. This is where Yeats lies "Under bare Ben Bulben's head," and his headstone bears the epitaph he composed for himself,

> Cast a cold eye
> On life, on death.
> Horseman, pass by!

PREHISTORIC SLIGO: Scattered over the face of County Sligo are traces of the **prehistoric races** who lived here during three main periods: the Late Stone Age (Neolithic, 2500–2000 B.C.); the Bronze Age (2000–500 B.C.); and the Early Iron Age (500 B.C. to A.D. 500). The Tourist Office has a marvelously detailed leaflet, *Prehistoric Sligo,* that tells you where to find the most important of these court cairns, portal dolmens, passage graves, ring forts, and gallery graves. In the immediate vicinity of Sligo town, you'll find **Carrowmore** (south of town near Ballysodare), a cemetery of about 65 megalithic tombs—one of the largest concentrations in Europe—in a one-mile-long, half-mile-wide area. And at the top of Knocknarea, there's the great **Misgaun Maeve,** an unopened cairn some 200 feet in diameter and about 80 feet high that archeologists believe covers a vast passage grave, but legend insists is the burial monument to Queen Maeve.

READERS' SIGHTSEEING SUGGESTION: "Seven miles south of Sligo on road N4 is the **Innisfree Hand Cut Crystal** factory (at the bridge). This crystal is similar to Waterford, but about 40% cheaper and they specialize in limited editions. They also ship anywhere" (Charles Burgh, Pittsburgh, Pa.).

6. SLIGO AFTER DARK

Just beside the Tourist Board building on Temple Street, the **Hawks Well Theatre** (tel. 071/61526 or 61518), has brought a resurgence to live theater in Sligo. As the first purpose-built theater in the West, it places a strong emphasis on Irish playwrights, productions are performed by leading Irish theater companies, and there's the occasional evening of poetry, musical concerts, or traditional song, dance, drama, and comedy. Past performances include *Playboy of the Western World, The Plough and the Stars,* and *Leopold Bloom: Heroic Moments.* It's a small, intimate theater with the most up-to-date equipment and, with advance notice, facilities in the stalls for the handicapped (toilets also have special facilities). Off-street parking is available at Cathedral car park. Tickets are quite inexpensive, and I urge you to call to check what's playing during your visit so you can book at least one night to see Irish theater in an environment like those that spawned one of the world's greatest theatrical traditions.

It's fairly easy to find traditional music and ballads in Sligo pubs and those nearby. However, since the "schedule" for such happenings is often a *non*-schedule, best check with the Tourist Office when you're there about days of the week the following are likely to have music. Even if there's no music, you can bet on good conversation any night of the week in any of these pubs, and who knows *where* that could lead!

From time to time, the **Sancta Maria Hotel** in Strandhill (tel. 071/68113) has a "Gaelic Night," and when that happens, natives from all around flock to the hotel in the sure knowledge there'll be good musicians on hand and a lot of singing and reciting of poetry. Brush up on your own party piece and go along if you happen on one of these very special evenings (call the hotel or check with the Tourist Board—weekend nights used to be the nights for music, but it changes).

C.C.E. usually holds sessions on Tuesday nights at the **United Trades Club** on Castle Street.

McLynn's Pub on Old Market Street frequently breaks out in song, almost always led by Donal McLynn, who carries on a tradition set by his late grandmother, who ran the pub for more than 30 years (the Ogham plaque by the doorway spells out "Granny" in the ancient script in her memory). The pub has the comfortable look of age, with a big hearth and lots of copper and old bar mirrors. The crowd tends to be on the young side, and you can usually count on ballads on Thursday.

Another gathering place where you can mingle with the locals from the surrounding countryside as traditional music is passed from one generation to the next is **The Thatch,** in Ballisodare. The small cottage pub has a huge fireplace and church-pew seats in one of its two rooms, and kitchen furnishings in the other. There's usually music on Thursday.

On the bridge at Drumcliffe, the **Yeats Tavern** has nightly musical goings-on all year in a very popular, modern setting. It's out the Donegal road, about five miles from town.

At Rosses Point, **Bruen's Pub** (known locally as "Austin Gillen's") is as nautical as Austin himself, filled with ship models, charts, and all sorts of other items related to the sea. Austin has a story to go with every one, and is a great one for the crack if you get him going. Pub grub is also available.

Not for music, but for a uniquely traditional Irish "local," where the crack is good and your company welcomed, is **Hargedon's** on O'Connell Street. It's over two centuries old and looks it, but is as authentic as they come.

7. SPECIAL EVENTS

For two weeks every August there's a glut of activity in Sligo centered around the works of William Butler Yeats. That's when the **Yeats International Summer School** presents seminars, lectures, workshops, poetry readings, and dramas for dedicated Yeats scholars. Afternoon tours are conducted, and evenings are filled with social and theatrical events. In 1988 tuition was IR£210 ($336), and the staff will help you find inexpensive accommodations. For full details, a brochure, and an application, contact the Secretary, Yeats Society Inc., Hyde Bridge, Sligo, Ireland (tel. 071/42693).

If you happen into Sligo while the summer school is in session, you can attend many of the events by buying individual tickets.

The week following Easter is dedicated to the **Feiseanna,** with competitions in traditional music, dancing, singing, plays, and all sorts of other activities. It draws the Irish from all over the country, and the town is alive with festivities day and night. **Sligo Midsummer Festival** takes place in June and a **Community Arts Festival** in October.

DONEGAL TOWN

□ □ □

1. USEFUL INFORMATION
2. ACCOMMODATIONS
3. WHERE TO EAT
4. THINGS TO SEE AND DO

Where other Irish towns have a square right in the middle of town, Donegal (Dun na nGall, "the Fort of the Foreigners") has a wide triangular space they call the Diamond. It's the meeting place of three major roadways from Derry, west Donegal, and Sligo, and it points up Donegal town's strategic location at the head of Donegal Bay and the mouth of the River Eske, a position of such importance that in ancient times the princes of Tir Chonaill (the O'Donnells) made this their chief seat. Red Hugh O'Donnell founded a Franciscan friary here in 1474, and when it was sacked in the 1600s and the monks were sent scurrying in fear of their lives, four went to Bundrowes for safety and set about compiling the scholarly *Annals of the Four Masters,* one of Ireland's most valuable sources of early church history. In the Diamond stands a 25-foot-high obelisk, inscribed with the names of the four monks at its base.

Today Donegal town is a friendly, thriving market town, famed for its woolens and as a touring base for the rest of this wildly beautiful county.

1. USEFUL INFORMATION

The **Tourist Office** is on Quay Street (tel. 073/21148), open May through September with hours of 10 a.m. to 6 p.m. . . . There's a bus pickup station on the Diamond for **Bus Eireann buses** with regular service to Derry, Dublin, Galway, Killybegs, Portnoo, and Belfast. . . . The **Post Office** is on Tir Conaill Street. . . . Doherty's on Main Street has **bicycles** for rent. . . . **Shops** close early on Wednesday. . . . Check with the Tourist Office for what's going on when you're in Donegal. The **telephone prefix** for Donegal is 073.

2. ACCOMMODATIONS

Note: Prices shown below are those in effect in 1989—expect them to be higher in 1990.

A HOSTEL: There's an excellent **hostel**—a former coast-guard station—three miles outside Donegal town (tel. Donegal 174).

BED-AND-BREAKFAST: Riverside House, Waterloo Place (tel. 073/ 21083), is just across the River Eske from Donegal Castle on a quiet residential terrace. The center of town is a quick walk away. Mrs. Kathleen Curristan and her pretty daughter, Elaine, welcome guests here and have decorated the five nice guest rooms in cheerful colors. All have handbasins, and there's one large family room with a double and two twin beds. Even the bathroom is bright, with matching floral wallpaper and shower curtains. The lounge frames the river and castle view through wide front windows, and its piano is often in use by guests as well as the Curristans. Bed-and-breakfast costs IR£10 ($16), with a 20% reduction for children.

In a secluded woodland setting, Mrs. Pearl Timony's **Drumcliffe House,** Coast Road, Donegal town (tel. 073/21200), is a lovely old home that dates back some 300 years. Both the house and its antique furnishings are interesting, and meals feature Mrs. Timony's home-baking. The four attractive guest rooms all have handbasins, and the house is centrally heated. The rate for bed-and-breakfast is IR£10 ($16).

Five miles outside Donegal town, **Ardeevin,** Lough Eske, Barnesmore, Co. Donegal (tel. 073/21790) sits on a rise overlooking Lough Eske and the Bluestack Mountains. There are five nice guest rooms, all with handbasins, and four have private bath with shower. Mrs. Mary McGinty is the charming hostess of the centrally heated dormer bungalow. B&B rate is IR£10 ($16), with a 20% reduction for children. Open April through October.

A HOTEL: You might have to call the **Hyland Central Hotel,** The Diamond (tel. 073/21027), a "Mini-Splurge"—it is a bit above our budget but has so much to recommend it represents the best rule of all budgeteering: value-for-money. This immaculately clean, family-run hotel is that rare combination of modern facilities with an old-fashioned, homey atmosphere. The dining room, overlooking the river, is lovely and serves moderately priced meals (see "Where to Eat"). Rooms here are spacious and have a light, airy look and comfortable modern furnishings. All have private bath, color TV, and direct-dial telephone. For a gorgeous view of Donegal Bay, ask for one on the back (the view in front is of the Diamond). Seasonal rates range from IR£20 ($32) to IR£32 ($51.25) per person.

READER'S ACCOMMODATIONS SELECTION: "Mrs. T. Timoney, **Castle View House,** Waterloo Place, Donegal town, Co. Donegal (tel. 073/22100), is a wonderful hostess; her home is one of the cleanest and prettiest we stayed in. If you stay you must have a meal. There were peat fires blazing in her living room and dining room" (Mrs. D. Doyle, Bricktown, N.J.).

3. WHERE TO EAT

The best budget meals are at the **Hyland Central Hotel** on the Diamond (see above). There's an excellent lunch special (hot meat and vegetables and ample portions) at under IR£5 ($8) served in the comfortable lounge, and in the evening, a mini-dinner menu is priced at IR£9.50 ($15.25) and there's a full dinner menu that runs about IR£14 ($22.50). Evening meals are in the cream-colored dining room, which has wide windows along one wall, lots of dark-wood trim and softly lighted, gold-framed oil paintings hung about.

Not much else to choose from, although there are scads of coffeeshops around the Diamond, all much the same except for décor.

4. THINGS TO SEE AND DO

Take a look at **Donegal Castle,** whose west tower dates from 1505, when Red Hugh O'Donnell rebuilt an earlier castle on the site and made this the chief O'Donnell stronghold. The rest was added by Sir Basil Brooke in 1607 and features a mammoth Jacobean fireplace and windows and gables in the handsome house he built around the old tower. Tip your hat to the **Four Masters Memorial,** then examine the large mounted anchor by the bay—it's from a French ship, perhaps one of those bringing troops to fight with Wolfe Tone in 1798, and was salvaged from the sea by fishermen in the mid-1800s. South of town at the river's estuary, there are the interesting, but slight ruins of **Donegal Abbey.** Lough Eske is roughly five miles northeast of Donegal town, with wooded shores and a backing of mountains.

Magee of Donegal, on the Diamond, is world-famous for its hand-woven Donegal Tweed, and there's a weaving demonstration right in the store. Tours to the factory are organized from time to time, and you can inquire at the store for specific dates and hours. The store has a wide selection of quality clothing for men and women and a good variety of linens, knitwear, and other Irish products.

For "after dark," traditional music is on frequently at the **Talk of the Town** lounge. And Donegal has some good pubs, many of which have a "country" air about them, with the usual group of devoted regulars who'll be glad to welcome visiting Yanks.

AROUND COUNTIES DONEGAL AND LEITRIM

□ □ □

1. ACCOMMODATIONS
2. WHERE TO STAY
3. THINGS TO SEE AND DO

County Donegal sits at the very top of Ireland, its jagged coastline ringed by wide strands backed by steep cliffs, its inland mountains cut by deep valleys, and its countryside filled with antiquities and legends. In the rhythmic patterns of Donegal speech can be heard the distinctive cadence of Ulster, and from Donegal cottages come some of the world's most beautiful hand-woven woolens. It is a county of vast uninhabited stretches, natives as rugged as the landscape in which they live, and an ancient culture kept alive in music, song, and story.

Long and narrow, County Leitrim is split down the middle by Lough Allen, an extension of the Shannon. North of the lake, tall mountains stretch to the borders of County Sligo, while to the south, the countryside is dotted with lovely lakes. In Lough Scur, there are remnants of prehistoric lake dwellings, called crannogs. The harbor at Carrick-on-Shannon is alive with cruisers, and there's good fishing both here and in nearby lakes.

1. ACCOMMODATIONS

Note: Prices shown below are those in effect in 1989—expect them to be higher in 1990.

County Donegal

HOSTELS. There are several An Oige hostels around County Donegal, ranging from simple accommodations to superior facilities. Between Killybegs and Ardara, basic facilities are at **The Red House,** Carrick, Co. Donegal (tel. Carrick 73); five miles from Dungloe, there's a good **hostel at Crohy Head,** Dungloe,

Co. Donegal (tel. 075/21330); good facilities at the **Youth Hostel,** Aranmore Island, Burtonport, Letterkenny, Co. Donegal (no phone), with regular ferry service between Burtonport and the island; near Glenveagh National Park, a good **hostel at Erigal,** Dunlewy, Gweedore, Letterkenny, Co. Donegal (tel. 075/31180); four miles from Downings, good facilities at the **Youth Hostel,** Tra na Rosann, Downings, Co. Donegal (tel. 074/55374); on the shores of Lough Swilly, good facilities at the **Youth Hostel,** Bunnaton, Glenvar, Co. Donegal (no phone); and on Tory Island (with irregular ferry service from Magheraroarty), basic facilities at the **Youth Hostel,** Tory Island, Co. Donegal (no phone).

BED-AND-BREAKFAST. Mrs. Mary McGee's **Killeadan,** Bundoran Road, Ballyshannon, Co. Donegal (tel. 072/51653 or 51377), is a marvelous touring base one mile outside Ballyshannon, and just four miles from the Belleek factory and 500 yards from the Donegal China factory. The centrally heated bungalow has six lovely guest rooms with handbasins, and four have private bath with shower. Mary is an officer in the Town & Country Homes Association and keenly interested in all her guests. Bed-and-breakfast costs IR£11 ($17.50), with a 25% reduction for children, and there's good parking. Open May through September.

Lismolin Country Home, Fintra Road, Killybegs, Co. Donegal (tel. 073/31035), is the home of Mrs. Bernie Cahill and sits right at the edge of a beautiful forest area. The modern, centrally heated bungalow is tastefully decorated, with six nice guest rooms, all with handbasins and private shower and toilet. The friendly Mrs. Cahill has been lauded by readers for her delicious breakfasts and homemade brown bread, as well as for her general helpfulness. Turf and log fires are often lit in the lounge. B&B rate is IR£11.50 ($18.50), with a one-third discount for children; dinner is IR£10 ($16).

Eileen and Ray Molloy are the delightful hosts at **Greenhaven,** Portnoo Road, Ardara, Co. Donegal (tel. 075/41174), which overlooks Loughross Bay and Slieve Tooey on the other side of the bay. There's a window-walled breakfast room open to the gorgeous view, and a large back garden. A modern extension holds seven comfortable guest rooms, all with handbasins, four with private bath and shower, and lovely, puffy eiderdown quilts on all beds. The Molloys are especially helpful in pointing their guests to the things to see and do in the area (visit local weavers, etc.). B&B costs IR£10.50 ($16.75), half that for children. Dinners many times feature fresh, locally caught seafood, and are priced at IR£9.50 ($15.25). Open March through November.

Bay View House, Portnoo Road, Ardara, Co. Donegal (tel. 075/41145), also has magnificent views of Loughros Bay and the Owenea River. Located a half mile outside town on the coast road, the centrally heated country home has a spacious lounge with picture windows and turf fires, and a large dining room, where dinners include traditional Irish dishes as well as fresh local fish. There are six comfortable bedrooms, all with private facilities and tea-making equipment. Marian and Charles Bennett are gracious, helpful hosts, and Charles (who plays traditional music in pubs with a local group) is chairman of the Ardara Tourism Committee. There's a games room and snooker table. The rate for bed-and-breakfast is IR£10.50 ($16.75), with a 25% reduction for children; dinner is IR£9.50 ($15.25).

Mrs. Rosleen Gill is the delightful, enthusiastic hostess at **Septora,** Convent Road, Letterkenny, Co. Donegal (tel. 074/22330). Her attractive, centrally heated bungalow is set in a quiet cul-de-sac and has three nicely decorated bedrooms, with built-in wardrobes and handbasins, two with private showers. Goose-down comforters are on each bed, and Mrs. Gill even furnishes hand tissues in all guest rooms. B&B rate is IR£10 ($16), with 25% off for children. Open March through October.

If you make it up to Malin Head, Ireland's most northerly point (which I strongly recommend if you can manage the time), **Mrs. Maire Doyle,** Barraicin, Malin Head, Co. Donegal (tel. 077/70184), will welcome you to her modern bungalow six miles outside Malin village, overlooking the sea. There are three nice guest rooms, all with handbasins. Hairdryers and a tea kettle are available on request. The B&B rate is IR£9 ($14.50), with 25% off for children; dinner is IR£8 ($12.75), and high tea is IR£6 ($9.50). Open Easter through October.

Mrs. McGuinness, **Conkay House,** Roshine Road, Killybegs, Co. Donegal (tel. 073/31273), will welcome you warmly to her modern bungalow which overlooks Killybegs Bay and is a short walk from town. The house is centrally heated and there is a garden which guests may use. The three comfortable bedrooms all have handbasins. The rate for bed-and-breakfast is IR£10 ($16) and there is a 25% reduction for children. Open Easter to October.

Mrs. Mary Ward, **Pinewood,** Straboy, Glenties, Co. Donegal (tel. 075/51223), is the friendly hostess of this modern bungalow located on the main Letterkenny road just two miles from Glenties. It is set in lovely surroundings and the house is centrally heated, with electric blankets supplied. Mary is an excellent cook and serves wonderful meals. Her husband, Michael, is a schoolteacher and familiar with historic and scenic sites all over Ireland. The four attractive bedrooms have handbasins and two have private facilities, for which there is no extra charge. The rate is IR£9 ($14.50) for bed-and-breakfast, and dinner costs IR£8 ($12.75); 40% reduction for children. Open March to October.

Mrs. Anne Campbell, Ardeen, Ramelton, Co. Donegal (tel. 074/51243), is the delightful hostess of a beautiful country home furnished with antiques and overlooking Lough Swilly. Mrs. Campbell and her family are all helpful and friendly. The house is centrally heated and the four pretty bedrooms all have handbasins. There's a hard-surface tennis court for guests to use. The rate for bed-and-breakfast is IR£11 ($17.50) and there is a 25% reduction for children. Open April to September.

A FARMHOUSE. The name tells a lot about **Lake and Seaview House,** Tubberkeen, Dungloe, Co. Donegal (tel. 075/21142). Mrs. Caroline Ward's modernized farmhouse is close to both, and the wild beauty of Glenveagh National Park is only 11 miles distant. Mrs. Ward can arrange fishing on the lake, and for swimmers (or those who just like to walk the seashore), beautiful deserted strands are right at hand. There are seven nice guest rooms, all with handbasins, and the B&B rate is IR£10.50 ($16.75), half that for children. Open from Easter through September.

SELF-CATERING. Ireland has many good self-catering cottages for visitors, but few with as breathtaking a location as the marvelous group known as the **Donegal Thatched Cottages** on Cruit Island, which sits just offshore (connected by a bridge) between Burtonport and Annagary. There are eight cottages, all traditional in design (with thatched roofs and turf-burning fireplaces as well as central heat), and all set on a sheltered clifftop with spectacular seascapes of Donegal's rugged coastline, with Aranmore and Owey Islands clearly visible. At the foot of the cliff, there's a lovely little half-moon of a beach, and at the other side of the cliff, a golden strand safe for swimming goes on for miles. The fishing, boating, and swimming around here are all superb—and it's a perfect place for just plain loafing! There are good local pubs and one very good restaurant nearby for those times you hanker for good company and good conversation (both in plentiful supply among the friendly locals). The cottages have been built and furnished with all Irish-made products, and while there's all the charm of bygone days in the décor, there are modern conveniences that would make any housewife of those days turn green with envy (like the automatic washer and dryer that are kept out of sight behind cabinet doors so as not to interfere with the traditional décor). Turf is furnished in generous quantities so you can indulge any penchant for the open hearth. Each cottage can sleep as many as seven adults comfortably, which makes the weekly rates fall easily within budget limits if you bring a full party. The seasonal rates range from IR£105 ($168) to IR£325 ($520), and can go as low as IR£75 ($120) for midweek and weekend stays from October through May. You can book into this very special place by contacting the charming owners, Conor and Mary Ward, Rosses Point, Co. Sligo (tel. 071/77197). They'll be glad to send you a brochure with full details.

BIG SPLURGES. The **Rathmullan Country House,** Rathmullan, Co. Donegal (tel. 074/58188), sits amid spacious, landscaped grounds that slope down to Lough Swilly, and in the more than 20 years that Robin and Bob Wheeler have been in residence, it has become a beloved favorite with the Irish from all over the Republic, as well as nearby Northern Ireland. The marvelous old house dates back to the early 1800s, and the Wheelers have brought back a graciousness and charm that disappeared during the years of its rather checkered career. The soft glow of turf or log fires in the drawing room and library lights furnishings that combine a tasteful mixture of period and comfortably overstuffed modern furnishings. The glass-enclosed dining pavilion looks out to award-winning gardens, and the cellar bar is a cozy spot for relaxed conviviality. Accommodations come in a wide range, from the large, almost luxuriously furnished guest rooms that look out to the Lough to plainer, somewhat smaller and less expensive rooms. All guest rooms have private facilities. The rate range is IR£20 ($32) to IR£32 ($51.25), with special weekly rates available. Sumptuous dinners, for which chef Bob has earned an international reputation, are priced at IR£13 ($20.75) for three courses, IR£16 ($25.50) for five. Rathmullan Country House is open from Easter through September, and advanced reservations for both accommodations and meals in this very popular place are absolutely essential. Most major credit cards are accepted. A special "Highly Recommended" to a Big Splurge that's cheap at the price! Open March to Christmas.

Bruckless House, Bruckless, Co. Donegal (tel. 073/37071), dates from the late 1700s and is set in 19 acres bordering Bruckless Bay. It is now the farmhouse home of Joan and Clive Evans, who took over on their return from several years in Hong Kong. Their years in the Orient are reflected in many of the furnishings, but the old house retains its traditional flavor, with a cobbled farmyard, kitchen garden, and log fires. Just 12 miles west of Donegal town on the main Killybegs road, Bruckless has gracious reception rooms with views of the bay, five comfortably fitted-out bedrooms (two doubles, one twin, and two singles) that share a large bathroom, and horses that can be booked by guests for riding. The Evanses serve breakfast and dinner (Joan does the cooking, with fresh garden vegetables, seafood fresh from nearby waters, and milk and cream from their dairy cow) around the kitchen table, just one indication of the informality and warm hospitality for which they are noted. Sightseeing along some of Donegal's most spectacular coastline, as well as in the tweed-weaving center of Ardara and the Glencolumbkille Folk Museum, is an easy matter using Bruckless House as a base. There are two golf courses within driving distance, and both coastal and deep-sea fishing can be arranged. Rates are IR£14 ($22.50) per person for bed-and-breakfast, and dinner is IR£11 ($17.60). Open April through September.

READERS' ACCOMMODATIONS SELECTIONS: "Mrs. G. McKelvey, **Seapoint House,** Quay Road, Dungloe, Co. Donegal (tel. 075/21250), welcomes you to her unpretentious home, at the water's edge of the narrow inlet, offering spacious accommodation and comfort to the weary traveler. Far from the clutches of big-city pressures, these environs offer a tranquility that is a rare commodity in today's world" (G. W. Howard, Silver Spring, Md.). . . . "We stay at the **Sportsman Hotel,** Co. Leitrim, every year and the hospitality and warmth of the owners, Mr. and Mrs. Bayliss, is unsurpassed" (Margaret Gallagher, Mineola, N.Y.).

County Leitrim

BED-AND-BREAKFAST. On the N4, **Corbally Lodge,** Dublin Road, Carrick-on-Shannon, Co. Leitrim (tel. 078/20228), is about a mile and a half south of town, set on its own spacious grounds. The pretty modern bungalow is the Rowley family home, and they are gracious hosts indeed. Open turf fires are the cozy centerpiece for evening gatherings. There are four nice guest rooms, all with handbasins, three with private facilities. The rate is IR£10 ($16) for bed-and-breakfast, and Corbally Lodge is open all year. Central heat and good parking.

FARMHOUSES. Violet and Raymond Thomas are the warm, friendly hosts at **Riversdale,** Ballinamore, Co. Leitrim (tel. 078/44122). The large farmhouse sits amid peaceful rural scenery on 85 acres of dairy and sheep farming. There are open fires on cool evenings, and fishing right on the property, as well as an indoor swimming pool, squash court, and sauna. About a mile and a half south of Ballinamore, this centrally heated house has six attractive and comfortable guest rooms, all with handbasins. Dinners, under the direction of the Thomases' daughter, who is Ballymaloe trained, feature fresh produce, meats, and fish, and there's a wine license. The rate is IR£10 ($16) for bed-and-breakfast, with a one-third reduction for children; dinners cost IR£9 ($14.50). Open year round, but advance reservations are required from November through February.

Mrs. Teresa Kennedy, **Glenview,** Aughoo, Ballinamore, Co. Leitrim (tel. 078/44157), is the warm and hospitable hostess of this lovely, modern farmhouse. There is a boat for hire and a pony, donkey, and cart which are free for children. The house is centrally heated and there is an attractive TV lounge with turf and log fires. The four bedrooms all have private facilities and dinner is available with advance notice. The rate for bed-and-breakfast is IR£10 ($16) and dinner is IR£9.50 ($15.25). 33% reduction for children. Open March to November.

SELF-CATERING. The **Breffni Holiday Cottages,** Dromahair, Co. Leitrim (tel. 071/64103), are grouped around a courtyard in the shadow of 17th-century castle ruins. Each of the eight cottages is nicely furnished, and while there's an open fireplace for cool-night comfort, each has central heating for those who don't want the fuss and bother of a fire. The three bedrooms, with one double and four single beds (plus a convertible couch in the living room), can accommodate six or seven comfortably, and one cottage has been adapted to the needs of the physically handicapped. Dromahair is a good base for touring the Yeats Country and most of the Northwest. Rates range from IR£75 ($120) to IR£175 ($280) per week, depending on the season.

2. WHERE TO EAT

The Northwest is filled with spots Mother Nature seems to have designed especially for picnics. Stop on a mountainside, spread your lunch on a sandy strand, or head for the lovely **Ards Forest Park** two miles north of Creeslough in County Donegal on Sheephaven Bay, where tables face the beach.

County Donegal

In Gortahork, **McFaddens Hotel** (tel. 074/35267) serves surprisingly good and varied meals in its dining room, specializing in fresh, local seafood like salmon, which comes with a beautifully done hollandaise sauce. Try the lemon mousse for dessert. Bar lunches are on tap from 1 to 2:15 p.m. every day, and the à la carte menu, with entrees priced at IR£5 ($8) to IR£12 ($19.25), is served from 6 to 9 p.m.

The **Woodhill House Restaurant** in Ardara (tel. 075/41112) is a country house in a beautiful setting, specializing in dishes that feature local produce and seafood at prices that start at IR£6 ($9.50). Bar snacks are also available. Hours are 6 to 10 p.m.

In Ballyshannon, two choices: Good bar food (soup and sandwiches, mostly) at **Sweeny's White Horse Bar** in the lounge bar, which features an open fire, with hours from 10:30 a.m. to 11:30 p.m.; and **McIntyre's Restaurant** on Castle Street (tel. 072/65245), a family-run eatery offering the Tourist Menu as well as an à la carte selection ranging from about IR£5 ($8) at lunch, IR£8 ($12.75) at dinner. Open from 10 a.m. to 10 p.m.

Fitzgerald's Hotel, Bundoran (tel. 072/41336), also offers a Tourist Menu from June through August, and an excellent five-course dinner for IR£7.50 ($12) and up. Hours are 5:30 to 8:30 p.m. (Tourist Menu only offered up to 7:30 p.m.).

County Leitrim

On the main Sligo–Dublin road, the **Breffni Inn,** Dromod, has a lovely lounge bar that serves homemade soup, sandwiches, and snacks at low prices.

3. THINGS TO SEE AND DO

The Northwest is not really a place to "do" as much as it's a region to be absorbed into your very soul, and that comes as naturally as breathing the clear, bracing air. There are special places you won't want to miss, but mostly you'll remember the sense of tuning in to a part of your inner self that all too often has been lost in the frenetic pace at which most of us gallop through modern life.

County Donegal

Base yourself at Donegal town or Ardara to explore the splendors of southern Donegal, then take the main roadway that circles the northern part of the county. You'll want to plan at least one overnight stop—the jagged, cliff-filled coastline, rocky mountain pastures, and breathtaking mountain passes that open a view that seems to go on to eternity can lead to an overload of the senses, and it's when you've reached saturation point that you'll welcome the warm and friendly company of the warm and friendly inhabitants of County Donegal.

Just outside Donegal town on the Ballyshannon–Sligo road, the **Donegal Craft Village** is a group of cottage-like buildings around a courtyard. Each is the workshop of a true artisan, and you'll find pottery, woodturnings, batik wallhangings, tweeds, etc.

Right around Donegal town, the three-mile-long **Barnesmore Gap** is seven miles to the northeast, through wild, mountainy country that once harbored highwaymen. North of town, **Eglish Glen** cuts between the Bluestack Mountains and Banagher Hill, and farther along you'll find the "Grey Mare's Tail" waterfall in **Srueił Glen.** The good St. Patrick knew Donegal well, and he once fasted for 40 days on an island in isolated **Lough Derg,** where pilgrims still come faithfully to observe a three-day fast.

Due west of Donegal town, in **Mountcharles,** stop by the little white shop with red trim that is **Gillespie Brothers.** Just meeting the Gillespies is a delight, but it can be profitable as well, for their tweed selections of suits and jackets, lap rugs, and blankets are exceptional (also sold by the length), and they also carry for the ladies a marvelous stock of hand-crocheted dresses, capes, and blouses. Prices are below most in other shops, and the brothers are happy to mail your purchases home.

If you can manage to get to the picturesque little harbor town of **Killybegs** in the late afternoon, go down to the pier to watch the fishing fleet come in—it's a memorable experience, with seagulls swarming and screeching overhead and half the town gathered to greet the fishermen. Farther along, in **Kilcar,** look for **Studio Donegal,** where the fabulous misty tones of Donegal tweed come in jacket, skirt, or pants lengths, as well as ready-made garments from such Irish manufacturers as Brian Boru. They also carry a good selection of local crafts. There's a hand-weaving workshop next door, and a spacious tea room serving home-baking.

The drive to **Glencolumbkille** ("St. Colmcille's Glen"), through lonely mountain country with occasional glimpses of the sea, is a journey through history and a culture that has changed little since the days when (or so local legend insists) Bonnie Prince Charlie hid out in the glen. The stony hills are dotted with more than 40 cairns, dolmens, souterrains, and other relics of a past that goes back as much as 5,000 years. At Glencolumbkille there's one of the most authentic **Folk Village Museums** in the country, with three cottages built and furnished to bring to life three different eras stretching from 1700 to 1900. There are guided tours every hour that explain the workings of each cottage. The home of a 1720 cotter is earthen-floored, and its open hearth has no chimney; by the 1820s the cotter's home has a flagstone floor, chimney, and oil-lamp lighting (as well as, sad to relate, a tin trunk that would carry the immigrating family's treasures to "Amerikay"); and the 1920 cottage is very like many you'll have seen in your travels around today's Irish countryside. The courtyard around which the cottages are grouped holds such everyday items as a peat cart and fishing boat, with the large "famine pot," a somber reminder of famine days, when starving peasants lined up to be served a meager ration. A schoolhouse from a century ago and a country pub, or "sheebeen" (where the drink sold was illegal poteen, more often than not!), complete the village. There's a cottage craft shop and tea room, where hot tea and scones are sold from June through September. The Folk Village has hours of 10 a.m. to 6 p.m. on weekdays from Easter to November, and 2 to 6 p.m. on Sunday.

Ardara has long been a center of the home-weaving industry, and its few streets are lined with shops selling tweeds at good prices. Three to look for are **Mołloys, Kennedy's** and **Bonners.**

Heading north, the cliff and coastal scenery is heart-stoppingly beautiful, with a haunting loneliness hovering over all. Drive through towns and villages with sonorous names like **Glenties** (Na Gleannta, "the valleys"), **Dongloe, Burtonport, Gweedore** (where there's always good traditional music), and **Dunfanaghy** (with a stop at **Alan Harley's Art Gallery,** which features Irish painter Tom Egginton's glowing landscape canvases and a huge stock of local crafts, and a detour around the clifftop Horn Head Drive). To the east, explore the shores of **Lough Swilly,** passing through historic **Rathmullen** and **Ramelton** and on to the cathedral town of **Letterkenny.** Drive on out to **Malin Head—**as far north as you can go on Ireland's mainland. Take time to go by the township of **Burt,** three miles south of **Bridgend,** and point your car (or walk) up the little road that leads to a great circular stone cashel known as **Grianan of Aileach** ("sun palace of Aileach"), once the royal seat of the O'Neills and a sacred meeting place for High Kings of Ireland. From its 800-foot-high summit there are vast panoramic views of **Lough Swilly, Lough Foyle,** and the distant sea.

At some point in your Donegal rambles, switch off (from Gweedore or Letterkenny) to take in the deeply wooded reaches of **Glenveagh National Park** and its impressive castle. Set in the very heart of the Donegal highlands, between the Derryveagh and Glendowan mountain ranges, the park covers 25,000 acres of wilderness, with the castle and its magnificent gardens set like a jewel on the edge of Lough Veagh. There's a very good audio-visual show, and tea and scones with homemade jam are available in the castle kitchen. At the main entrance near **Churchill Village,** the **Glebe Gallery** houses the art collection of noted painter Derek Hill, who has willed the property and the paintings to the nation.

A newcomer on the Irish handcraft scene is the delicately beautiful **Donegal Irish Parian China** (much like porcelain) made in Ballyshannon. Look for the graceful shapes and soft green shamrock design, then inquire locally about visiting the factory. As we go to press, no formal arrangements have been made for such visits, but this is such exquisite china that I have no doubt it will prove popular enough to stimulate some sort of display right on the scene.

While I can't vouch for this personally, I'm told that **Nancy's Pub,** on the Portnoo road in Ardara, is "very large in local character." You might want to check it out.

County Leitrim

Dromahair (Druim Dha Eithiar, "The Ridge of the Two Air-Demons") is where a royal lady inadvertently set in motion the first Norman invasion of Ireland. It seems that back in the 12th century, Dervogilla, wife of Tiernan O'Rourke, eloped with the King of Leinster, who was promptly outlawed by his fellow chieftains. When he went to England's Henry II for assistance, the king gave his royal consent for any of his vassals who so chose to join up with the Irish king to win back his lost lands. When a bevy of barons from South Wales threw in with the Irish chieftain, they formed the group of Anglo-Normans who landed near Wexford in 1169. The ruins of the lady's residence, **Breffni Castle,** are found on the riverbank adjacent to the 1626 Old Hall, built by Sir William Villiers. On the other side of the river there are ruins of the 1508 **Creevelea Abbey,** and the remains of an even older church nearby are thought to be those of one founded by St. Patrick when he spent some time here.

If your Irish roots are in Leitrim soil, the **Leitrim Heritage Centre,** County Library, Ballinamore, Co. Leitrim (tel. 078/44012), stands ready to help you trace your ancestry. The centre maintains a full-time professional genealogical service for the county, and you can write ahead with all the details you can furnish, or call in when you come to Ireland. Fees are based on the amount of work involved, and the knowledgeable staff will let you know before any charge is made whether or not there is a high probability of success in your search. The centre is open Monday through Friday from 10 a.m. to 1 p.m. and 2 to 5 p.m.

Carrick-on-Shannon (Cara Droma Ruisg, "The Weir of the Marshy Ridge") is a center for fishing and boating on the River Shannon.

READER'S SHOPPING SUGGESTION: "Just outside Ramelton on the road to Milford, I came across a wonderful craft shop owned by **Mrs. S. Browne,** Black's Glen. The Aran sweaters on display were knit by Mrs. Browne and her neighbors and she sells them at substantial savings. They're as beautiful and well crafted as you'd find anywhere. There were lots of other interesting handcrafts in her shop also" (Arthur Rubin, Bergenfield, N.J.).

CHAPTER XXVII

THE MIDLANDS

□ □ □

1. INTRODUCING THE MIDLANDS
2. AROUND COUNTIES CAVAN, LAOIS, LONGFORD, MONAGHAN, OFFALY, ROSCOMMON, AND WESTMEATH

Ireland's Midland counties are often called Lakeland, and indeed the landscape is dotted with lakes. The Rivers Shannon and Erne glide between broad banks, spreading here and there into Lough Ree and Lough Sheelin.

1. INTRODUCING THE MIDLANDS

This is the land of fishing, boating, and hunting, and in ancient days it was the land of the lake dwellers, who built artificial islands called crannogs on which to raise their round huts, protected from enemy attack by the surrounding waters. At the geographical heart of the country, the great monastic community of Clonmacnois was settled near Athlone, withstood assaults by Vikings, Normans, and Cromwell, and has left us a rich heritage of Celtic crosses and round towers.

The great Irish poet Patrick Kavanagh was born in the Midlands, but "escaped" to live out most of his life in Dublin. Although Kavanagh wrote of his birthplace, "O stoney grey soil of Monaghan,/You burgled my bank of youth," there is something in the nearly flat, faintly rolling land of Ireland's innards that must nurture literary talent. Oliver Goldsmith spent much of his life here, and you can trace his footsteps, guided by the *Goldsmith Country* booklet published by the Tourist Board. The blind harper O'Carolan lies buried in County Roscommon. William Percy French was born in County Roscommon. County Longford was home to Maria Edgeworth, an 18th-century writer and angel of mercy during the famine years. Padraic Colum—poet, playwright, novelist, and essayist— was a product of County Longford, and chronicled the lives of its peasantry with an honest eye.

The **Lakeland Regional Tourist Office** is just off the Dublin road in Mullingar (tel. 044/48761), and the good folk there can furnish an amazing amount of literature to steer you to the treasures of the Midland counties.

2. AROUND COUNTIES CAVAN, LAOIS, LONGFORD, MONAGHAN, OFFALY, ROSCOMMON, AND WESTMEATH

ACCOMMODATIONS: Unfortunately, the Midlands Region does not have hostel facilities, but good bed-and-breakfast homes and farmhouses abound.

Note: Prices shown below are those in effect in 1989—expect them to be higher in 1990.

County Cavan

BED-AND-BREAKFAST. Gardens surround **Ker Maria,** Station Road, Cootehill, Co. Cavan (tel. 049/52293), the pretty Georgian-style home of Mrs. Teresa Colhoun. Cootehill is just about midway between Donegal and Dublin, and Mrs. Colhoun has four nice guest rooms, all with handbasins and one with private bath and shower. Rates are IR£9 ($14.50), with a 20% reduction for children. Central heating and good parking. Open April to mid-October.

SELF-CATERING. One of the prettiest sites for getting away from it all in Ireland is Killykeen Forest Park in County Cavan, and the Forest Service has worked hand-in-glove with tourism people to develop a group of log-cabin units for holiday-makers. The beautifully wooded park also contains good fishing. For detailed information on facilities, rates, and booking, contact the Department of Energy, Forest Service (Amenity Section), Leeson Lane, Dublin 2 (tel. 01/615666, ext. 551).

County Laois

BED-AND-BREAKFAST. In a pretty, wooded setting on the Portlaoise–Carlow road, **Aspen,** Rock of Dunamase, Portlaoise, Co. Laois (tel. 0502/25405), is about four miles outside of town. Mrs. Noreen Llewellyn is the gracious hostess in this spacious, centrally heated bungalow, and she has four attractive guest rooms with handbasins, two with private bathroom. There are lovely woodland walks just outside the door. The rate is IR£11 ($17.50), with a 20% discount for children.

County Longford

BED-AND-BREAKFAST. Mrs. Breege O'Donnell is a longtime favorite hostess with readers. Her large two-story home, **Tivoli,** Dublin Road, Longford (tel. 043/46898), is immaculate and well appointed, and her warm friendliness makes guests feel like members of her family. There are 11 guest rooms with handbasins (three also have private shower), and the house is centrally heated. The rate is IR£10.50 ($16.75), half that for children, and there's a car park.

County Monaghan

BED-AND-BREAKFAST. Surrounded by woods and nearby lakes, **Rose-Linn-Lodge,** Lurgans, Carrickmacross, Co. Monaghan (tel. 042/61035), is a centrally heated bungalow about a mile from Carrickmacross. Mrs. Rosaleen Haworth has three nice guest rooms with handbasins, and takes a personal interest in all her guests. B&B rate is IR£10 ($16), with 20% off for children. Open all year.

County Offaly

BED-AND-BREAKFAST. Mrs. Bridie Casey, **Padraig Villa,** Glaskill, Screggan, Tullamore, Co. Offaly (tel. 0506/55962), is a charming, hospitable hostess and her modern country home, surrounded by pretty gardens, is just one mile off the

Tullamore–Birr road. You will be welcomed here with tea or coffee and home-baked cakes. The house is centrally heated and there is a private car park. Four of the five bedrooms have handbasins, and Mrs. Casey serves a lovely dinner. The rate for bed-and-breakfast is IR£11 ($17.50) and dinner is the same price; 20% reduction for children. Open all year.

A HOTEL. The **County Arms Hotel,** Birr, Co. Offaly (tel. 050/20791), is a graceful old (1810) Georgian house that has been transformed into a comfortable and relatively inexpensive hotel. Set in a wooded lawn, with gardens to the side and back, the hotel has been owned and operated by the Loughnane family for many years, and there's an air of friendly, personal service that's sometimes hard to come by in larger establishments. Bed-and-breakfast rates range from IR£23 ($36.75) to IR£28 ($44.75).

County Roscommon

BED-AND-BREAKFAST. The **Hillside House,** Doon, Corrigeenroe, Boyle, Co. Roscommon (tel. 079/66075), is the comfortable, slightly old-fashioned home of Mrs. Taylor. It's in a beautiful, scenic location with views of Lough Key and handy to the Forest Park. Of the six homey bedrooms, five have handbasins. The rate is IR£9.50 ($15.25), with 25% off for children. There's central heating, and the evening meal is supplied if required. Dinner is IR£8 ($12.75); tea is IR£6 ($9.60).

Mrs. Delia Dolan, **Munsboro House,** Sligo Road, Roscommon, Co. Roscommon (tel. 0903/26375), is a gracious and helpful hostess. Located just two miles outside Roscommon, her home is a very attractive, three-story, Georgian house situated on 150 acres of farmland. There is horseback riding on the farm for both adults and children. Evening meals are available with advance notice and five lovely bedrooms all have handbasins. The rate is IR£11 ($17.50) for bed-and-breakfast and IR£10 ($16) for dinner; 25% reduction for children. Open April through October.

BIG SPLURGE. The **Abbey Hotel,** Abbeytown, Galway Road, Roscommon, Co. Roscommon (tel. 0903/26240), is worth a short detour. Within the lovely lawns and gardens that surround this marvelous 18th-century turreted mansion, ruins of a medieval monastery bear mute witness to the history of this part of Roscommon. Only 90 miles from Dublin and 50 miles from Galway, the Abbey is a perfect base for a stopover to explore other monastic ruins and Norman castles en route cross country. Owners Tommy and Anya Grealy carry on a family tradition of gracious hospitality that began back in 1878 when the Grealy family opened a coaching inn. The hotel today provides all modern comforts, but retains such mementos of the past as the curved twin staircase with its stained-glass window at the landing, whose pattern the Grealys are having duplicated in panels for the front entry and lounge. Bedrooms are of good size, with attractive décor and comfortable furnishings, and come with private bath, telephone, radio, and color TV. The bright, window-walled dining room overlooks the back lawn and specializes in fresh Irish produce and a good wine list. Roscommon is a short detour off the main Dublin–Galway road, and rewarding not only for its own sightseeing attractions, but because the 50 miles from Roscommon to Galway go through lovely rural scenery too often missed by visitors who stick to the highways. Rates at the Abbey start at IR£30 ($48) single, IR£48 ($76.75) double for bed-and-breakfast. If you're traveling with a party of four or more, or if you plan a stay of several days, be sure to ask about special discounts.

County Westmeath

BED-AND-BREAKFAST. Dympna and Sean Casey's modern split-level home, **Hilltop,** Delvin Road, Rathconnell, Mullingar, Co. Westmeath (tel. 044/48958), is in a beautiful setting two miles from Mullingar and adjacent to Lough Sheever. Dympna is an official of the Town & Country Homes Association and warmly interested in seeing that all her guests are comfortable and get the most from their holidays. All five guest rooms are nicely furnished, and all have private toilets and showers as well as handbasins. The rate is IR£10 ($16), and they are open from March through October.

FARMHOUSES. One of my favorite farmhouses in Ireland is **Woodlands Farm,** Streamstown, Co. Westmeath (tel. 044/26414), some ten miles from Mullingar and quite convenient to Clonmachoise. Maybe it's because serenity sets in the moment you approach the rambling two-story by way of an avenue of aged trees which often shade grazing horses. More likely, it's the warm, friendly hospitality of Mary and Willy Maxwell and their attractive children that draws me back. The house itself is charming, with a 200-year-old section to which a wing was added about a century ago that is still called the "new" addition. Parlor windows look out onto wooded grounds, and a fire is lit most evenings when a tea tray is rolled into the gracious room, which is furnished with antiques. Breakfasts are truly special, featuring fresh milk from their own cows and Mary's home-baked bread. The house has central heating, and the six bedrooms include one cozy single. Donkeys and pet sheep are an added attraction, and guests are given the run of the farmyard and grounds. The rate is IR£10 ($16), with half off for children. Mary's delicious evening meals are IR£8.50 ($13.50). Open March through October. To find Woodlands, leave Mullingar via the Galway road, then take the road to Athlone; at Streamstown, look for the sign near the school. If you get hopelessly lost, just stop and ask—the Maxwells are well known in the Streamstown area.

Eight miles from Mullingar is John and Marian Finucane-Clarke's **Reynella House,** Bracklyn, Mullingar, Co. Westmeath (tel. 044/74134), a beautiful, 200-year-old Georgian farmhouse situated in woodlands and overlooking their own private fishing lake. There is a game room and a library with log fires and the house is centrally heated. The five pretty bedrooms all have handbasins and the meals are excellent, made with home-grown produce. The rate for bed-and-breakfast is IR£9.50 ($15.20) and dinner is the same price; 20% reduction for children. Open all year except Christmas.

READERS' ACCOMMODATIONS SELECTIONS: "Joe and Mabel Barrett, **Lynton,** Ballinderry, Mullingar, Co. Westmeath (tel. 044/40383), have a very comfortable, modern home which caters to hunters as well as regular tourists. There is a large hunting preserve nearby. The most interesting aspect of the house is the private museum displaying old Viking swords, Finian pikes, rifles, etc., collected by the owners from the surrounding countryside" (D. McGrath, Long Island, N.Y., and E. S. Morley, Mamaroneck, N.Y.). . . . "Mrs. M. Martin, **Nocdale House,** 9 Ard Rois Ave., Cloughvalley, Carrickmacross, Co. Monaghan (tel. 042/61608), was the nicest and most accommodating hostess of any we encountered—she even did our laundry for us—and her home is modern, clean, and pretty. The breakfasts were grand affairs served overlooking a beautiful mountain view" (E. and M. Rogers, Long Island, N.Y.).

WHERE TO EAT: Picnics are a joy in the Midland region, with woodlands and lake shores galore. Country pubs can also be a "discovery," although your best bet for pub grub is in any one of the little market towns you pass through.

County Cavan

In Butlersbridge, about four miles north of Cavan town, the **Derragarra Inn** (tel. 049/31003 or 31205) sits by the side of the River Annalee. While it no longer provides accommodations, it has won just about every food award in the book, and its interior décor is a marvelous hodgepodge of items that range from old farm implements to exotic souvenirs owner John Clancey collected in his years of wandering the world. In addition to bar food (steakburgers, cheese snacks, etc.) priced under £3 ($4.75), there are full dinners consisting of hors d'oeuvres, main course (such as a T-bone steak, ham, roast beef, chicken, or fish), vegetables, and dessert. Beautifully arranged salad plates with ample portions are also available. Prices range from IR£5.60 ($9) for the three-course Tourist Menu to IR£9 ($14.50). There's continuous service from 10:30 a.m. to 11:30 p.m. every day except Sunday, when hours are 12:30 to 2 p.m. and 4 to 10 p.m.

County Laois

In Portlaoise, **Egan's Hostelry Inn,** 24 Main St., a fully licensed restaurant, serves snacks all day, as well as an à la carte menu, at moderate prices.

County Longford

The **Edgeworth Hotel,** Edgeworthstown, serves both Irish and continental dishes on the à la carte lunch and dinner menus, with moderate prices. Hours are 12:30 to 2:30 p.m. and 6:30 to 9 p.m. daily.

County Offaly

In Birr, the **County Arms Hotel** (tel. 0509/20791) serves a superior "mini-luncheon" menu in the bar lounge, as well as very good full meals in the pleasant dining room, all at moderate prices. Meals are served seven days a week, very handy should you be driving through the Midlands on Sunday, when so many restaurants are closed.

County Roscommon

Combine sightseeing with lunching at the **Lakeshore Restaurant** (tel. 079/62214) in Lough Key Forest Park just outside Boyle. Picture windows overlook the boat basin, and you can choose from light meals (salads and sandwiches) or more substantial grills. Take-aways are available, and there's a wine license. The price range is IR£3 ($4.75) to IR£8 ($12.75). Open weekends only in April, daily from May to September.

In Boyle, the **Royal Hotel** on Bridge Street has a comfortable, family-run hotel dining room that serves a variety of good Irish-style meals, priced from IR£7 ($11.25) at lunch, IR£12 ($19.25) at dinner. The lower-priced Tourist Menu is available from 12:30 to 3 p.m.

County Westmeath

The **Gramby Restaurant,** 9 Dominic St., in Mullingar (tel. 044/40280), is a cozy place, with open fires and friendly service. The food is good, honest fare well prepared, with moderate prices on the à la carte menu. The lower Tourist Menu is available year round. Hours are 8 a.m. to 10 p.m.

THINGS TO SEE AND DO: Outdoors types will love the Midlands: **fishing** is excellent and free in most places; **hikers** and just plain **walkers** can tramp forest parks and lakeshores; there's **golf** in Mullingar and Athlone; and there are miles and miles of water for dedicated **boaters.** For **history buffs,** there are ecclesiastical ruins and stately homes.

County Cavan

Plan to spend some time in the 600 acres of **Killykeen Forest Park,** located between Killeshandra and Cavan town. There's plenty to enjoy: fishing, swimming, boating, shady nature trails, and picnic sites, as well as a self-catering holiday village. Within its grounds you'll also find crannogs, ring forts, and the ruined **Lough Oughter Castle,** where in 1649 the great chieftain Owen Roe O'Neil died (to this day some say he was poisoned by a treacherous hand).

County Laois

There's a perfectly preserved round tower at **Timahoe,** some five miles south of Stradbally.

Nine miles south of Portlaoise, a **Cistercian abbey** was founded by Conor O'More in 1183 at Abbeyleix. The **de Vesci demesne,** adjoining the town, holds the tomb of Malachi O'More, a Laois chieftain.

County Longford

In **Edgeworthstown,** there's a small **museum** dedicated to the Edgeworth family, of whom the most notable members were Maria, English-born novelist and essayist who spent most of her life in Ireland and did much to relieve suffering during the worst famine years, and her father, an inventor and author. The town's historical museum is open during summer months.

County Monaghan

Stop by the **Carrickmacross Lace Co-op** (tel. 042/62506 or 62085) in the charming little town of Carrickmacross. The lace makers sketch out original designs to be worked in the sheerest lawn appliquéd to even sheerer net. The tiny, invisible hand-stitching is done in some 20 cottages by skillful and patient women, whose numbers are dwindling every year, with few young girls willing to learn the ancient art. The world-famous Carrickmacross lace, introduced to the Monaghan area in the 1800s, has continued as a cottage industry from 1846 to this day. A Miss Reid built the first schoolhouse for the lace. Then the founding of the St. Louis Convent ensured the development of the lace and it has remained the center for the lace for many years. The toll house at the end of town is the display center run by the Carrickmacross Lace Co-op for the lace today. It is to this historic little building that the lace makers, after many patient hours of sewing their elegant lace, bring the fruits of their labor. The toll house is well worth a visit, to view the display of such items as a collar and cuff set at IR£40 ($64), or go all out and invest in an heirloom veil for IR£75 ($120) to IR£600 ($960).

It was in County Monaghan that the poet Patrick Kavanagh first saw the light of day. Although he lived for 30 years in Dublin and considered that city to be the place that transformed him from a "happily unhappy, ordinary countryman" into the "abnormally normal" poet, much of his poetry had to do with the place of his birth. In the end, he was brought back to his native county, and his grave is in **Inishkeen** just opposite a small stone church and the remains of an ancient round tower.

When in Monaghan town, stop by the award-winning **Monaghan County Museum** to see the medieval processional Cross of Clogher, which dates from the 14th century, as well as other artifacts from this county's rich past.

County Offaly

The gardens at **Birr Castle** in the town of Birr (Biorra, "Spring Wells") are open to the public. The castle was a much besieged stronghold during the 16th and 17th centuries, and was later the seat of the Earls of Rosse. The third earl had an observatory in the castle, where he designed a telescope that was, for some 80 years, the largest in the world.

One of Ireland's most holy sites is **Clonmacnois** (Cluain Mic Nois, "meadow of the son of Nos"), where St. Ciaran founded a monastery in 548. It was plundered by Irish chieftains, Vikings, and Anglo-Normans and finally gave up the ghost when Cromwell's forces desecrated it beyond restoration. Today you'll find among its ruins a cathedral, eight churches, two round towers, the remains of a castle, more than 200 monumental slabs, and three sculptured high crosses. There are guided tours during the summer months.

County Roscommon

Near Castlerea, **Clonalis House** (tel. 0907/20014) dates from the 19th century and is home of the O'Conor Don, chieftain of the Clan O'Conor, onetime High Kings of Ireland, traditional Kings of Connaught, and Europe's oldest family, whose descent can be traced back through 60 generations to 75 B.C. It is furnished with Sheraton pieces and a collection of artifacts that includes O'Carolan's harp, rare glass and china, paintings, and Gaelic manuscripts. From May through June it opens only on Saturday and Sunday from 2 to 5:30 p.m.; from July through early September it is open Monday through Saturday from 11 a.m. to 5:50 p.m. and on Sunday 2 to 5:30 p.m.; other times by arrangement. Admission for adults is IR£1.50 ($2.50); for children (over 7), 70p ($1). There's an exhibition of horse-drawn farm machinery and carriages, plus antique lace. Afternoon tea is available, as well as a craft shop.

In **Boyle,** the ruins of a 12th-century **Cistercian abbey** are impressive, and if you'd like to see the interior, look up the caretaker whose home is just next door.

Two miles east of Boyle, visit the **Lough Key Forest Park.** It's one of the country's loveliest, and especially interesting are the Bog Gardens, with heathers and other small plants that grow well in peat.

Lovers of traditional Irish music may want to make a pilgrimage to **Kilronan,** where the revered blind harper, composer, and poet Turlough O'Carolan lies in a cemetery above whose arched gateway is inscribed: "Within this churchyard lie the remains of Carolan, the last of the Irish bards who departed this life 25 March, 1738. R.I.P."

In the village of Knockcroghery, look for **Cromleach Crafts Ltd.,** Mill House Pottery (tel. 0903/7079). This is the home studio in which artist/sculptor/potter Anne Lally hand-makes the traditional clay pipes (or "dudeen"). Be sure to phone her, however, before you drop in. Besides the pipes, Anne also has paintings for sale.

County Westmeath

In **Athlone** (Ath Luain, "The Ford of Luan"), **King John's Castle,** which dates from the 13th century, is fascinating, and there's a museum within its walls. Athlone is where John McCormack, the famous Irish tenor, was born, and his birthplace is marked by a bronze plaque in the Bawn, off Mardyke Street.

From an Athlone base, no fewer than five stately homes and gardens are less than an hour's drive: **Birr Castle** is 28 miles; **Clonalis House,** Castlerea, is 40 miles; **Tullynally Castle,** Castlepollard, is 43 miles; **Emo court** is 48 miles; and **Abbeyleix,** Woodland Gardens, 55 miles.

CHAPTER XXVIII

INTRODUCING NORTHERN IRELAND

□ □ □

1. THE PRACTICALITIES
2. A SUGGESTED ITINERARY

Yet another face of Ireland lies across the border that marks the six-county province of Northern Ireland. Its green fields, cliff-studded and cove-indented coastline, forest-clad mountains, and above all its hospitable inhabitants are reasons enough to cross that border. Beyond those, there are elements found *only* in the North that will add an extra, very special dimension to your Irish experience.

To begin with the obvious, this is where you'll find the famed Giant's Causeway—mighty Fionn MacCumhaill's rocky pathway across to Scotland—along with a curving stretch of green glens, secluded inlets, towering cliffs (two of which are connected in summer months by the ingenious Carrick-a-Rede rope bridge high above a chasm between a salmon fishery island and the mainland), pleasant resort towns with safe beaches, and quiet, quaint little villages. So spectacular is the Antrim Coast that many of the 40,000 American visitors each year settle into this part of the province for their entire stay.

But what a pity to miss the gentler shoreline of County Down with its romantic Mountains of Mourne that sweep down to a sea replete with wide, curving strands fronted by charming holiday towns, and its firm claim on a good part of Saint Patrick's Irish sojourn, from his first footsteps on Irish soil to his last. Quiet little villages on the Ards Peninsula look across to Scotland (clearly visible in many places), and the countryside is dotted with Norman castles, forest parks beckoning the hiker, and even a windmill still whirling away at harvest time, plus Strangford Lough and palm-tree-bordered Carlingford Lough.

And who would want to miss County Fermanagh's Lough Erne and its 300 square miles of boating or fishing amid exquisite scenery? Or the fabulous Marble Arch Caves? Devenish Island with its ancient abbey and tower and White Island's mysterious Celtic stone figures, just two of the lough's 154 islands, entice the sightseer. Or Armagh's two cathedrals—one Protestant, one Catholic, and both named for Saint Patrick? Or the Sperrin Mountains of County Tyrone, as well as the unique folk park that so vividly depicts the rural lives of Irish immigrants on both sides of the Atlantic? Or Derry's massive old city walls? Or—well, read on and you'll find a wealth of other scenic splendors spread throughout all six counties.

All that gorgeous scenery is not only a delight to the eye, but serves as well as a mighty spur to the imagination, for it has spawned a good many of Ireland's legends. It was in this part of Ireland that the brave Cuchulainn roamed and, singlehanded, guarded the border against the onslaught of Queen Maeve when she set out to capture the Brown Bull of Cooley. This was home territory for Fionn MacCumhaill (whom you may know as Finn MacCoul) and his faithful Fianna warriors. And the beautiful Deirdre o' the Sorrows played out her life's tragedy within the borders of Ulster.

If the above mention of these heroes has set your mind soaring, let me recommend a marvelous little paperback on sale in most bookstores in Ireland: it's titled *Heroic Tales from the Ulster Cycle* and is published by O'Brien Educational Press (with offices at 20 Victoria Rd., Dublin 6).

And if the landscape and legends of Northern Ireland are magical, its people are no less so. Because of all that history related back in an early chapter of this book, the accents of the North will fall on your ears with the soft burr of Scotland, mingled with the clipped speech of native English and the lilting Irish brogue of the Republic. "Och, it's not a bad day at all," the Ulsterman will remark; to which his Republican neighbor will reply, "Sure, and isn't that God's truth." It's an enchanting mix, and don't be at all surprised if you find yourself ending sentences with the distinctive lift that characterizes so much of what you hear.

Along with their speech, these descendants of Great Britain's plantation-era families have put into the mix strong elements of their cultures. Squash and cricket are sports you'll rarely find in the Republic, but they flourish above the border; the strains of traditional Irish music are interspersed with music of a distinctly British or Scottish flavor; Belfast's magnificent Opera House is as likely to play an English drawing-room comedy as an Irish classic by O'Casey or Synge. And while Orangemen parade in great numbers and with great gusto on July 12th to celebrate their beloved King Billy's victory at the Battle of the Boyne, there is no less a festive air about Catholic parades and celebrations on the 15th of August, when the Ancient Order of Hibernian crowds take over to celebrate the Feast of the Assumption.

Aha! you say, those two celebrations may be equally festive, but don't they reflect the politics and the *troubles* that make one hesitate to plan a trip to Northern Ireland? Sadly, I cannot answer an unqualified "No" to that question. As we go to press, the strife that has infected Northern Ireland since 1969 goes on, sometimes with long no-incident intervals, other times with headline-grabbing frequency. From time to time there are signs that a peaceful solution may yet be found to the problems that beleaguer the province. The latest—and many believe most hopeful—is the Anglo-Irish Agreement signed in 1985. But, again, I cannot tell you that an end is in sight for these tragic "troubles."

What I *can* tell you is that in those two decades, no tourist has come to any harm (a comforting thought!); that the U.S. State Department has never issued a travel warning regarding Northern Ireland, as it does to destinations deemed unsafe to visit; that in all my own ramblings around Northern Ireland I have never felt endangered; and that the one guarantee I can unhesitatingly make is that the people of the province will welcome you warmly, delighted that you've come to visit.

That is not to say, of course, that you will be totally unaware of the tensions. Border checkpoints, posted guards at hotels and other public gathering places, and the occasional armed road patrol you meet on country roads all indicate that this is indeed a troubled area. However, body and purse searches of the past have, happily, almost disappeared and at most checkpoints you are passed quickly through with a polite wave. There *are* some very simple rules designed to ensure your safety—I'll tell you about those in detail later in this chapter—that will become automatic soon after your arrival.

In short, my best advice is: Don't miss this other—different—face of Ireland.

1. THE PRACTICALITIES

THE CURRENCY: Northern Ireland's currency is that of Great Britain's, the pound sterling. As we go to press, the exchange rate against the American dollar is £1 = $1.75, and all prices quoted in these pages are based on that rate. In these uncertain days, exchange rates fluctuate with amazing frequency, so be sure to check the current situation when you come.

Americans will be well advised to buy pounds sterling with dollars rather than Irish punts, since the exchange rate is much more favorable—you can do that at banks in the Republic before you cross the border if it's more convenient. One caution: If you're arriving in the North on a weekend or bank holiday, be sure to buy pounds sterling before you come. And, of course, it is always best to change your currency at a bank rather than in department stores or hotels. In Belfast, the Thomas Cook office (11 Donegal Pl., Belfast 1) can also convert currency at the official rate.

The following table will give you an idea of how your dollars compare to the exchange rate quoted above:

£	U.S. $	£	U.S. $
1p	.02	£6	10.50
5p	.08	£7	12.25
10p	.18	£8	14.00
25p	.44	£9	15.75
50p	.88	£10	17.50
75p	1.31	£12.50	21.88
£1	1.75	£15	26.25
£2	3.50	£17.50	30.63
£2.50	4.38	£20	35.00
£3	5.25	£22.50	39.38
£4	7.00	£25	43.75
£5	8.75	£30	52.50

ABOUT THOSE RULES AND REGULATIONS: There aren't that many, but you should know them in advance. The single most important regulation if you're driving is that concerning parking. When you see an area signposted "Control Zone," it means that cars must *not be left parked and unattended, even for a short time.* In those areas, it is felt that cars left empty (even if locked) are a security risk, and the regulation is strictly enforced. There will usually be a parking lot close at hand with an attendant on duty.

You'll also see some hotels, public offices, or shopping areas fenced off with security personnel on duty. Only rarely will you be stopped when entering these areas, and even then you'll be sent through with a courteous smile after a quick look at your purse or shopping bag.

When coming from the Republic, it is always advisable to enter through one of the approved checkpoints, which are clearly marked on tourist maps. You won't have to show your passport or produce a visa.

TOURIST INFORMATION: There are about 30 Tourist Information Offices around the province, with helpful, friendly personnel anxious to help with any problem and make sure you see the highlights of their area. The Northern Ireland Tourist Board's main office is at River House, 48-52 High St., Belfast (tel. 0232/246609), with hours of 9 a.m. to 5:15 p.m. weekdays and 9 a.m. to 2 p.m. on Saturday from Easter to September and public holidays.

ACCOMMODATIONS: You'll find the same high standards for accommodations as in the Republic, with the Northern Ireland Tourist Board maintaining just as strict an inspection program as their counterpart to the south. Bed-and-breakfast homes, guesthouses, farmhouses, and moderately priced hotels are in generous supply, and it is generally not necessary to book in advance—you can meander around the province pretty much at will without the worry of being stuck without a bed. A time-saving idea is to come armed with the Tourist Board's directory, *Where to Stay*, which you can obtain for £1 ($1.75) by writing to Northern Ireland Tourist Board, River House, 48-52 High St., Belfast, Northern Ireland, or at bookshops and any Tourist Office once you've arrived. There's also a helpful illustrated *Farm & Country Holidays* booklet with about 100 listings; *Town & Seaside House Holidays*, also illustrated and listing some 50 homes; *The Disabled Tourist in Northern Ireland*, which lists places to stay as well as accessible sightseeing attractions; and for campers, *Caravan & Camp Sites*, with more than 100 approved sites.

Note: During off-seasons (March to mid-June and mid-September to December), many Northern Ireland accommodations have special weekend and midweek packages. If you plan to visit during those periods, write to the Northern Ireland Tourist Board for their *Holiday Breakaways* booklet, which details all such specials in all six counties.

MEALS: The Tourist Board also publishes a directory of eateries, *Where to Eat*, that covers all price ranges, from pub grub to posh restaurants, in all six counties. A money-saver is the 6 p.m. high tea served in many hotels and some restaurants —portions are ample, and the menu usually includes eggs, sausage, ham, or fish and chips. High tea is less expensive than the regular dinner menu (which most often goes on at 7 p.m.). Best make reservations in the better hotel dining rooms and restaurants on weekends and holidays.

PUB HOURS: The last drinks are served in Northern Ireland pubs at 11 p.m., although the doors don't close until 11:30 p.m. They open at 11:30 a.m. every day except Sunday, when most open only from 12:30 to 2:30 p.m. and 7 to 10 p.m. (the only remedy for a terrible thirst during other hours on Sunday is to get yourself to a licensed restaurant or a hotel bar).

DRIVING: As in the Republic, driving is on the left. Northern Ireland has an excellent network of highways, with speed limits of 30 mph in town (unless a slower speed is posted), 60 mph on highways and country roads, and 70 mph on

NORTHERN IRELAND

dual carriageways (divided highways). Traffic circles are called "round-abouts," and exits are well marked.

If you're driving a rental car from the Republic, you should check to see that the insurance covers your stay above the border—and the same, of course, applies if you're going the other way. In the North, the leading car-rental firms are **Avis, Hertz,** and **Godfrey Davis,** with offices in Belfast and at Belfast International Airport.

PUBLIC TRANSPORT: You can travel around the North quite easily and inexpensively using the rail and bus services. Day trips are also available to almost all sightseeing highlights. Northern Ireland Railways (NIR) has a seven-day, unlimited travel, **Rail Runabout pass** good April through October at a cost of £22 ($38.50) for adults, £11 ($19.25) for children. It's available at most railway stations. Primary rail service is from Belfast to Londonderry via Ballymena and Coleraine; Belfast to Bangor; and Belfast to Dublin (a two-hour trip). Information on all NIR services is available at the **Travel and Information Centre** in Belfast's Central Station, or by calling 0232/230310 or 230671. Good bus service will get you almost anywhere there's no train.

There are taxi ranks at the Belfast International Airport, harbor ports, and the principal rail and bus stations. For other taxi service, check the local telephone directory for numbers to call. Some of the black, London-style cabs are not metered, and you should agree on a fare to your destination when you start out.

SHOPPING: Prices are generally lower in Northern Ireland than in the Republic for such items as Belleek, hand-woven tweeds, crystal, and many other fine products. Folks from below the border, in fact, often make shopping forays to the six counties to take advantage of the price difference. Two shopping expeditions that can be enjoyable and profitable are those to **Belleek Pottery,** Belleek, County Fermanagh (tel. 036/565501), and **Tyrone Crystal,** Dungannon, County Tyrone (tel. 086/872-5335), but you should telephone ahead to make arrangements for your visit.

2. A SUGGESTED ITINERARY

The six counties of Northern Ireland are all good rambling country, and this section is by no means meant to be a rigid, not-to-be-deviated-from itinerary. It is, however, a convenient circular tour of the province that will get you to most of the highlights. As in the Republic, you're sure to discover some places not mentioned in the county-by-county chapters that follow.

If you're coming from Donegal, the following route is recommended (and, of course, it can be reversed should your departure point be Belfast). From Londonderry, head north through Limavady and the Roe Valley to Coleraine and the Bann Valley. Then go on to Portrush and the Giant's Causeway. Bushmills distillery is a short detour south from this point. Drive on through Ballycastle and enter the Antrim Coast Road, which takes you through the Nine Glens of Antrim, Larne, and Carrickfergus to Belfast. Then it's south to Downpatrick (if time permits, cut east around the Ards Peninsula) and west to Armagh, Enniskillen, and Belleek. Outstanding sightseeing points in each county are listed in Chapter XXX.

CHAPTER XXIX

BELFAST AND LONDONDERRY

□ □ □

1. BELFAST
2. LONDONDERRY

In ancient times, Belfast was a fort set at a ford of the River Lagan (it's name in Irish is Beal Feirste, "Mouth of the Sandy Ford"). Around it a small village developed, and in the 17th century Protestant settlers from Scotland and parts of England moved in (and native villagers were moved out) by order of English rulers, thus establishing the character of the city that grew at a steady pace until the end of the 1700s, thanks in large part to a thriving linen industry. In 1791 Wolfe Tone founded the United Irish Society in Belfast to bring together Protestants and Catholics who chafed under the repressive Penal Laws, and in 1798 their efforts led to an uprising, one which was quickly squelched by English forces. The shipyard that was to contribute so much to the city's growth was opened in 1791. By the time the Industrial Revolution was in full bloom during the 19th century, both shipbuilding and the linen trade welcomed newer, more modern operating methods. Both prospered, and Belfast's population grew by leaps and bounds.

1. BELFAST

The city today is a bustling, energetic center of industry, yet for the visitor it is easy to get around and holds many points of interest—most prominent of which has to be the good Queen Victoria, whose statue adorns Donegall Square and whose architectural style is in evidence all around the city.

ACCOMMODATIONS: The Queen's University area is a happy hunting ground for good bed-and-breakfast accommodations, and those listed outside the city are close enough to serve as a good base for exploring Belfast while enjoying the scenic countryside.

Note: Prices shown below are those in effect in 1989—expect them to be higher in 1990.

Bed-and-Breakfast

Liserin Guest House, 17 Eglantine Ave., Belfast BT9 6DW (tel. 0232/660769), is set on a quiet street shaded by lime trees. It's about a 15-minute walk into the city center, and there's good bus service at the end of the block. The brick

Victorian-style town house dates back to 1892, and original woodwork, high ceilings, and spacious rooms add to its charm. That charm comes in large part, too, from Mrs. Joan Walker, its gracious hostess, and she takes a personal interest in guests, serving evening tea and, upon request, a simple evening meal for about £6 ($10.50). The seven guest rooms include five singles, all attractively furnished and all with handbasins. Those in the back catch more sun than the ones in front, but all are light and cheerful. B&B rates are £13 ($22.75) single, £25 ($43.75) double.

Beaumont Lodge, 237 Stranmillis Rd., Belfast BT9 5EE (tel. 0232/ 667965), is tucked away in lawns surrounded by green hedges, a sparkling white guesthouse with a feeling of seclusion that belies its setting just off a busy road beside the New Ulster Clinic. There is good bus transportation into the city center, a real convenience for nondrivers or for drivers who wish to leave their cars parked on the grounds. The ground-floor lounge is a striking, two-story room with floor-to-ceiling windows looking out to the lawn, which is given a rather whimsical air by one of those fast-disappearing classic red telephone booths of Northern Ireland, placed there by owner Valerie Kidd. The lounge has an interesting hooded fireplace, TV for guests, and tea and coffee makings (with biscuits always in supply). All seven bedrooms are bright and cheerful, and one of the family rooms has private facilities (all others share two toilets and shower rooms). Bed-and-breakfast rates are £11 ($19.25) per person, and Mrs. Kidd will provide the evening meal if requested the day before, although there are several good restaurants nearby.

Miss Angela Drumm, a native of County Meath who has lived in Belfast for many years, is the attractive and gracious hostess at **Camera House,** 44 Wellington Park, Belfast BT9 6DP (tel. 0232/660026 or 667856). This lovely guesthouse is just a few minutes' walk from the city center. The red-brick Victorian-style house has bay windows in the guest lounge and dining room, giving a light, airy look to both. All rooms, in fact, are quite bright, and all have showers and toilets, and TVs. Of the 11, four are singles. Miss Drumm will furnish a light supper if you request it early in the day at a cost of £7 ($12.25). Bed-and-breakfast rates are £19 ($33.25) single, and £27 ($47.25) double.

Your enchantment with **The Cottage,** 377 Comber Rd., Dundonald BT16 0XB, Co. Down (tel. 0247/878189), is likely to begin even as you drive into the parking area out back, for the driveway brings you into full view of a lovely lawn and colorful flowerbeds that beckon the traveler to sit awhile and enjoy such outdoors beauty. Once inside the traditional, sparkling white cottage, however, you'll be sorely tempted never to set foot outside again. Mrs. Elizabeth Muldoon has realized every cottage-lover's dream—she has lovingly retained (and even enhanced) all the original charm of the house and at the same time she installed every modern convenience. The living room is picture-pretty, as is the rustic dining area, and bedrooms are beautifully furnished with many antiques scattered about. Décor throughout is in keeping with a traditional country home. Just a short drive from Belfast, the Cottage is one of the most inviting accommodations in the area. Bed-and-breakfast rates are £12 ($21) single, £23 ($40.25) double.

Queens University of Belfast Common Room, 1 College Gardens, Belfast BT9 6BQ (tel. 0232/665938), can provide excellent accommodations in a university environment. There are lounges and catering and recreational facilities set in a pleasant, quiet, yet central, part of Belfast. The recently refurbished bedrooms range in price from £10 ($17.50) to £18.50 ($32.50) per night single, and £33.50 ($53.50) double, including a full breakfast. All rooms have tea- and coffee-making facilities. Special rates are available for long stays. Contact Mr. E. P. Black, accommodation manager.

Farmhouse

A comfortable old farmhouse that's been thoroughly modernized, **Greenlea Farm,** 48 Dunover Rd., Ballywalter BT22 2LE, Co. Down (tel. 02477/58218), looks out from its hilltop to the Ards Peninsula and across to the misty coast of Scotland and the Isle of Man. Mrs. Evelyn McIvor is its warm, friendly hostess who teaches crafts and enjoys sharing her considerable knowledge of the area with guests. Both the lounge and dining room have picture windows that frame the spectacular view, and the dining room holds lovely antique pieces, with lots of silver and crystal on display. Recreational amenities include tennis and bowling. Mrs. McIvor has one large family room with bunk beds for two children and a double for parents, as well as accommodations for singles and doubles. Her rates for bed-and-breakfast are £10 ($17.50) per person for one night only, £9 ($15.75) per person per night for longer stays, with a 25% reduction for children under 12 and 50% for those under 8.

A Big Splurge

Ash-Rowan Guest House, 12 Windsor Ave., Belfast BT9 6EE (tel. 0232/661758), is a real treat. After a career in award-winning restaurants, Evelyn and Sam Hazlette acquired this lovely old late-Victorian residence and have turned it into a Grade A guesthouse serving (as you might expect) superb evening meals. Set back from the street in a quiet residential area between Lisburn Road and Malone Road, Ash-Rowan is only ten minutes from the center of the city and provides private parking on the grounds. Each bedroom is beautifully decorated in individual style, has a private toilet and shower, vanity unit, color TV, and razor points. An added feature is the dressing gown provided each guest—color-keyed to the room, no less! There's also a paperback library for the use of guests. The Hazlettes are the very soul of hospitality, and offer their guests a choice of either a full traditional or continental breakfast. As for evening meals, they are very special, with both cuisine and service rivaling those in a first-class restaurant. Rates for bed-and-breakfast are £28 ($49) single, £46 ($80.50) double.

WHERE TO EAT: From pub grub to elegant Big Splurges, you'll find meals to suit your mood and your pocketbook in Belfast. Pick up a copy of *Where to Eat* to supplement the selections below.

Thompsons Restaurant, 47 Arthur St. (tel. 223762), is one of those unobtrusive little places you sometimes—if you're very, very lucky—stumble across right in the heart of the city simply going about the business of supplying good food in ample portions at reasonable prices in a friendly, unpretentious setting. Because its front room is a pub, it might, in fact, be listed in the pub-grub paragraph below; but because its food goes so far beyond the usual, it warrants much more attention. Food service is in a room just beyond the bar, but you're likely to spend at least one drink's time out front waiting to be seated, for this is a popular place with Belfast natives who work in the inner city. Cordiality reigns, however, in both the pub and the restaurant sections, and any wait is bound to be a pleasant one. The extensive (and surprising) menu, concentrating mainly on such Irish offerings as seafood, steak, ham, and chicken, covers just about anything you could want, and far more than you could expect in this kind of eatery. There's plaice or sole poached with fresh prawns in cheese and wine sauce or in a mornay sauce or fried in bread crumbs with banana and chutney (as well as less exotic choices); scampi that comes in several forms (Newburg, provençale, grilled, or deep-fried); fresh Irish trout baked or grilled; prime filet steaks (au poivre or tournedos Rossini); sirloin steaks; etc. A la carte prices for main courses range from £4 ($7) to £6 ($10.50), with omelets in the £2 ($3.50) to £3 ($5.25) range, and appetizers (from which I happily assembled an excellent lunch) running from under £1 ($1.75) to £3 ($5.25) for smoked salmon. All come with home-made Ulster wheaten bread and butter. Hours are 12:15 to 3:15 p.m. and 6 to 9:30 p.m. Monday through Saturday. As you may have guessed, this is a personal favorite and one I wouldn't want you to miss!

Just behind the Law Courts, **The Strand at the Buttery,** 89 Chichester St. (tel. 0232/321744), is a large licensed establishment that serves light meals, steaks, chicken Kiev, etc., at prices not much above £5 ($8.75). As you might expect, it has a large following among the legal fraternity. Hours are noon to 9:30 p.m. Monday through Saturday.

Over in the university area, near the Ulster Museum and Botanic Gardens, **The Strand,** 12 Stranmillis Rd. (tel. 0232/682266), has won several awards for its outstanding food with dishes such as crabmeat-stuffed courgettes and chicken roulade with tomato sauce. Prices are in the £10 ($17.50) to £15 ($24) range, hours are 11:30 a.m. to 11 p.m., and it's best to reserve.

La Belle Époque, 103 Great Victoria St. (tel. 0232/223244), is considered by many to be the best restaurant in Belfast. Cuisine here is of the French persuasion, with steak, pheasant, and lobster among the specialties. Prices run £10 ($17.50) to £15 ($24), and it's open from 6 p.m. to midnight. Reservations recommended.

Good pub grub is to be found from noon to 2:30 p.m. at the following: **Linenhall Bar,** 9 Clarence St.; **Rumpoles,** 81 Chichester St.; **Beaten Docket,** 48 Great Victoria St.; **Botanic Inn,** 23 Malone Rd. (university area); **Elbow,** 49 Dublin Rd.; **Garrick,** 11 Montgomery St.; The **Front Page,** 106 Donegall St.; and on the outskirts of town, **King's Head,** Lisburn Road, Balmoral (opposite King's Hall).

THINGS TO SEE AND DO: Your first stop should be the **Northern Ireland Tourist Board Information Office** in River House, 48 High St. (tel. 0232/246609). They can give you a good, free street map of Belfast and brochures on sightseeing highlights, city bus tours, day trips, and sports such as fishing, golf, cruising for Belfast and for all of Northern Ireland.

You can't miss the **City Hall,** a massive Portland stone building crowned with a copper dome in Donegall Square. It was ten years abuilding and its interior is elegant with Greek and Italian marble. The city's industrial history is traced in a large mural. If you don't recognize it otherwise, you'll know it by the bust of Queen Victoria out front (she was a guest of the city in 1846 and is much revered). A Great War Memorial sits on the west side, with a memorial sculpture to the *Titanic,* which was built in Belfast and went to the bottom in 1912.

Look for the **Albert Memorial** toward the river on High Street—it pays tribute, of course, to Queen Victoria's consort and is affectionately known as Belfast's "leaning tower" because it is slightly less than straight.

An interesting collection of stained glass, paintings, and sculptures—all dealing with Belfast's seafaring connections—is on display at the **Harbour Office** in Corporation Square. You can see it on weekdays from 9:30 a.m. to 4:30 p.m. if you call the administration officer at 234422, ext. 205, in advance.

On Lower Donegall Street, the **Belfast Cathedral** (St. Anne's) was built between 1899 and 1904. It has a particularly fine mosaic showing St. Patrick landing at Saul in A.D. 432, which you will find over the entrance to the Chapel of the Holy Spirit.

Bend an elbow at least once, or go by for a pub lunch, at the **Crown Liquor Saloon** on Great Victoria Street. It's a marvelous old Victorian pub, the ultimate in casual elegance with its carved woodwork, snugs lining one wall, flickering gaslights, and painted ceramic tiles. Some "chrome and mirror" addicts got their hands on it a few years back and nearly modernized the character out of it, but the National Trust came to the rescue and it is now back to its original state.

Try to get to a performance in the **Grand Opera House,** on Great Victoria Street (tel. 0232/240411). It's a marvel of rich, rococo eccentricity, with 24 gilt elephant heads separating boxes sporting canopies, Buddhas scattered about the draperies, and lots of gold and maroon. Closed from 1972 to 1981, it's been beautifully restored.

A morning or afternoon at the **Belfast Zoo** is a delight. It's out on Antrim Road in a mountain park with good views of the city and the lough. Open every day from 10 a.m. to 5 p.m., until 3 p.m. in winter.

Some eight miles from Belfast on the road to Bangor, the **Ulster Folk and Transport Museum,** Cultra Manor, Holywood, Co. Down (tel. 428428), is a unique museum of folklife and transport set on some 176 acres. The manor house holds a tea room and conference facilities, and there are interesting permanent and temporary exhibitions in the Folk Gallery and the Transport Gallery (which has a branch on Witham Street in Belfast). The open-air museum is composed of a fascinating collection of buildings of all types, rural and urban, from the 18th century to the 19th, all furnished in the style of about 1900—a microcosm of Ulster life of that period. Farms, an old church, a flax-scutching mill, schools, and many other buildings make this enchanting place well worth a visit of half a day (more if you can spare it). Admission is £1 ($1.75) for adults, 50p (90¢) for children; under 5 years old, free. Hours are 11 a.m. to 6 p.m. Monday through Saturday and 2 to 6 p.m. on Sunday, May through September (open until 9 p.m. May through June); other months it closes at 5 p.m.

Tracing Your Roots

For help in tracking down Irish ancestors, contact the **Irish Heritage Association,** 162A Kingsway, Dunmurry, Belfast BT17 9AD (tel. 0232/629595). They'll research on a mail-order basis or provide professional help while you are in Ireland, both north and south of the border. They can also arrange personal "roots" tours for individuals or groups, and organize All-Ireland Heritage Tours and clan gatherings.

2. LONDONDERRY

There's the aura of the ages about Londonderry—in ancient times, it was known as Doire Calgach ("Calgach's Oak wood"), later simply as Doire ("Oak Grove"); then came St. Columba in A.D. 546 to found a monastic settlement which became Cholomcille Doire ("St. Columba's oakgrove"). Some ten centuries later, after years of seesaw battles to conquer it, King James succeeded in 1613 and promptly transferred it by charter to the City of London to be administered by the Honourable Irish Society, and its name became Londonderry. After all that, it is still affectionately called simply Derry by most of the Irish on both sides of the border.

Strong city walls 20 to 25 feet high and 14 to 37 feet high with seven gates went up soon after the society took over things, and despite siege after siege, those walls are largely intact today. This old, walled section of modern-day Londonderry is west of the River Foyle, as are the main business and shopping districts, with ancient winding lanes and rows of charming Georgian and Victorian buildings. In the northeastern portion of the walls, Shipquay Gate is only two blocks from the river, and the historic old Guildhall with its turrets and tower clock is midway between river quays and this gate. Most of what you'll want to see will be within a short walk of these two points, including the bus station, Tourist Office, and inexpensive places to eat. Surrounding the original, walled city and across Craigavon Bridge (south of the Guildhall), modern Londonderry has sprouted along the river and hillsides, covering almost ten times the area that spawned it.

You'll find the **Tourist Office** on Foyle Street (tel. 0504/267284), with hours of 9 a.m. to 5:15 p.m. weekdays and 10 a.m. to 5 p.m. on Saturday from May to September. The helpful staff will arrange accommodations (no charge) and walking tours, and provide sightseeing information for the city and its immediate vicinity.

The **railway station** is on Duke Street, Waterside (tel. 0504/42228); the **Ulsterbus station,** on Foyle Street (tel. 0504/262261).

ACCOMMODATIONS: Most city accommodations are well beyond the reach of budgeteers, but the Tourist Office can help you find nearby places within our price range.

Note: Prices shown below are those in effect in 1989—expect them to be higher in 1990.

Bed-and-Breakfast

In the city itself, Mrs. Eleonora Slevin operates **Clarence House,** 15 Northland Rd., Londonderry (tel. 0504/265342), with singles, doubles, twin rooms, and family rooms available. The rate is £10 ($17.50) per person.

Florence House, 16 Northland Rd., Londonderry (tel. 0504/268093), offers five doubles and two family rooms. Mrs. McGinley is hostess here, and her rate for bed-and-breakfast is £10 ($17.50) per person.

A Farmhouse

Friendly Mrs. Emma Craig presides over **Ballycarton Farm,** Bellarena, Limavady BT49 0HZ, Co. Londonderry (tel. Bellarena 05047/50216), which is beautifully situated about 17 miles outside Londonderry in 50 acres of mountain and coastal scenery. The comfortably furnished guest rooms are all of ample size, many with good views. Mrs. Craig can arrange babysitting, and she doesn't mind travelers with dogs. The rate is £10 ($17.50), and the evening meal costs the same (with advance booking, Mrs. Craig will prepare dinner for nonresidents).

A Hotel

One of the nicest inexpensive hotels I've run across in Ireland is the **White Horse Inn,** 68 Clooney Rd., Campsie BT47 3PA, Co. Londonderry (tel. 0504/860606). It's four miles outside town on the Limavady road, with good, frequent bus service into Londonderry. The owners of this modern, attractive hotel/motel, Alwyn and Irish Kydd, have put into effect per-room pricing, which means your room costs the same whether you use it as a single or a double. Each room has tea- and coffee-making equipment, direct-dial telephone, color TV, and an alarm clock. Attached to the hotel is a block of motel-like chalets with a fridge and cooking facilities. On the premises you'll also find the Carousel Restaurant, Yesterdays grill room (see "Where to Eat"), and a sophisticated bar and lounge—with these complete facilities, the out-of-town location is no inconvenience at all, and the White Horse has my high recommendation (especially for two traveling together, when rates become budget). Rates begin at £31.50 ($55.25) for hotel rooms, and around £35 ($61.25) for chalets.

WHERE TO EAT: The aforementioned **White Horse Inn** offers exceptional value with lunches for under £5 ($8.75), and evening meals for under £10 ($17.50).

For pub grub between noon and 2:30 p.m., try the following: **Bells,** 60 Victoria Rd.; **The Venue,** Northland Road; the **Inn at the Cross,** 171 Glenshane Rd.; and **New Monico,** 4 Custom House St.

THINGS TO SEE AND DO: The Tourist Office has background information on points of interest in the city.

One thing you should *not* miss in Londonderry is a walk along the old **city walls.** They are the only unbroken city walls in the British Isles, and Londonderry was the last city in Europe to build protective wall fortifications. Check with the Tourist Office about days and times of their guided walking tours along the walls, and go along if you can—the narrative adds a lot to the city scene below and the landscape beyond. If you go on your own, enter at the Shipquay Gate.

You can visit the imposing Gothic **Guildhall** on a tour with a guide (call the superintendent at 265151). It dates from 1890, but had to be almost completely reconstructed after a terrible fire in 1908. Look for the window in the marble vestibule that depicts *The Relief of Derry*. The lovely stained-glass windows are the work of local artisans. The Guildhall is open Monday through Friday from 9 a.m. to 4 p.m.

St. Columb's Cathedral was built in the mid-1600s, but much of what you'll see today has been added since. One of its most important features is the memorial window showing the relief of the siege in 1689. You can visit any day between 9 a.m. and 12:30 p.m. and 2 and 4:30 p.m.; closed Thursday afternoon.

Outside the walls, take time to stroll down narrow little streets such as Albert and Nailor Row, both lined with interesting and quaint houses and buildings.

Londonderry is rich in traditional Irish music, with musicians from neighboring County Donegal often coming over to join in. Check with the Tourist Office, or go by the following pubs to see if and when there will be music: **Phoenix Bar,** Park Avenue, Rosemount; **Gweedore Bar,** Waterloo Street; **Castle Bar,** Waterloo Street; and **Dungloe Bar,** Waterloo Street. Another hangout of traditional musicians is **The Quaver,** 31 Carlisle Rd., where its owner, young Doreen Rice, sells music and instruments (pick up a tin whistle for little or nothing—you'll be surprised how soon you'll be tooting a tune!).

CHAPTER XXX

AROUND NORTHERN IRELAND

□ □ □

1. COUNTY ANTRIM
2. COUNTY ARMAGH
3. COUNTY DOWN
4. COUNTY FERMANAGH
5. COUNTY LONDONDERRY
6. COUNTY TYRONE

The six counties that make up Northern Ireland hold some of the island's true scenic wonders, as well as a wealth of sightseeing attractions. We'll take them county by county.

1. COUNTY ANTRIM

ACCOMMODATIONS: My personal choice of accommodations in County Antrim is almost any of the friendly farmhouses, but there are two rather special hotels that definitely deserve consideration.

Note: Prices shown below are those in effect in 1989—expect them to be higher in 1990.

Farmhouses

Mrs. Ria Johnston, **White Gables,** 83 Dunluce Rd., Portballintrae, Co. Antrim, BT57 8SJ (tel. Bushmills 02657/31611), is the charming hostess of this attractive country house set in pretty countryside. The house is centrally heated and there is a radio in each room. There are washing and ironing facilities available and some major credit cards are accepted here. Three of the five comfortable bedrooms have private facilities. The rate for bed-and-breakfast is £12.50 ($22) with a discount for stays of more than two days, and there is a reduction for children. Open April to September.

Within easy reach of the Glens of Antrim, airport, boats, and trains, Mrs. Catharine Scally's **Tudor farmhouse,** 185 Torr Rd., Cushendun BT44 (tel.

Cushendun 252), has an inviting and old-fashioned air, with stained-glass windows and antiques. The house has five very comfortably furnished bedrooms with beautiful views overlooking Cushendun. Bed-and-breakfast costs £10 ($17.50); 25% reduction for children.

Ardnaree, 105 Dunluce Rd., White Rocks, Portrush BT56 8ND (tel. Portrush 0265/823407), overlooks the sea, with the hills of Donegal in the distance. A beautiful beach is just a few minutes' walk away, and there's a good golf course in the vicinity. The centrally heated modern bungalow is the home of Mrs. Elsie Rankin, who takes a personal interest in her guests. The attractive guest rooms include two on the ground floor, one with private toilet and shower and one large family room. The bed-and-breakfast rate is £12.50 ($22).

Ben Neagh House, 11 Crumlin Rd., Crumlin BT29 4AD (tel. Crumlin 084/94-22271), has a grass tennis court and an indoor games room among its amenities. The Georgian-style farmhouse in its park-like setting is the home of Mr. and Mrs. Peel, who make their guests feel right at home. Rates for bed-and-breakfast are £12 ($21) single, £24 ($42) double.

Mrs. Mary Aiken's **Bethany Christian Guest House,** 5 Bay Rd., Carnlough, BT44 0HQ (tel. 0574/85667), is a pleasant, homey place with five bedrooms, all but two of which have private showers or baths. Religious paintings throughout the house attest to Mrs. Aiken's deep Christian faith, and as a practical measure of her concern for her fellow human beings, she has provided on the ground floor one room especially suited to those who are wheelchair-bound, with a ground-level entrance from the outside and wide doors to both the bedroom and bath. There's a no-smoking rule in the lounge, dining room, and some bedrooms. The bed-and-breakfast rate is £11 ($19.25).

On the coastal drive between Ballygally and Glenarm, **Drumnagreach Lodge,** 406 Shore Rd., Glenarm, Co. Antrim (tel. 057/484529), was once the gate lodge for the Drumnagreach manor house that is now a first-class hotel (see below). These days it's the home in which Marie Poland welcomes guests for bed-and-breakfast and provides two bright, attractive bedrooms. The hotel grill room is only a short, pleasant walk away for reasonably priced meals, and the coastal scenery along here is spectacular. The rate for bed-and-breakfast is £8 ($14).

Hotels

Dobbins Inn Hotel, 6-8 High St., Carrickfergus, Co. Antrim (tel. 096/03-51905), will probably look familiar at first sight. In fact, if you carry around in your heart a secret picture of the perfect little Irish country inn, you'll be certain you've found it when you see the Dobbins Inn Hotel, with its pretty window boxes flanking the simple entrance. Inside, you're met with warm, friendly hospitality in a setting that reveals something of the history of this old building. The street on which it stands was once part of the grounds of the 16th-century Dobbins Castle, and during renovations, a great stone fireplace was uncovered in the present-day Coffee Room, as well as a short, walled-up escape passage and another passageway that connected Carrickfergus Castle to St. Nicholas Church by way of this building, a residence at that time. Be sure to ask about "Maud," a ghostly presence said to haunt the castle/church passage. In an upstairs conference room there are framed documents also discovered during renovations. The 13 bedrooms are simply but tastefully furnished, and each has private bath, color TV, telephone, radio, and tea and coffee maker. The lounge bar serves snacks and light lunches, and the De Courcy restaurant has an inexpensive grill menu at lunch and a moderately priced dinner menu. High tea is available in the Coffee Room for £3 ($5.25) to £8 ($14). Bed-and-breakfast rates are £26 ($45.50) single, £46 ($80.50) double, and there are special weekend rates.

Drumnagreagh Hotel, Coast Road, Glenarm, Co. Antrim (tel.

057/484651)—it means "the ridge on the marshy flat"—has one of the most spectacular settings along the Antrim coast, high on a bluff overlooking the sea in front and the sweeping mountainsides of Glen Arn out back. Originally built for a linen merchant around the turn of the century, it was willed to his housekeeper in 1926, and in the years since has seen service as a private residence, convalescent home, and hotel. Its present incarnation is that of a small hotel decorated and managed very much in the grand manner. A semi-Victorian flavor dominates the décor in the public rooms, from the reception area to the elegant octagonal Victorian conservatory-style dining room. An old-world-style grill room serves moderately priced meals in a more informal ambience. Bedrooms are all well done-up, with private baths, telephones, radios, and TVs—ask for front or back locations depending on your preference for sea or country views. Bed-and-breakfast rates are £36 ($63) single, £50 ($87.50) double, for rooms with a sea view and £43 ($75.25) double for those in back. Dinner in the lovely dining room runs around £16 ($28), grill room meals are in the £7 ($12.25) to £8 ($14) range, and there's an excellent Sunday carvery at £7 ($12.25).

The **Londonderry Arms Hotel,** Carnlough, Co. Antrim (tel. 0574/85255, 85458, or 85459), sits right across the road from Carnlough Harbour, and began life back in 1854 as a coaching inn. The O'Neill family has owned the pretty ivy-covered hotel since 1947, and Frank (the present O'Neill manager) continues the tradition of graciousness and home-style hospitality. There are beautiful antique furnishings scattered about, the tavern has a traditional décor, and the spacious lounge is warmed by a copper-hooded fireplace. Both the tavern and the lounge draw lots of locals, making a stop here even more interesting for us visitors. Guest rooms are beautifully done-up, and hand-woven Avoca bedspreads are a nice touch. All have private bath, telephone, radio, and TV. The rather modest rates (for this type of accommodation) include a full Irish breakfast and run £19.50 ($34.25) single, £34 ($59.50) double, from May through December, lower from January to May. Highly recommended, both for the high standards and for the O'Neills.

The **Bayview Hotel,** Portballintrae, Bushmills, Co. Antrim (tel. Bushmills 026/57-31453), is another small hotel whose hospitality and homey comfort seems to come from another era. It faces the seafront, and is a great favorite with locals, who regularly patronize both its Porthole Lounge Bar and Watch House Restaurant. In a brilliant concept of renovation, the hotel's owners have given all guest rooms a view of the curving bayfront, and all are nicely furnished and decorated. Bed-and-breakfast rates begin at £26 ($45.50) for singles, £36 ($63) for doubles.

The old-fashioned, country-Victorian-style **Causeway Hotel,** Bushmills, Co. Antrim (tel. 026/57-31210 or 57-31226), is the perfect place for an overnight stop to see the Giant's Causeway—it's just next door, a very short walk to the Visitor's Centre. It was built in 1836 to accommodate visitors who arrived back then by jaunting car. In recent years it operated only as a bar and restaurant until Stanley Armstrong and his wife, Doreen, set about to restore it as a functioning hotel, which opened its doors in May 1988. Doreen has done most of the decorating and made exhaustive searches to find Victorian furniture in keeping with the hotel's history. An especially appealing room is the upstairs Resident Lounge, with its sweeping views of the sea and the causeway. Its 16 bedrooms vary in size and décor, but all come with private baths, tea and coffee makers, telephones, radios, and TVs. There's a large public bar and a dining room overlooking the sea. Bed-and-breakfast rates are £23 ($40.25) single, £40 ($70) double, and there are excellent dinner, bed, and breakfast rates, as well as a mini-weekend special (two nights dinner, bed, and breakfast).

Although **O'Malley's Edgewater Hotel,** 88 Strand Rd., Portstewart, Co.

Londonderry (tel. 026/583-3314 or 583-3688), is actually not in County Antrim, its proximity to the Giant's Causeway (only nine miles away) and the Causeway Coast makes it a good touring base for this part of Northern Ireland. This is the kind of old-style hotel with a homey atmosphere that you dream of and seldom find. The Michelin-rated hotel is situated right on the beach, with a panoramic view of the Donegal Hills. All bedrooms have private bathrooms and are fitted out with coffee and tea makers, color TVs with video, and direct-dial telephones. Amenities include a games room, sauna, Jacuzzi, and sunbed. Portstewart golf course is only 700 yards from the hotel, and there are five others in the vicinity. Bed-and-breakfast rates are £30 ($52.50) single, £46 ($80.50) double, during summer months; lower in winter. Children under 12 stay free in the room with their parents. Suites are also available.

WHERE TO EAT: When driving the Antrim Coast road, plan to stop for lunch or dinner at the **Londonderry Arms Hotel** in Carnlough (see above). Meals are served in a dining room replete with period pieces, and if you can get a table in the front dining room, you'll have a view of the harbor as you dine. Lunch will run about £7.50 ($13.25), and dinner is about £11 ($19.25).

A good, inexpensive lunch stop as you set out on the County Antrim coastal drive is the **Courtyard Coffee House,** Scotch Quarter, Carrickfergus (tel. 096/03-69881). It's just north of the town hall and library, facing the waterfront. The self-service menu features light lunches such as soup, sandwiches, salad plates, quiche, and pastries for £4 ($7) and under. You can eat in the light, bright indoor room or outside in the inner courtyard. Hours are 9:30 a.m. to 4:30 p.m., and it closes Sunday.

Ballygally Castle Hotel, Ballygally, Co. Antrim (tel. 0574/83212), serves inexpensive bar food from 12:30 to 2:15 p.m. every day but Sunday, and its restaurant features moderately priced lunches those same hours, plus dinners from 6:30 to 9:15 p.m. seven days a week. Very popular with people in the locality are the Saturday-night dinner dances and Sunday high teas (5:30 to 8:15 p.m.).

Between Ballygally and Glenarm on the Shore Road, the **Drumnagreagh Hotel,** Shore Road, Glenarm (tel. 057/484651) serves moderately priced lunch and dinner in its Grill Room seven days a week. A good stop on your way to the Giants Causeway via the Glens of Antrim.

Begin or end your visit to the Giant's Causeway with a meal at the **Causeway Hotel,** Giant's Causeway, Bushmills, Co. Antrim (tel. 026/57-31226). Service is available in the bar, as well as in the restaurant, and prices are moderate. Open daily.

The award-winning **Ramore Wine Bar and Restaurant,** The Harbour, Portrush, Co. Antrim (tel. 0265/824313), offers excellent value, with full lunches of seafood, lamb cutlets with tarragon, duck breast with honey, filet or sirloin steak, and suprême of chicken for prices of £6 ($10.50) to £8 ($14), as well as less expensive burgers, sandwiches, etc. Needless to say, there's an extensive wine list, and you can order by the glass or the bottle. Hours for the Wine Bar are noon to 3 p.m. Monday through Saturday. The upstairs restaurant (with higher prices in a more elegant setting) serves from 6 to 10 p.m. Tuesday through Saturday.

Also in Portrush, **O'Neill's,** 36 Ballyreagh Rd., Portrush, Co. Antrim (tel. 0265/822435), serves an excellent carvery for £7 ($12.25) for the full meal, £4 ($7) for the main course only. Hours are 5 to 10 p.m. Monday through Saturday and 12:30 to 3 p.m. and 5 to 10 p.m. on Sunday.

For pub grub, stop in Portballintrae at the **Bayview Hotel's Porthole Lounge Bar** and lunch with the locals.

In Portstewart, **O'Malley's Edgewater Hotel,** 88 Strand Rd. (tel.

026/583-2224 or 583-3688), serves excellent lunches and dinners in a glass-walled dining room overlooking the sea and a curving beach. Prices run about the same as at the Londonderry Arms above. Open daily.

In Portrush, **The Harbour Bar** is a good place for a before- or after-dinner libation. It sits on the wharf overlooking the boat-filled harbor, and it's mostly locals you'll find in the plain, old-style bar. Very Irish.

THINGS TO SEE AND DO: County Antrim has perhaps the largest concentration of sightseeing attractions of any of the six counties.

Americans will be interested to know that the following presidents had County Antrim roots: Andrew Jackson's parents came from Carrickfergus; Andrew Johnson's grandfather was from Larne; Chester A. Arthur's father was born near Ballymena; Grover Cleveland's grandfather was a County Antrim merchant; William McKinley's great-great-grandfather emigrated from Conagher, near Ballymoney; and Theodore Roosevelt's maternal ancestors were from Larne. Quite an impressive score for one county!

In **Carrickfergus,** there's another American connection: Commander John Paul Jones stood offshore just below **Carrickfergus Castle** in 1778 in the *Ranger* and mounted an attack on the British *Drake* that ended with his capture of the larger vessel. The massive castle dates from the late 12th and early 13th centuries, there's an interesting museum inside, with a small admission charge. In June, medieval banquets are held in the castle (call 096/03-63604 for reservations), and in July there's a medieval fair and crafts market. Hours are 10 a.m. to 6 p.m. Monday through Saturday and on Sunday from 2 to 6 p.m. In winter, 4 p.m. is closing time.

The ancestral home of Andrew ("Old Hickory") Jackson, U.S. president from 1829 to 1837, was just beyond the north end of Carrickfergus's seafront promenade at Boneybefore, a site now marked by a plaque. Just a few yards away, the Andrew Jackson Centre gives an insight into the life of his forebears.

Driving north from Carrickfergus, you'll pass through—and slowly, please, so you won't miss one whit of some pretty gorgeous scenery—the nine **Glens of Antrim,** which open to the sea.

The **Giant's Causeway,** east of Portrush, is much more impressive when you walk its basalt columns (there are some 37,000!) than any photograph can possibly convey. How they came to be packed so tightly together that they form a sort of bridge from the shoreline out into the sea, submerge, and then surface on the Hebrides island of Staffa, is a matter of conjecture. Scientists will tell you unequivocally that they're the result of a massive volcanic eruption about 60 million years ago, when molten lava cooled and formed into geometric shapes. But, after all, what do *they* know—as far as the *Irish* are concerned, the causeway would still be above water all the way across had it not been for a ferocious tiff between the Ulster giant, Finn MacCoul, and his Scottish counterpart, Finn Gall. You see, it was the Ulsterman who built the causeway in the first place, and when he went home to rest up a bit from his labors, the wily Scotsman tripped across, club in hand, to catch his foe unawares. Now, *Mrs.* MacCoul was busy at the hearth with the dinner, and when Finn Gall burst into her kitchen and demanded to know if the sleeping giant were her husband, she—in a master stroke of quick thinking—assured him, "Ooh, no, sor, 'tis only ma wee babe." Well, the very thought of what the father of such a gigantic babe must be like put such a fright into the Scotsman that he hightailed it back across the water, destroying the causeway behind him to keep Finn MacCoul in Ireland where he belonged. Choose your own version (I, personally, favor the giants!), but don't miss a stop by this curiosity. It's free, and there's even a minibus (with a very small fare) down to the bottom of the cliff for those who don't care to make the short walk.

If you happen along the Antrim Coast Drive between May and September, stop about five miles northwest of Ballycastle to take a look at the **Carrick-a-Rede Rope Bridge.** It's strung across a 25-yard chasm to connect two clifftops that are separated by seas too treacherous to be crossed any other way. If you're not the faint-hearted type, you'll not be charged to cross over the wooden planks as you grip the rope handrails. There's a roadside car park from which you walk to the bridge.

Just east of Portrush, look for a rocky headland crowned by the great lump of ruined **Dunluce Castle.** Some say its name means "mermaid's fort," and they might well be right—there's a deep cave that penetrates the rock on which the castle sits at the sea's edge. There are too many tales and legends surrounding Dunluce to recount here, but you can read them in the official guide available at the entrance. From April through September you can visit the castle between the hours of 10 a.m. and 7 p.m. Monday through Saturday, from 2 to 7 p.m. on Sunday. During other months, closing time is 4 p.m. and all day Monday.

A short detour off the coast road will take you to the village of Bushmills and the oldest licensed distillery in the world. The **Old Bushmills Distillery** is a fascinating place, and still turning out "the wine of the country" after all these centuries. People in Northern Ireland will urge you to try Black Bush—do! To see a marvelous exhibition of its history and follow a guided tour through the distilling process, book with one of the free tours every Monday through Thursday morning and afternoon or Friday morning. There are sometimes schedule changes, however, so it's best to phone ahead to make sure (tel. Bushmills 026/57-31521).

The farmhouse from which President Chester Arthur's father left for America in 1816 is at **Dreen,** near Cullybackey, Ballymena, and the white-washed thatched cottage is worth a drive through beautiful countryside to meet the delightful people who maintain it for visitors like you and me. They'll greet you Monday through Friday from April through September from 2 to 6 p.m.

In the town of **Antrim,** look for the perfectly preserved round tower that is 49 feet around and over 90 feet tall.

If you're an island lover, you will want to reserve an overnight to spend on **Rathlin Island,** a rugged outpost off the Antrim coast that is Ireland's largest inhabited island. It has a fascinating history, and can only be reached via the mail boat that makes trips daily May through August, leaving Ballycastle Harbour about 10:30 a.m. and not returning to the mainland until 9 a.m. the following day. The 35-minute open motorboat trip costs £4 ($7) round trip. The island's only accommodation is the **Rathlin Guest House,** The Quay, Rathlin, Co. Antrim (tel. Rathlin 63917), run by Mrs. Kay McCurdy. Bed-and-breakfast rate is £9 ($15.75), with the evening meal costing £6 ($10.50). There are marvelous cliff walks, magnificent views of Ireland's northern coast, and the fun of topping off the day at the one pub in the company of some of the 100 inhabitants.

2. COUNTY ARMAGH

ACCOMMODATIONS: *Note: Prices listed below are those in effect in 1989—expect them to be higher in 1990.*

A Guesthouse

For bed-and-breakfast accommodations in Northern Ireland's smallest county, try **Mary and Michael Murphy's guesthouse,** 63 Drumcairn Rd., Armagh, Co. Armagh (tel. Armagh 0861/525074). It's about a mile and a half from town, set on 16 pleasant rural acres. The modern bungalow is centrally heated, and all the attractive guest rooms are on the ground level and have handbasins. Mary can arrange for a babysitter. Rates are £10 ($17.50) single, £20 ($35) double.

A Farmhouse

In Portadown, **Redbrick House,** Corbrackey Lane, Portadown BT62 1PQ (tel. Portadown 0762/335268), is three miles out of town and, with enough advance notice, Mrs. Moreen Stephenson, the accommodating hostess, will arrange to meet first-time visitors. At this country house, guests will enjoy traditional home-cooking, free laundry, and a huge welcome. The centrally heated modern bungalow counts one large family room among its nice guest rooms, all of which are on the ground floor. Rates are £12 ($21) per person, £16 ($28) for bed, breakfast, and dinner.

WHERE TO EAT: In Armagh town, the **Archway,** 5 Hartford Pl., has inexpensive set lunches as well as pastries and light snacks. Hours are 10 a.m. to 5 p.m. Tuesday through Saturday. **Spider's Rest,** 2 Scotch St., serves sandwiches from 12:30 to 2:30 p.m. every day except Sunday. Excellent evening meals are available at the **Gallery Restaurant,** Ulster Inn, 147 Railway St. (tel. Armagh 0861/522103), with à la carte prices for a four-course meal running from £7.50 ($13.15) to £11 ($19.25). Hours are 7 to 9:45 p.m., and it's fully licensed.

In Portadown, look for inexpensive lunches at **Allen's Coffee House,** West Street, and the **Crown Bar,** Woodhouse Street.

THINGS TO SEE AND DO: Armagh is Northern Ireland's most interesting cathedral town, with imposing edifices of both the Catholic and Protestant faiths facing each other from their respective hilltops. According to a tablet on the north side of the **Church of Ireland cathedral** (which was restored in the 18th and 19th centuries), this is the final resting place of Brian Boru. Red hats of every cardinal archbishop of Armagh and medallions for each of Ireland's saints are part of what you'll find in the Gothic-style **Catholic cathedral,** which dates from the mid-1800s.

On **The Mall** in Armagh town, there's a fine small **museum** that holds an exceptionally good collection of prehistoric relics, historical costumes, and natural-history exhibits as well as an art gallery. It's free, and hours are 10 a.m. to 1 p.m. and 2 to 5 p.m. Monday through Saturday. Also on the Mall is the **Royal Irish Fusiliers Regimental Museum,** housed in the Sovereign's House and open weekdays from 10 a.m. to 12:30 p.m. and 2 to 4:30 p.m.

About two miles outside Newry on the Newtownhamilton road, there's an interesting 18th-century thatched manor house. **Derrymore House** is reputed to have been the setting for the Act of Union between Great Britain and Ireland, and you can go through the house by calling ahead (tel. Saintfield 0238/510721) for an appointment.

3. COUNTY DOWN

ACCOMMODATIONS: During summer months, many accommodations in County Down offer special-interest (fishing, golf, etc.) "Super Summer Saver" midweek and weekend rates. For details, contact the Tourist Officer, Down District Council, Strangford Road, Downpatrick, Co. Down (tel. Downpatrick 4331).

In addition to the County Down accommodations listed in Chapter XXIX in Belfast, the farmhouses below are highly recommended.

Note: Prices listed below are those in effect in 1989—expect them to be higher in 1990.

Farmhouses

Just on the edge of Newcastle (off the Bryansford–Newcastle road, the B180), you'll find the modern bungalow presided over by Mrs. Jean Hart, **Grasmere,** 16 Marguerite Park, Bryansford Road, Newcastle BT33 0PE (tel. Newcastle 039/67-22450). This charming lady has two double rooms and one single, all with handbasins. Surrounded by green fields, Grasmere is only a ten-minute walk from the beach. Bed-and-breakfast rate is £10 ($17.50).

Mrs. Margaret Deering, **Ballycastle House,** 20 Mountstewart Rd., Newtownards, Co. Down BT22 2AL (tel. Greyabbey 024/774357), is a friendly, generous woman and her home is a beautiful 300-year-old farmhouse, which has been recently and elegantly refurbished. The house is centrally heated, and washing and ironing facilities are available for guests to use. There are four comfortable bedrooms, one of which has private facilities. The rate is £11 ($19.25) for bed-and-breakfast and there is a reduction for children. Open all year.

Mrs. Joan McKee, **Beechhill,** Loughries Road, Newtownards, Co. Down, BT23 3RN (tel. 024/817526), is the hospitable hostess of this country guesthouse located in a pretty country setting. The house is centrally heated and an evening meal is available with advance notice. There are washing and ironing facilities and five attractive guest bedrooms, one of which is a family room. The rate for bed-and-breakfast is £10 ($17.50) and there is a reduction for children. Open year round.

A Hotel

In the pleasant seaside resort of Kilkeel, the **Kilmorey Arms Hotel,** Greencastle Street, Kilkeel (tel. Kilkeel 62220 or 62801), is a delightful small inn, with the sort of homey atmosphere that draws Irish families back year after year. Its attractive public rooms are much favored by people in the town, and you're likely to find Miss Hopper, the friendly manager, scurrying around attending to last-minute details for a local wedding dinner or some other function. There's a nice cocktail lounge, and the flagstone-floored public bar is full of character, both from its relic-hung walls and from the faces passing the time of day at the bar (if you're just passing through Kilkeel, do stop by this interesting bar for a pint). There are 18 nice bedrooms, all with private bath. Rates are £15 ($26.25) single, £29 ($50.75) double.

READERS' ACCOMMODATION SELECTION: "Irene and Robert Adair, **Wyncrest Guest House,** 30 Main Rd., Ballymartin, Kilkeel, Co. Down (tel. 069/37-63012), work hard to make Americans feel welcome. The days we have spent in Northern Ireland have been delightful and very safe. Too bad more Americans don't visit and enjoy as we have" (G. and P. Curten, Austin, Tex.).

WHERE TO EAT: **Rea's,** 78 Market St., Downpatrick (tel. 2017), is an old-style place, with two small front rooms crammed full of an eclectic collection of old objects (like the pottery bottle that was once used to hold Guinness, a marble for its stopper). Second, it always has the contented hum of a good crowd—many of them obviously regulars—enjoying good company and good food. There's a more modern dining room back of those character-filled front rooms, and an almost-formal dining room upstairs (fireplace, gilt mirrors, etc.). Fresh seafood is the specialty here, and dinner prices run £10 ($17.50) to £15 ($26.25). Lunch is served from noon to 3 p.m. Monday through Saturday; dinner, from 6:30 to 9:30 p.m. Wednesday through Saturday.

Just offshore (connected by a causeway) on Skettrick Island, **Whiterock,** Co. Down, Daft Eddies (tel. 541615), serves an excellent buffet lunch from

12:45 to 2 p.m. Monday through Saturday all year for as little as £3 ($5.25) to £5 ($8.75). À la carte dinners feature seafood, local meats, and excellent steaks at prices of £5 ($8.75) to £10 ($17.50) from 7:30 to 9:30 p.m.

For superior pub grub, stop in the **Primrose Bar,** 30 Main St., Ballynahinch. It's known locally for its steak casseroles and open-face prawn sandwiches. Other offerings include fresh trout, salmon, and a variety of salads. There's always a nice fire blazing, and as a Northern Ireland friend assured me, "The crack [talk] is always good." Hours are 12:30 to 11 p.m. Monday through Saturday and 12:30 to 2:30 p.m. on Sunday.

THINGS TO SEE AND DO: County Down has been immortalized by William Percy French for its Mountains of Mourne which "sweep down to the sea." One of the places you can best see that sweep is the resort town of **Newcastle,** which curves around a gorgeous bay with a wide, golden strand. (A little trivia item: Actress Greer Garson was born in Castlelarne.)

A delightful County Down exploration takes in the **Ards Peninsula,** 23 miles of unspoiled countryside dotted with picture-postcard villages, windmills, and ancient ring forts. Drive out to the little 19th-century village of **Kearney** and you drive back through the centuries. There's a car-ferry that crosses from **Portaferry** to **Strangford** in about four minutes and lets you look straight out to sea (if, that is, you look quick enough).

St. Patrick's first stone church is thought to have been erected on the site of the present-day **Down Cathedral** in Downpatrick, and a stone in the churchyard purports to be his gravestone (it's the one under a gigantic weeping willow tree), as well as that of St. Brigid and of St. Columba. The fact that those assertions are a matter of much dispute does little to dispel the sense of the continuity of the centuries when you stand on the peaceful hillside site—certainly it would take a heart of stone not to believe that they could be true!

The **Newry Arts Centre and Museum,** 1a Bank Parade (tel. Newry 0693/ 61244), features exhibitions of ancient archeological items, folk art, and pottery as well as touring exhibitions of interest. There's no admission charge, and hours are 11 a.m. to 4:30 p.m. Monday through Friday.

Near Strangford Village, **Castle Ward** is a fascinating house that's a sort of architectural hodgepodge, part pseudo-Gothic and part classical. The estate, administered by the National Trust, sits on the shores of Strangford Lough and includes formal gardens, a Victorian laundry and theater in the stableyard, and a sawmill. A tea room is open in the stableyard from April through October. The house is also open from April through October for a small admission charge; the grounds are open to the public without charge from dawn to sunset daily year round.

Bang in the middle of County Down, **Ballynahinch** might have been the setting for a dramatic change in the course of Irish history had not the 7,000 United Irishmen (led by a linen draper from Lisburn named Henry Munroe) been roundly defeated in their battle to take the town. The bloody battle raged the length of Ballynahinch's broad main street until, in the end, the royal forces were the victors. Munroe was executed, as was a young Presbyterian girl named Betsy Gray who had seized an old, rusty sword, mounted a horse, and joined in the fray. It was a last, desperate stand for the United Irishmen, and you might give a tip of the hat to their memory as you pass through.

4. COUNTY FERMANAGH

ACCOMMODATIONS: *Note: Prices listed below are those in effect in 1989— expect them to be higher in 1990.*

A Farmhouse

About 20 miles from Enniskillen and 12 miles from good beaches, **Manville House,** Aughnablaney, Letter (tel. Kesh 036/56-31668), is the centrally heated, lakeside home of Mrs. Pearl Graham. There are marvelous views of Lough Erne and the Sligo Mountains, and there's good fishing right at hand. All the well-appointed guest rooms have handbasins. The rate for bed-and-breakfast is £11 ($19.25). To reach Manville House, take the A47 from Kesh and turn right at the signpost for Letter.

Self-Catering

The **Carlton Cottages,** Belleek, Co. Fermanagh (tel. 036/565282), are well-planned three-bedroom cottages set in wooded grounds on the banks of the River Erne. It's hard to imagine a more beautiful setting, and each cottage is fitted with twin beds, bath and shower, fully equipped kitchen, and a large lounge with an open-hearth fireplace. Patio doors open to the outside. Seasonal rates range from £140 ($245) to £275 ($481) per week, and there are special weekend rates available. Highly recommended.

WHERE TO EAT: The **Encore Steak House,** Main Street, Ballinamallard (tel. Ballinamallard 606), is just a short drive from Enniskillen. There's an air of intimacy in the beautifully appointed, two-centuries-old building, and the menu features steak (what else!), duck, trout, and other seafood as well as a very good beef curry. Table d'hôte dinner prices run about £10 ($17.50), and hours are 5 to 11 p.m.; closed Monday. Definitely worth a detour to have dinner here.

In Bellanaleck, **The Sheelin** (tel. Florencecourt 232) is a small, picturesque house, and dining there is like eating with friends in a family dining room. Open from 10 a.m. to 9:30 p.m. Monday through Saturday and 1:30 to 6:30 p.m. on Sunday, the Sheelin offers morning coffee, lunches, afternoon teas (all at moderate prices) and, once a week, usually Saturday, gourmet dinners (pricey).

THINGS TO SEE AND DO: The **River Erne** and its **Upper and Lower Loughs** are tourist centers for County Fermanagh. The river and the loughs are dotted with interesting and historical islands, and a holiday cruising their waters is a very special experience. You can book a variety of watery accommodations in Enniskillen, and the **Lakeland Visitor Centre,** Shore Road, Enniskillen (tel. Enniskillen 0365/23110), publishes a detailed *Holidays Afloat and Ashore* booklet with illustrations of many of the cruisers available.

To learn more about this fascinating part of Northern Ireland (some of the mountainy country around the loughs is quite mysterious and wild, and there are historic monastic ruins on many of the islands), go by the Visitor Centre and browse through the mountain of literature they can provide to help you plan an itinerary. If possible, try to get on the water, even if only for a brief time.

In Enniskillen, the **Royal Inniskilling Fusiliers Regimental Museum** and the **County Museum** are in the **Castle Keep,** Castle Barracks (tel. Enniskillen 0365/25050). The castle keep dates from the 16th century, was built by the Maguires, and was remodeled in the 18th century. The Regimental Museum features battle trophies of the Dragoons and Fusiliers from the Napoleonic Wars, arms, and a host of colorful uniforms. In the County Museum, the history of the county is traced through archeological relics from the Middle Stone Age to the end of the early Christian period. Hours are 10 a.m. to 12:30 p.m. and 2 to 5 p.m. daily (weekends only in winter), and there's a small admission charge. Hours are subject to change, so call ahead.

On the shores of Lough Coole, about a mile and a half southeast of

Enniskillen, **Castle Coole** is a splendid neoclassical mansion set in its own parkland. The house is open from April through September every day except Friday, from 2 to 6 p.m.

Another stately home worth a visit is **Florence Court,** about eight miles southwest of Enniskillen. The three-story 18th-century mansion has pavilions on each side, connected to the house by open, arched walkways. The woodland setting is as romantic as the house, with a landscaped "pleasure garden" and walled garden. Open from noon to 6 p.m. every day except Tuesday, April through September.

Telephone ahead to arrange a guided tour of the **Belleek** chinaware factory (tel. 0365/65501). It's not only interesting, but fun—the skilled workers always welcome a bit of a chat with visitors. Tours are available on weekdays only.

One of the most awesome sights in all of Europe is the **Marble Arch caves,** Marbank Scenic Loop Road, Florencecourt, Co. Fermanagh (tel. 036/582777), signposted off the Enniskillen–Sligo road (the A509). Your underground boat travels through this vast cave system, through a spectacular underground world of rivers, waterfalls, lakes, lofty chambers, and winding passages. It's chilly down there, if not downright cold, so bring along a sweater, plus good walking shoes with low heels for dealing with uneven surfaces. Open from 11 a.m. to 7 p.m. every day (till 7:30 p.m. from June to August). Adults pay £2.50 ($4.50); children, £1 ($1.75). However, these hours can vary—best call ahead to be sure the caves are open.

5. COUNTY LONDONDERRY

See Chapter XXIX for the city of Londonderry.

ACCOMMODATIONS: *Note: Prices listed below are those in effect in 1989—expect them to be higher in 1990.*

Guesthouses

At **Camus House,** 27 Curragh Rd., Coleraine BT51 3RY, Co. Londonderry (tel. 0265/2982), it's hard to say which is the more attractive, the 1685 country home (overlooking the River Bann) or its owner, vivacious Mrs. Josephine King (known to all and sundry as "Joey"). The gracious old house would be attraction enough on its own, but then there's Joey, who welcomes guests with tea (or something a little stronger) and scones with fresh cream in a cozy sitting room in front of a fieldstone fireplace. The room's warmth is enhanced by lots of wood and the 125 handmade horse brasses that line the walls. Elsewhere, period furnishings are punctuated by comfortable sofas and easy chairs. Bedrooms are beautifully furnished and have handbasins, spacious closets, and lamps placed strategically to give good light for reading. One family room sleeps four, one has three singles, and one has a double bed as well as a single. In the sunny dining room, guests help themselves to fresh fruit and juices, after which they tuck into a hearty Ulster fry of eggs and ham or bacon and wheaten bread. Joey is an avid—and very good!—fisherwoman and will direct her guests to the best spots on the river. Best of all, her bright personality lights up evening gatherings around the fire or early-morning conferences on just how to spend the day. It's no wonder at all that Camus House has won numerous country-house awards and gained a widespread reputation for hospitality. Rates for bed-and-breakfast are £15 ($26.25) single, £25 ($43.75) double. Highest recommendation.

Mrs. Irwin, **Blackheath House,** 112 Killeague Rd., Coleraine, Co. Londonderry, BT51 4HH (tel. Aghadowey 026/585-433), is the hostess of this lovely country house set in rural surroundings and located near an excellent restaurant, although Mrs. Irwin will prepare dinner with advance notice. The house is centrally heated and most rooms have a radio, TV, and telephone. A packed lunch is available should you want it, and washing and ironing facilities are there for guests to use. Five of the six attractive bedrooms have private facilities. The rate for bed-and-breakfast is £25 ($43.75) and dinner costs £11 ($19.25). Open year round. A bit of a Big Splurge, but worth it.

READER'S ACCOMMODATIONS SELECTION: "Every amenity, from good food to entertainment is available at the **Gorteen House Hotel,** 187 Roe Mill Rd., Limavady, Co. Derry (tel. 05047/63333), a mansion of yesteryear brought up-to-date by additions to both sides and back. Superior rooms make the night a comfort to be remembered" (G. W. Howard, Silver Spring, Md.).

THINGS TO SEE AND DO: Go by the **Bellarena Smokery** in Limavady (tel. Limavady 05047/50481), where fish are smoked by traditional methods. It's a good place to buy oak-smoked fish for a picnic farther along the road. The smokery is open Monday through Friday from 9:30 a.m. to 4:30 p.m.

6. COUNTY TYRONE

ACCOMMODATIONS: *Note: Prices listed below are those in effect in 1989—expect them to be higher in 1990.*

A Bed-and-Breakfast

The **Grange,** 15 Grange Rd., Ballygawley BT70 (tel. Ballygawley 066/266-8053, or 253-8053 after 6 p.m.), is a charming little cottage that dates back to 1720, but has been thoroughly modernized, even to central heating. Mrs. Lyttle is hostess here, and her attractive guest rooms (one is a family room with private facilities) all have handbasins. Rates are £9.50 ($16.75) single, £18 ($31.50) double.

A Farmhouse

Set on a 150-acre farm, **Greenmount Lodge,** 58 Greenmount Rd., Gortaclare, Omagh BT79 0YE (tel. Fintona 0662/841325), is a large two-story farmhouse with nicely appointed guest rooms. Mrs. Frances Reid, the friendly hostess, is a superb cook and evening meals are a delight. Bed-and-breakfast rates are £9.50 ($16.75) single, £18 ($31.50) double.

A Hotel

Convenience, comfort, and a friendly, accommodating staff make the **Royal Arms Hotel,** Main Street, Omagh, Co. Tyrone (tel. 0662/42119, 3262, or 44860), an ideal base. Family-owned and -operated, it exudes a homey warmth, and there's an old-world charm about its Tavern Lounge and the adjoining dining room. There's also an attractive lounge, a coffeeshop, a hairdressing salon, and a travel agency. All 21 bedrooms are nicely appointed and comfortably furnished, and all have a direct-dial telephone, TV, radio, and private bath. Rates for bed-and-breakfast start at £17 ($29.75) single, £35.50 ($62.25) double.

A Big Splurge

Augher Castle (Spur Royal Castle), Augher, Co. Tyrone BT77 0BE (tel. 066/25-48589), was built in 1610 by the Earl of Londonderry and down through the centuries has been a gracious private residence. Now owned by Maureen and Joe Beattie, it welcomes paying guests with the hospitality of their own home. This engaging couple has furnished the castle as befits its titled history, with antiques, historic and whimsical artifacts, paintings, etc. With scarcely a ripple on the face of all its antiquity, they have installed modern bathrooms and a marvelous country kitchen looking out over lawns that slope down to the private lake. A log fire adds even more warmth to the elegant drawing room, where before-dinner drinks are served, and the dining room is nothing short of baronial, with a mammoth fireplace around which guests often cluster for after-dinner libations following a leisurely dinner prepared from the freshest ingredients and perfectly served.

The five spacious bedrooms are furnished with antiques and interesting bits and pieces you'd expect to find in just this sort of country-gentleman residence. There are even real Irish linens on the beds, and each bedroom has good views of the grounds.

The castle is set in wooded parklands, with Joe's horses grazing out front (he can arrange riding, as well as hunting with local hunt clubs in season), and fishing is good in the lake out back, which has become a virtual wildlife refuge. The Beatties are very knowledgeable of the historic Clogher Valley in which Augher is located and are delighted to direct guests to sightseeing, which includes several National Trust properties, as well as historic and prehistoric sites. A special attraction, though not in any guidebook, is Jimmy Johnson's Pub in the village, a friendly and colorful gathering place.

Bed-and-breakfast rates are £35 ($61.25) per person, and dinner (highly recommended) is £18 ($31.50). This one is a charmer, as are its owners!

WHERE TO EAT: In Omagh, the **Mellon Country Inn,** 134 Beltany Rd. (tel. Newtownstewart 06626/61224), is only a mile from the Ulster-American Folk Park and offers inexpensive meals all through the day. Morning coffee is served from 11:30 a.m. to 12:30 p.m.; snacks, grills, and a table d'hôte menu from 12:30 to 2:30 p.m.; hot or cold snacks from 2:30 to 5:30 p.m.; high tea from 5:30 to 7:30 p.m.; and extensive à la carte or table d'hôte menus from 5:30 to 9:30 p.m. The food is good, and prices reasonable.

THINGS TO SEE AND DO: The **Ulster-American Folk Park** is an outdoor museum which has as its main theme the history of 18th- and 19th-century emigration from Ulster to North America. Life in rural Ulster and in the New World is re-created through exhibits that include the ancestral home of the Mellon family of Pittsburgh, whose forefathers were from Ulster and who endowed the folk park. There's a pioneer farm and gallery exhibitions. Hours are 11 a.m. to 6:30 p.m. daily in summer, weekdays only from 10:30 a.m. to 5 p.m. other months, and there's a small admission charge.

CHAPTER XXXI

P.S.—MORE BIG SPLURGES

□ □ □

Yes, this *is* a book about budget travel. And, yes, budget travel in Ireland *is* a fun way to go. But as I have also said earlier in this book, you will find the same Irish friendliness and charm in large, luxury establishments as in the bed-and-breakfast homes and farmhouses so dear to our budgeteering hearts. And which of us has not yearned, at one time or another, to indulge a penchant for—as the Irish would say—"upmarket" accommodations, or to be pampered over dinners in posh restaurants.

So for those of you who may have won the Irish Sweepstakes, inherited a fortune, or simply saved enough to forget the budget (be it for only a day or for your entire trip), I'm adding this postscript of additional places in which your "splurge" dollars will buy as good value in the upper range as your budget dollars will in my foregoing recommendations. Together with those listed in earlier chapters, they should provide you a luxury pad in just about any region in Ireland. All this is organized first by region, and then by county or city within this chapter.

As you read through the following, bear in mind that in many cases (though not all, by any means), I'm talking not just Big Splurge, but BIG Splurge!

THE EASTERN REGION (COUNTIES DUBLIN, WICKLOW, LOUTH, KILDARE, AND MEATH)

---

1. COUNTY DUBLIN

ACCOMMODATIONS: The **Westbury Hotel,** Grafton Street, Dublin 2 (tel. 01/791122), is not only Dublin's newest luxury hotel, but it's one of the city's most convenient. Tucked away just off Grafton Street right in the heart of the city center, it is also without doubt one of the most beautiful. Its white marble entrance leads into a lower foyer carpeted in pale pink, and that same Navan/Youghal carpet leads up a sweeping staircase of cream marble and brass to the upper foyer, lobby, dining room and other public spaces. Soft shades of peach, lots of marble, walnut panels, peach silk wall coverings, oil paintings, valuable artifacts, wing-back Chinese Chippendale chairs mixed companionably with modern furniture—all are tastefully combined to create an atmosphere of spacious elegance. The upper foyer Terrace provides soft music throughout the evening and for afternoon tea; the Russell Room's peach-and-mint-green décor is the setting for fine dining; the Seafood Restaurant Bar features shellfish from Dublin Bay; and the Polo Bar is hung wall-to-wall with hunting prints.

Guest rooms and suites all are furnished in mahogany and brass, have canopies over beds, marble bathrooms, built-in hairdryers, and bathrobes for guests. They're also among the most spacious I've encountered in Ireland, and there are even some suites with Jacuzzis. Rates start at IR£85 ($136) single, IR£110 ($176) double, plus 15% service charge.

For many international travelers, the **Shelbourne Hotel,** St. Stephen's Green, Dublin 2 (tel. 01/766471), is synonymous with Dublin. The lovely old red-and-white brick hotel has been an Irish "home" for heads of state, entertainment celebrities, and literary lights (Thackeray praised it highly in his account of an 1843 visit) from the time it opened its doors in 1824. Its lobby and Horseshoe Bar continue to be among the city's most popular gathering spots for Dubliners as well as visitors. There's an old-world elegance and graciousness about the public rooms, and its haute cuisine restaurant is just the place for one of those "pampered" dinners. A recent major refurbishing put a new gleam to guest rooms whose furnishings differ in décor from period pieces to the poshest modern. Rates for such luxury range from IR£95 ($152) and up for a single, IR£140 ($224) and up for a double, with a one-third reduction for children and a 15% service charge. For a superb view of St. Stephen's Green, ask for a room on the front.

Buswell's Hotel, 25 Molesworth St., Dublin 2 (tel. 01/764013), is a Dublin institution. Over the years Buswell's has hosted such Irish notables as Sir Roger Casement and Eamon de Valera. Located just up from the Dail, it offers center-city convenience, superb accommodations at reasonable rates and a dining room / pub lunch / drinking clientele liberally sprinkled with politicians, leading Dublin business people and colorful personalities. And small wonder, for since 1925 the hotel has been owned and operated by the Duff family with the sort of personal involvement that has led to possibly the lowest staff turnover in the city and an enviable guest list of "regulars" who return year after year. More and more conferences are being held here, also, with the addition of several attractive meeting rooms.

Georgian elegance surrounds you in the lobby, the Leinster Room Restaurant and the Georgian Bar, while the Tudor-style Molesworth Cellar Bar offers conviviality along with excellent lunch and evening snack selections. As for guest rooms, all 70 come equipped with private bath and shower, tea and coffee makers, hairdryers, direct-dial telephone, radio, and color TV. Best of all, few are a "standard" size and shape, and each is individually decorated—there are quaint, old-fashioned rooms up under the eaves and others that are brightly modern. Rates run IR£45 ($72) single, IR£70 ($112) double, and IR£81 ($129.50) triple, with special winter weekend offers at considerable discounts.

A great favorite with Americans is **Jurys Hotel,** Pembroke Road, Ballsbridge, Dublin 4 (tel. 01/605000). It's very near the American Embassy, and a long walk or short bus ride from the city center. While in many respects its exterior resembles luxury hotels around the world (not much character to the straight up-and-down concrete-and-glass structure), inside there are delightful touches of a distinctive Irish flavor, such as the Dubliner Bar in the lobby (which serves an excellent, moderately priced lunch). A glass-roofed pavilion holds lounges, a sunken bar, indoor/outdoor pool, and a quality seafood restaurant. Jurys Embassy garden restaurant is a favorite for lunch and dinner among the city's business people and diplomats, and its Coffee Dock Grill serves moderately priced meals and snacks (as well as wine) 23 hours a day (5 to 6 a.m. is when it's closed). And during summer months its huge ballroom is the setting for Jurys

Irish Cabaret, one of the longest running in the country. Every conceivable convenience for travelers has been provided, with a car-rental desk, airline desk, same-day laundry and dry cleaning, beauty salon, barbershop, boutique, and newsstand.

Prints of Old Dublin are hung in the beautifully appointed guest rooms, which all have direct-dial telephones, TV, radio, and private bath. There's a comfortable and attractive seating area in each. Rates: IR£75 ($120) to IR£79 ($126.50) single, IR£82 ($131.25) to IR£88 ($140.75) double, with a one-third discount for children from 4 to 12 and no charge for those under 4. Service charge is 12½%.

Also in the embassy area, the **Berkeley Court,** Landsdowne Road, Ballsbridge, Dublin 4 (tel. 01/601711), sits in four acres of beautifully landscaped grounds. Pampering begins the minute you drive up to its awning-covered car porch, where you're protected from inclement weather by an enclosure. The elegant lobby features marble pillars, a fountain, wall hangings, impressive antique pieces that include an 18th-century Kingwood marquetry bombo commode, lots of plants, and luxurious Youghal carpeting. There's a lovely lobby bar replete with wood paneling, etched glass panels, and cane-backed chairs, and a gourmet, international cuisine restaurant done in the formal, Louis XIV style. Guest rooms are a bit on the small side, but nicely appointed and decorated, with half-canopies over the beds. TVs come with remote controls to be operated from bed, and telephones are all direct-dial. Needless to say, each room has its own private bath. Rates begin at IR£85 ($136) single, IR£112 ($179.25) double, with one-third off for children, and a 15% service charge.

RESTAURANTS: First of all, review the Big Splurges recommended in Chapter VI. These will provide a wider choice for luxury dining.

The **Lord Edward,** 23 Christchurch Pl. (tel. 01/542420), has already been recommended as an exceptionally good pub-grub source in Dublin. But for a memorable seafood lunch or dinner, make your way to the small upstairs restaurant, with a stop at the middle-floor bar where you imbibe before a glowing fireplace in a white-stucco-walled room with beamed ceiling. The cozy, bay-windowed dining room one floor above is a haven of soft lights, velvet chairs, and intimacy, with seating for only 36 diners. Relaxed elegance is the tone, with expert service and a menu that can offer as many as eight different prawn dishes and main courses you'll know are the freshest possible, since the knowledgeable and caring proprietors make shopping forays twice daily—once for lunch and again for dinner. There's a wide range of specialty coffees, including Calypso (with Tía Maria), Cossack (with vodka) and one of Dublin's best Irish coffees. Lunch hours are 12:30 to 2:30 p.m. Tuesday through Friday, and dinner is from 6 to 10:45 p.m. Tuesday through Saturday. For a five-course dinner, count on spending about IR£25 ($40) without wine. You can raise or lower that estimate from the extensive à la carte menu, and there are set dinners at IR£12.50 ($20) and IR£17.50 ($28), but reservations are a must in the popular and highly recommended eatery. Closed Sunday and Monday.

If it's sophisticated French cuisine you yearn for, head for **Le Coq Hardi,** 35 Pembroke Rd., Ballsbridge (tel. 01/689070), where owner-chef John Howard features a blend of haute, bourgeois, and nouvelle cuisine. In the warm, inviting atmosphere of a Georgian house, surrounded by a décor of rosewood and brass, you can choose from such specialties as filet of spring lamb with fresh tomato and tarragon; milk-fed veal with sauce of wild mushrooms, apple brandy, and cream; and a good selection of seafood. The star of the menu is undoubtedly the Coq Hardi (what else!), a mouthwatering breast of chicken stuffed with mashed potato, mushrooms, and secret seasonings, wrapped in bacon, baked and flamed with Irish whiskey at your table. This sort of culinary expertise has won the restaurant several well-deserved awards. With seating for only 45, this is another place where advance booking is absolutely essential. Lunch is served from 12:30 to 3 p.m.; dinner, from 7:30 to 11 p.m. The table d'hôte lunch runs IR£14 ($22.50); a four-course, à la carte dinner will average IR£30 ($48) without wine; and there's a 12½% service charge. It's closed the first two weeks in August, Saturday for lunch, Sunday, and bank holidays. Highest recommendation.

Out in Howth, set right on the edge of Dublin Bay in the old harbormaster's house, the **King Sitric,** East Pier, Howth Harbour (tel. 01/32535 or 326729), is one of the best seafood restaurants in the country. The owner/managers, Joan and Aidan McManus, personally oversee the entire operation, with Joan very much in evidence in the dining room, and Aidan (whose background includes extensive training on the Continent) negotiating seafood purchases directly from the trawlers that put into the harbor. The décor is Georgian, with antique chairs and sofas in the charming two-room lounge. As for the menu, it all depends on the season. Your best bet is to ask the waiter about the day's catch, and from time to time you can expect to see dishes featuring salmon, bass, plaice, turbot, brill, scallops, prawns, and lobster (with more exotic fish depending on just what the trawlers have snared that day). There's lunch at IR£10 ($16) to IR£11.50 ($18.50), a set dinner at IR£18.75 ($30), and an à la carte menu with prices from IR£10 ($16) to IR£16.50 ($26.50). Hours are 12:30 to 2:30 p.m. (weekdays only) and 6:30 to 11 p.m. Monday through Saturday; closed Sunday. Be sure to book ahead.

South of the city, the freshest of seafood is also a specialty of the **Restaurant na Mara,** Marine Road, Dun Laoghaire (tel. 01/806767 or 800509). It's an attractive place with an interesting history that began as the result of a seafood festival a few years back when the Great Southern Hotel was requested to cater a seafood menu in the buffet room of the old railway station. The success of that short-term venture was so great that the Great Southern set about a transformation of the Victorian-style room with its high, vaulted ceiling. Using the softness of salmon-pink walls, turf-brown carpeting, and candlelight, the managers have created a relaxing and inviting restaurant that serves mostly seasonal seafood dishes, with creative cooking turning out such specialties as the popular poached sole filets in white-wine sauce with prawns. Lobster comes in several guises, and *the* dessert in my own humble opinion is an elegant crêpe flambé that serves two. It's fully licensed, with an extensive wine list. Lunch is from 1 to 2:30 p.m., with a set, four-course seafood lunch at IR£12 ($19.25) and up; dinner hours are 7 to 10:30 p.m., with à la carte prices from IR£11 ($17.50) to IR£14 ($22.50). Closed Sunday, Monday, Christmas, and Easter. About 90% of their business comes from locals who eat here regularly, so best to reserve.

2. COUNTY WICKLOW

ACCOMMODATIONS: Just 28 miles from Dublin, **Hunter's Hotel,** Rathnew, Co. Wicklow (tel. 0404/4106), is a lovely old coaching inn situated on the banks of the River Vartry. Its beautifully landscaped gardens have won awards, and they're the perfect place to relax in the late afternoon or early evening. In fine weather, pre-lunch and pre-dinner drinks, as well as afternoon tea, are served in these serene outdoor surroundings. The restaurant is superb (see below) and much patronized by locals and Dubliners. Mrs. Maureen Gelletlie is the fifth generation of her family to own and manage Hunter's, and she takes great pride in seeing to the personal comfort of all the guests. There are only 17 guest rooms, all charmingly decorated in country-house style, and some come with private bath. The rate, which includes breakfast, is IR£23 ($36.75) per person, single or double, with a 25% reduction for children and a 10% service charge.

At the **Old Rectory Country House,** Wicklow town, Co. Wicklow (tel. 0404/67048; or in the U.S. 212/832-2277, or toll free 800/223-6510, 800/223-5077 in the northeastern states), Linda and Paul Saunders welcome guests to their lovely 1870s Greek Revival–style rectory with a complimentary coffee tray with chocolates, tourist information, fresh flowers, and a welcome card. Set in landscaped grounds and gardens, the Old Rectory features Victorian wood paneling, high ceilings, log fires in marble fireplaces, and individually decorated guest rooms with private bath facilities, tea and coffee trays, radios, stationery, and assorted toiletries. Your full breakfast can be of the Irish, Scottish, or Swiss variety, and is accompanied by *The Irish Times*—it's even possible to have breakfast served in bed! Evening meals here have gained the Saunders an enviable reputation (see below). Dublin is only an hour's drive away, and County Wicklow's many sightseeing attractions are right at hand, including Glendalough, Avoca, and no fewer than five Heritage properties (stately homes, gardens, museums, etc.). Golf and riding are nearby, and Leopardstown racecourse is only 25 miles away. Bed-and-breakfast rates are IR£32 ($51.25) per person sharing. Open April through October.

RESTAURANTS: In Wicklow town, the **Old Rectory Country House** (tel. 0404/2048) is an 1870s, Georgian-style rectory that has blossomed as one of County Wicklow's premier eateries under the loving guidance of Paul and Linda Saunders. Set in its own gardens on the edge of town, the house exudes tranquil elegance, with spacious public rooms, high ceilings, and cheerful log fires. Dinner is served by candlelight, with Linda in the kitchen and Paul attending to the very personal service in the lovely dining room. Fresh seafoods and local produce and meats are the basis of the gourmet menu, and there's a good wine list. There's a table d'hôte dinner for IR£19 ($30.50), and an à la carte menu with selections from IR£15 ($24) to IR£25 ($40). From Sunday to Thursday there's only one seating, at 7:30 p.m.; on Friday and Saturday hours are 7:30 to 9 p.m.; and advance booking is absolutely essential. Accommodations are also available in bright, attractive guest rooms with private bath and telephone, at rates of IR£28 ($44.80) per person for bed-and-breakfast.

Hunter's Hotel, Rathnew (tel. 0404/4106), recommended above, is a terrific place for a Big Splurge meal, with lunch served from 1 to 3 p.m., dinner from 7:30 to 9:30 p.m., and afternoon tea in between. Vegetables come straight from the hotel's own garden, seafood is freshly caught, and roasts, steaks, and other meats are locally produced. Service is the pampering kind. Lunch runs about IR£10 ($16), dinner will cost about IR£17 ($27.25), and there's a 10% service charge. Be sure to book ahead.

3. COUNTY LOUTH

ACCOMMODATIONS: Set in 130 wooded acres and surrounded by green lawns, **Ballymascanlon House Hotel,** Dundalk, Co. Louth (tel. 042/71124), has twice won awards for its lovely gardens. The peaked-gabled old country mansion has high ceilings and spacious rooms in the original house, and there's a modern extension with more standardized guest rooms. A sports center that includes a heated indoor swimming pool, sauna, solarium, gym, children's playground, and squash and tennis courts makes it an all-round, self-contained resort, with golf and the seaside nearby. All 36 guest rooms have a telephone and private bath and are attractively decorated. Its location just about at midway on the main Dublin–Belfast road makes this a convenient stopping point. Seasonal rates range from IR£28 ($44.75) to IR£30 ($48).

4. COUNTY KILDARE

RESTAURANTS: Set in a Georgian-style country house, the dining room at **Curryhills House,** Prosperous, Naas, Co. Kildare (tel. 045/68150), is the pride and joy of owner/managers Bridie and Bill Travers. Décor is Tudor, and the cuisine features gourmet dishes prepared from local, fresh ingredients. On Friday there's traditional Irish music, and on Saturday you're invited to an old-fashioned sing-along. Hours are 12:30 to 2 p.m. for lunch, 6:30 to 11 p.m. for dinner; lunch prices begin at IR£8 ($12.75); dinner prices, at IR£15 ($24). Closed Sunday.

THE SOUTHEAST (COUNTIES WEXFORD, WATERFORD, KILKENNY, CARLOW, AND SOUTH TIPPERARY)

---

5. COUNTY WEXFORD

ACCOMMODATIONS: Marlfield House, Gorey, Co. Wexford (tel. 055/ 21124 or 21572), was once the home of the Earl of Courtown. Surrounded by some 35 acres of wooded countryside and landscaped gardens, the stately Regency house is filled with antiques, gilt-framed mirrors, and crystal chandeliers. Log fires in the public rooms add a gracious note of warmth, and a lovely curved staircase sweeps up to elegantly decorated and furnished guest rooms. Wallpapers, draperies, and bedspreads are all coordinated, antiques are used lavishly, and all 11 rooms have a private bath. Mary and Ray Bowe, the charming owners who have brought the old home back to its former glory, go out of their way to see that guests are catered to. There's an excellent restaurant (see below). Rates, which include a full Irish breakfast, are IR£45 ($72) to IR£55 ($88), and children under 7 are discouraged.

The **Ferrycarrig Hotel,** Ferrycarrig Bridge (P.O. Box 11), Wexford (tel. 053/22999), was described by one reviewer as "a modern lump of concrete," and I'd have to go along with that description except for several things that make it quite exceptional (as, indeed, that reviewer went on to do).

First of all, it is situated just across the Ferrycarrig Bridge on the Enniscorthy side of the Slaney Estuary, and although it is very close to a main thoroughfare, it is nestled right down on the riverbank, out of sight and sound of traffic, with green lawns that give it a true country setting. Then there's that terrific view of the river and the scores of sailing and fishing boats busily pursuing pleasure or profit. Not only that, but every single room faces the river with broad picture windows to take advantage of those river views. And best of all, I'd have to count personable Matt and Olive Britton, who run the hotel (Olive's in charge of the kitchen and dining room) with the sort of hospitality you expect in Ireland, but not in a modern hotel. Add to all those reasons for staying at the Ferrycarrig the fact that Wexford is just two miles away, and they make this an ideal touring base for the Wexford area.

Actually, an outstanding sightseeing attraction is almost at the doorstep of the hotel. A wooded river walk from the hotel grounds leads (in about three minutes) to a ruined tower perched atop a craggy cliff at the northern edge of the bridge which crosses the Slaney. Some historians claim this is all that remains of the first Anglo-Norman castle erected in Ireland, although others dispute that. No matter, it's certainly ancient (all agree it dates at least to the 15th century), and the short climb up to the tower rewards you with unbounded admiration for its builders as well as a superb overview of the Slaney rushing through a narrow gorge below. There's also the unique Wexford Heritage Park on the south side of the river.

As for the hotel, bedrooms are all attractively furnished, with comfortable chairs arranged to add living-room comfort. All have private bath. There's a cozy bar, and the Conservatory Restaurant (a favorite with locals as well as guests) specializes in the freshest of local seafood, meats, and vegetables.

Rates for bed-and-breakfast run from IR£35 ($56) to IR£40 ($64) single, IR£60 ($96) to IR£66 ($105.60) double, depending on the season (high rates apply during Wexford Festival as well as July and August). Special weekend and package rates are available. Children under 10 sharing a room with their parents stay free. Send an IR£20 ($32) deposit to confirm all bookings. Open Easter through October.

RESTAURANTS: If you can't manage to *stay* in **Marlfield House** (see above), do try to have at least one Big Splurge meal there. Mary Bowe is known for her expertise with seafoods, although any choice from the menu will consist of home-grown or locally produced ingredients prepared with a gourmet cook's touch. The restaurant is set in a Victorian-style conservatory, with sweeping views of the lawns and gardens. It's altogether charming and the epitome of luxury dining. Lunch is served from 1 to 2:30 p.m., with prices beginning at IR£15 ($24); dinner hours are 7:30 to 9:30 p.m., at prices of IR£21 ($33.50) and up. Closed three days at Christmas and the month of January. Reservations essential.

6. COUNTY WATERFORD

ACCOMMODATIONS: **Waterford Castle,** The Island, Ballinakill, Waterford (tel. 051/78203), is one castle whose setting and history push romance right to the brink of fantasy—it sits on its own wooded island, and castles just don't come much more romantic than that! Waterford Castle's 311 island acres divide the River Suir at a point leading to Waterford city's deep-water port 1½ miles upstream. Its strategic location accounts for a long and colorful history, but it's the sheer beauty of that location that overwhelms when you board the small flat-bottomed, chain-link-driven car-ferry to cross some 300 yards of the Suir. Then up the curving avenue to the fine stone castle itself, which was a Fitz-Gerald family stronghold from 1160 to 1958. Somewhat modest in size, the castle's Great Hall is a bit on the small side. Small it may be, but it *is* impressive, with a large stone fireplace at one end. Its stone crossbeam sports the FitzGerald coat-of-arms, along with those of other clans who had joined them as allies in ancient wars, and hanging at the opposite end is one of the castle's original tapestries, depicting a hunting scene that might well have taken place right on the island.

Bedrooms are in the two Elizabethan-style wings that were added in the 1800s, and all have magnificent views onto the Suir, woodlands, or the landscaped lawn out front. All are beautifully furnished and decorated. There's a magnificent oak-paneled dining room (once the ballroom), where superb meals are served with flowers and candles on the table, Waterford crystal glassware, and Wedgwood dinnerware bearing the FitzGerald crest. And the former drawing room, now named the FitzGerald Room, has the clan war cry, "Crom a Boo," inscribed on the fireplace stonework. On the castle grounds there are lovely wooded walks, horseback riding, fishing, and hunting, with golf and tennis facilities near by, as well as the historic city of Waterford and the rugged Dunmore East coast to explore.

Waterford Castle is open year round, with rates that range from IR£80 ($128) to IR£100 ($160) for singles, IR£100 ($160) to IR£135 ($216) for doubles, IR£220 ($352) to IR£250 ($400) for suites.

7. COUNTY KILKENNY

ACCOMMODATIONS: On the outskirts of town, set in spacious grounds, the **Hotel Kilkenny,** College–Callan road, Kilkenny, Co. Kilkenny (tel. 056/62000), is a two-story, red-and-white country house to which a modern extension has been added. The public rooms reflect the character of the original home, with gracious furnishings, high ceilings, and tall windows. Elsewhere, every conceivable modern convenience has been added to make this a truly luxury establishment. There are 60 top standard guest rooms with private bath, color TV, video films, radio, and tea- and coffee-making facilities. A health and leisure center holds a heated swimming pool, turbo Jacuzzi, gym, saunas, and tennis courts. A restaurant and the Olde World Bar complete the amenities. Rates (which include breakfast) are IR£44.50 ($71.25) single, IR£66.75 ($106.75) double, with a 25% reduction for children and a 10% service charge.

8. SOUTH TIPPERARY

ACCOMMODATIONS: The **Knocklofty House Hotel,** Clonmel, Co. Tipperary (tel. 052/38222), is four miles from Clonmel on the scenic Ardfinnan road, and is surely one of the most beautifully situated stately homes in Ireland's southeastern region. Approached by a shaded avenue, the Georgian mansion enjoys superb views of landscaped lawns and gardens, and terraces lead down to the River Suir, which winds through the 105-acre estate. It has a long history, with strong connections to America, since it, along with vast landholdings in Counties Tipperary and Waterford, was presented to one Richard P. Hutchinson in the mid-1600s. A kinsman, Thomas Hutchinson, was the first governor of the Massachusetts Bay Colony, and Richard himself had sojourned in New England from 1633 to 1648. In 1783 his descendants became the Earls of Donoughmore, and Knocklofty House remained their family seat until the end of 1983. The beautiful galleried library dates from 1650, although the original house was considerably altered and refurbished in the mid-1700s, when a second floor was added. By the end of that century, north and south wings had been added. Records of all that history, along with photograph albums recording illustrious visitors, remain in the library to this day.

Nowadays, it is Joyce and Paddy O'Keeffe who extend the gracious hospitality that is a tradition at Knocklofty House. Widely traveled, they have brought their expertise to bear in creating luxurious bedrooms and suites, as well as a recreation center that transforms the estate into a virtual self-contained holiday resort. There's a gymnasium, a 50-foot indoor heated swimming pool, Jacuzzi, sunbed, tennis court, squash court, table tennis, and clay pigeon trap. And there's excellent salmon and trout fishing just steps away in the River Suir, the mature woodlands invite leisurely walks, and horseback riding can be arranged. Within easy driving distance are the sightseeing attractions of Waterford city, Kilkenny, Ardmore, and Cashel.

It is perhaps in the beautiful oak-paneled dining room overlooking the river that the O'Keeffes have outdone themselves, for it has gained no little renown as a first-class restaurant that draws bookings from far and near (see below).

Seasonal rates for bed-and-breakfast range from IR£30 ($48) to IR£40 ($64) per person, and there are special three-day and weekend rates available. Open year round.

RESTAURANTS: The **Knocklofty House Hotel,** Clonmel, Co. Tipperary (tel. 052/38222), is some four miles from Clonmel, out a scenic country road, and offers superb dining in a splendid room paneled in mellow oak overlooking lawns and gardens that slope down to the River Suir. The room is beautifully appointed, with a truly sophisticated elegance, and the menu features traditional dishes that reflect a French flavor in preparation. While selections change according to availability of fresh ingredients, typical choices are noisettes of lamb provençale, loin of veal with lemon and ginger, fresh local salmon with dill-cream sauce, and filet of mullet with a rosemary-butter sauce. Vegetables are always fresh and cooked to perfection, and vegetarians are catered to. There's a nice selection of wines at moderate prices. If you'd like a pre- or après-dinner drink, you'll be served in the balconied library that dates back to 1650, where a pianist often entertains during the high season.

A five-course table d'hôte dinner is IR£16 ($25.50) and is served from 7 to 10:30 p.m. (last orders at 9:30 p.m.); lunch, from 12:30 to 2:30 p.m., runs about IR£9 ($14.50). Reservations are strongly advised for dinner. Open daily. Highly recommended.

THE SOUTHERN REGION (COUNTIES CORK AND KERRY)

9. COUNTY CORK

ACCOMMODATIONS: In Chapter XV you'll find an enthusiastic endorsement of **Arbutus Lodge,** Montenotte, Cork, Co. Cork (tel. 021/501237), as a Big Splurge place to eat. Now, let me add my heartfelt recommendation of this special place as a Big Splurge accommodation. The elegant 1802 town house overlooking Cork city is surrounded by gardens, features a surprising and excellent collection of the works of modern Irish artists, and holds only 20 guest rooms, each of which is beautifully and individually decorated and furnished. Owner/Manager Declan Ryan personally oversees the comfort of his guests, and a stay at Arbutus is much like a visit in a private home. Guest rooms overlook either the garden or the city (the cityscape is stunning!). The rate, which includes breakfast, starts at IR£59 ($94.50).

The **Fitzpatrick Silver Springs Hotel,** Tivoli, Cork (tel. 021/507533; in the U.S., 212/684-1820, or toll free 800/221-1074, 800/268-9051 in Canada), is a tall white hotel overlooking the River Lee in a beautiful setting of some 40 acres of wooded and landscaped grounds, has long been a Cork city landmark. Since coming under the ownership of the Fitzpatrick family (see Fitzpatrick's Castle in Killiney, Co. Dublin, and the Shannon Shamrock, in Bunratty, Shannonside), it is fast taking its place as one of the city's leading hostelries. Under a massive renovation program the 110 bedrooms have been decorated in cool pastels, with two double beds or one double and one twin bed in each. Most have lovely views of the Lee, the city, or the shady grounds from large picture windows. There are also elegant one- and two-bedroom suites. Superb meals are served in the attractive River Room, and there's a more informal Waterfront Grill Room for less expensive dining. You can order afternoon tea in the spacious lobby lounge, something stronger from the lobby bar or the cozy downstairs Blarney Bar, both of which are favorite gathering places for Cork business people as well as guests. After dark, repair to Fitzies downstairs nightclub. The Silver Springs is an ideal touring base, since the attractions of Cork city are just minutes away, and Fota House only a short drive, as are Blarney, Kinsale, and other County Cork sightseeing highlights. In the leisure complex, there's an Olympic-size heated pool, two tennis courts, a squash court, and a gymnasium. A nine-hole golf course is being laid out and should be in use by the end of 1989. Seasonal rates range from IR£35 ($56) to IR£57 ($91.25) single, IR£55 ($88) to IR£77 ($123.25) double.

Ballylickey Manor House and Garden Cottages, Ballylickey, Bantry Bay, Co. Cork (tel. 027/50071), overlooking Bantry Bay, is a lovely old country manor set in landscaped lawns and gardens. In the main house, four pretty garden suites have been installed and decorated in gracious country style. Each has a living room, bedroom, and bath, with fridge and tea-making facilities, and can accommodate up to three. Down by the swimming pool and outstanding restaurant, cottages reflect a more rustic style, although both they and the garden suites are the last word in luxury. Most luxurious of all, breakfast will be brought in from the restaurant if you just can't face the world without that morning meal— not your usual B&B, even though rates include either a full Irish or continental breakfast. Cottage rooms may be booked single or as suites with connecting bedrooms, and though there's no separate living room, each is spacious enough to accommodate a table and chairs and provide comfortable seating. Built by Lord Kenmare as a shooting lodge over 300 years ago, the beautifully restored home is centrally located for touring the southwest of Ireland, there are two golf courses nearby, private salmon and trout fishing is available, and on the grounds there's an outdoor swimming pool. Rates for Manor House suites begin at IR£85 ($136) for two; garden cottages range from IR£57 ($91.25) to IR£65 ($104) double; and there are weekly and three-day half-board special rates.

Set in a 500-acre farmland estate, **Longueville House,** Longueville, Mallow, Co. Cork (tel. 022/27156), is three miles west of Mallow, overlooking the Blackwater River valley. Off in the distance are visible the ruins of 16th-century Dromaneen Castle, ancestral home of owner Michael O'Callaghan, and on the front lawn, rows of huge oaks are planted in the same formation as French and English troops at the Battle of Waterloo. There's significance in both these views, for the castle was forfeited to Cromwell in 1641 by an O'Callaghan and the land only repurchased by Michael's father (who served in the Irish Senate some 30 years) in 1938, thus reclaiming his family heritage and passing it along to Michael and his charming wife, Jane. The battle-line oaks were planted when the land and house were in English hands.

The handsome 1720 Georgian mansion sports a wide entrance hall whose walls are hung with O'Callaghan portraits, and a lounge that is surely one of the loveliest in the country, with plush, soft gold armchairs pulled up to face the carved fireplace and a beautifully detailed stucco ceiling. The lounge bar is Victorian in style, with wine-red upholstery, and in the gourmet restaurant (see below), portraits of every Republic of Ireland president dub it the President's Room. All 20 guest rooms are attractively furnished, and all have a private bath. There's trout and salmon fishing in the Blackwater right on the estate, and free golf three miles away. A decided bonus to those of a literary bent is the excellent library. Rates for bed-and-breakfast are IR£35 ($56) single, IR£98 ($156.75) double, and there are weekly rates available. Open from Easter to late October. Note: Children are not encouraged as guests, since Longueville House is essentially an adult retreat.

At **Assolas Country House,** Kanturk, Co. Cork (tel. 029/50015), you're only about an hour's drive (through scenic and historic countryside) from Killarney to the west and Cork to the east. The 17th-century Queen Anne–style house is set in 100 acres of parkland, and its flower gardens have won more than one award, including the 1985 Ireland Garden Award. Towering old trees and green lawns lead down to the edge of the Blackwater River (where guests fish free). Inside the wide front doors there are spacious public rooms with a traditional country-house décor and open fires, and a large rumpus room with stone fireplace, and upstairs guest rooms come in a variety of sizes and shapes, all done up in country fabrics and colors. There's a comfortable, relaxed air about the place that is the direct result of Eleanor and Hugh Bourke's gracious hospitality. Dining is superb (the restaurant is recognized internationally—see below). In addition to fishing, guests have access to tennis, boating, and croquet. Rates for bed-and-breakfast range from IR£38 ($60.75) to IR£65 ($104) with a 25% reduction for children and a 10% service charge. Open from Easter through October.

RESTAURANTS: See above for a full description of **Longueville House,** Mallow (tel. 022/27156). Its President's Room restaurant is one of the best in the country, and even if you're only passing through this part of the Southern Region, you'll be in for a very special treat if you phone ahead to book a meal here. Meals are served in the stately Georgian dining room under the gaze of Ireland's presidents since it became a Republic and beneath an ornate plaster ceiling adorned with the delicate work of an Italian artist. In fine weather the Victorian conservatory, with its massed greenery, white ironwork, and glorious views of the garden, is open to diners as well. As for the food, it's won just about every award and international recognition going, as well it should. Cordon Bleu–trained Jane O'Callaghan oversees the preparation of gourmet selections that utilize produce grown in their own fields, as well as their own lamb and fish fresh from waters that flow through Longueville estate. Mallard and venison are featured in season, and the wine list includes wines produced from Michael's own vineyards (among the first—and only ones—in Ireland). Dinner will run about IR£22 ($35.25) and the restaurant is fully licensed. Dinner hours are 7 to 9 p.m. Open March to December 20.

Assolas Country House (see above), Kanturk (tel. 029/50015), is another good choice for a Big Splurge meal in the Southern Region. The dining room is a real gem, with Queen Anne period furnishings, Dresden china, mahogany tables, and a comfortable lounge for before- or after-dinner drinks. The pâté maison is homemade, and the menu always features home-grown fresh vegetables, often salmon fresh from the Blackwater. The Irish coffee is excellent, and there's a good, extensive wine list. The set dinner price is IR£21 ($33.50), plus a 10% service charge, and it's served from 7:30 p.m. every day from Easter through October. Again, you must book ahead.

10. COUNTY KERRY

ACCOMMODATIONS: Hotel Ard-na-Sidhe, Caragh Lake, Killorglin, Co. Kerry (tel. 064/31262), is a real find for those who value a scenic, tranquil holiday base. You may find it hard to believe that this grand red sandstone Victorian mansion was built more than a century and a half ago by one Lady O'Connell as a private guesthouse! And the lady certainly knew how to accommodate guests, a tradition which has not eroded over the years that have seen the magnificent structure perched above the shores of Caragh Lake evolve into a professional guesthouse that combines traditional elegance with all the amenities of a modern luxury hotel.

It should be pointed out that the hotel's location is a bit isolated, and I can only echo what the management, itself, tries to impress on prospective guests: Ard-na-Sidhe (which means "height of the fairies") is strictly for those who enjoy a quiet holiday—wooded walks, fishing (boats and guides are available), and reading or other such pursuits are the main activities here. Personally, I can't think of a more beautiful spot for a retreat with loved ones—or better yet, for a honeymoon! However, I should also add that Killarney is only 17 miles away for those whose tastes are a bit more lively. Also, golf links are only 3 miles away and all the sporting facilities of the Hotel Dunloe Castle and Hotel Europe (under the same ownership) are free to all guests here.

Spacious public rooms are decorated in soft tones of blues and browns and beige, furnished with antiques, and feature open fireplaces. The dining room is an intimate and restful setting for fine dining. As for bedrooms, they're a far cry from your standard hotel room—no two are the same size or shape. There are some without bath, and views are either of the lake or the beautifully landscaped gardens. A short distance from the main house, there's a modern block where rooms and suites are more uniform and of a different character than in the older building. Per-room rates range from IR£27 ($43.25) for a single room without bath to IR£54 ($86.50) for a double with garden view. Rates include a full Irish breakfast, plus all taxes and service charges. Open May to September.

The **Park Hotel,** Kenmare, Co. Kerry (tel. 064/41200), is set in some 11 garden acres, and was originally built as an upmarket hostelry for railway passengers, but a few years ago it had reached a rather sad state of deterioration. That's when a new owner, Francis Brennan, took things in hand and restored it to a standard far higher than it had known even in its glory days. Its public rooms are furnished with lovely antiques, and down the wide corridors of the main hotel, each of the spacious bedrooms is individually styled, while in a newer wing, luxurious uniformity is maintained. All 50 come with private baths, radios, direct-dial telephones, and individual heat control. Both the hotel and its dining room have won several international awards of distinction, including a Michelin star. Kenmare is an excellent starting point for a Ring of Kerry tour, and to the south, Glengarrif, Bantry, and West Cork are within easy driving distance. In addition, golf, tennis, fishing, and croquet are available. Rates start at IR£80 ($128) single, IR£165 ($264) double. Open April to Christmas.

SHANNONSIDE (COUNTIES CLARE AND LIMERICK)

11. COUNTY CLARE

ACCOMMODATIONS: Its location alone would qualify **Fitzpatrick's Shannon Shamrock Hotel,** Bunratty, Co. Clare (tel. 061/361177), as a Big Splurge—five miles from Shannon Airport, nine miles from Limerick, and just next door to Bunratty Castle. The Folk Park, the medieval banquet, and Durty Nellie's are all just a short walk away, and there's courtesy coach service to the airport upon request as well as to Limerick twice daily. There's much more than location, however, to recommend this lovely hotel. It's a sister to Fitzpatrick's Castle Hotel in Killiney, and while the two bear no outward resemblance, they are both looked over with the same personal care and attention by the Fitzpatrick family. The exceptionally efficient and friendly staff reflects that same sort of personal concern.

The Shannon Shamrock, a low, rambling stone building, exudes low-key informality in a setting of pure luxury. The stone-floor lobby leads into a large lounge whose focal point is a huge stone fireplace (ablaze on cool evenings). Comfortable seating arranged for intimate groupings make this an inviting place to have morning coffee, afternoon tea, or late-night drinks. The pretty cocktail bar, with dark-blue velvet upholstering, skylights, and lots of dark wood and green plants, has music Wednesday through Sunday during summer months. Shades of soft green and rose dominate the dining room. There's an indoor heated swimming pool and a sauna on the premises and plenty of parking space.

All 110 guest rooms come with private bath, radio, TV, and telephone. Décor and furnishings are outstanding in all, but for a sumptuous break from the rigors of travel, treat yourself to a stay in one of the beautiful and spacious River Suites—velvet chair-and-sofa coverings, king-size beds, and windows with a view are featured in bed-sitting rooms for two and separate bedroom and bed-sitting room for four. Depending on the season, rates range from IR£44 ($70.50) to IR£52 ($83.25) for singles, IR£53 ($84.75) to IR£72 ($115.25) for doubles. Service charge is 10%.

The **Old Ground Hotel,** Ennis, Co. Clare (tel. 065/28127), is an ivy-covered, two-story brick building set behind an iron fence in spacious grounds right in the heart of Ennis, just 12 miles north of Shannon Airport. It is known for its happy blend of old-world elegance and charm with modern comfort and efficiency. Its interior is an intriguing mixture of contemporary and period décor and furnishings, with a luxurious restaurant in the traditional manner and open fires when there's a chill in the air, and guest rooms furnished with the latest in guest conveniences. For example, in addition to private bath, direct-dial telephone, and color TV, each room also has facilities for making tea or coffee. Some are decorated pretty much as standard hotel rooms are around the world; others have such Victorian touches as occasional tables with delicately curved legs, gold-framed mirrors, touches of old brass on chests, and mini-chandeliers. All have hand-woven Donegal bedspreads. The Celtic Bar, with its tweed-cushioned chairs and tables of teak inset with woven rushwork, is a relaxing meeting place for locals as well as guests. The Old Ground is a Trust House Forte property, assuring the highest standards in service as well as amenities. It's also a very convenient base for exploring the glories of Shannonside. Rates, which include a full Irish breakfast, start at IR£42 ($67.25) single, IR£54 ($86.50) double, with a one-third reduction for children.

RESTAURANTS: See Chapter XX for Big Splurge recommendations of restaurants and castle banquets—those listed are absolute top value-for-money in the Shannonside region.

12. COUNTY LIMERICK

ACCOMMODATIONS: On the edge of what has been called Ireland's prettiest village, **Dunraven Arms Hotel,** Adare, Co. Limerick (tel. 061/94209), is a two-story, traditional-style, gold-colored hotel that has the look of an old time inn. Indeed, that small-inn-type hospitality greets you at the door and never diminishes throughout your stay. There's the pleasant glow of being a welcome guest in a comfortable, country-style hostelry where friendliness and courtesy are outstanding. The spacious lounge bar overlooks pretty gardens and offers excellent bar lunches at inexpensive rates, and the dining room features French cuisine, using fresh ingredients from local farms. Comfortable, traditional furnishings add a homey touch. Both public rooms and guest rooms are attractively done up in country prints, and all guest rooms have a private bath and telephone. This is where Princess Grace and Prince Rainier stayed during their 1963 visit. Not only is this a great sightseeing base—only 10 miles from Limerick, 16 from Bunratty Castle, 25 from Shannon Airport, 61 from Killarney, and 60 from Cork—but there are fishing, horseback riding, and golf close at hand. Rates, which include breakfast, start at IR£35 ($56) single, IR£54 ($86.50) double, during high season, lower other months. There's a 50% discount for children and a 12½% service charge.

THE WESTERN REGION (COUNTIES GALWAY AND MAYO)

---

13. COUNTY GALWAY

ACCOMMODATIONS: Set in 50 acres of gardens and woodland walks at the head of Cashel Bay among the jagged peaks and rocky headlands of Connemara, the **Cashel House Hotel,** Cashel Bay, Connemara, Co. Galway (tel. 095/31001), has a delightful country-house atmosphere. Among the notables who have chosen to come here for holidays were Gen. and Madame Charles de Gaulle in 1969, who turned out to be enthusiastic boosters of the warm Irish hospitality shown them by owners Kay and Dermot McEvilly. The stylish 19th-century house blends antique pieces with comfortable modern furnishings, and the cozy bar is the setting for many a friendly crack at the end of a day of sightseeing. The pretty dining room overlooks the gardens, and crackling peat and log fires add to the hominess of this utterly charming place. The dining room, which is open to nonresidents as well as guests, enjoys a countrywide reputation for its fine food (see below). The McEvillys are happy to arrange trout and salmon fishing for their guests, as well as horseback riding and picnic itineraries. And there is all of Connemara to be explored.

There are 30 guest rooms, all with private bath, heated towel racks, and superb views. Nine have sitting areas that transform them into small suites. Rates, including breakfast, are IR£33.50 ($53.50) to IR£35 ($56), with a 12½% service charge. Open March through October, and reservations may be made in the U.S. by calling 212/714-2323, or toll free 800/223-6764, 800/522-5568 in New York State.

Guests at **Currarevagh House,** Oughterard, Co. Galway (tel. 091/82313), often feel as if they're visiting in a private home, as indeed they are, for this is the family home of the present owner, Harry Hodgson, who manages the small inn with his lovely wife, June. The mid-19th-century country house sits in 150 wooded acres on the shores of Lough Corrib, and the Hodgsons provide boats and ghillies (guides) if you wish for some of the best trout fishing in the country. There's a tennis court on the grounds, golf and horseback riding close by. Furnishings and décor carry out the relaxed informality of the place, and spacious guest rooms look out to splendid views. Rates, including breakfast, are IR£29 ($46.50) per person, plus a 10% service charge. A marvelous country dinner will run about IR£14 ($22.50). Open Easter through October.

A former shooting lodge, **Rock Glen Country House,** Clifden, Connemara, Co. Galway (tel. 095/21035), is beautifully situated about a mile and a half out the Roundstone–Ballyconneely road from Clifden. Its low, rambling profile belies the spaciousness inside, where a large, lovely drawing room sets a gracious and informal tone. There's also a cozy bar and a dining room which features excellent meals prepared by the friendly owner/manager, John Roche. All 31 bedrooms have private baths, and 15 of them are on the ground floor (a boon to the handicapped and those of us who tote around tons of luggage!). Rates, which include a hearty Irish breakfast, range from IR£22 ($35.25) to IR£34 ($54.50) per person, with a one-third reduction for children and a 12½% service charge.

Right in the middle of the ruggedly beautiful Connemara region, **Rosleague Manor Country House,** Letterfrack, Co. Galway (tel. 095/41101 or 41102), overlooks Ballinakill Bay and is one mile from Connemara's new national park. The fine old Georgian mansion has the high ceilings, tall windows, and spacious rooms typical of this style, and its furnishings include many fine period pieces and works of art. Open turf fires complement the central heating. Anne and Patrick Foyle are the friendly owners who run the small hotel with special regard for guests' comfort and enjoyment of the area, giving it a distinctly "family" flavor. Bedrooms all have private bath and are nicely decorated and furnished. Rates range from IR£25 ($40) to IR£33 ($52.75) per person, with a 20% reduction for children and a 10% service charge. Open from Easter through October.

RESTAURANTS: Cashel House (tel. 095/21252 or 31001), recommended above as a Big Splurge accommodation, is also one of Ireland's best places to splurge on a memorable meal. The pretty, cheerful dining room overlooks colorful gardens, and meals here are simple, but beautifully prepared, with Irish seafood and lamb high on the list of menu specialties. Traditional dishes such as boiled bacon and cabbage appear from time to time as well, and Cashel House serves salmon caught and smoked in the area. There's a good wine list, and dinner will run around IR£20 ($32). From March through October, lunch hours are 1 to 2 p.m. (with an à la carte menu), and dinner is at 7:30 p.m. Advance reservations are absolutely essential.

14. COUNTY MAYO

ACCOMMODATIONS: Ashford Castle, Cong, Co. Mayo (tel. 092/46003), is the stuff of which dreams are made—at least, for Americans with nary a castle to call their own. In 1984 it was the place President and Mrs. Reagan chose to stay during their Irish visit. The gray stone pile, with its towers and turrets, sprawls across great green lawns that slope down to Lough Corrib, surrounded by 500 acres of woodlands and landscaped grounds (including a nine-hole golf course). The original castle was built here in 1228, and those surrounding acres have seen plenty of military action in their day. A member of the Guinness family, however, changed things in the 19th century, when he erected two large wings in the style of a French château, and today's modernized castle-hotel is a delightful blending of the two.

A medieval touch greets you in the reception hall, where suits of armor and coats-of-arms line the walls. A truly magnificent staircase sweeps upward, and huge, gilt-framed oil paintings add to the opulence. There is nothing overpoweringly formal about Ashford Castle, however, and the guest lounge is downright inviting (not quite small enough to call cozy), with thick carpeting and comfortable seating and a huge, baronial fireplace just to remind you that it began life as a noble abode. The downstairs lounge bar has a distinctly modern feel, even though it is fitted out as a dungeon, and the palatial dining room is worthy of a Big Splurge in anyone's book (see below). Guest rooms have all been modernized, with not a hint of medieval beginnings, but with contemporary furnishings and décor to cater to guests' comfort—even the bathrooms are carpeted! All have gorgeous views of lake, river, or gardens, with such luxurious touches as bedside panel controls for radio and lights.

Sports people will find some of the country's best fishing right on the grounds, and hunters come from all over Europe to stalk pheasant, snipe, and duck during winter months. Sightseers find this an ideal base for exploring the west of Ireland.

Rates begin at IR£60 ($96) single, IR£86 ($137.50) double; and if you want to go all out in your splurging, there are weekly rates available. Closed February and March.

Breaffy House Hotel, Castlebar, Co. Mayo (tel. 094/22033), also has a regal air, and is one of the most beautiful stone mansion houses in Ireland. The large gabled house sits in 60 park-like acres, and under a caring management manages to infuse warmth and charm into a setting that is nothing less than baronial. There's enough to do right on the grounds to keep you entertained—lake fishing, pony trekking, shooting in season, and tree-lined walks. For more sedentary types (or the final retreat for sporty types after all that activity), there's a Tudor-style lounge bar with wooden rafters, pewter dishes, and hanging lanterns, and another more in the style of an urban cocktail lounge, with big armchairs, a fireplace, and TV. Meals are so superb that I'm going to recommend the dining room as a Big Splurge (see below), and breakfasts (included in the rates) are outstanding, with grilled kippers, sausages or bacon, homemade brown bread, black pudding, and even doughnuts!

As for guest rooms, they reflect the very personal attention given to guests' needs, with such extras as facilities for making tea or coffee, hot-water bottles (though there's central heating and not much need for them), mending kits, writing desks, and conveniently placed hooks for bathrobes. Décor is pastel, walls are paneled, and views are lovely. All, of course, have a private bath. Rates are IR£25 ($40) per person sharing (singles pay a supplement of IR£5, or $8), with no service charge, and a one-third discount for children. There are good special rates for stays of three to seven nights.

More a country mansion than a true castle, **Mount Falcon Castle Country House,** Ballina, Co. Mayo (tel. 096/21172), is a place of quiet tranquility, set in wooded grounds not far from lovely deserted beaches. Fishermen can choose between the River Moy, Lough Conn, or the sea; other sports-minded guests will find golf, pony trekking, and horseback riding close by and a tennis court on the grounds; a game room will keep you occupied indoors. The lovely gabled house has spacious rooms, high ceilings, and log fires. Best of all, it has the friendly management of Mrs. Aldridge, who takes a personal interest in all guests and is especially proud of meals that come to her table with vegetables, fruit, milk, and cream straight from her own gardens. The attractive guest rooms have private baths. Rates for bed-and-breakfast begin at IR£28 ($44.75) per person, with a 50% reduction for children 4 to 10, no charge for those under 4. Closed Christmas week, February, and March.

RESTAURANTS: If you're not going to go all out and stay in **Ashford Castle,** described above, let me suggest that you book in for dinner (tel. 094/22644) in a dining room that is splendid to look at and where the service matches the elegance of the setting. It's a large room (seats 200), with sparkling crystal chandeliers, Doric pillars, and tall Gothic windows overlooking the lake. Dinners are flawlessly prepared, often with fish fresh from the waters outside, and you'll find such specialties as poached turbot with hollandaise sauce, escalope de veau Tipperary, and beef Stroganoff among menu selections. There's a large dessert and cheese menu to finish things off. There's an à la carte menu, but the best value is the set dinner at IR£22 ($35.25). One thing more: even with its large capacity, the dining room is not prepared for drop-ins, so be sure to reserve.

I can recommend a Big Splurge meal at **Breaffy House,** Castlebar (tel. 094/22033), with equal enthusiasm (see above for full description). The lovely dining room is modern in décor, but made intimate by soft lighting and thick carpeting. A measure of the care taken with all meals is the fact that everything is cooked to order, making this a place to relax and dine at a leisurely pace (allow at least 20 minutes for your order to arrive). The menu selection is quite extensive, with such regional specialties as seafood, pork, lamb, and beef, as well as curried prawns, chicken Maryland, and several French dishes. Aylesbury duckling with orange sauce comes crackly crisp. You can dine à la carte or opt for the set dinner that starts at IR£12 ($19.25), and hours are 7 to 9 p.m. seven days a week.

THE NORTHWESTERN REGION (COUNTIES SLIGO, DONEGAL, AND LEITRIM)

---

15. COUNTY SLIGO

ACCOMMODATIONS: **Coopershill Country House,** Riverstown, Co. Sligo (tel. 071/65108), is a great stone Georgian family mansion built back in 1774 amid more than 500 acres of woodlands and pastures grazed by sheep and cattle. The graciousness of its original era are reflected in the large rooms, high ceilings and beautiful furnishings, as well as the charming manner of its owners, Brian and Lindy O'Hara. There are only six bedrooms, but all are special, with private bathrooms and most with either four-poster or canopy beds. There's fishing for pike and perch on the river that flows through the grounds (Mrs. O'Hara has a small boat available to guests), and beautiful beaches are close by. The rates, which include breakfast, are IR£25 ($40) to IR£28 ($44.75). Open from Easter to mid-October.

When you head for Yeats Country, consider treating yourself to Big Splurge accommodations at **Ballincar House Hotel,** Rosses Point Road, Sligo (tel. 071/45361). Helen O'Brien is the friendly hostess at this small hotel (only 20 bedrooms) located about midway between Sligo town and Rosses Point. Once a comfortable country home, the hotel is surrounded by mature gardens, and the sports-minded will find a leisure complex that includes a sauna, a tennis court, and squash courts. Golfers are close to the Rosses Point course, and there's safe swimming at the Rosses Point beach. Bedrooms all are nicely appointed and have private baths, and the dining room serves award-winning meals in a lovely setting. Rates, including breakfast, range from IR£24 ($38.50) to IR£29 ($46.50) per person, depending on the season, with a 15% reduction for children and a 10% service charge.

16. COUNTY DONEGAL

ACCOMMODATIONS: You'll find **Rathmullan House,** my personal first choice for a County Donegal Big Splurge, fully described in Chapter XXVI.

Up near County Donegal's spectacular Bloody Forelands, the **Ostan Gweedore,** Bunbeg, Co. Donegal (tel. Bunbeg 85 or 86), is a modern hotel perched on a small hill that gives it a gorgeous view of miles and miles of sandy beaches and offshore islands. Charles Boyle manages it for his family, and among the amenities they provide are a health complex, tennis courts, golf, and fishing. All rooms have a private bath and picture windows to take advantage of the views, and the dining room is outstanding, featuring local seafoods. Rates for bed-and-breakfast are IR£30 ($48) single, IR£50 ($80) double, with a 25% discount for children and no service charge.

In one of the most beautiful settings in County Donegal—on Donegal Bay, midway between Connemara and the Donegal highlands—the **Sand House Hotel,** Rossnowlagh, Co. Donegal (tel. 072/51777), is a modern, three-story hotel that looks out onto a two-mile crescent beach to the front and a nine-hole golf course to the back. So modern is the hotel in appearance that I was somewhat surprised to learn that it was once a fishing lodge—its metamorphic expansion is undoubtedly due to the indefatigable Mary Britton, the charming manager. The attractive pub is often filled with enthusiastic surfers, since the Sand House has its own surf club (surfboards are furnished at no charge for guests), and its theme is fittingly nautical. It is also the setting for weekend ballad sessions. Another pleasant lounge features a stained-glass wall and scenes of Ireland executed in beaten copper. Antique pieces are scattered throughout public areas. Fresh seafood shares menu honors with continental and traditional Irish selections. Guest rooms are nicely done in warm earth tones, all with private bath, and those in front have smashing sea views. Rates for bed-and-breakfast begin at IR£35 ($56) for singles, IR£60 ($96) for doubles, with a service charge of 10%. There's a one-third reduction for children during July and August, 50% in May, June, and September. Closed October to Easter.

THE MIDLANDS (COUNTIES CAVAN, LAOIS, LONGFORD, OFFALY, MONAGHAN, ROSCOMMON, AND WESTMEATH)

---

17. COUNTY MONAGHAN

ACCOMMODATIONS: The family-owned and operated **Nuremore Hotel,** Carrickmacross, Co. Monaghan (tel. 042/61438), is only about 50 miles from

Dublin, and its 100 acres of surrounding woodlands, green lawns, gardens, and smooth golf course provide a restful country setting for sightseeing in either the Midlands or the Eastern Region. There's also an indoor heated swimming pool, a spa pool, snooker room, sauna, and squash court, as well as good fishing in the hotel's own lakes. The thoroughly modern guest rooms all have private bath, TV, video, and telephone, and there's an excellent restaurant. Rates, which include breakfast, begin at IR£33 ($52.75) single and IR£54 ($86.50) double, with a 25% reduction for children.

Lucy and Johnny Madden carry on an eight-generation tradition as owners of **Hilton Park,** Clones, Scotshouse, Co. Monaghan (tel. 047/56007), a stately mansion set in a wooded 600-acre estate that holds three lakes and a nine-hole golf course. Throughout the house are those exquisite architectural details (elegant woodwork, ceilings, etc.) of more gracious times. Furnishings and memorabilia from the past are very much a part of the present at Hilton Park, and three of the bedrooms hold four-poster or canopied beds. Some bedrooms have dressing rooms, and there are two with private bath. Best of all, each one looks out over the surrounding parkland. Meals consist of typical country-house fare, almost all of which utilizes meats, fish, vegetables, and fruits from the estate itself. The lakes afford good fishing, boating, and swimming, and riding is available nearby, as well as shooting during season. Lough Erne provides cruising and fishing, and there are plenty of other stately homes, museums, and historic sites to be visited. Rates are IR£35 ($56) for bed-and-breakfast for a room with bath, IR£27 ($43.25) for those without. Dinner costs IR£16 ($25.50), and the 10% service charge is waived if you stay more than one night.

18. COUNTY LONGFORD

ACCOMMODATIONS: As small as it is, Ireland tempts travelers to dash cross country in a matter of hours, thereby missing out on all the Midlands have to offer. Consider, instead, a stopover of at least one night in a magnificent Tudor Gothic mansion, **Carrigglas Manor,** Longford (tel. 45165), three miles from Longford town, the home of Jeffry and Tessa Lefroy. The house itself has a romantic history—its builder was Lord Chief Justice of Ireland in 1837, who counted Jane Austen among his close friends (some think he was the model for Darcy in *Pride and Prejudice*). This is, in fact, literary countryside, with connections to Goldsmith and the Edgeworths. For the sports-minded, riding, fishing, and golf are available in the vicinity, and sightseers will find a wealth of ancient ruins, stately homes, and gardens.

Reception rooms are the epitome of elegance, filled with heirloom furniture, artifacts, and family portraits. As for the five guest bedrooms, the two doubles come with canopied beds, a bit more luxurious than the one twin-bedded and two single rooms. Attractive self-catering apartments are presently under construction in the renovated stables and may be available by the time this book is in print.

Guests are only booked Tuesday through Friday, since the house and garden are open to the public Saturday through Monday. Rates for dinner (including a before-dinner drink and wine with the meal), bed-and-breakfast are IR£75 ($120), and the Lefroys ask that guests not plan to arrive before 6 p.m. the first evening.

NORTHERN IRELAND (COUNTIES ANTRIM, LONDONDERRY, DOWN, ARMAGH, TYRONE, AND FERMANAGH)

19. COUNTY ANTRIM

ACCOMMODATIONS: Just a short drive from the city center, yet set in its own wood park-like grounds overlooking Belfast Lough and the County Antrim coastline, the **Culloden Hotel,** 142 Bangor Rd., Holywood, BT18 0EX (tel. 023/17-5223), was built in the 1800s as the official palace for the bishops of Down. It's a magnificent building of Scottish baronial architecture, and its public rooms are filled with beautiful antiques, elegant woodwork and detailed plasterwork, stained glass, and Louis XV chandeliers. As for guest rooms and suites, all enjoy marvelous views and luxurious appointments, as well as telephones, radios, and TVs. A newer wing has been skillfully designed to fit in with the original architecture and holds some 40 luxury bedrooms and a roof garden.

Cuisine in the lovely dining room has won accolades from international food critics, and for less formal meals there's the Cultra Inn, just a short walk from the main building, which has a pub in which to enjoy lunch as well as libations and a grill room for evening meals.

Recreation facilities include two squash courts, an all-weather tennis court, a putting green, lawn croquet, table tennis, a pool table, and a rowing machine. The Royal Belfast Golf Club is within walking distance and is open to Culloden guests.

Rates at this delightful haven from city hustle and bustle are IR£75 ($131.25) single, IR£100 ($175) double, and IR£120 ($210) for suites.

The **Dunadry Inn,** Dunadry, Co. Antrim (tel. Templepatrick 32474), is farther out from Belfast city center (15 miles), but handy to the airport (4 miles) and to the town of Antrim (3 miles). It's an ideal touring base and a restful and interesting place to end sightseeing days. Because of its out-of-town location the Dunadry offers a unique car-hire service that allows you to pick up and drop off your car there, and they'll pick you up and deliver you back to the airport. The hotel's name translates to "The Middle Fort," since it was the center of three fortifications between Tara and Dunseverick. Over its long history it's been a paper mill and a linen mill, surrounded by a village of some 20 cottages (a site now covered by the inn, whose restaurant is built right over the old mill stream). The Copper Bar is a striking, two-story baronial hall with a fireplace at one end, exposed wooden rafters, and a wood-railed mezzanine leading off to second-story guest rooms. The copper-hooded bar offers a good buffet lunch and draws a convivial group of late-night drinkers. At one side of the courtyard there's a two-foot-wide stone wall left from the old mill. There's good fishing (free to guests) in the river. All guest rooms are luxuriously furnished, with a private bath, color TV, radio, and direct-dial telephone—many have French windows that open to the garden or courtyard. Bedspreads are of locally woven tweeds. Rates begin at £55 ($88) single, £68 ($108.75) double. The special weekend rates offer particularly good value.

See also the recommendation in Chapter XXX for the **Londonderry Arms Hotel,** Carnlough, Co. Antrim—another personal favorite.

Ballygally Castle Hotel, Ballygally, Co. Antrim (tel. 0574-83212) is only 25 miles from Belfast and five miles from Larne on the North Antrim coast and dates from 1625. Facing the beach of Ballygally Bay, with fine views that reach as far as the Scottish coast, the castle is constructed of local stone, in the Scottish style, and has remained unaltered in virtually every respect. Amazingly, modern plumbing, central heating, and other creature comforts have been added without destroying the character of this interesting old fortress. A modern extension housing hotel public rooms and additional bedrooms makes no effort to emulate the castle architecture, but the dungeon cocktail bar in the cellars of the castle is totally in keeping with its setting.

All 29 bedrooms (some in the turrets of the original building, more in the extension) are individually decorated, and each comes with private bath, telephone, TV, and radio. The dining room here has gained a wide-spread reputation, and its Saturday night "Candlelight" dinner dances are very popular, as is the Sunday high tea.

There's a trout stream right on the grounds, many walks past streams and waterfalls, and less than a mile away, there's an 18-hole golf course. Just across the road, at the edge of the beach, the Ballygally Craft Shop offers a wide array of handcrafts at good-value prices.

Rates for bed and a full Irish breakfast are £31 ($54.25) single, £47 ($82.25) double.

The **Bushmills Inn,** 25 Main St., Bushmills, Co. Antrim (tel. 026/57-32339), is a lovely little inn that has been rescued from almost total deterioration by owners Roy Bolton and Richard Wilson, who have brought it back far beyond its beginnings as a coaching inn during the early 1800s. Its style these days is one that might be called "country elegant," with a small lobby that perfectly emulates a private drawing room, with lots of wood and rich carpeting—charming! Upstairs there's a good library in the old round tower, with a whimsical concealed door. A Victorian bar, complete with flickering gas lights, serves bar food from the adjacent open kitchen. The 12 luxury bedrooms all have private baths, with color TVs, radios, and direct-dial telephones. Two family rooms have intriguing "balcony beds" for the children—and the kids love them! Meals are served in a lovely dining room, with dinner averaging about IR£10 ($17.50) and a less expensive menu available from 5 to 6:30 p.m. Bed-and-breakfast rates are IR£27 ($47.25) single, IR£42 ($73.50) double.

20. COUNTY LONDONDERRY

ACCOMMODATIONS: Set in its own grounds at the edge of town, the **Everglades Hotel,** Prehen Road, Londonderry BT47 2PA (tel. 0504/46722), is one of Northern Ireland's leading luxury hotels, and you're likely to find a fair sprinkling of locals in the bar and restaurant on any given day. Guest rooms are attractively furnished with cane chairs, tables, and beds and have private bath, color TV, in-house movies, radio, direct-dial telephone, and facilities for making tea and coffee. There's an inviting cocktail lounge, the Buttery Bar for quick meals, snacks, or drinks, and the lovely Seminole Restaurant for excellent full-meal service. Rates begin at £40 ($64) for singles, £55 ($88) for doubles.

21. COUNTY DOWN

ACCOMMODATIONS: At the **Slieve Donard Hotel,** Newcastle, Co. Down (tel. Newcastle 23681), you can look across Dundrum Bay to where the Mountains of Mourne sweep down to the sea and then you can walk along the four-mile curving sandy strand to their very feet. You can also live out any latent Victorian fantasies in the turreted, red-brick hotel set in its acres of green lawn. When it was built, back in 1897, there were coal fires in every bath. These days every modern convenience is incorporated into public and guest rooms, somehow leaving intact a genteel atmosphere that evokes an era of sweeping long skirts and frock-coated gentlemen. Front rooms overlooking the sea are especially nice, and I am particularly fond of nos. 103 and 104, both singles with curved windows and the bath up a short flight of steps (a perfect retreat for the single traveler). The Dogs Head pub and restaurant at the entrance gates is a white-washed gate lodge serving food at moderate prices, and the hotel's main dining room excels in fresh seafood creations. Rates begin at £33 ($57.75) single, £50 ($87.50) double, during summer months (lower other times), and it's a good idea to book ahead in this popular hostelry.

CHAPTER XXXII

THE ABC'S OF IRELAND

□ □ □

Although much of the information listed below is also contained in the foregoing chapters, I hope this will serve as a quick reference when you need to know the nitty-gritty of traveling in Ireland.

AMERICAN EMBASSY/CONSULATE: In the Republic, the U.S. Embassy is in Dublin, at 42 Elgin Rd. (tel. 01/688777). In Northern Ireland, it's the U.S. Consulate General, Queen's House, 14 Queen's St., Belfast BT1 (tel. 0232/228239).

AMERICAN EXPRESS: You'll find the American Express office at 116 Grafton St., Dublin (tel. 01/772874), with a full range of services, including accepting mail for members. The same is true of the Northern Ireland office, which is located at Hamilton Travel, 23 Waring St., Belfast (tel. 0232/230321).

BANKING HOURS: Banks close for the lunch hour all over the country, and observe weekday opening hours of 10 a.m. to 12:30 p.m. and 1:30 to 3 p.m. They're closed Saturday, Sunday, and bank holidays. Airport banks are open every day except Christmas from 7:30 a.m. to 11 p.m.

ELECTRIC CURRENT: Ireland's current is 220 volts A.C., so if you must bring small appliances (like hairdryers), you should also pack a voltage converter and a variety of plug adapters (you'd be *amazed* how many different-shaped plugs and outlets there are!). Electric shavers using 110 volts should present no problem, since there will be shaver points in virtually every accommodation.

EMERGENCIES: Throughout the country, the number to call for police, ambulance, firemen, or any other type of emergency assistance is **999.**

HAIRDRESSING: There are branches of the excellent **Peter Mark** salons throughout the country, with Dublin addresses at 74 Grafton St. (tel. 714399), 36 Grafton St. (tel. 715000), and 11a Upper O'Connell St. (tel. 745580). They specialize in international standards of cutting and styling, as well as all regular salon services. Men will find barbershop prices moderate to inexpensive by American standards.

HOLIDAYS: In the Republic, national holidays fall on: January 1 (New Year's Day), March 17 (St. Patrick's Day), Good Friday and Easter Monday, the first Monday in June, the first Monday in August, the last Monday in October, Christmas Day, and December 26 (St. Stephen's Day). The whole country shuts down for these days (well, shops and banks, anyway). Northern Ireland observes the same holiday schedule, with the exception that the August bank holiday is replaced by the first Monday in September and the Battle of the Boyne is celebrated on July 12. Also, some towns observe an "Early Closing Day," with shops closing at 1 p.m.; since the day of the week varies from community to community, be sure to inquire if you have shopping to do.

MAIL DELIVERY: General Delivery in Ireland is known as **Poste Restante,** and it is received at the General Post Office, O'Connell Street, Dublin, and the GPO in other large cities around the country. Hours for pickup of mail in Dublin are 10:30 a.m. to 6:30 p.m. Monday through Saturday and 9 a.m. to 8 p.m. on Sunday; in other locations, it's 9 a.m. to 5:30 p.m. Monday through Friday. Mail will be held a maximum of two months.

MEDICAL ATTENTION: Medical facilities in Ireland are excellent (in fact, I plan *always* to be sick only when I'm on Irish soil!). If you need a doctor, dentist, or hospital service, the first source of information should be your accommodations hostess or someone on the local scene. Failing that, the **Irish Medical Association,** 10 Fitzwilliam Pl., Dublin (tel. 01/762550), can put you in touch with local medical help.

METRIC MEASURES: Ireland uses the metric system, so become familiar with the equivalents, or follow the formula instructions if you feel the need to convert.

Length
    1 millimeter = 0.04 inches (*or* less than 1/16 in)
    1 centimeter = 0.39 inches (*or* just under ½ in)
    1 meter   = 1.09 yards (*or* about 39 inches)
    1 kilometer   = 0.62 mile (*or* about ⅔ mile)

To convert kilometers to miles, take the number of kilometers and multiply by .62 (for example, 25 km × .62 = 15.5 mi).

To convert miles to kilometers, take the number of miles and multiply by 1.61 (for example, 50 mi × 1.61 = 80.5 km).

Capacity
    1 liter = 33.92 ounces
           = 1.06 quarts
           = 0.26 gallons

To convert liters to gallons, take the number of liters and multiply by .26 (for example, 50 l × .26 = 13 gallons).

To convert gallons to liters, take the number of gallons and multiply by 3.79 (for example, 10 gal × 3.79 = 37.9 l).

Weight
    1 gram   = 0.04 ounces (*or* about a paperclip's weight)
    1 kilogram = 2.2 pounds

To convert kilograms to pounds, take the number of kilos and multiply by 2.2 (for example, 75 kg × 2.2 = 165 pounds).

To convert pounds to kilograms, take the number of pounds and multiply by .45 (for example, 90 lb × .45 = 40.5 kg).

Area

1 hectare (100m²) = 2.47 acres

To convert hectares to acres, take the number of hectares and multiply by 2.47 (for example, 20 ha × 2.47 = 49.4 acres).

To convert acres to hectares, take the number of acres and multiply by .41 (for example, 40 acres × .41 = 16.4 hectare).

Temperature

To convert degrees C to degrees F, multiply degrees C by 9, divide by 5, then add 32 (for example 9/5 × 20°C + 32 = 68°F).

To convert degrees F to degrees C, subtract 32 from degrees F, then multiply by 5, and divide by 9 (for example, 85°F − 32 × 5/9 = 29°C).

PHOTOGRAPHIC SUPPLIES: Film of most types is readily available in Ireland, even in small towns (usually at the chemist's outside large cities), and Dublin, Cork, and Limerick have good camera shops. You'll find film more costly than at home, however, and as a young American told me with great earnestness, "In Ireland, you're going to need about three times the film you thought you would—there's another good shot around every bend in the road!" So keep that in mind and save money by coming prepared.

POLICE: Garda Siochana, "protector of the peace," is the Gaelic name for the Irish police force, and they're familiarly known as Garda (if there's just one), and Gardai ("gard-ee," collectively). Except for special detachments, they're unarmed, and they wear dark-blue uniforms. In Northern Ireland, the police are known as the Royal Ulster Constabulary.

POSTAGE: In the Republic, airmail postage to the U.S. for letters is 46p (75¢) for the first half ounce, 17p (25¢) for each additional half ounce. The less expensive air letters (available from post offices) cost 40p (65¢) per letter. Postcards require postage of 30p (50¢). Street mailboxes are painted green. In Northern Ireland, United Kingdom postal rates apply, and their street mailboxes are painted red.

REST ROOMS: Even the smallest Irish town usually has public rest rooms, as do most hotels, department stores, pubs, restaurants, and theaters—gas (petrol) stations do not. A helpful tip: Some public toilets are not as well equipped as they might be, and it's a good idea to carry paper tissues in your handbag for emergencies. Rest rooms are usually marked with the Gaelic **Mna** (women) and **Fir** (men).

STUDENT DISCOUNTS: Any student traveling to Ireland should bring an **International Student Identity Card.** You must, however, arm yourself with this valuable document *before you leave home.* The cost in 1988 was $10, and you can obtain your card through **CIEE** (the **Council on International Educational Exchange),** 205 E. 42nd St., New York, NY 10017 (tel. 212/661-1414). The **Irish Student Travel Service (USIT),** 7 Anglesea St., Dublin (tel. 01/778117), is the place to go for discount transportation tickets and information on other student reductions. There are USIT offices in several other locations around the country (see Chapter I). For student exchange arrangements and home stays in Ireland, pick up a copy of the *Discover Young Ireland* booklet from any Tourist Office.

TAXIS: You'll find taxi ranks at bus and railway stations, airports, ferry ports, major hotels, and along the main street of some cities. Don't expect to be able to hail them on the street, but the telephone directory will list numbers to call under the heading "Taxi-cab Ranks and Shelters." In rural areas, if there is taxi service available, *everybody* knows the number!

TELEGRAMS: No Western Union—telegrams are sent through the post office, and even if regular postal services are not available on weekends, there is usually telegraph service for several hours on Saturday and Sunday (call the local telephone operator for specific information).

TELEPHONES: Well, they're better than they *used* to be—but still a far cry from the service you're probably accustomed to at home. It can be an adventure to make a call in Ireland, and I must confess to a certain amount of enjoyment if it happens to entail a bit of conversation with the helpful (and witty) operators. Coinboxes use 2p and 5p coins, and you should have an ample supply if you're making a toll call.

TIME: A good part of the charm of the Irish is due to their almost total disregard for time (the monster that drives the rest of us to distraction). They firmly believe that "When God made time, he made plenty of it," yet in my experience, after spending several months in Ireland each year, everything seems to get attended to in *good* time, even though many times not in the time *I* had in mind! Be that as it may, Ireland's official time is Greenwich Mean Time in winter and Summer Time (Daylight Savings) from April to October. Summer days are brilliantly light (or mistily light, depending on the whimsical showers) until 10:30 or 11 p.m., while in winter darkness descends as early as 4 p.m.

TIPPING: There really is no hard-and-fast rule for tipping in Ireland—the tradition of no tipping at all still clings to some rural areas and in some social situations (such as pubs, where you *never* tip the man behind the stick), but in most cases the waitress, taxi driver, or anyone else rendering a service will accept your tip with courteous appreciation. As a general rule, you'd want to tip porters carrying bags, waitresses, parking-lot attendants, hairdressers, and barbers. As for amount, observe the 10% to 15% rule, with one exception—your *minimum* tip should be 50p, whether or not a percentage of the bill amounts to that much. Actually, whether you tip or not, it's the sincere "thank you" that the Irish value most.

TRANSPORTATION: The **Eurailpass** is good for unlimited rail travel in Ireland and on the Continent (but not in Great Britain or Northern Ireland), as well as on Irish Continental lines ferries between Ireland and France. It can also be used on Ireland's Expressway Bus Network. If you're not using a Eurailpass, Bus Eireann will sell you a money-saving **Rambler Pass** for unlimited travel on rail or bus. See Chapter II for details.

There is good bus transport in both the Republic and in Northern Ireland, making it possible to reach virtually every hamlet in the country. Rail service to all major destinations is good, also, but can be spotty in rural and outlying areas. Students are eligible for the **Youth Student Pass.** All passes are available from mainline railway stations in Ireland, or you may purchase them through travel agents in the States or CIE Tours International, 590 Fifth Ave., New York, NY 10036 (tel. 212/944-8828). Northern Ireland Railways has a seven-day, unlimited travel **Rail Runabout pass** good April through October, available at most railway stations.

WEATHER FORECAST: The weather in Ireland is fickle, and must give forecasters fits. You can, however, get their best judgment and a report on weather conditions at the moment for the country as a whole by calling 01/743320, and for the Dublin area forecast the number is 01/1199.

YOUTH HOSTELS: There are 54 hostels around the Republic, ranging from basic facilities to simple-but-adequate to a good deal more than adequate. They're available to members of the **International Youth Hostel Association,** and the Irish hostel association **(An Oige)** issues a comprehensive handbook of the country's hostels, rules and regulations, charges, etc. You can pick up a copy from their Dublin headquarters at 39 Mountjoy Square (tel. 01/745734) or by writing for one before you leave home. In Northern Ireland, contact the **Youth Hostel Association of Northern Ireland,** 56 Bradbury Pl., Belfast BT7 1RV (tel. 0232/224733).

Index

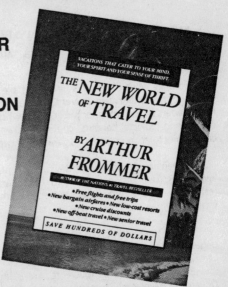

NOW, SAVE MONEY ON ALL YOUR TRAVELS!
Join Frommer's™ Dollarwise® Travel Club

Saving money while traveling is never a simple matter, which is why, over 27 years ago, the **Dollarwise Travel Club** was formed. Actually, the idea came from readers of the Frommer publications who felt that such an organization could bring financial benefits, continuing travel information, and a sense of community to economy-minded travelers all over the world.

In keeping with the money-saving concept, the annual membership fee is low—$18 (U.S. residents) or $20 U.S. (Canadian, Mexican, and foreign residents)—and is immediately exceeded by the value of your benefits which include:

1. The latest edition of any TWO of the books listed on the following pages.
2. A copy of any Frommer City Guide.
3. An annual subscription to an 8-page quarterly newspaper *The Dollarwise Traveler* which keeps you up-to-date on fastbreaking developments in good-value travel in all parts of the world—bringing you the kind of information you'd have to pay over $35 a year to obtain elsewhere. This consumer-conscious publication also includes the following columns:
    Hospitality Exchange—members all over the world who are willing to provide hospitality to other members as they pass through their home cities.
    Share-a-Trip—requests from members for travel companions who can share costs and help avoid the burdensome single supplement.
    Readers Ask . . . Readers Reply—travel questions from members to which other members reply with authentic firsthand information.
4. Your personal membership card which entitles you to purchase through the club all Frommer publications for a third to a half off their regular retail prices during the term of your membership.

So why not join this hardy band of international Dollarwise travelers now and participate in its exchange of information and hospitality? Simply send $18 (U.S. residents) or $20 U.S. (Canadian, Mexican, and other foreign residents) along with your name and address to: Frommer's Dollarwise Travel Club, Inc., Gulf + Western Building, One Gulf + Western Plaza, New York, NY 10023. Remember to specify which *two* of the books in section (1) and which *one* in section (2) above you wish to receive in your initial package of member's benefits. Or tear out the next page, check off your choices, and send the page to us with your membership fee.

FROMMER BOOKS
PRENTICE HALL PRESS
ONE GULF + WESTERN PLAZA
NEW YORK, NY 10023

Date_____

Friends:
Please send me the books checked below:

FROMMER'S™ $-A-DAY® GUIDES

(In-depth guides to sightseeing and low-cost tourist accommodations and facilities.)

☐ Europe on $30 a Day	$14.95	☐ New Zealand on $40 a Day	$12.95
☐ Australia on $30 a Day	$12.95	☐ New York on $50 a Day	$12.95
☐ Eastern Europe on $25 a Day	$13.95	☐ Scandinavia on $60 a Day	$13.95
☐ England on $40 a Day	$12.95	☐ Scotland and Wales on $40 a Day	$12.95
☐ Greece on $30 a Day	$12.95	☐ South America on $30 a Day	$13.95
☐ Hawaii on $50 a Day	$13.95	☐ Spain and Morocco (plus the Canary Is.)	
☐ India on $25 a Day	$12.95	on $40 a Day	$13.95
☐ Ireland on $35 a Day	$13.95	☐ Turkey on $25 a Day	$12.95
☐ Israel on $30 & $35 a Day	$12.95	☐ Washington, D.C., & Historic Va. on	
☐ Mexico (plus Belize & Guatemala)		$40 a Day	$12.95
on $25 a Day	$13.95		

FROMMER'S™ DOLLARWISE® GUIDES

(Guides to sightseeing and tourist accommodations and facilities from budget to deluxe, with emphasis on the medium-priced.)

☐ Alaska	$13.95	☐ Cruises (incl. Alask, Carib, Mex, Hawaii,	
☐ Australia	$14.95	Panama, Canada, & US)	$14.95
☐ Austria & Hungary	$14.95	☐ California & Las Vegas	$14.95
☐ Belgium, Holland, Luxembourg	$13.95	☐ Florida	$13.95
☐ Brazil	$14.95	☐ Mid-Atlantic States	$13.95
☐ Egypt	$13.95	☐ New England	$13.95
☐ France	$14.95	☐ New York State	$13.95
☐ England & Scotland	$14.95	☐ Northwest	$14.95
☐ Germany	$13.95	☐ Skiing in Europe	$14.95
☐ Italy	$14.95	☐ Skiing USA—East	$13.95
☐ Japan & Hong Kong	$13.95	☐ Skiing USA—West	$13.95
☐ Portugal, Madeira, & the Azores	$13.95	☐ Southeast & New Orleans	$13.95
☐ South Pacific	$13.95	☐ Southeast Asia	$14.95
☐ Switzerland & Liechtenstein	$13.95	☐ Southwest	$14.95
☐ Bermuda & The Bahamas	$13.95	☐ Texas	$13.95
☐ Canada	$13.95	☐ USA	$15.95
☐ Caribbean	$13.95		

FROMMER'S™ TOURING GUIDES

(Color illustrated guides that include walking tours, cultural & historic sites, and other vital travel information.)

☐ Australia	$9.95	☐ Paris	$8.95
☐ Egypt	$8.95	☐ Scotland	$9.95
☐ Florence	$8.95	☐ Thailand	$9.95
☐ London	$8.95	☐ Venice	$8.95

TURN PAGE FOR ADDITONAL BOOKS AND ORDER FORM.

FROMMER'S™ CITY GUIDES

(Pocket-size guides to sightseeing and tourist accommodations and facilities in all price ranges.)

☐ Amsterdam/Holland $5.95	☐ Minneapolis/St. Paul $5.95
☐ Athens $5.95	☐ Montreal/Quebec City $5.95
☐ Atlantic City/Cape May $5.95	☐ New Orleans $5.95
☐ Belgium $5.95	☐ New York $5.95
☐ Boston $5.95	☐ Orlando/Disney World/EPCOT $5.95
☐ Cancún/Cozumel/Yucatán $5.95	☐ Paris $5.95
☐ Chicago $5.95	☐ Philadelphia $5.95
☐ Dublin/Ireland $5.95	☐ Rio $5.95
☐ Hawaii $5.95	☐ Rome $5.95
☐ Las Vegas $5.95	☐ San Francisco $5.95
☐ Lisbon/Madrid/Costa del Sol $5.95	☐ Santa Fe/Taos (avail. May 1989) $5.95
☐ London $5.95	☐ Sydney $5.95
☐ Los Angeles $5.95	☐ Washington, D.C. $5.95
☐ Mexico City/Acapulco $5.95	

SPECIAL EDITIONS

☐ A Shopper's Guide to the Caribbean $12.95	☐ Motorist's Phrase Book (Fr/Ger/Sp) $4.95
☐ Beat the High Cost of Travel $6.95	☐ Paris Rendez-Vous $10.95
☐ Bed & Breakfast—N. America $11.95	☐ Swap and Go (Home Exchanging) $10.95
☐ California with Kids $14.95	☐ The Candy Apple (NY for Kids) $11.95
☐ Guide to Honeymoon Destinations	☐ Travel Diary and Record Book $5.95
(US, Canada, Mexico, & Carib) $12.95	☐ Where to Stay USA (Lodging from $3
☐ Manhattan's Outdoor Sculpture $15.95	to $30 a night) $10.95

☐ Marilyn Wood's Wonderful Weekends (NY, Conn, Mass, RI, Vt, NH, NJ, Del, Pa) $11.95

☐ The New World of Travel (Annual sourcebook by Arthur Frommer previewing: new travel trends, new modes of travel, and the latest cost-cutting strategies for savvy travelers) $12.95

SERIOUS SHOPPER'S GUIDES

(Illustrated guides listing hundreds of stores, conveniently organized alphabetically by category)

☐ Italy $15.95	☐ Los Angeles $14.95
☐ London $15.95	☐ Paris $15.95

GAULT MILLAU

(The only guides that distinguish the truly superlative from the merely overrated.)

☐ The Best of Chicago (avail. June 1989) $15.95	☐ The Best of New England (avail. June 1989) . .$15.95
☐ The Best of France (avail. July 1989) $15.95	☐ The Best of New York $15.95
☐ The Best of Italy (avail. July 1989) $15.95	☐ The Best of San Francisco $15.95
☐ The Best of Los Angeles $15.95	☐ The Best of Washington, D.C. $15.95

ORDER NOW!

In U.S. include $1.50 shipping UPS for 1st book; 50¢ ea. add'l book. Outside U.S. $2 and 50¢, respectively.

Allow four to six weeks for delivery in U.S., longer outside U.S.

Enclosed is my check or money order for $_____

NAME_____

ADDRESS_____

CITY_____ STATE_____ ZIP_____